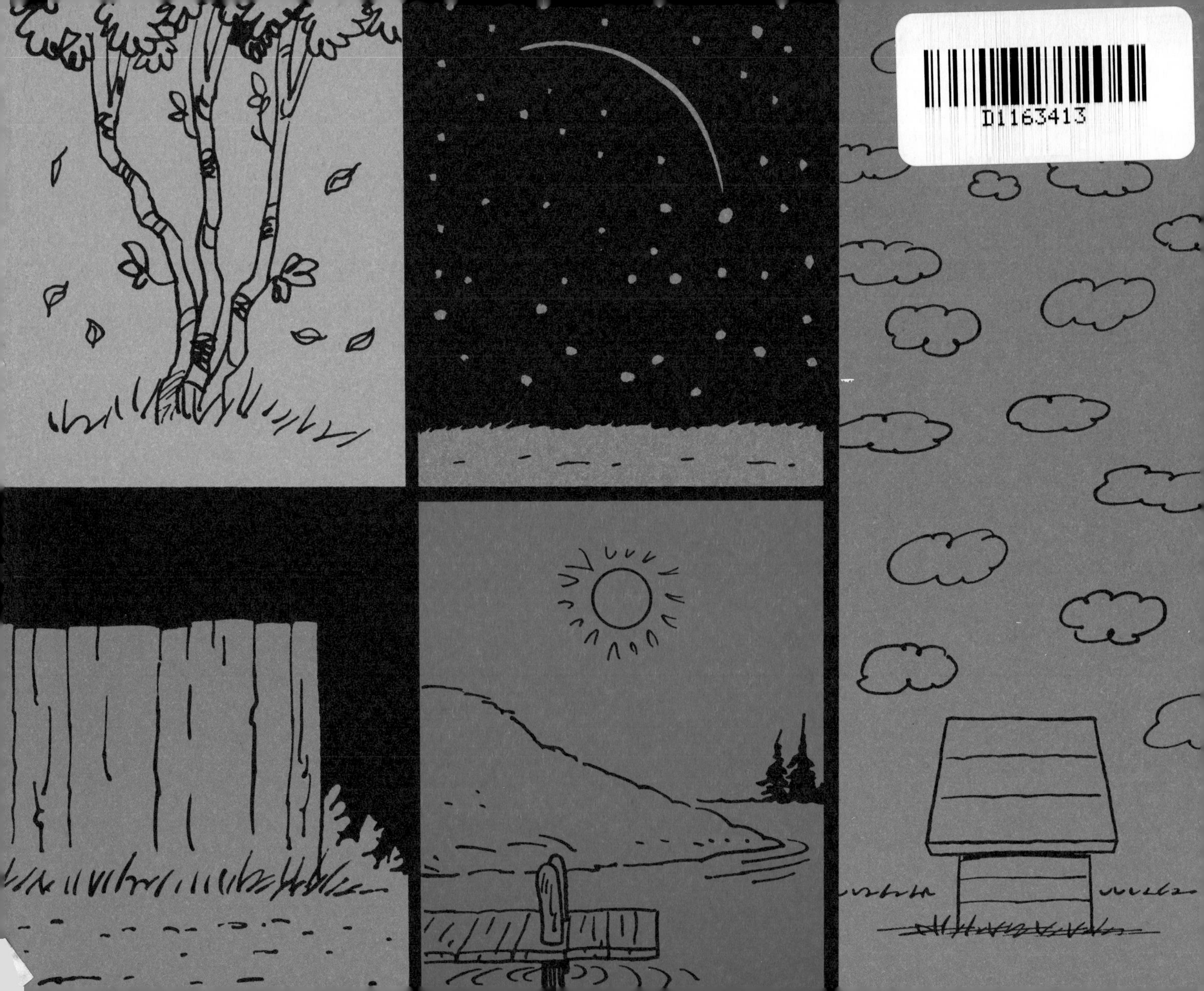

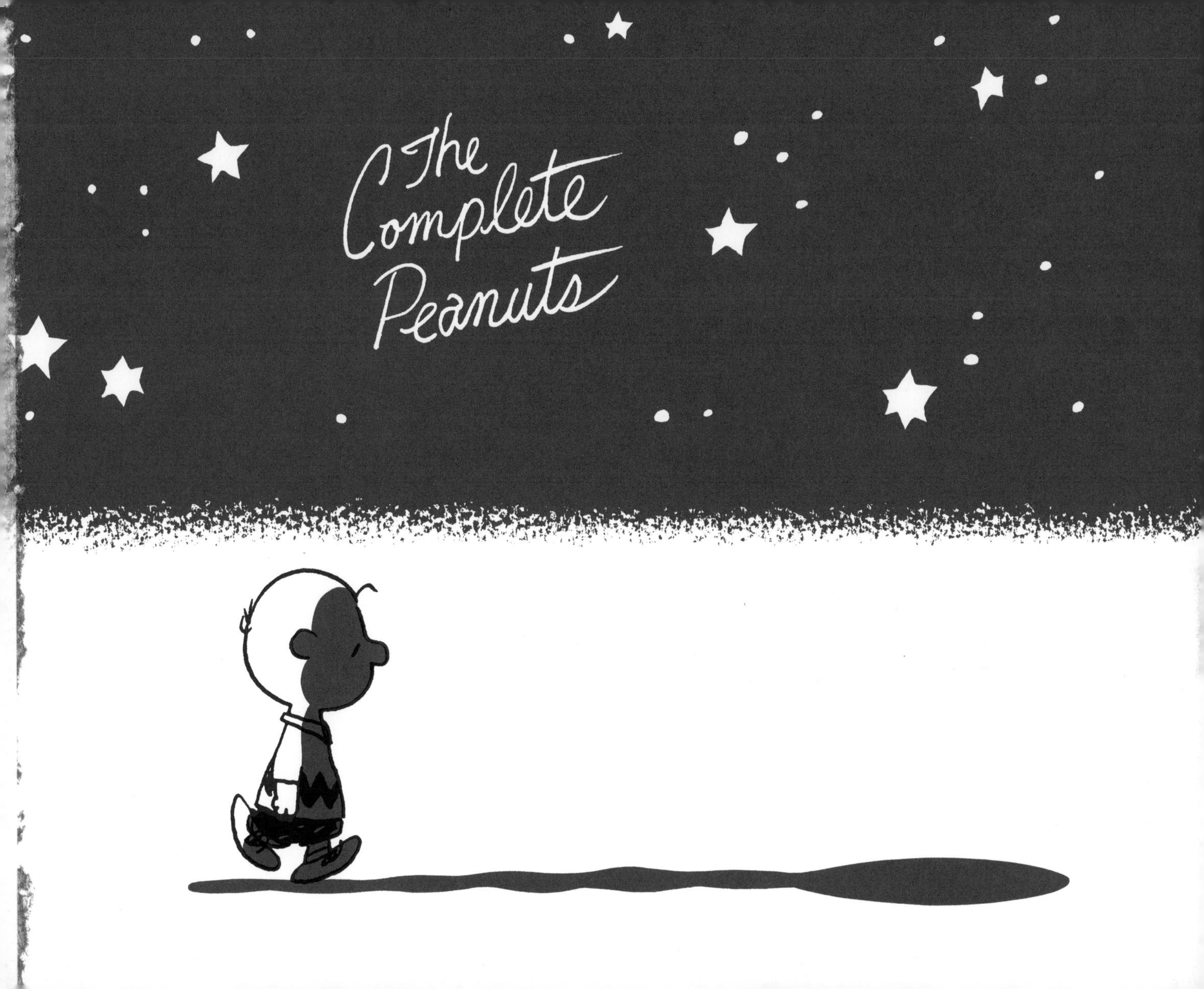
The Complete Peanuts

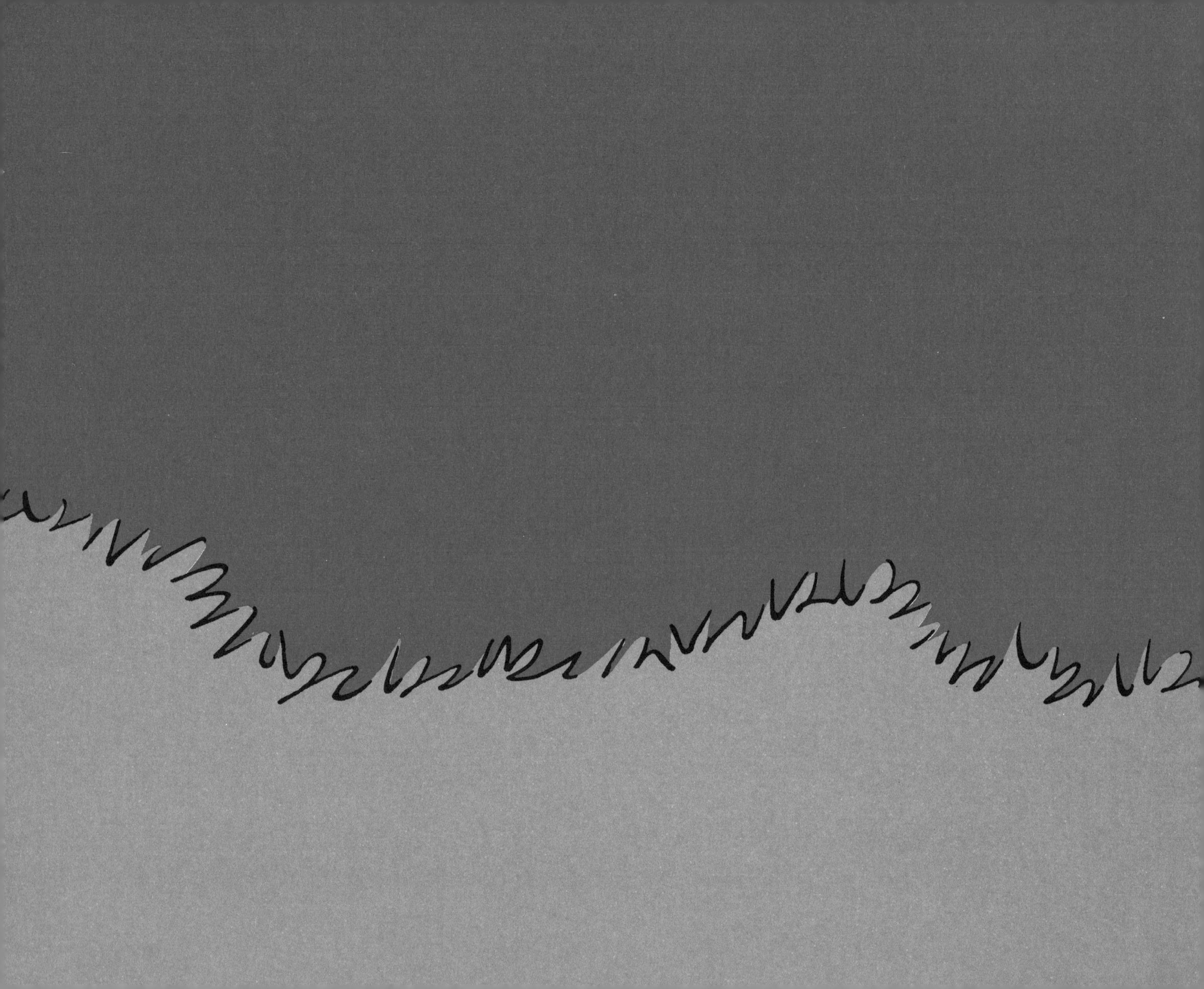

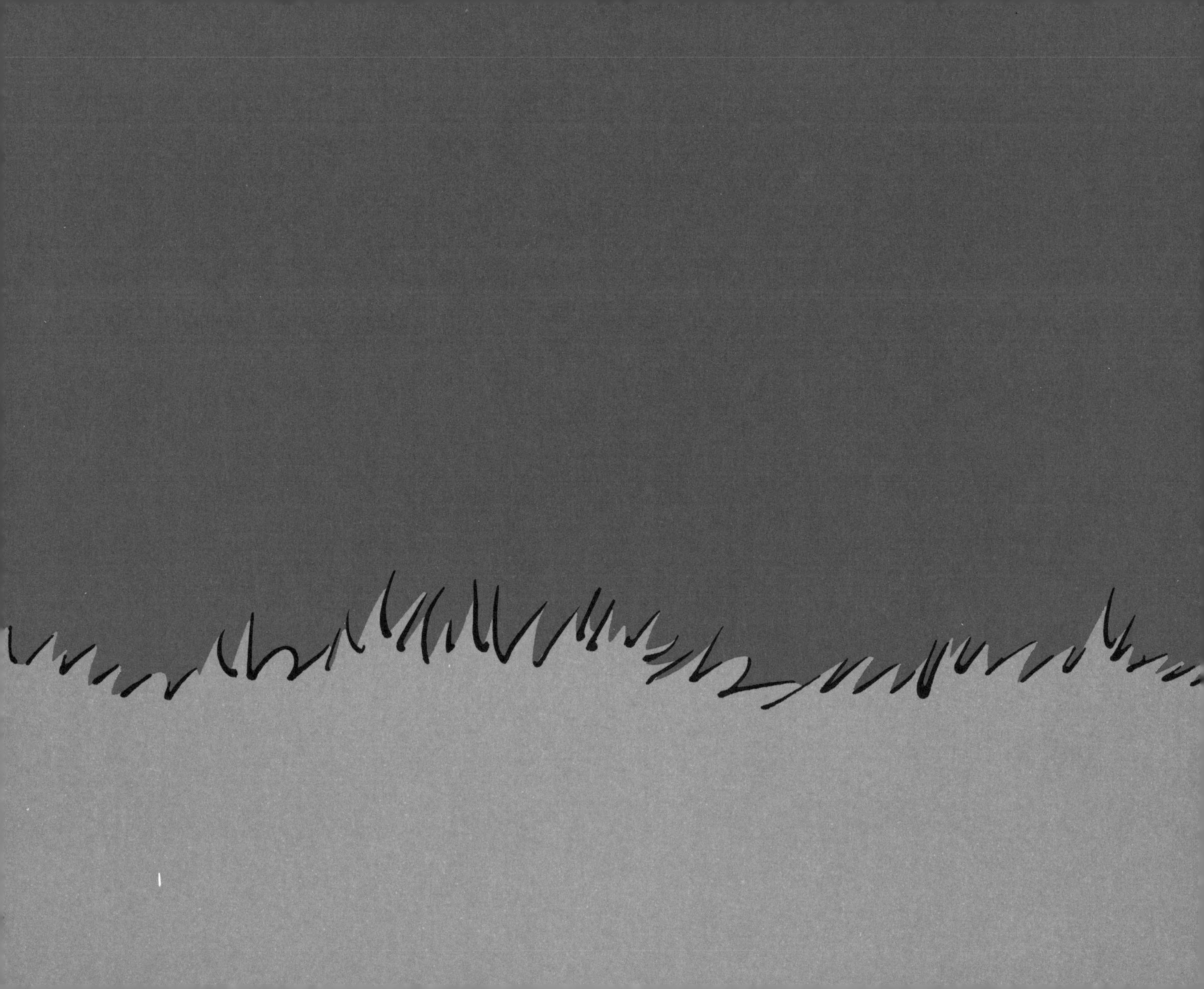

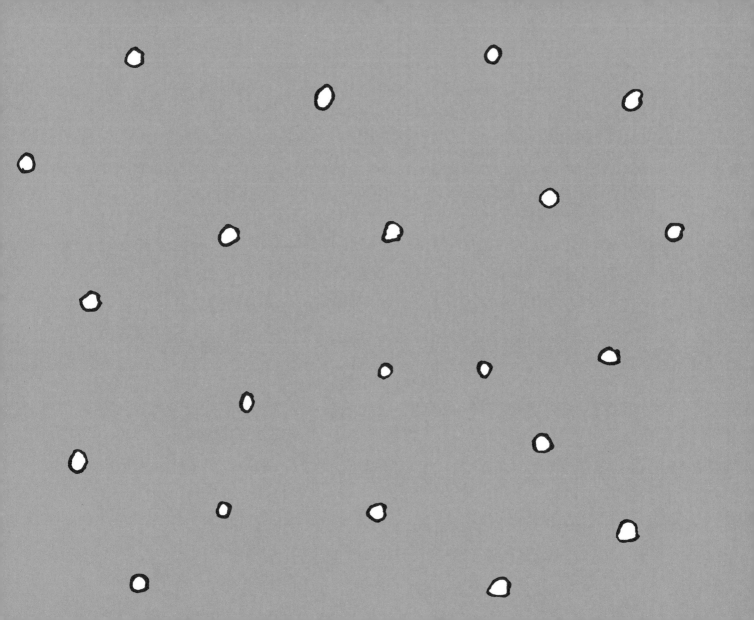

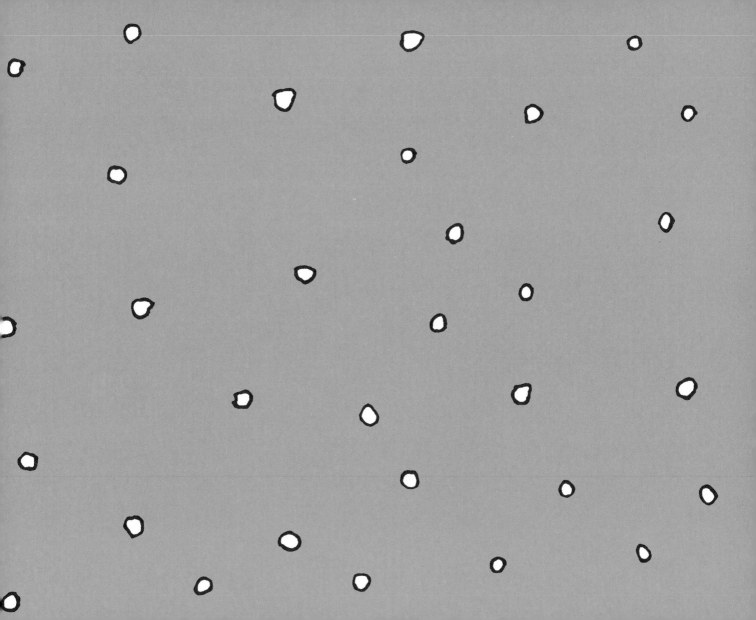

THE COMPLETE PEANUTS
by Charles M. Schulz
published by
Fantagraphics Books

Editor: Gary Groth
Designer: Seth
Production Manager: Kim Thompson
Production, assembly, and restoration: Paul Baresh
Archival and production assistance: Marcie Lee and Alexa Koenings
Index compiled by Jenna Allen and Ian Burns
Associate Publisher: Eric Reynolds
Publishers: Gary Groth & Kim Thompson

Special thanks to Jeannie Schulz, without whom
this project would not have come to fruition.
Thanks also to John R. Troy and the
Charles M. Schulz Creative Associates,
especially Paige Braddock and Kim Towner.
Thanks for special support from United Media.

Fantagraphics Books, 7563 Lake City Way, Seattle, WA 98115, USA. For a free full-color catalogue of comics,
call 1-800-657-1100. Our books may be viewed on our website at www.fantagraphics.com.

Distributed to the book trade by:

USA: W.W. Norton and Company, Inc.
500 Fifth Avenue, New York, NY 10010
212-354-5500
Order Department: 800-233-4830

CANADA: Canadian Manda Group
165 Dufferin Street, Toronto, Ontario CANADA M6K 3H6
Order department: 416-516-0911

ISBN: 978-1-60699-375-0
First printing: June, 2010   Printed in China

CHARLES M. SCHULZ

THE COMPLETE PEANUTS

1977 to 1978

"WHY ME,
LORD?"

FANTAGRAPHICS BOOKS

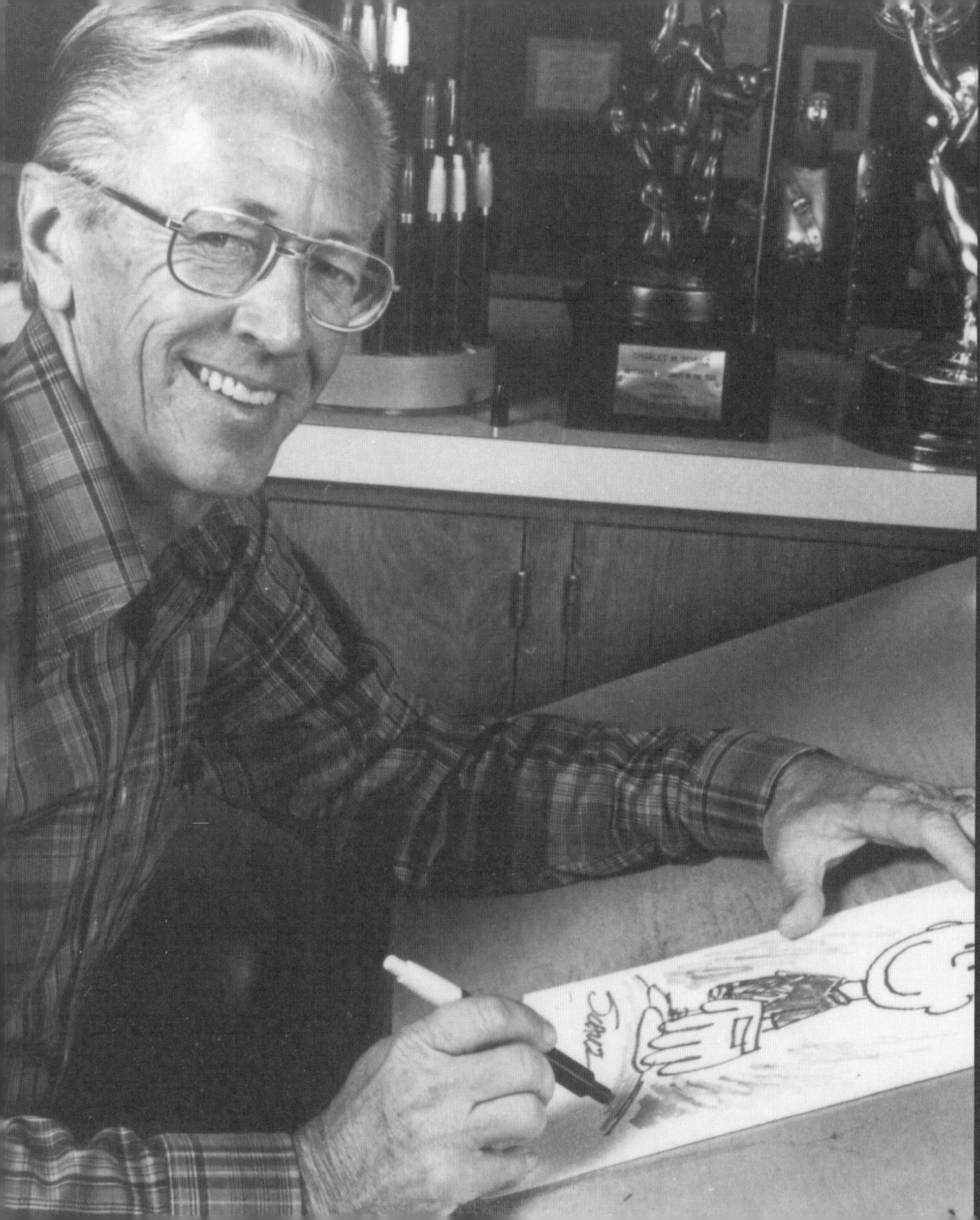

Charles M. Schulz at his drawing board at 1 Snoopy Place, circa 1975. Courtesy of the Schulz Family.

FOREWORD by ALEC BALDWIN

Peanuts has always been about two opposing human frailties to me. Floating like a comic strip's balloon over my childhood and beyond, Charles Schulz's characters have symbolized the innocence and anxiety of youth and how they affect each other. Charlie Brown was probably the first "person" I was introduced to who wanted things in life that I wanted, that I assume we all wanted; yet, at the same time, I wondered why he wanted them. He brought an existential view of the world to my attention, however simply, long before I would read Nietzsche and Sartre.

Surrounding Charlie Brown was every kind of dream, loss, hope, temptation, provocation, and frustration life has to offer. Charlie Brown did not face all of those events and challenges by himself. Schulz created boys and girls and even a dog, with an urge toward self-examination that Salinger would admire. Serving as both friends and foils for Charlie Brown, these characters would eventually forge their own identities and become icons used to distinguish personality types we have all lived among, wrestled with, and loved.

There was a woman in my life that I nicknamed Lucy. She was corrosively honest, controlling, confrontational, and the love of my life. Underneath her bluster and her rigid view of the world was a decent, caring, loyal friend. Schulz's Lucy was an element in my former girlfriend's personality as strong as any personality trait in Charlotte Brontë's women. Or Tennessee Williams' women. Or Candace Bushnell's women. Lucy foreshadowed the empowered alpha female personified by contemporary women like Billie Jean King, Margaret Thatcher, Helen Gurley Brown, and Hillary Clinton. In *Peanuts*, behind every great and greatly neurotic man is a woman coaxing you, kicking you or cooing at you, all without reservations, yet always with the best of intentions.

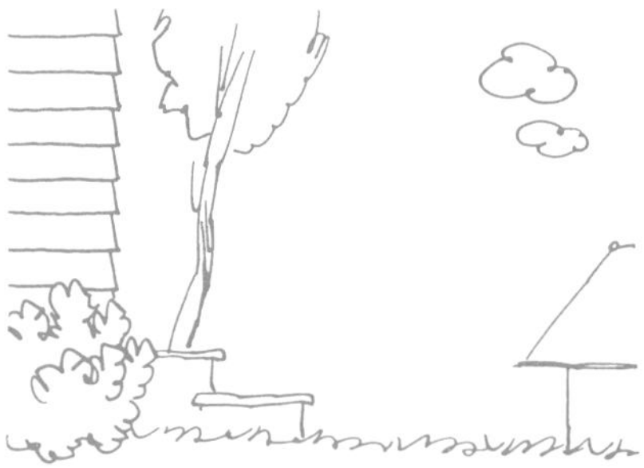

Schulz introduced me to Schroeder (perhaps the first "person" I ever met whose name began with four consecutive consonants) and Schroeder introduced me to Beethoven. Not just the name, but the man and his monolithic aura. Beethoven's bust sat atop Schroeder's piano (both scowling at the world) and compelling Schroeder onward to practice, practice, practice. Eventually, in the *Peanuts* television specials, Beethoven's actual music would emanate from that piano and, along with Vince Guaraldi's original compositions, pieces like Beethoven's monumental Hammerklavier Sonata (opus 106) became a part of my world as well.

Everyone knows a Pig-Pen, a Linus. Everyone has walked to the mirror first thing in the morning, with bed hair shooting in all directions, and thought, "It's Woodstock!" Everyone has faced, even embraced, within himself (even in middle-age!) the Walter Mitty-ish inner life of Snoopy. Snoopy is, perhaps, Schulz's most advanced, most complicated character. Whereas Charlie Brown brings his trudging, Jimmy Stewart-like decency and predictability to each one of his quixotic endeavors, Snoopy, in his own mind, is more Wright Brothers, more Bill Gates, more "I see things that never were and say why not" than any of the other *Peanuts* troupe. Snoopy is brave to the point of stupidity — in his own mind. He is cool in a manner only Ian Fleming could capture — in his own mind. On the fifty-yard line of life, he can score at will with seconds on the clock — in his own mind. Part Chuck Yeager, part James Bond, part Johnny Unitas, Snoopy is that part of us that will not rest, will not resign, will not retire until all of the Red Barons have been eliminated from our skies. Whereas Charlie Brown is faith, Snoopy is hope. Whereas Charlie Brown believes all will end well, Snoopy will make it so. At least in his own mind.

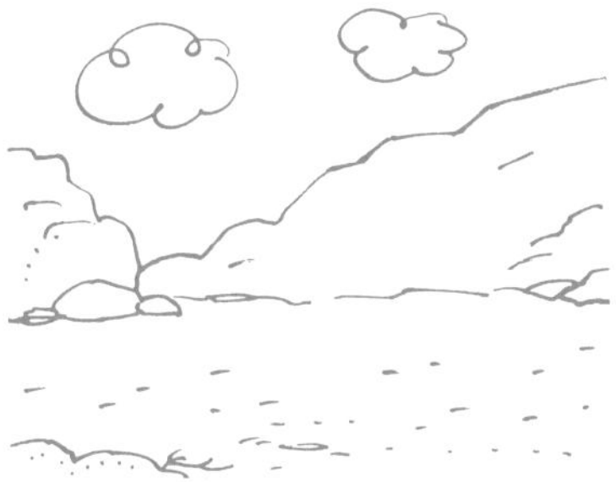

When Schulz's characters appeared on TV, Schulz was taking an enormous risk. His unimaginably successful creations seemed, on the surface, ineluctably "written": to be seen and read, but not heard. Then Lee Mendelson, Bill Melendez, and Schulz pulled off something that was nothing less than magical. They gave voice and music and design to an animated *Peanuts*. The result was programming that joins Frank Capra and Andy Williams and cranberry sauce as emblematic of what the holidays could be, and often are, if only in our hearts.

Charles Schulz is like Twain to me. Simple characters, simple settings, simple stories. But their impact is enormous, it is moving, and it is forever. And though I can only speculate that if Mark Twain lived in our more desperately self-rationalizing times and had decided he wanted to draw his characters, he'd have created something like *Peanuts*, thank God Schulz actually did.

1977
TO
1978

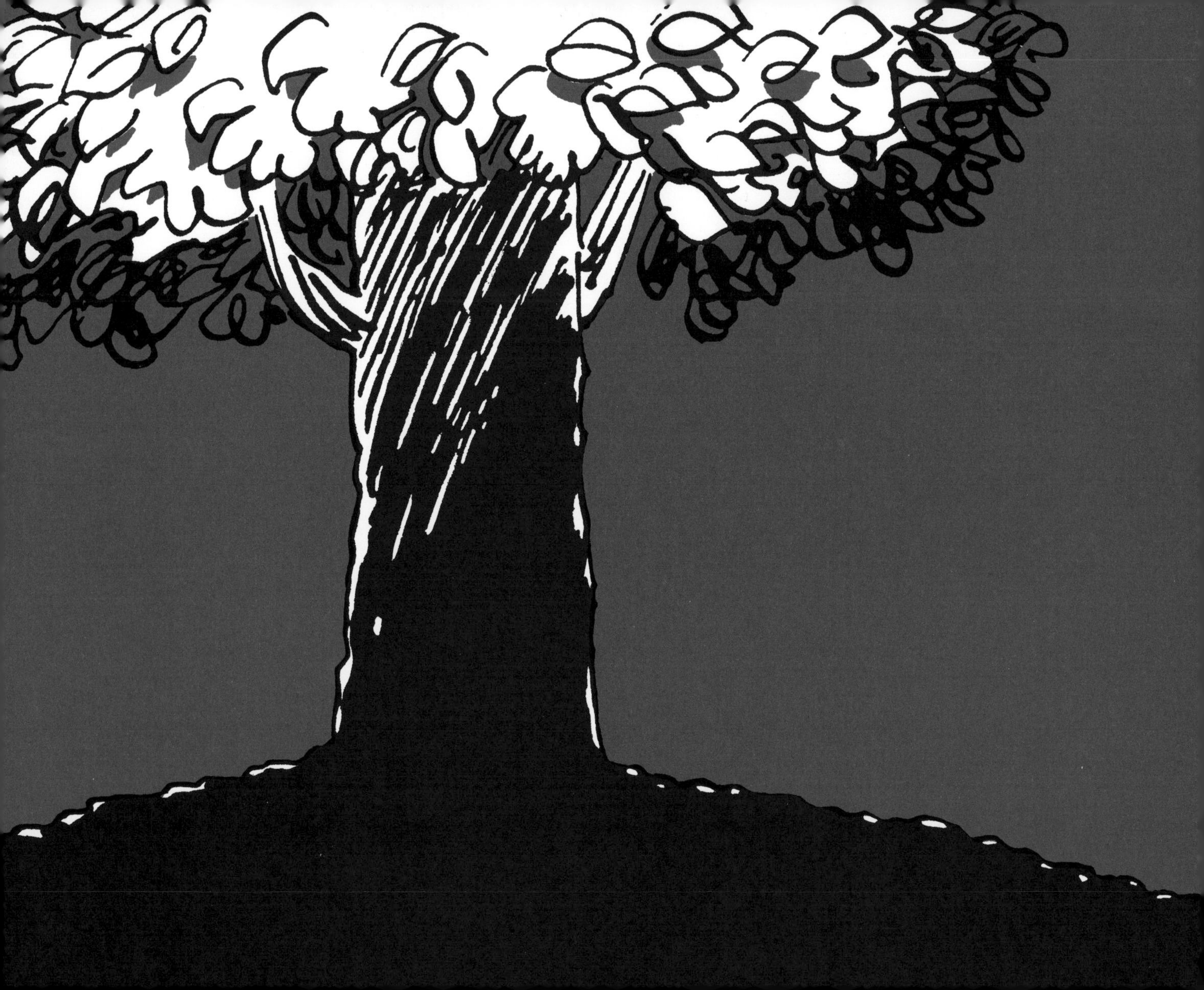

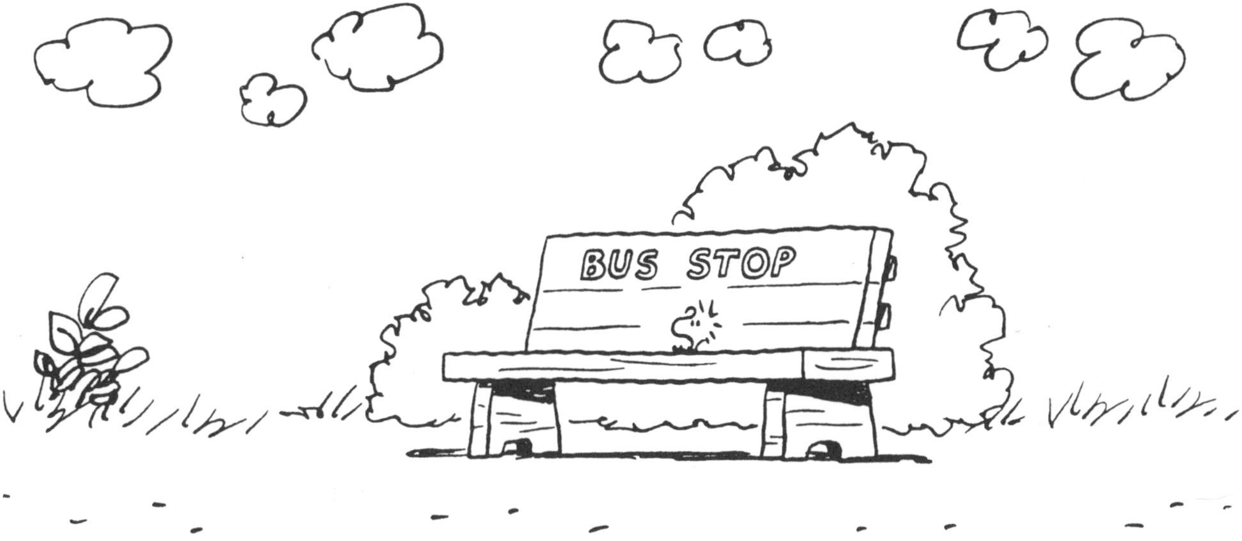
BUS STOP

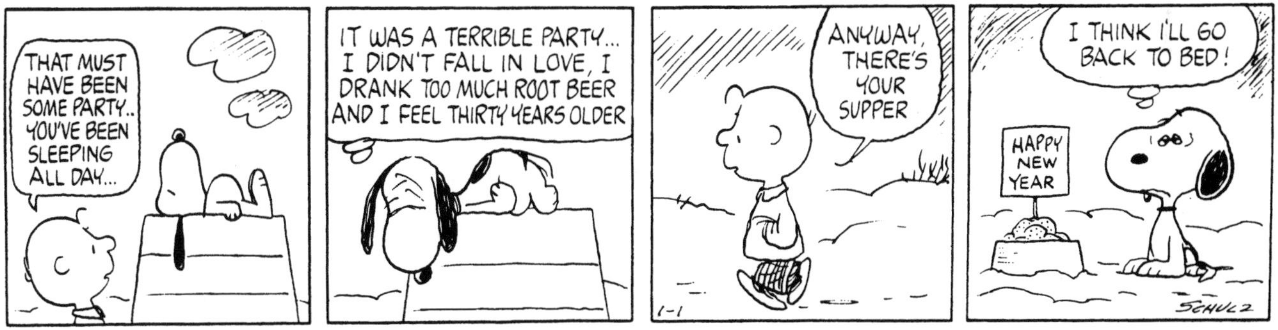
THAT MUST HAVE BEEN SOME PARTY.. YOU'VE BEEN SLEEPING ALL DAY...
IT WAS A TERRIBLE PARTY... I DIDN'T FALL IN LOVE, I DRANK TOO MUCH ROOT BEER AND I FEEL THIRTY YEARS OLDER
1-1
ANYWAY, THERE'S YOUR SUPPER
I THINK I'LL GO BACK TO BED!
HAPPY NEW YEAR
SCHULZ

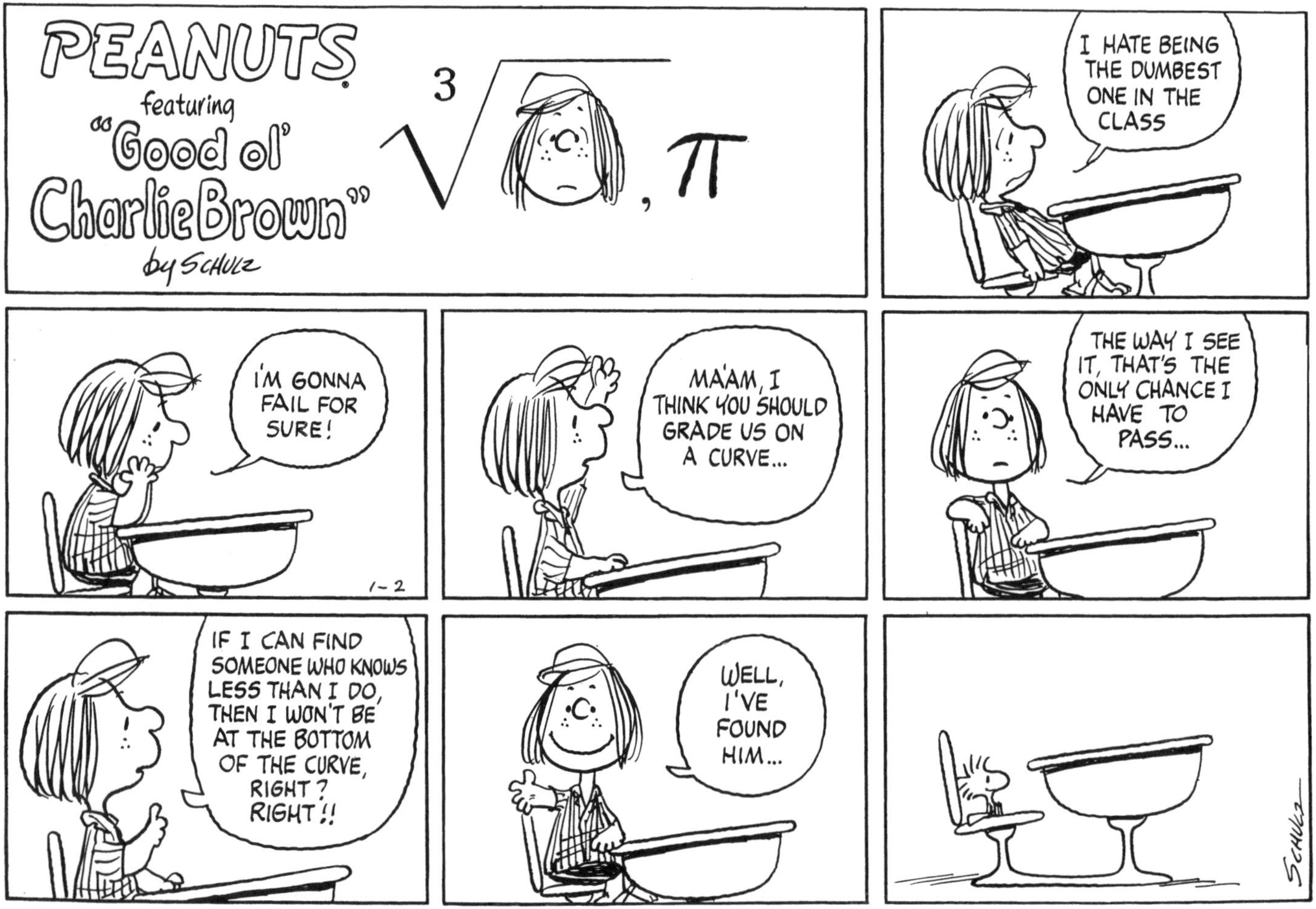
PEANUTS
featuring
"Good ol' CharlieBrown"
by SCHULZ
3
I HATE BEING THE DUMBEST ONE IN THE CLASS
I'M GONNA FAIL FOR SURE!
1-2
MA'AM, I THINK YOU SHOULD GRADE US ON A CURVE...
THE WAY I SEE IT, THAT'S THE ONLY CHANCE I HAVE TO PASS...
IF I CAN FIND SOMEONE WHO KNOWS LESS THAN I DO, THEN I WON'T BE AT THE BOTTOM OF THE CURVE, RIGHT? RIGHT!!
WELL, I'VE FOUND HIM...
SCHULZ

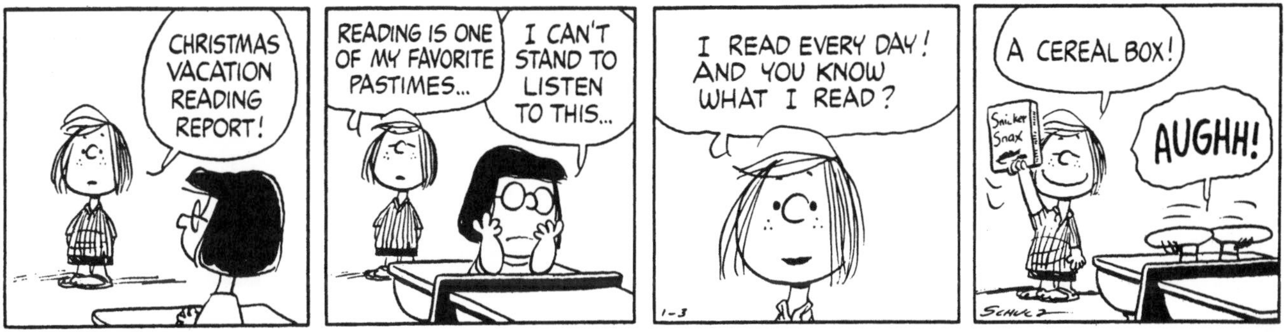
CHRISTMAS VACATION READING REPORT!
READING IS ONE OF MY FAVORITE PASTIMES...
I CAN'T STAND TO LISTEN TO THIS...
I READ EVERY DAY! AND YOU KNOW WHAT I READ?
1-3
A CEREAL BOX!
AUGHH!
Snicker Snax

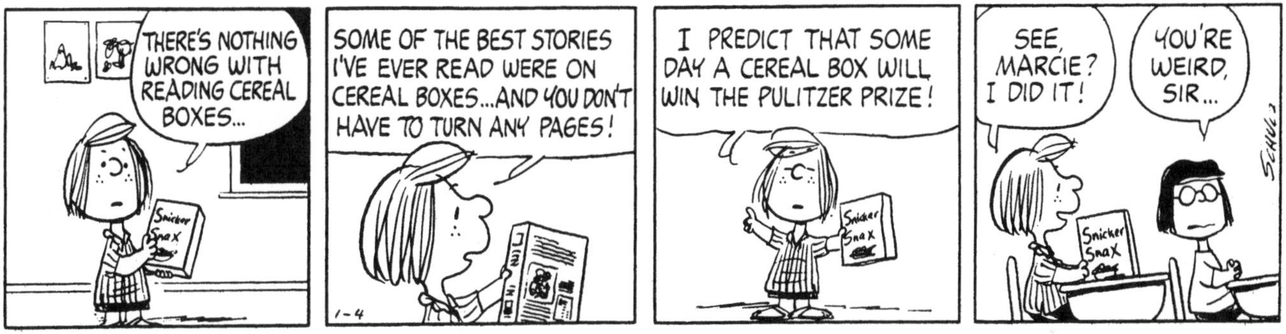
THERE'S NOTHING WRONG WITH READING CEREAL BOXES...
SOME OF THE BEST STORIES I'VE EVER READ WERE ON CEREAL BOXES...AND YOU DON'T HAVE TO TURN ANY PAGES!
1-4
I PREDICT THAT SOME DAY A CEREAL BOX WILL WIN THE PULITZER PRIZE!
SEE, MARCIE? I DID IT!
YOU'RE WEIRD, SIR...

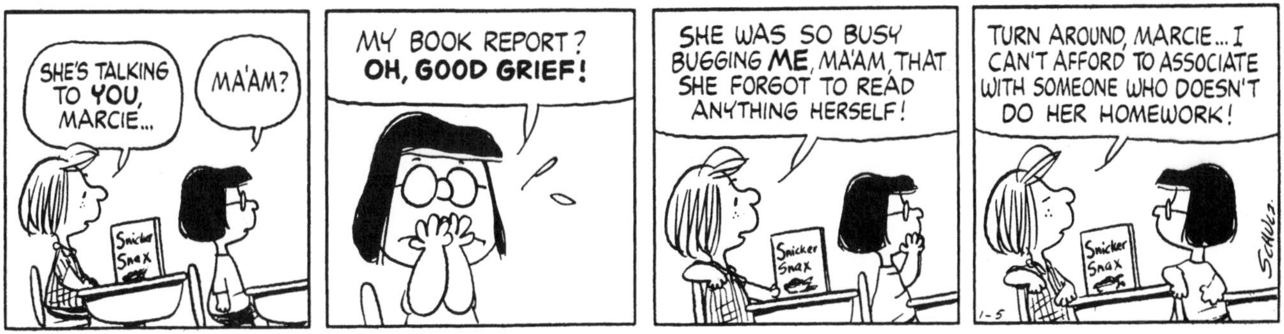
SHE'S TALKING TO **YOU**, MARCIE...
MA'AM?
MY BOOK REPORT? **OH, GOOD GRIEF!**
SHE WAS SO BUSY BUGGING **ME**, MA'AM, THAT SHE FORGOT TO READ ANYTHING HERSELF!
TURN AROUND, MARCIE... I CAN'T AFFORD TO ASSOCIATE WITH SOMEONE WHO DOESN'T DO HER HOMEWORK!
1-5

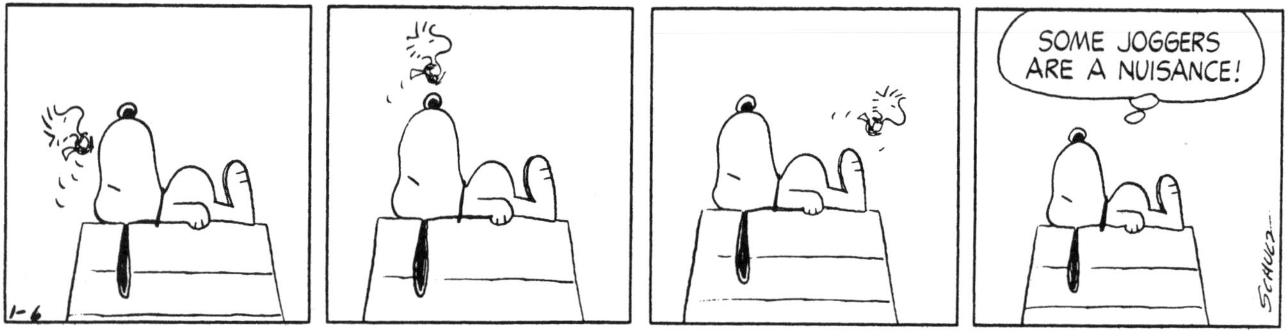
1-6
SOME JOGGERS ARE A NUISANCE!

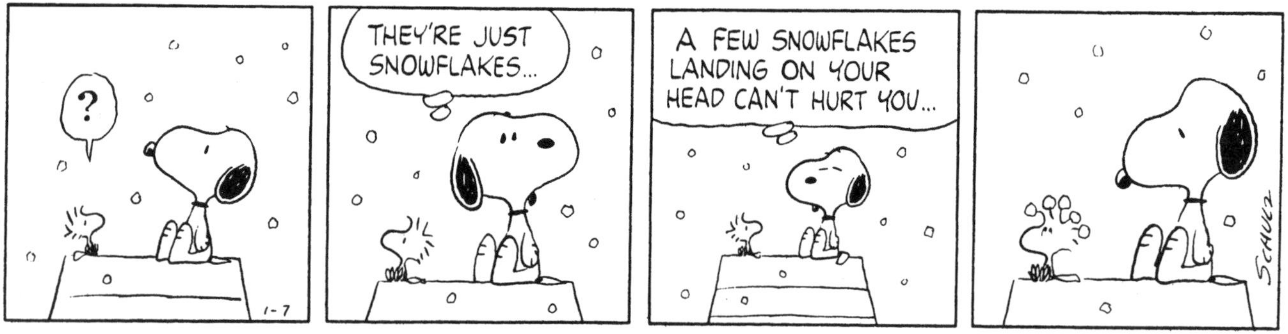
?
1-7
THEY'RE JUST SNOWFLAKES...
A FEW SNOWFLAKES LANDING ON YOUR HEAD CAN'T HURT YOU...

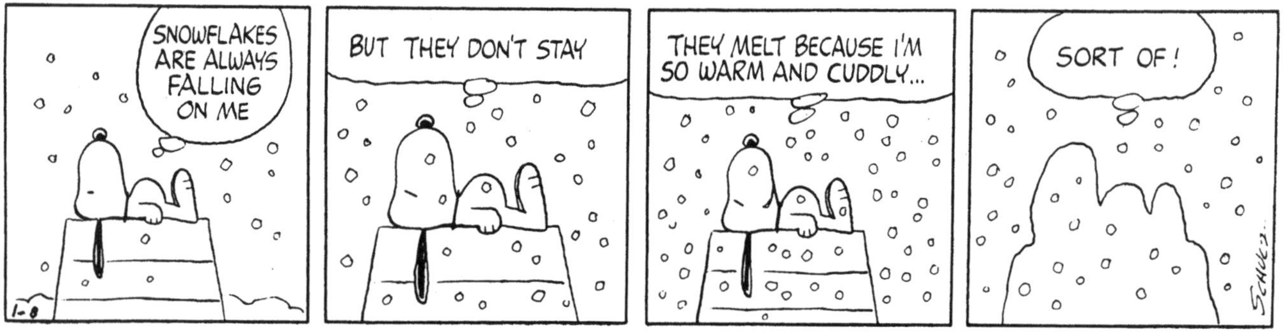
1-8
SNOWFLAKES ARE ALWAYS FALLING ON ME
BUT THEY DON'T STAY
THEY MELT BECAUSE I'M SO WARM AND CUDDLY...
SORT OF!

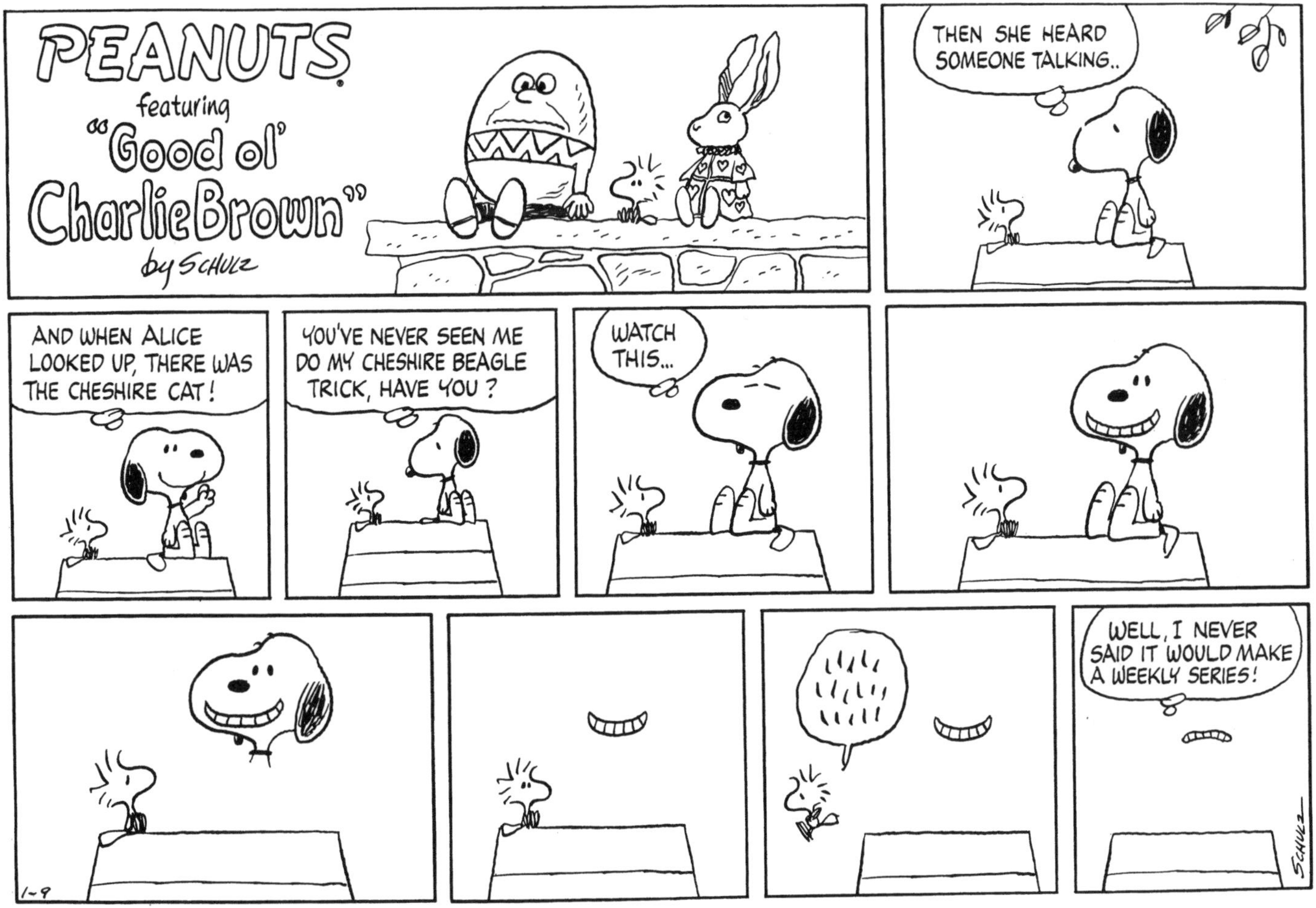
PEANUTS
featuring
"Good ol' Charlie Brown"
by SCHULZ
THEN SHE HEARD SOMEONE TALKING..
AND WHEN ALICE LOOKED UP, THERE WAS THE CHESHIRE CAT!
YOU'VE NEVER SEEN ME DO MY CHESHIRE BEAGLE TRICK, HAVE YOU?
WATCH THIS...
1-9
WELL, I NEVER SAID IT WOULD MAKE A WEEKLY SERIES!
SCHULZ

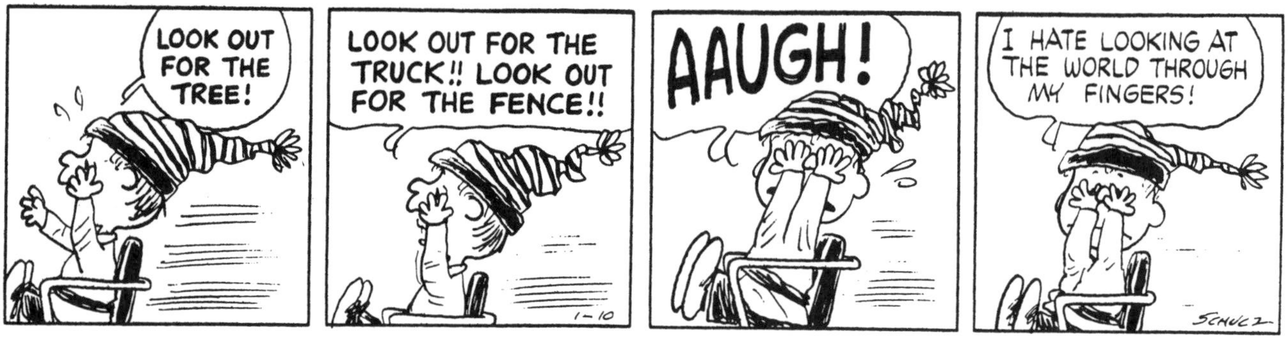
LOOK OUT FOR THE TREE!
LOOK OUT FOR THE TRUCK!! LOOK OUT FOR THE FENCE!!
AAUGH!
I HATE LOOKING AT THE WORLD THROUGH MY FINGERS!

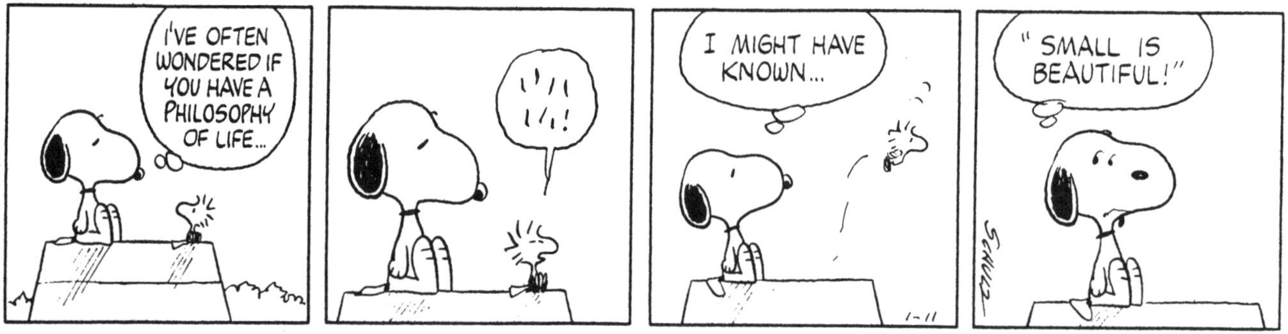
I'VE OFTEN WONDERED IF YOU HAVE A PHILOSOPHY OF LIFE...
I MIGHT HAVE KNOWN...
"SMALL IS BEAUTIFUL!"

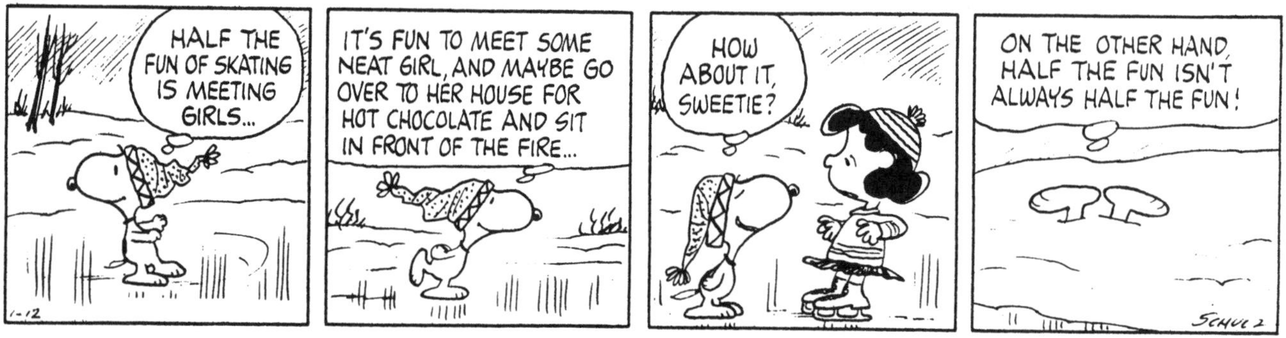
HALF THE FUN OF SKATING IS MEETING GIRLS...
IT'S FUN TO MEET SOME NEAT GIRL, AND MAYBE GO OVER TO HER HOUSE FOR HOT CHOCOLATE AND SIT IN FRONT OF THE FIRE...
HOW ABOUT IT, SWEETIE?
ON THE OTHER HAND, HALF THE FUN ISN'T ALWAYS HALF THE FUN!

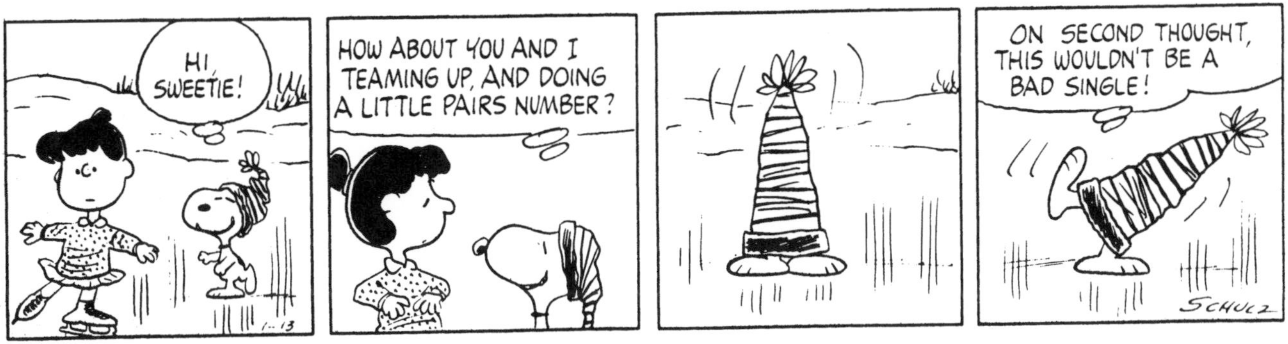
HI SWEETIE!
HOW ABOUT YOU AND I TEAMING UP, AND DOING A LITTLE PAIRS NUMBER?
ON SECOND THOUGHT, THIS WOULDN'T BE A BAD SINGLE!

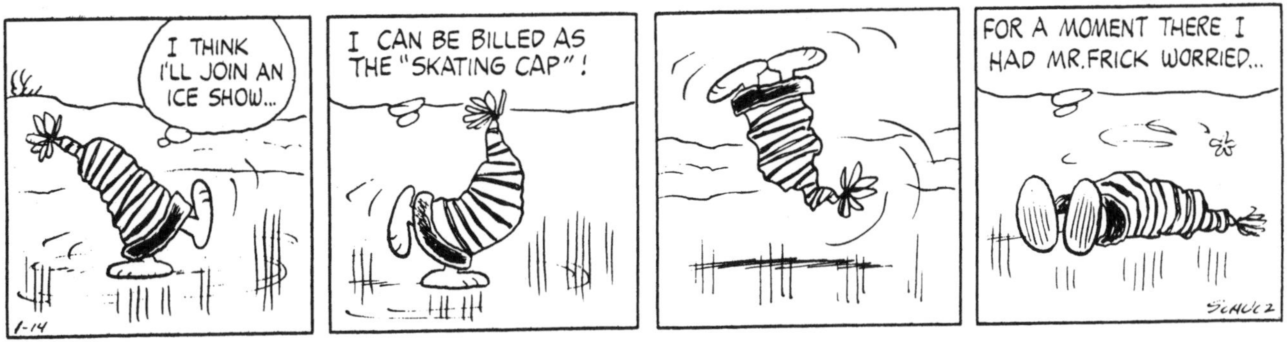
I THINK I'LL JOIN AN ICE SHOW...
I CAN BE BILLED AS THE "SKATING CAP"!
FOR A MOMENT THERE I HAD MR. FRICK WORRIED...

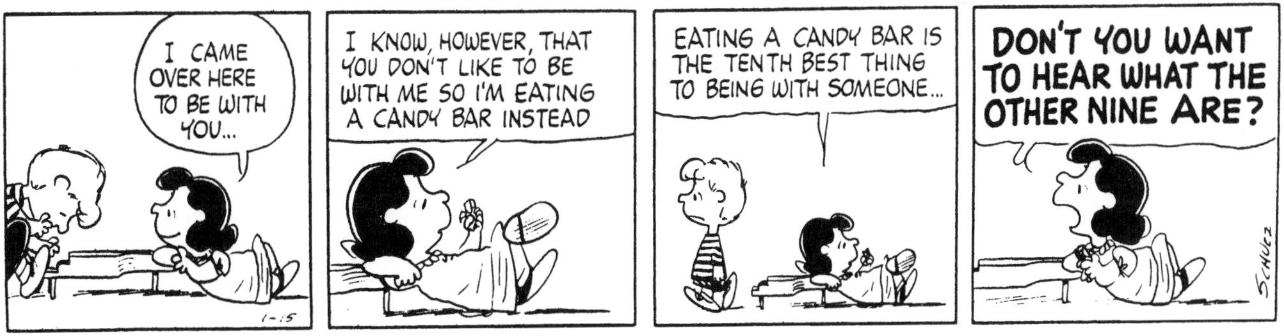
I CAME OVER HERE TO BE WITH YOU...
I KNOW, HOWEVER, THAT YOU DON'T LIKE TO BE WITH ME SO I'M EATING A CANDY BAR INSTEAD
EATING A CANDY BAR IS THE TENTH BEST THING TO BEING WITH SOMEONE...
DON'T YOU WANT TO HEAR WHAT THE OTHER NINE ARE?

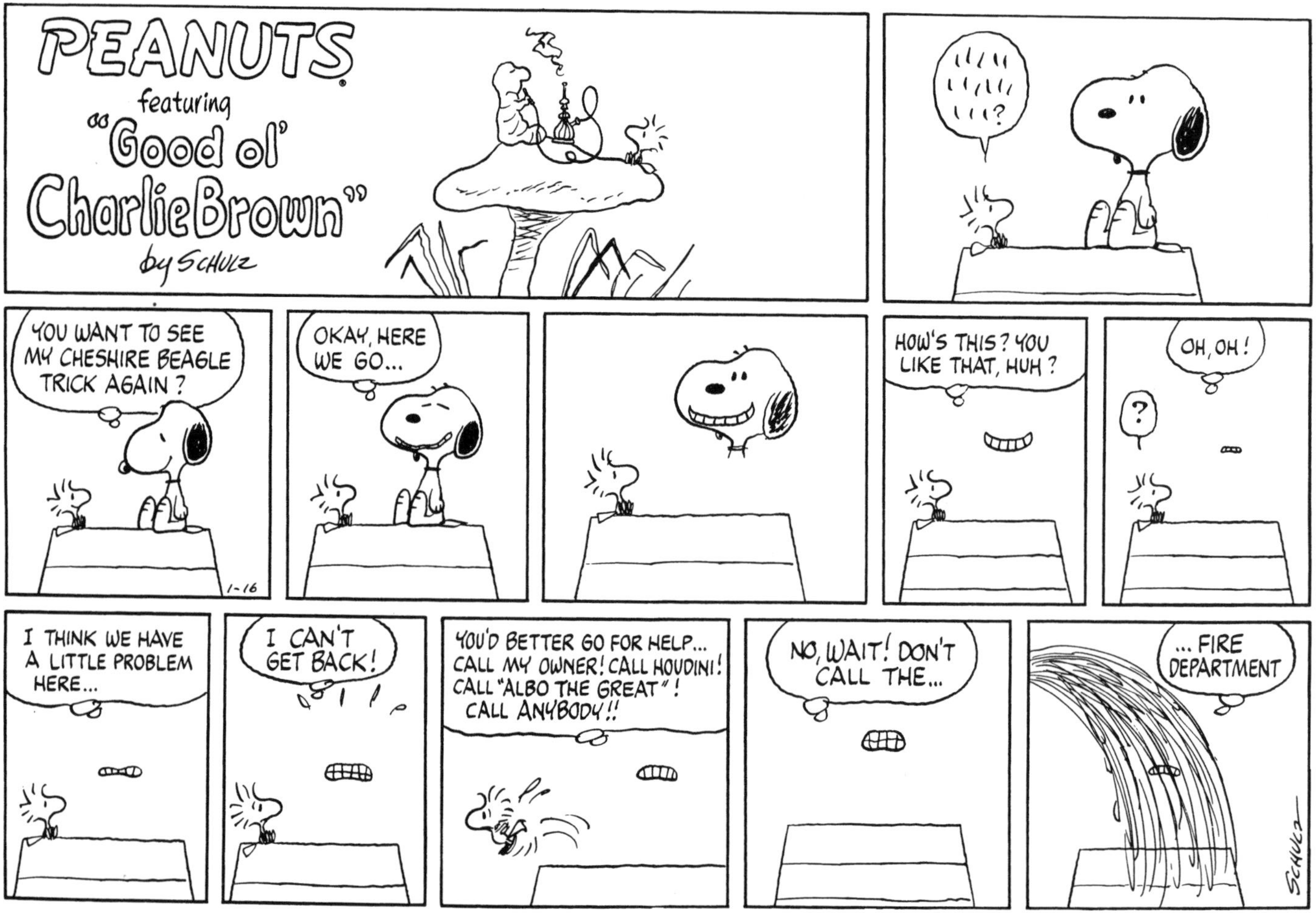
PEANUTS
featuring
"Good ol' CharlieBrown"
by SCHULZ
YOU WANT TO SEE MY CHESHIRE BEAGLE TRICK AGAIN ?
1-16
OKAY, HERE WE GO...
HOW'S THIS ? YOU LIKE THAT, HUH ?
?
OH, OH !
I THINK WE HAVE A LITTLE PROBLEM HERE...
I CAN'T GET BACK !
YOU'D BETTER GO FOR HELP... CALL MY OWNER! CALL HOUDINI! CALL "ALBO THE GREAT" ! CALL ANYBODY !!
NO, WAIT! DON'T CALL THE...
...FIRE DEPARTMENT
SCHULZ

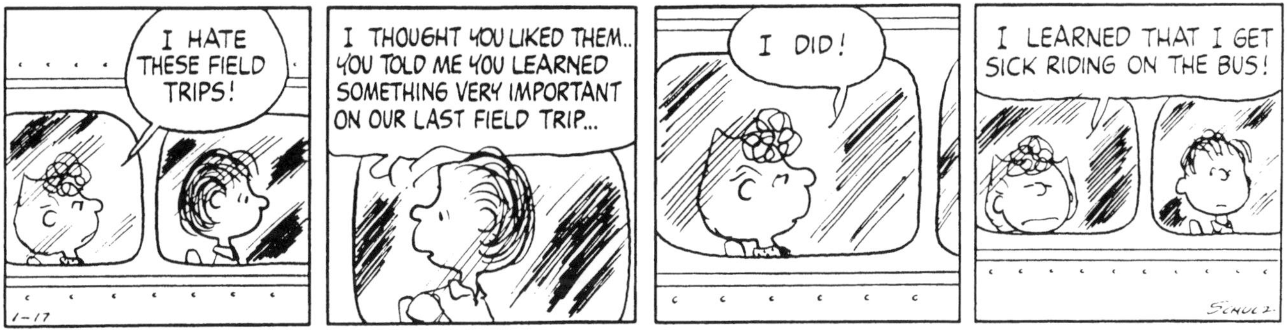
I HATE THESE FIELD TRIPS!
I THOUGHT YOU LIKED THEM.. YOU TOLD ME YOU LEARNED SOMETHING VERY IMPORTANT ON OUR LAST FIELD TRIP...
I DID!
I LEARNED THAT I GET SICK RIDING ON THE BUS!
SCHULZ

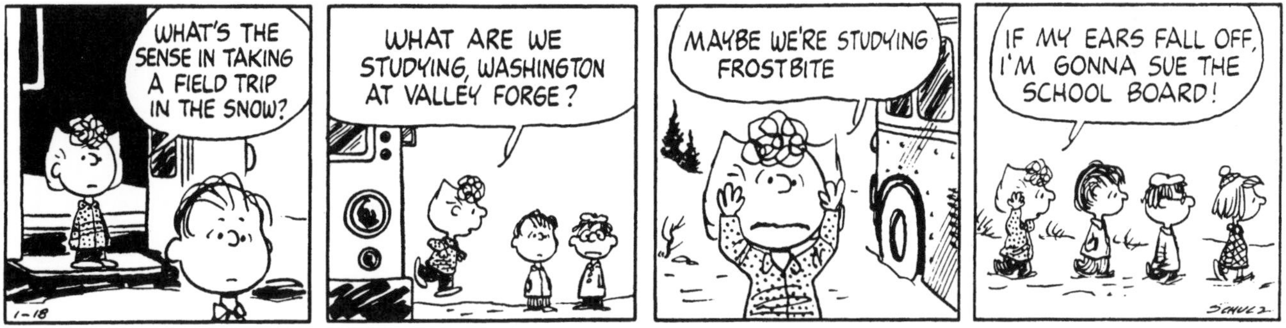
WHAT'S THE SENSE IN TAKING A FIELD TRIP IN THE SNOW?
WHAT ARE WE STUDYING, WASHINGTON AT VALLEY FORGE?
MAYBE WE'RE STUDYING FROSTBITE
IF MY EARS FALL OFF, I'M GONNA SUE THE SCHOOL BOARD!
SCHULZ

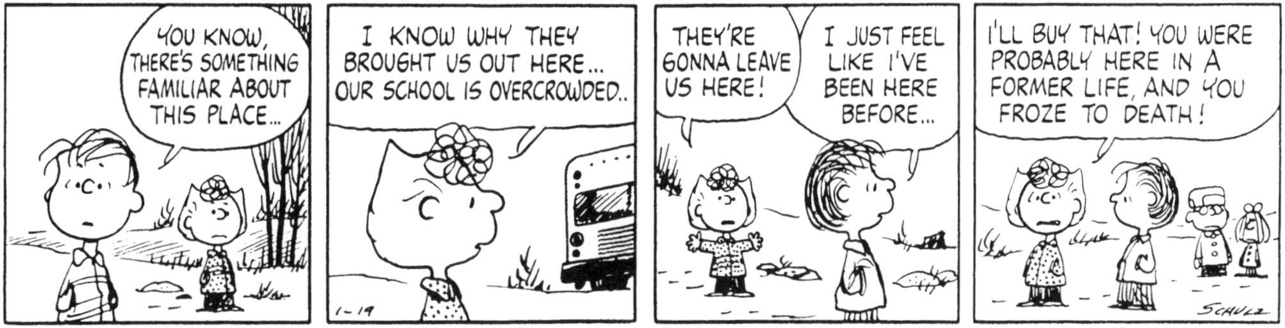
YOU KNOW, THERE'S SOMETHING FAMILIAR ABOUT THIS PLACE...
I KNOW WHY THEY BROUGHT US OUT HERE... OUR SCHOOL IS OVERCROWDED..
THEY'RE GONNA LEAVE US HERE!
I JUST FEEL LIKE I'VE BEEN HERE BEFORE...
I'LL BUY THAT! YOU WERE PROBABLY HERE IN A FORMER LIFE, AND YOU FROZE TO DEATH!
SCHULZ

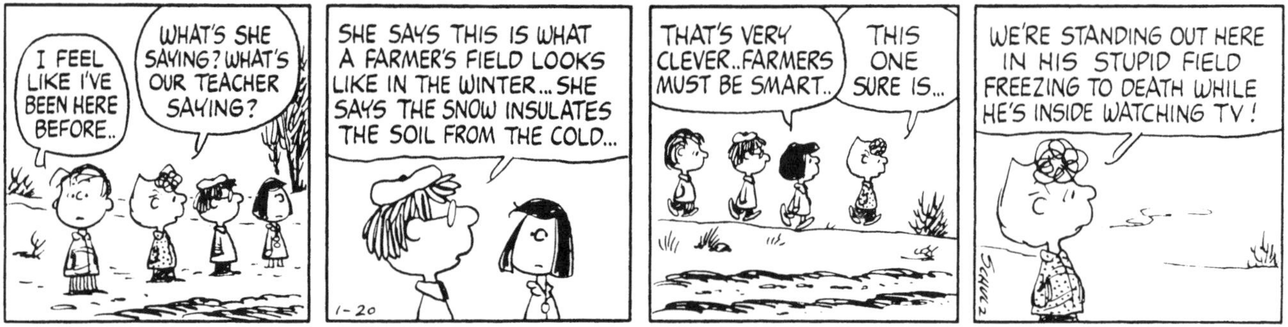
I FEEL LIKE I'VE BEEN HERE BEFORE..
WHAT'S SHE SAYING? WHAT'S OUR TEACHER SAYING?
SHE SAYS THIS IS WHAT A FARMER'S FIELD LOOKS LIKE IN THE WINTER... SHE SAYS THE SNOW INSULATES THE SOIL FROM THE COLD...
1-20
THAT'S VERY CLEVER..FARMERS MUST BE SMART..
THIS ONE SURE IS...
WE'RE STANDING OUT HERE IN HIS STUPID FIELD FREEZING TO DEATH WHILE HE'S INSIDE WATCHING TV!

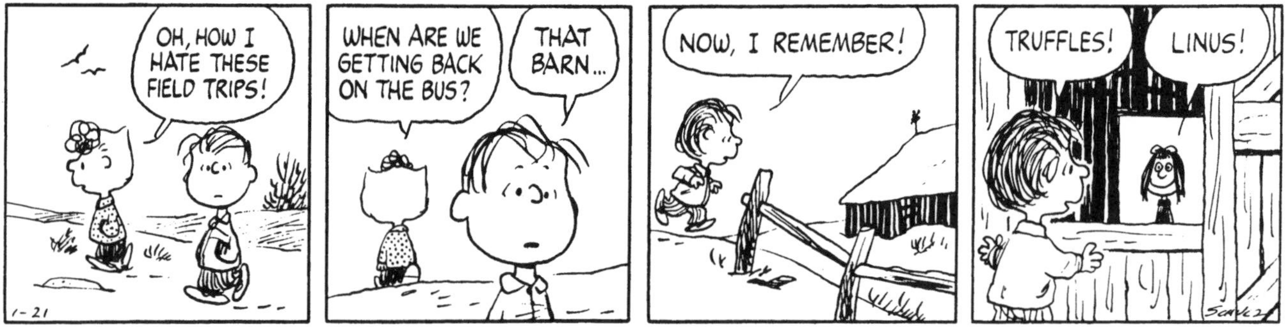
OH, HOW I HATE THESE FIELD TRIPS!
1-21
WHEN ARE WE GETTING BACK ON THE BUS?
THAT BARN...
NOW, I REMEMBER!
TRUFFLES!
LINUS!

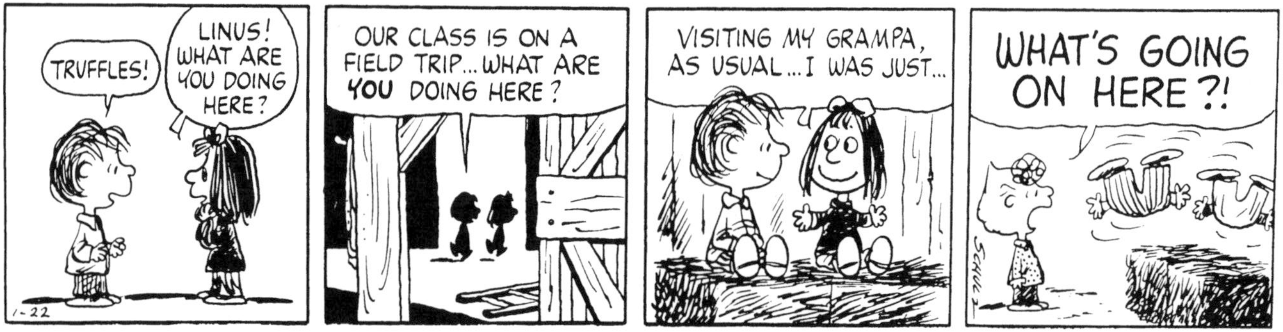
TRUFFLES!
LINUS! WHAT ARE YOU DOING HERE?
1-22
OUR CLASS IS ON A FIELD TRIP... WHAT ARE YOU DOING HERE?
VISITING MY GRAMPA, AS USUAL... I WAS JUST...
WHAT'S GOING ON HERE?!

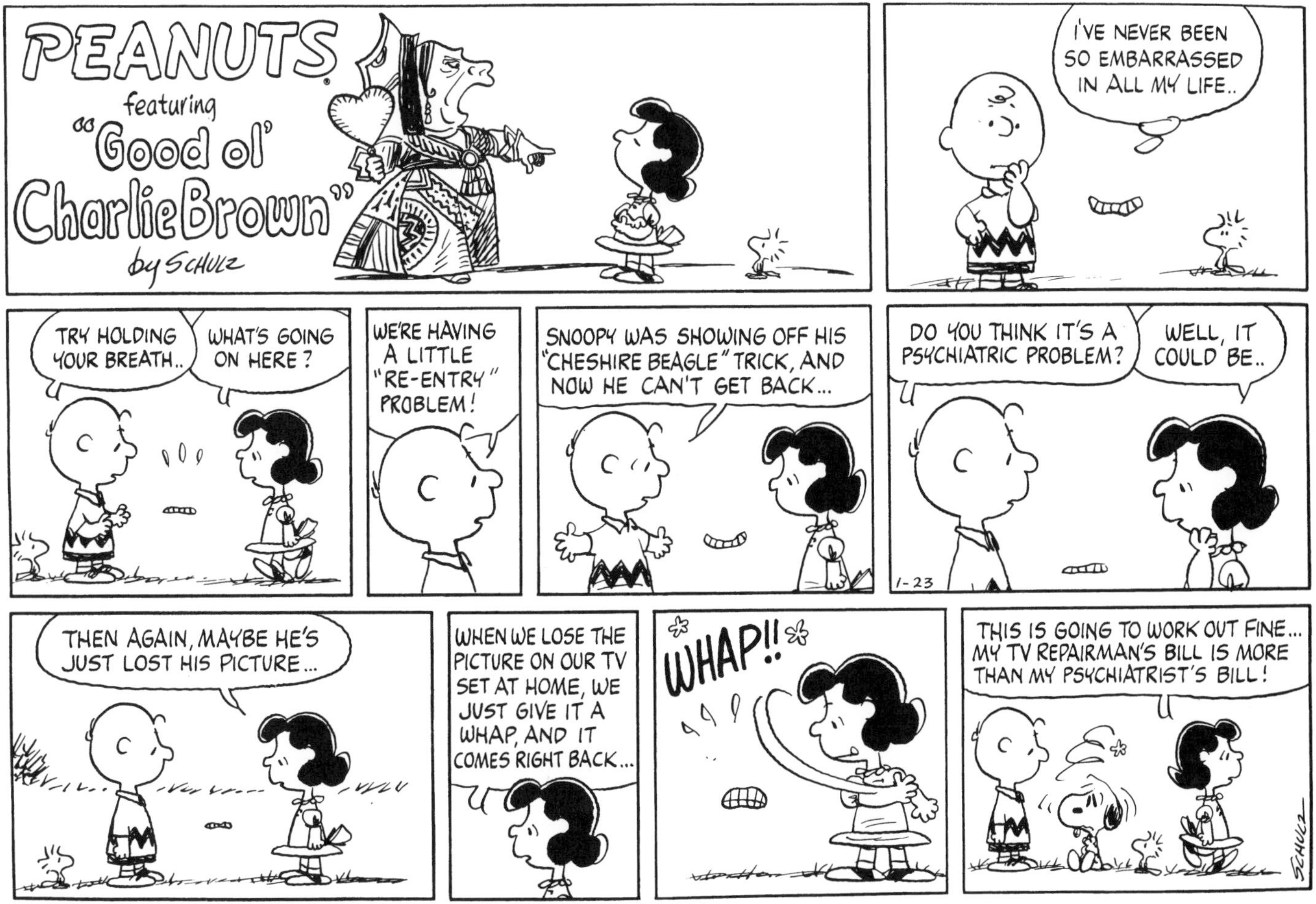
PEANUTS
featuring "Good ol' CharlieBrown"
by SCHULZ
I'VE NEVER BEEN SO EMBARRASSED IN ALL MY LIFE..
TRY HOLDING YOUR BREATH..
WHAT'S GOING ON HERE?
WE'RE HAVING A LITTLE "RE-ENTRY" PROBLEM!
SNOOPY WAS SHOWING OFF HIS "CHESHIRE BEAGLE" TRICK, AND NOW HE CAN'T GET BACK...
DO YOU THINK IT'S A PSYCHIATRIC PROBLEM?
WELL, IT COULD BE..
1-23
THEN AGAIN, MAYBE HE'S JUST LOST HIS PICTURE...
WHEN WE LOSE THE PICTURE ON OUR TV SET AT HOME, WE JUST GIVE IT A WHAP, AND IT COMES RIGHT BACK...
WHAP!!
THIS IS GOING TO WORK OUT FINE... MY TV REPAIRMAN'S BILL IS MORE THAN MY PSYCHIATRIST'S BILL!
SCHULZ

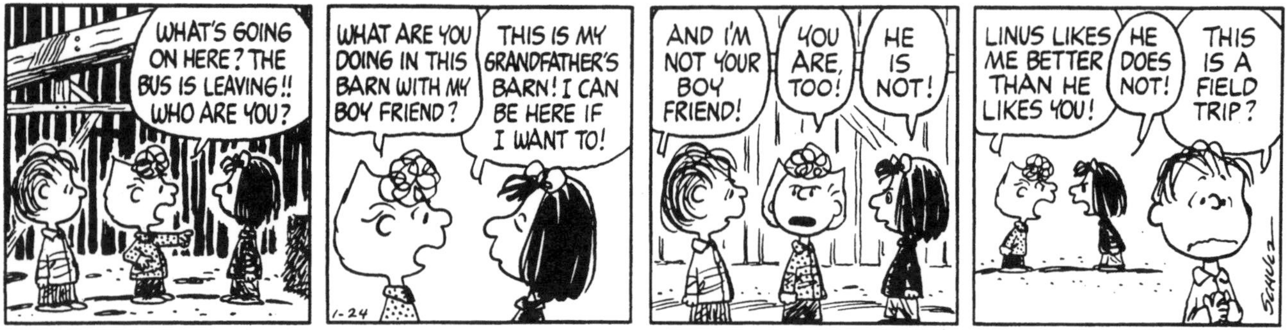
WHAT'S GOING ON HERE? THE BUS IS LEAVING!! WHO ARE YOU?
WHAT ARE YOU DOING IN THIS BARN WITH MY BOY FRIEND?
THIS IS MY GRANDFATHER'S BARN! I CAN BE HERE IF I WANT TO!
AND I'M NOT YOUR BOY FRIEND!
YOU ARE, TOO!
HE IS NOT!
LINUS LIKES ME BETTER THAN HE LIKES YOU!
HE DOES NOT!
THIS IS A FIELD TRIP?

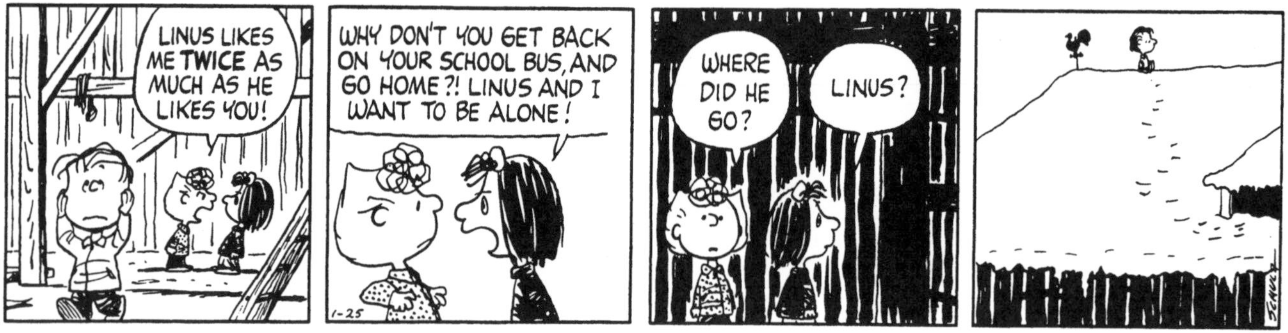
LINUS LIKES ME **TWICE** AS MUCH AS HE LIKES YOU!
WHY DON'T YOU GET BACK ON YOUR SCHOOL BUS, AND GO HOME?! LINUS AND I WANT TO BE ALONE!
WHERE DID HE GO?
LINUS?

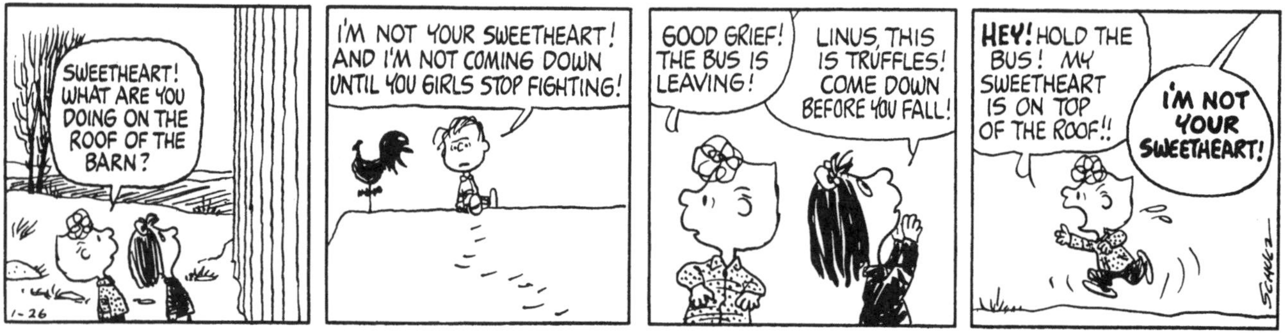
SWEETHEART! WHAT ARE YOU DOING ON THE ROOF OF THE BARN?
I'M NOT YOUR SWEETHEART! AND I'M NOT COMING DOWN UNTIL YOU GIRLS STOP FIGHTING!
GOOD GRIEF! THE BUS IS LEAVING!
LINUS, THIS IS TRUFFLES! COME DOWN BEFORE YOU FALL!
HEY! HOLD THE BUS! MY SWEETHEART IS ON TOP OF THE ROOF!!
I'M NOT YOUR SWEETHEART!

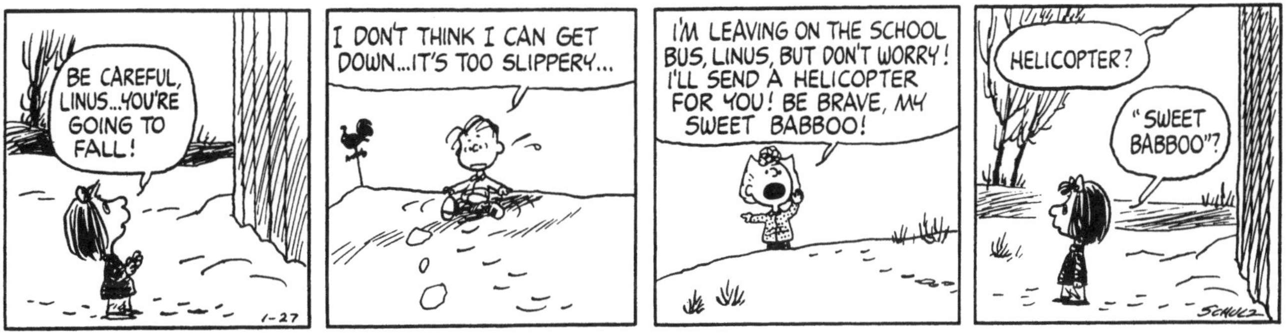
BE CAREFUL, LINUS...YOU'RE GOING TO FALL!
1-27
I DON'T THINK I CAN GET DOWN...IT'S TOO SLIPPERY...
I'M LEAVING ON THE SCHOOL BUS, LINUS, BUT DON'T WORRY! I'LL SEND A HELICOPTER FOR YOU! BE BRAVE, MY SWEET BABBOO!
HELICOPTER?
"SWEET BABBOO"?
SCHULZ

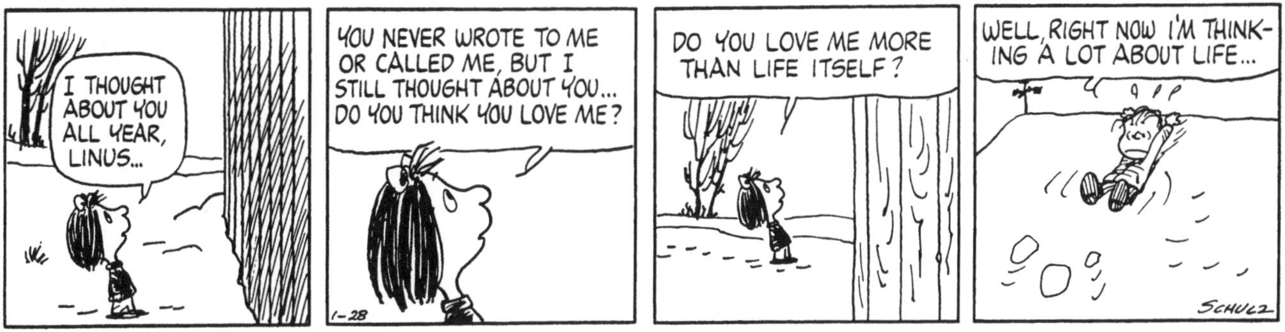
I THOUGHT ABOUT YOU ALL YEAR, LINUS...
YOU NEVER WROTE TO ME OR CALLED ME, BUT I STILL THOUGHT ABOUT YOU... DO YOU THINK YOU LOVE ME?
1-28
DO YOU LOVE ME MORE THAN LIFE ITSELF?
WELL, RIGHT NOW I'M THINKING A LOT ABOUT LIFE...
SCHULZ

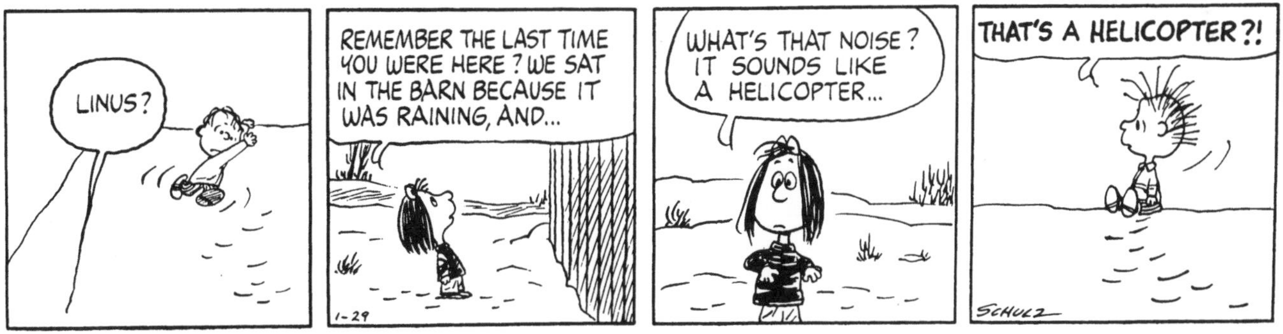
LINUS?
REMEMBER THE LAST TIME YOU WERE HERE? WE SAT IN THE BARN BECAUSE IT WAS RAINING, AND...
1-29
WHAT'S THAT NOISE? IT SOUNDS LIKE A HELICOPTER...
THAT'S A HELICOPTER?!
SCHULZ

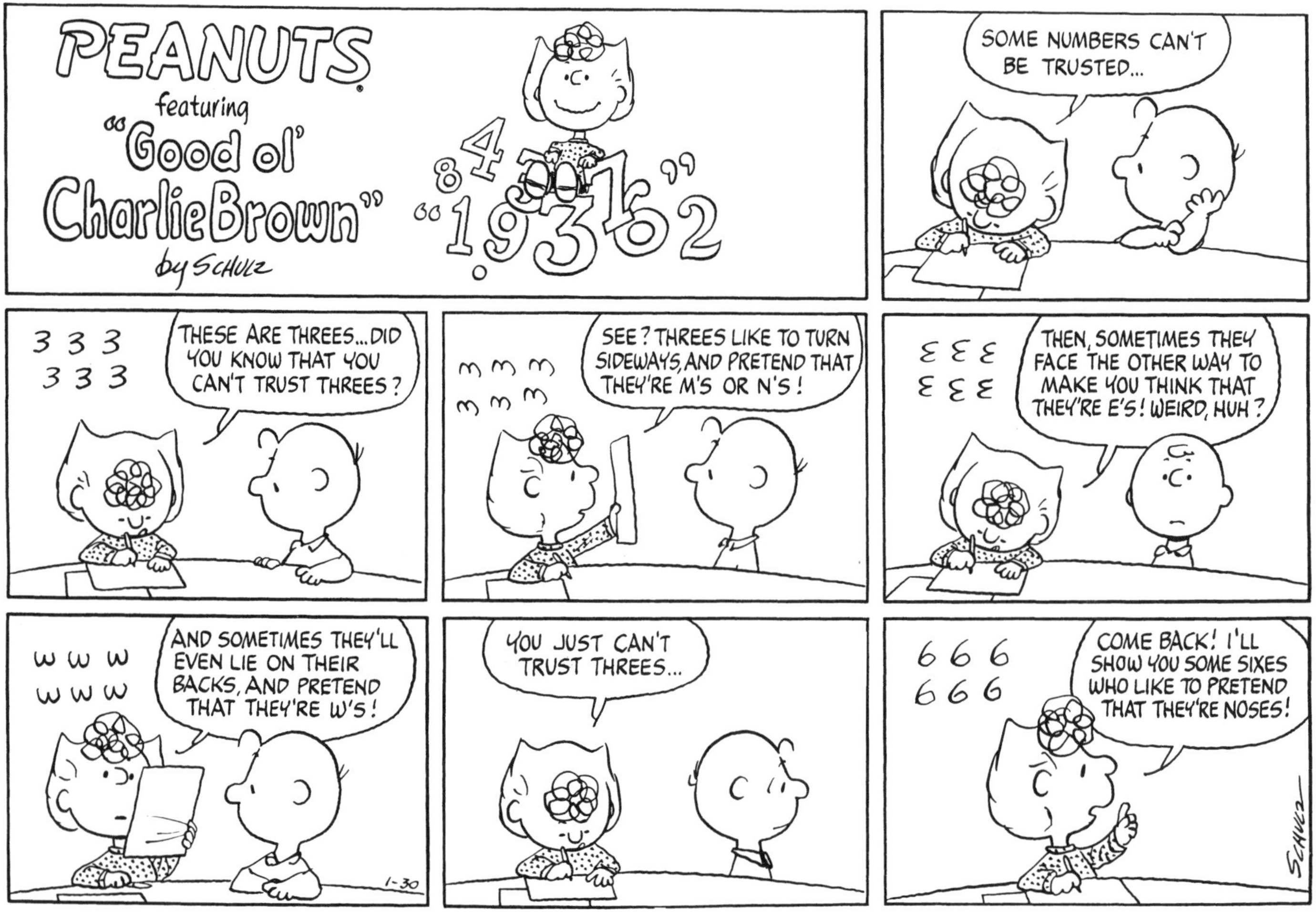
PEANUTS
featuring "Good ol' Charlie Brown"
by SCHULZ
"1962"
SOME NUMBERS CAN'T BE TRUSTED...
3 3 3
3 3 3
THESE ARE THREES...DID YOU KNOW THAT YOU CAN'T TRUST THREES?
SEE? THREES LIKE TO TURN SIDEWAYS, AND PRETEND THAT THEY'RE M'S OR N'S!
THEN, SOMETIMES THEY FACE THE OTHER WAY TO MAKE YOU THINK THAT THEY'RE E'S! WEIRD, HUH?
AND SOMETIMES THEY'LL EVEN LIE ON THEIR BACKS, AND PRETEND THAT THEY'RE W'S!
1-30
YOU JUST CAN'T TRUST THREES...
6 6 6
6 6 6
COME BACK! I'LL SHOW YOU SOME SIXES WHO LIKE TO PRETEND THAT THEY'RE NOSES!
SCHULZ

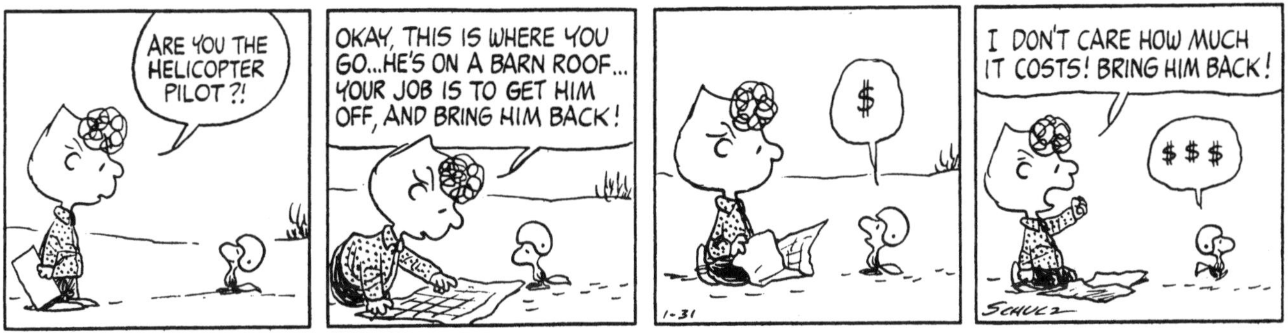
ARE YOU THE HELICOPTER PILOT?!
OKAY, THIS IS WHERE YOU GO...HE'S ON A BARN ROOF... YOUR JOB IS TO GET HIM OFF, AND BRING HIM BACK!
$
1-31
I DON'T CARE HOW MUCH IT COSTS! BRING HIM BACK!
$ $ $
SCHULZ

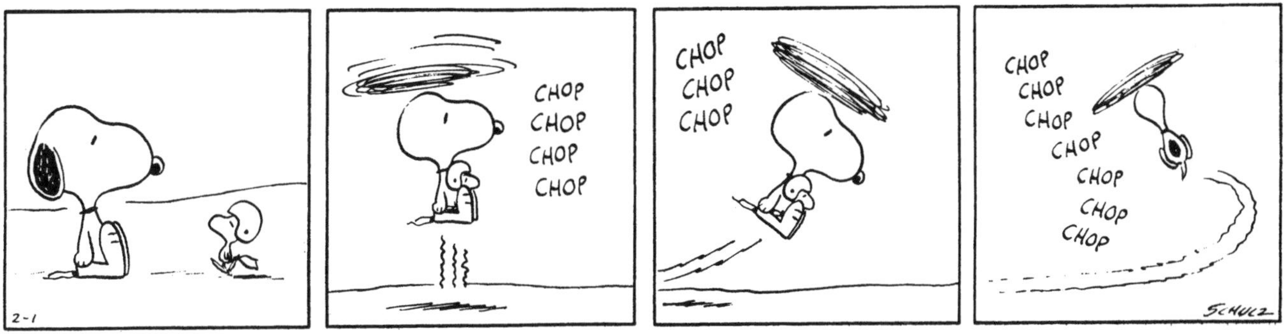
2-1
CHOP
CHOP
CHOP
CHOP
CHOP
CHOP
CHOP
CHOP
CHOP
CHOP
CHOP
CHOP
CHOP
CHOP
SCHULZ

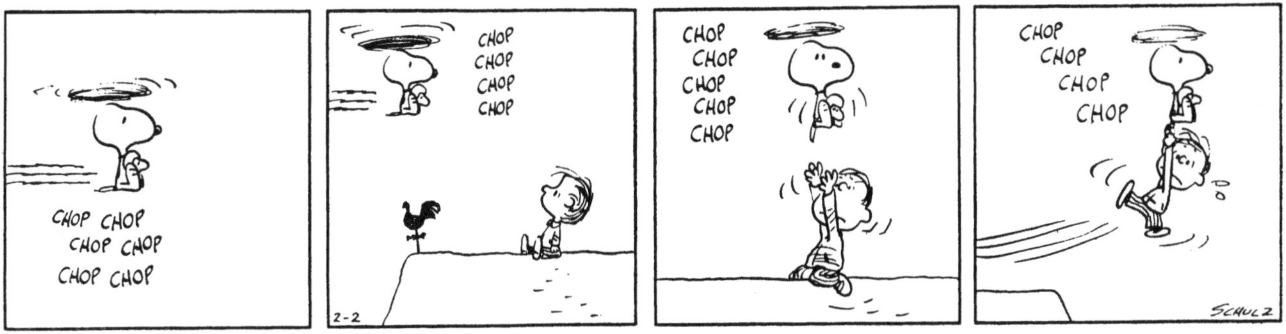
CHOP CHOP
CHOP CHOP
CHOP CHOP
CHOP
CHOP
CHOP
CHOP
2-2
CHOP
CHOP
CHOP
CHOP
CHOP
CHOP
CHOP
CHOP
CHOP
SCHULZ

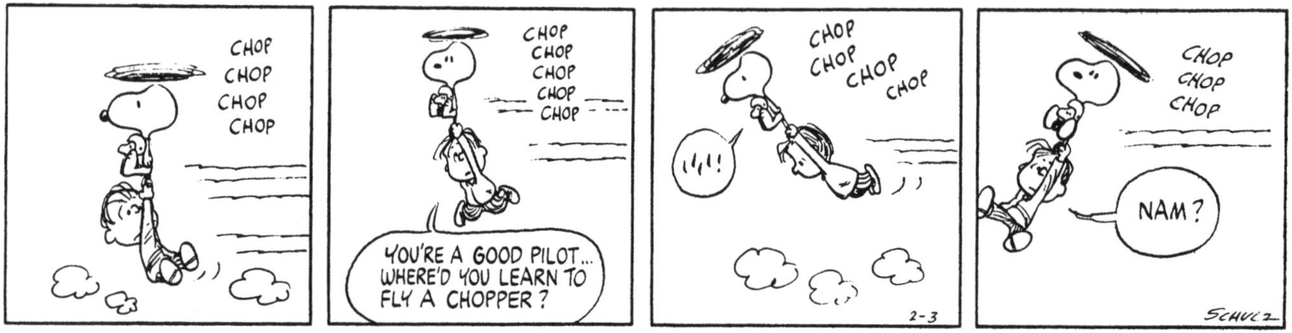
CHOP
CHOP
CHOP
CHOP
CHOP
CHOP
CHOP
CHOP
CHOP
YOU'RE A GOOD PILOT... WHERE'D YOU LEARN TO FLY A CHOPPER?
CHOP
CHOP
CHOP
CHOP
2-3
CHOP
CHOP
CHOP
NAM?
SCHULZ

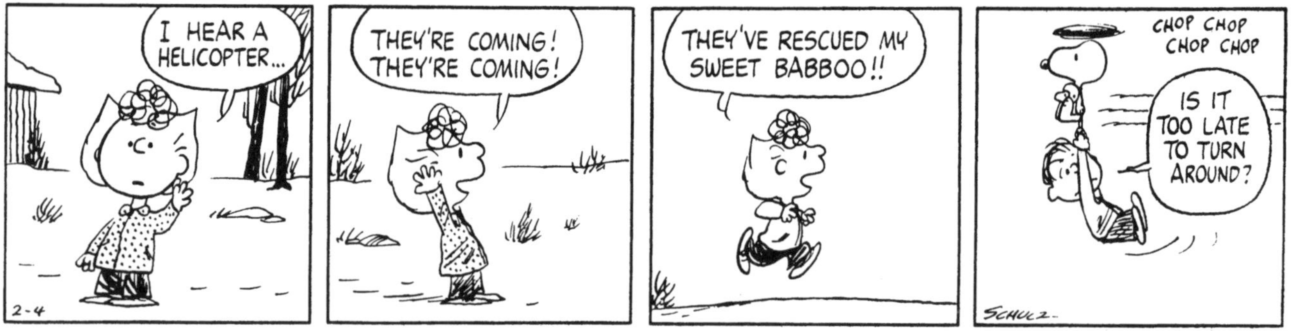
I HEAR A HELICOPTER...
2-4
THEY'RE COMING! THEY'RE COMING!
THEY'VE RESCUED MY SWEET BABBOO!!
CHOP CHOP
CHOP CHOP
IS IT TOO LATE TO TURN AROUND?
SCHULZ

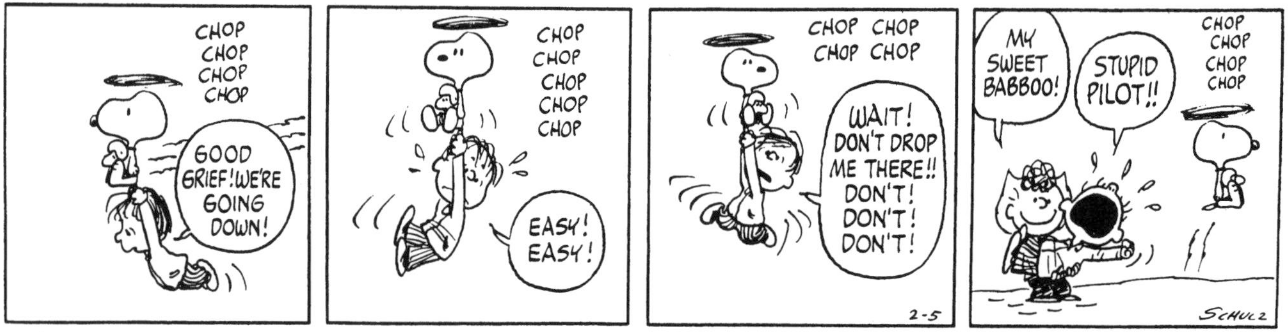
CHOP
CHOP
CHOP
CHOP
GOOD GRIEF! WE'RE GOING DOWN!
CHOP
CHOP
CHOP
CHOP
CHOP
EASY! EASY!
CHOP CHOP
CHOP CHOP
WAIT! DON'T DROP ME THERE!! DON'T! DON'T! DON'T!
2-5
MY SWEET BABBOO!
STUPID PILOT!!
CHOP
CHOP
CHOP
CHOP
SCHULZ

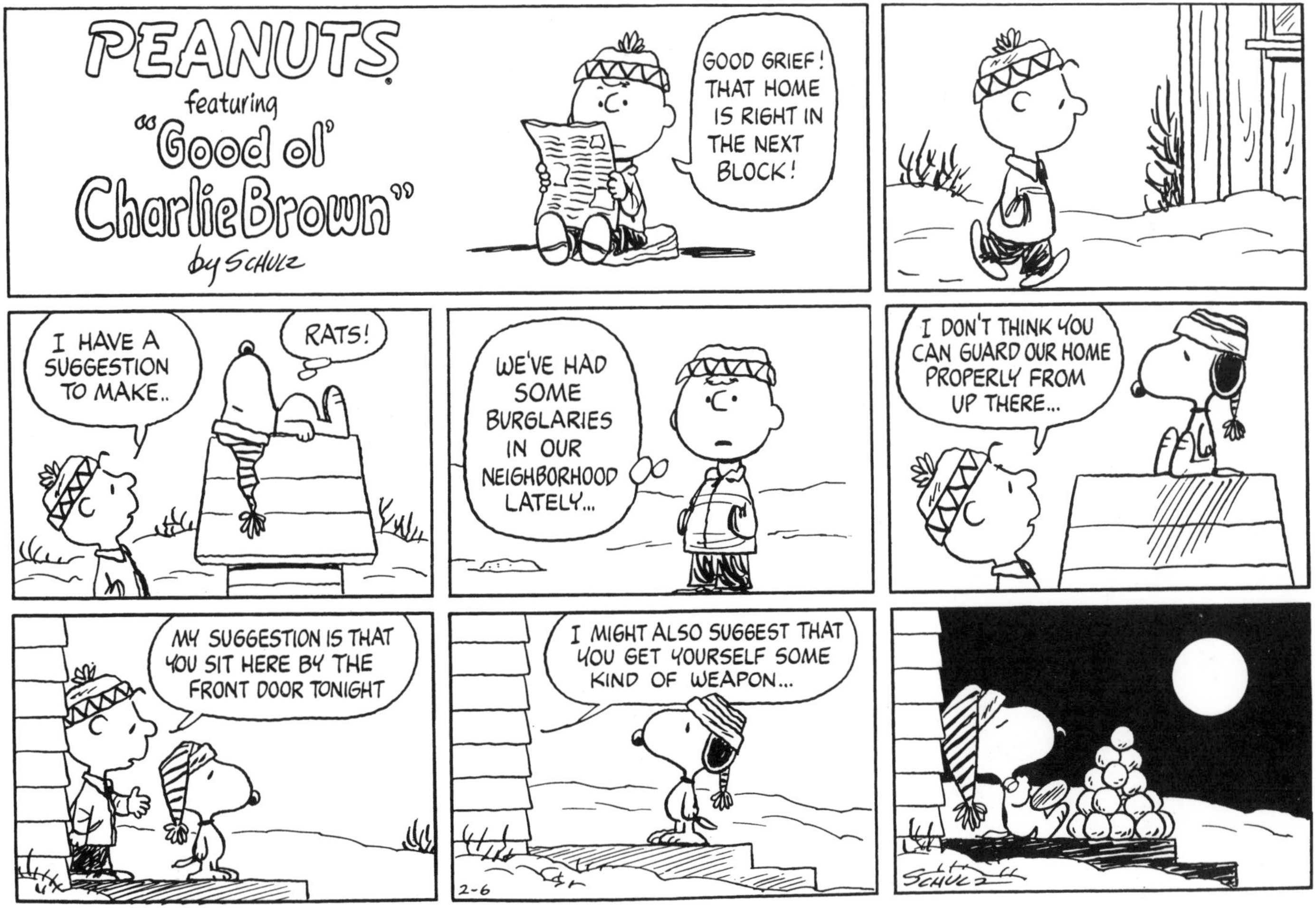
PEANUTS®
featuring "Good ol' CharlieBrown"
by SCHULZ
GOOD GRIEF! THAT HOME IS RIGHT IN THE NEXT BLOCK!
I HAVE A SUGGESTION TO MAKE..
RATS!
WE'VE HAD SOME BURGLARIES IN OUR NEIGHBORHOOD LATELY...
I DON'T THINK YOU CAN GUARD OUR HOME PROPERLY FROM UP THERE...
MY SUGGESTION IS THAT YOU SIT HERE BY THE FRONT DOOR TONIGHT
I MIGHT ALSO SUGGEST THAT YOU GET YOURSELF SOME KIND OF WEAPON...
2-6
SCHULZ

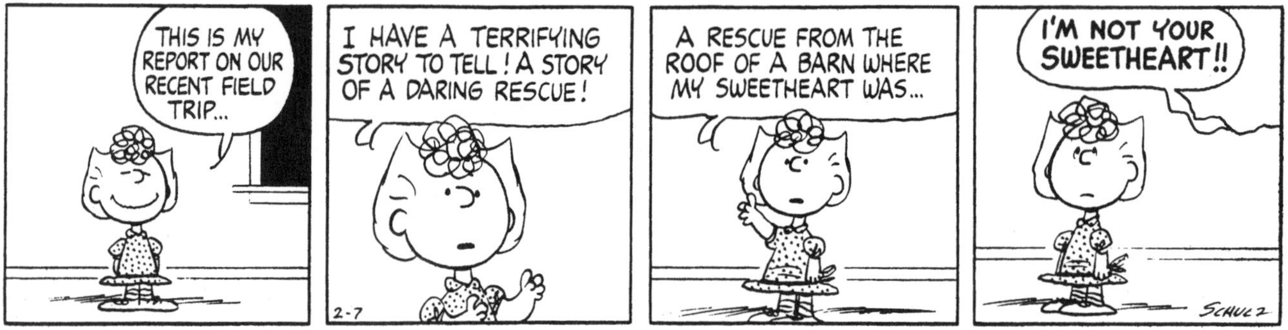
THIS IS MY REPORT ON OUR RECENT FIELD TRIP...
I HAVE A TERRIFYING STORY TO TELL! A STORY OF A DARING RESCUE!
2-7
A RESCUE FROM THE ROOF OF A BARN WHERE MY SWEETHEART WAS...
I'M NOT YOUR SWEETHEART!!
SCHULZ

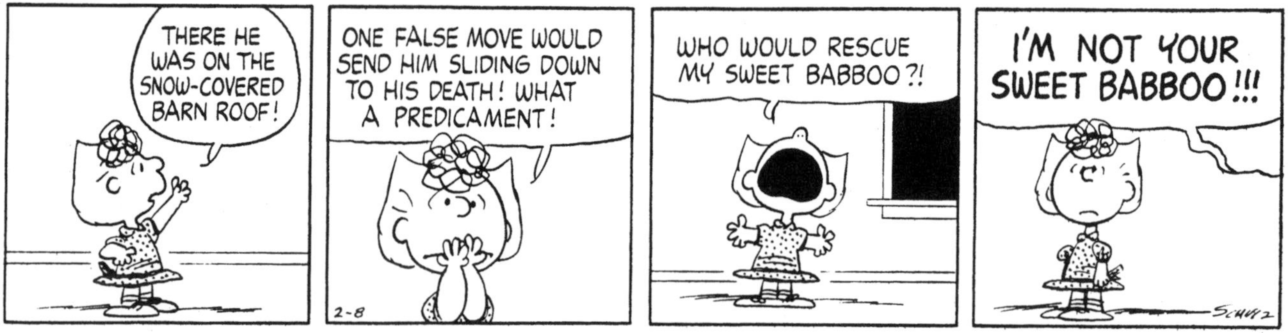
THERE HE WAS ON THE SNOW-COVERED BARN ROOF!
ONE FALSE MOVE WOULD SEND HIM SLIDING DOWN TO HIS DEATH! WHAT A PREDICAMENT!
2-8
WHO WOULD RESCUE MY SWEET BABBOO?!
I'M NOT YOUR SWEET BABBOO!!!
SCHULZ

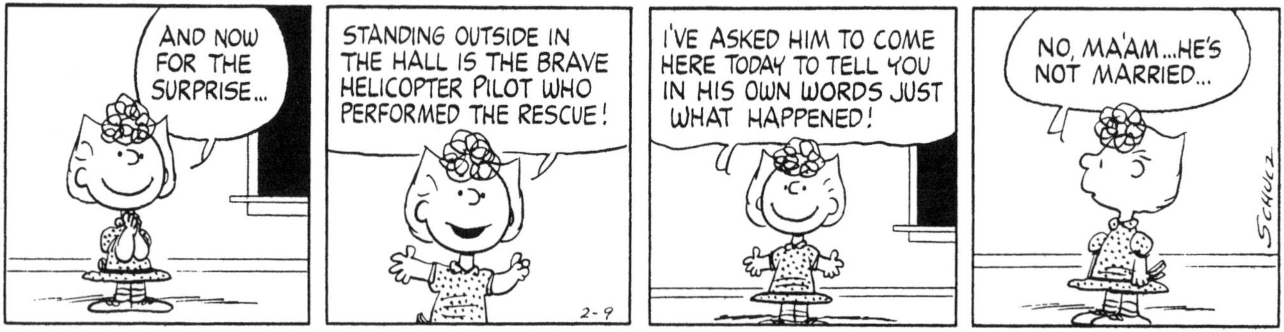
AND NOW FOR THE SURPRISE...
STANDING OUTSIDE IN THE HALL IS THE BRAVE HELICOPTER PILOT WHO PERFORMED THE RESCUE!
2-9
I'VE ASKED HIM TO COME HERE TODAY TO TELL YOU IN HIS OWN WORDS JUST WHAT HAPPENED!
NO, MA'AM...HE'S NOT MARRIED...
SCHULZ

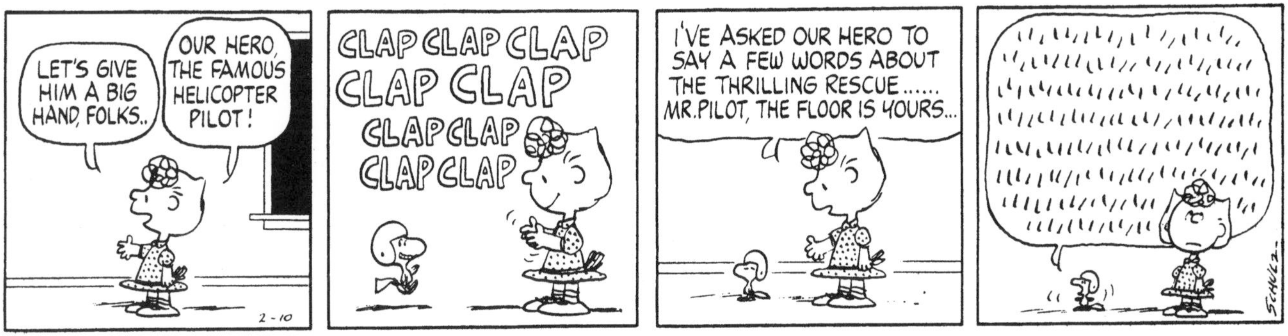
LET'S GIVE HIM A BIG HAND, FOLKS..
OUR HERO, THE FAMOUS HELICOPTER PILOT!
2-10
CLAP CLAP CLAP
CLAP CLAP
CLAPCLAP
CLAPCLAP
I'VE ASKED OUR HERO TO SAY A FEW WORDS ABOUT THE THRILLING RESCUE...... MR.PILOT, THE FLOOR IS YOURS...
SCHULZ

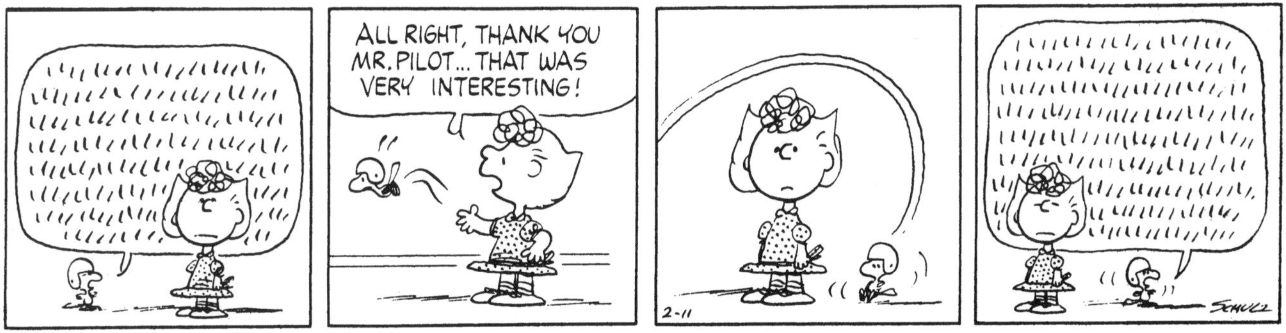
ALL RIGHT, THANK YOU MR.PILOT...THAT WAS VERY INTERESTING!
2-11
SCHULZ

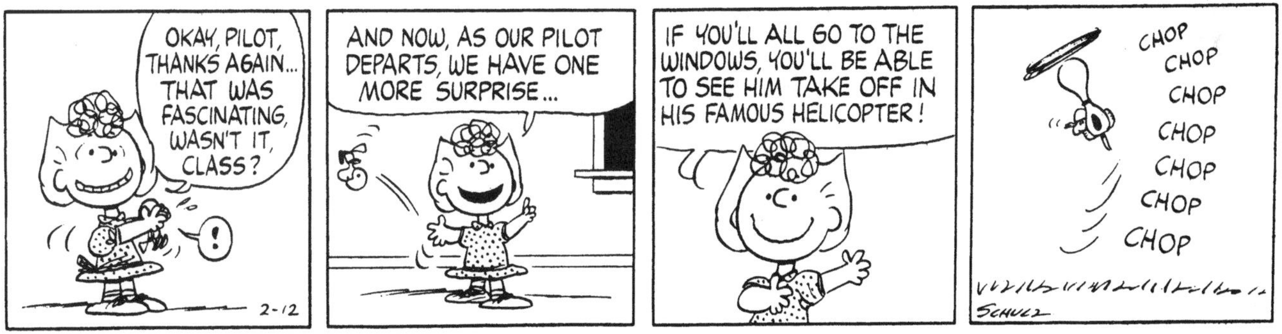
OKAY, PILOT, THANKS AGAIN... THAT WAS FASCINATING, WASN'T IT, CLASS?
!
2-12
AND NOW, AS OUR PILOT DEPARTS, WE HAVE ONE MORE SURPRISE...
IF YOU'LL ALL GO TO THE WINDOWS, YOU'LL BE ABLE TO SEE HIM TAKE OFF IN HIS FAMOUS HELICOPTER!
CHOP
CHOP
CHOP
CHOP
CHOP
CHOP
CHOP
SCHULZ

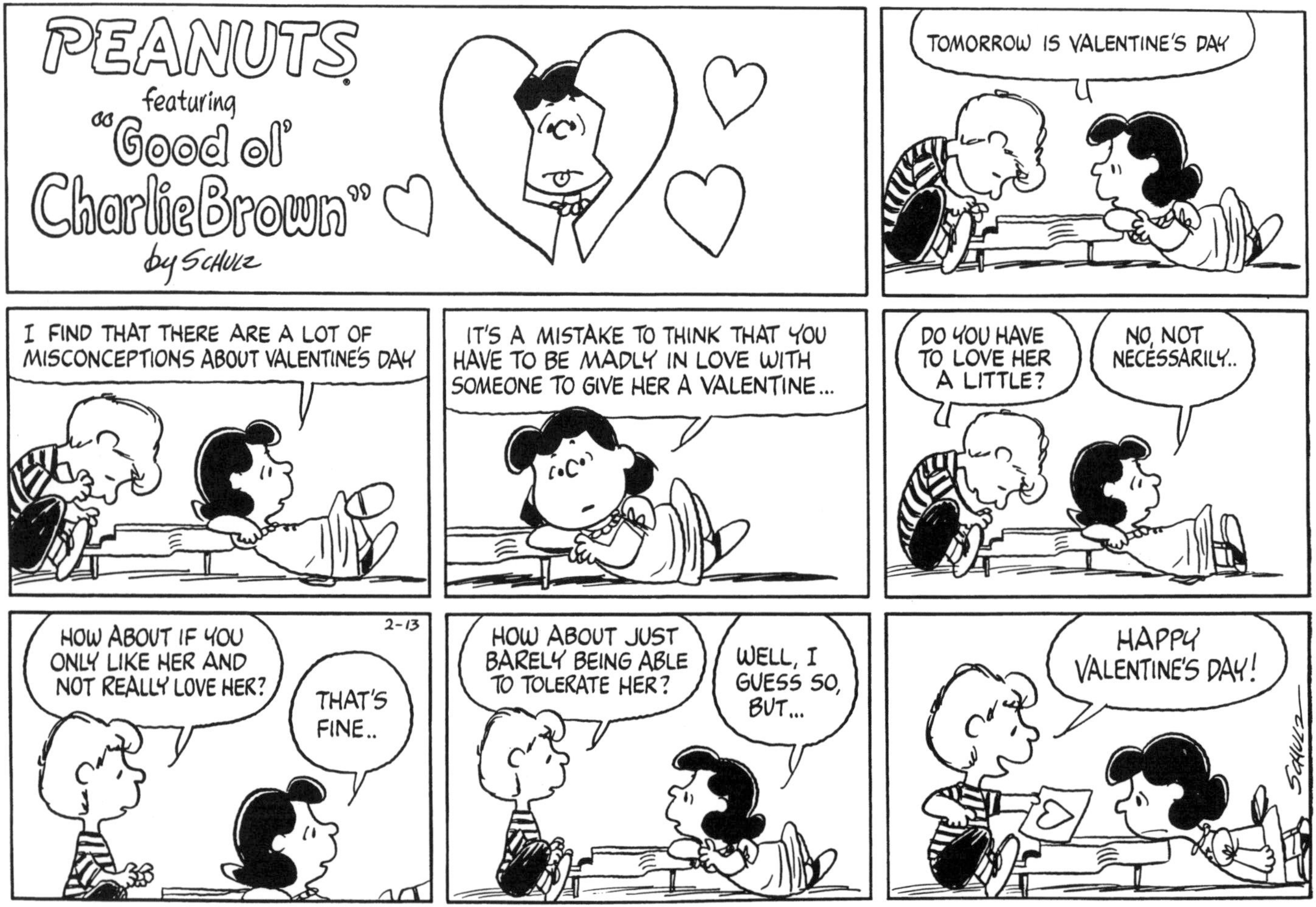
PEANUTS
featuring
"Good ol' Charlie Brown"
by SCHULZ
TOMORROW IS VALENTINE'S DAY
I FIND THAT THERE ARE A LOT OF MISCONCEPTIONS ABOUT VALENTINE'S DAY
IT'S A MISTAKE TO THINK THAT YOU HAVE TO BE MADLY IN LOVE WITH SOMEONE TO GIVE HER A VALENTINE...
DO YOU HAVE TO LOVE HER A LITTLE?
NO, NOT NECESSARILY..
2-13
HOW ABOUT IF YOU ONLY LIKE HER AND NOT REALLY LOVE HER?
THAT'S FINE..
HOW ABOUT JUST BARELY BEING ABLE TO TOLERATE HER?
WELL, I GUESS SO, BUT...
HAPPY VALENTINE'S DAY!
SCHULZ

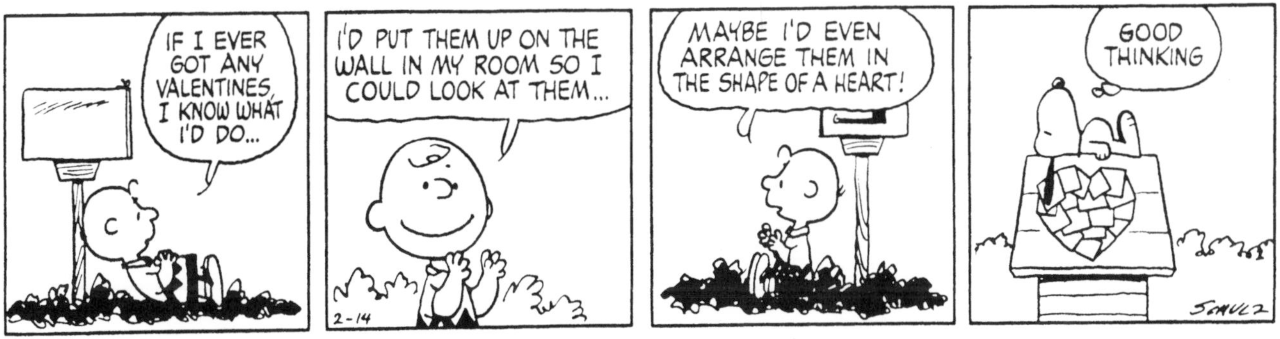
IF I EVER GOT ANY VALENTINES, I KNOW WHAT I'D DO...
2-14
I'D PUT THEM UP ON THE WALL IN MY ROOM SO I COULD LOOK AT THEM...
MAYBE I'D EVEN ARRANGE THEM IN THE SHAPE OF A HEART!
GOOD THINKING
SCHULZ

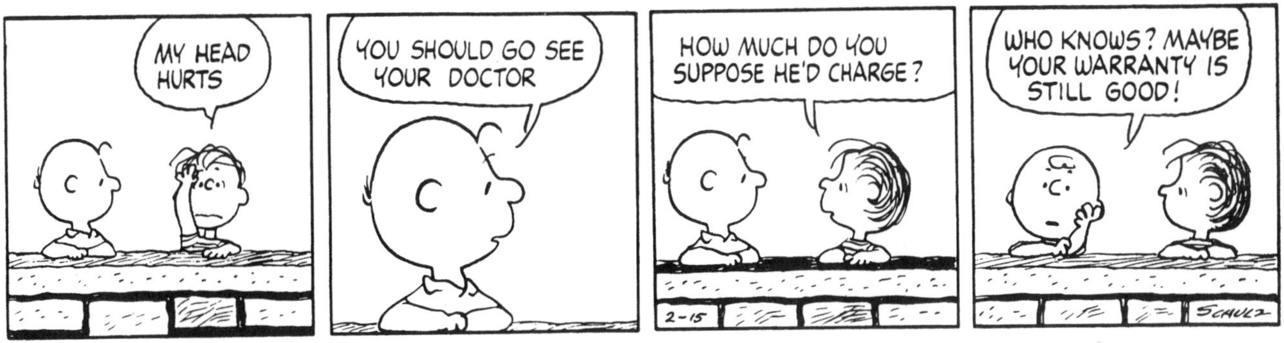
MY HEAD HURTS
YOU SHOULD GO SEE YOUR DOCTOR
HOW MUCH DO YOU SUPPOSE HE'D CHARGE?
2-15
WHO KNOWS? MAYBE YOUR WARRANTY IS STILL GOOD!
SCHULZ

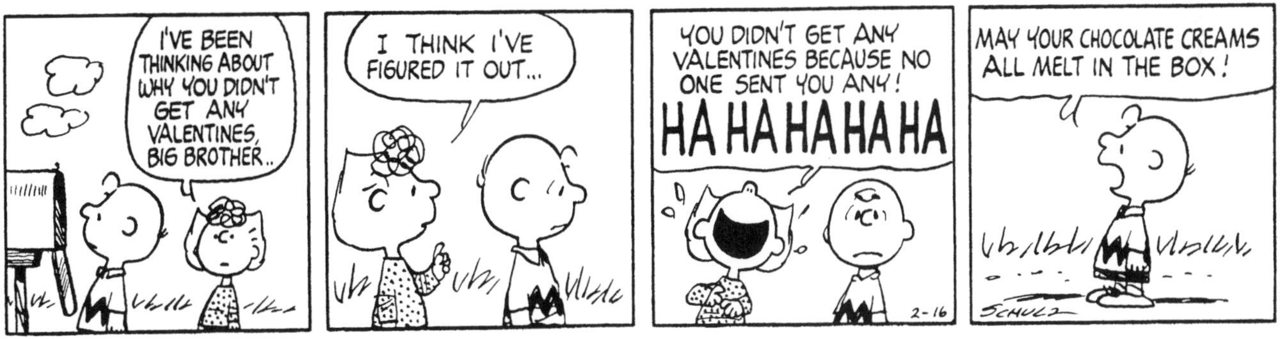
I'VE BEEN THINKING ABOUT WHY YOU DIDN'T GET ANY VALENTINES, BIG BROTHER..
I THINK I'VE FIGURED IT OUT...
YOU DIDN'T GET ANY VALENTINES BECAUSE NO ONE SENT YOU ANY!
HA HA HA HA HA
2-16
MAY YOUR CHOCOLATE CREAMS ALL MELT IN THE BOX!
SCHULZ

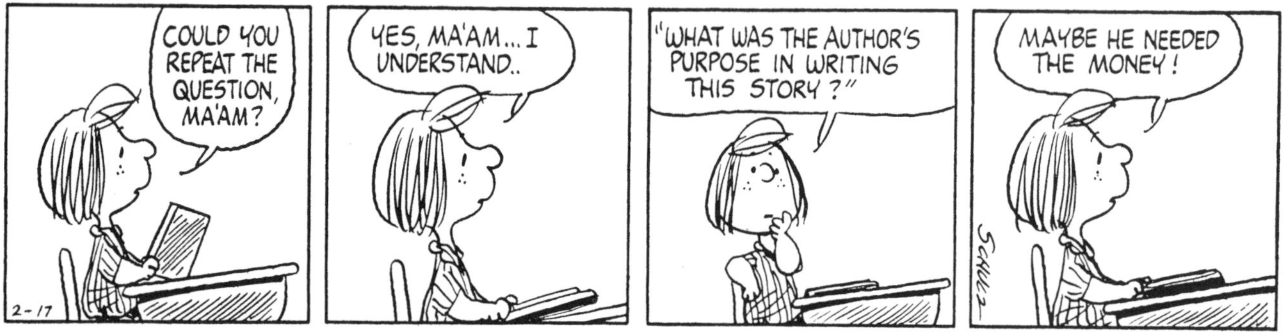
COULD YOU REPEAT THE QUESTION, MA'AM?
YES, MA'AM... I UNDERSTAND..
"WHAT WAS THE AUTHOR'S PURPOSE IN WRITING THIS STORY?"
MAYBE HE NEEDED THE MONEY!
2-17
SCHULZ

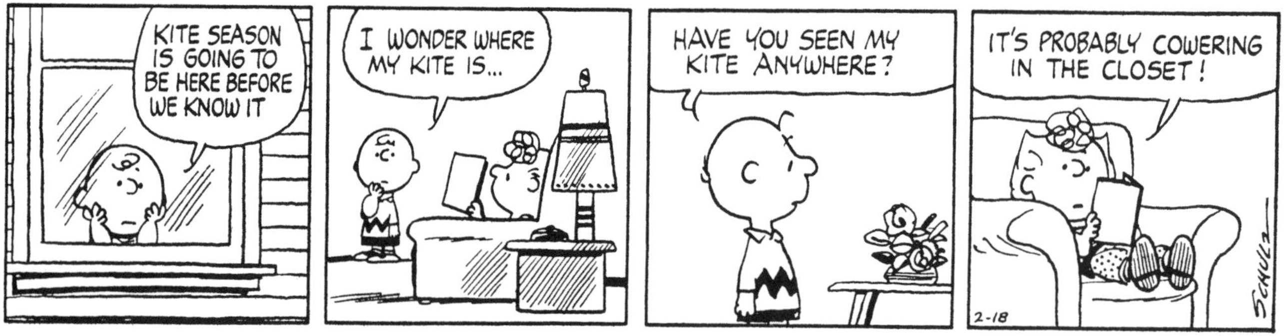
KITE SEASON IS GOING TO BE HERE BEFORE WE KNOW IT
I WONDER WHERE MY KITE IS...
HAVE YOU SEEN MY KITE ANYWHERE?
IT'S PROBABLY COWERING IN THE CLOSET!
2-18
SCHULZ

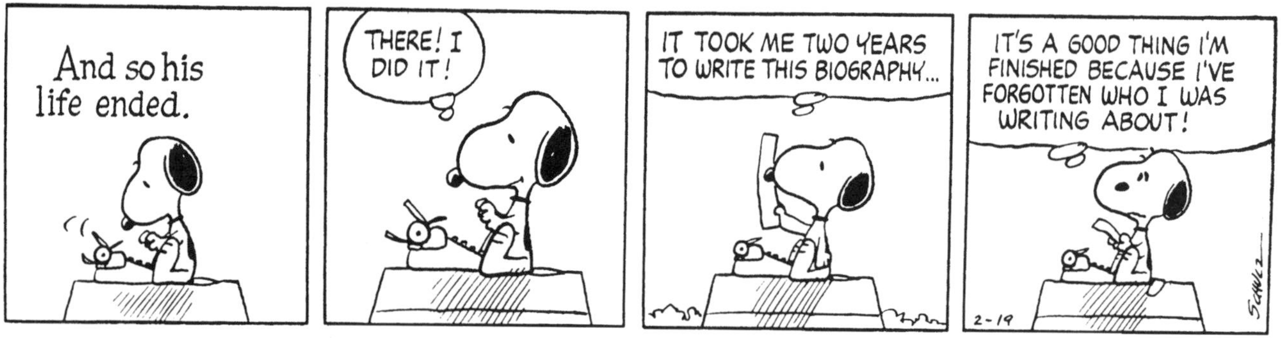
And so his life ended.
THERE! I DID IT!
IT TOOK ME TWO YEARS TO WRITE THIS BIOGRAPHY...
IT'S A GOOD THING I'M FINISHED BECAUSE I'VE FORGOTTEN WHO I WAS WRITING ABOUT!
2-19
SCHULZ

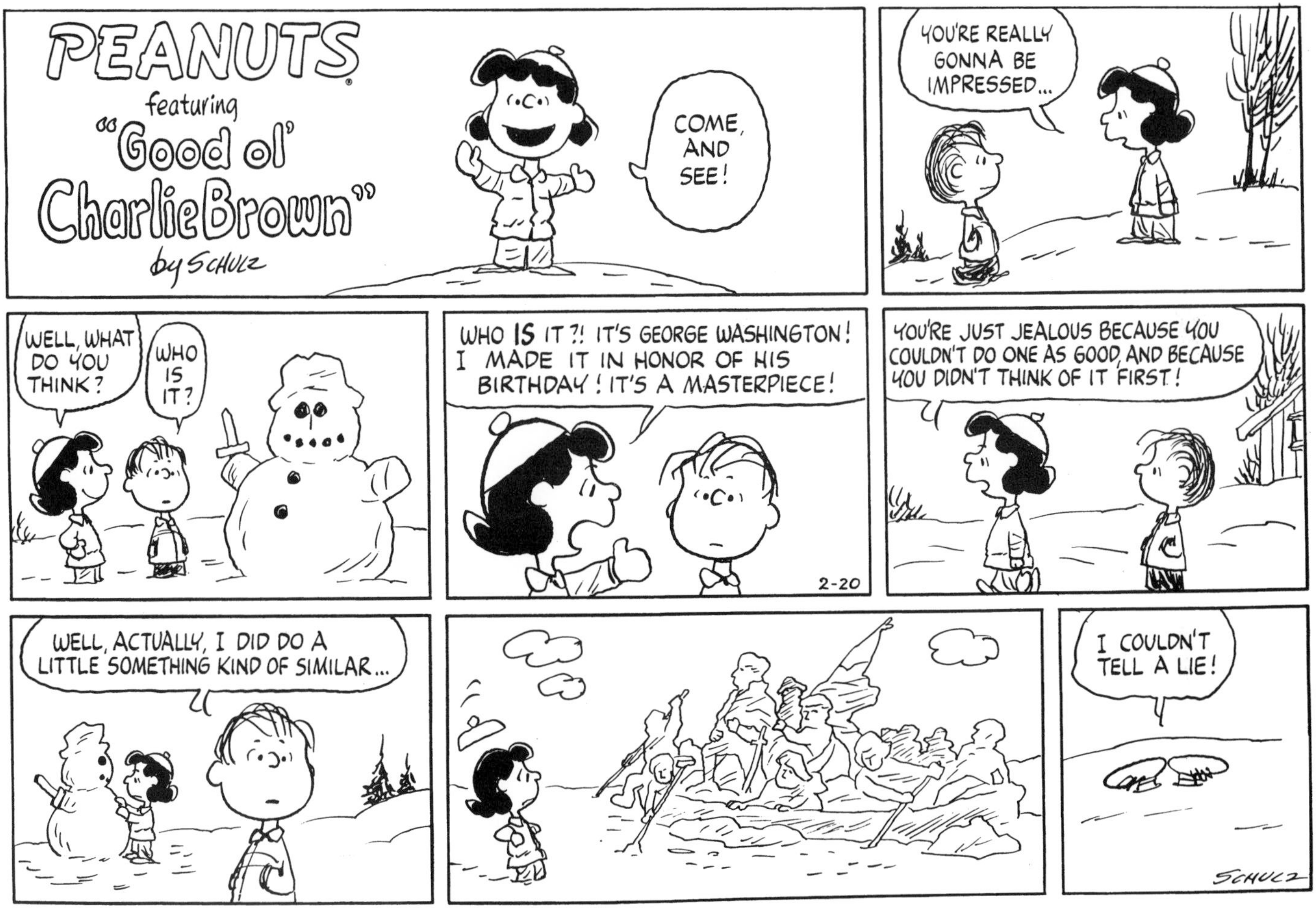
PEANUTS
featuring "Good ol' Charlie Brown"
by SCHULZ
COME, AND SEE!
YOU'RE REALLY GONNA BE IMPRESSED...
WELL, WHAT DO YOU THINK?
WHO IS IT?
WHO IS IT?! IT'S GEORGE WASHINGTON! I MADE IT IN HONOR OF HIS BIRTHDAY! IT'S A MASTERPIECE!
2-20
YOU'RE JUST JEALOUS BECAUSE YOU COULDN'T DO ONE AS GOOD, AND BECAUSE YOU DIDN'T THINK OF IT FIRST!
WELL, ACTUALLY, I DID DO A LITTLE SOMETHING KIND OF SIMILAR...
I COULDN'T TELL A LIE!
SCHULZ

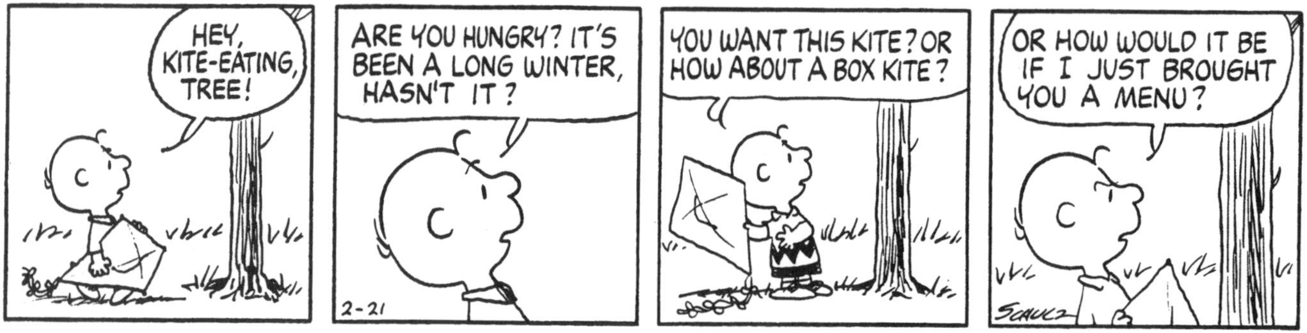
HEY, KITE-EATING, TREE!
ARE YOU HUNGRY? IT'S BEEN A LONG WINTER, HASN'T IT?
2-21
YOU WANT THIS KITE? OR HOW ABOUT A BOX KITE?
OR HOW WOULD IT BE IF I JUST BROUGHT YOU A MENU?
SCHULZ

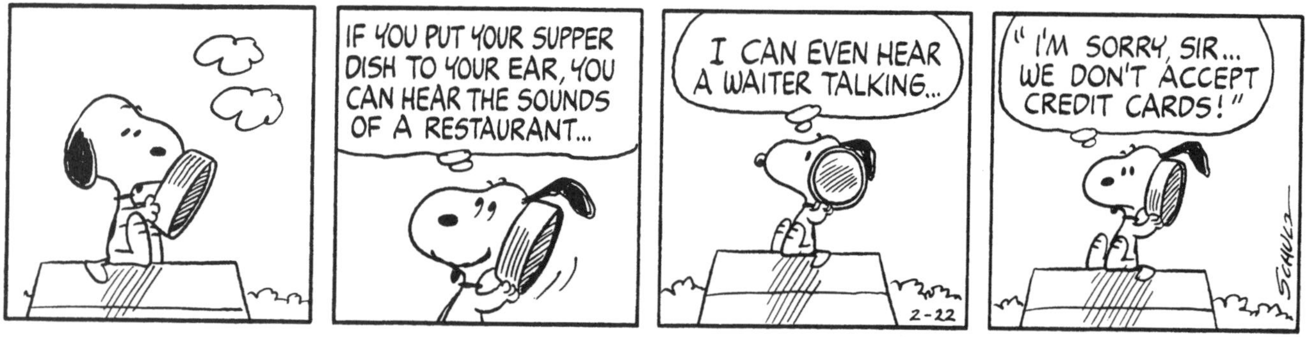
IF YOU PUT YOUR SUPPER DISH TO YOUR EAR, YOU CAN HEAR THE SOUNDS OF A RESTAURANT...
I CAN EVEN HEAR A WAITER TALKING...
2-22
"I'M SORRY, SIR... WE DON'T ACCEPT CREDIT CARDS!"
SCHULZ

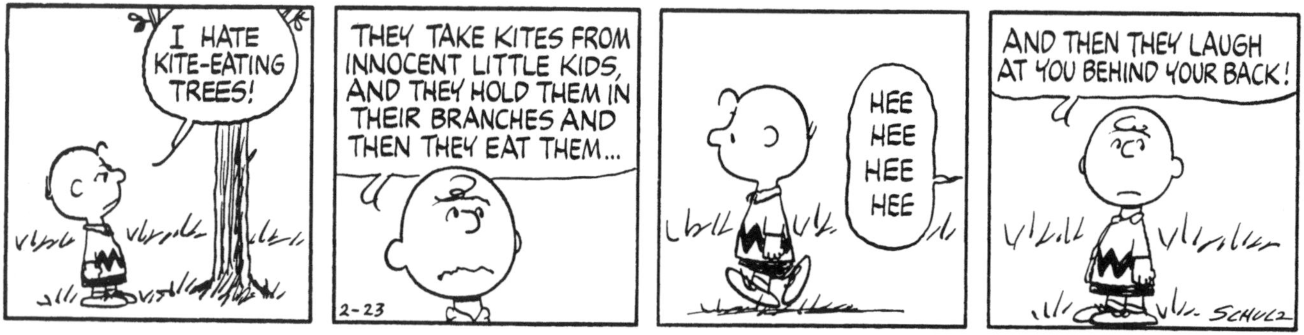
I HATE KITE-EATING TREES!
THEY TAKE KITES FROM INNOCENT LITTLE KIDS, AND THEY HOLD THEM IN THEIR BRANCHES AND THEN THEY EAT THEM...
2-23
HEE HEE HEE HEE
AND THEN THEY LAUGH AT YOU BEHIND YOUR BACK!
SCHULZ

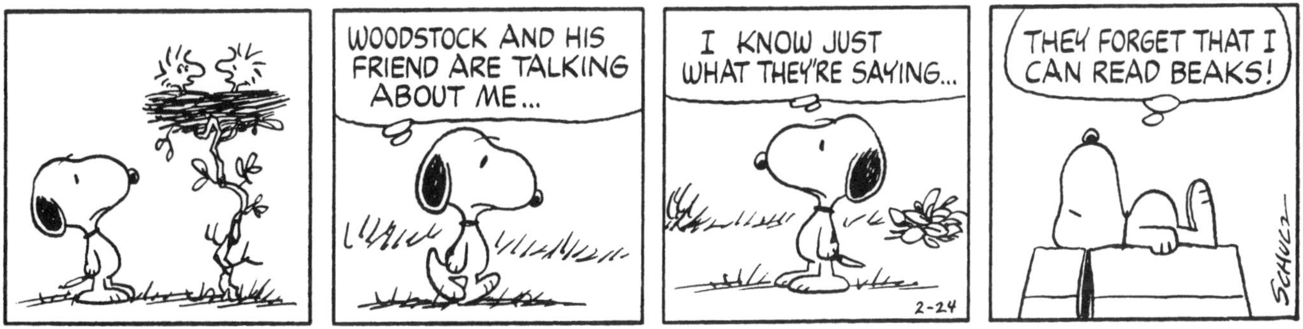
WOODSTOCK AND HIS FRIEND ARE TALKING ABOUT ME...
I KNOW JUST WHAT THEY'RE SAYING...
2-24
THEY FORGET THAT I CAN READ BEAKS!
SCHULZ

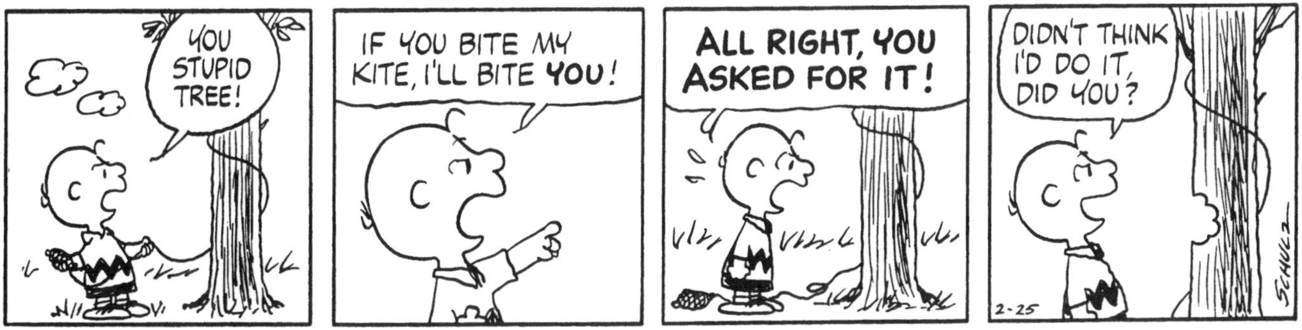
YOU STUPID TREE!
IF YOU BITE MY KITE, I'LL BITE **YOU**!
ALL RIGHT, YOU ASKED FOR IT!
DIDN'T THINK I'D DO IT, DID YOU?
2-25
SCHULZ

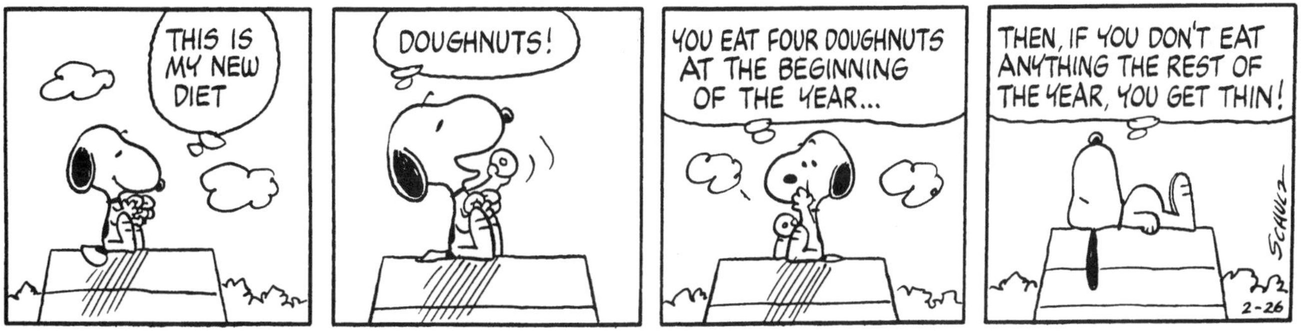
THIS IS MY NEW DIET
DOUGHNUTS!
YOU EAT FOUR DOUGHNUTS AT THE BEGINNING OF THE YEAR...
THEN, IF YOU DON'T EAT ANYTHING THE REST OF THE YEAR, YOU GET THIN!
SCHULZ
2-26

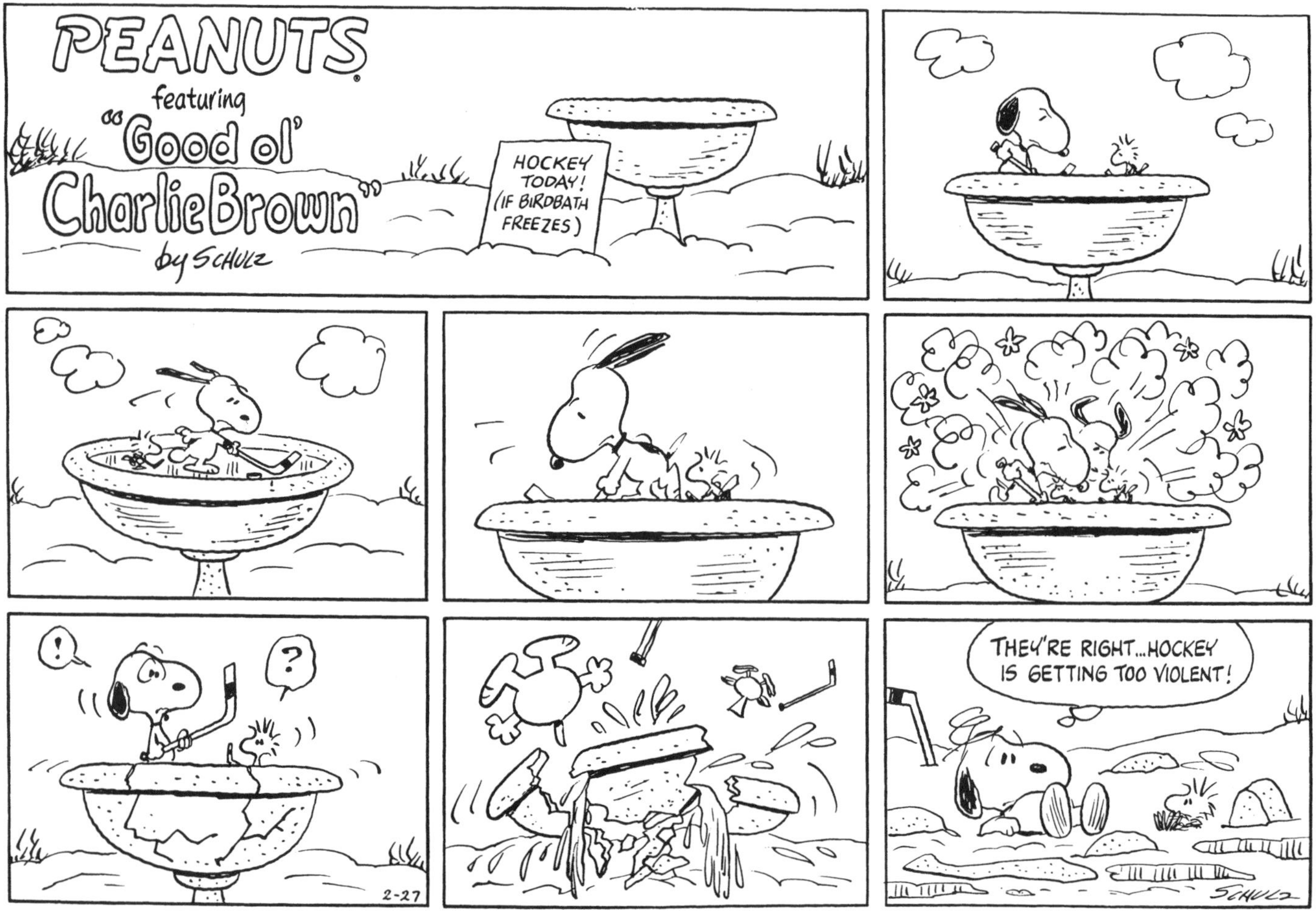
PEANUTS
featuring "Good ol' Charlie Brown"
by SCHULZ
HOCKEY TODAY! (IF BIRDBATH FREEZES)
!
?
2-27
THEY'RE RIGHT...HOCKEY IS GETTING TOO VIOLENT!
SCHULZ

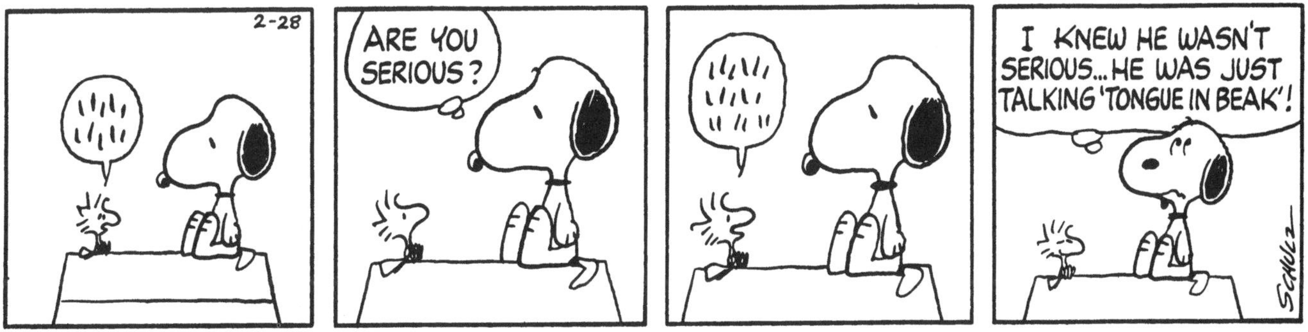
2-28
ARE YOU SERIOUS?
I KNEW HE WASN'T SERIOUS... HE WAS JUST TALKING 'TONGUE IN BEAK'!
SCHULZ

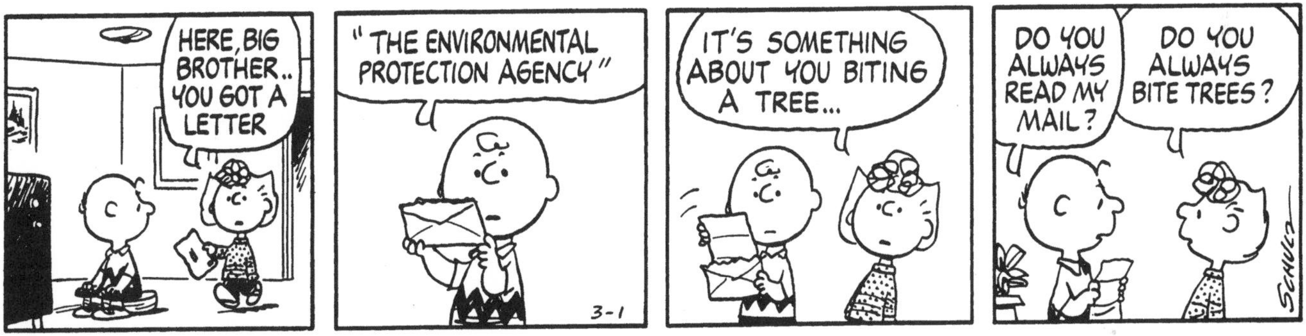
HERE, BIG BROTHER.. YOU GOT A LETTER
"THE ENVIRONMENTAL PROTECTION AGENCY"
3-1
IT'S SOMETHING ABOUT YOU BITING A TREE...
DO YOU ALWAYS READ MY MAIL?
DO YOU ALWAYS BITE TREES?
SCHULZ

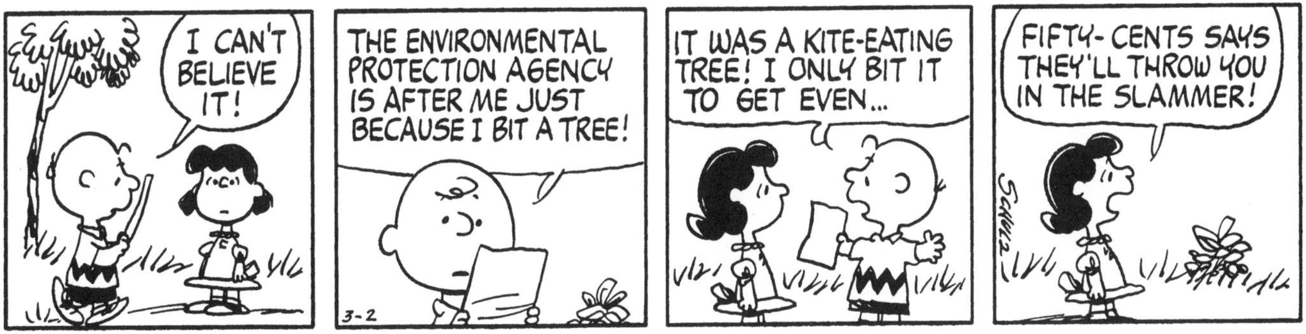
I CAN'T BELIEVE IT!
THE ENVIRONMENTAL PROTECTION AGENCY IS AFTER ME JUST BECAUSE I BIT A TREE!
3-2
IT WAS A KITE-EATING TREE! I ONLY BIT IT TO GET EVEN...
FIFTY-CENTS SAYS THEY'LL THROW YOU IN THE SLAMMER!
SCHULZ

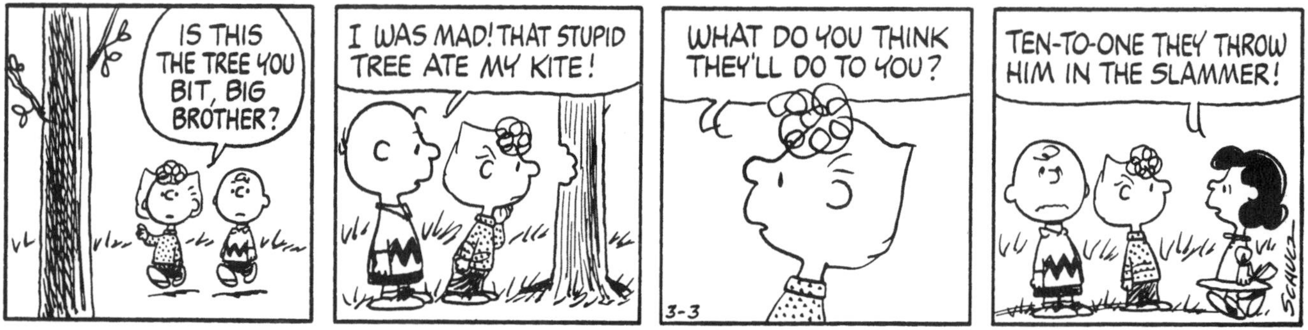
IS THIS THE TREE YOU BIT, BIG BROTHER?
I WAS MAD! THAT STUPID TREE ATE MY KITE!
WHAT DO YOU THINK THEY'LL DO TO YOU?
3-3
TEN-TO-ONE THEY THROW HIM IN THE SLAMMER!
SCHULZ

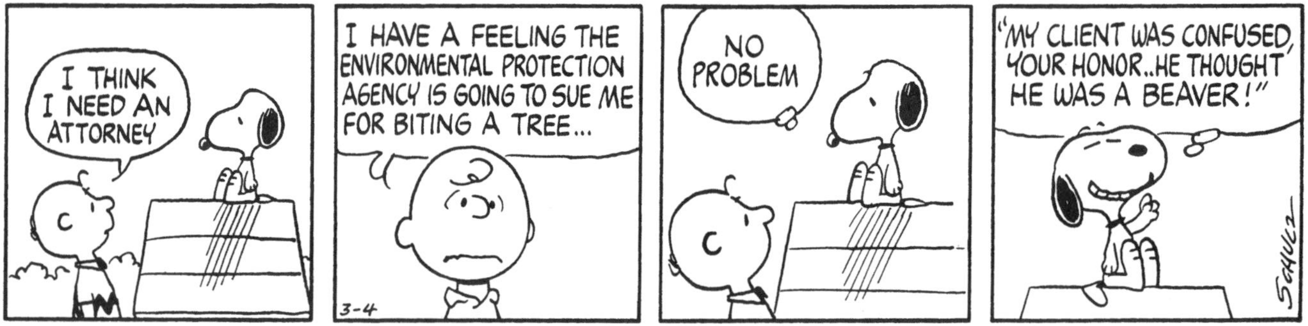
I THINK I NEED AN ATTORNEY
I HAVE A FEELING THE ENVIRONMENTAL PROTECTION AGENCY IS GOING TO SUE ME FOR BITING A TREE...
3-4
NO PROBLEM
"MY CLIENT WAS CONFUSED, YOUR HONOR..HE THOUGHT HE WAS A BEAVER!"
SCHULZ

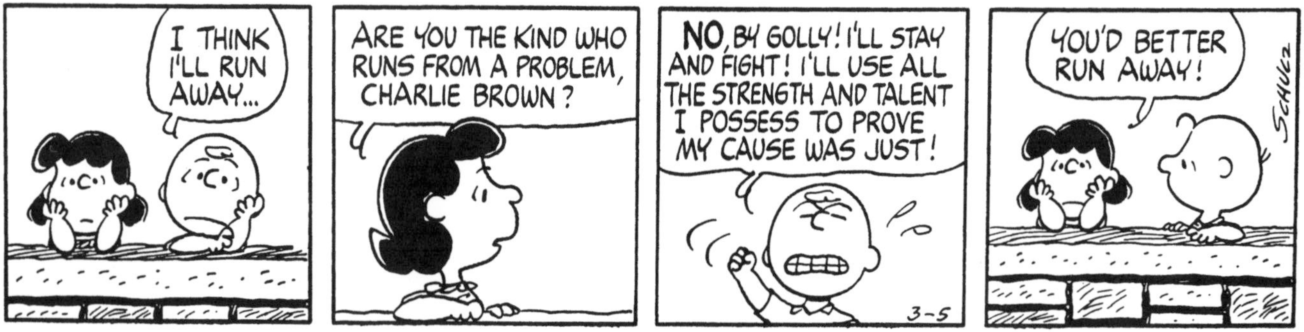
I THINK I'LL RUN AWAY...
ARE YOU THE KIND WHO RUNS FROM A PROBLEM, CHARLIE BROWN?
NO, BY GOLLY! I'LL STAY AND FIGHT! I'LL USE ALL THE STRENGTH AND TALENT I POSSESS TO PROVE MY CAUSE WAS JUST!
3-5
YOU'D BETTER RUN AWAY!
SCHULZ

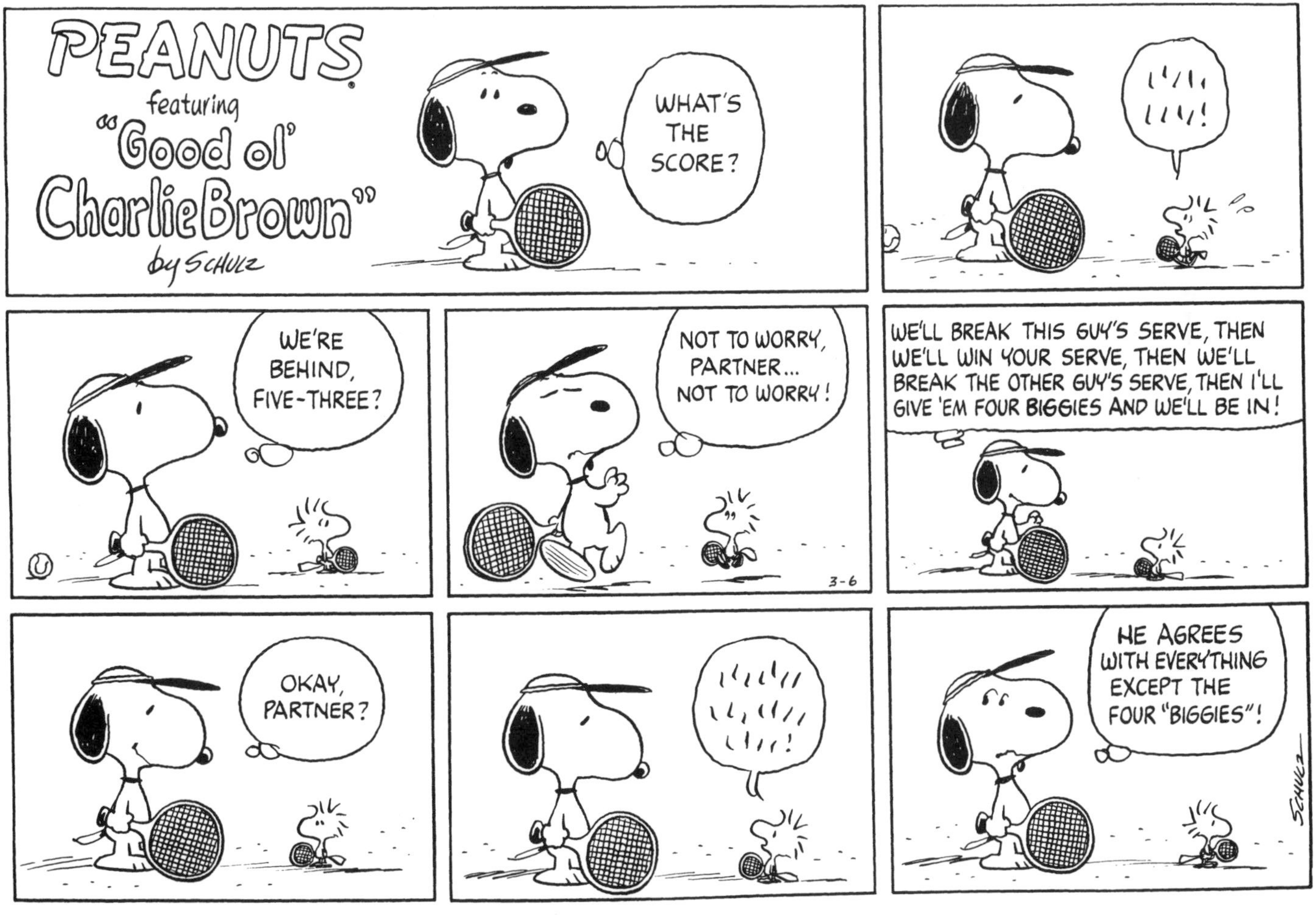
PEANUTS
featuring
"Good ol' Charlie Brown"
by SCHULZ
WHAT'S THE SCORE?
WE'RE BEHIND, FIVE-THREE?
NOT TO WORRY, PARTNER... NOT TO WORRY!
3-6
WE'LL BREAK THIS GUY'S SERVE, THEN WE'LL WIN YOUR SERVE, THEN WE'LL BREAK THE OTHER GUY'S SERVE, THEN I'LL GIVE 'EM FOUR BIGGIES AND WE'LL BE IN!
OKAY, PARTNER?
HE AGREES WITH EVERYTHING EXCEPT THE FOUR "BIGGIES"!
SCHULZ

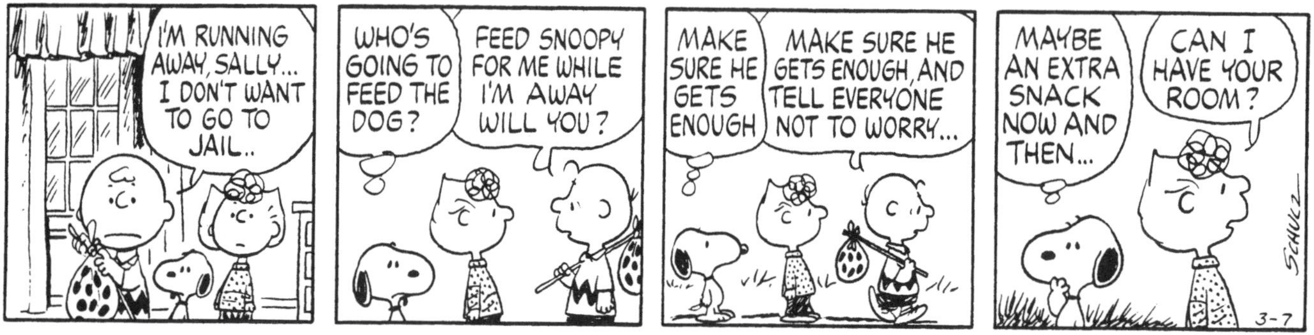
I'M RUNNING AWAY, SALLY... I DON'T WANT TO GO TO JAIL..
WHO'S GOING TO FEED THE DOG?
FEED SNOOPY FOR ME WHILE I'M AWAY WILL YOU?
MAKE SURE HE GETS ENOUGH
MAKE SURE HE GETS ENOUGH, AND TELL EVERYONE NOT TO WORRY...
MAYBE AN EXTRA SNACK NOW AND THEN...
CAN I HAVE YOUR ROOM?
SCHULZ
3-7

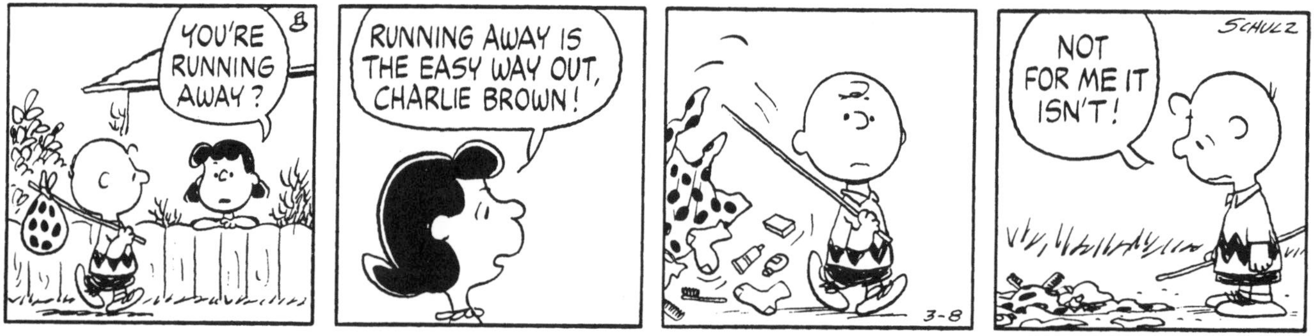
YOU'RE RUNNING AWAY?
RUNNING AWAY IS THE EASY WAY OUT, CHARLIE BROWN!
3-8
SCHULZ
NOT FOR ME IT ISN'T!

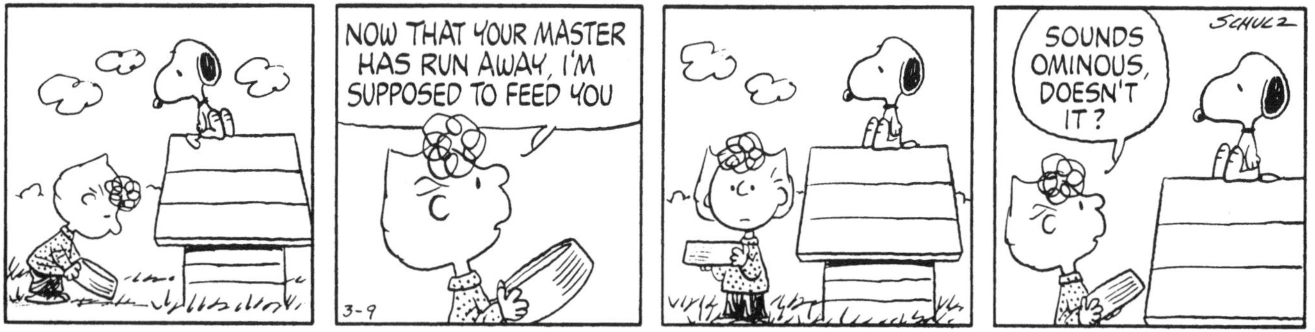
NOW THAT YOUR MASTER HAS RUN AWAY, I'M SUPPOSED TO FEED YOU
3-9
SCHULZ
SOUNDS OMINOUS, DOESN'T IT?

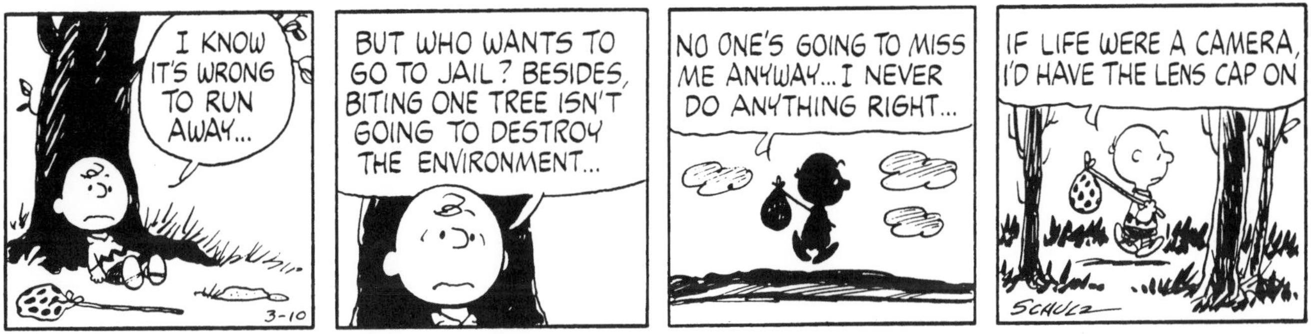
I KNOW IT'S WRONG TO RUN AWAY...
3-10
BUT WHO WANTS TO GO TO JAIL? BESIDES, BITING ONE TREE ISN'T GOING TO DESTROY THE ENVIRONMENT...
NO ONE'S GOING TO MISS ME ANYWAY... I NEVER DO ANYTHING RIGHT...
IF LIFE WERE A CAMERA, I'D HAVE THE LENS CAP ON
SCHULZ

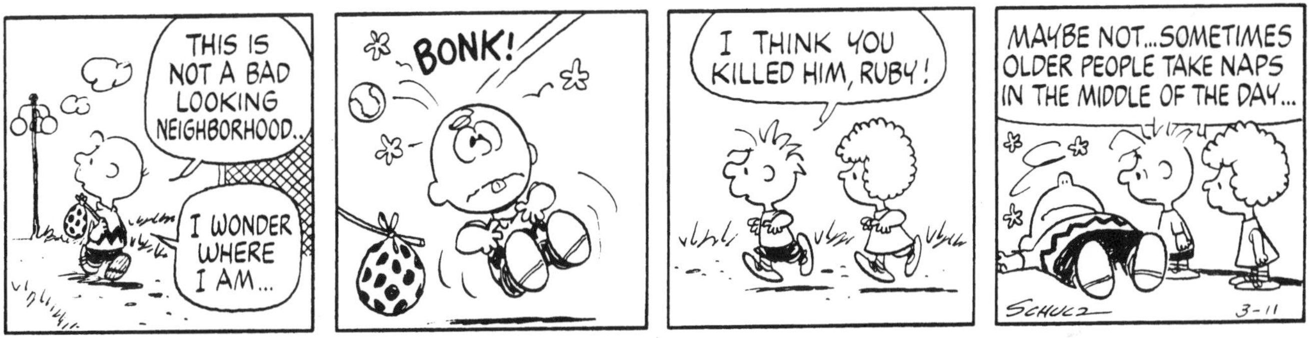
THIS IS NOT A BAD LOOKING NEIGHBORHOOD..
I WONDER WHERE I AM...
BONK!
I THINK YOU KILLED HIM, RUBY!
MAYBE NOT...SOMETIMES OLDER PEOPLE TAKE NAPS IN THE MIDDLE OF THE DAY...
SCHULZ
3-11

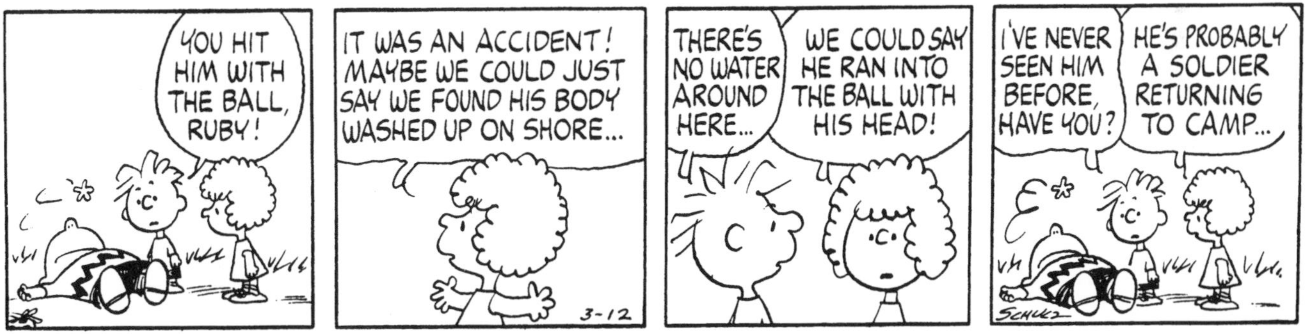
YOU HIT HIM WITH THE BALL, RUBY!
IT WAS AN ACCIDENT! MAYBE WE COULD JUST SAY WE FOUND HIS BODY WASHED UP ON SHORE...
3-12
THERE'S NO WATER AROUND HERE...
WE COULD SAY HE RAN INTO THE BALL WITH HIS HEAD!
I'VE NEVER SEEN HIM BEFORE, HAVE YOU?
HE'S PROBABLY A SOLDIER RETURNING TO CAMP...
SCHULZ

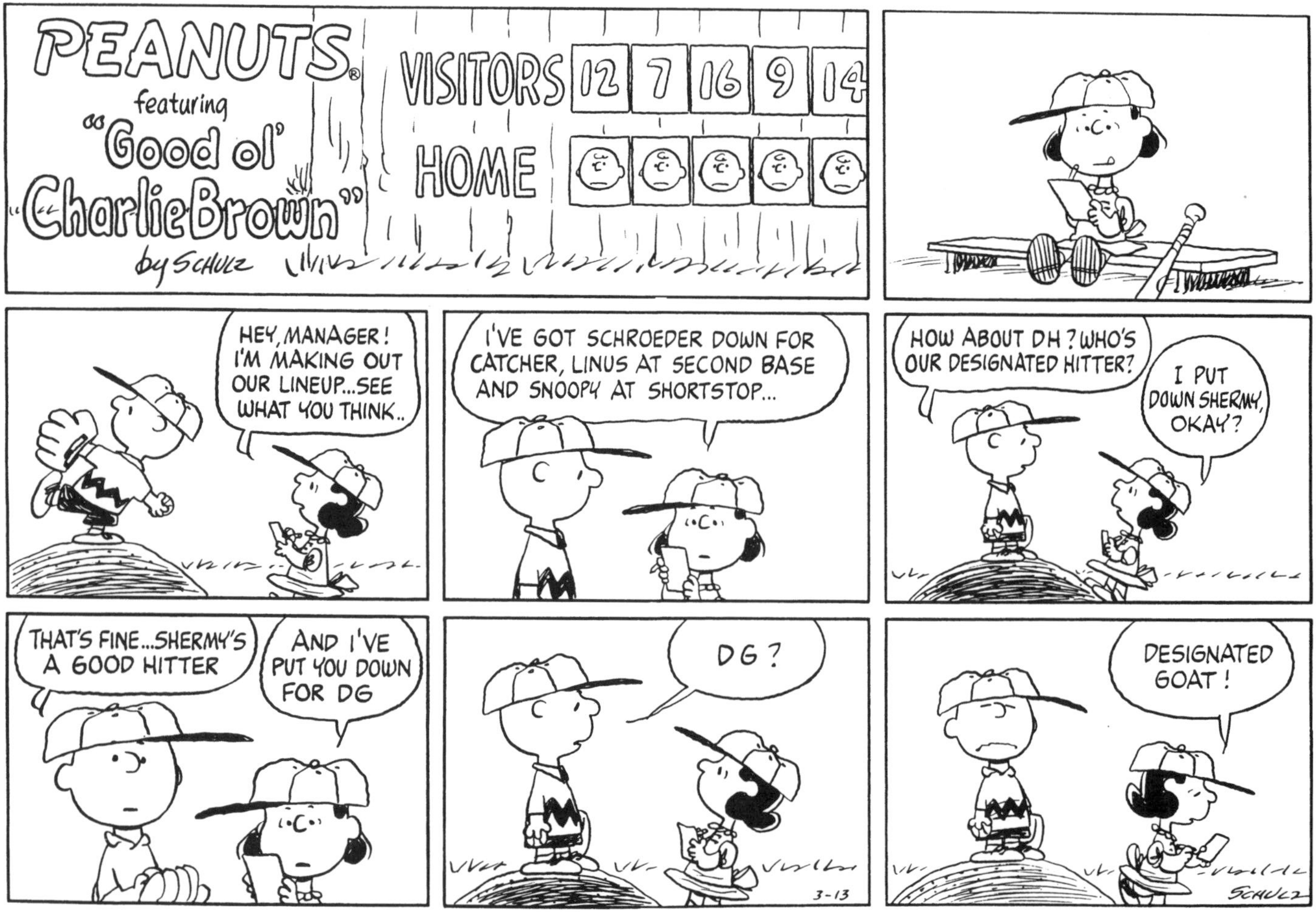
PEANUTS®
featuring
"Good ol' CharlieBrown"
by SCHULZ
VISITORS 12 7 16 9 14
HOME
HEY, MANAGER! I'M MAKING OUT OUR LINEUP...SEE WHAT YOU THINK..
I'VE GOT SCHROEDER DOWN FOR CATCHER, LINUS AT SECOND BASE AND SNOOPY AT SHORTSTOP...
HOW ABOUT DH? WHO'S OUR DESIGNATED HITTER?
I PUT DOWN SHERMY, OKAY?
THAT'S FINE...SHERMY'S A GOOD HITTER
AND I'VE PUT YOU DOWN FOR DG
DG?
DESIGNATED GOAT!
3-13
SCHULZ

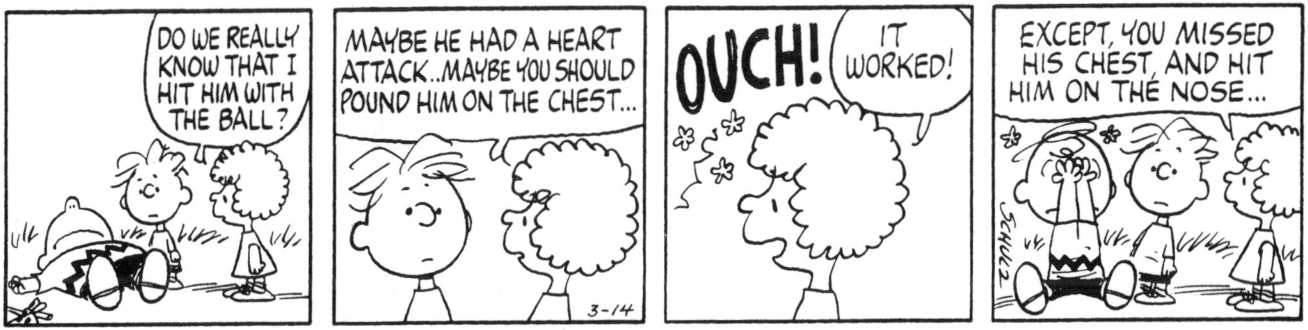
DO WE REALLY KNOW THAT I HIT HIM WITH THE BALL?
MAYBE HE HAD A HEART ATTACK..MAYBE YOU SHOULD POUND HIM ON THE CHEST...
3-14
OUCH!
IT WORKED!
EXCEPT, YOU MISSED HIS CHEST, AND HIT HIM ON THE NOSE...
SCHULZ

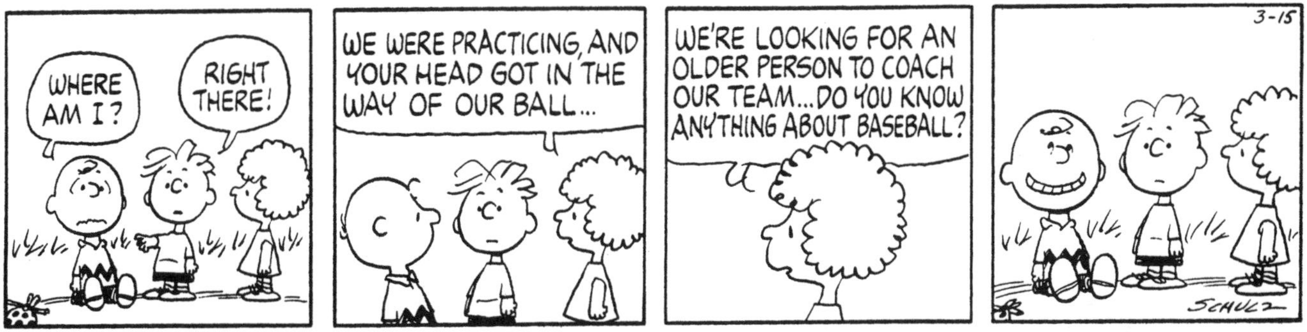
WHERE AM I?
RIGHT THERE!
WE WERE PRACTICING, AND YOUR HEAD GOT IN THE WAY OF OUR BALL...
WE'RE LOOKING FOR AN OLDER PERSON TO COACH OUR TEAM...DO YOU KNOW ANYTHING ABOUT BASEBALL?
3-15
SCHULZ

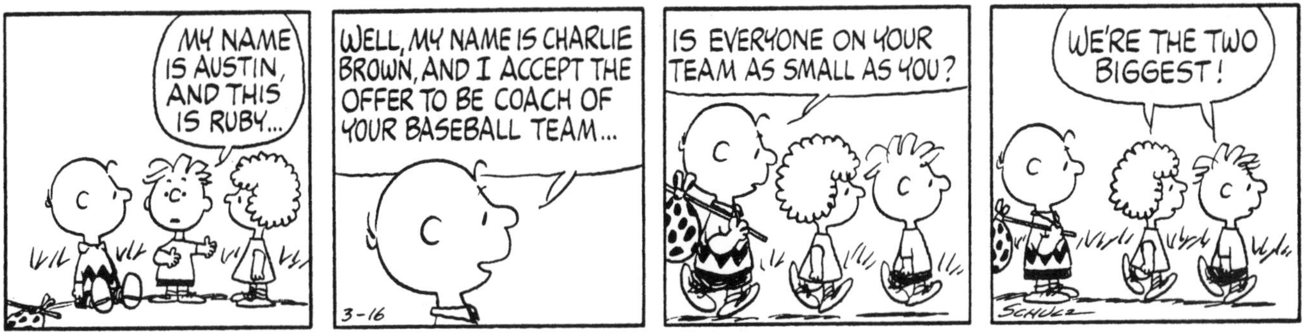
MY NAME IS AUSTIN, AND THIS IS RUBY...
WELL, MY NAME IS CHARLIE BROWN, AND I ACCEPT THE OFFER TO BE COACH OF YOUR BASEBALL TEAM...
3-16
IS EVERYONE ON YOUR TEAM AS SMALL AS YOU?
WE'RE THE TWO BIGGEST!
SCHULZ

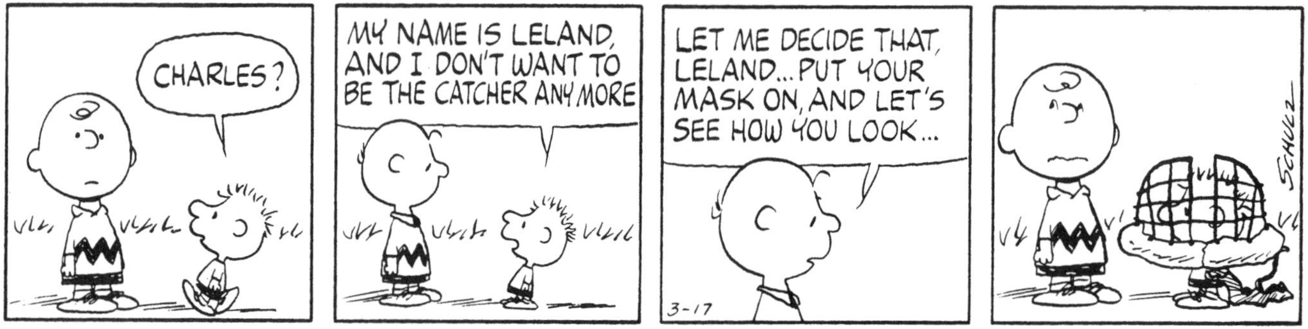
CHARLES?
MY NAME IS LELAND, AND I DON'T WANT TO BE THE CATCHER ANY MORE
LET ME DECIDE THAT, LELAND... PUT YOUR MASK ON, AND LET'S SEE HOW YOU LOOK...
3-17
SCHULZ

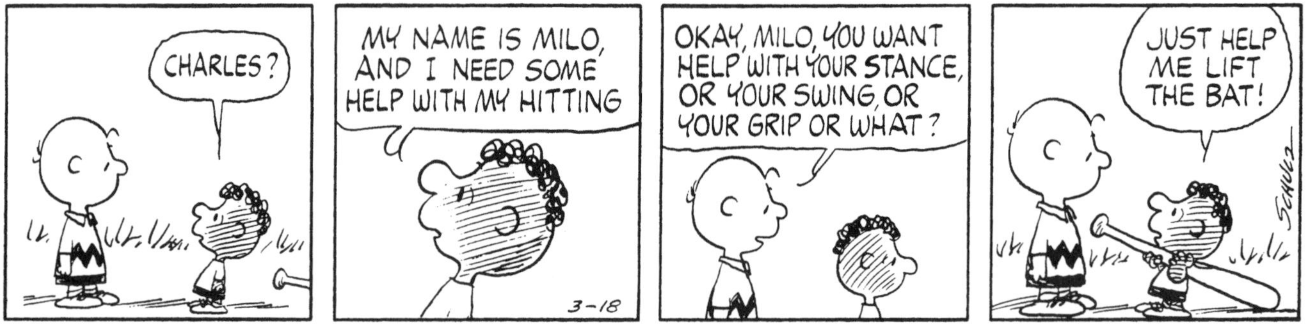
CHARLES?
MY NAME IS MILO, AND I NEED SOME HELP WITH MY HITTING
3-18
OKAY, MILO, YOU WANT HELP WITH YOUR STANCE, OR YOUR SWING, OR YOUR GRIP OR WHAT?
JUST HELP ME LIFT THE BAT!
SCHULZ

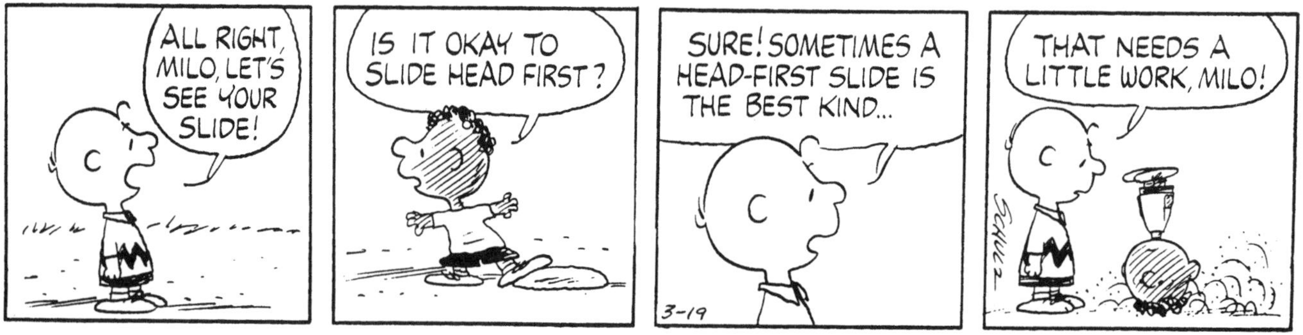
ALL RIGHT, MILO, LET'S SEE YOUR SLIDE!
IS IT OKAY TO SLIDE HEAD FIRST?
SURE! SOMETIMES A HEAD-FIRST SLIDE IS THE BEST KIND...
3-19
THAT NEEDS A LITTLE WORK, MILO!
SCHULZ

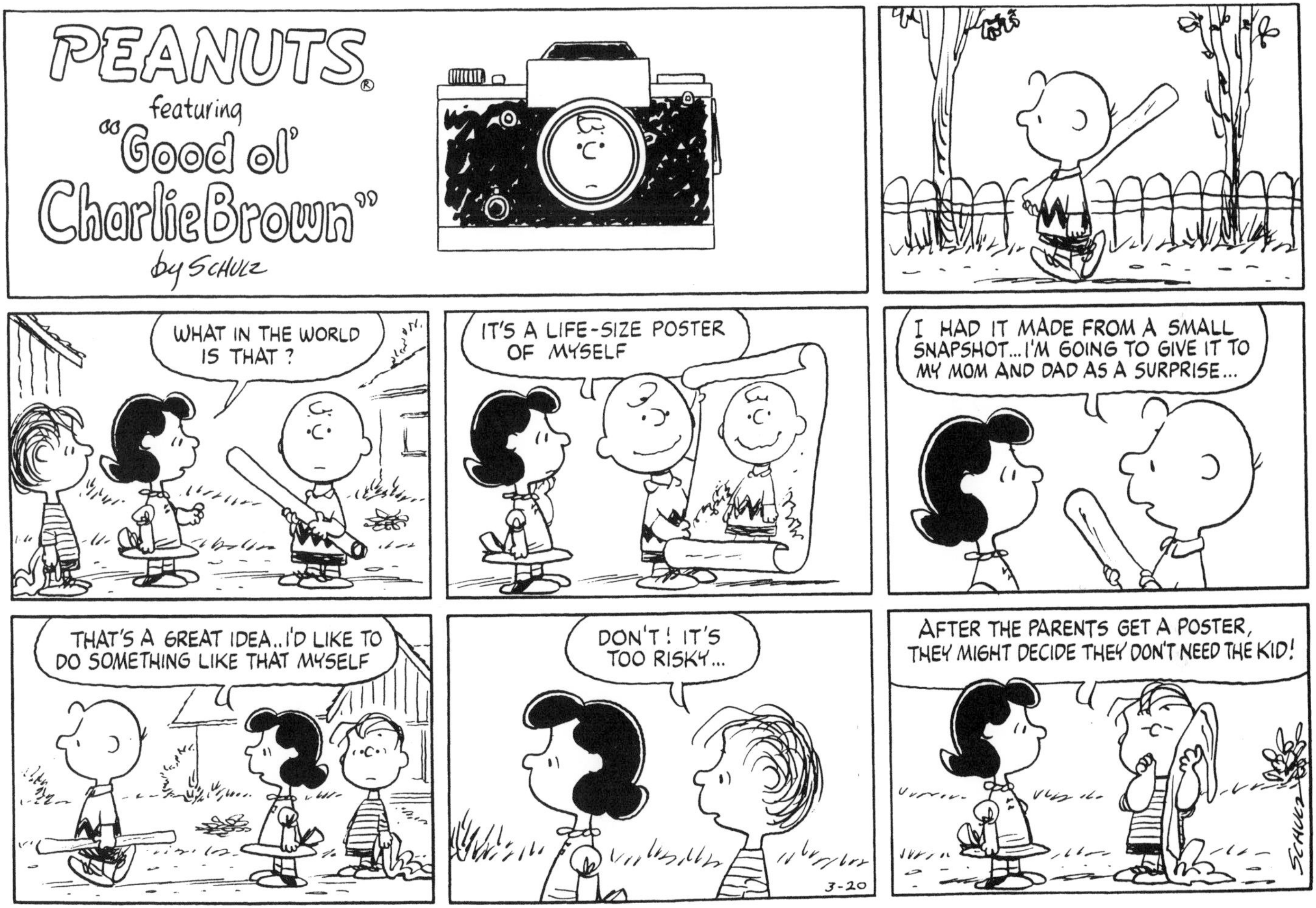
PEANUTS®
featuring "Good ol' Charlie Brown"
by SCHULZ
WHAT IN THE WORLD IS THAT ?
IT'S A LIFE-SIZE POSTER OF MYSELF
I HAD IT MADE FROM A SMALL SNAPSHOT...I'M GOING TO GIVE IT TO MY MOM AND DAD AS A SURPRISE...
THAT'S A GREAT IDEA..I'D LIKE TO DO SOMETHING LIKE THAT MYSELF
DON'T ! IT'S TOO RISKY...
AFTER THE PARENTS GET A POSTER, THEY MIGHT DECIDE THEY DON'T NEED THE KID!
3-20
SCHULZ

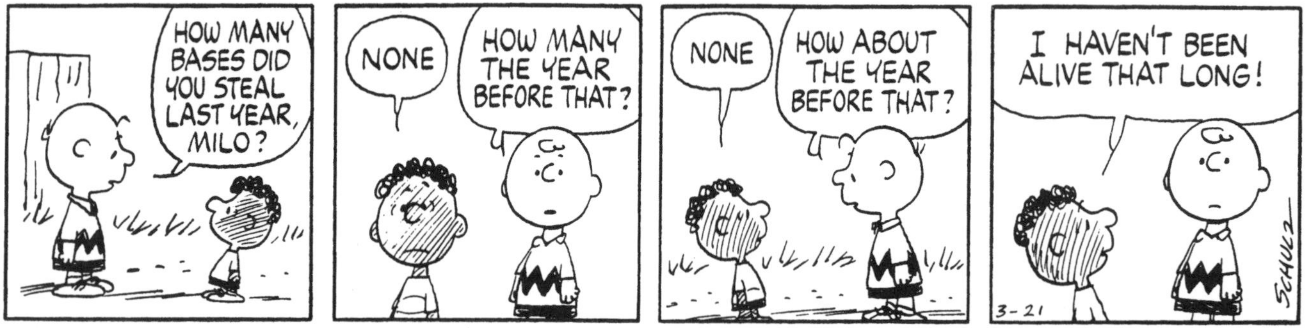
HOW MANY BASES DID YOU STEAL LAST YEAR, MILO?
NONE
HOW MANY THE YEAR BEFORE THAT?
NONE
HOW ABOUT THE YEAR BEFORE THAT?
I HAVEN'T BEEN ALIVE THAT LONG!
3-21
SCHULZ

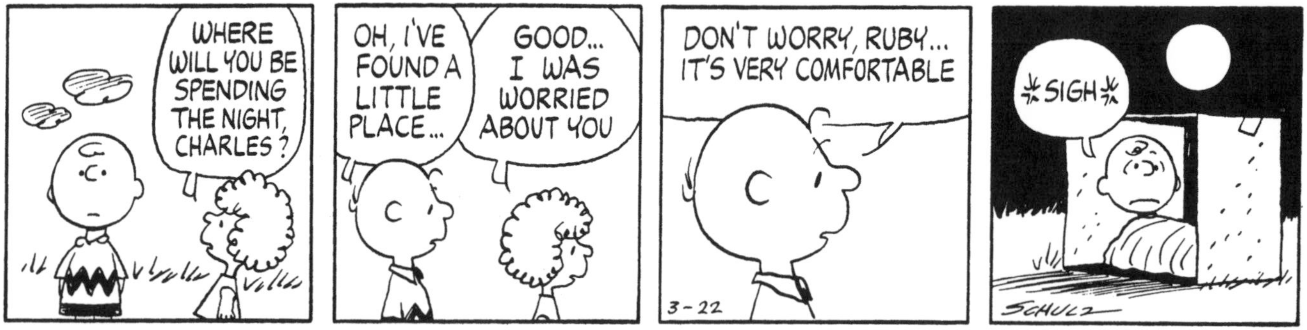
WHERE WILL YOU BE SPENDING THE NIGHT, CHARLES?
OH, I'VE FOUND A LITTLE PLACE...
GOOD... I WAS WORRIED ABOUT YOU
DON'T WORRY, RUBY... IT'S VERY COMFORTABLE
3-22
SIGH
SCHULZ

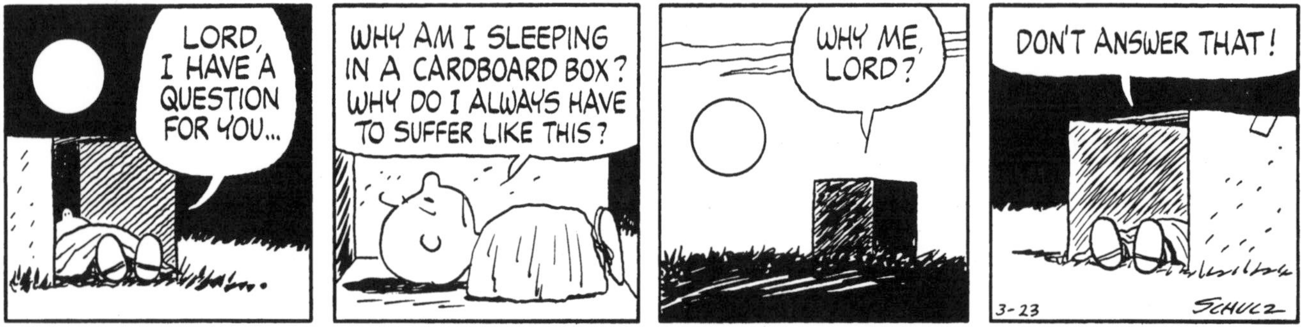
LORD, I HAVE A QUESTION FOR YOU...
WHY AM I SLEEPING IN A CARDBOARD BOX? WHY DO I ALWAYS HAVE TO SUFFER LIKE THIS?
WHY ME, LORD?
DON'T ANSWER THAT!
3-23
SCHULZ

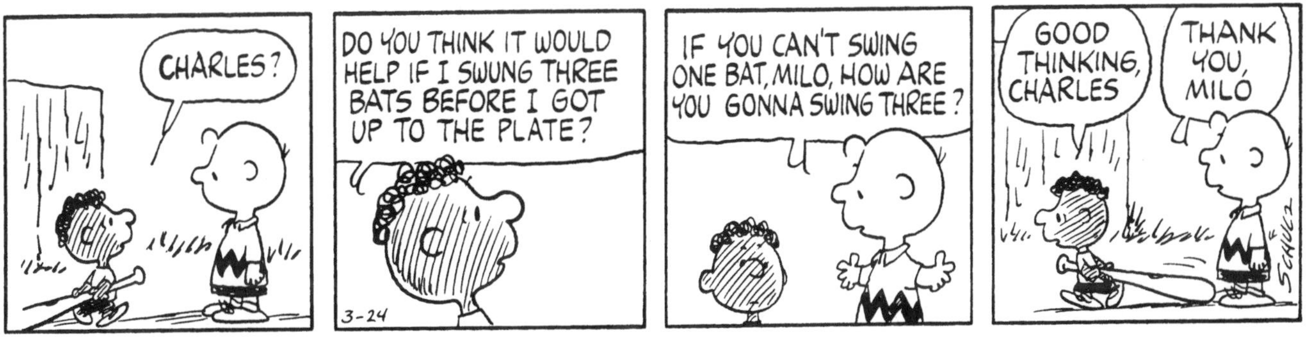
CHARLES?
DO YOU THINK IT WOULD HELP IF I SWUNG THREE BATS BEFORE I GOT UP TO THE PLATE?
3-24
IF YOU CAN'T SWING ONE BAT, MILO, HOW ARE YOU GONNA SWING THREE?
GOOD THINKING, CHARLES
THANK YOU, MILO
SCHULZ

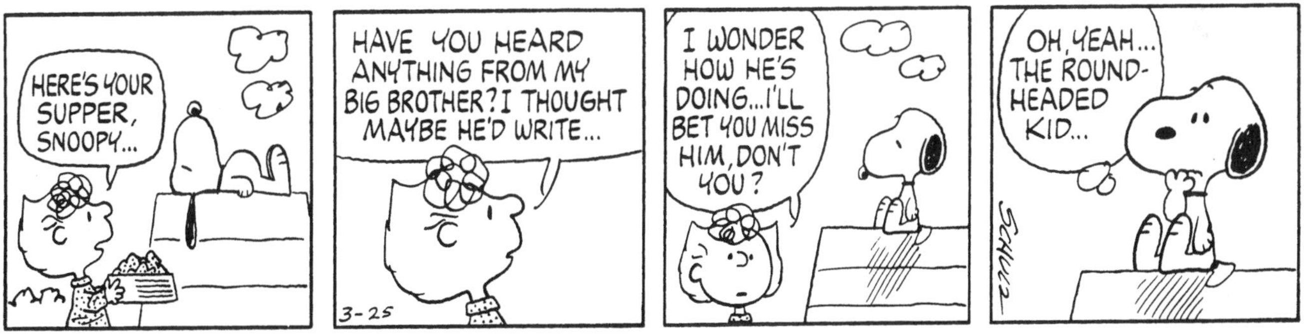
HERE'S YOUR SUPPER, SNOOPY...
HAVE YOU HEARD ANYTHING FROM MY BIG BROTHER? I THOUGHT MAYBE HE'D WRITE...
3-25
I WONDER HOW HE'S DOING...I'LL BET YOU MISS HIM, DON'T YOU?
OH, YEAH... THE ROUND-HEADED KID...
SCHULZ

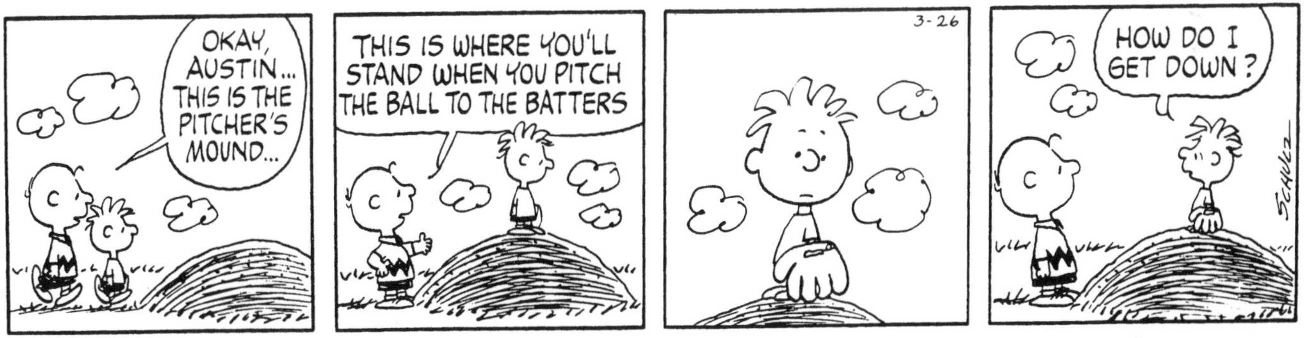
OKAY, AUSTIN... THIS IS THE PITCHER'S MOUND...
THIS IS WHERE YOU'LL STAND WHEN YOU PITCH THE BALL TO THE BATTERS
3-26
HOW DO I GET DOWN?
SCHULZ

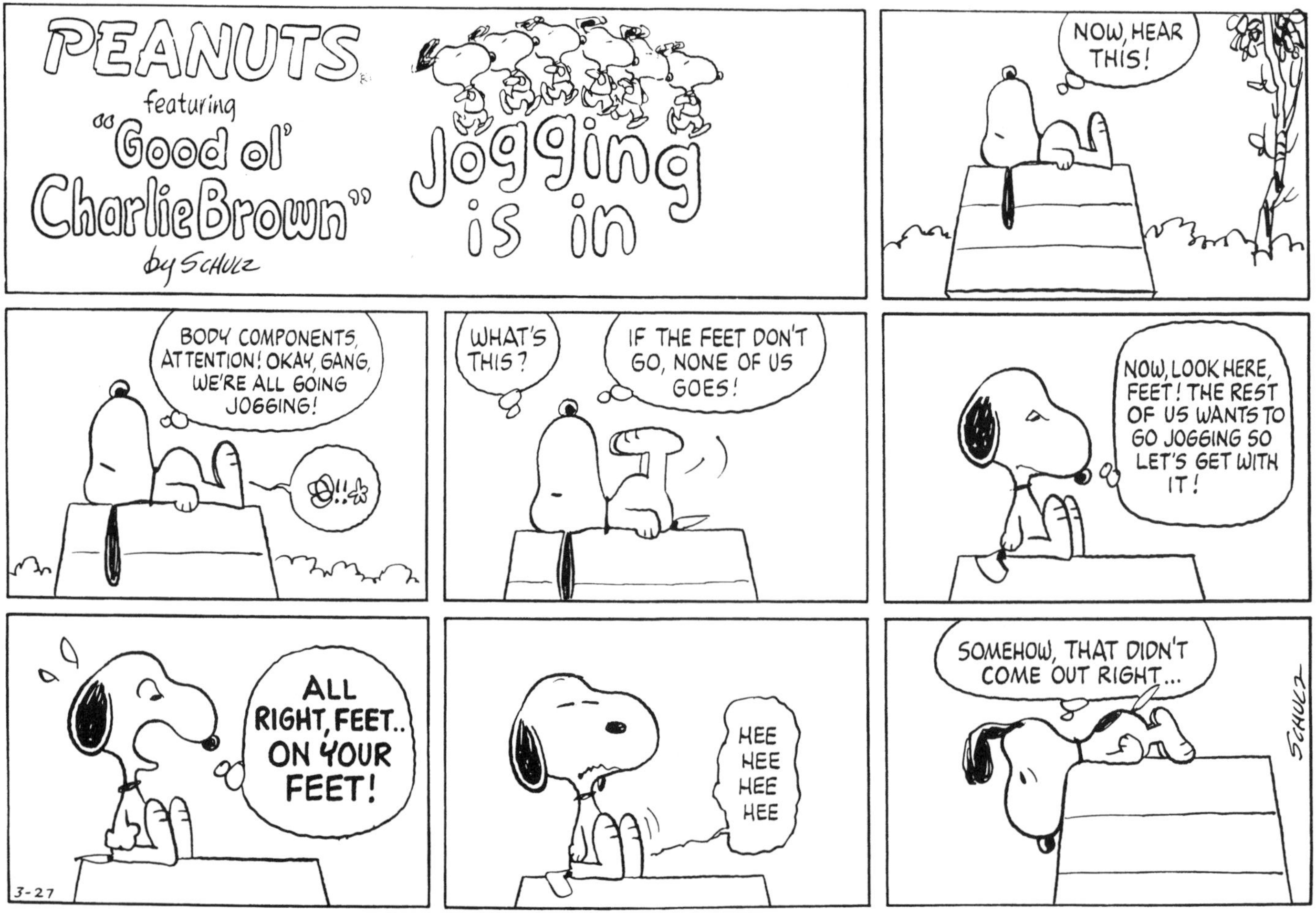
PEANUTS
featuring "Good ol' Charlie Brown"
by SCHULZ
Jogging is in
NOW, HEAR THIS!
BODY COMPONENTS, ATTENTION! OKAY, GANG, WE'RE ALL GOING JOGGING!
WHAT'S THIS?
IF THE FEET DON'T GO, NONE OF US GOES!
NOW, LOOK HERE, FEET! THE REST OF US WANTS TO GO JOGGING SO LET'S GET WITH IT!
ALL RIGHT, FEET.. ON YOUR FEET!
HEE HEE HEE HEE
SOMEHOW, THAT DIDN'T COME OUT RIGHT...
SCHULZ
3-27

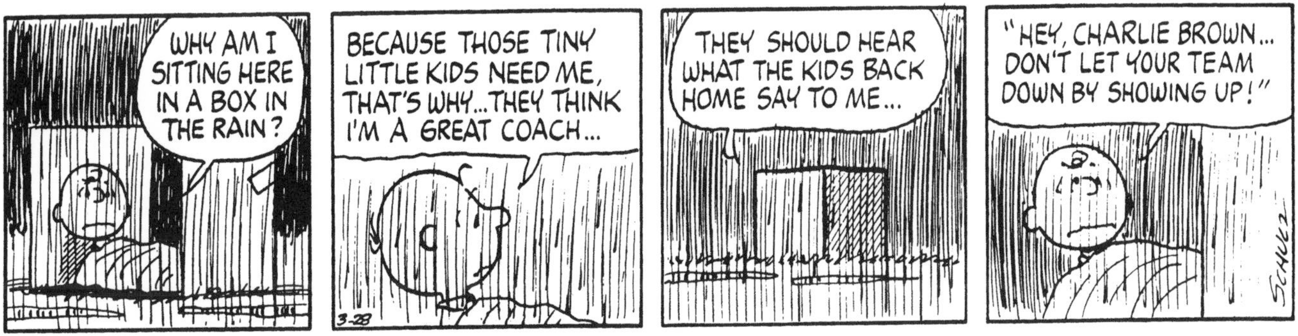
WHY AM I SITTING HERE IN A BOX IN THE RAIN?
BECAUSE THOSE TINY LITTLE KIDS NEED ME, THAT'S WHY...THEY THINK I'M A GREAT COACH...
THEY SHOULD HEAR WHAT THE KIDS BACK HOME SAY TO ME...
"HEY, CHARLIE BROWN... DON'T LET YOUR TEAM DOWN BY SHOWING UP!"

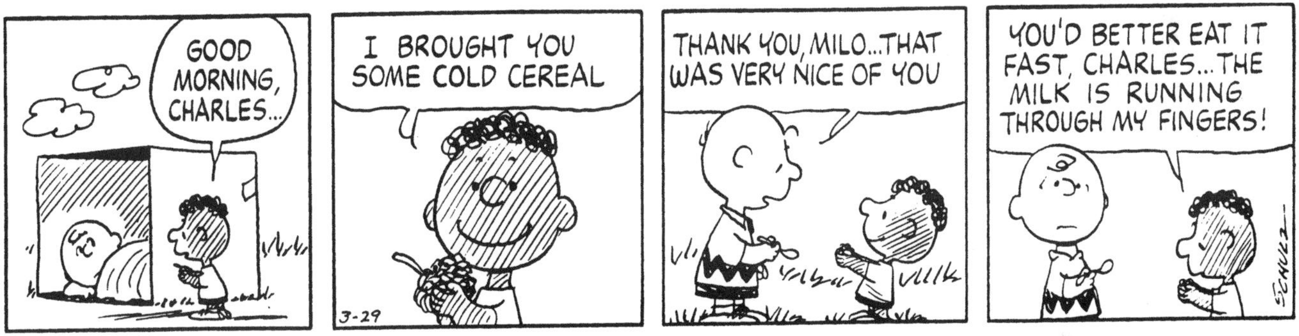
GOOD MORNING, CHARLES...
I BROUGHT YOU SOME COLD CEREAL
THANK YOU, MILO...THAT WAS VERY NICE OF YOU
YOU'D BETTER EAT IT FAST, CHARLES...THE MILK IS RUNNING THROUGH MY FINGERS!

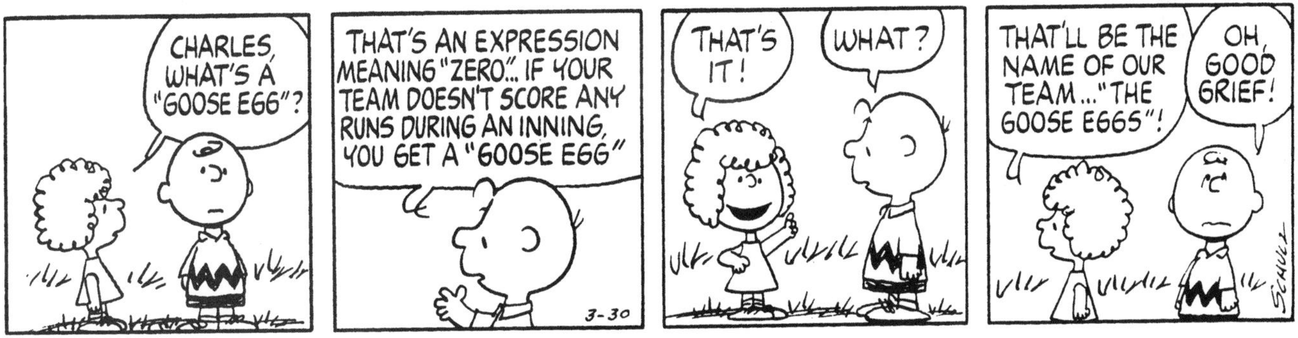
CHARLES, WHAT'S A "GOOSE EGG"?
THAT'S AN EXPRESSION MEANING "ZERO"... IF YOUR TEAM DOESN'T SCORE ANY RUNS DURING AN INNING, YOU GET A "GOOSE EGG"
THAT'S IT!
WHAT?
THAT'LL BE THE NAME OF OUR TEAM..."THE GOOSE EGGS"!
OH, GOOD GRIEF!

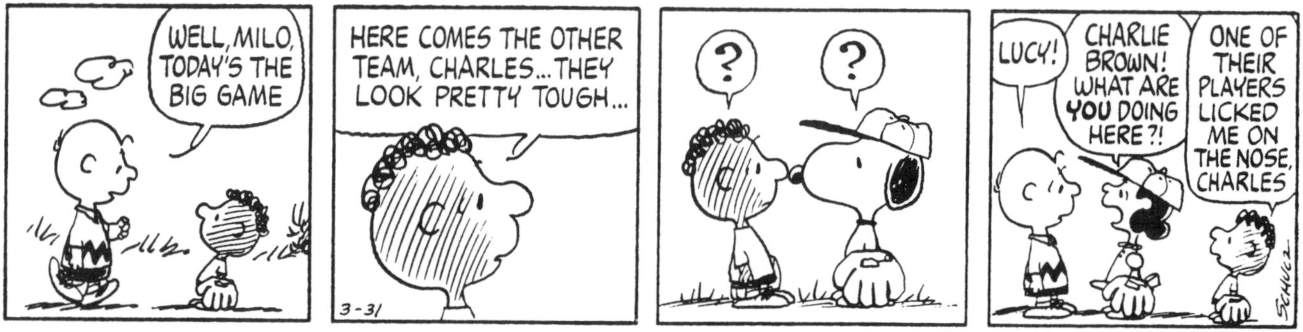
WELL, MILO, TODAY'S THE BIG GAME
HERE COMES THE OTHER TEAM, CHARLES...THEY LOOK PRETTY TOUGH...
3-31
?
?
LUCY!
CHARLIE BROWN! WHAT ARE **YOU** DOING HERE?!
ONE OF THEIR PLAYERS LICKED ME ON THE NOSE, CHARLES

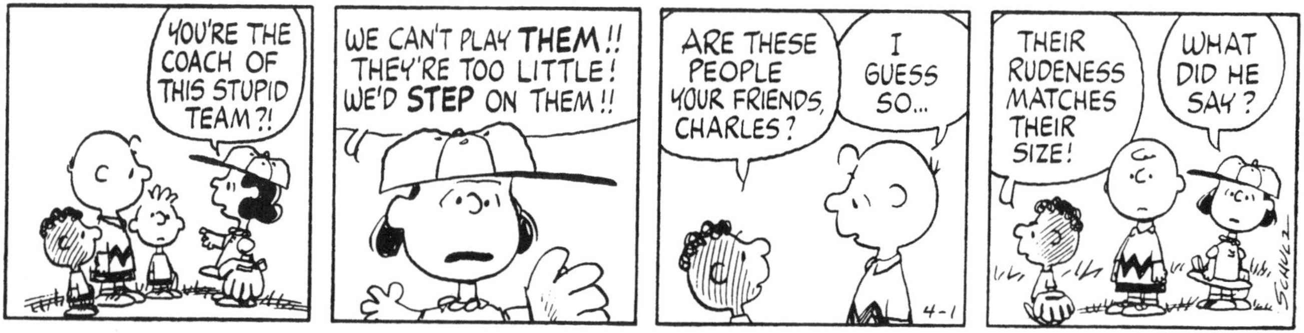
YOU'RE THE COACH OF THIS STUPID TEAM?!
WE CAN'T PLAY **THEM**!! THEY'RE TOO LITTLE! WE'D **STEP** ON THEM!!
ARE THESE PEOPLE YOUR FRIENDS, CHARLES?
I GUESS SO...
4-1
THEIR RUDENESS MATCHES THEIR SIZE!
WHAT DID HE SAY?

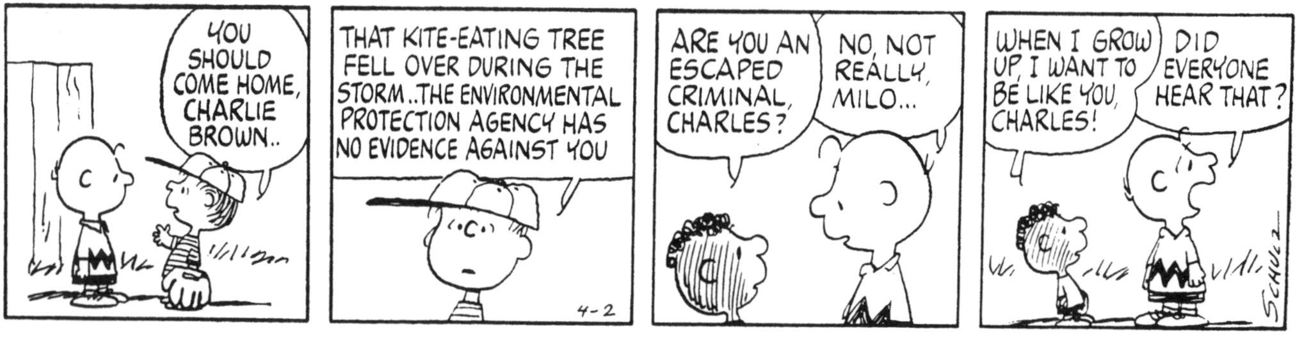
YOU SHOULD COME HOME, CHARLIE BROWN..
THAT KITE-EATING TREE FELL OVER DURING THE STORM..THE ENVIRONMENTAL PROTECTION AGENCY HAS NO EVIDENCE AGAINST YOU
4-2
ARE YOU AN ESCAPED CRIMINAL, CHARLES?
NO, NOT REALLY, MILO...
WHEN I GROW UP, I WANT TO BE LIKE YOU, CHARLES!
DID EVERYONE HEAR THAT?

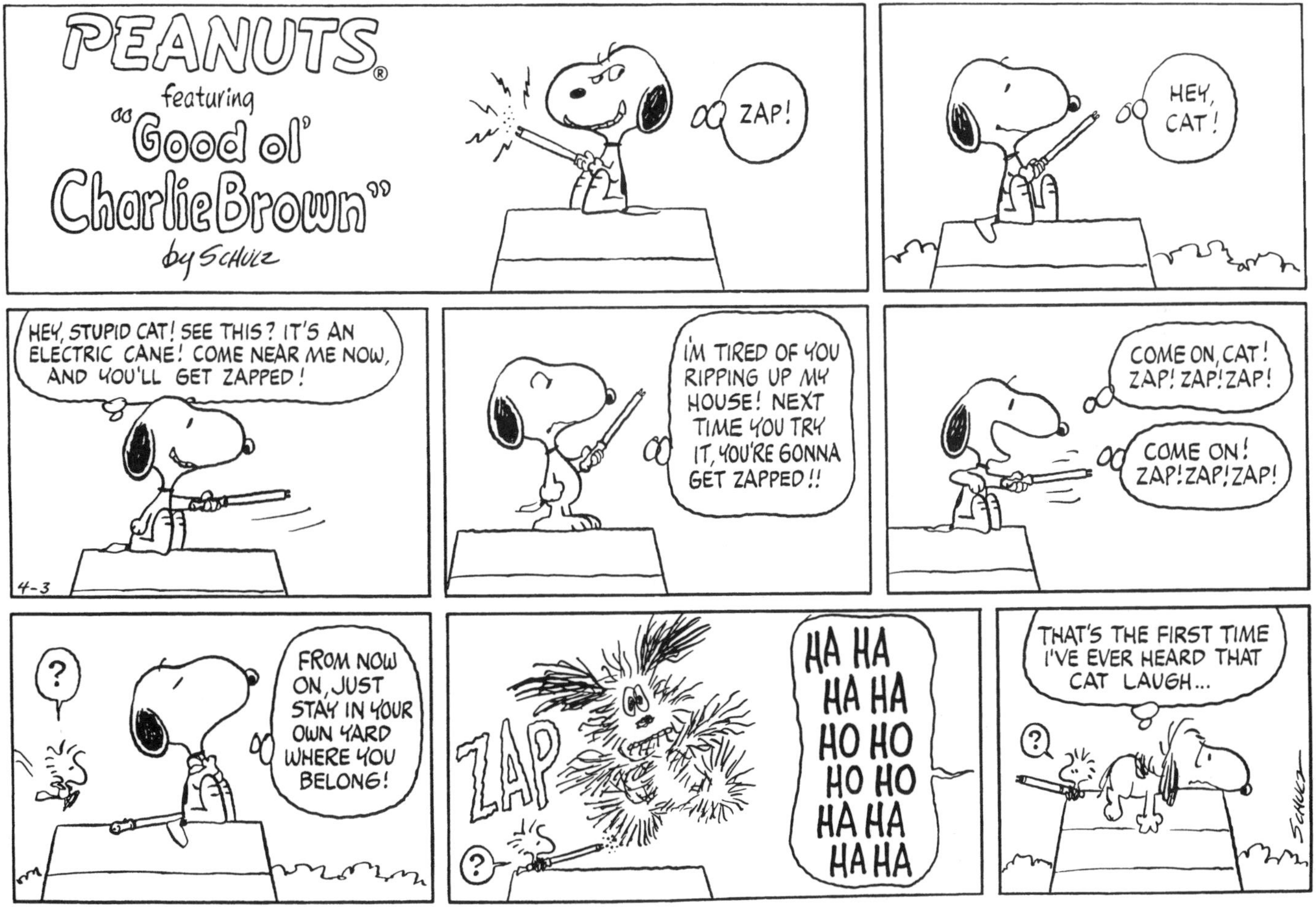
PEANUTS®
featuring "Good ol' Charlie Brown"
by SCHULZ
ZAP!
HEY, CAT!
HEY, STUPID CAT! SEE THIS? IT'S AN ELECTRIC CANE! COME NEAR ME NOW, AND YOU'LL GET ZAPPED!
4-3
I'M TIRED OF YOU RIPPING UP MY HOUSE! NEXT TIME YOU TRY IT, YOU'RE GONNA GET ZAPPED!!
COME ON, CAT! ZAP! ZAP! ZAP!
COME ON! ZAP! ZAP! ZAP!
?
FROM NOW ON, JUST STAY IN YOUR OWN YARD WHERE YOU BELONG!
ZAP
?
HA HA HA HA HO HO HO HO HA HA HA HA
THAT'S THE FIRST TIME I'VE EVER HEARD THAT CAT LAUGH...
?
SCHULZ

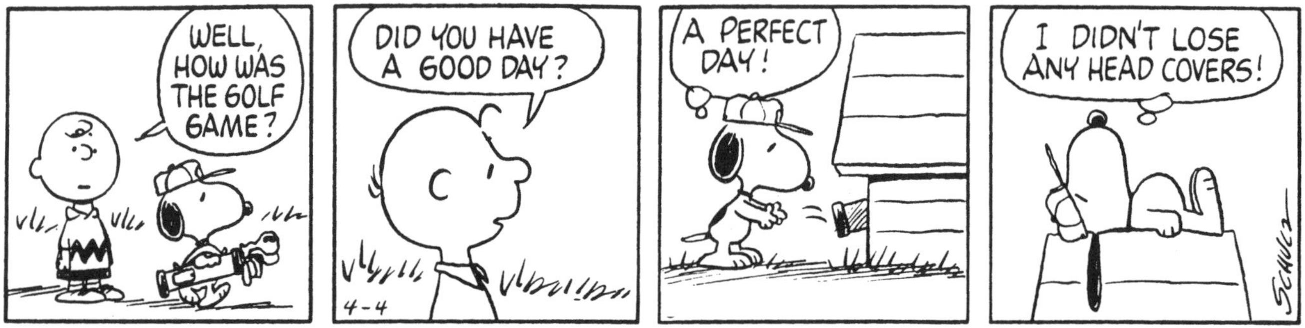
WELL, HOW WAS THE GOLF GAME?
DID YOU HAVE A GOOD DAY?
4-4
A PERFECT DAY!
I DIDN'T LOSE ANY HEAD COVERS!
SCHULZ

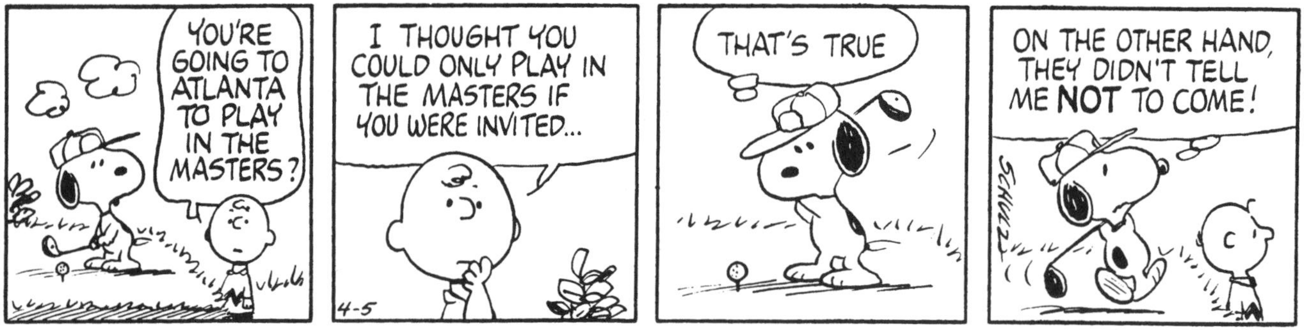
YOU'RE GOING TO ATLANTA TO PLAY IN THE MASTERS?
I THOUGHT YOU COULD ONLY PLAY IN THE MASTERS IF YOU WERE INVITED...
4-5
THAT'S TRUE
ON THE OTHER HAND, THEY DIDN'T TELL ME **NOT** TO COME!
SCHULZ

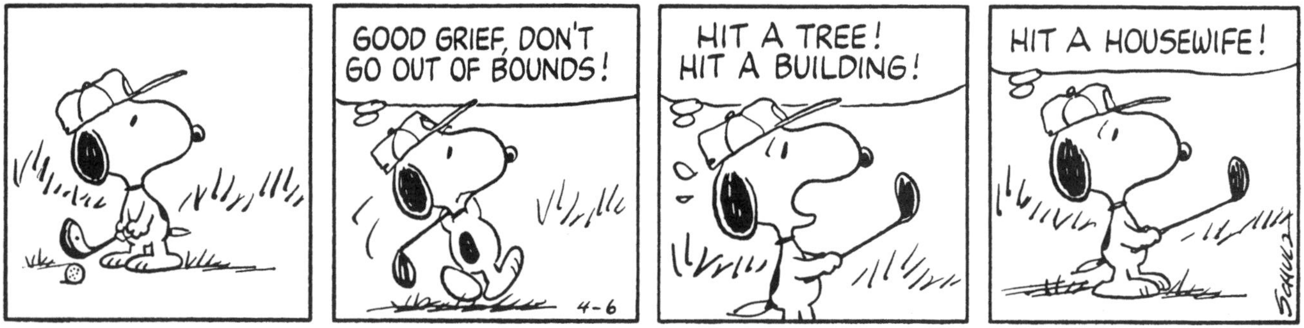
GOOD GRIEF, DON'T GO OUT OF BOUNDS!
4-6
HIT A TREE! HIT A BUILDING!
HIT A HOUSEWIFE!
SCHULZ

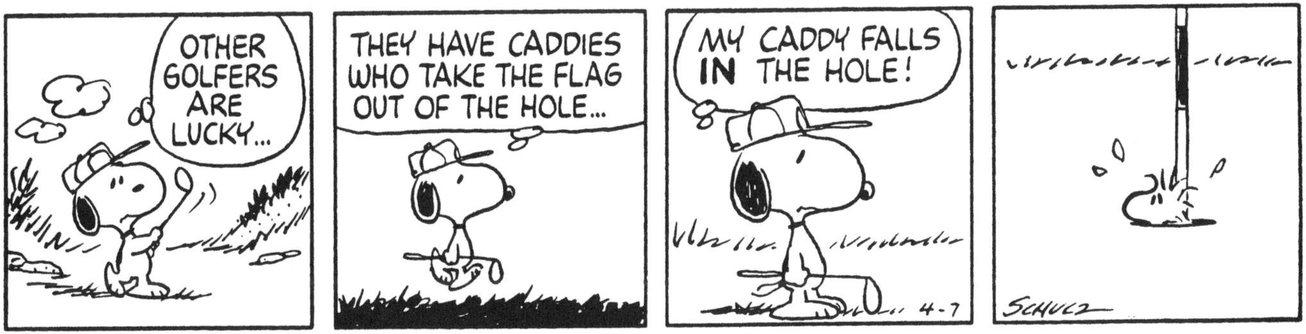
OTHER GOLFERS ARE LUCKY...
THEY HAVE CADDIES WHO TAKE THE FLAG OUT OF THE HOLE...
MY CADDY FALLS **IN** THE HOLE!

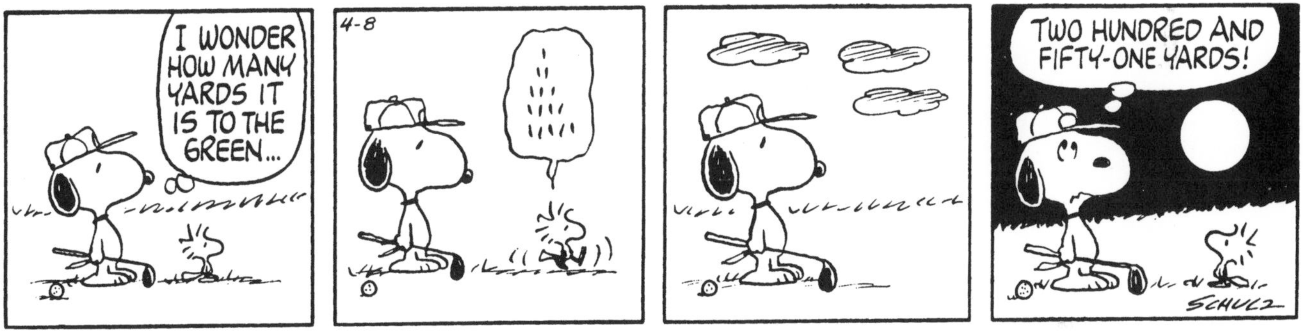
I WONDER HOW MANY YARDS IT IS TO THE GREEN...
TWO HUNDRED AND FIFTY-ONE YARDS!

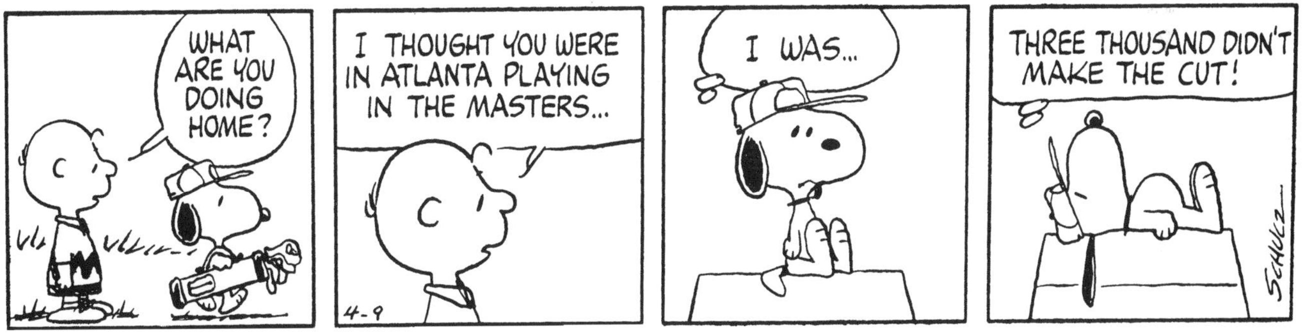
WHAT ARE YOU DOING HOME?
I THOUGHT YOU WERE IN ATLANTA PLAYING IN THE MASTERS...
I WAS...
THREE THOUSAND DIDN'T MAKE THE CUT!

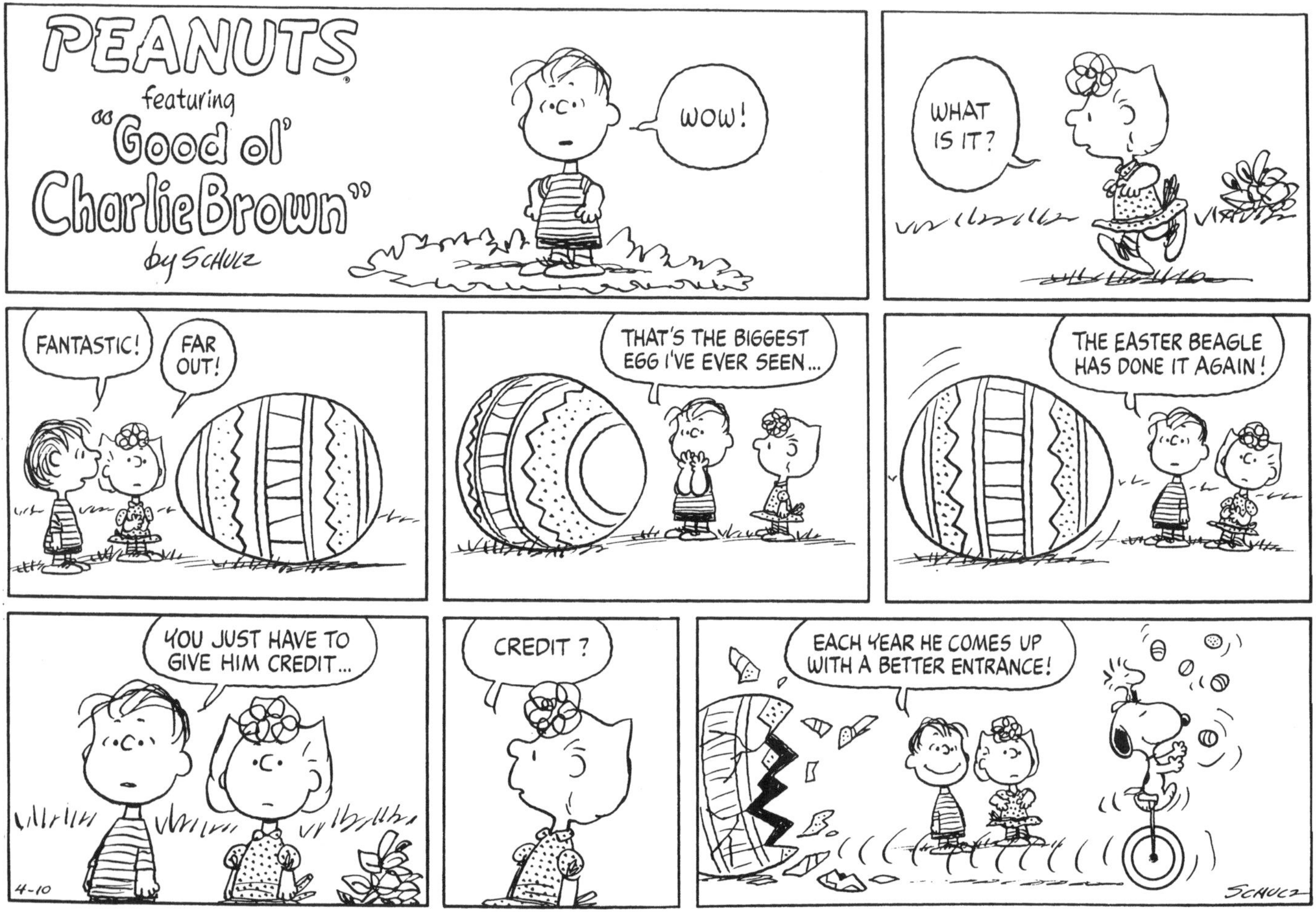
PEANUTS
featuring
"Good ol' Charlie Brown"
by SCHULZ
WOW!
WHAT IS IT?
FANTASTIC!
FAR OUT!
THAT'S THE BIGGEST EGG I'VE EVER SEEN...
THE EASTER BEAGLE HAS DONE IT AGAIN!
YOU JUST HAVE TO GIVE HIM CREDIT...
CREDIT ?
EACH YEAR HE COMES UP WITH A BETTER ENTRANCE!
4-10
SCHULZ

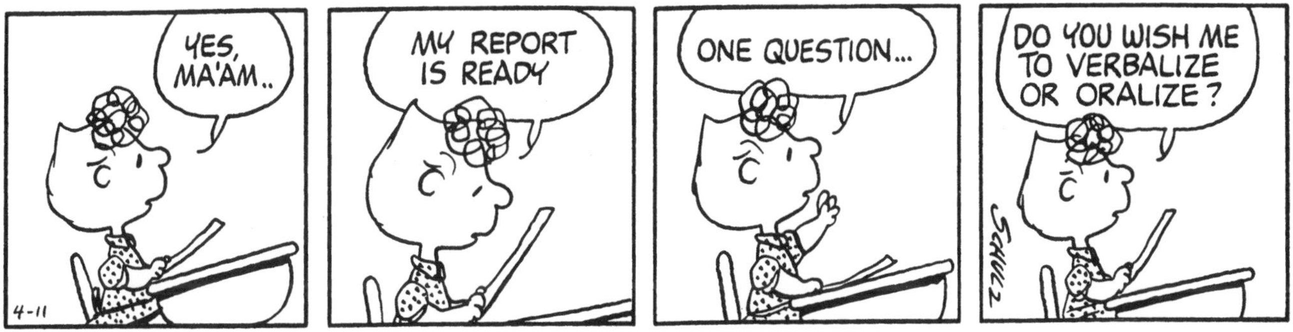
YES, MA'AM..
MY REPORT IS READY
ONE QUESTION...
DO YOU WISH ME TO VERBALIZE OR ORALIZE?
4-11
SCHULZ

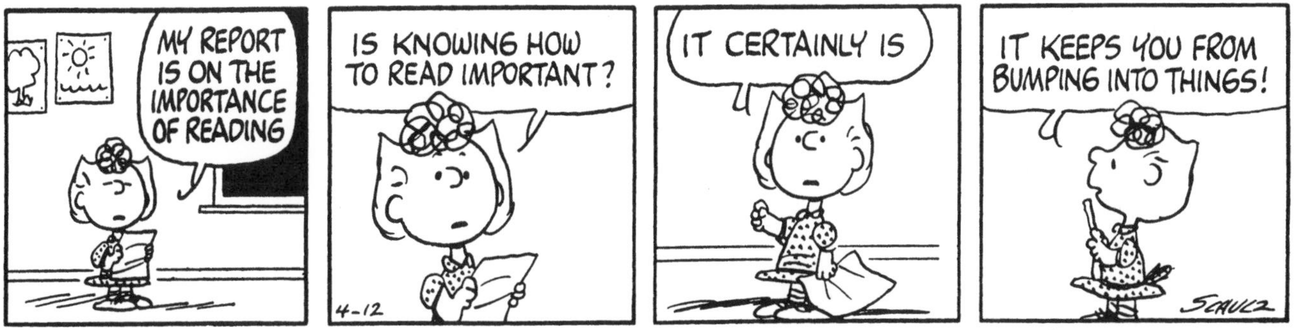
MY REPORT IS ON THE IMPORTANCE OF READING
IS KNOWING HOW TO READ IMPORTANT?
IT CERTAINLY IS
IT KEEPS YOU FROM BUMPING INTO THINGS!
4-12
SCHULZ

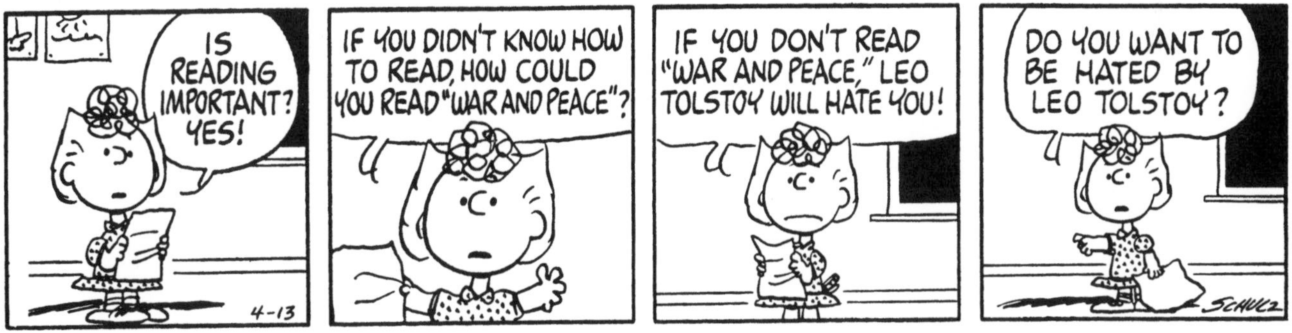
IS READING IMPORTANT? YES!
IF YOU DIDN'T KNOW HOW TO READ, HOW COULD YOU READ "WAR AND PEACE"?
IF YOU DON'T READ "WAR AND PEACE," LEO TOLSTOY WILL HATE YOU!
DO YOU WANT TO BE HATED BY LEO TOLSTOY?
4-13
SCHULZ

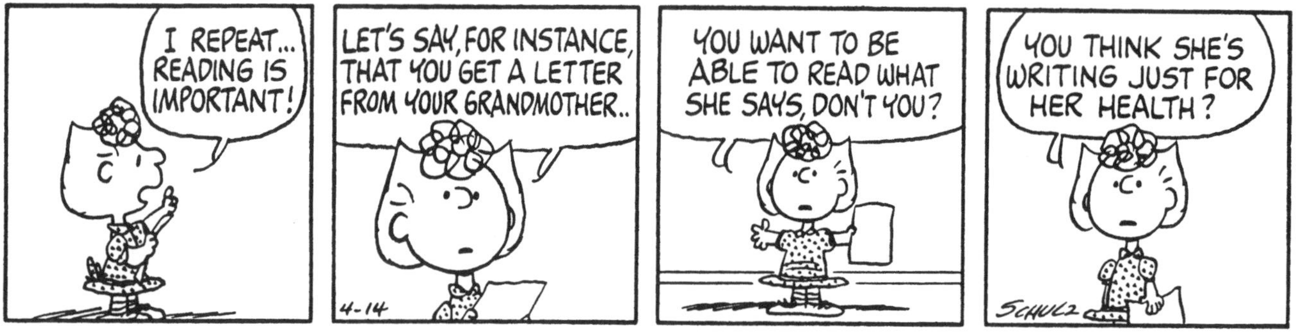
I REPEAT... READING IS IMPORTANT!
LET'S SAY, FOR INSTANCE, THAT YOU GET A LETTER FROM YOUR GRANDMOTHER..
4-14
YOU WANT TO BE ABLE TO READ WHAT SHE SAYS, DON'T YOU?
YOU THINK SHE'S WRITING JUST FOR HER HEALTH?
SCHULZ

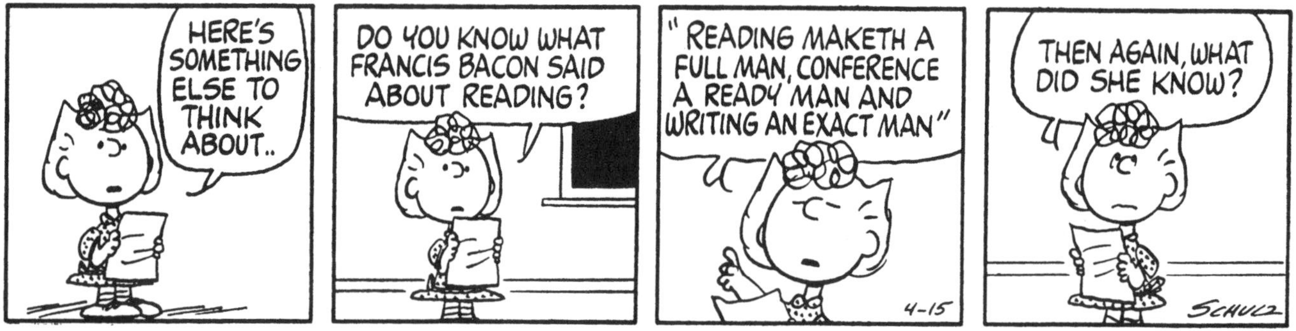
HERE'S SOMETHING ELSE TO THINK ABOUT..
DO YOU KNOW WHAT FRANCIS BACON SAID ABOUT READING?
"READING MAKETH A FULL MAN, CONFERENCE A READY MAN AND WRITING AN EXACT MAN"
4-15
THEN AGAIN, WHAT DID SHE KNOW?
SCHULZ

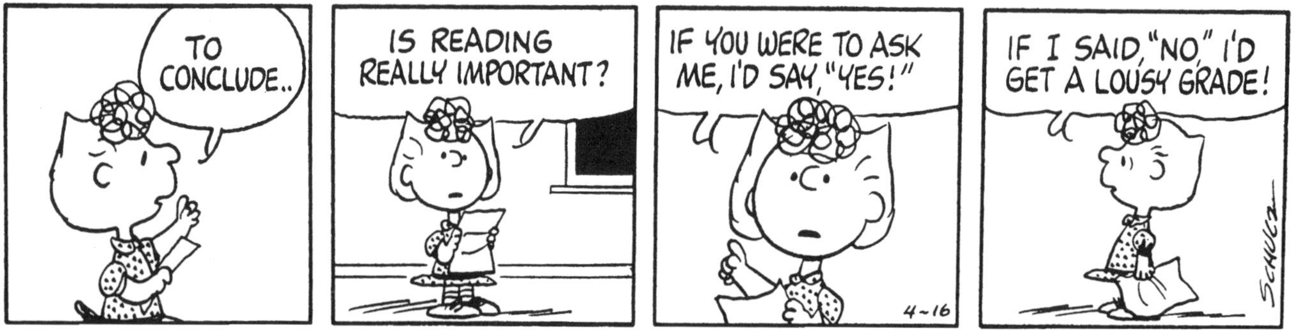
TO CONCLUDE..
IS READING REALLY IMPORTANT?
IF YOU WERE TO ASK ME, I'D SAY, "YES!"
4-16
IF I SAID, "NO," I'D GET A LOUSY GRADE!
SCHULZ

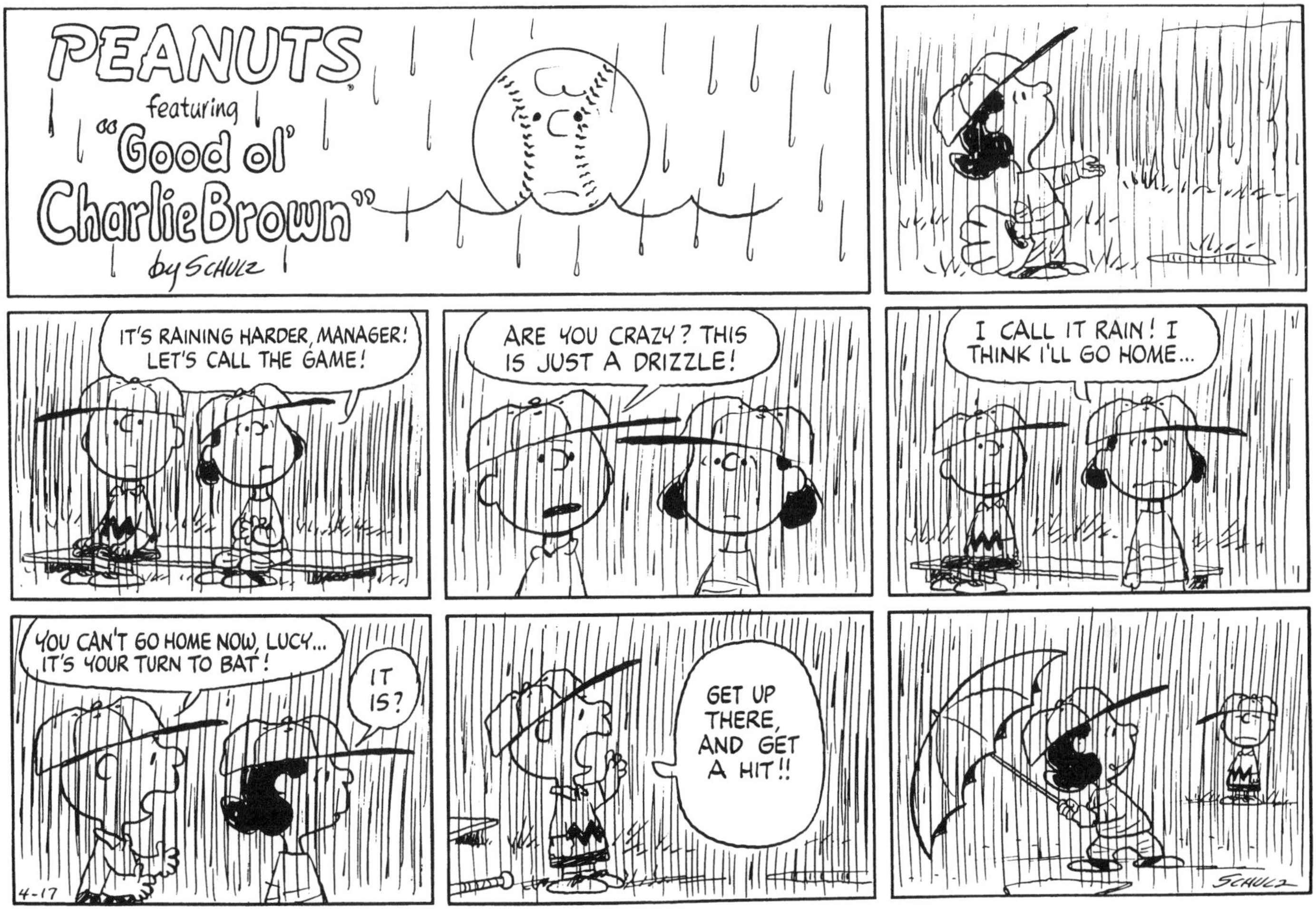
PEANUTS
featuring "Good ol' CharlieBrown"
by SCHULZ
IT'S RAINING HARDER, MANAGER! LET'S CALL THE GAME!
ARE YOU CRAZY? THIS IS JUST A DRIZZLE!
I CALL IT RAIN! I THINK I'LL GO HOME...
YOU CAN'T GO HOME NOW, LUCY... IT'S YOUR TURN TO BAT!
IT IS?
GET UP THERE, AND GET A HIT!!
4-17
SCHULZ

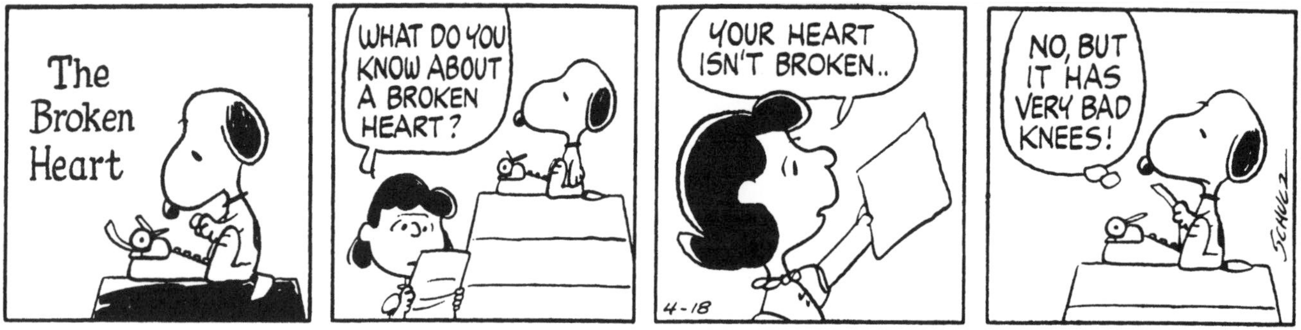
The Broken Heart
WHAT DO YOU KNOW ABOUT A BROKEN HEART?
YOUR HEART ISN'T BROKEN..
4-18
NO, BUT IT HAS VERY BAD KNEES!
SCHULZ

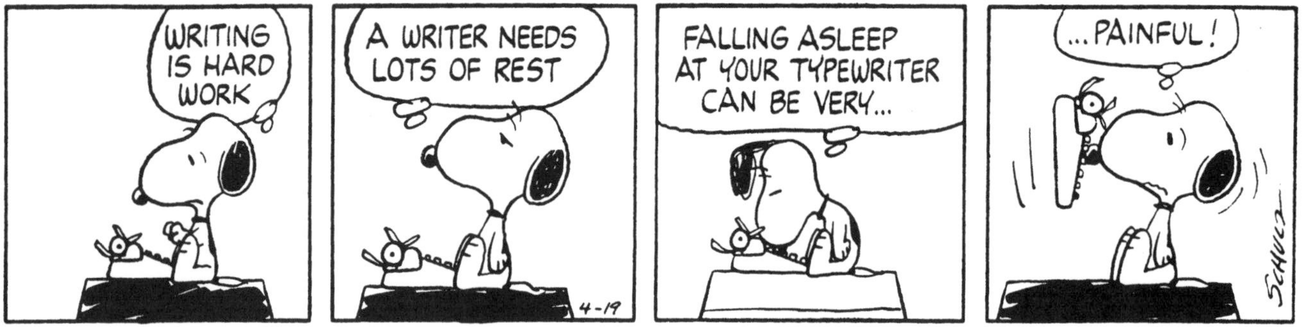
WRITING IS HARD WORK
A WRITER NEEDS LOTS OF REST
4-19
FALLING ASLEEP AT YOUR TYPEWRITER CAN BE VERY...
...PAINFUL!
SCHULZ

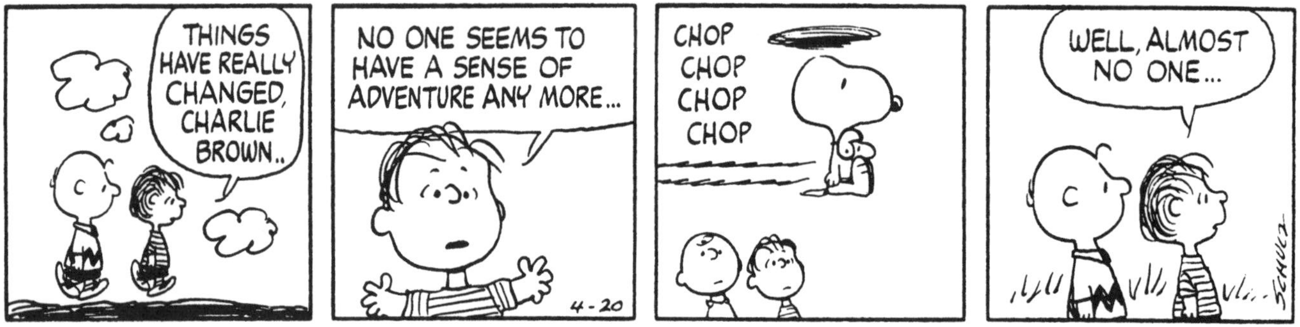
THINGS HAVE REALLY CHANGED, CHARLIE BROWN..
NO ONE SEEMS TO HAVE A SENSE OF ADVENTURE ANY MORE...
4-20
CHOP
CHOP
CHOP
CHOP
WELL, ALMOST NO ONE...
SCHULZ

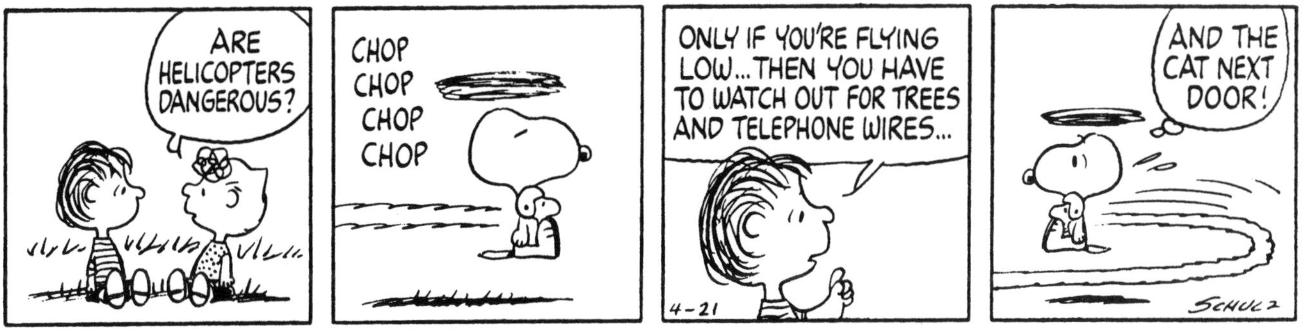
ARE HELICOPTERS DANGEROUS?
CHOP CHOP CHOP CHOP
ONLY IF YOU'RE FLYING LOW...THEN YOU HAVE TO WATCH OUT FOR TREES AND TELEPHONE WIRES...
4-21
AND THE CAT NEXT DOOR!
SCHULZ

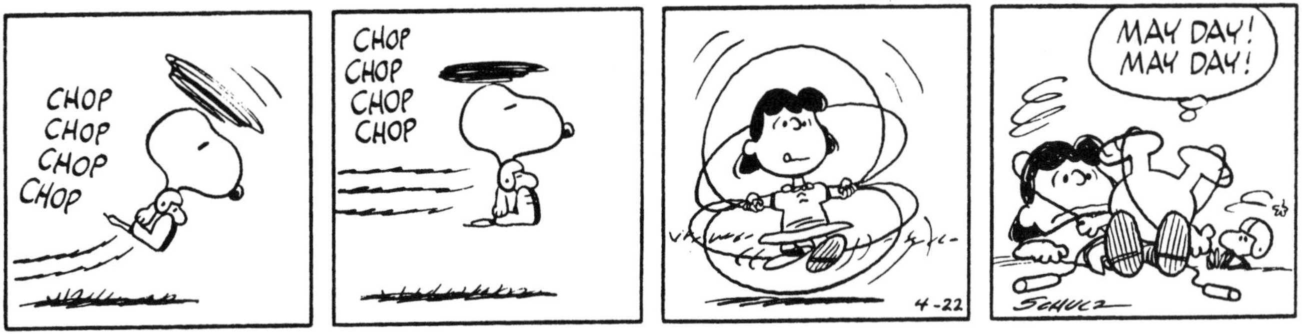
CHOP CHOP CHOP CHOP
CHOP CHOP CHOP CHOP
4-22
MAY DAY! MAY DAY!
SCHULZ

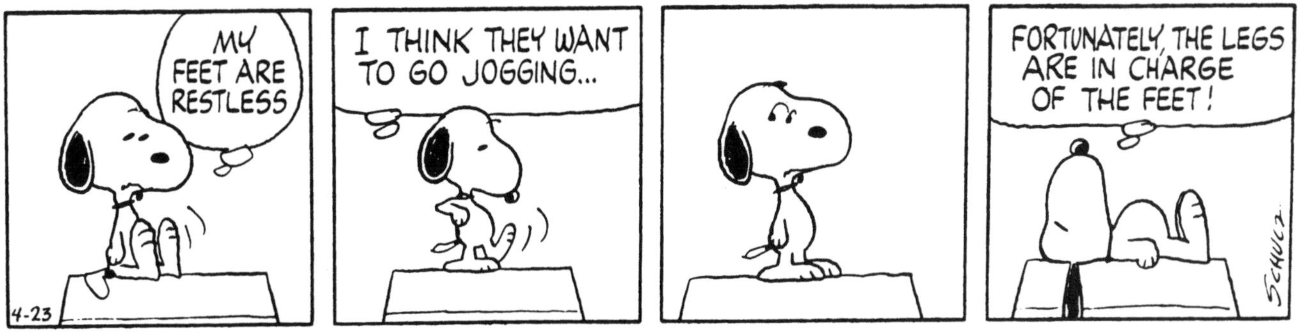
MY FEET ARE RESTLESS
4-23
I THINK THEY WANT TO GO JOGGING...
FORTUNATELY, THE LEGS ARE IN CHARGE OF THE FEET!
SCHULZ

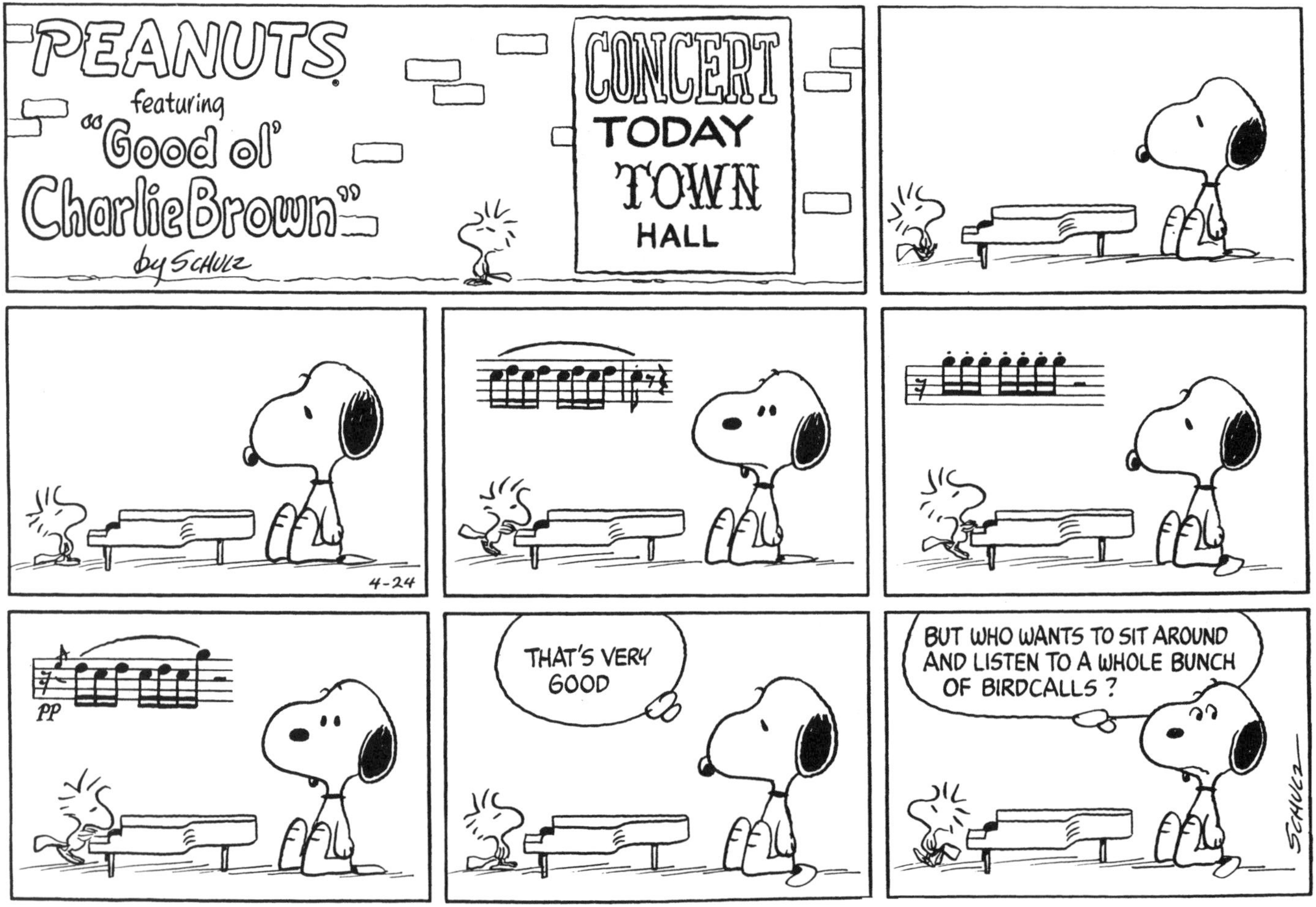
PEANUTS
featuring
"Good ol' Charlie Brown"
by SCHULZ
CONCERT
TODAY
TOWN
HALL
4-24
PP
THAT'S VERY GOOD
BUT WHO WANTS TO SIT AROUND AND LISTEN TO A WHOLE BUNCH OF BIRDCALLS ?
SCHULZ

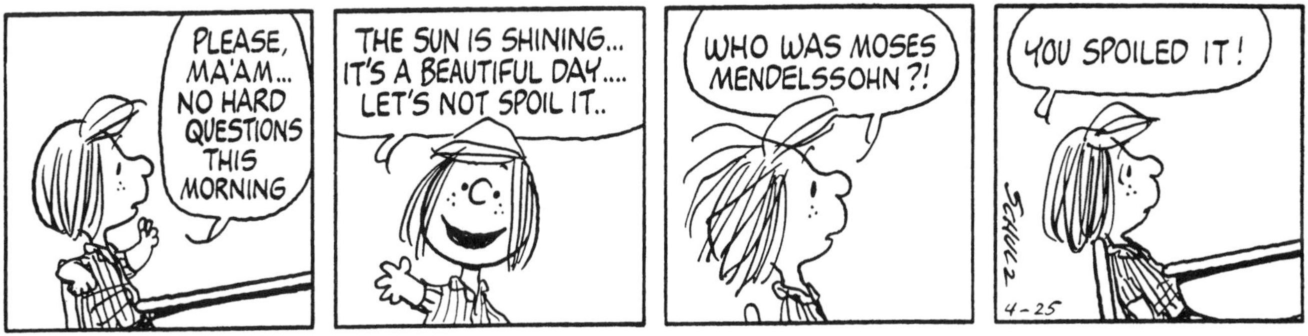
PLEASE, MA'AM... NO HARD QUESTIONS THIS MORNING
THE SUN IS SHINING... IT'S A BEAUTIFUL DAY.... LET'S NOT SPOIL IT..
WHO WAS MOSES MENDELSSOHN ?!
YOU SPOILED IT !
SCHULZ
4-25

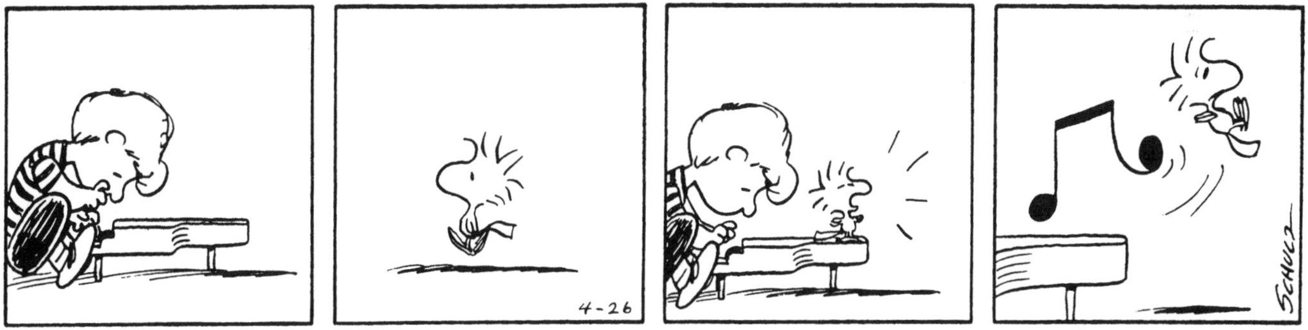
4-26
SCHULZ

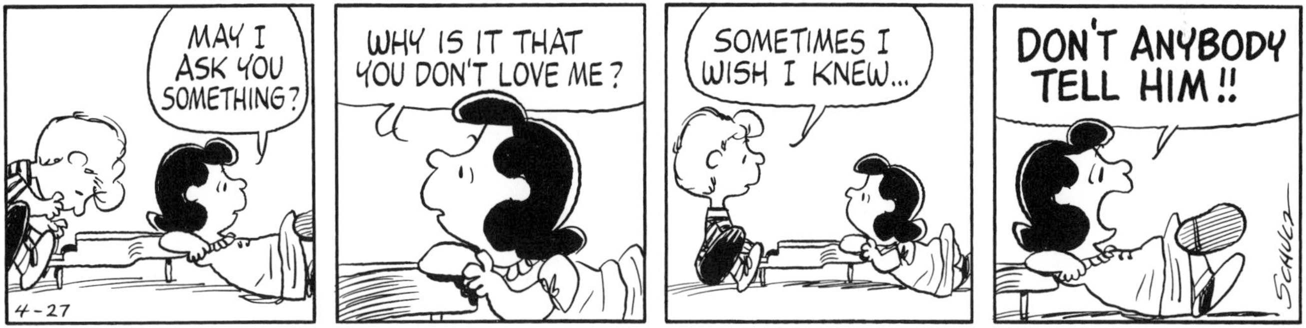
MAY I ASK YOU SOMETHING?
4-27
WHY IS IT THAT YOU DON'T LOVE ME?
SOMETIMES I WISH I KNEW...
DON'T ANYBODY TELL HIM !!
SCHULZ

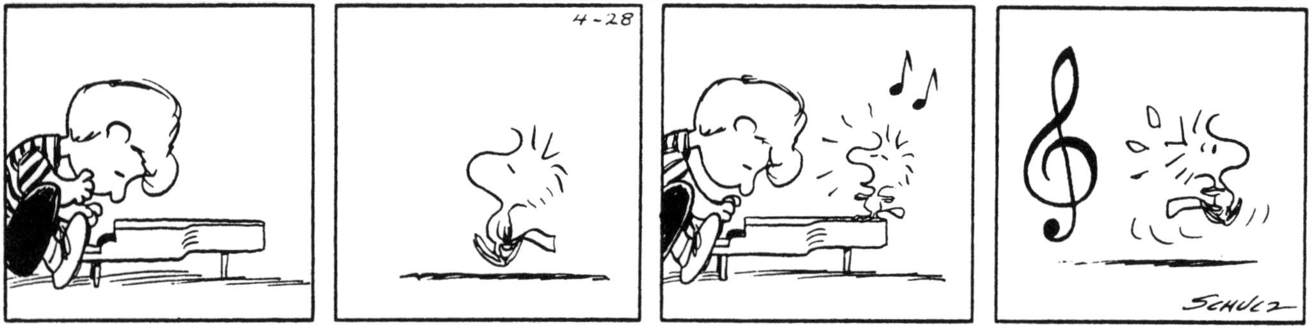
4-28
SCHULZ

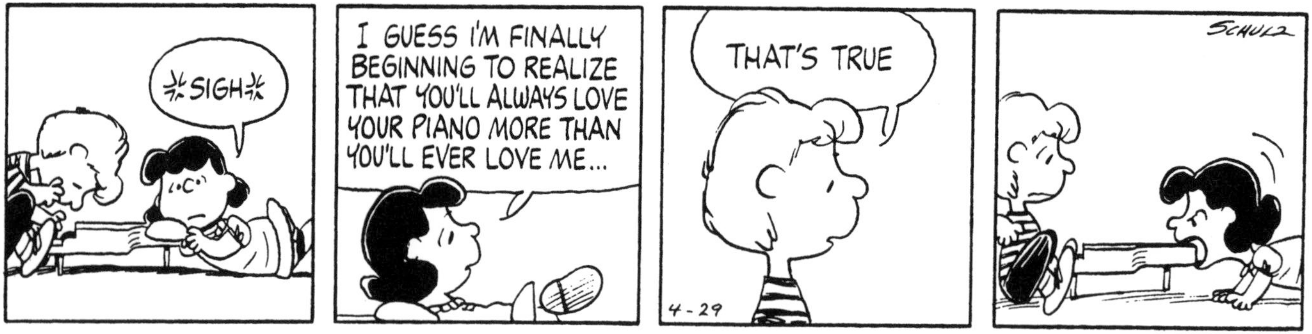
SIGH
I GUESS I'M FINALLY BEGINNING TO REALIZE THAT YOU'LL ALWAYS LOVE YOUR PIANO MORE THAN YOU'LL EVER LOVE ME...
THAT'S TRUE
4-29
SCHULZ

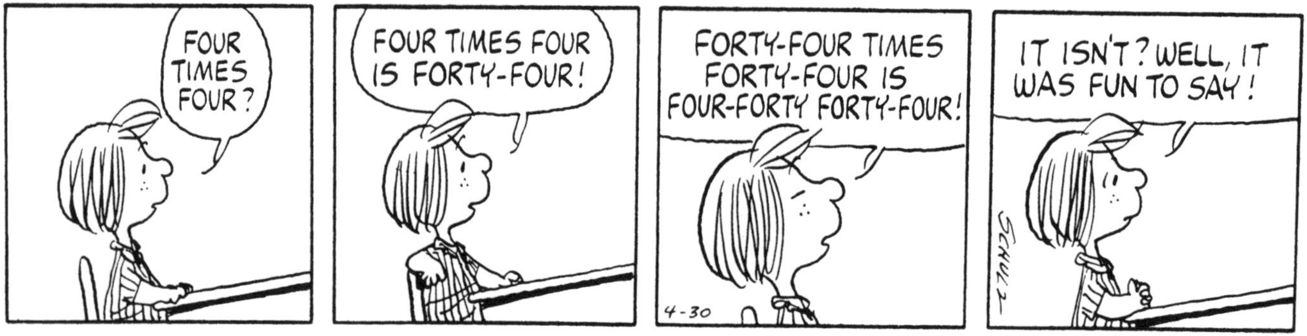
FOUR TIMES FOUR?
FOUR TIMES FOUR IS FORTY-FOUR!
FORTY-FOUR TIMES FORTY-FOUR IS FOUR-FORTY FORTY-FOUR!
4-30
IT ISN'T? WELL, IT WAS FUN TO SAY!
SCHULZ

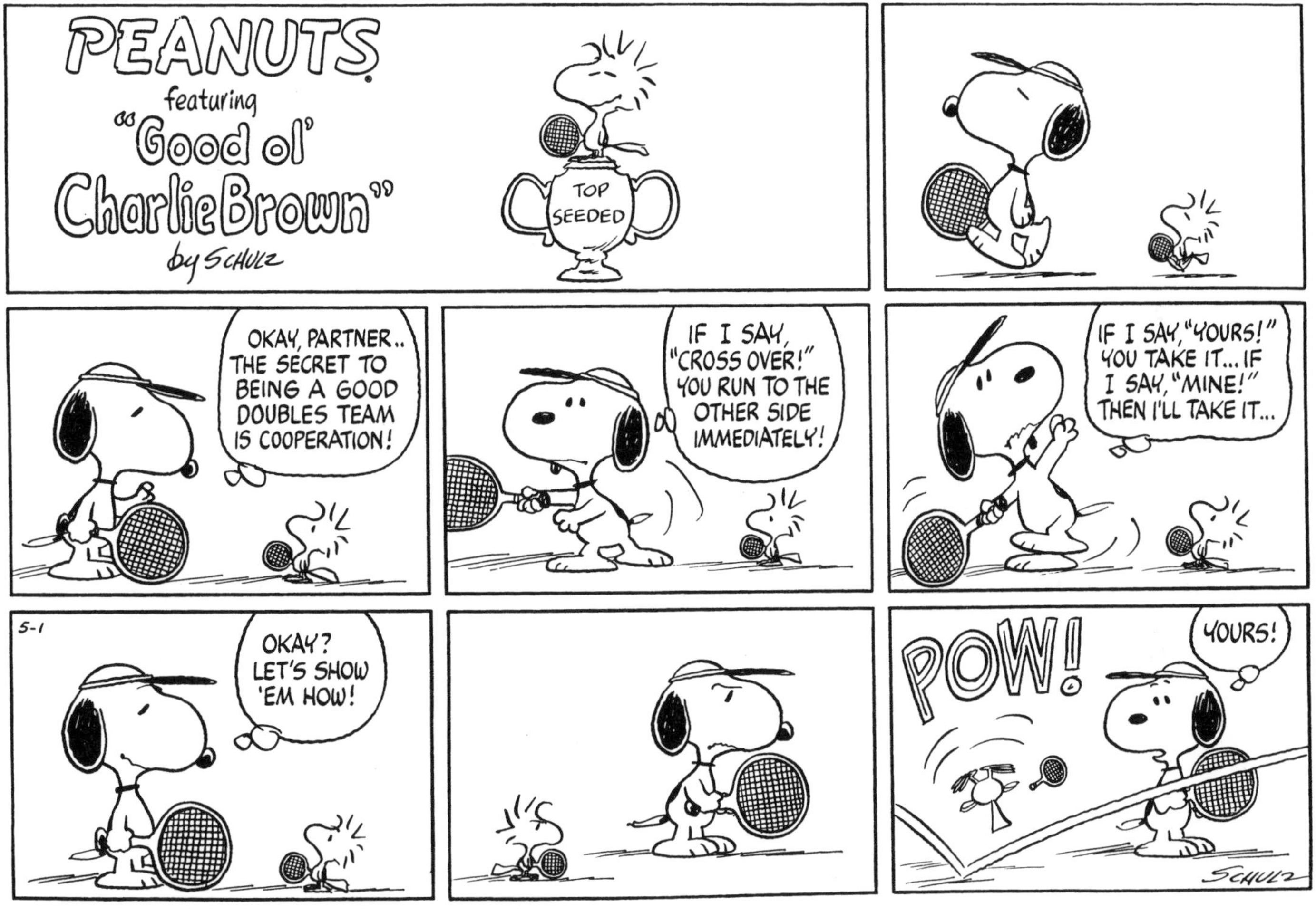
PEANUTS
featuring
"Good ol' CharlieBrown"
by SCHULZ
TOP SEEDED
OKAY, PARTNER.. THE SECRET TO BEING A GOOD DOUBLES TEAM IS COOPERATION!
IF I SAY, "CROSS OVER!" YOU RUN TO THE OTHER SIDE IMMEDIATELY!
IF I SAY, "YOURS!" YOU TAKE IT... IF I SAY, "MINE!" THEN I'LL TAKE IT...
5-1
OKAY? LET'S SHOW 'EM HOW!
POW!
YOURS!
SCHULZ

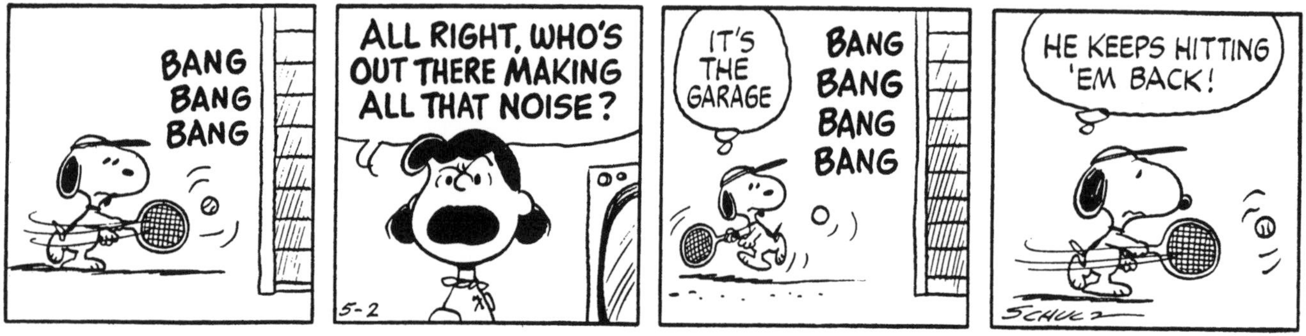
BANG
BANG
BANG
ALL RIGHT, WHO'S OUT THERE MAKING ALL THAT NOISE?
5-2
IT'S THE GARAGE
BANG
BANG
BANG
BANG
HE KEEPS HITTING 'EM BACK!
SCHULZ

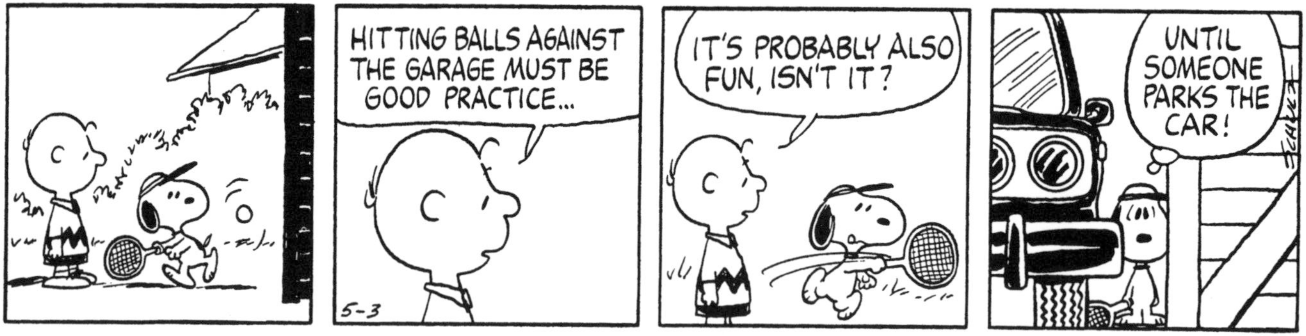
HITTING BALLS AGAINST THE GARAGE MUST BE GOOD PRACTICE...
5-3
IT'S PROBABLY ALSO FUN, ISN'T IT?
UNTIL SOMEONE PARKS THE CAR!
SCHULZ

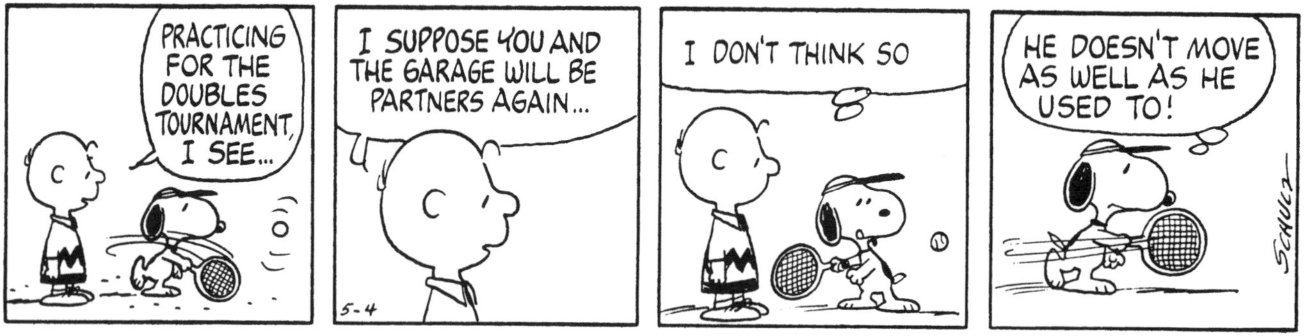
PRACTICING FOR THE DOUBLES TOURNAMENT, I SEE...
I SUPPOSE YOU AND THE GARAGE WILL BE PARTNERS AGAIN...
5-4
I DON'T THINK SO
HE DOESN'T MOVE AS WELL AS HE USED TO!
SCHULZ

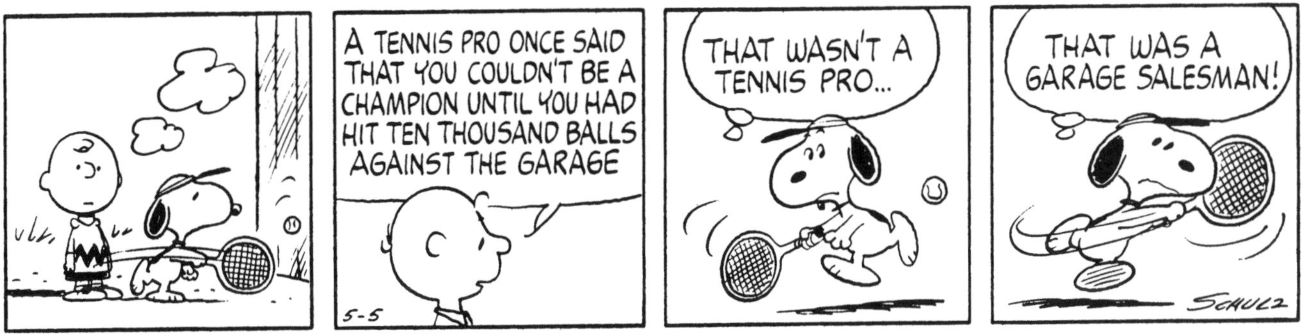
A TENNIS PRO ONCE SAID THAT YOU COULDN'T BE A CHAMPION UNTIL YOU HAD HIT TEN THOUSAND BALLS AGAINST THE GARAGE
5-5
THAT WASN'T A TENNIS PRO...
THAT WAS A GARAGE SALESMAN!
SCHULZ

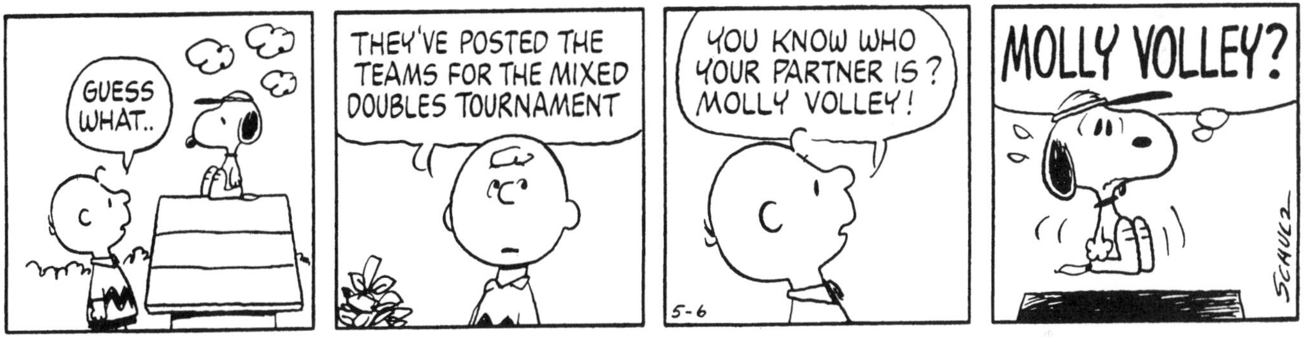
GUESS WHAT..
THEY'VE POSTED THE TEAMS FOR THE MIXED DOUBLES TOURNAMENT
YOU KNOW WHO YOUR PARTNER IS? MOLLY VOLLEY!
5-6
MOLLY VOLLEY?
SCHULZ

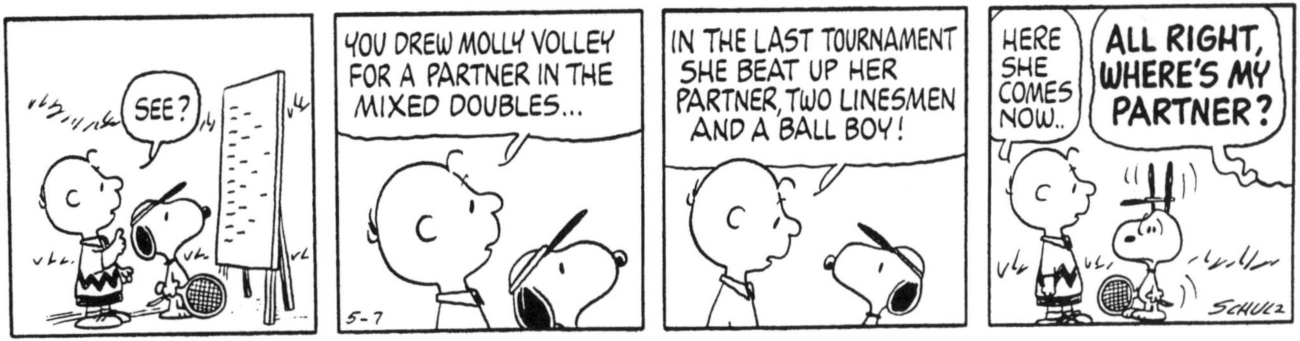
SEE?
YOU DREW MOLLY VOLLEY FOR A PARTNER IN THE MIXED DOUBLES...
5-7
IN THE LAST TOURNAMENT SHE BEAT UP HER PARTNER, TWO LINESMEN AND A BALL BOY!
HERE SHE COMES NOW..
ALL RIGHT, WHERE'S MY PARTNER?
SCHULZ

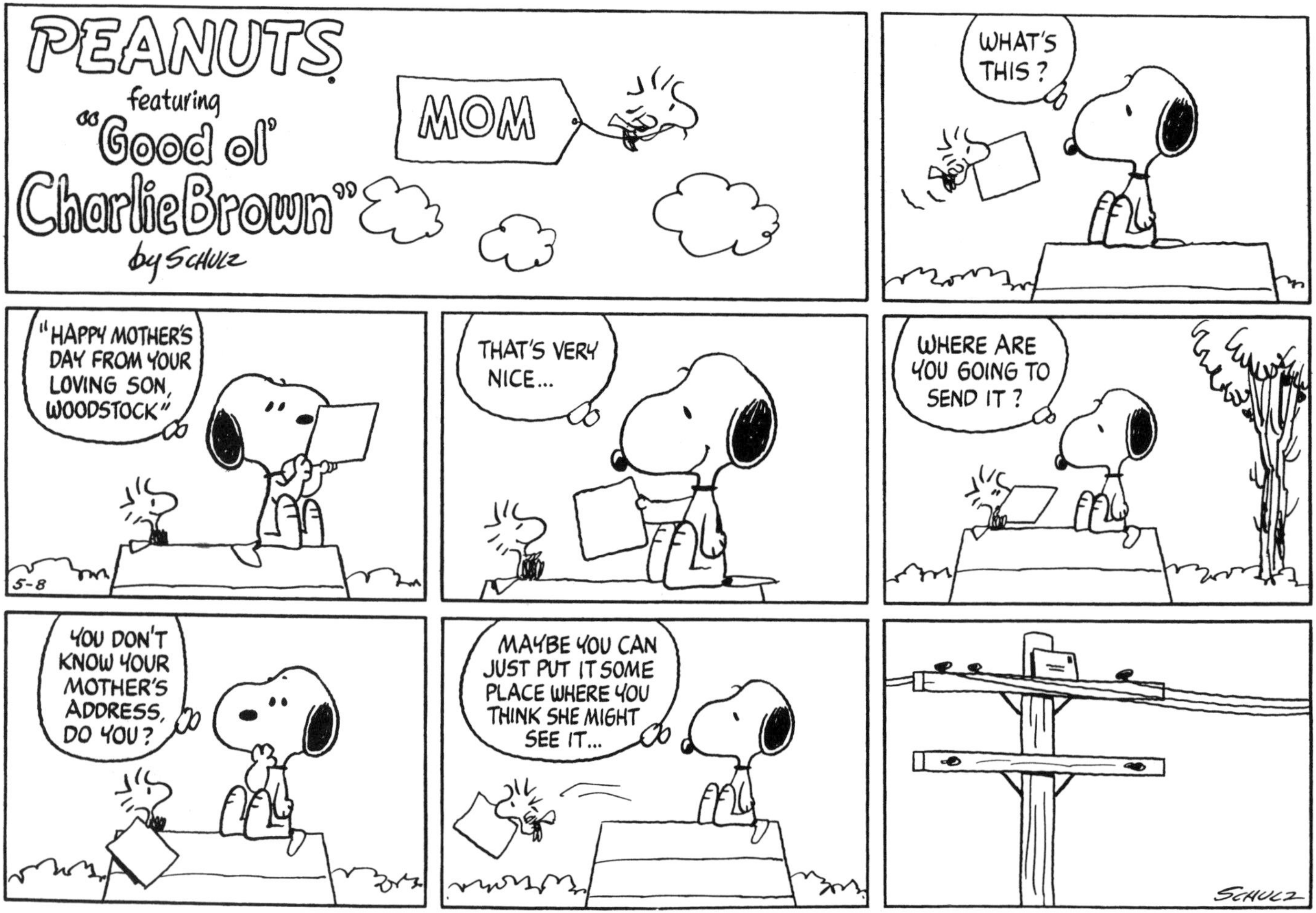
PEANUTS
featuring
"Good ol' Charlie Brown"
by SCHULZ
MOM
WHAT'S THIS ?
"HAPPY MOTHER'S DAY FROM YOUR LOVING SON, WOODSTOCK"
5-8
THAT'S VERY NICE...
WHERE ARE YOU GOING TO SEND IT ?
YOU DON'T KNOW YOUR MOTHER'S ADDRESS, DO YOU ?
MAYBE YOU CAN JUST PUT IT SOME PLACE WHERE YOU THINK SHE MIGHT SEE IT...
SCHULZ

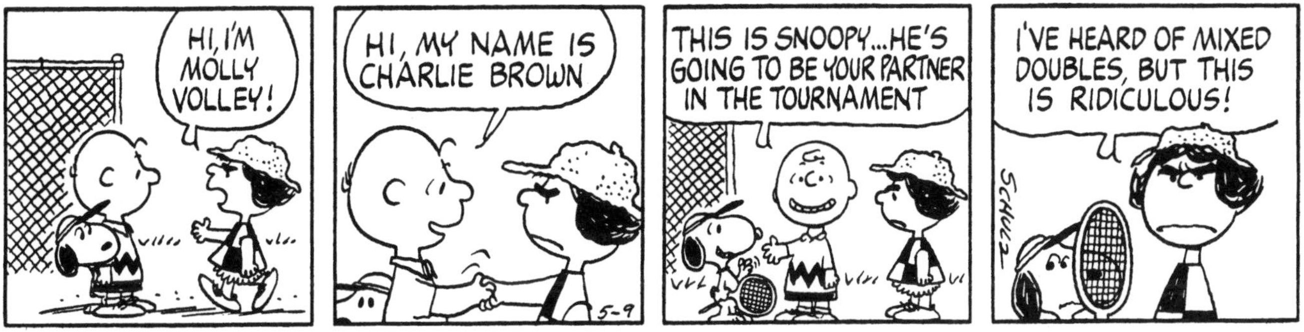
HI, I'M MOLLY VOLLEY!
HI, MY NAME IS CHARLIE BROWN
THIS IS SNOOPY...HE'S GOING TO BE YOUR PARTNER IN THE TOURNAMENT
I'VE HEARD OF MIXED DOUBLES, BUT THIS IS RIDICULOUS!

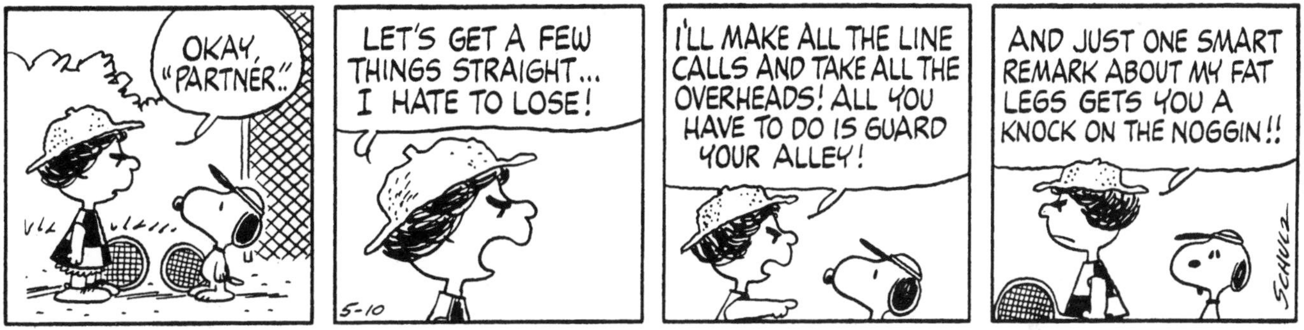
OKAY, "PARTNER."
LET'S GET A FEW THINGS STRAIGHT... I HATE TO LOSE!
I'LL MAKE ALL THE LINE CALLS AND TAKE ALL THE OVERHEADS! ALL YOU HAVE TO DO IS GUARD YOUR ALLEY!
AND JUST ONE SMART REMARK ABOUT MY FAT LEGS GETS YOU A KNOCK ON THE NOGGIN!!

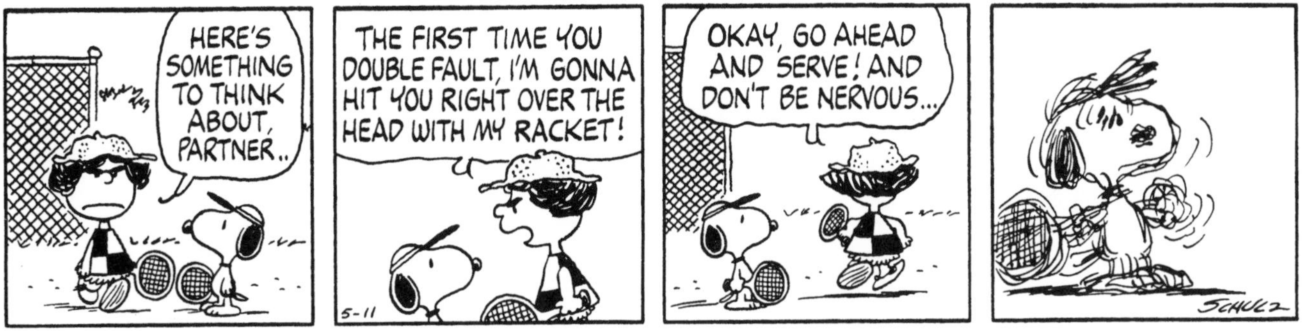
HERE'S SOMETHING TO THINK ABOUT, PARTNER..
THE FIRST TIME YOU DOUBLE FAULT, I'M GONNA HIT YOU RIGHT OVER THE HEAD WITH MY RACKET!
OKAY, GO AHEAD AND SERVE! AND DON'T BE NERVOUS...

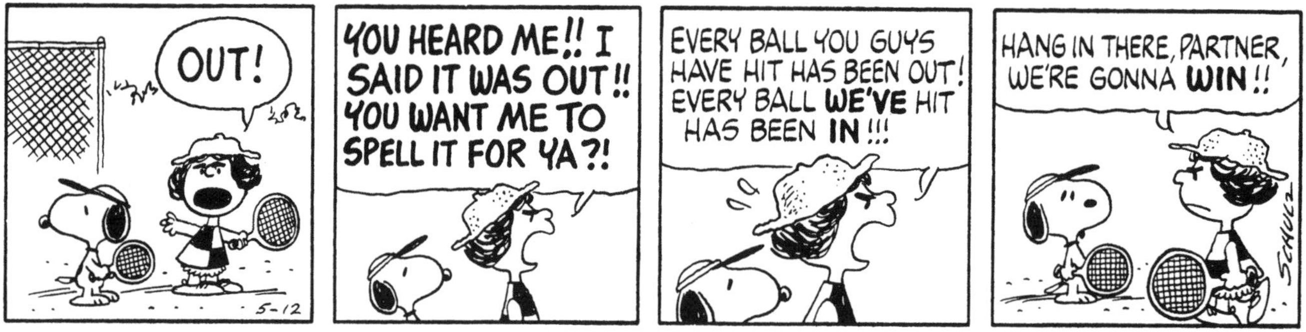
OUT!
YOU HEARD ME!! I SAID IT WAS OUT!! YOU WANT ME TO SPELL IT FOR YA?!
EVERY BALL YOU GUYS HAVE HIT HAS BEEN OUT! EVERY BALL WE'VE HIT HAS BEEN IN!!!
HANG IN THERE, PARTNER, WE'RE GONNA WIN!!
5-12
SCHULZ

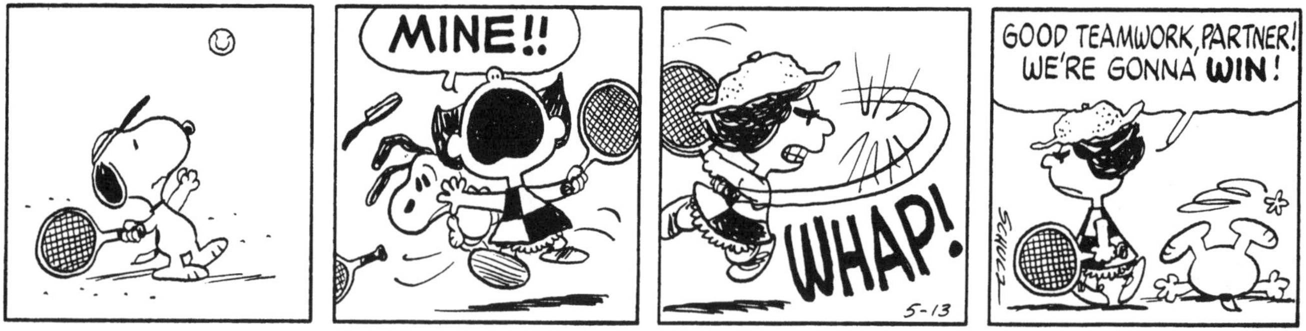
MINE!!
WHAP!
5-13
SCHULZ
GOOD TEAMWORK, PARTNER! WE'RE GONNA WIN!

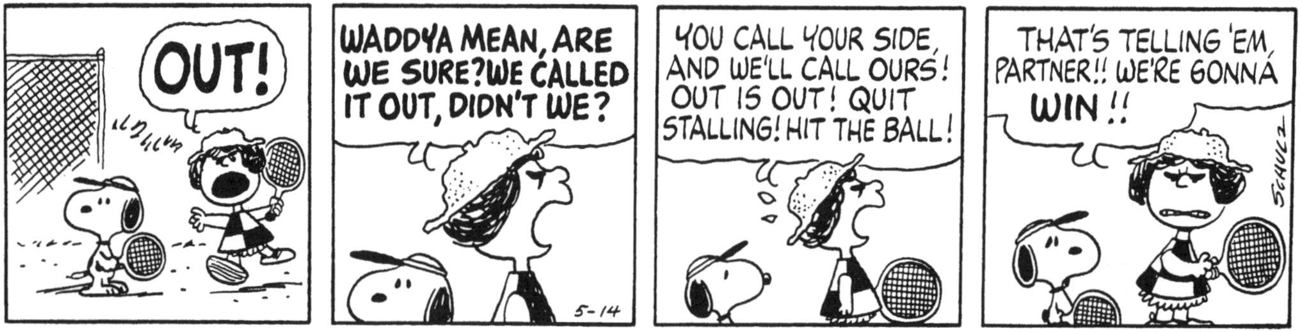
OUT!
WADDYA MEAN, ARE WE SURE? WE CALLED IT OUT, DIDN'T WE?
5-14
YOU CALL YOUR SIDE, AND WE'LL CALL OURS! OUT IS OUT! QUIT STALLING! HIT THE BALL!
THAT'S TELLING 'EM, PARTNER!! WE'RE GONNA WIN!!
SCHULZ

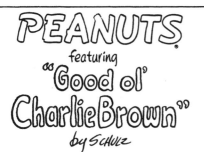

PEANUTS featuring "Good ol' Charlie Brown" by SCHULZ

TIME OUT!

NOW WHAT?

HEY, MANAGER, I HAVE A GREAT IDEA!

AFTER WE'VE LOST A GAME, WHY DON'T WE RUN AN AD IN THE NEWSPAPER?

AN AD?

SURE, WE COULD OFFER A REWARD FOR THE LOST GAME!

5-15

WHEN THE LOST GAME WAS FOUND, IT WOULDN'T BE A LOST GAME ANY MORE!

IF I GET ANOTHER GREAT IDEA, I'LL LET YOU KNOW..

MAYBE OUTFIELDERS SPEND TOO MUCH TIME STANDING IN THE SUN...

SCHULZ

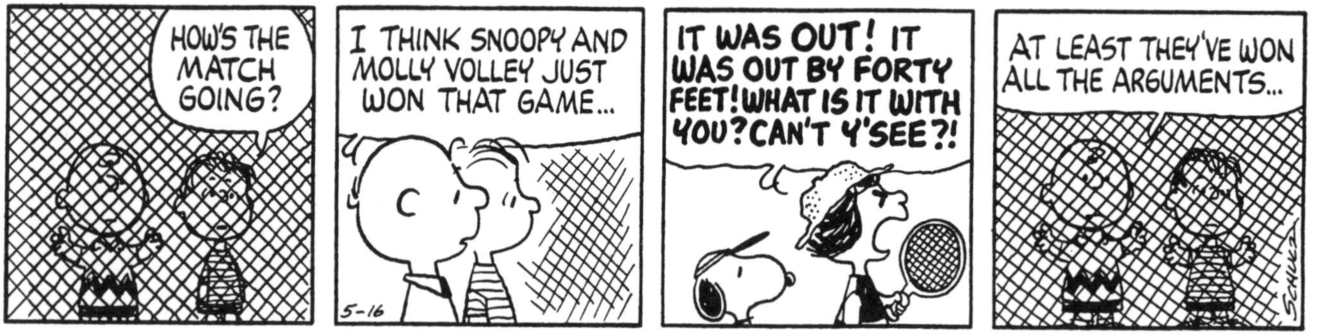
HOW'S THE MATCH GOING?
I THINK SNOOPY AND MOLLY VOLLEY JUST WON THAT GAME...
5-16
IT WAS OUT! IT WAS OUT BY FORTY FEET! WHAT IS IT WITH YOU? CAN'T Y'SEE?!
AT LEAST THEY'VE WON ALL THE ARGUMENTS...
SCHULZ

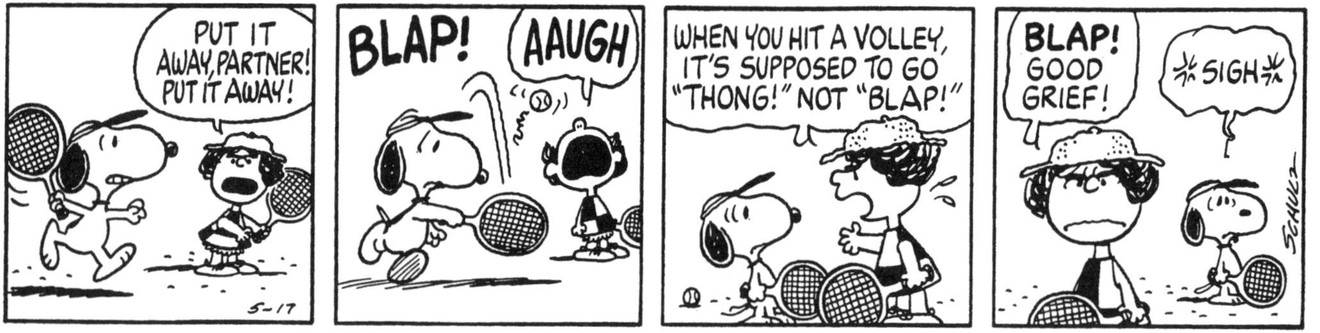
PUT IT AWAY, PARTNER! PUT IT AWAY!
5-17
BLAP!
AAUGH
WHEN YOU HIT A VOLLEY, IT'S SUPPOSED TO GO "THONG!" NOT "BLAP!"
BLAP! GOOD GRIEF!
SIGH
SCHULZ

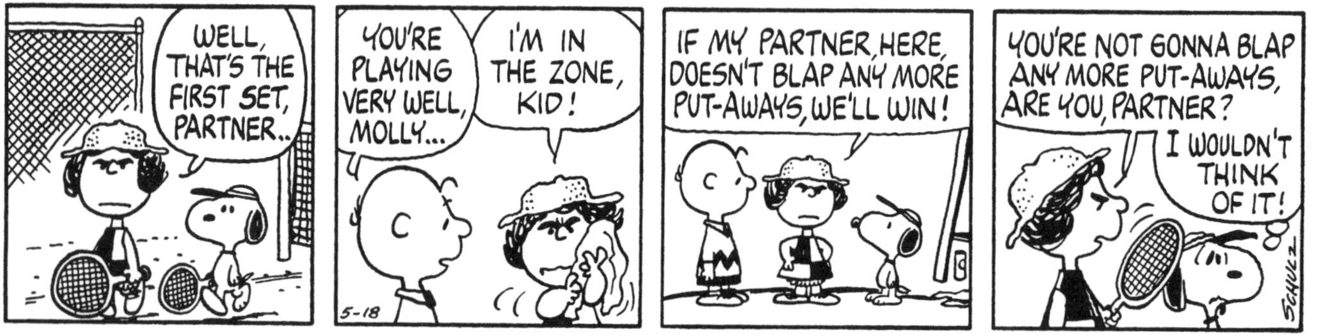
WELL, THAT'S THE FIRST SET, PARTNER..
YOU'RE PLAYING VERY WELL, MOLLY...
I'M IN THE ZONE, KID!
5-18
IF MY PARTNER, HERE, DOESN'T BLAP ANY MORE PUT-AWAYS, WE'LL WIN!
YOU'RE NOT GONNA BLAP ANY MORE PUT-AWAYS, ARE YOU, PARTNER?
I WOULDN'T THINK OF IT!
SCHULZ

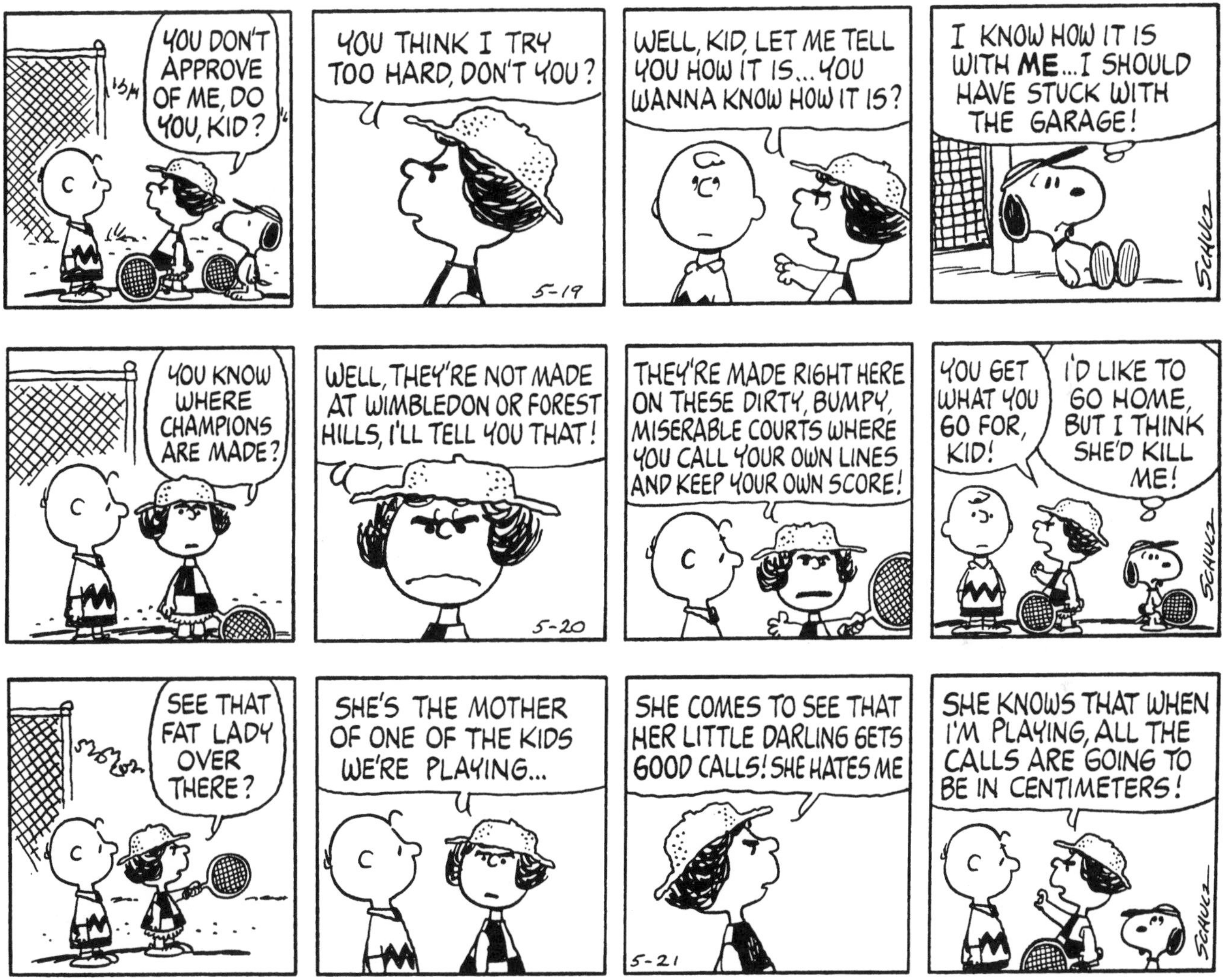
YOU DON'T APPROVE OF ME, DO YOU, KID?
YOU THINK I TRY TOO HARD, DON'T YOU?
5-19
WELL, KID, LET ME TELL YOU HOW IT IS...YOU WANNA KNOW HOW IT IS?
I KNOW HOW IT IS WITH ME...I SHOULD HAVE STUCK WITH THE GARAGE!
SCHULZ
YOU KNOW WHERE CHAMPIONS ARE MADE?
WELL, THEY'RE NOT MADE AT WIMBLEDON OR FOREST HILLS, I'LL TELL YOU THAT!
5-20
THEY'RE MADE RIGHT HERE ON THESE DIRTY, BUMPY, MISERABLE COURTS WHERE YOU CALL YOUR OWN LINES AND KEEP YOUR OWN SCORE!
YOU GET WHAT YOU GO FOR, KID!
I'D LIKE TO GO HOME, BUT I THINK SHE'D KILL ME!
SCHULZ
SEE THAT FAT LADY OVER THERE?
SHE'S THE MOTHER OF ONE OF THE KIDS WE'RE PLAYING...
SHE COMES TO SEE THAT HER LITTLE DARLING GETS GOOD CALLS! SHE HATES ME
5-21
SHE KNOWS THAT WHEN I'M PLAYING, ALL THE CALLS ARE GOING TO BE IN CENTIMETERS!
SCHULZ

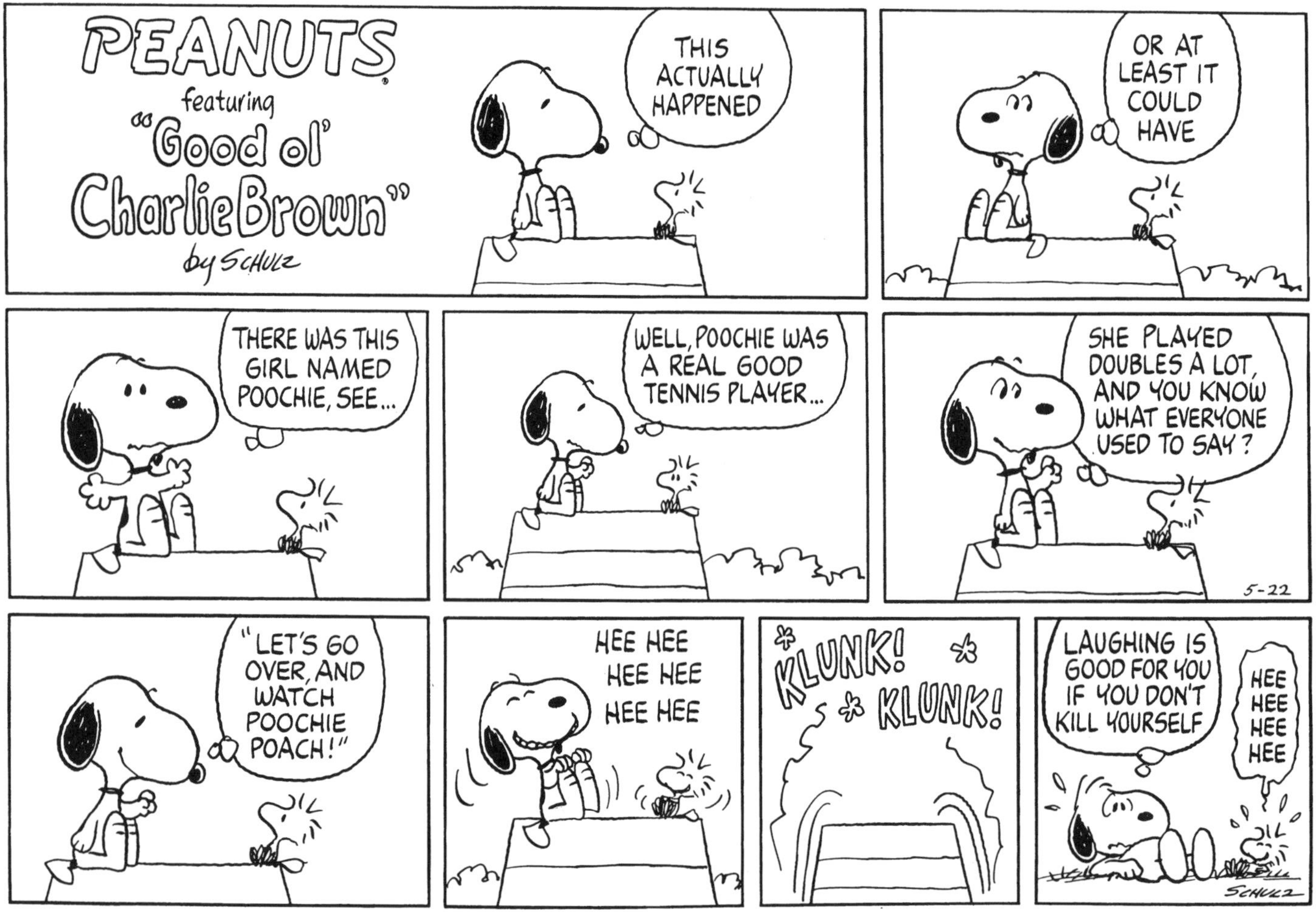
PEANUTS
featuring
"Good ol' Charlie Brown"
by SCHULZ
THIS ACTUALLY HAPPENED
OR AT LEAST IT COULD HAVE
THERE WAS THIS GIRL NAMED POOCHIE, SEE...
WELL, POOCHIE WAS A REAL GOOD TENNIS PLAYER...
SHE PLAYED DOUBLES A LOT, AND YOU KNOW WHAT EVERYONE USED TO SAY?
5-22
"LET'S GO OVER, AND WATCH POOCHIE POACH!"
HEE HEE HEE HEE HEE HEE
KLUNK!
KLUNK!
LAUGHING IS GOOD FOR YOU IF YOU DON'T KILL YOURSELF
HEE HEE HEE HEE
SCHULZ

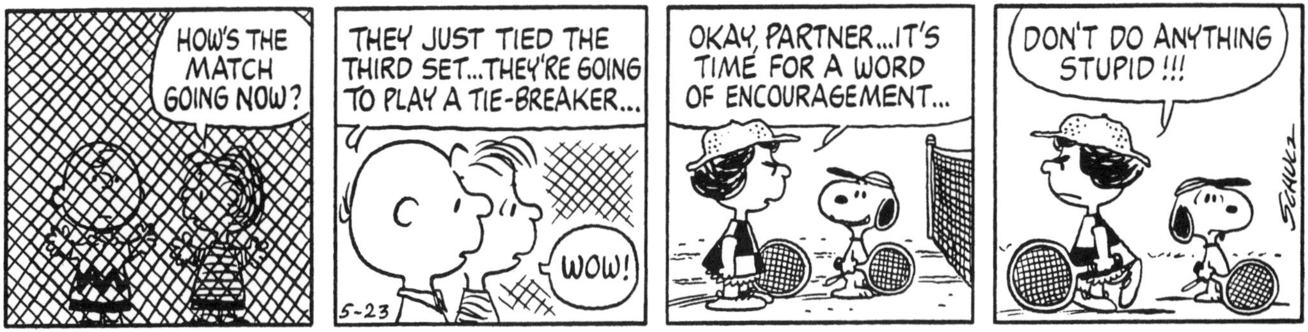
HOW'S THE MATCH GOING NOW?
THEY JUST TIED THE THIRD SET...THEY'RE GOING TO PLAY A TIE-BREAKER...
WOW!
5-23
OKAY, PARTNER...IT'S TIME FOR A WORD OF ENCOURAGEMENT...
DON'T DO ANYTHING STUPID!!!
SCHULZ

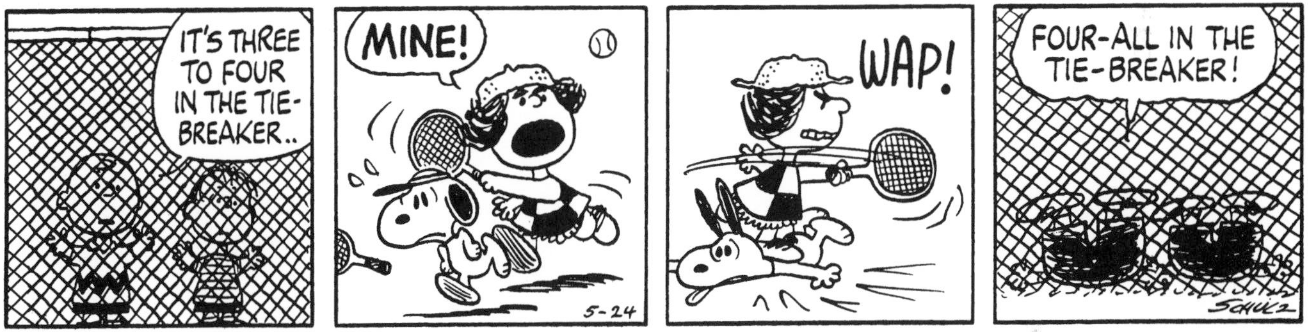
IT'S THREE TO FOUR IN THE TIE-BREAKER..
MINE!
5-24
WAP!
FOUR-ALL IN THE TIE-BREAKER!
SCHULZ

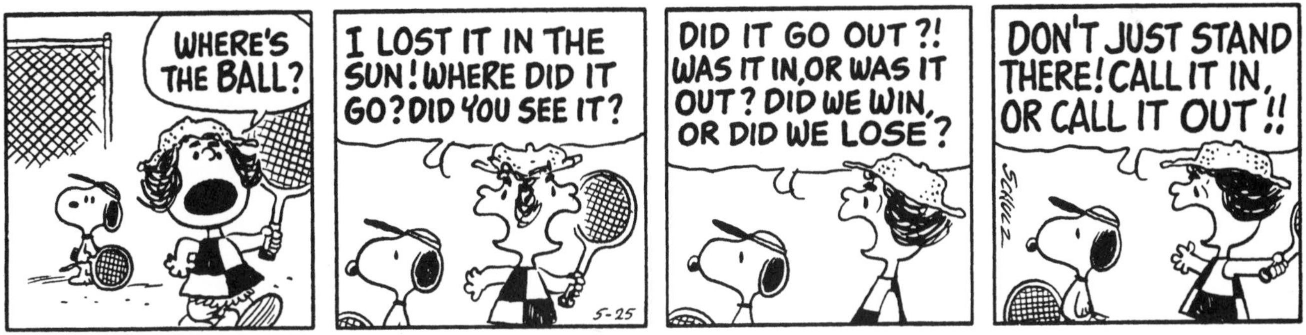
WHERE'S THE BALL?
I LOST IT IN THE SUN! WHERE DID IT GO? DID YOU SEE IT?
5-25
DID IT GO OUT?! WAS IT IN, OR WAS IT OUT? DID WE WIN, OR DID WE LOSE?
DON'T JUST STAND THERE! CALL IT IN, OR CALL IT OUT!!
SCHULZ

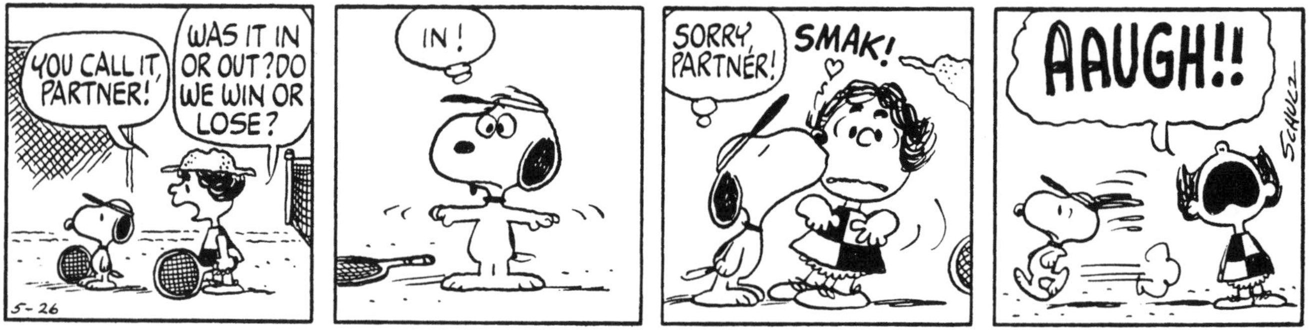

YOU CALL IT, PARTNER!
WAS IT IN OR OUT? DO WE WIN OR LOSE?
5-26
IN!
SORRY, PARTNER!
SMAK!
AAUGH!!
SCHULZ

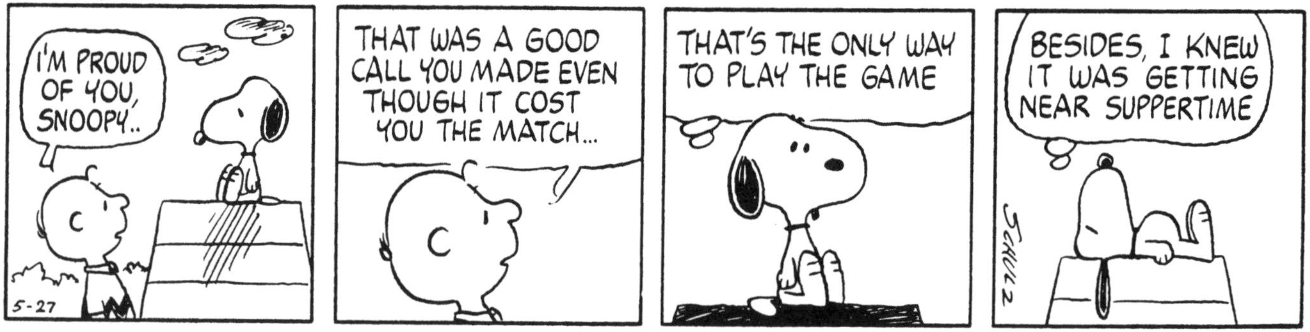

I'M PROUD OF YOU, SNOOPY..
5-27
THAT WAS A GOOD CALL YOU MADE EVEN THOUGH IT COST YOU THE MATCH...
THAT'S THE ONLY WAY TO PLAY THE GAME
BESIDES, I KNEW IT WAS GETTING NEAR SUPPERTIME
SCHULZ

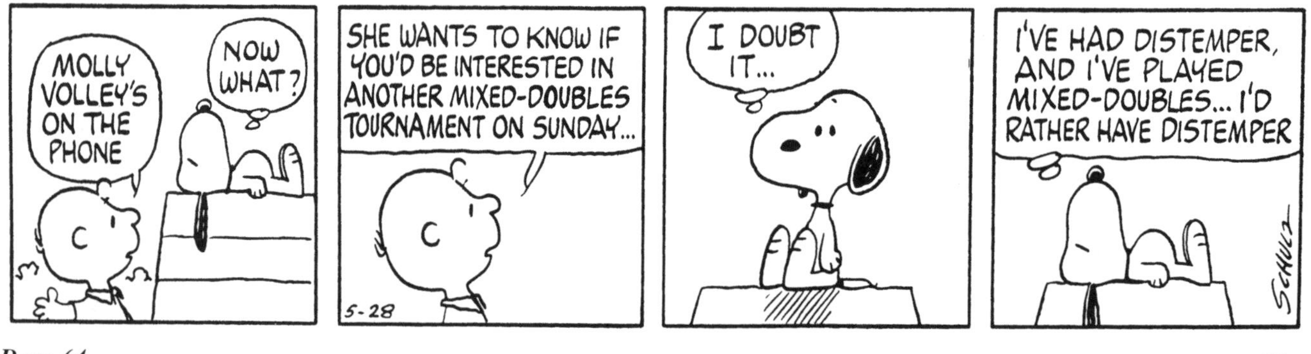

MOLLY VOLLEY'S ON THE PHONE
NOW WHAT?
SHE WANTS TO KNOW IF YOU'D BE INTERESTED IN ANOTHER MIXED-DOUBLES TOURNAMENT ON SUNDAY...
5-28
I DOUBT IT...
I'VE HAD DISTEMPER, AND I'VE PLAYED MIXED-DOUBLES... I'D RATHER HAVE DISTEMPER
SCHULZ

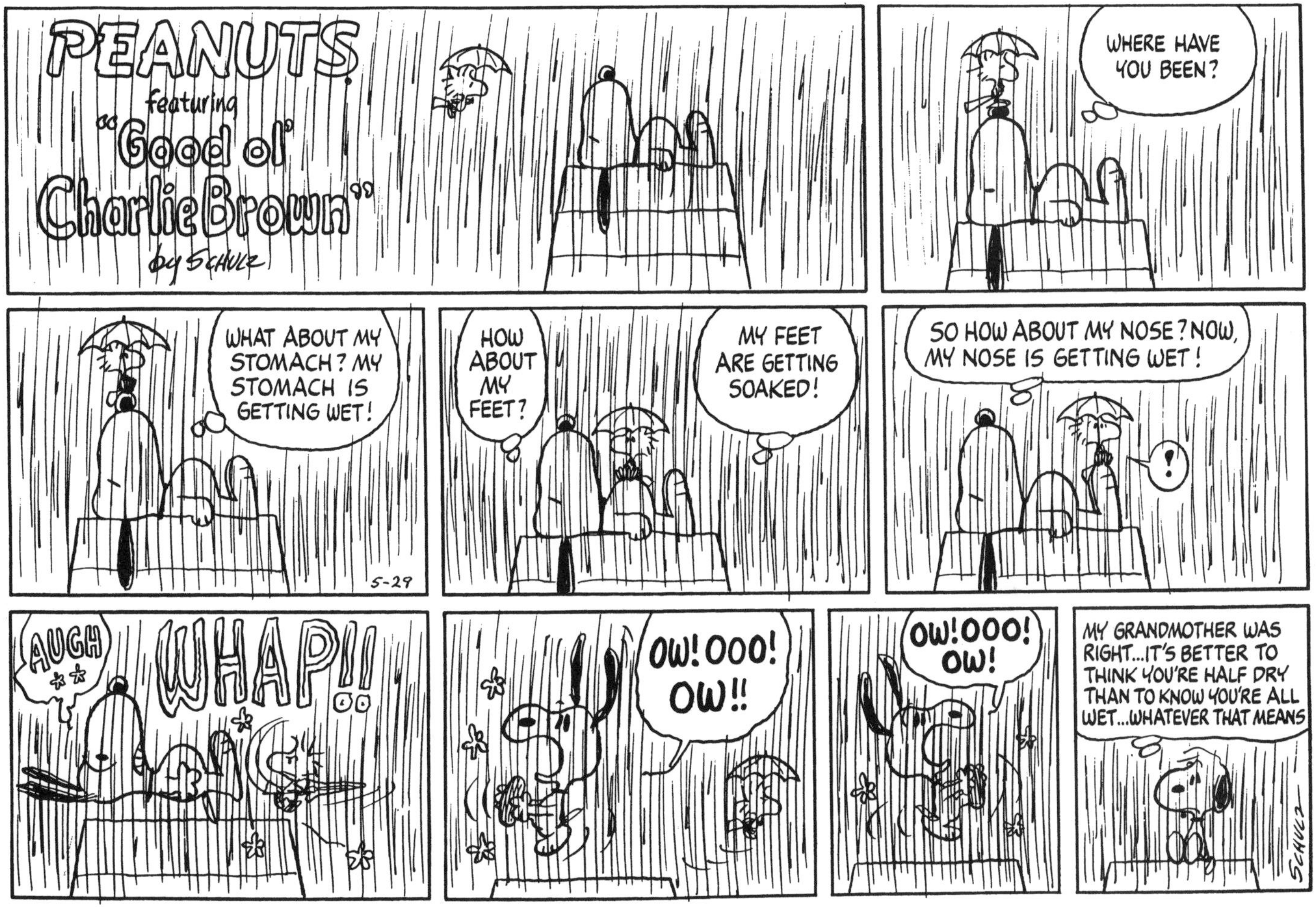
PEANUTS
featuring
"Good ol' Charlie Brown"
by SCHULZ
WHERE HAVE YOU BEEN?
WHAT ABOUT MY STOMACH? MY STOMACH IS GETTING WET!
5-29
HOW ABOUT MY FEET?
MY FEET ARE GETTING SOAKED!
SO HOW ABOUT MY NOSE? NOW, MY NOSE IS GETTING WET!
!
AUGH
WHAP!!
OW! OOO! OW!!
OW! OOO! OW!
MY GRANDMOTHER WAS RIGHT...IT'S BETTER TO THINK YOU'RE HALF DRY THAN TO KNOW YOU'RE ALL WET...WHATEVER THAT MEANS
SCHULZ

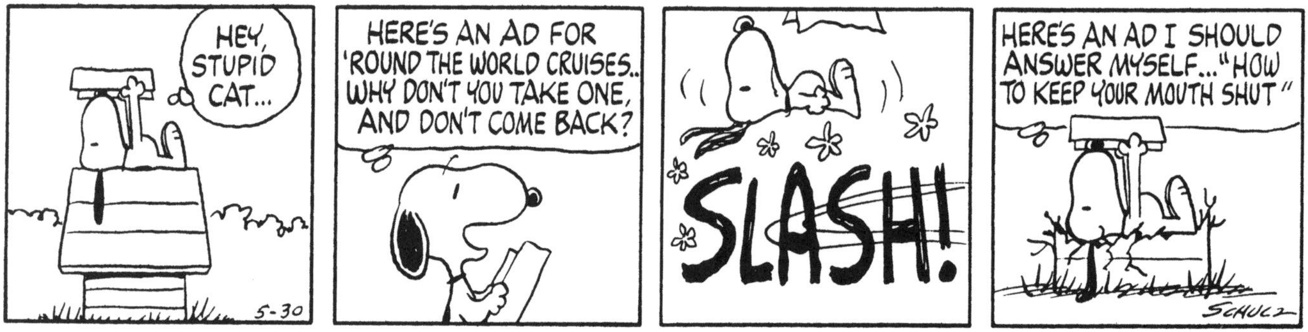
HEY, STUPID CAT...
5-30
HERE'S AN AD FOR 'ROUND THE WORLD CRUISES.. WHY DON'T YOU TAKE ONE, AND DON'T COME BACK?
SLASH!
HERE'S AN AD I SHOULD ANSWER MYSELF..."HOW TO KEEP YOUR MOUTH SHUT"
SCHULZ

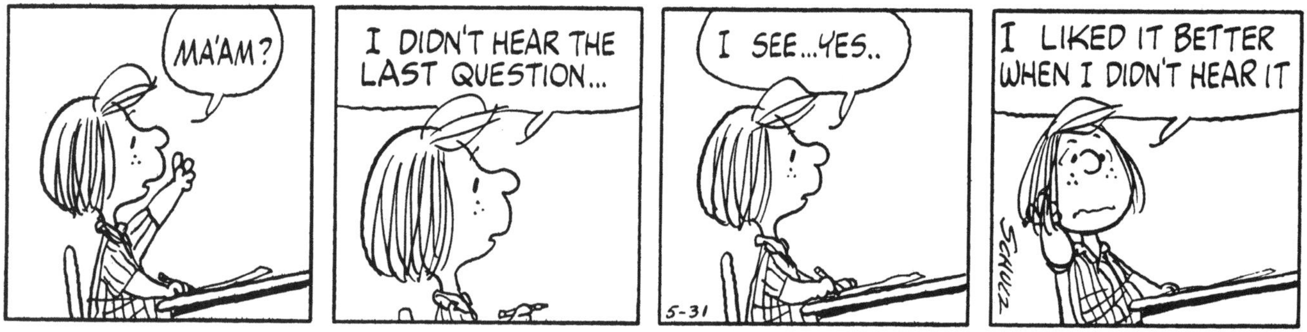
MA'AM?
I DIDN'T HEAR THE LAST QUESTION...
I SEE...YES..
5-31
I LIKED IT BETTER WHEN I DIDN'T HEAR IT
SCHULZ

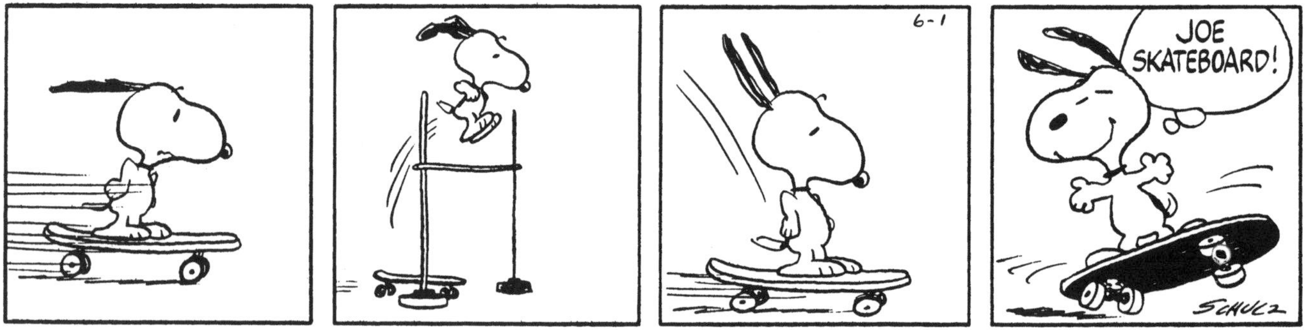
6-1
JOE SKATEBOARD!
SCHULZ

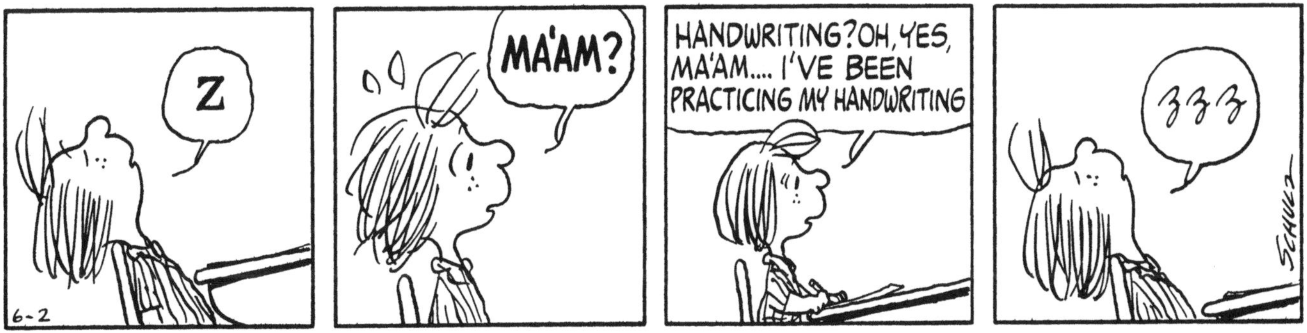
Z
6-2
MA'AM?
HANDWRITING? OH, YES, MA'AM.... I'VE BEEN PRACTICING MY HANDWRITING
ZZZ
SCHULZ

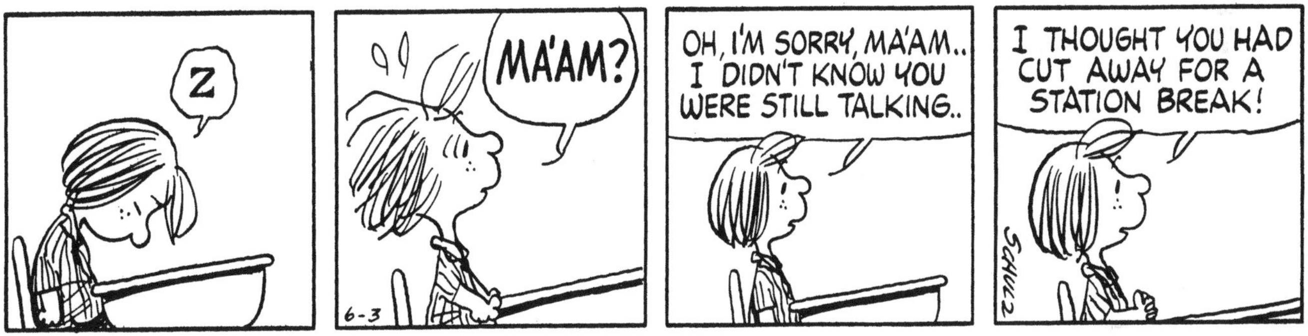
Z
MA'AM?
6-3
OH, I'M SORRY, MA'AM.. I DIDN'T KNOW YOU WERE STILL TALKING..
I THOUGHT YOU HAD CUT AWAY FOR A STATION BREAK!
SCHULZ

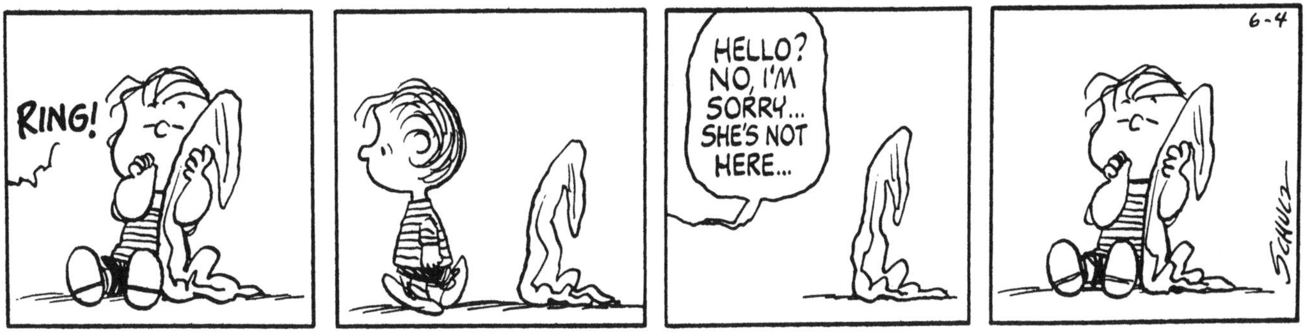
RING!
HELLO? NO, I'M SORRY... SHE'S NOT HERE...
6-4
SCHULZ

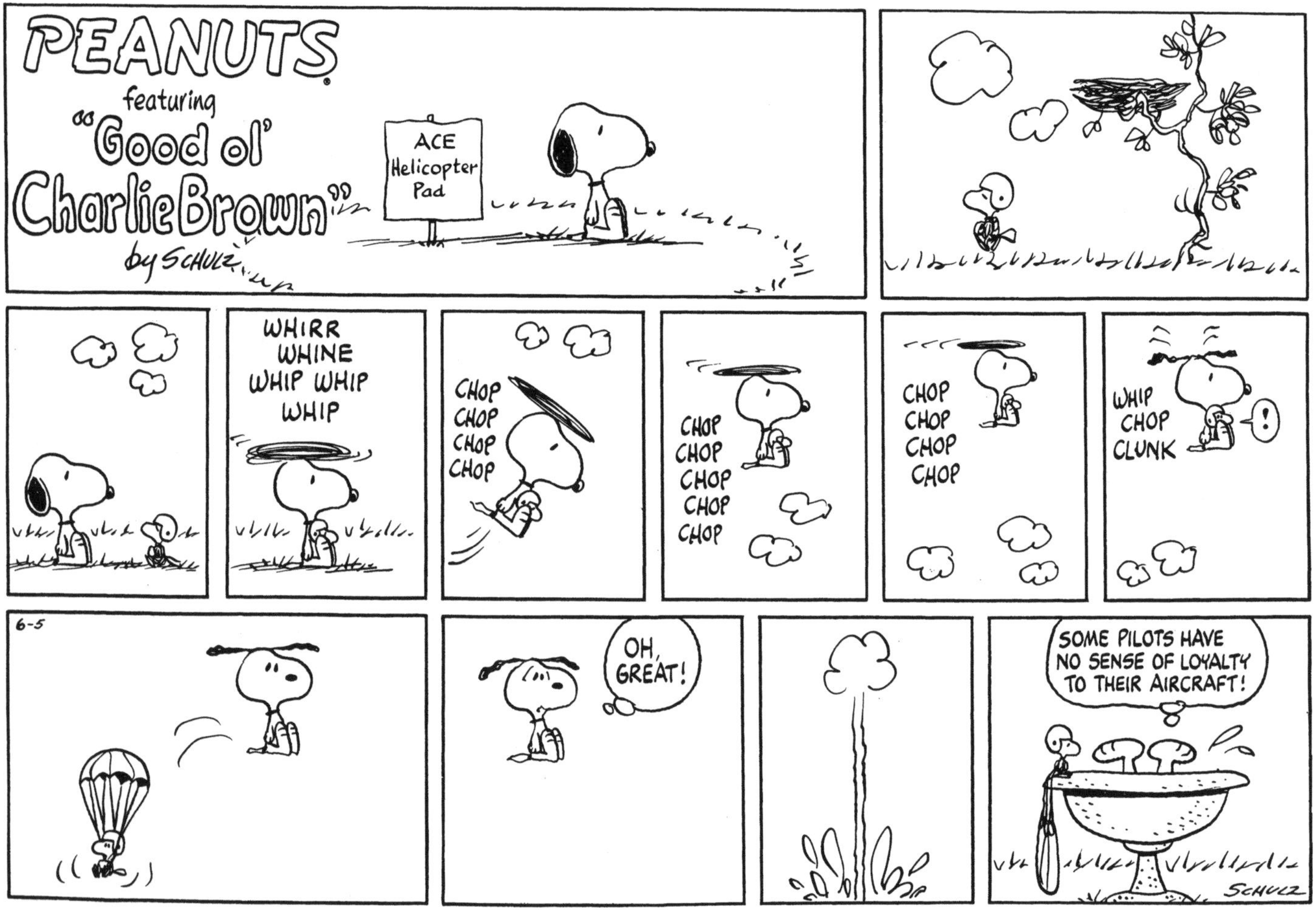
PEANUTS
featuring "Good ol' CharlieBrown"
by SCHULZ
ACE Helicopter Pad
WHIRR WHINE WHIP WHIP WHIP
CHOP CHOP CHOP CHOP
CHOP CHOP CHOP CHOP CHOP
CHOP CHOP CHOP CHOP
WHIP CHOP CLUNK
!
6-5
OH, GREAT!
SOME PILOTS HAVE NO SENSE OF LOYALTY TO THEIR AIRCRAFT!
SCHULZ

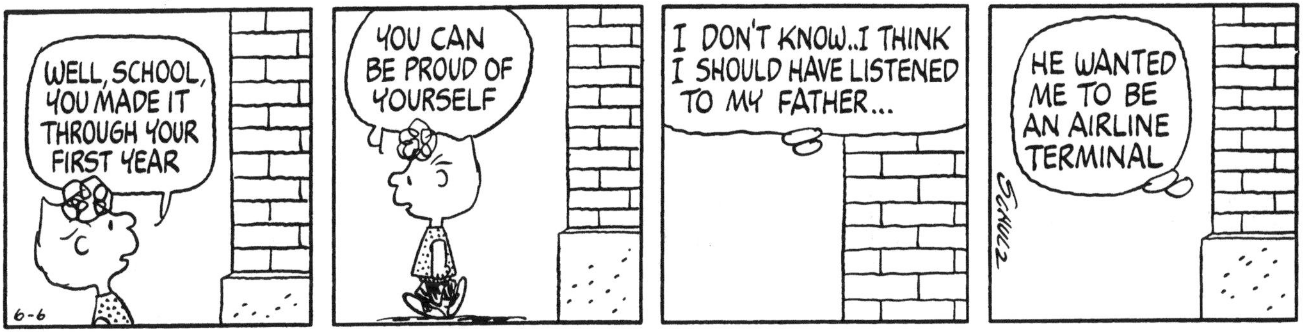
WELL, SCHOOL, YOU MADE IT THROUGH YOUR FIRST YEAR
6-6
YOU CAN BE PROUD OF YOURSELF
I DON'T KNOW..I THINK I SHOULD HAVE LISTENED TO MY FATHER...
HE WANTED ME TO BE AN AIRLINE TERMINAL

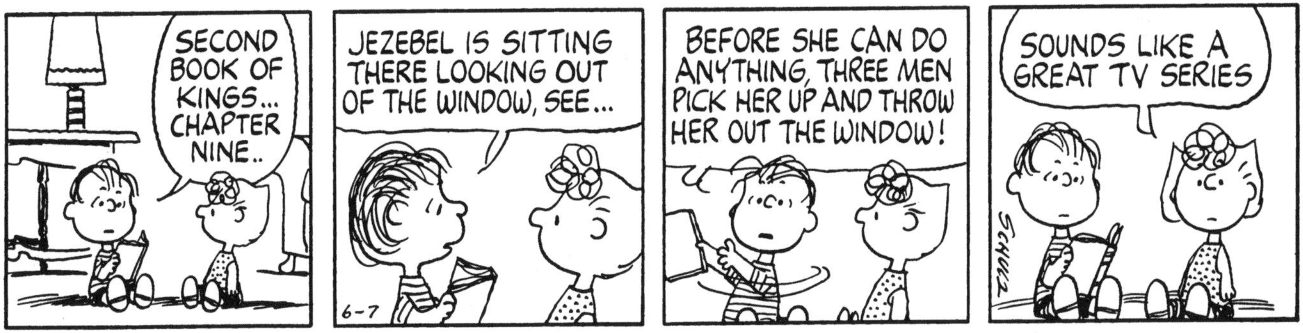
SECOND BOOK OF KINGS... CHAPTER NINE..
JEZEBEL IS SITTING THERE LOOKING OUT OF THE WINDOW, SEE...
6-7
BEFORE SHE CAN DO ANYTHING, THREE MEN PICK HER UP AND THROW HER OUT THE WINDOW!
SOUNDS LIKE A GREAT TV SERIES

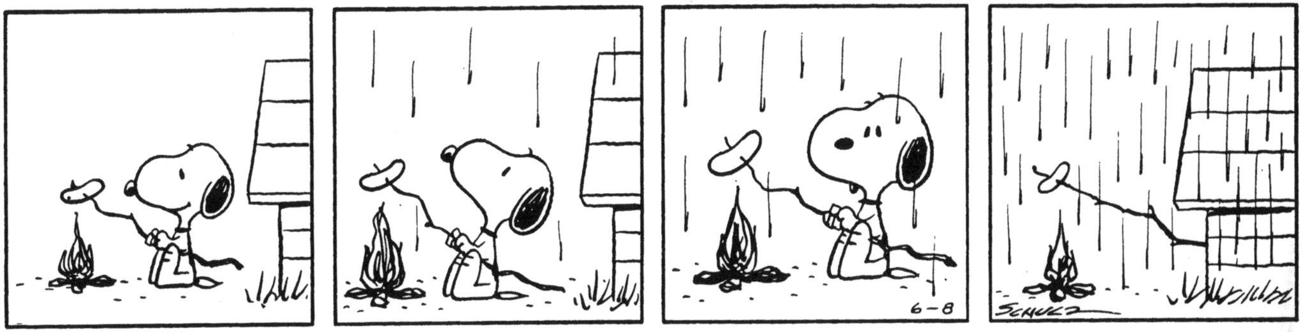
6-8

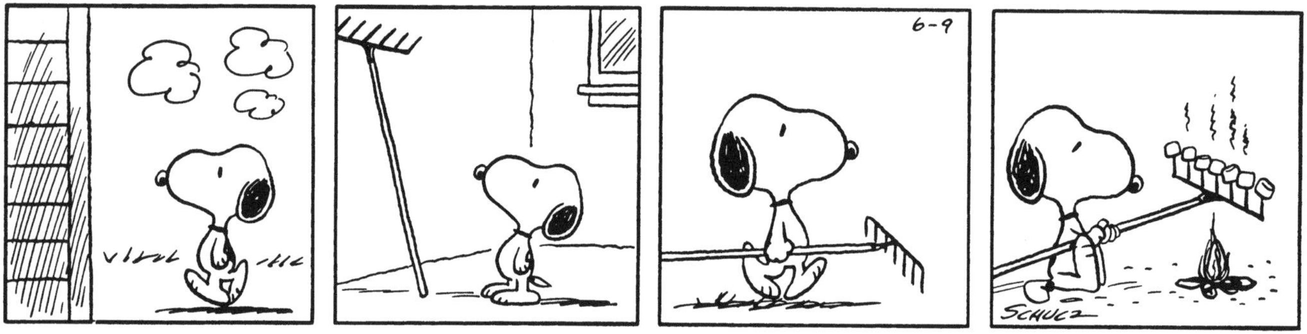
6-9
SCHULZ

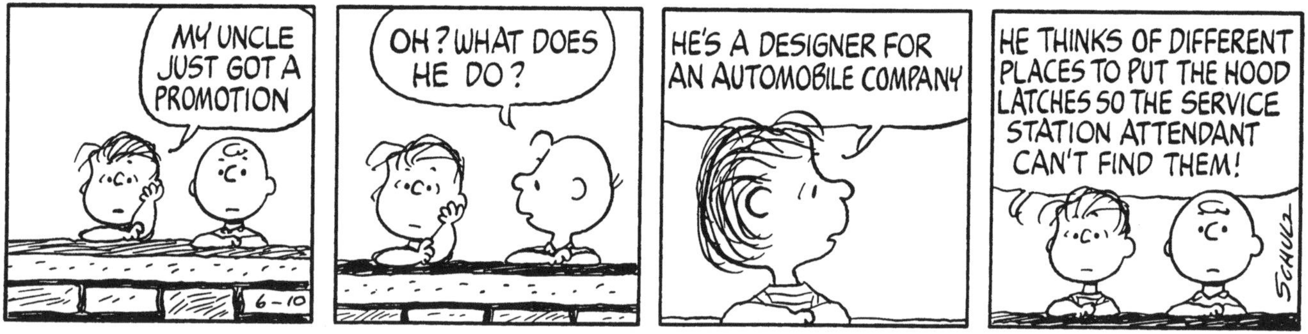
MY UNCLE JUST GOT A PROMOTION
6-10
OH? WHAT DOES HE DO?
HE'S A DESIGNER FOR AN AUTOMOBILE COMPANY
HE THINKS OF DIFFERENT PLACES TO PUT THE HOOD LATCHES SO THE SERVICE STATION ATTENDANT CAN'T FIND THEM!
SCHULZ

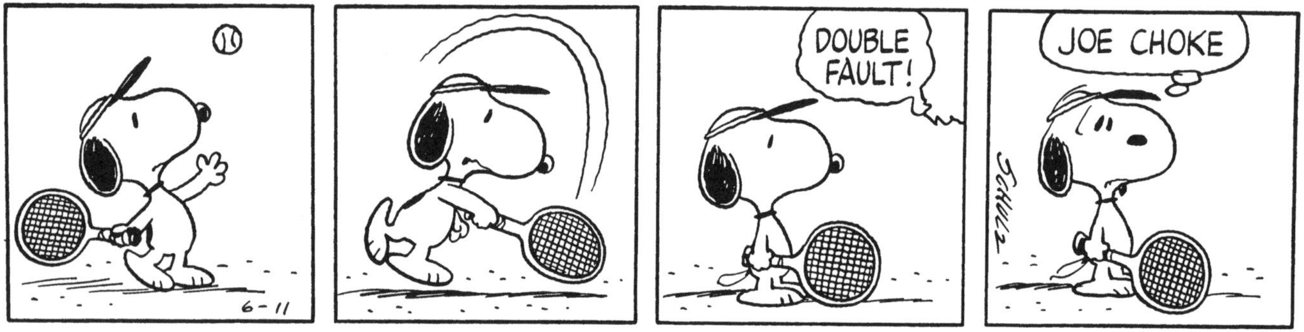
6-11
DOUBLE FAULT!
SCHULZ
JOE CHOKE

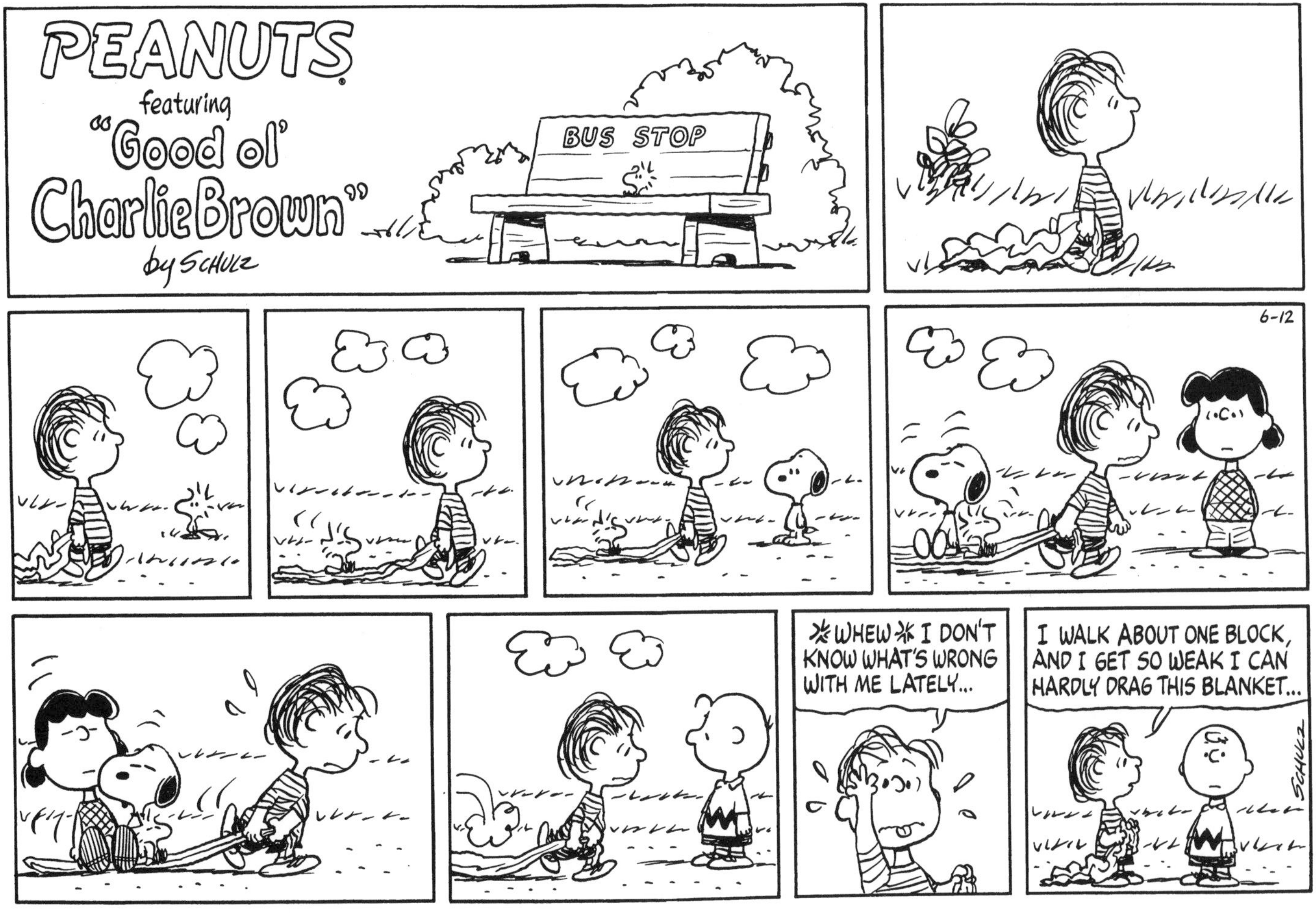
PEANUTS
featuring
"Good ol' Charlie Brown"
by SCHULZ
BUS STOP
6-12
WHEW I DON'T KNOW WHAT'S WRONG WITH ME LATELY...
I WALK ABOUT ONE BLOCK, AND I GET SO WEAK I CAN HARDLY DRAG THIS BLANKET...
SCHULZ

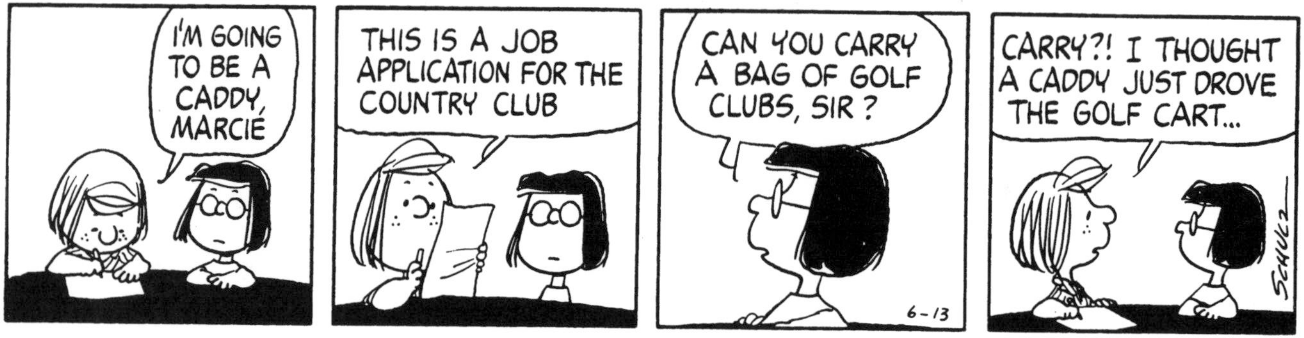
I'M GOING TO BE A CADDY, MARCIE
THIS IS A JOB APPLICATION FOR THE COUNTRY CLUB
CAN YOU CARRY A BAG OF GOLF CLUBS, SIR ?
6-13
CARRY?! I THOUGHT A CADDY JUST DROVE THE GOLF CART...
SCHULZ

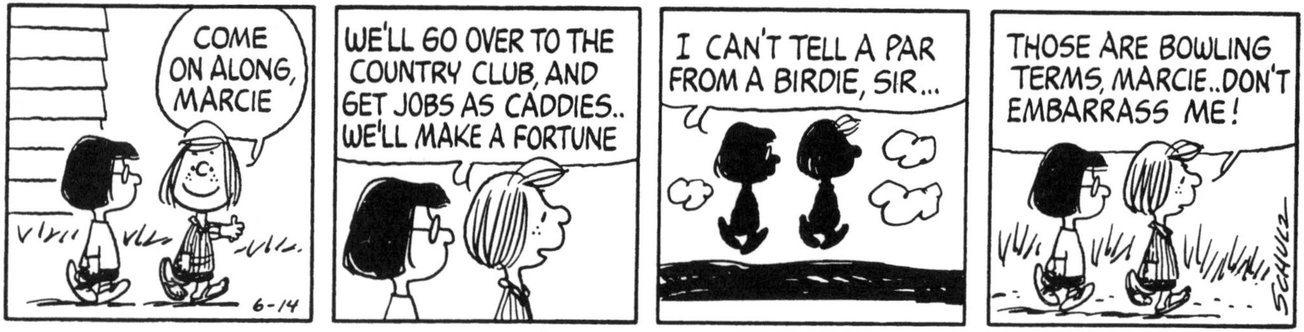
COME ON ALONG, MARCIE
6-14
WE'LL GO OVER TO THE COUNTRY CLUB, AND GET JOBS AS CADDIES.. WE'LL MAKE A FORTUNE
I CAN'T TELL A PAR FROM A BIRDIE, SIR...
THOSE ARE BOWLING TERMS, MARCIE..DON'T EMBARRASS ME!
SCHULZ

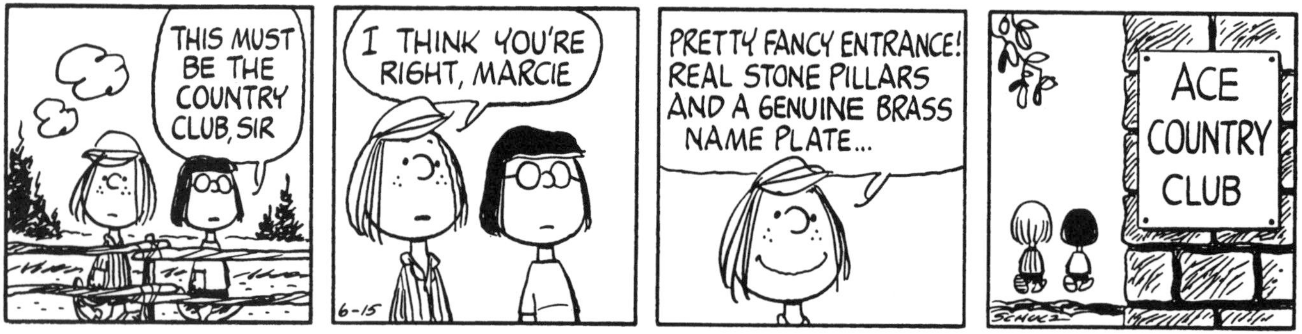
THIS MUST BE THE COUNTRY CLUB, SIR
I THINK YOU'RE RIGHT, MARCIE
6-15
PRETTY FANCY ENTRANCE! REAL STONE PILLARS AND A GENUINE BRASS NAME PLATE...
ACE COUNTRY CLUB
SCHULZ

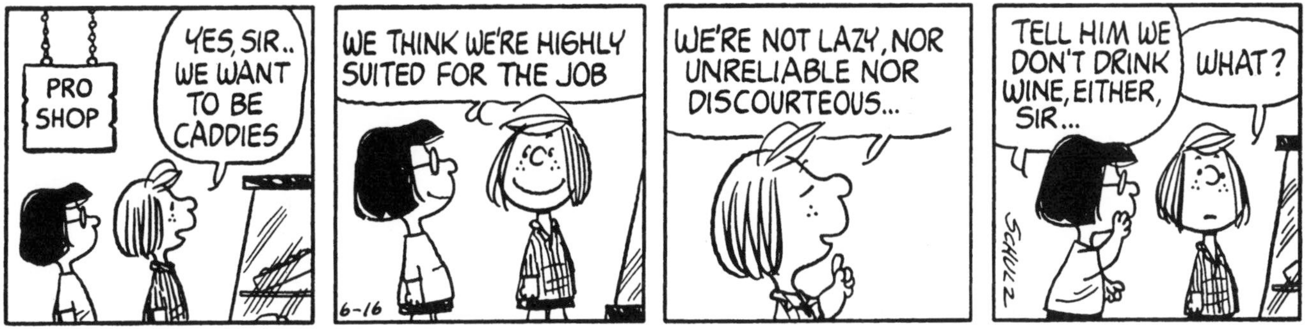
PRO SHOP
YES, SIR.. WE WANT TO BE CADDIES
WE THINK WE'RE HIGHLY SUITED FOR THE JOB
6-16
WE'RE NOT LAZY, NOR UNRELIABLE NOR DISCOURTEOUS...
TELL HIM WE DON'T DRINK WINE, EITHER, SIR...
WHAT?
SCHULZ

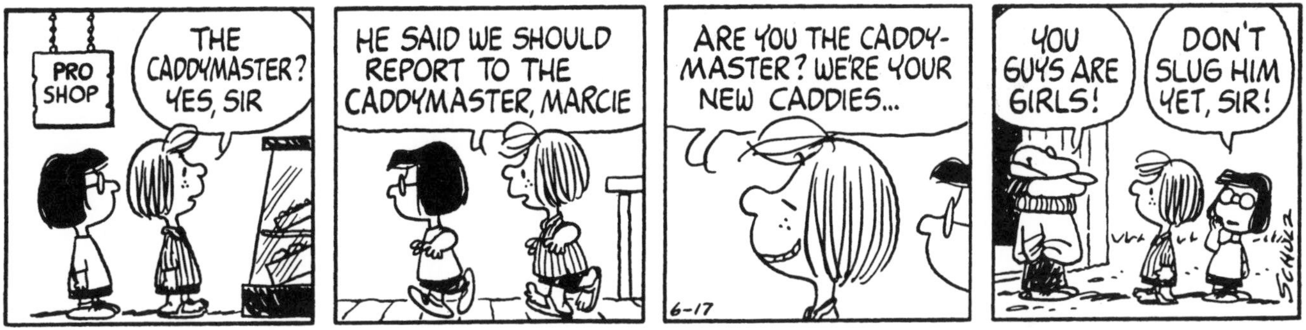
PRO SHOP
THE CADDYMASTER? YES, SIR
HE SAID WE SHOULD REPORT TO THE CADDYMASTER, MARCIE
ARE YOU THE CADDY-MASTER? WE'RE YOUR NEW CADDIES...
6-17
YOU GUYS ARE GIRLS!
DON'T SLUG HIM YET, SIR!
SCHULZ

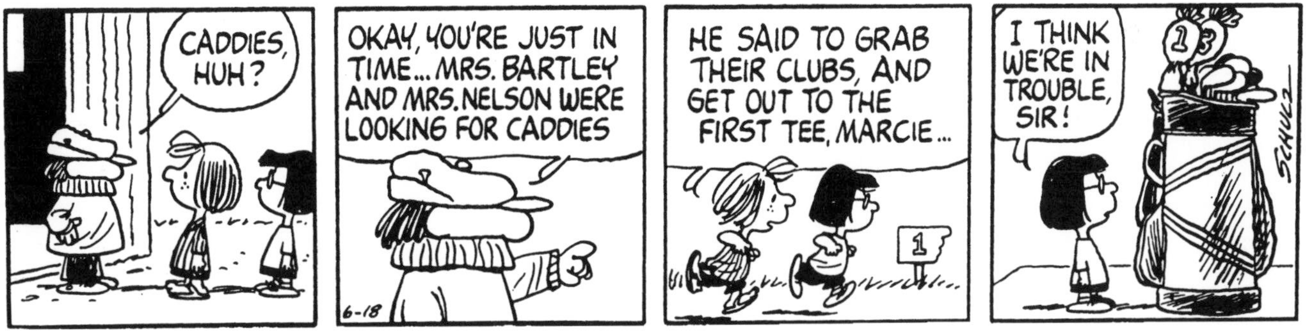
CADDIES, HUH?
OKAY, YOU'RE JUST IN TIME... MRS. BARTLEY AND MRS. NELSON WERE LOOKING FOR CADDIES
6-18
HE SAID TO GRAB THEIR CLUBS, AND GET OUT TO THE FIRST TEE, MARCIE...
1
I THINK WE'RE IN TROUBLE, SIR!
SCHULZ

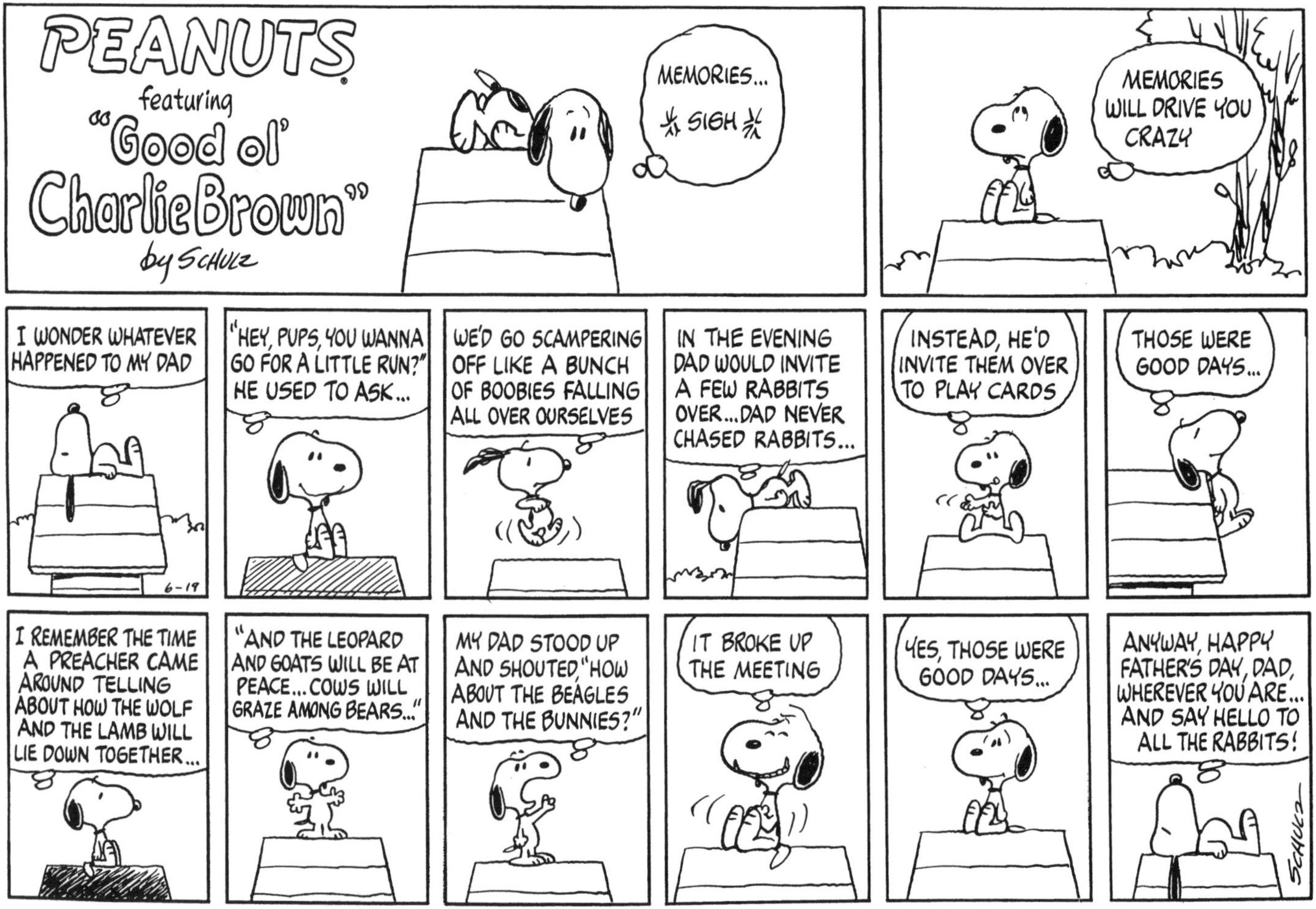
PEANUTS
featuring
"Good ol' Charlie Brown"
by SCHULZ
MEMORIES... SIGH
MEMORIES WILL DRIVE YOU CRAZY
I WONDER WHATEVER HAPPENED TO MY DAD
6-19
"HEY, PUPS, YOU WANNA GO FOR A LITTLE RUN?" HE USED TO ASK...
WE'D GO SCAMPERING OFF LIKE A BUNCH OF BOOBIES FALLING ALL OVER OURSELVES
IN THE EVENING DAD WOULD INVITE A FEW RABBITS OVER...DAD NEVER CHASED RABBITS...
INSTEAD, HE'D INVITE THEM OVER TO PLAY CARDS
THOSE WERE GOOD DAYS...
I REMEMBER THE TIME A PREACHER CAME AROUND TELLING ABOUT HOW THE WOLF AND THE LAMB WILL LIE DOWN TOGETHER...
"AND THE LEOPARD AND GOATS WILL BE AT PEACE...COWS WILL GRAZE AMONG BEARS..."
MY DAD STOOD UP AND SHOUTED, "HOW ABOUT THE BEAGLES AND THE BUNNIES?"
IT BROKE UP THE MEETING
YES, THOSE WERE GOOD DAYS...
ANYWAY, HAPPY FATHER'S DAY, DAD, WHEREVER YOU ARE... AND SAY HELLO TO ALL THE RABBITS!
SCHULZ

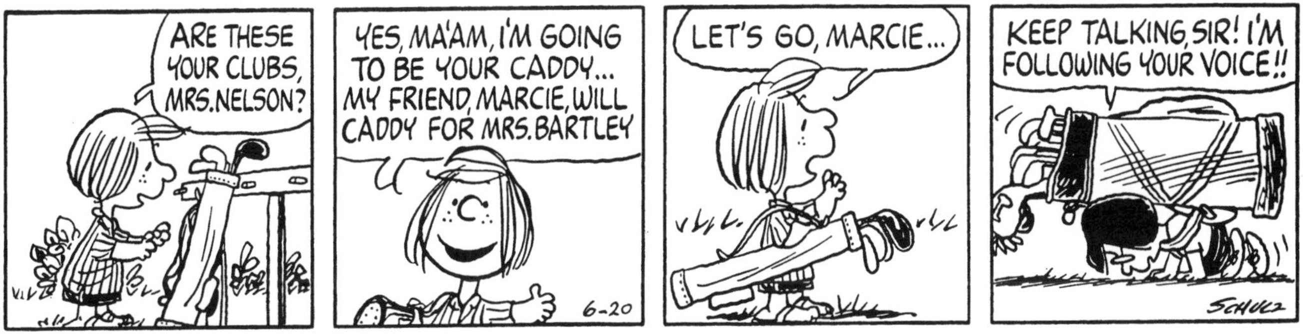
ARE THESE YOUR CLUBS, MRS.NELSON?
YES, MA'AM, I'M GOING TO BE YOUR CADDY... MY FRIEND, MARCIE, WILL CADDY FOR MRS.BARTLEY
6-20
LET'S GO, MARCIE...
KEEP TALKING, SIR! I'M FOLLOWING YOUR VOICE!!
SCHULZ

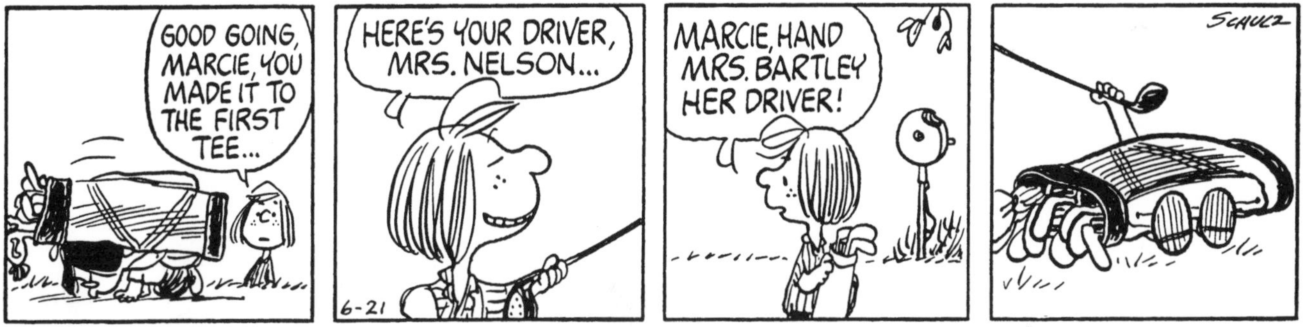
GOOD GOING, MARCIE, YOU MADE IT TO THE FIRST TEE...
HERE'S YOUR DRIVER, MRS. NELSON...
6-21
MARCIE, HAND MRS. BARTLEY HER DRIVER!
SCHULZ

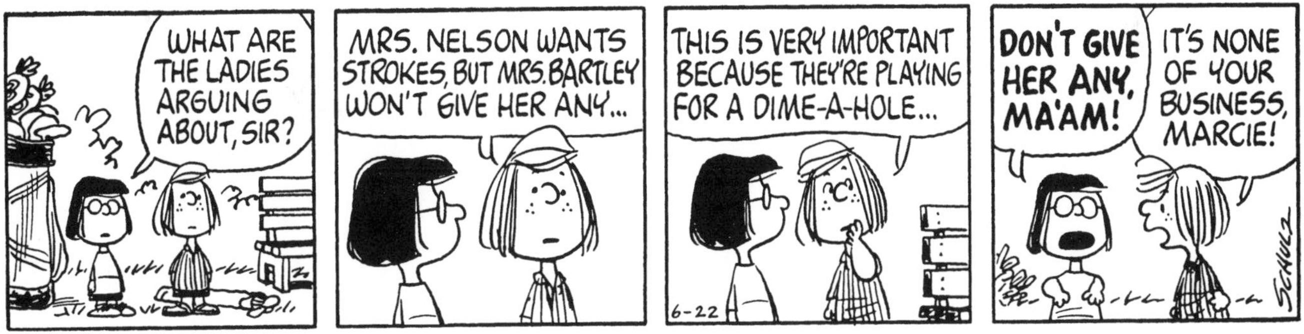
WHAT ARE THE LADIES ARGUING ABOUT, SIR?
MRS. NELSON WANTS STROKES, BUT MRS.BARTLEY WON'T GIVE HER ANY...
THIS IS VERY IMPORTANT BECAUSE THEY'RE PLAYING FOR A DIME-A-HOLE...
6-22
DON'T GIVE HER ANY, MA'AM!
IT'S NONE OF YOUR BUSINESS, MARCIE!
SCHULZ

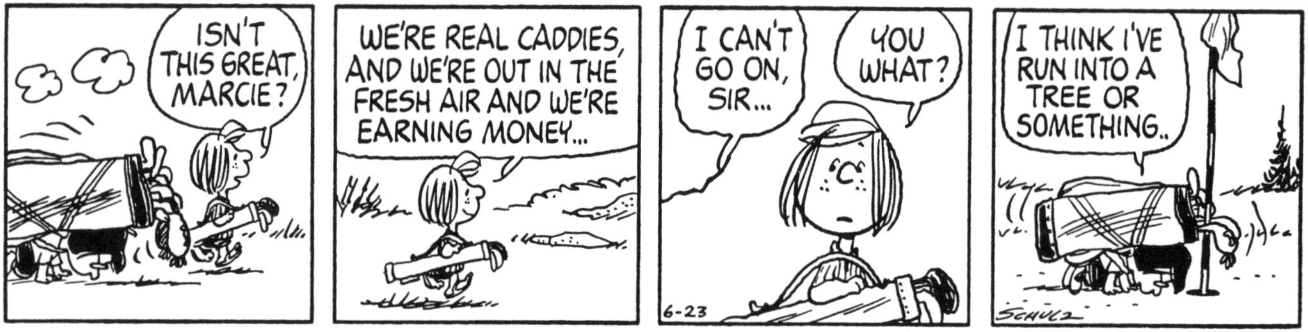
ISN'T THIS GREAT, MARCIE?
WE'RE REAL CADDIES, AND WE'RE OUT IN THE FRESH AIR AND WE'RE EARNING MONEY...
I CAN'T GO ON, SIR...
YOU WHAT?
6-23
I THINK I'VE RUN INTO A TREE OR SOMETHING..
SCHULZ

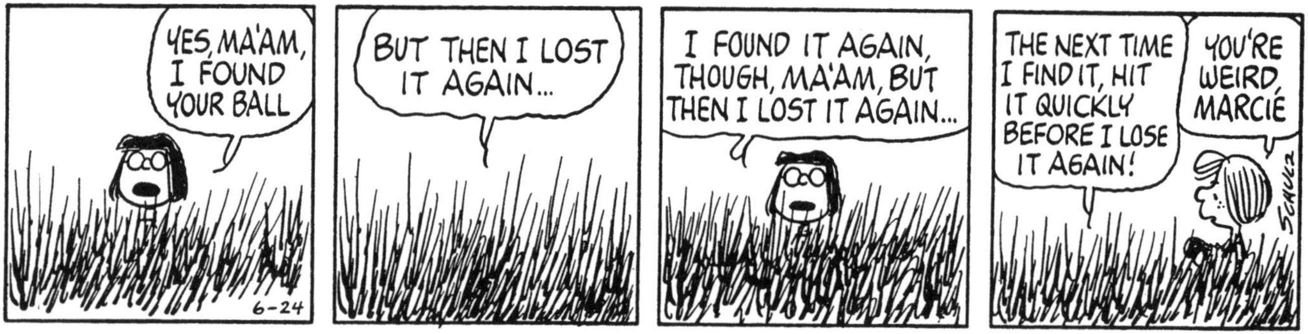
YES, MA'AM, I FOUND YOUR BALL
6-24
BUT THEN I LOST IT AGAIN...
I FOUND IT AGAIN, THOUGH, MA'AM, BUT THEN I LOST IT AGAIN...
THE NEXT TIME I FIND IT, HIT IT QUICKLY BEFORE I LOSE IT AGAIN!
YOU'RE WEIRD, MARCIE
SCHULZ

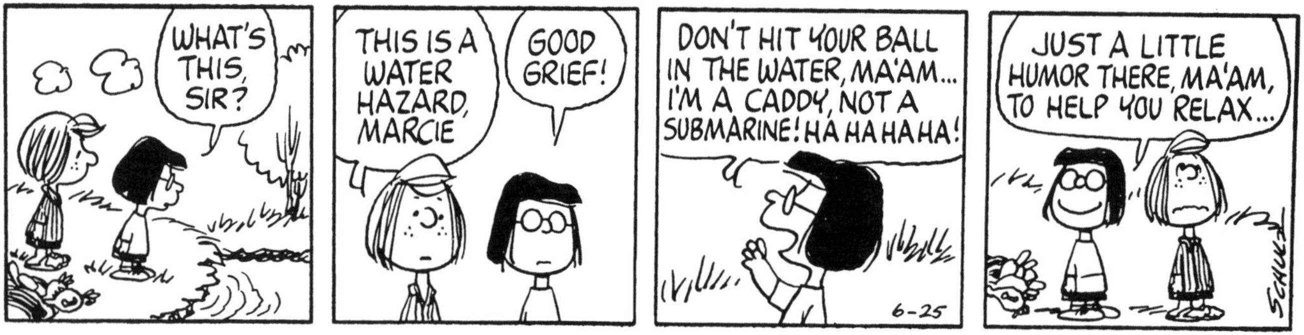
WHAT'S THIS, SIR?
THIS IS A WATER HAZARD, MARCIE
GOOD GRIEF!
DON'T HIT YOUR BALL IN THE WATER, MA'AM... I'M A CADDY, NOT A SUBMARINE! HA HA HA HA!
6-25
JUST A LITTLE HUMOR THERE, MA'AM, TO HELP YOU RELAX...
SCHULZ

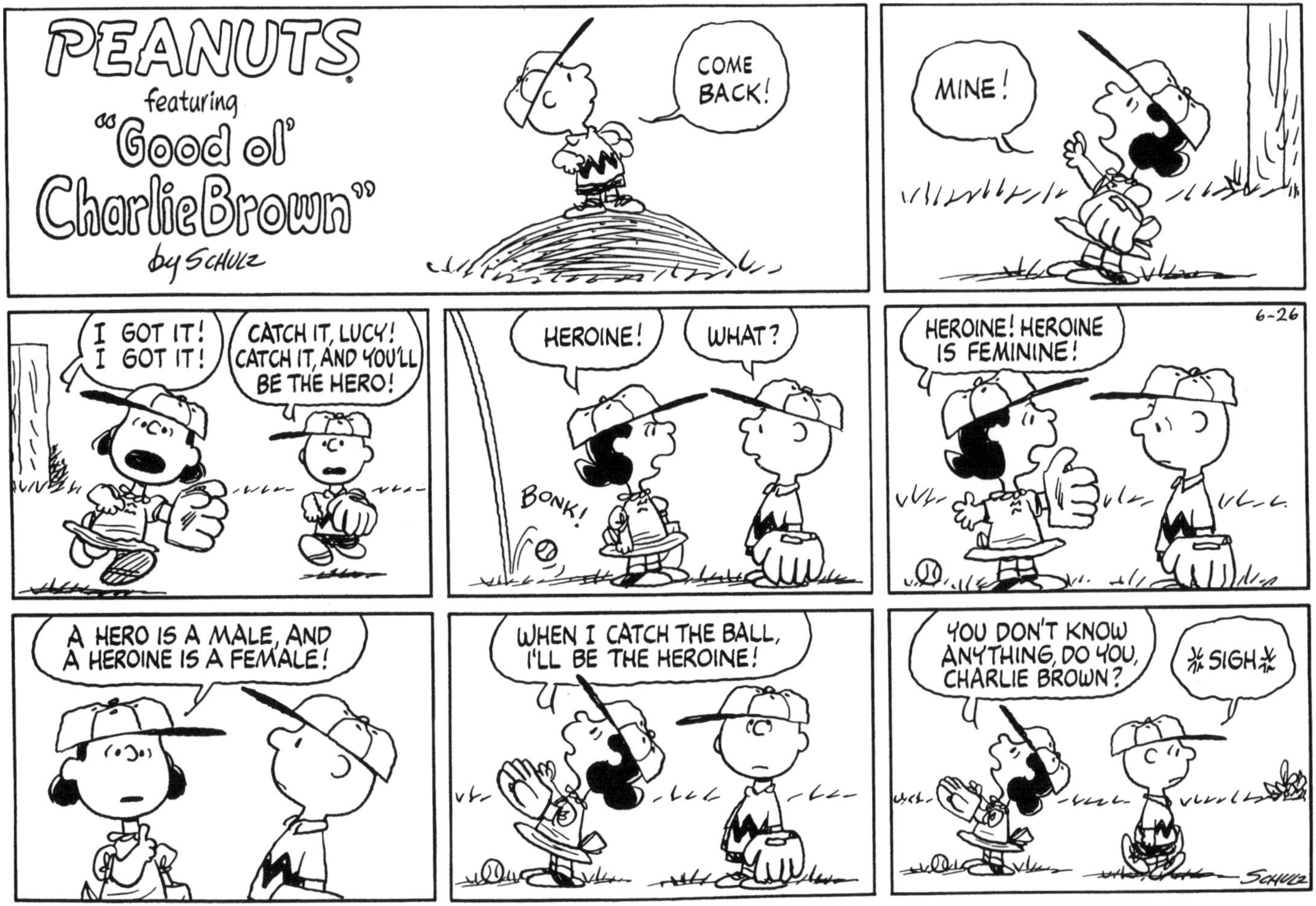
PEANUTS
featuring
"Good ol' Charlie Brown"
by SCHULZ
COME BACK!
MINE!
I GOT IT! I GOT IT!
CATCH IT, LUCY! CATCH IT, AND YOU'LL BE THE HERO!
HEROINE!
WHAT?
BONK!
HEROINE! HEROINE IS FEMININE!
6-26
A HERO IS A MALE, AND A HEROINE IS A FEMALE!
WHEN I CATCH THE BALL, I'LL BE THE HEROINE!
YOU DON'T KNOW ANYTHING, DO YOU, CHARLIE BROWN?
SIGH
SCHULZ

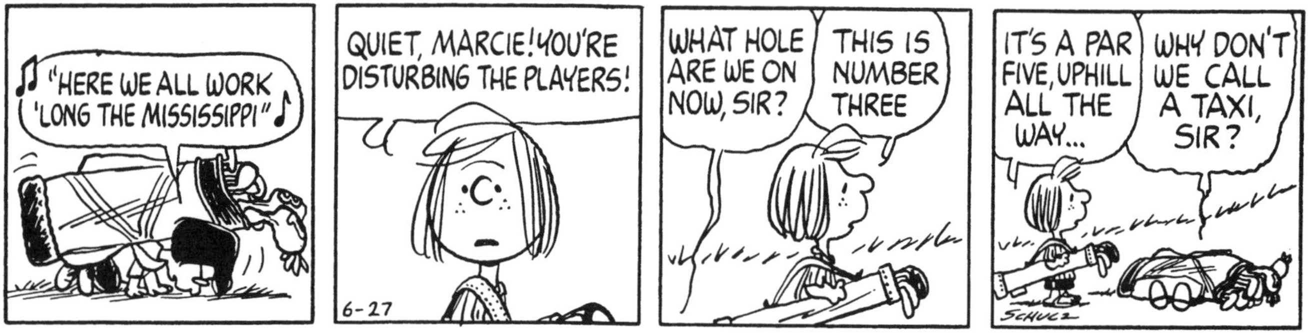
♫ "HERE WE ALL WORK 'LONG THE MISSISSIPPI" ♪
QUIET, MARCIE! YOU'RE DISTURBING THE PLAYERS!
6-27
WHAT HOLE ARE WE ON NOW, SIR?
THIS IS NUMBER THREE
IT'S A PAR FIVE, UPHILL ALL THE WAY...
WHY DON'T WE CALL A TAXI, SIR?
SCHULZ

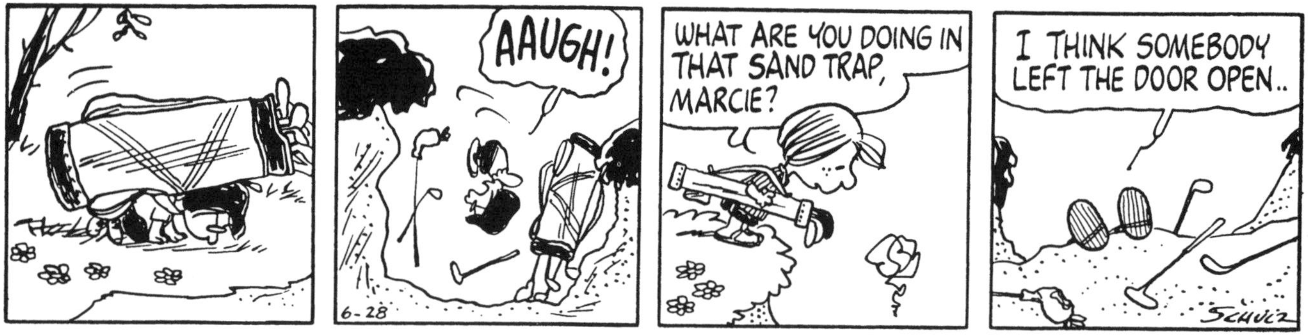
AAUGH!
6-28
WHAT ARE YOU DOING IN THAT SAND TRAP, MARCIE?
I THINK SOMEBODY LEFT THE DOOR OPEN..
SCHULZ

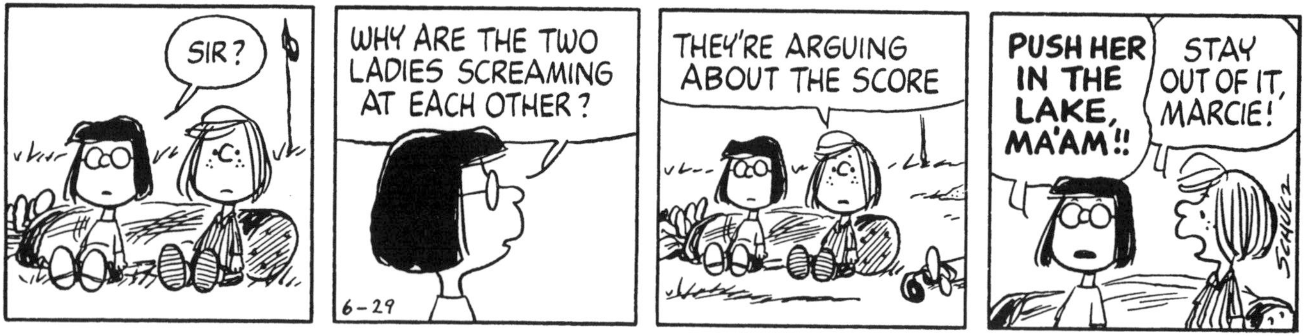
SIR?
WHY ARE THE TWO LADIES SCREAMING AT EACH OTHER?
6-29
THEY'RE ARGUING ABOUT THE SCORE
PUSH HER IN THE LAKE, MA'AM!!
STAY OUT OF IT, MARCIE!
SCHULZ

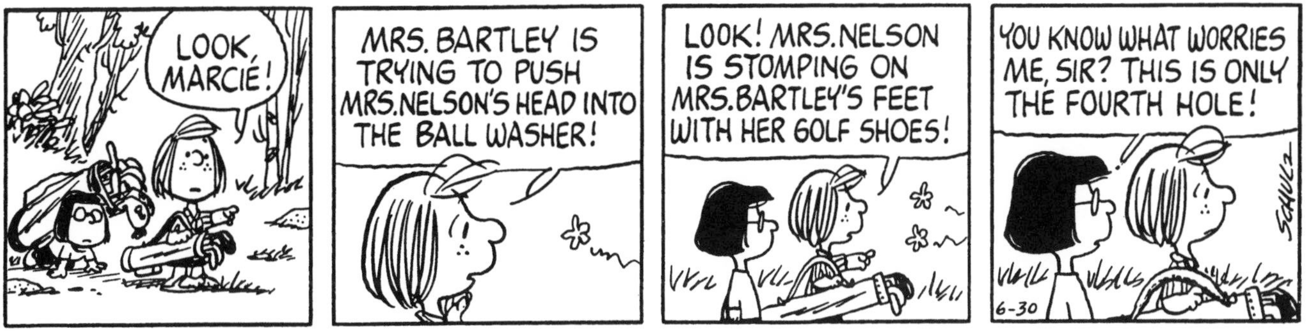
LOOK, MARCIE!
MRS. BARTLEY IS TRYING TO PUSH MRS. NELSON'S HEAD INTO THE BALL WASHER!
LOOK! MRS. NELSON IS STOMPING ON MRS. BARTLEY'S FEET WITH HER GOLF SHOES!
YOU KNOW WHAT WORRIES ME, SIR? THIS IS ONLY THE FOURTH HOLE!
SCHULZ
6-30

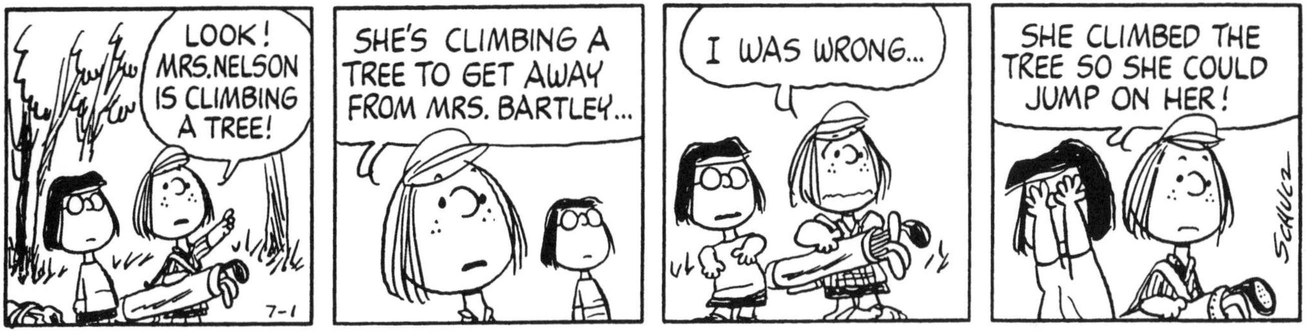
LOOK! MRS. NELSON IS CLIMBING A TREE!
7-1
SHE'S CLIMBING A TREE TO GET AWAY FROM MRS. BARTLEY...
I WAS WRONG...
SHE CLIMBED THE TREE SO SHE COULD JUMP ON HER!
SCHULZ

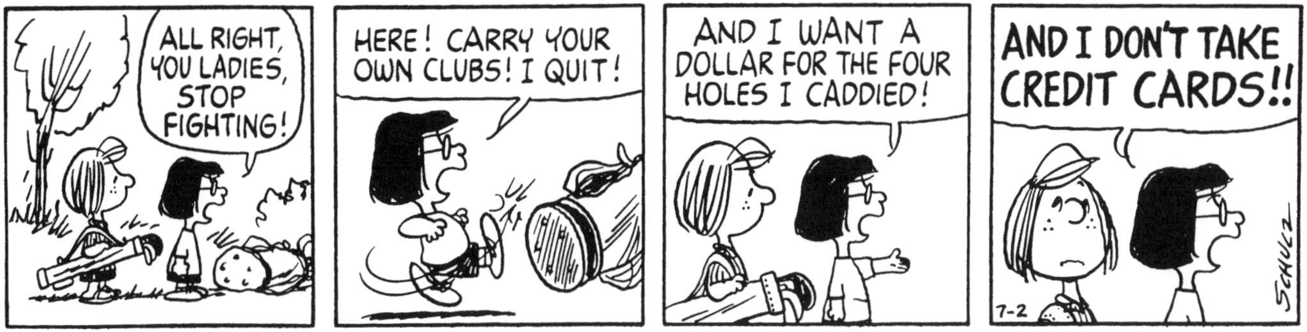
ALL RIGHT, YOU LADIES, STOP FIGHTING!
HERE! CARRY YOUR OWN CLUBS! I QUIT!
AND I WANT A DOLLAR FOR THE FOUR HOLES I CADDIED!
AND I DON'T TAKE CREDIT CARDS!!
SCHULZ
7-2

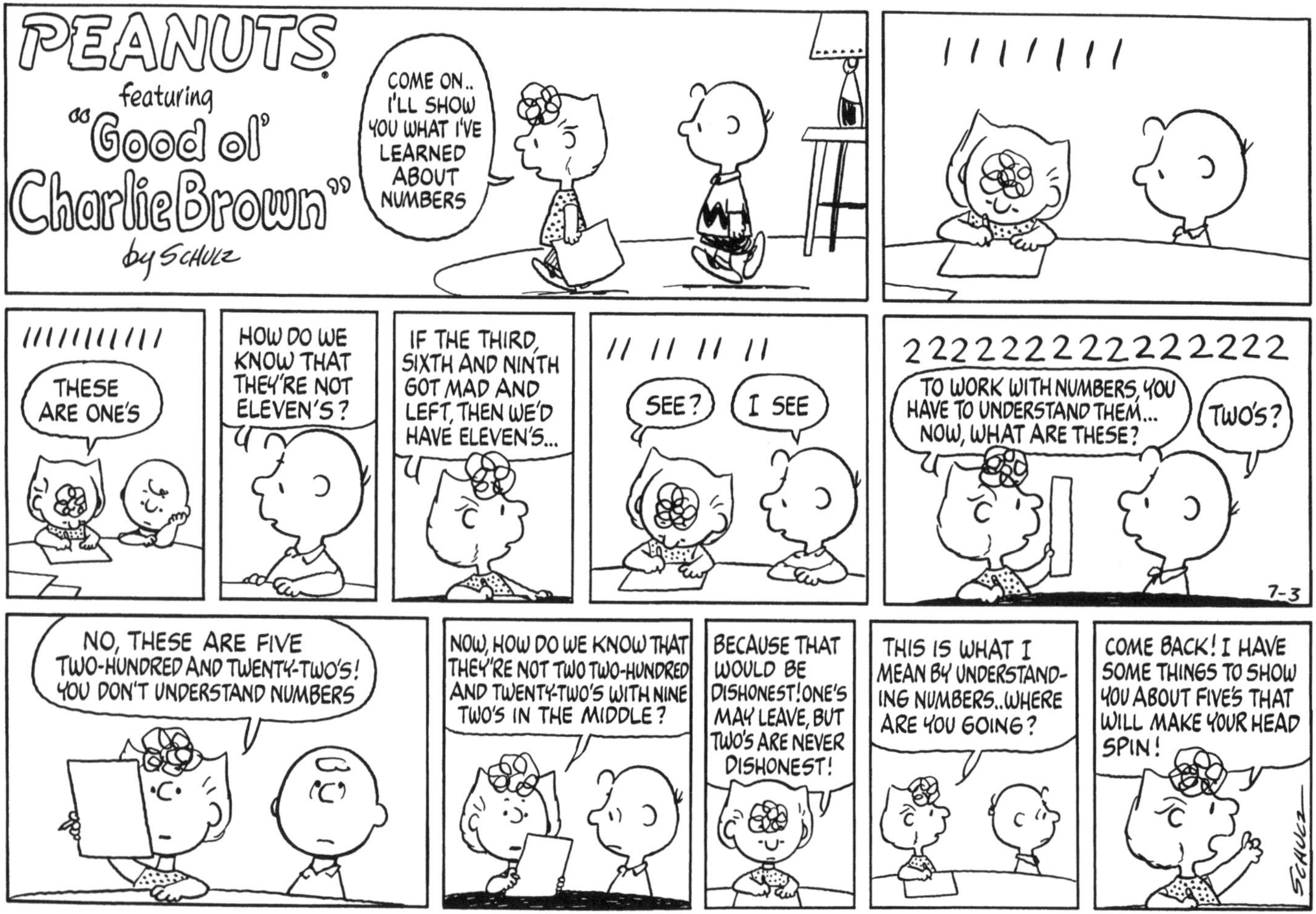
PEANUTS
featuring "Good ol' Charlie Brown"
by SCHULZ
COME ON.. I'LL SHOW YOU WHAT I'VE LEARNED ABOUT NUMBERS
I I I I I I I I
I I I I I I I I I I I
THESE ARE ONE'S
HOW DO WE KNOW THAT THEY'RE NOT ELEVEN'S ?
IF THE THIRD, SIXTH AND NINTH GOT MAD AND LEFT, THEN WE'D HAVE ELEVEN'S...
II II II II
SEE?
I SEE
222222222222222
TO WORK WITH NUMBERS, YOU HAVE TO UNDERSTAND THEM... NOW, WHAT ARE THESE?
TWO'S?
7-3
NO, THESE ARE FIVE TWO-HUNDRED AND TWENTY-TWO'S! YOU DON'T UNDERSTAND NUMBERS
NOW, HOW DO WE KNOW THAT THEY'RE NOT TWO TWO-HUNDRED AND TWENTY-TWO'S WITH NINE TWO'S IN THE MIDDLE?
BECAUSE THAT WOULD BE DISHONEST! ONE'S MAY LEAVE, BUT TWO'S ARE NEVER DISHONEST!
THIS IS WHAT I MEAN BY UNDERSTANDING NUMBERS..WHERE ARE YOU GOING?
COME BACK! I HAVE SOME THINGS TO SHOW YOU ABOUT FIVE'S THAT WILL MAKE YOUR HEAD SPIN!
SCHULZ

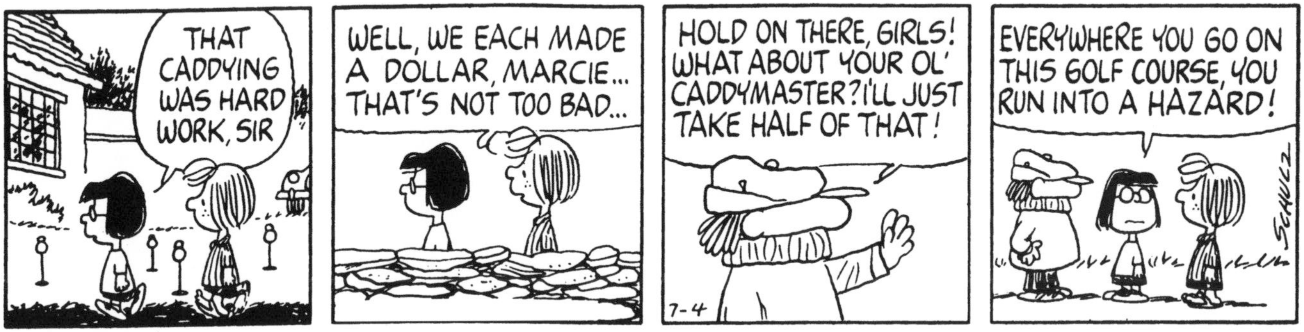
THAT CADDYING WAS HARD WORK, SIR
WELL, WE EACH MADE A DOLLAR, MARCIE... THAT'S NOT TOO BAD...
HOLD ON THERE, GIRLS! WHAT ABOUT YOUR OL' CADDYMASTER? I'LL JUST TAKE HALF OF THAT!
7-4
EVERYWHERE YOU GO ON THIS GOLF COURSE, YOU RUN INTO A HAZARD!
SCHULZ

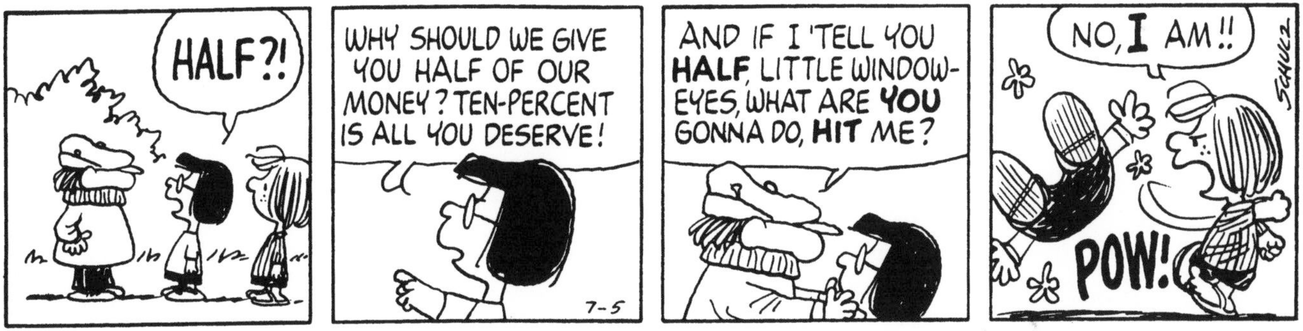
HALF?!
WHY SHOULD WE GIVE YOU HALF OF OUR MONEY? TEN-PERCENT IS ALL YOU DESERVE!
7-5
AND IF I TELL YOU HALF, LITTLE WINDOW-EYES, WHAT ARE YOU GONNA DO, HIT ME?
NO, I AM!!
SCHULZ
POW!

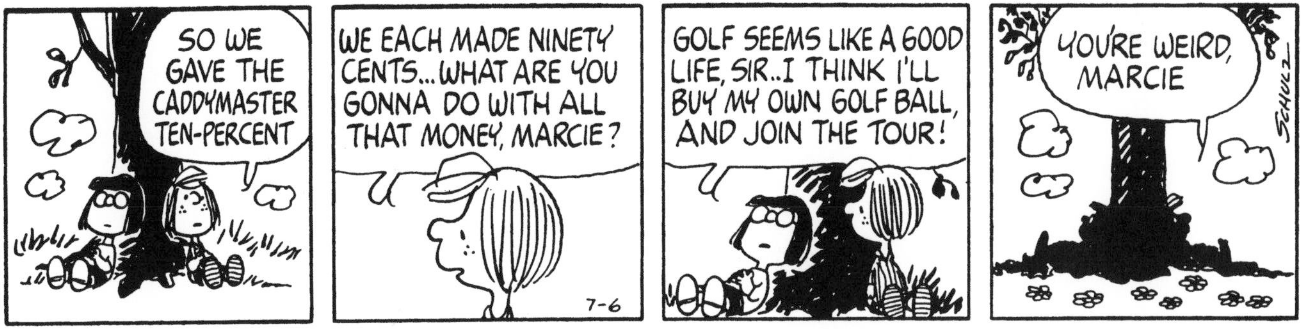
SO WE GAVE THE CADDYMASTER TEN-PERCENT
WE EACH MADE NINETY CENTS... WHAT ARE YOU GONNA DO WITH ALL THAT MONEY, MARCIE?
7-6
GOLF SEEMS LIKE A GOOD LIFE, SIR.. I THINK I'LL BUY MY OWN GOLF BALL, AND JOIN THE TOUR!
YOU'RE WEIRD, MARCIE
SCHULZ

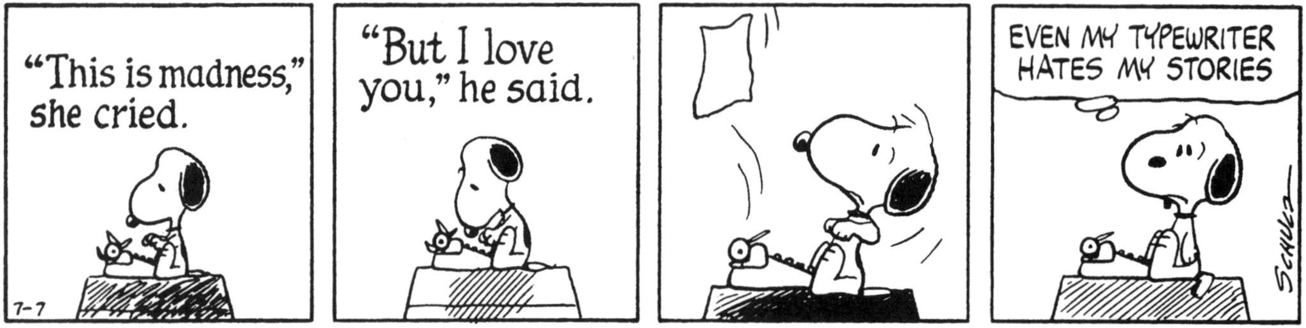
"This is madness," she cried.
"But I love you," he said.
EVEN MY TYPEWRITER HATES MY STORIES
7-7
SCHULZ

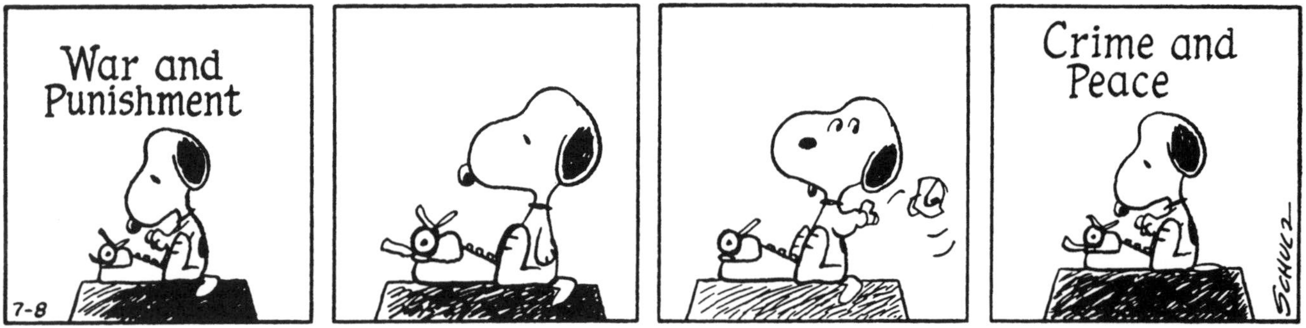
War and Punishment
Crime and Peace
7-8
SCHULZ

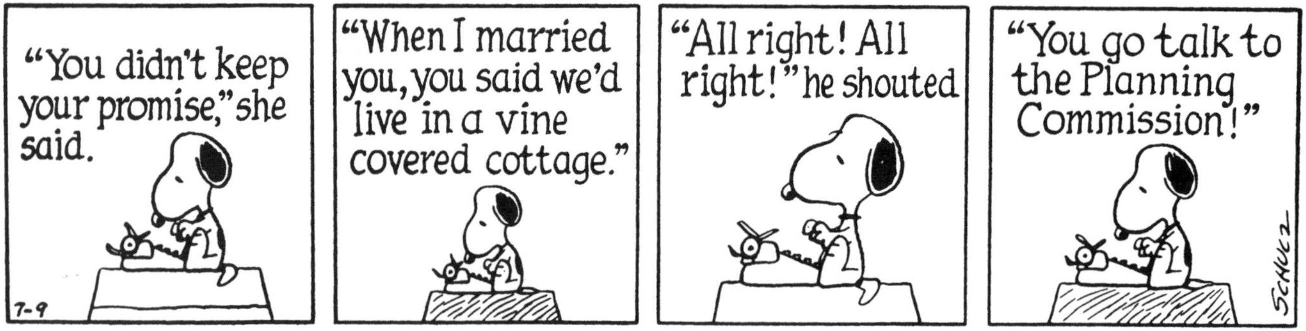
"You didn't keep your promise," she said.
"When I married you, you said we'd live in a vine covered cottage."
"All right! All right!" he shouted
"You go talk to the Planning Commission!"
7-9
SCHULZ

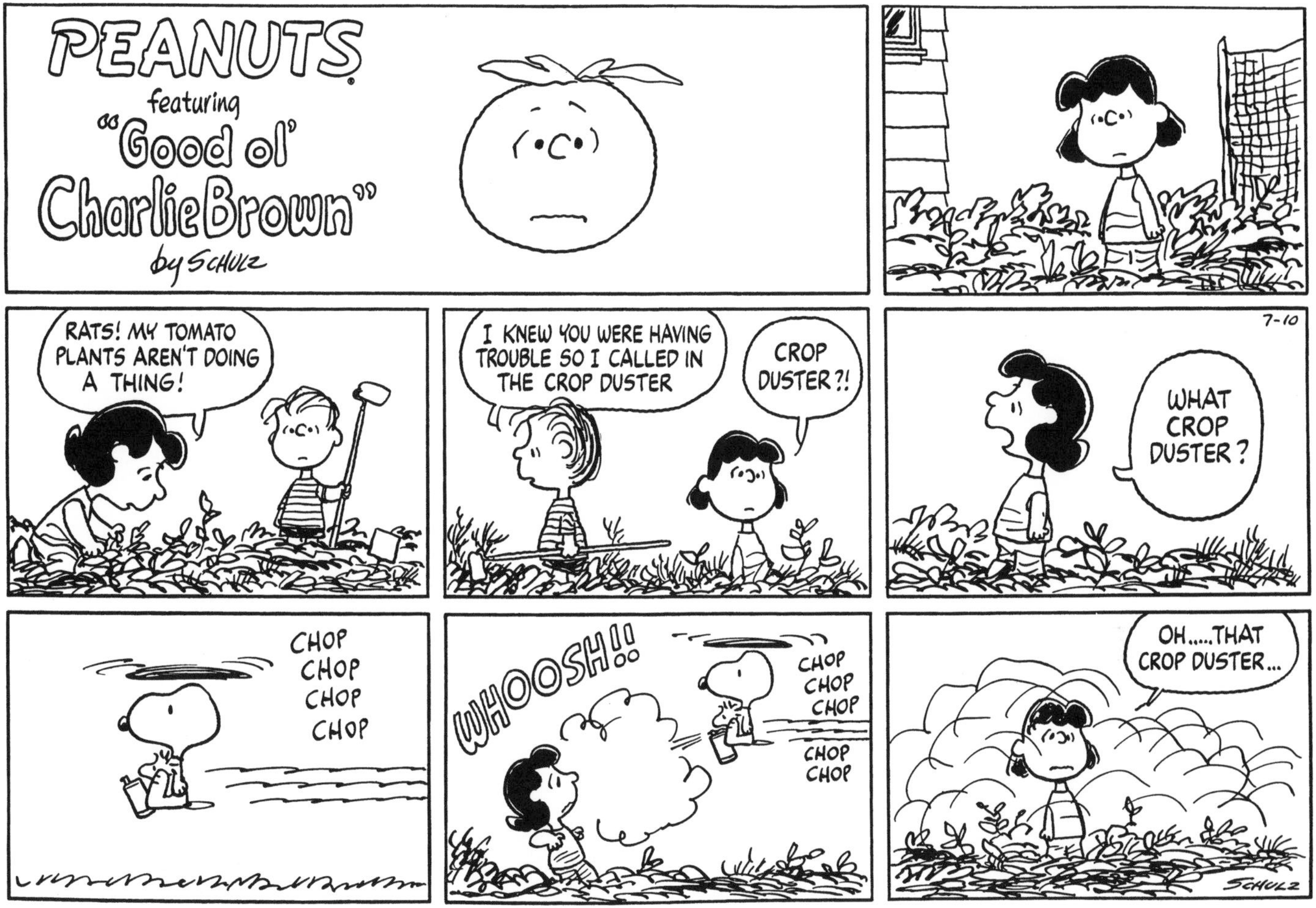
PEANUTS
featuring
"Good ol' Charlie Brown"
by SCHULZ
RATS! MY TOMATO PLANTS AREN'T DOING A THING!
I KNEW YOU WERE HAVING TROUBLE SO I CALLED IN THE CROP DUSTER
CROP DUSTER?!
7-10
WHAT CROP DUSTER?
CHOP CHOP CHOP CHOP
WHOOSH!!
CHOP CHOP CHOP
CHOP CHOP
OH.....THAT CROP DUSTER...
SCHULZ

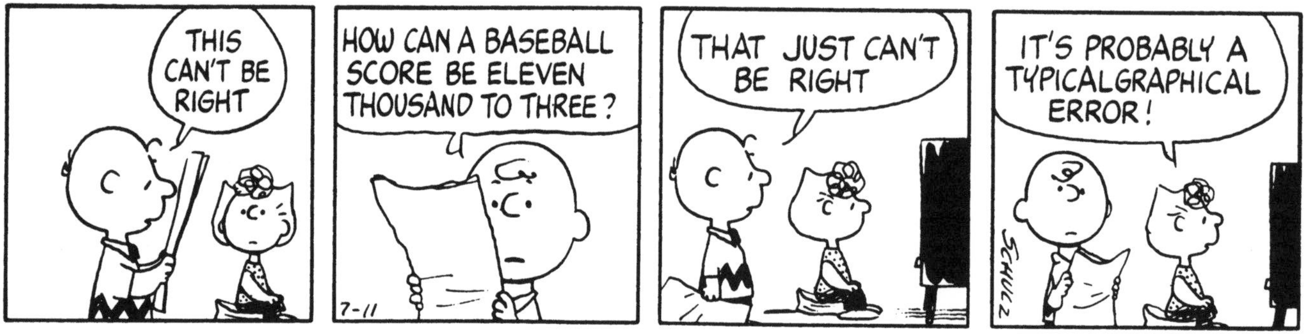
THIS CAN'T BE RIGHT
HOW CAN A BASEBALL SCORE BE ELEVEN THOUSAND TO THREE?
7-11
THAT JUST CAN'T BE RIGHT
IT'S PROBABLY A TYPICALGRAPHICAL ERROR!
SCHULZ

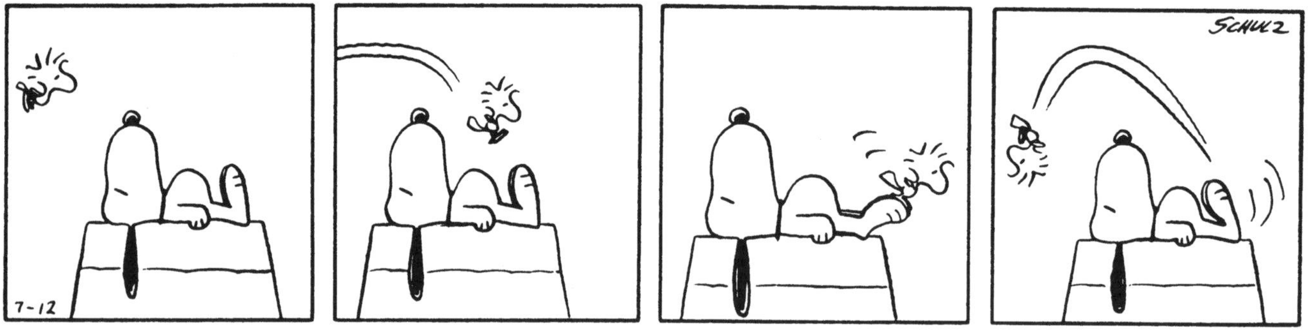
7-12
SCHULZ

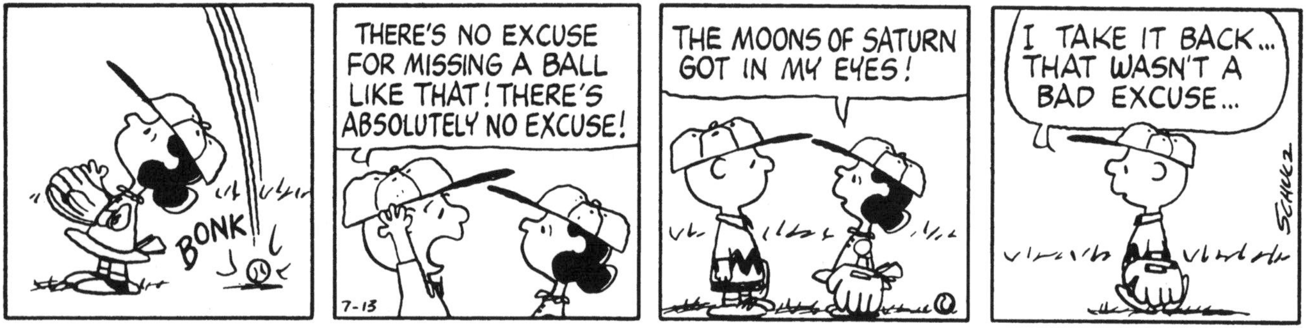
BONK
THERE'S NO EXCUSE FOR MISSING A BALL LIKE THAT! THERE'S ABSOLUTELY NO EXCUSE!
7-13
THE MOONS OF SATURN GOT IN MY EYES!
I TAKE IT BACK... THAT WASN'T A BAD EXCUSE...
SCHULZ

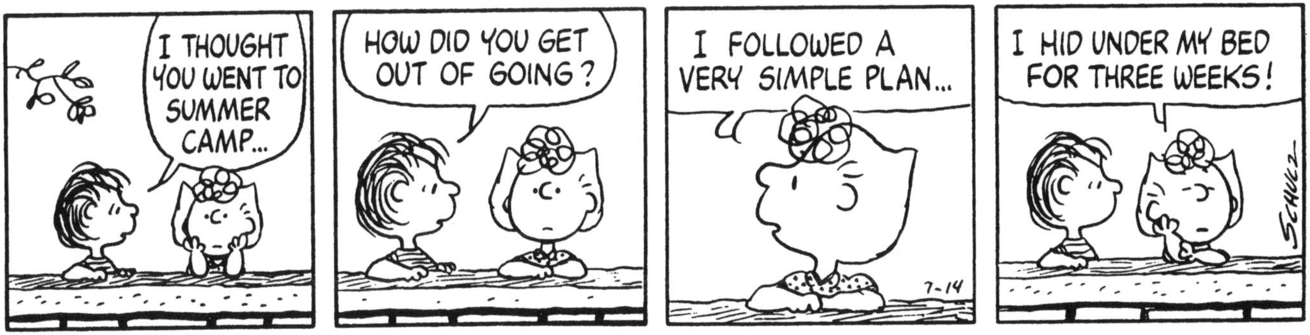
I THOUGHT YOU WENT TO SUMMER CAMP...
HOW DID YOU GET OUT OF GOING?
I FOLLOWED A VERY SIMPLE PLAN...
7-14
I HID UNDER MY BED FOR THREE WEEKS!
SCHULZ

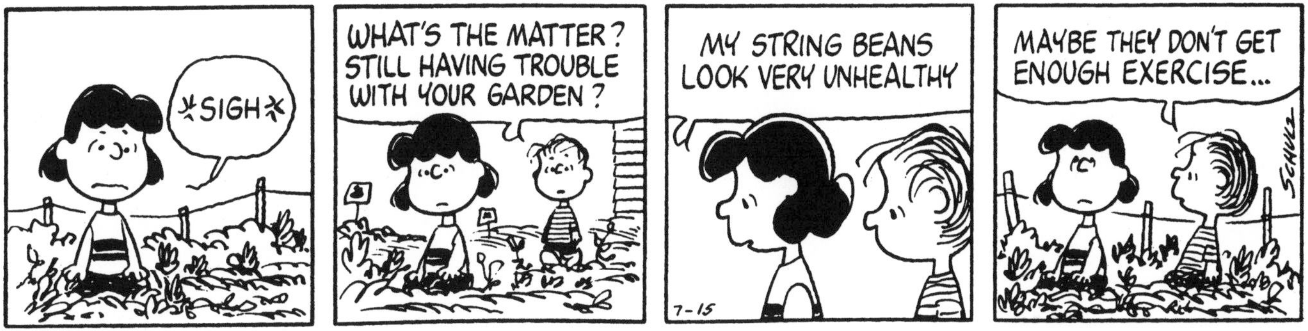
SIGH
WHAT'S THE MATTER? STILL HAVING TROUBLE WITH YOUR GARDEN?
MY STRING BEANS LOOK VERY UNHEALTHY
7-15
MAYBE THEY DON'T GET ENOUGH EXERCISE...
SCHULZ

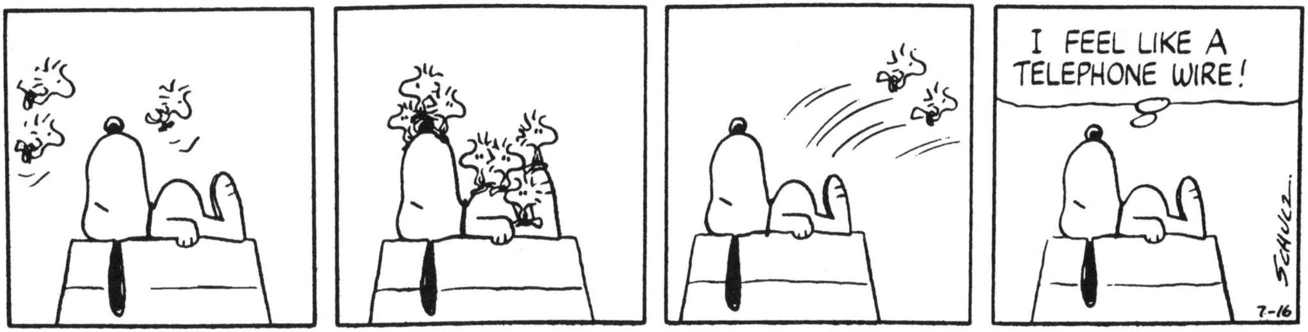
I FEEL LIKE A TELEPHONE WIRE!
SCHULZ
7-16

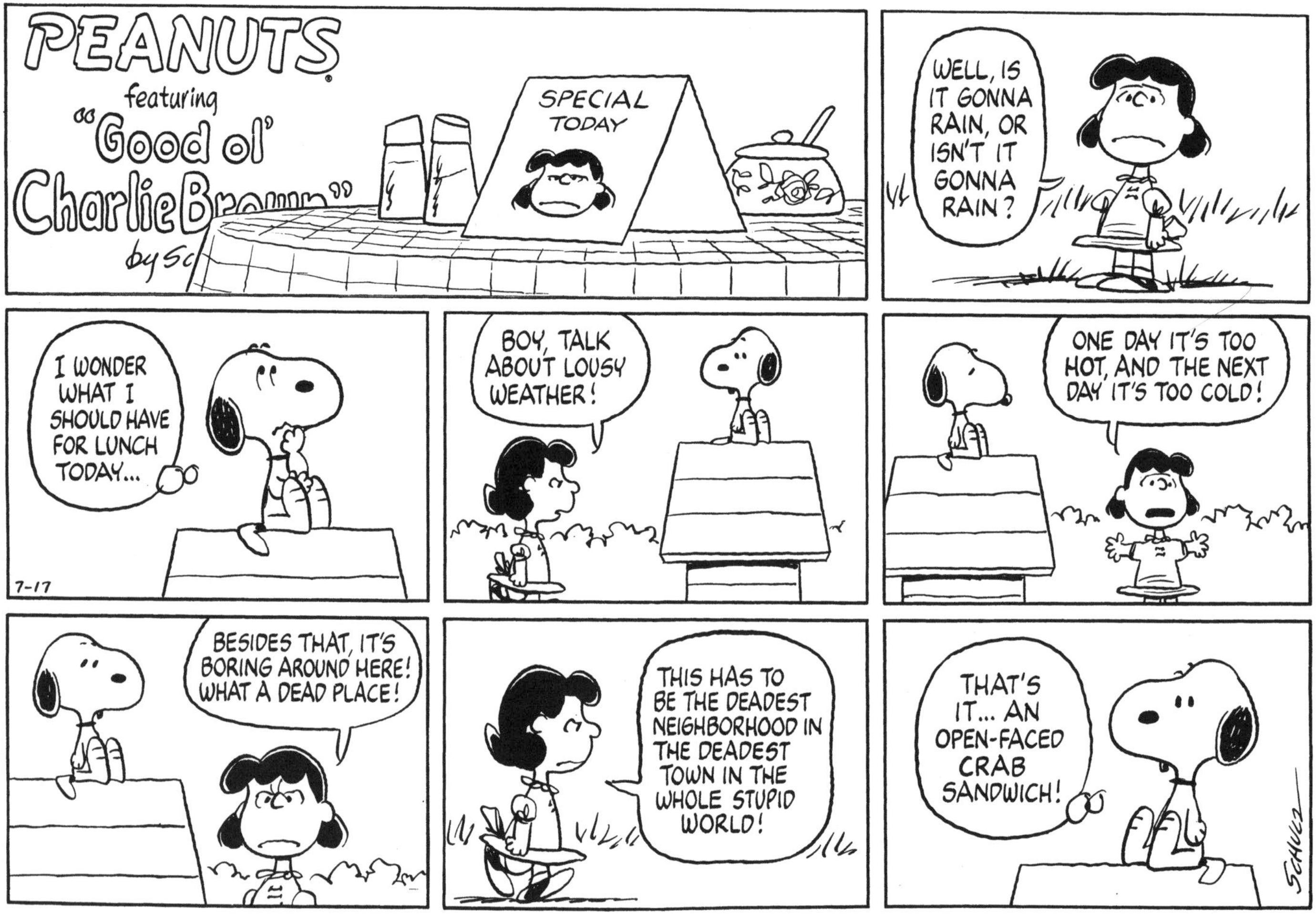
PEANUTS
featuring "Good ol' Charlie Brown"
by Sc
SPECIAL TODAY
WELL, IS IT GONNA RAIN, OR ISN'T IT GONNA RAIN?
I WONDER WHAT I SHOULD HAVE FOR LUNCH TODAY...
7-17
BOY, TALK ABOUT LOUSY WEATHER!
ONE DAY IT'S TOO HOT, AND THE NEXT DAY IT'S TOO COLD!
BESIDES THAT, IT'S BORING AROUND HERE! WHAT A DEAD PLACE!
THIS HAS TO BE THE DEADEST NEIGHBORHOOD IN THE DEADEST TOWN IN THE WHOLE STUPID WORLD!
THAT'S IT... AN OPEN-FACED CRAB SANDWICH!
SCHULZ

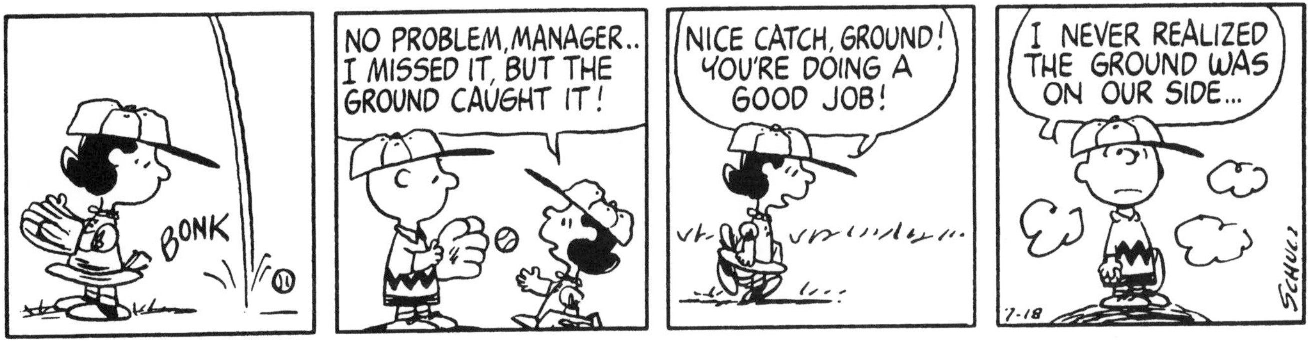
BONK
NO PROBLEM, MANAGER.. I MISSED IT, BUT THE GROUND CAUGHT IT!
NICE CATCH, GROUND! YOU'RE DOING A GOOD JOB!
I NEVER REALIZED THE GROUND WAS ON OUR SIDE...
7-18
SCHULZ

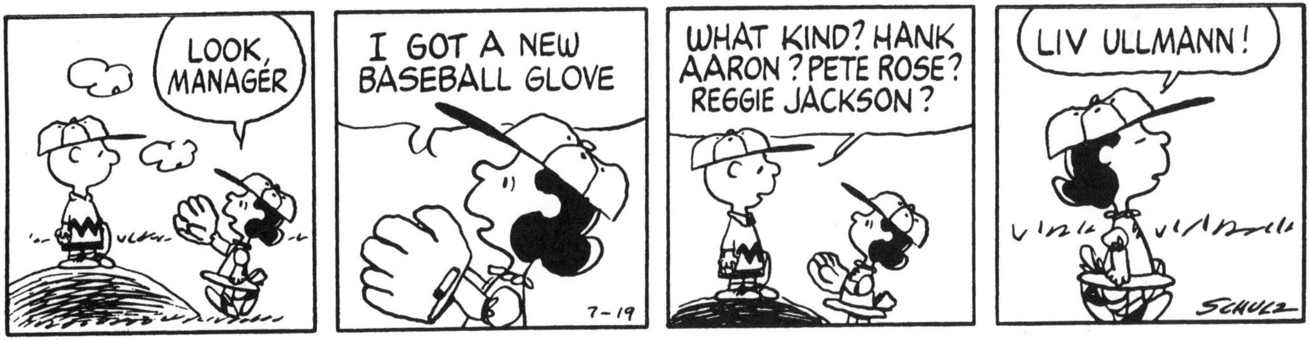
LOOK, MANAGER
I GOT A NEW BASEBALL GLOVE
7-19
WHAT KIND? HANK AARON? PETE ROSE? REGGIE JACKSON?
LIV ULLMANN!
SCHULZ

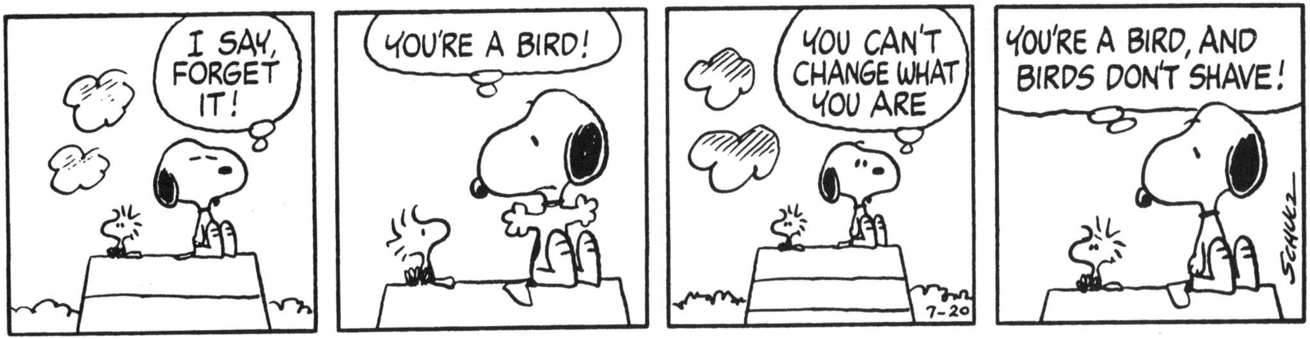
I SAY, FORGET IT!
YOU'RE A BIRD!
YOU CAN'T CHANGE WHAT YOU ARE
7-20
YOU'RE A BIRD, AND BIRDS DON'T SHAVE!
SCHULZ

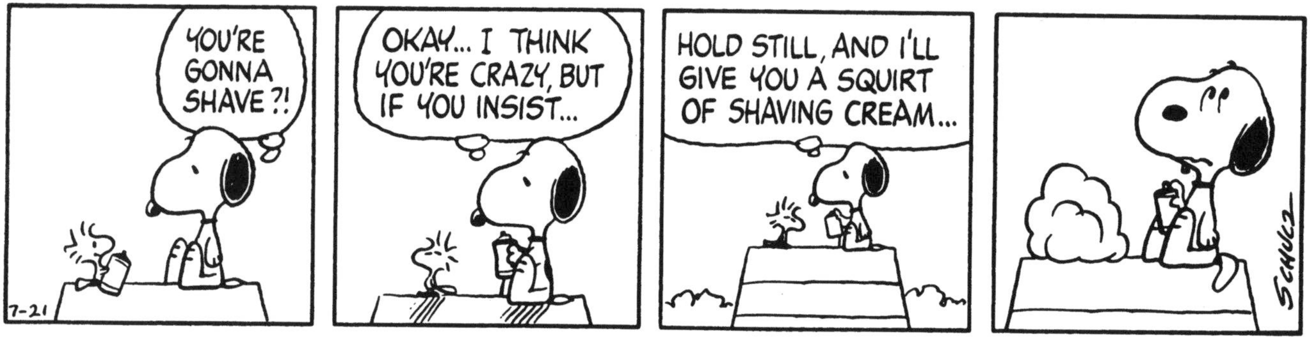
7-21
YOU'RE GONNA SHAVE ?!
OKAY... I THINK YOU'RE CRAZY, BUT IF YOU INSIST...
HOLD STILL, AND I'LL GIVE YOU A SQUIRT OF SHAVING CREAM...
SCHULZ

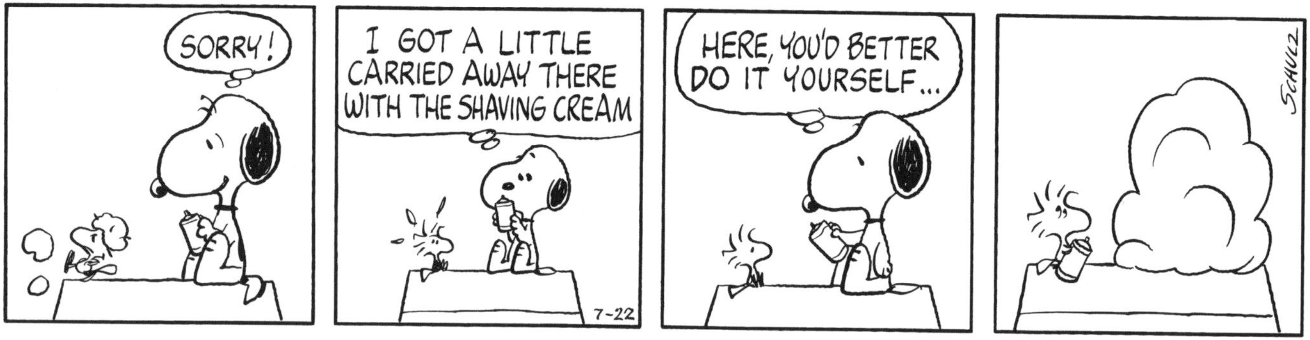
SORRY!
I GOT A LITTLE CARRIED AWAY THERE WITH THE SHAVING CREAM
7-22
HERE, YOU'D BETTER DO IT YOURSELF...
SCHULZ

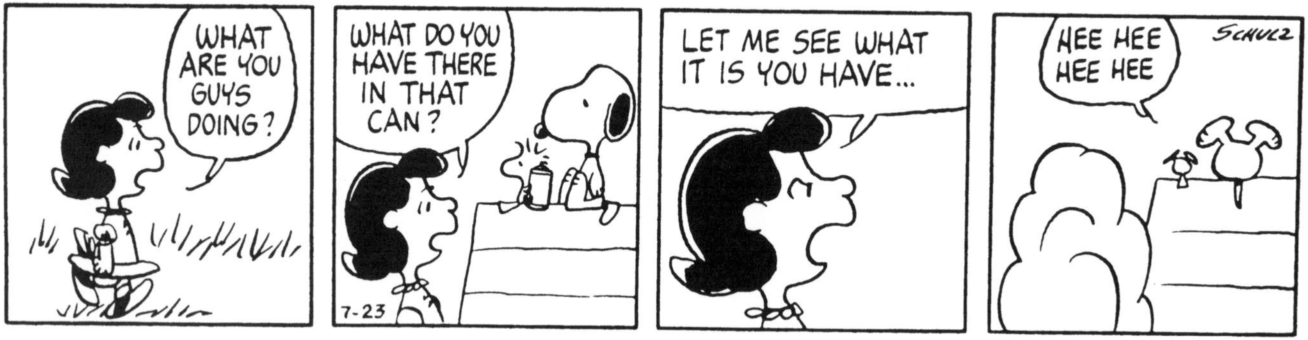
WHAT ARE YOU GUYS DOING?
WHAT DO YOU HAVE THERE IN THAT CAN?
7-23
LET ME SEE WHAT IT IS YOU HAVE...
SCHULZ
HEE HEE HEE HEE

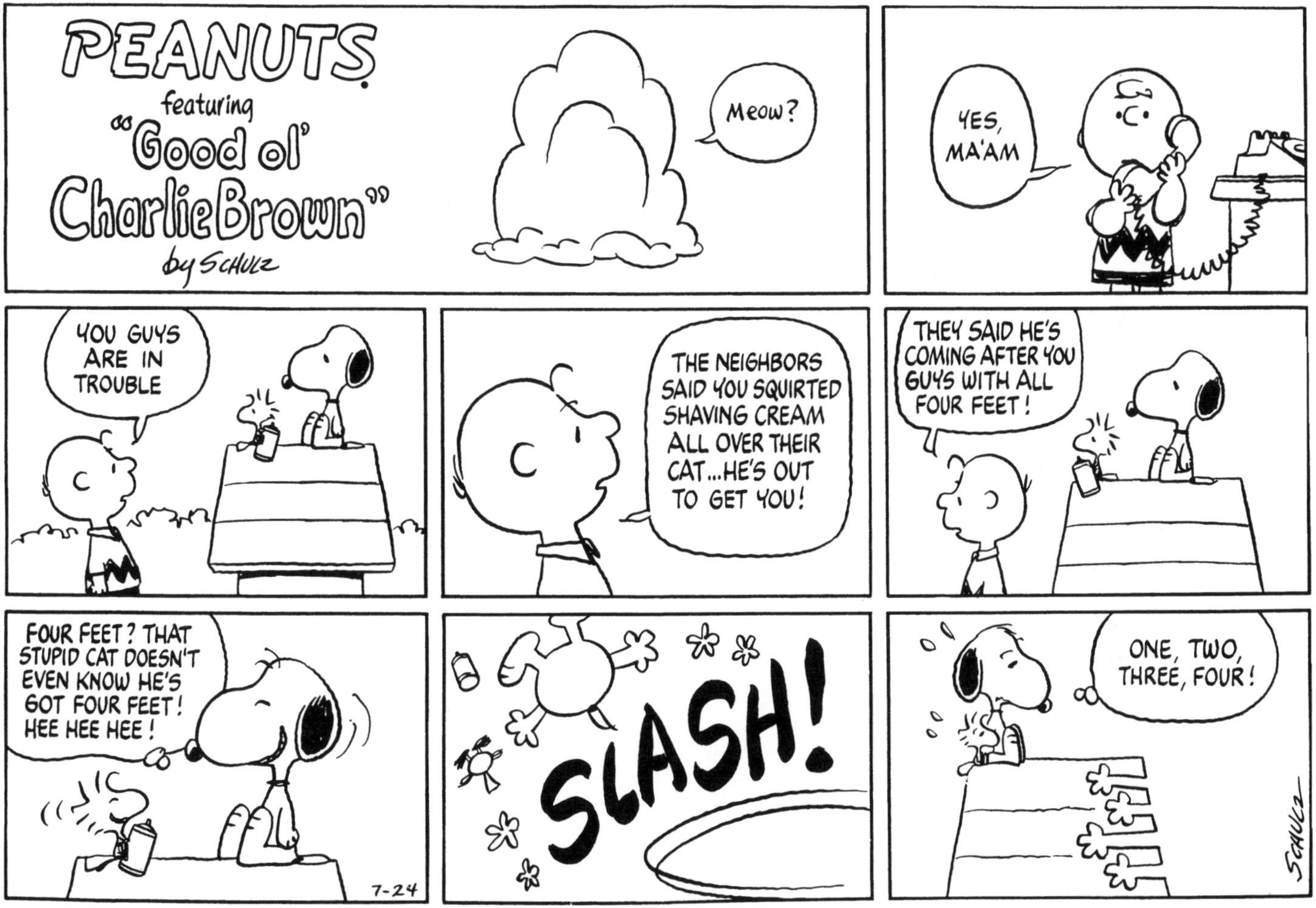
PEANUTS
featuring
"Good ol' Charlie Brown"
by SCHULZ
Meow?
YES, MA'AM
YOU GUYS ARE IN TROUBLE
THE NEIGHBORS SAID YOU SQUIRTED SHAVING CREAM ALL OVER THEIR CAT...HE'S OUT TO GET YOU!
THEY SAID HE'S COMING AFTER YOU GUYS WITH ALL FOUR FEET!
FOUR FEET? THAT STUPID CAT DOESN'T EVEN KNOW HE'S GOT FOUR FEET! HEE HEE HEE!
7-24
SLASH!
ONE, TWO, THREE, FOUR!
SCHULZ

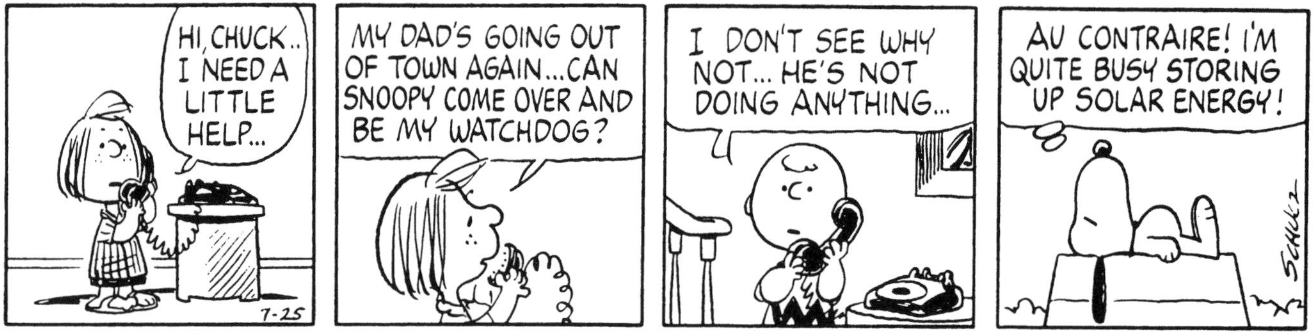
HI, CHUCK.. I NEED A LITTLE HELP...
7-25
MY DAD'S GOING OUT OF TOWN AGAIN...CAN SNOOPY COME OVER AND BE MY WATCHDOG?
I DON'T SEE WHY NOT... HE'S NOT DOING ANYTHING...
AU CONTRAIRE! I'M QUITE BUSY STORING UP SOLAR ENERGY!
SCHULZ

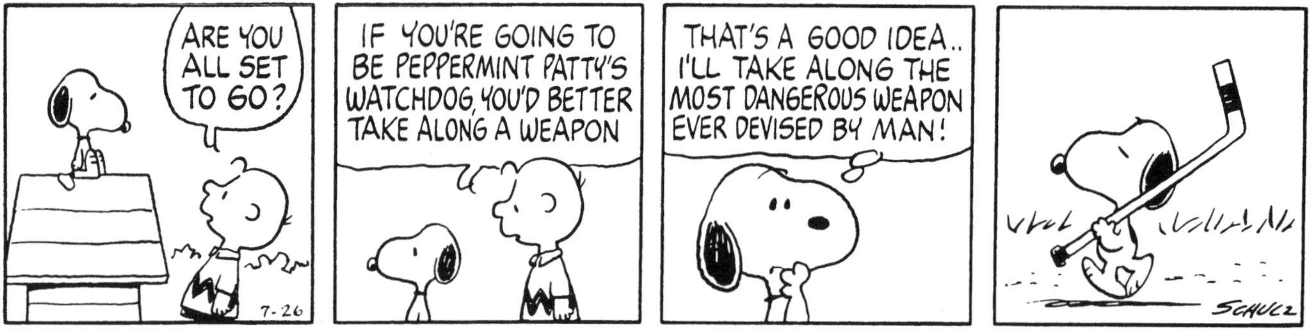
ARE YOU ALL SET TO GO?
7-26
IF YOU'RE GOING TO BE PEPPERMINT PATTY'S WATCHDOG, YOU'D BETTER TAKE ALONG A WEAPON
THAT'S A GOOD IDEA.. I'LL TAKE ALONG THE MOST DANGEROUS WEAPON EVER DEVISED BY MAN!
SCHULZ

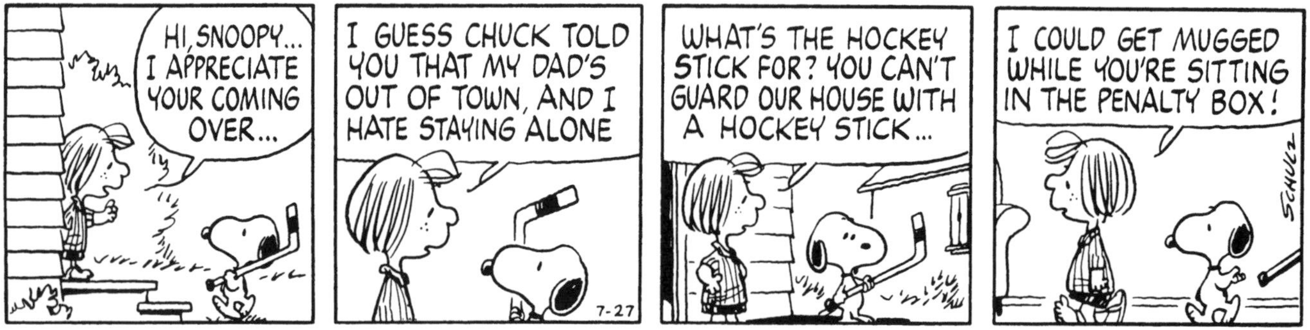
HI, SNOOPY... I APPRECIATE YOUR COMING OVER...
I GUESS CHUCK TOLD YOU THAT MY DAD'S OUT OF TOWN, AND I HATE STAYING ALONE
7-27
WHAT'S THE HOCKEY STICK FOR? YOU CAN'T GUARD OUR HOUSE WITH A HOCKEY STICK...
I COULD GET MUGGED WHILE YOU'RE SITTING IN THE PENALTY BOX!
SCHULZ

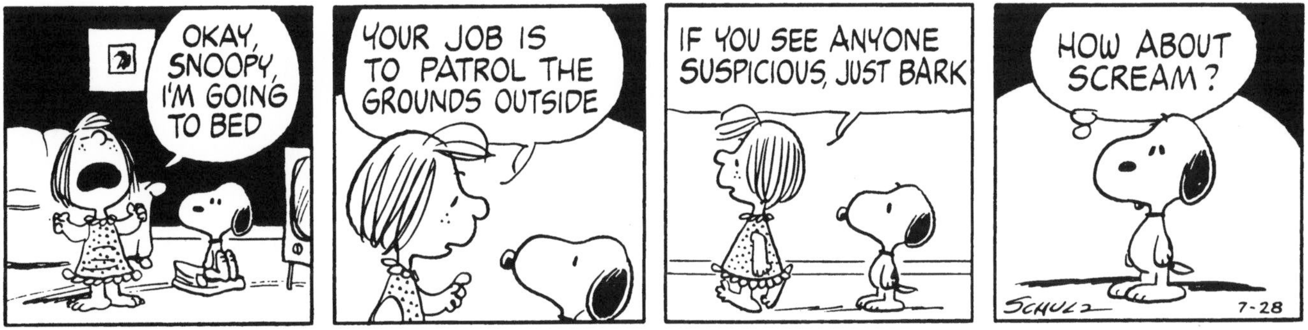
OKAY, SNOOPY, I'M GOING TO BED
YOUR JOB IS TO PATROL THE GROUNDS OUTSIDE
IF YOU SEE ANYONE SUSPICIOUS, JUST BARK
HOW ABOUT SCREAM?
SCHULZ
7-28

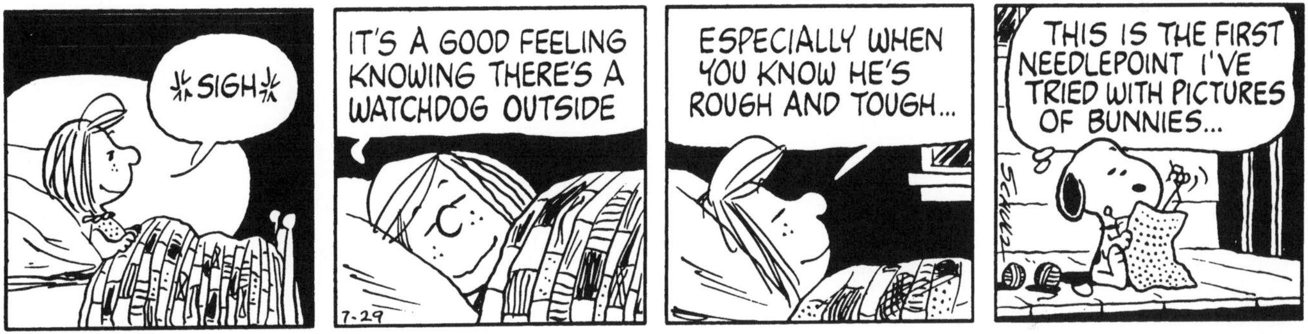
SIGH
IT'S A GOOD FEELING KNOWING THERE'S A WATCHDOG OUTSIDE
7-29
ESPECIALLY WHEN YOU KNOW HE'S ROUGH AND TOUGH...
THIS IS THE FIRST NEEDLEPOINT I'VE TRIED WITH PICTURES OF BUNNIES...
SCHULZ

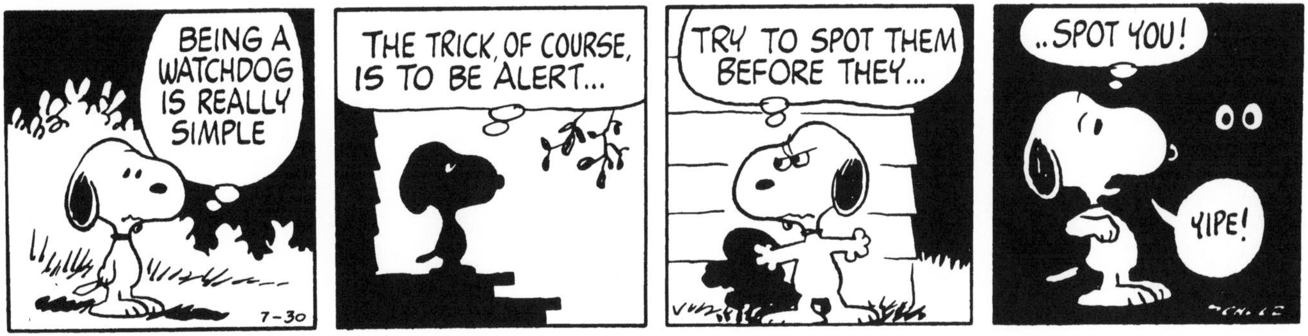
BEING A WATCHDOG IS REALLY SIMPLE
7-30
THE TRICK, OF COURSE, IS TO BE ALERT...
TRY TO SPOT THEM BEFORE THEY...
..SPOT YOU!
YIPE!

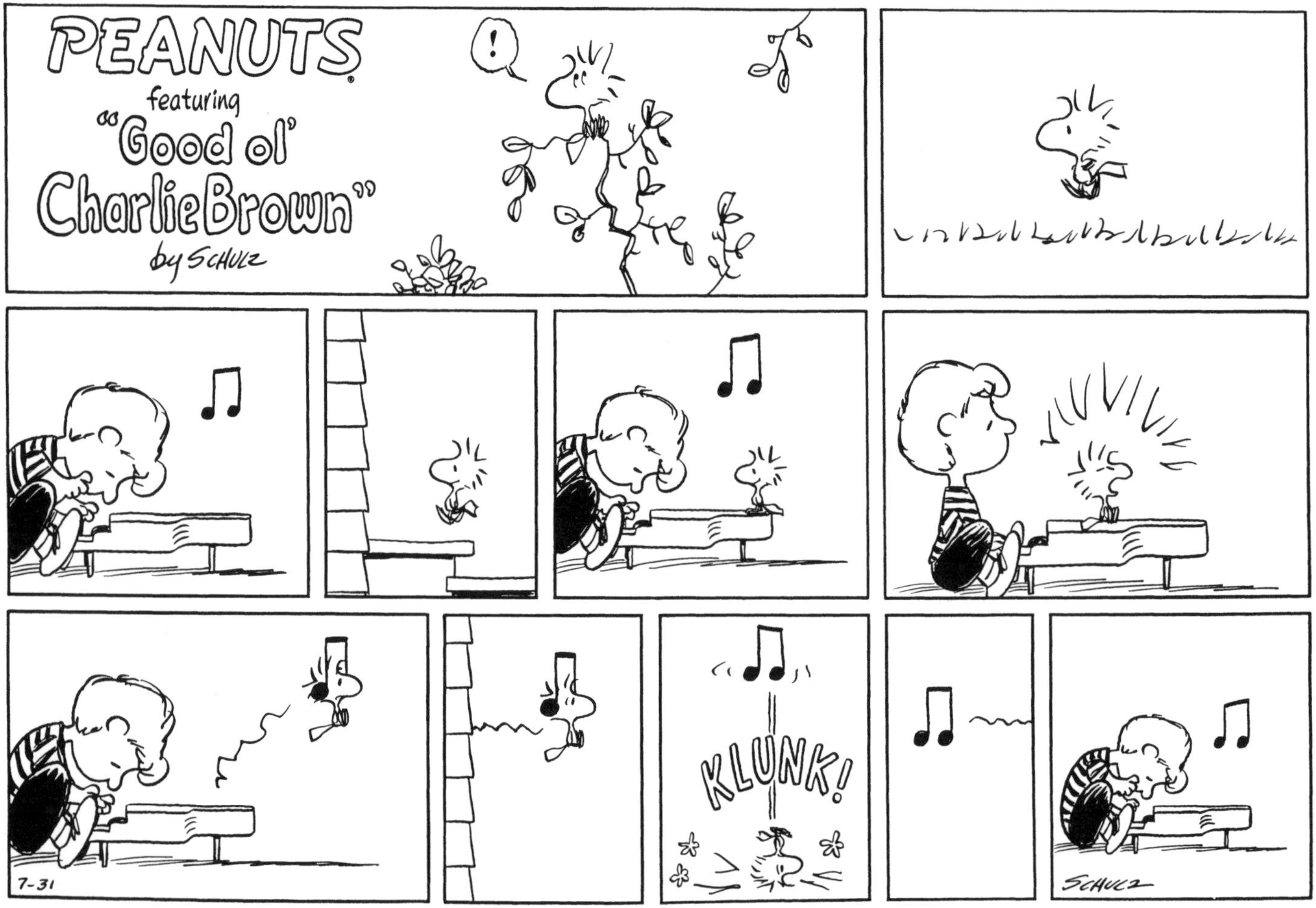
PEANUTS
featuring
"Good ol' Charlie Brown"
by SCHULZ
!
KLUNK!
7-31
SCHULZ

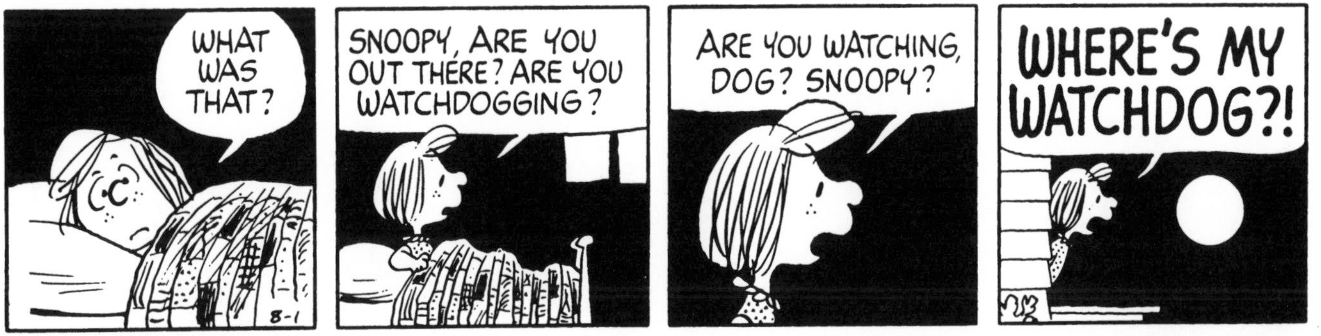
WHAT WAS THAT?
8-1
SNOOPY, ARE YOU OUT THERE? ARE YOU WATCHDOGGING?
ARE YOU WATCHING, DOG? SNOOPY?
WHERE'S MY WATCHDOG?!

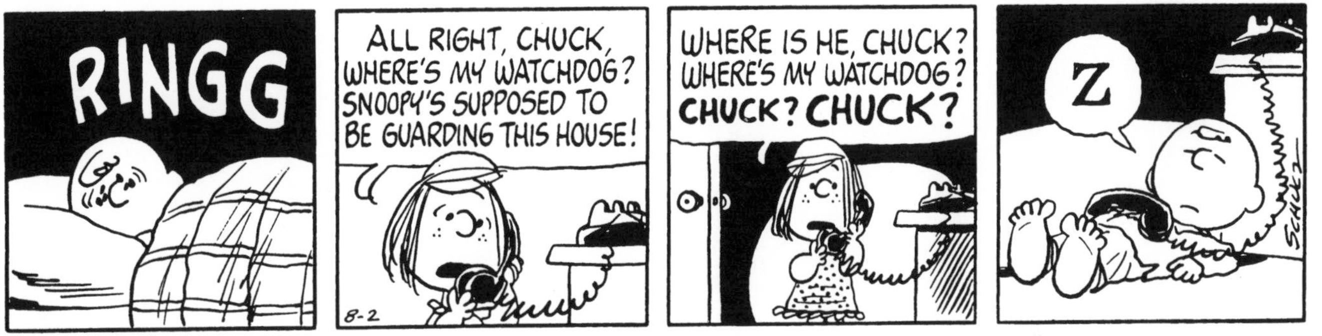
RINGG
ALL RIGHT, CHUCK, WHERE'S MY WATCHDOG? SNOOPY'S SUPPOSED TO BE GUARDING THIS HOUSE!
8-2
WHERE IS HE, CHUCK? WHERE'S MY WATCHDOG? CHUCK? CHUCK?
Z
SCHULZ

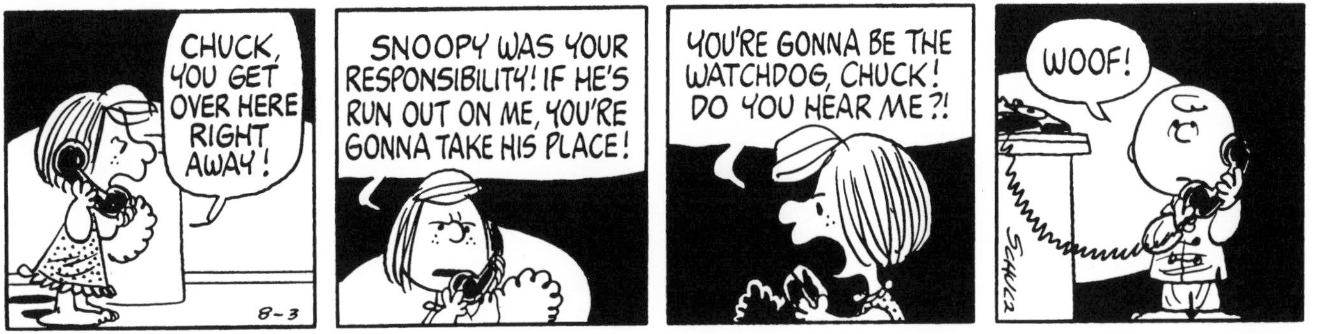
CHUCK, YOU GET OVER HERE RIGHT AWAY!
8-3
SNOOPY WAS YOUR RESPONSIBILITY! IF HE'S RUN OUT ON ME, YOU'RE GONNA TAKE HIS PLACE!
YOU'RE GONNA BE THE WATCHDOG, CHUCK! DO YOU HEAR ME?!
WOOF!
SCHULZ

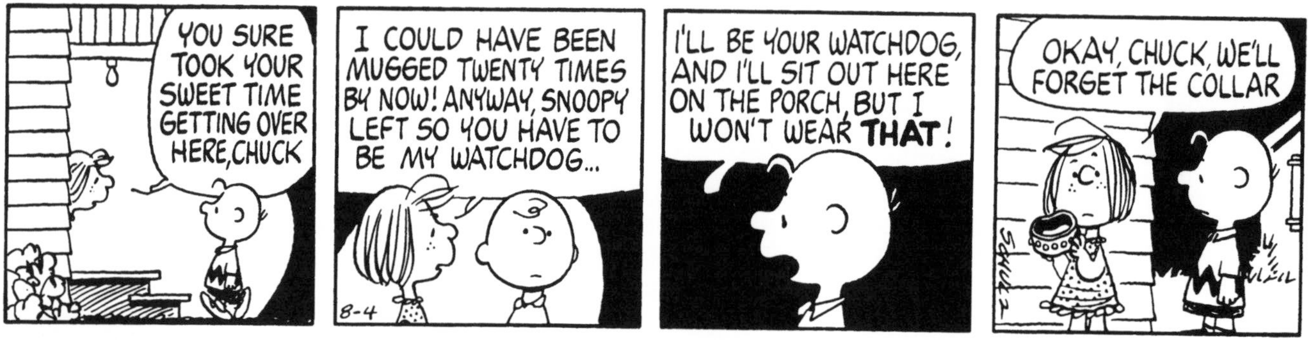
YOU SURE TOOK YOUR SWEET TIME GETTING OVER HERE, CHUCK
I COULD HAVE BEEN MUGGED TWENTY TIMES BY NOW! ANYWAY, SNOOPY LEFT SO YOU HAVE TO BE MY WATCHDOG...
8-4
I'LL BE YOUR WATCHDOG, AND I'LL SIT OUT HERE ON THE PORCH, BUT I WON'T WEAR **THAT**!
OKAY, CHUCK, WE'LL FORGET THE COLLAR
SCHULZ

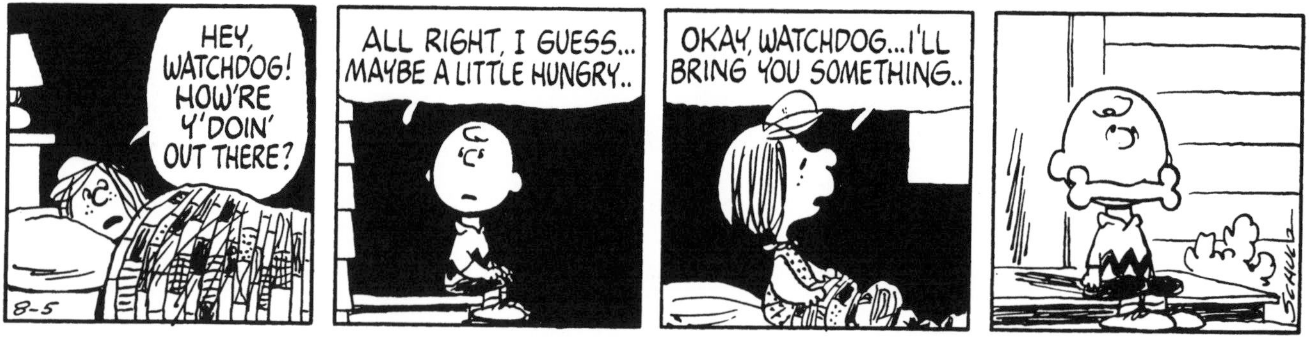
HEY, WATCHDOG! HOW'RE Y'DOIN' OUT THERE?
8-5
ALL RIGHT, I GUESS... MAYBE A LITTLE HUNGRY..
OKAY, WATCHDOG...I'LL BRING YOU SOMETHING..
SCHULZ

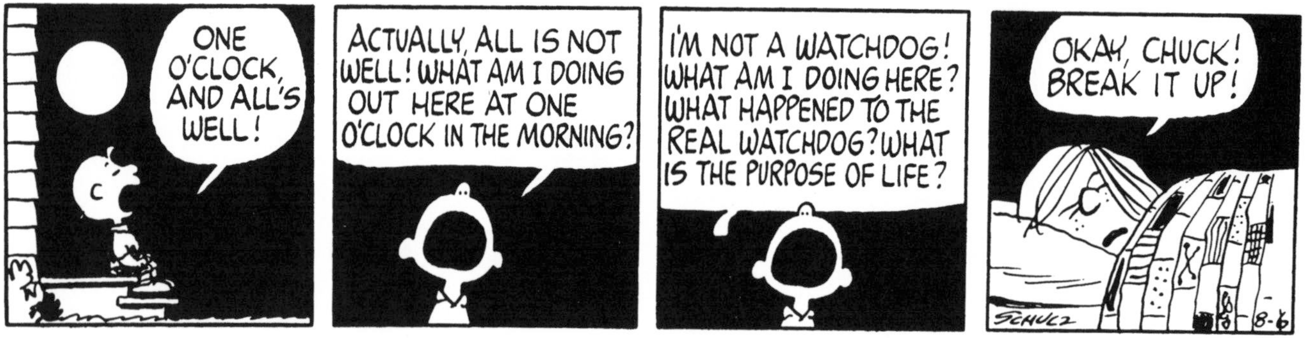
ONE O'CLOCK, AND ALL'S WELL!
ACTUALLY, ALL IS NOT WELL! WHAT AM I DOING OUT HERE AT ONE O'CLOCK IN THE MORNING?
I'M NOT A WATCHDOG! WHAT AM I DOING HERE? WHAT HAPPENED TO THE REAL WATCHDOG? WHAT IS THE PURPOSE OF LIFE?
OKAY, CHUCK! BREAK IT UP!
SCHULZ
8-6

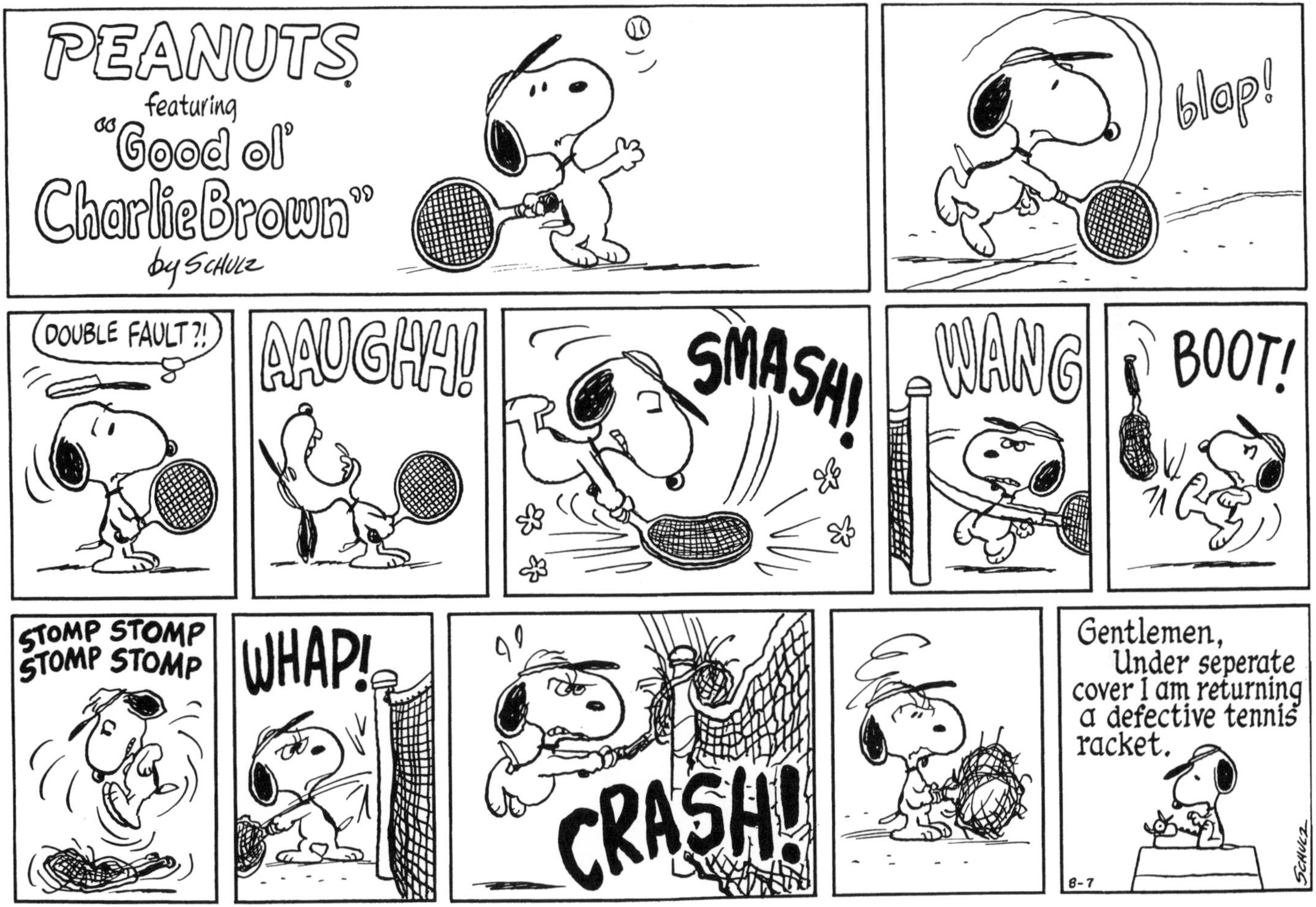
PEANUTS
featuring
"Good ol' CharlieBrown"
by SCHULZ
blap!
DOUBLE FAULT?!
AAUGHH!
SMASH!
WANG
BOOT!
STOMP STOMP
STOMP STOMP
WHAP!
CRASH!
Gentlemen,
Under seperate cover I am returning a defective tennis racket.
8-7
SCHULZ

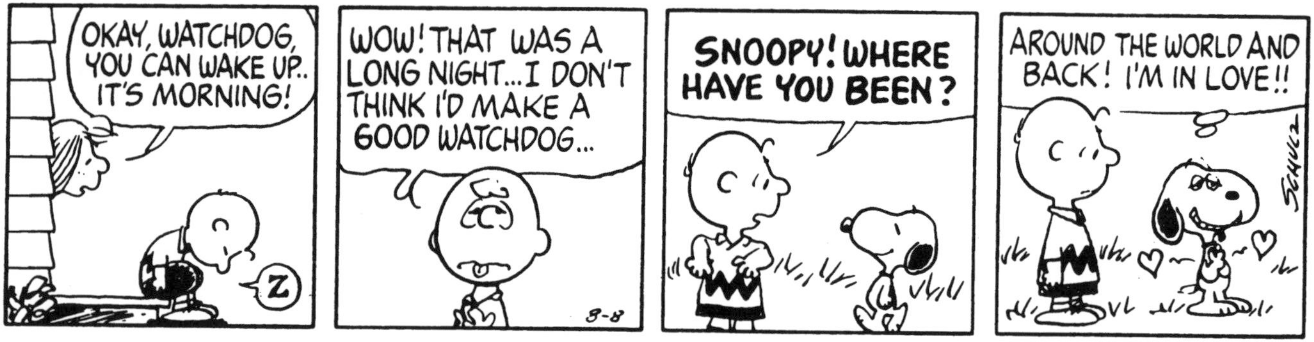
OKAY, WATCHDOG, YOU CAN WAKE UP.. IT'S MORNING!
Z
WOW! THAT WAS A LONG NIGHT...I DON'T THINK I'D MAKE A GOOD WATCHDOG...
8-8
SNOOPY! WHERE HAVE YOU BEEN?
AROUND THE WORLD AND BACK! I'M IN LOVE!!
SCHULZ

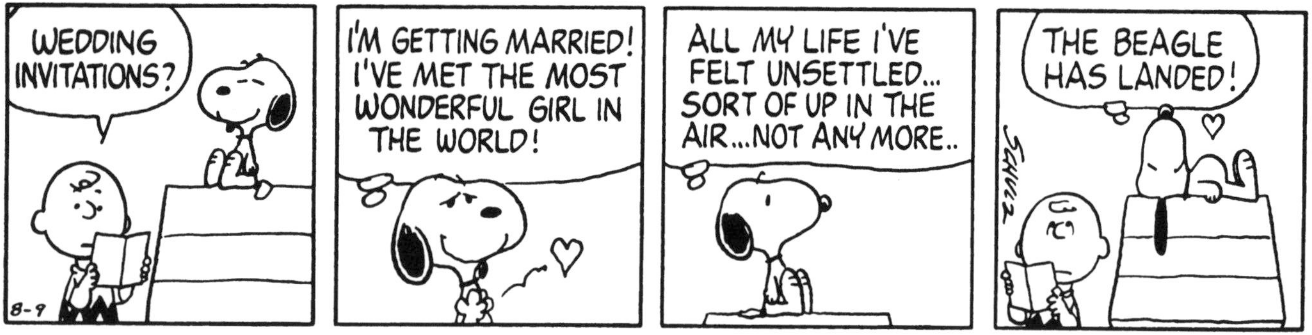
WEDDING INVITATIONS?
8-9
I'M GETTING MARRIED! I'VE MET THE MOST WONDERFUL GIRL IN THE WORLD!
ALL MY LIFE I'VE FELT UNSETTLED... SORT OF UP IN THE AIR...NOT ANY MORE..
SCHULZ
THE BEAGLE HAS LANDED!

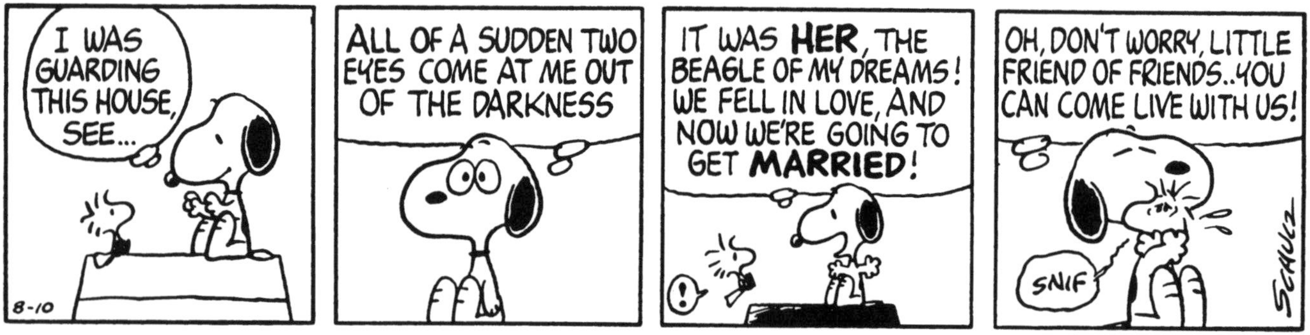
I WAS GUARDING THIS HOUSE, SEE...
8-10
ALL OF A SUDDEN TWO EYES COME AT ME OUT OF THE DARKNESS
IT WAS HER, THE BEAGLE OF MY DREAMS! WE FELL IN LOVE, AND NOW WE'RE GOING TO GET MARRIED!
!
OH, DON'T WORRY, LITTLE FRIEND OF FRIENDS..YOU CAN COME LIVE WITH US!
SNIF
SCHULZ

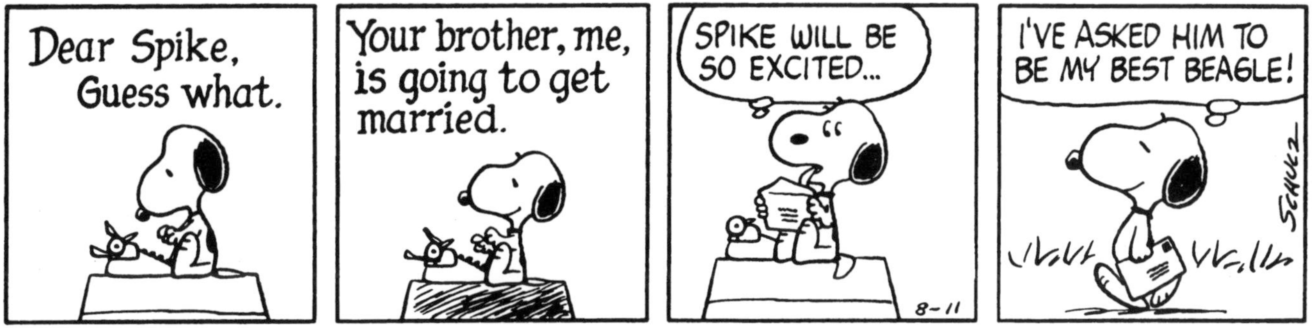
Dear Spike,
Guess what.
Your brother, me, is going to get married.
SPIKE WILL BE SO EXCITED...
I'VE ASKED HIM TO BE MY BEST BEAGLE!
SCHULZ
8-11

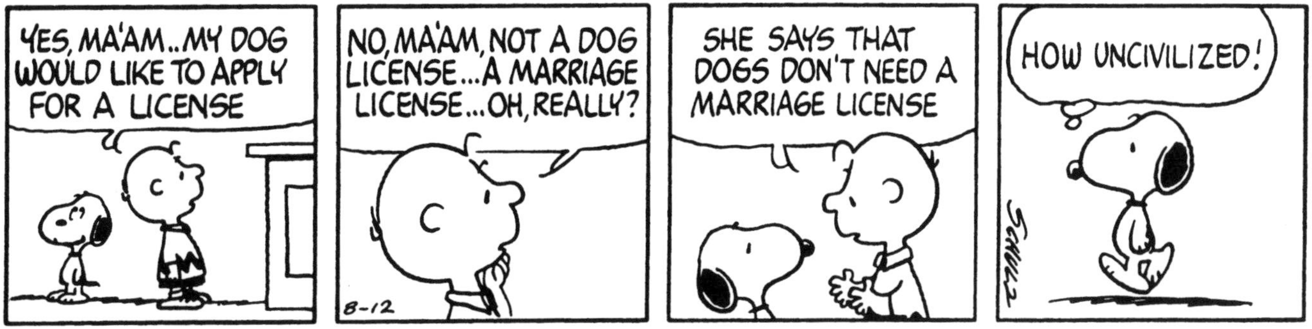
YES, MA'AM...MY DOG WOULD LIKE TO APPLY FOR A LICENSE
NO, MA'AM, NOT A DOG LICENSE...A MARRIAGE LICENSE...OH, REALLY?
8-12
SHE SAYS THAT DOGS DON'T NEED A MARRIAGE LICENSE
HOW UNCIVILIZED!
SCHULZ

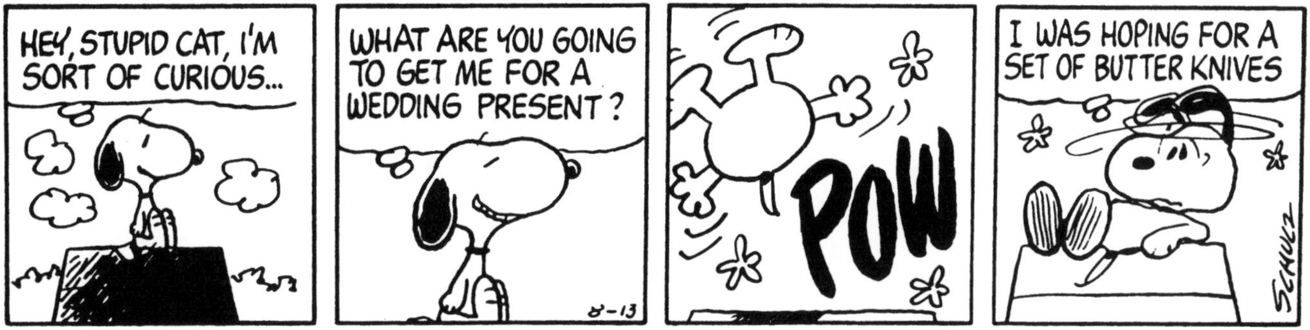
HEY, STUPID CAT, I'M SORT OF CURIOUS...
WHAT ARE YOU GOING TO GET ME FOR A WEDDING PRESENT?
8-13
POW
I WAS HOPING FOR A SET OF BUTTER KNIVES
SCHULZ

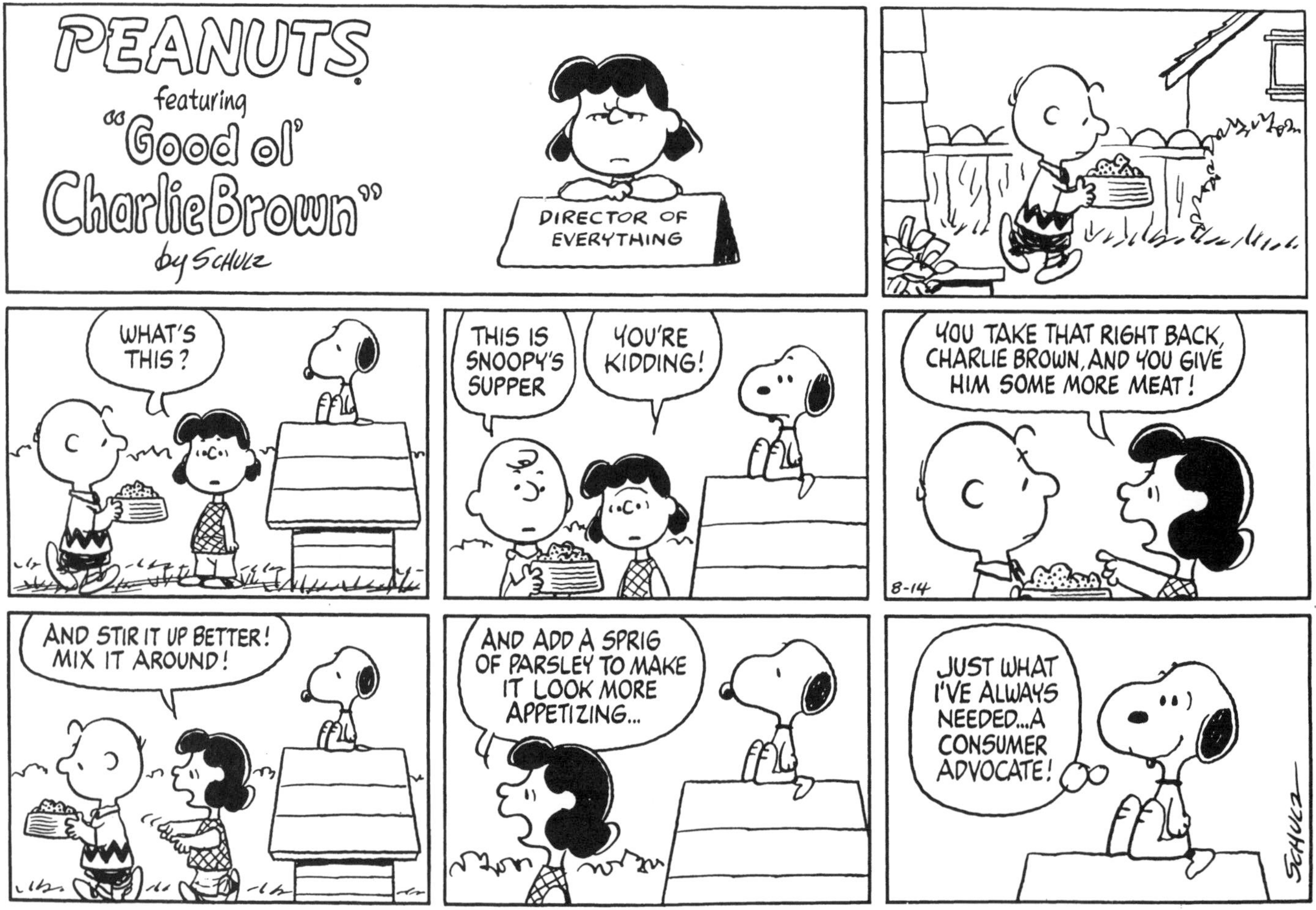
PEANUTS
featuring
"Good ol' Charlie Brown"
by SCHULZ
DIRECTOR OF EVERYTHING
WHAT'S THIS?
THIS IS SNOOPY'S SUPPER
YOU'RE KIDDING!
YOU TAKE THAT RIGHT BACK, CHARLIE BROWN, AND YOU GIVE HIM SOME MORE MEAT!
8-14
AND STIR IT UP BETTER! MIX IT AROUND!
AND ADD A SPRIG OF PARSLEY TO MAKE IT LOOK MORE APPETIZING...
JUST WHAT I'VE ALWAYS NEEDED...A CONSUMER ADVOCATE!
SCHULZ

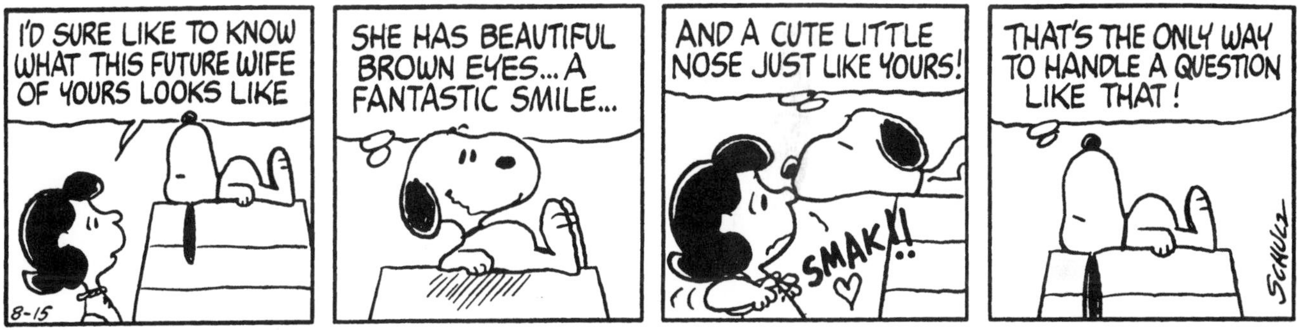
8-15
I'D SURE LIKE TO KNOW WHAT THIS FUTURE WIFE OF YOURS LOOKS LIKE
SHE HAS BEAUTIFUL BROWN EYES... A FANTASTIC SMILE...
AND A CUTE LITTLE NOSE JUST LIKE YOURS!
SMAK!!
THAT'S THE ONLY WAY TO HANDLE A QUESTION LIKE THAT!
SCHULZ

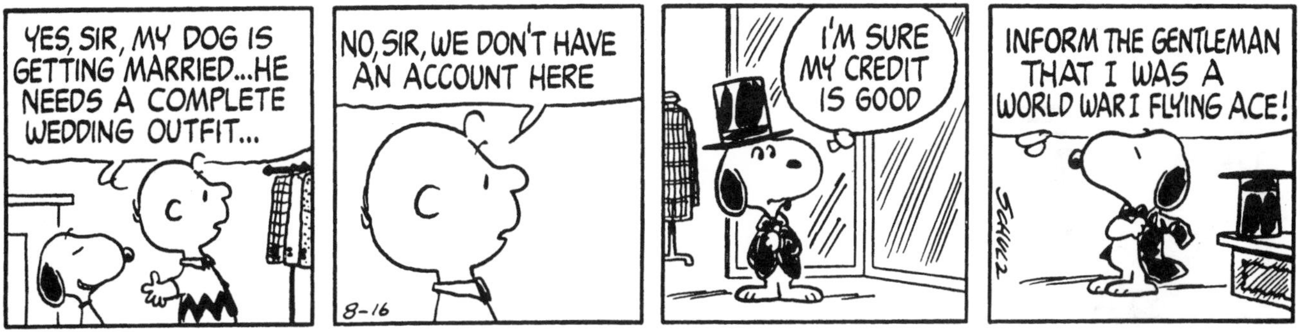
YES, SIR, MY DOG IS GETTING MARRIED...HE NEEDS A COMPLETE WEDDING OUTFIT...
NO, SIR, WE DON'T HAVE AN ACCOUNT HERE
8-16
I'M SURE MY CREDIT IS GOOD
INFORM THE GENTLEMAN THAT I WAS A WORLD WAR I FLYING ACE!
SCHULZ

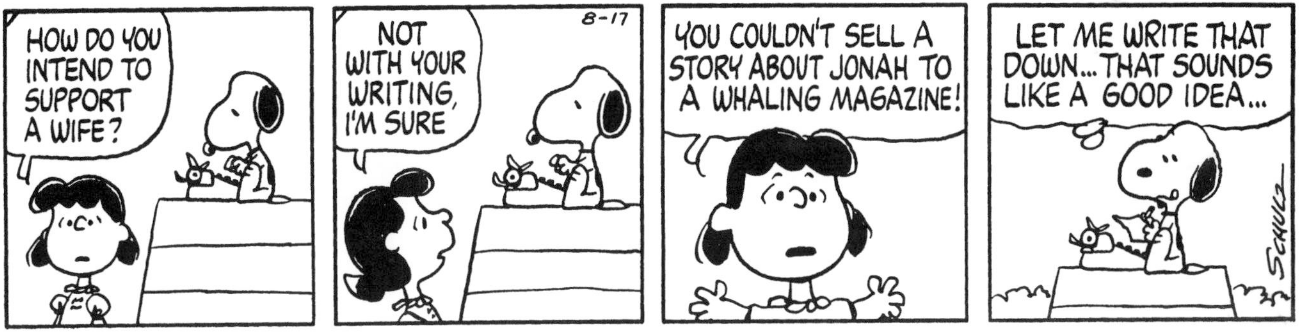
HOW DO YOU INTEND TO SUPPORT A WIFE?
8-17
NOT WITH YOUR WRITING, I'M SURE
YOU COULDN'T SELL A STORY ABOUT JONAH TO A WHALING MAGAZINE!
LET ME WRITE THAT DOWN... THAT SOUNDS LIKE A GOOD IDEA...
SCHULZ

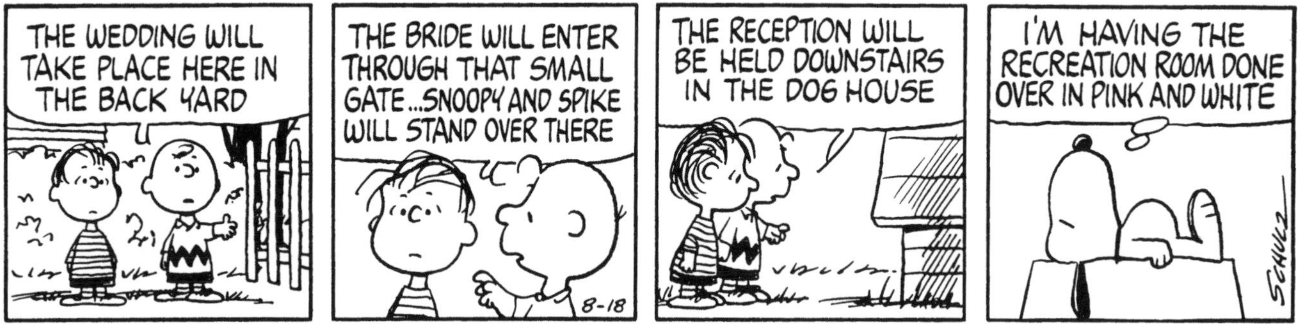
THE WEDDING WILL TAKE PLACE HERE IN THE BACK YARD
THE BRIDE WILL ENTER THROUGH THAT SMALL GATE...SNOOPY AND SPIKE WILL STAND OVER THERE
8-18
THE RECEPTION WILL BE HELD DOWNSTAIRS IN THE DOG HOUSE
I'M HAVING THE RECREATION ROOM DONE OVER IN PINK AND WHITE
SCHULZ

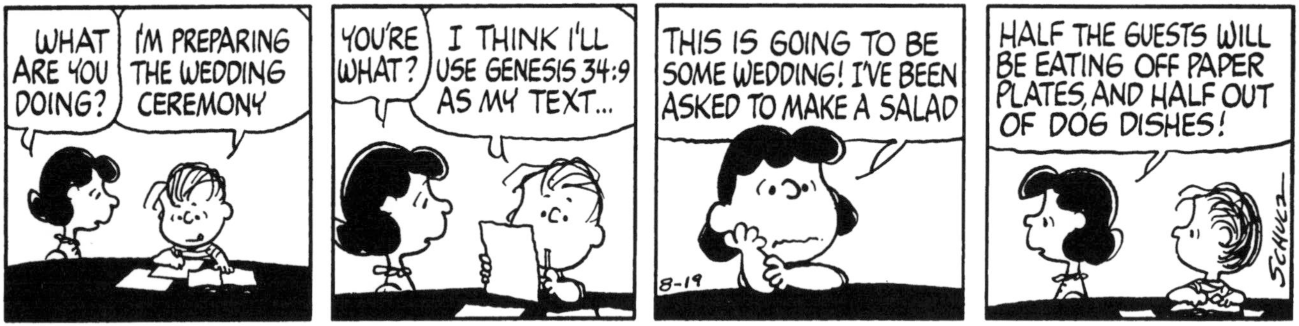
WHAT ARE YOU DOING?
I'M PREPARING THE WEDDING CEREMONY
YOU'RE WHAT?
I THINK I'LL USE GENESIS 34:9 AS MY TEXT...
THIS IS GOING TO BE SOME WEDDING! I'VE BEEN ASKED TO MAKE A SALAD
8-19
HALF THE GUESTS WILL BE EATING OFF PAPER PLATES, AND HALF OUT OF DOG DISHES!
SCHULZ

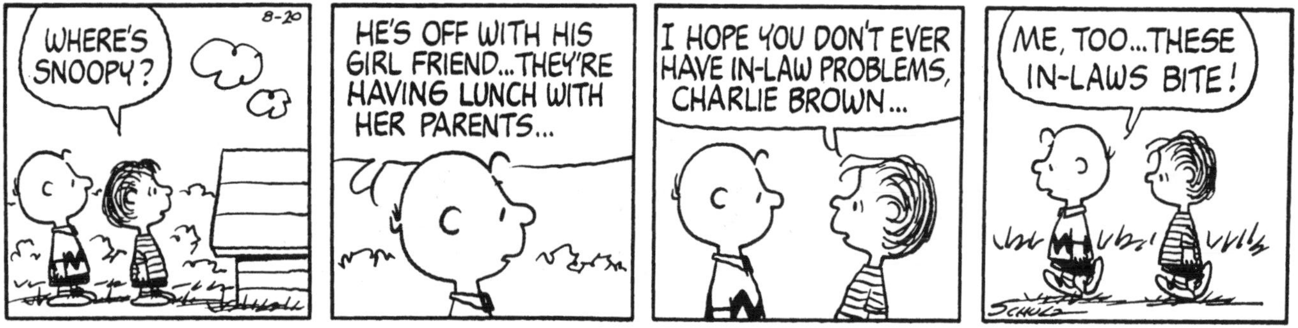
8-20
WHERE'S SNOOPY?
HE'S OFF WITH HIS GIRL FRIEND...THEY'RE HAVING LUNCH WITH HER PARENTS...
I HOPE YOU DON'T EVER HAVE IN-LAW PROBLEMS, CHARLIE BROWN...
ME, TOO...THESE IN-LAWS BITE!
SCHULZ

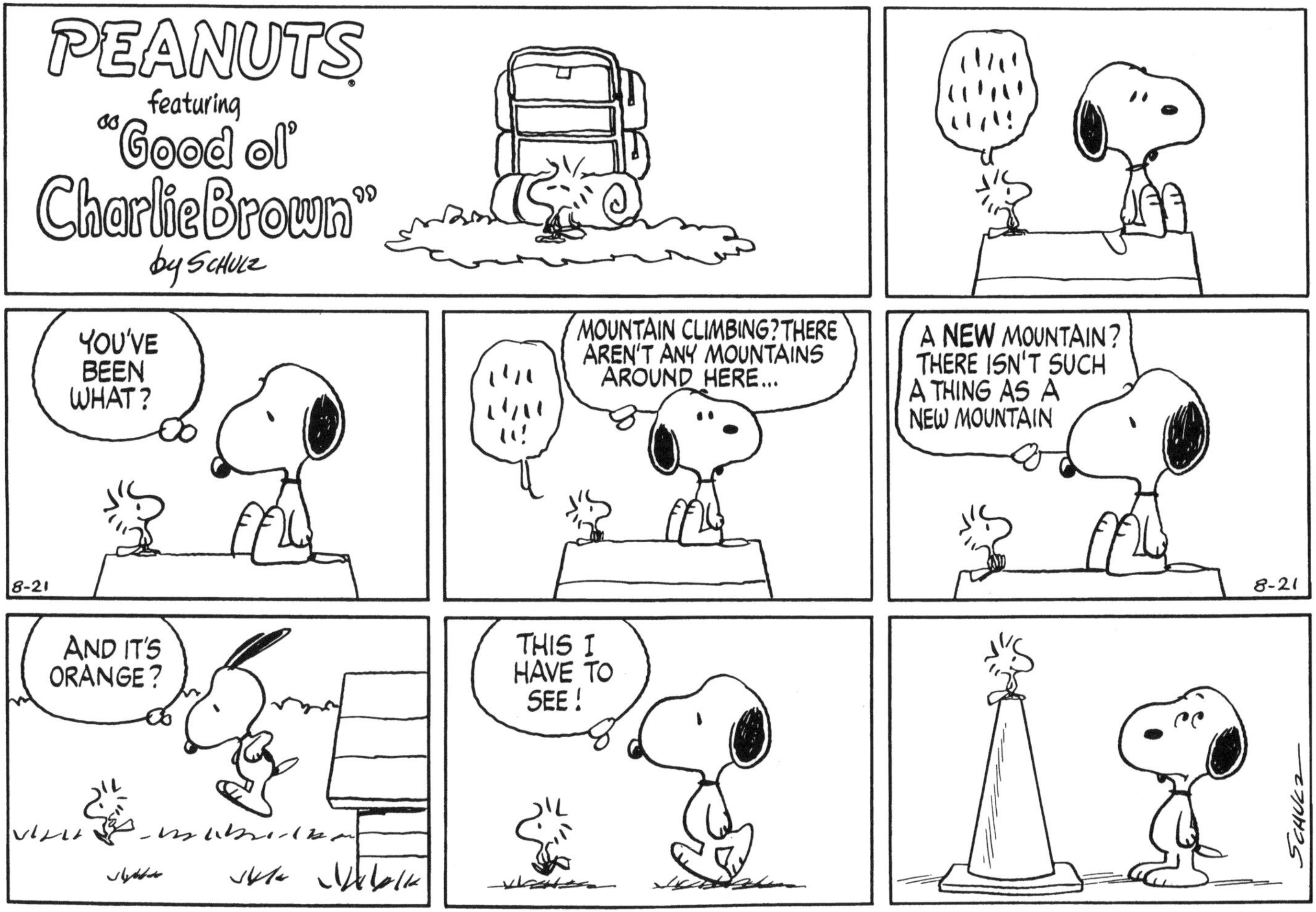
PEANUTS
featuring
"Good ol' CharlieBrown"
by SCHULZ
YOU'VE BEEN WHAT?
8-21
MOUNTAIN CLIMBING? THERE AREN'T ANY MOUNTAINS AROUND HERE...
A NEW MOUNTAIN? THERE ISN'T SUCH A THING AS A NEW MOUNTAIN
8-21
AND IT'S ORANGE?
THIS I HAVE TO SEE!
SCHULZ

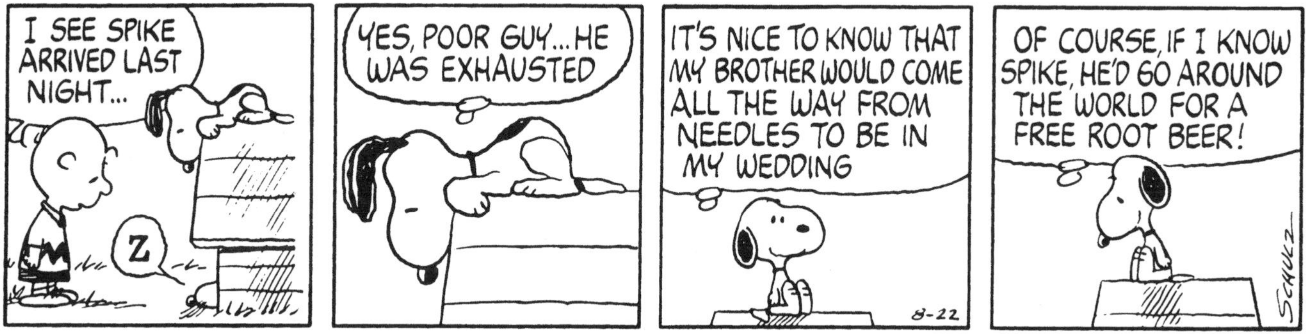
I SEE SPIKE ARRIVED LAST NIGHT...
Z
YES, POOR GUY... HE WAS EXHAUSTED
IT'S NICE TO KNOW THAT MY BROTHER WOULD COME ALL THE WAY FROM NEEDLES TO BE IN MY WEDDING
8-22
OF COURSE, IF I KNOW SPIKE, HE'D GO AROUND THE WORLD FOR A FREE ROOT BEER!
SCHULZ

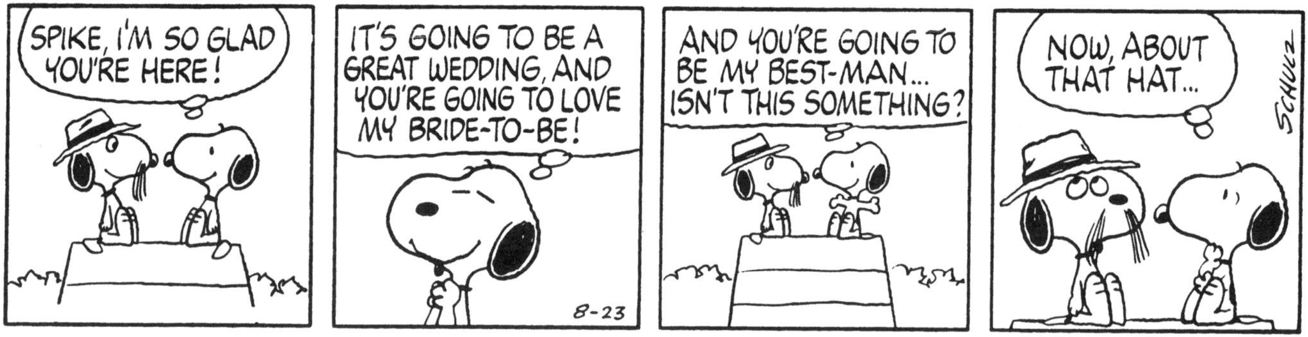
SPIKE, I'M SO GLAD YOU'RE HERE!
IT'S GOING TO BE A GREAT WEDDING, AND YOU'RE GOING TO LOVE MY BRIDE-TO-BE!
8-23
AND YOU'RE GOING TO BE MY BEST-MAN... ISN'T THIS SOMETHING?
NOW, ABOUT THAT HAT...
SCHULZ

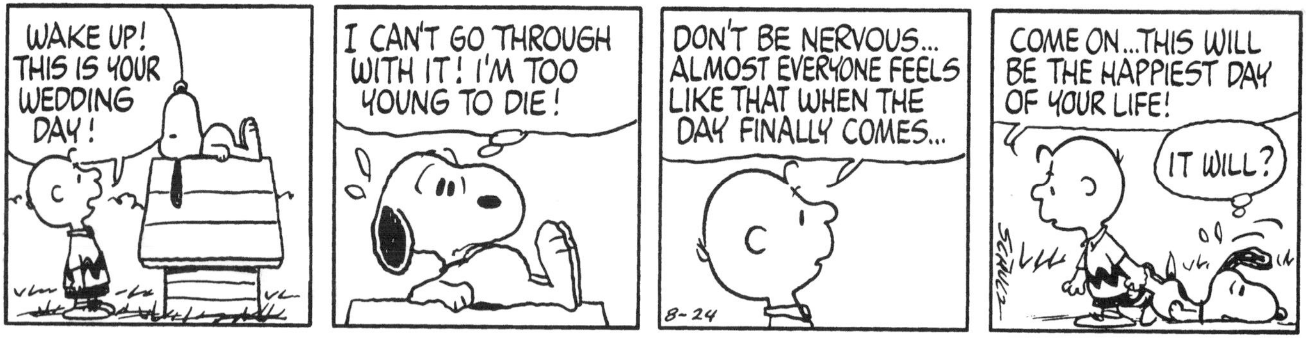
WAKE UP! THIS IS YOUR WEDDING DAY!
I CAN'T GO THROUGH WITH IT! I'M TOO YOUNG TO DIE!
DON'T BE NERVOUS... ALMOST EVERYONE FEELS LIKE THAT WHEN THE DAY FINALLY COMES...
8-24
COME ON...THIS WILL BE THE HAPPIEST DAY OF YOUR LIFE!
IT WILL?
SCHULZ

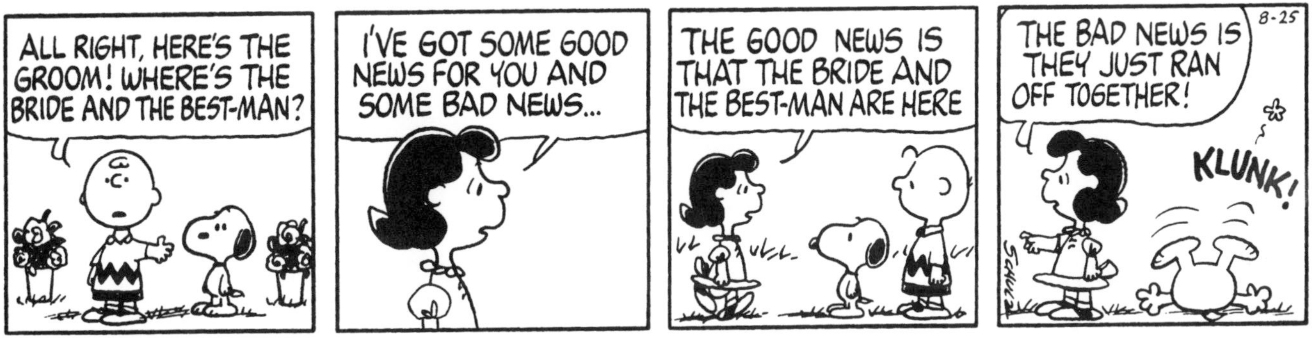
ALL RIGHT, HERE'S THE GROOM! WHERE'S THE BRIDE AND THE BEST-MAN?
I'VE GOT SOME GOOD NEWS FOR YOU AND SOME BAD NEWS...
THE GOOD NEWS IS THAT THE BRIDE AND THE BEST-MAN ARE HERE
8-25
THE BAD NEWS IS THEY JUST RAN OFF TOGETHER!
KLUNK!

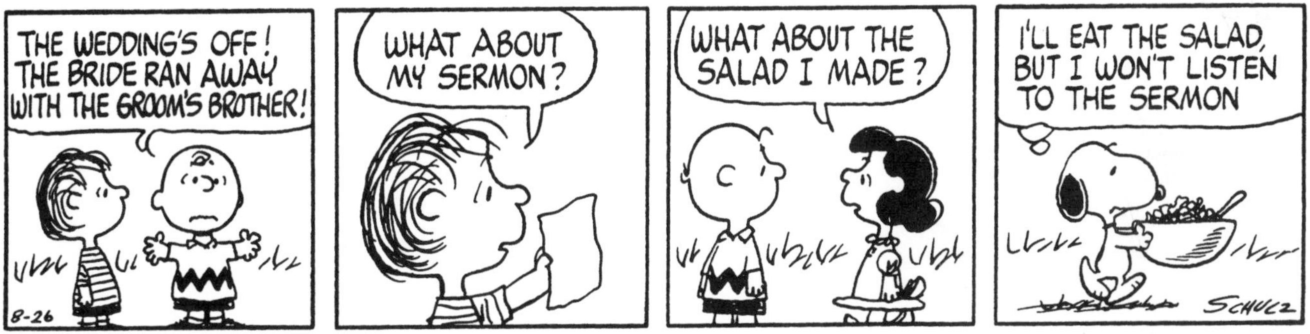
THE WEDDING'S OFF! THE BRIDE RAN AWAY WITH THE GROOM'S BROTHER!
8-26
WHAT ABOUT MY SERMON?
WHAT ABOUT THE SALAD I MADE?
I'LL EAT THE SALAD, BUT I WON'T LISTEN TO THE SERMON

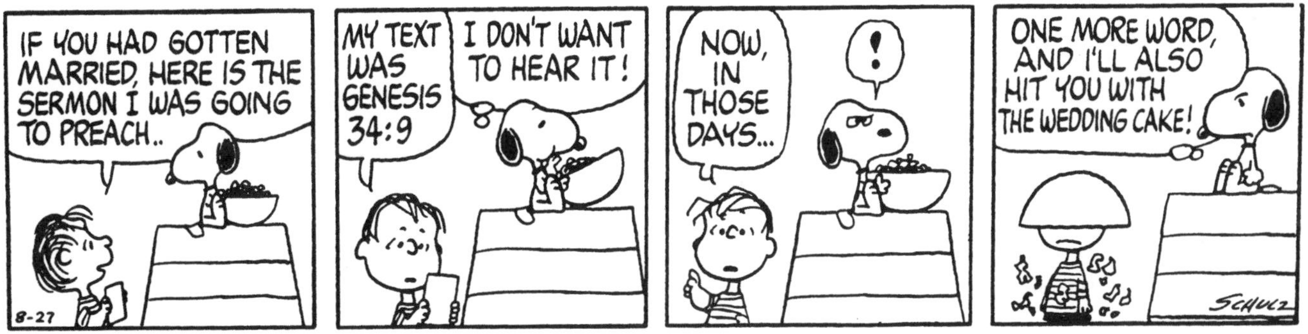
IF YOU HAD GOTTEN MARRIED, HERE IS THE SERMON I WAS GOING TO PREACH..
8-27
MY TEXT WAS GENESIS 34:9
I DON'T WANT TO HEAR IT!
NOW, IN THOSE DAYS...
!
ONE MORE WORD, AND I'LL ALSO HIT YOU WITH THE WEDDING CAKE!

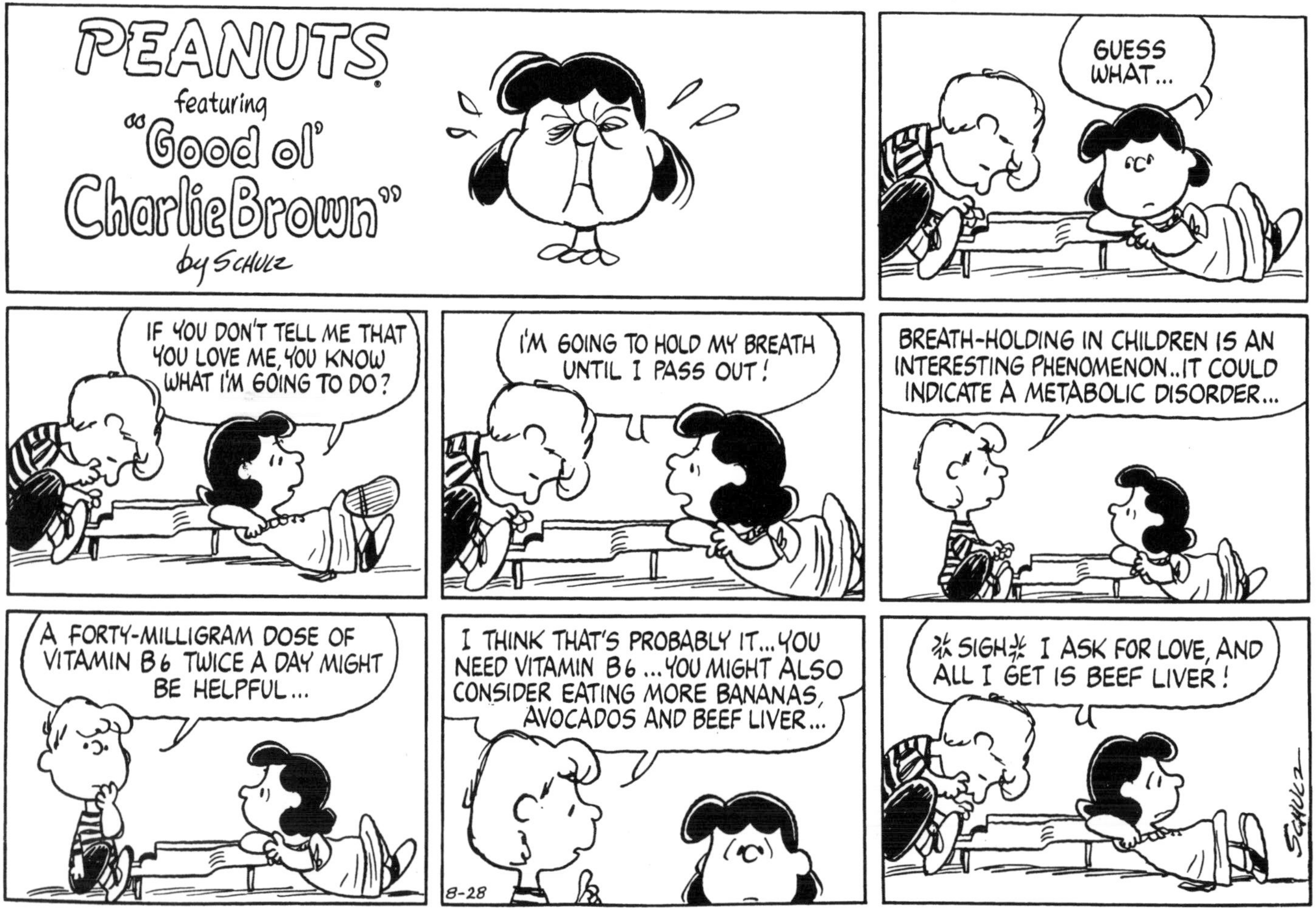
PEANUTS
featuring "Good ol' Charlie Brown"
by SCHULZ
GUESS WHAT...
IF YOU DON'T TELL ME THAT YOU LOVE ME, YOU KNOW WHAT I'M GOING TO DO?
I'M GOING TO HOLD MY BREATH UNTIL I PASS OUT!
BREATH-HOLDING IN CHILDREN IS AN INTERESTING PHENOMENON..IT COULD INDICATE A METABOLIC DISORDER...
A FORTY-MILLIGRAM DOSE OF VITAMIN B6 TWICE A DAY MIGHT BE HELPFUL...
I THINK THAT'S PROBABLY IT...YOU NEED VITAMIN B6 ...YOU MIGHT ALSO CONSIDER EATING MORE BANANAS, AVOCADOS AND BEEF LIVER...
8-28
SIGH I ASK FOR LOVE, AND ALL I GET IS BEEF LIVER!
SCHULZ

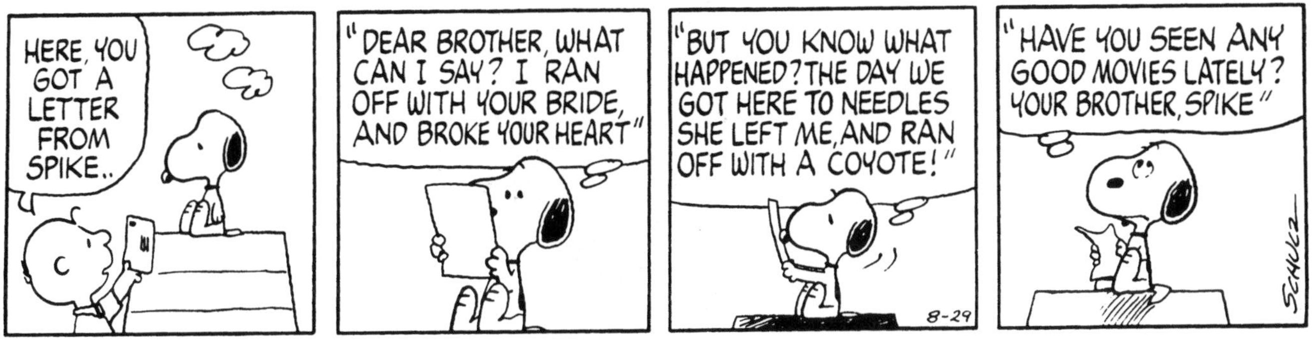
HERE, YOU GOT A LETTER FROM SPIKE..
"DEAR BROTHER, WHAT CAN I SAY? I RAN OFF WITH YOUR BRIDE, AND BROKE YOUR HEART"
"BUT YOU KNOW WHAT HAPPENED? THE DAY WE GOT HERE TO NEEDLES SHE LEFT ME, AND RAN OFF WITH A COYOTE!"
8-29
"HAVE YOU SEEN ANY GOOD MOVIES LATELY? YOUR BROTHER, SPIKE"
SCHULZ

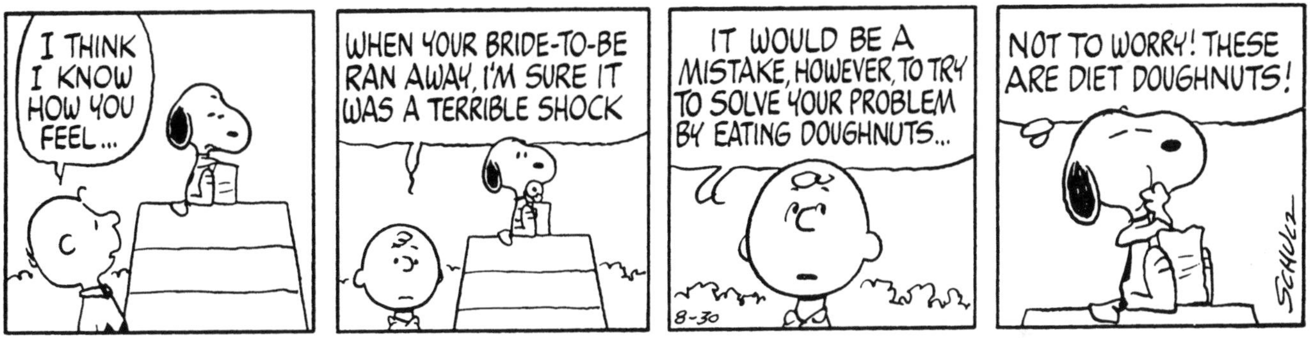
I THINK I KNOW HOW YOU FEEL...
WHEN YOUR BRIDE-TO-BE RAN AWAY, I'M SURE IT WAS A TERRIBLE SHOCK
IT WOULD BE A MISTAKE, HOWEVER, TO TRY TO SOLVE YOUR PROBLEM BY EATING DOUGHNUTS...
8-30
NOT TO WORRY! THESE ARE DIET DOUGHNUTS!
SCHULZ

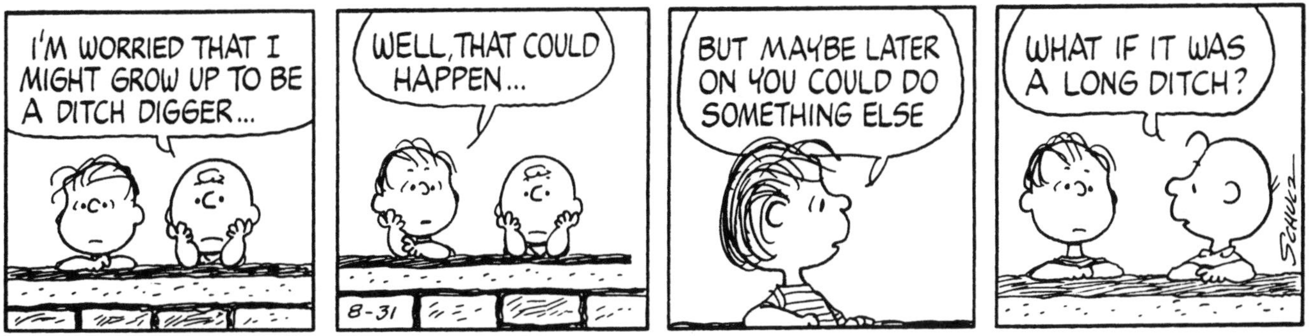
I'M WORRIED THAT I MIGHT GROW UP TO BE A DITCH DIGGER...
WELL, THAT COULD HAPPEN...
8-31
BUT MAYBE LATER ON YOU COULD DO SOMETHING ELSE
WHAT IF IT WAS A LONG DITCH?
SCHULZ

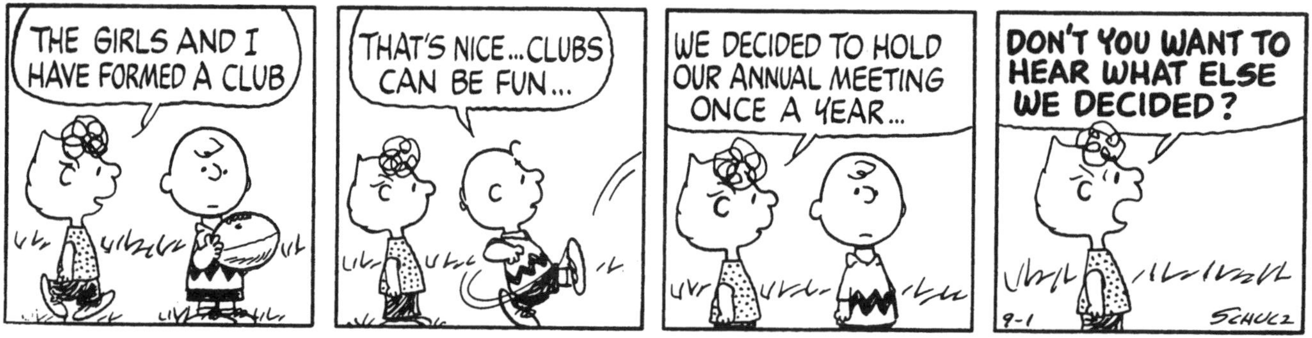
THE GIRLS AND I HAVE FORMED A CLUB
THAT'S NICE...CLUBS CAN BE FUN...
WE DECIDED TO HOLD OUR ANNUAL MEETING ONCE A YEAR...
DON'T YOU WANT TO HEAR WHAT ELSE WE DECIDED?

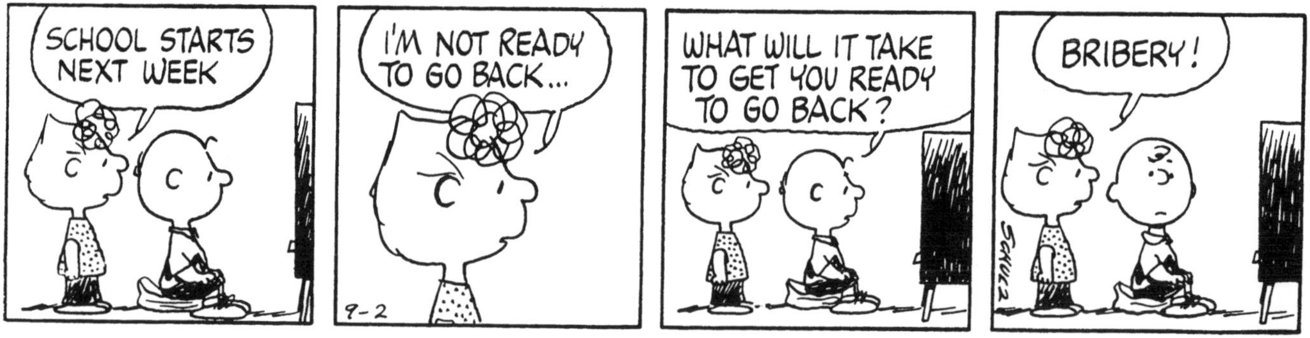
SCHOOL STARTS NEXT WEEK
I'M NOT READY TO GO BACK...
WHAT WILL IT TAKE TO GET YOU READY TO GO BACK?
BRIBERY!

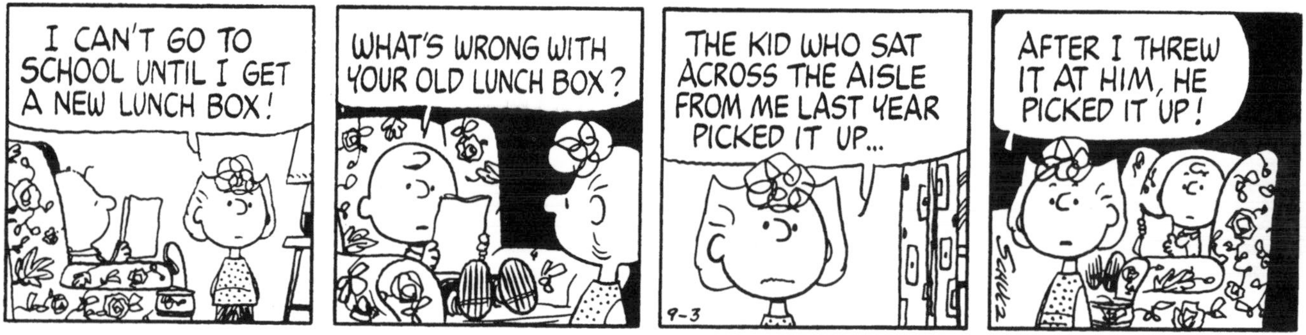
I CAN'T GO TO SCHOOL UNTIL I GET A NEW LUNCH BOX!
WHAT'S WRONG WITH YOUR OLD LUNCH BOX?
THE KID WHO SAT ACROSS THE AISLE FROM ME LAST YEAR PICKED IT UP...
AFTER I THREW IT AT HIM, HE PICKED IT UP!

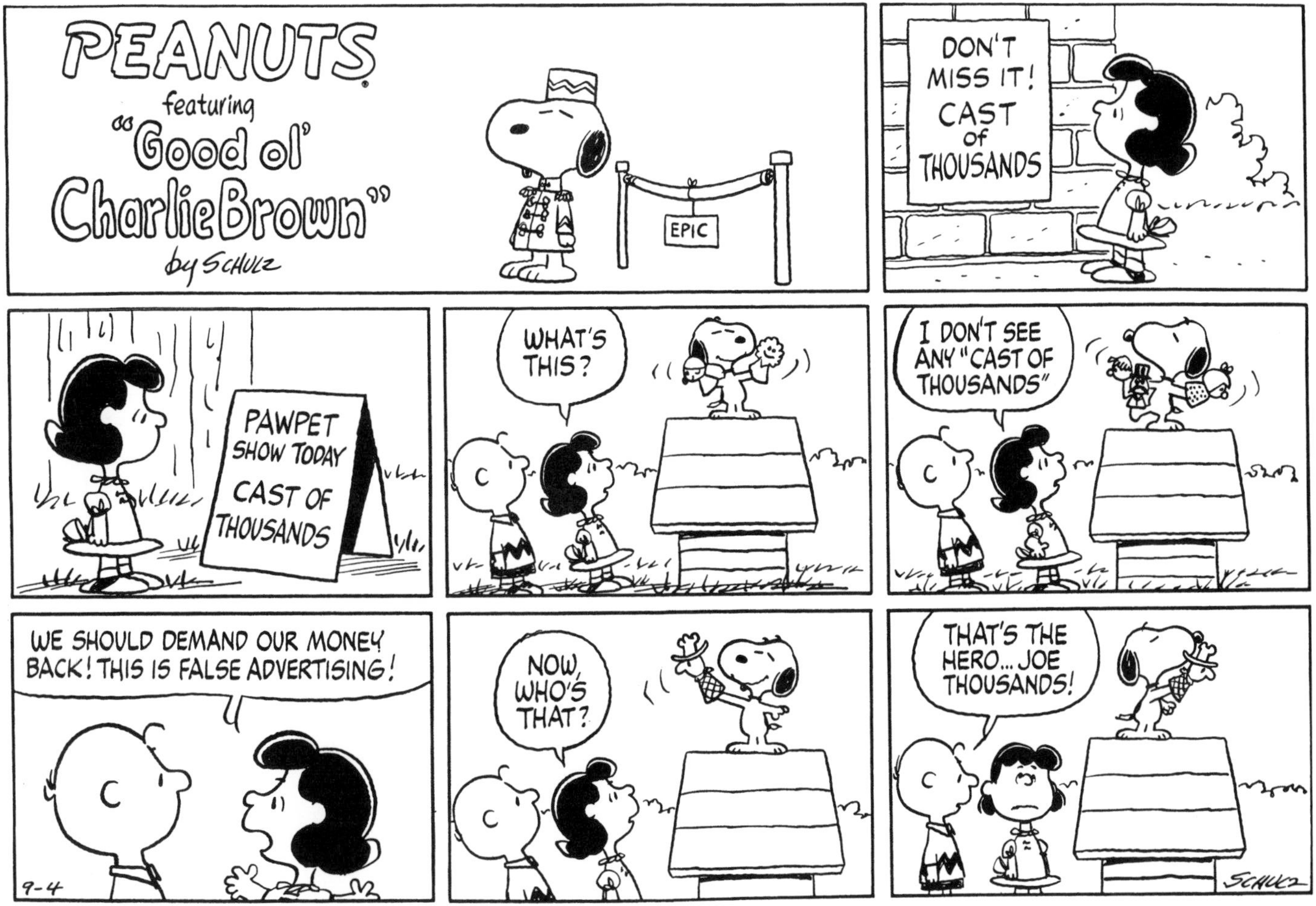
PEANUTS
featuring
"Good ol' Charlie Brown"
by SCHULZ
EPIC
DON'T MISS IT! CAST of THOUSANDS
PAWPET SHOW TODAY CAST OF THOUSANDS
WHAT'S THIS?
I DON'T SEE ANY "CAST OF THOUSANDS"
WE SHOULD DEMAND OUR MONEY BACK! THIS IS FALSE ADVERTISING!
9-4
NOW, WHO'S THAT?
THAT'S THE HERO... JOE THOUSANDS!
SCHULZ

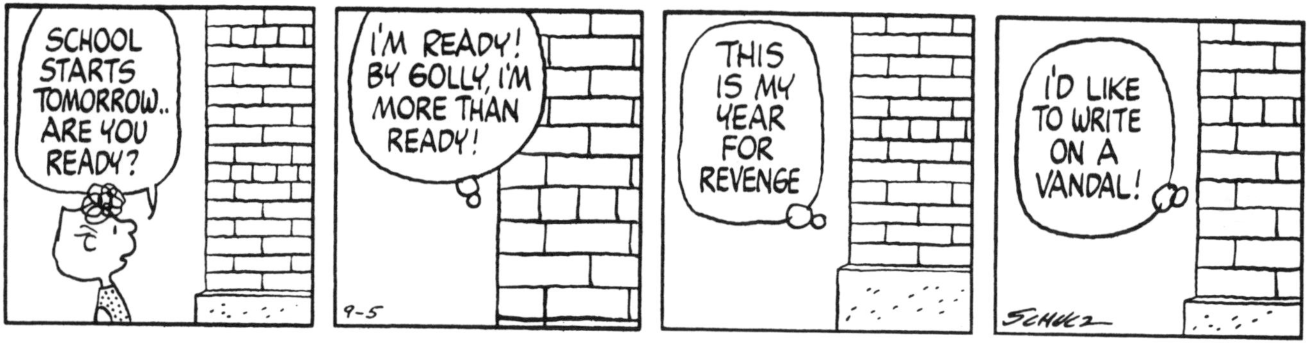
SCHOOL STARTS TOMORROW.. ARE YOU READY?
I'M READY! BY GOLLY, I'M MORE THAN READY!
9-5
THIS IS MY YEAR FOR REVENGE
I'D LIKE TO WRITE ON A VANDAL!
SCHULZ

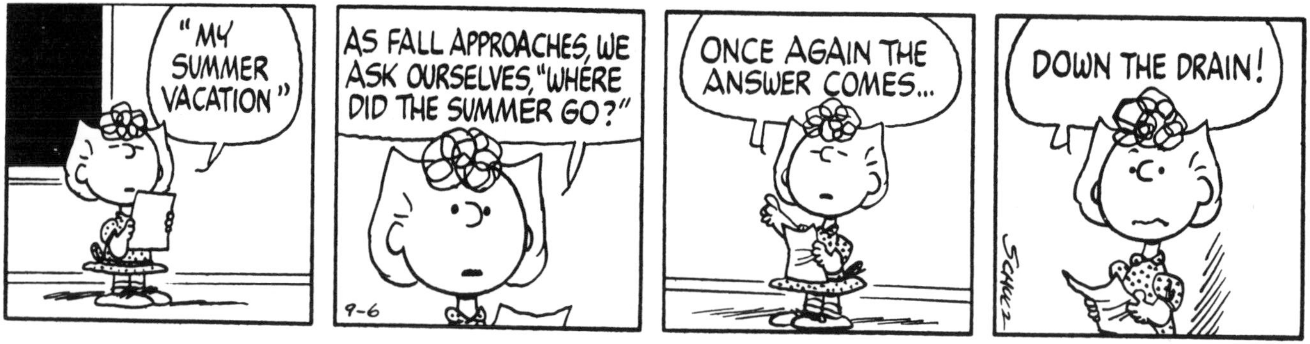
"MY SUMMER VACATION"
AS FALL APPROACHES, WE ASK OURSELVES, "WHERE DID THE SUMMER GO?"
9-6
ONCE AGAIN THE ANSWER COMES...
DOWN THE DRAIN!
SCHULZ

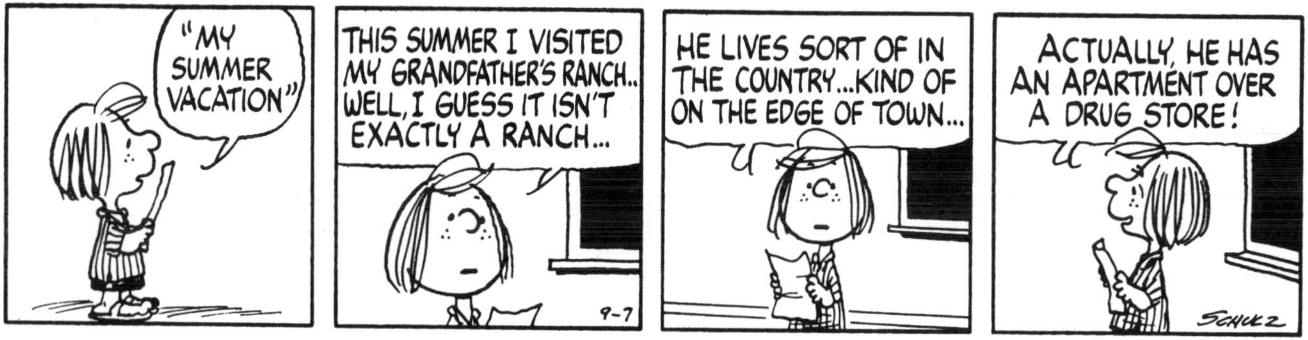
"MY SUMMER VACATION"
THIS SUMMER I VISITED MY GRANDFATHER'S RANCH.. WELL, I GUESS IT ISN'T EXACTLY A RANCH...
9-7
HE LIVES SORT OF IN THE COUNTRY...KIND OF ON THE EDGE OF TOWN...
ACTUALLY, HE HAS AN APARTMENT OVER A DRUG STORE!
SCHULZ

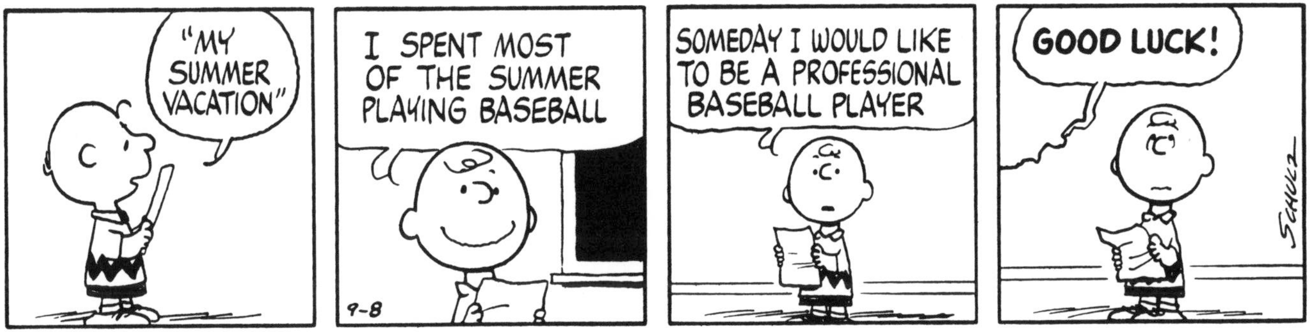
"MY SUMMER VACATION"
I SPENT MOST OF THE SUMMER PLAYING BASEBALL
9-8
SOMEDAY I WOULD LIKE TO BE A PROFESSIONAL BASEBALL PLAYER
GOOD LUCK!
SCHULZ

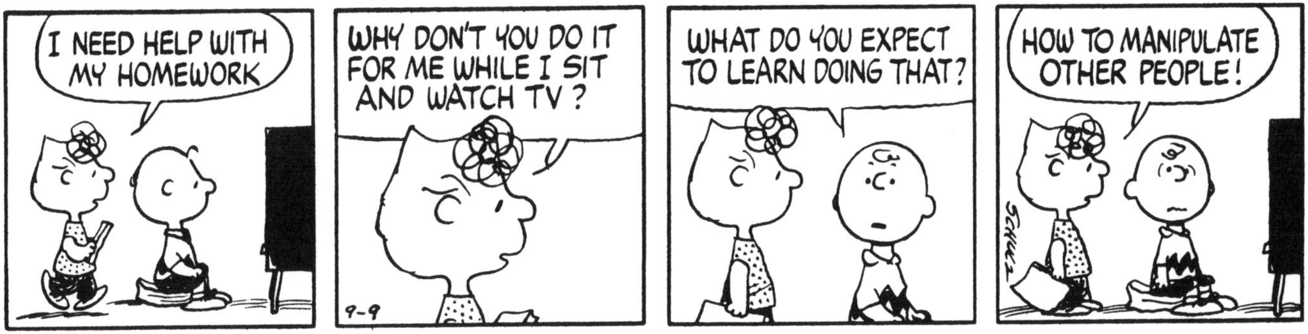
I NEED HELP WITH MY HOMEWORK
WHY DON'T YOU DO IT FOR ME WHILE I SIT AND WATCH TV?
9-9
WHAT DO YOU EXPECT TO LEARN DOING THAT?
HOW TO MANIPULATE OTHER PEOPLE!
SCHULZ

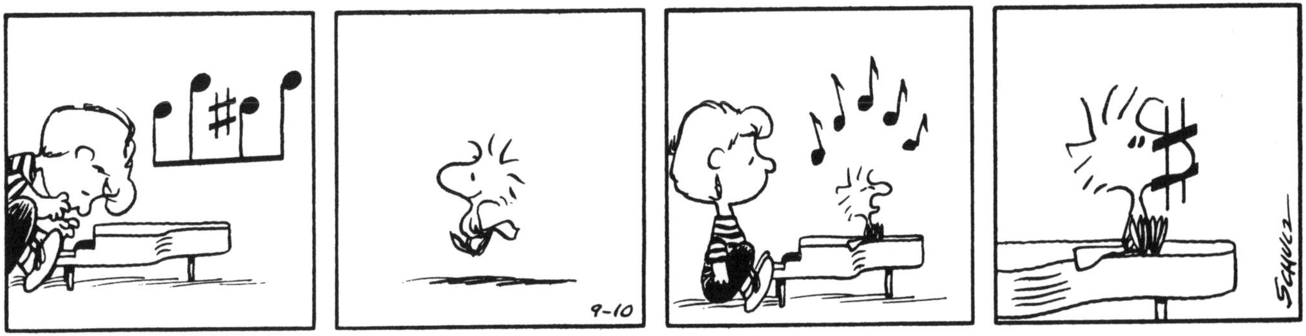
9-10
SCHULZ

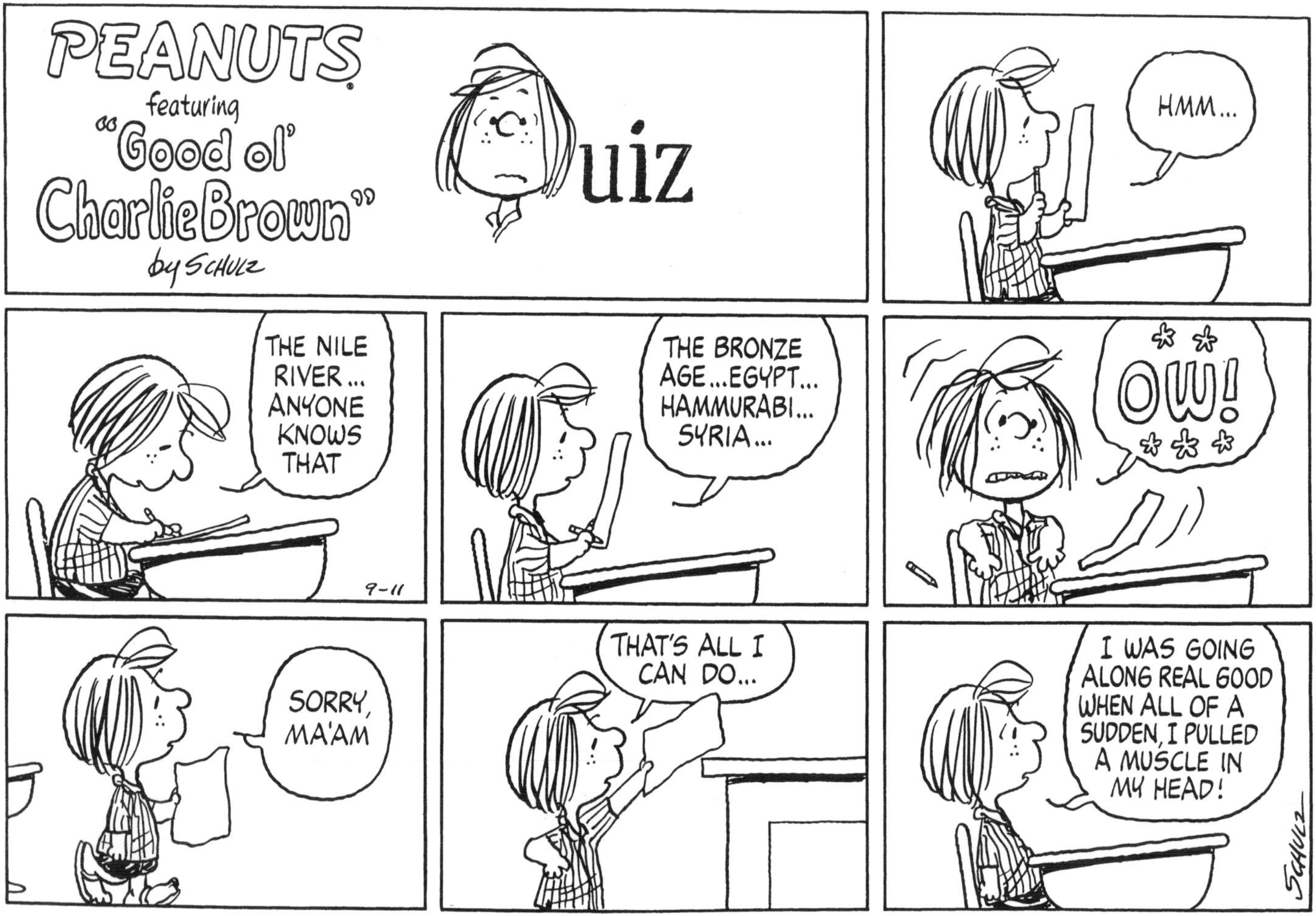
PEANUTS
featuring "Good ol' Charlie Brown"
by SCHULZ
Quiz
HMM...
THE NILE RIVER... ANYONE KNOWS THAT
9-11
THE BRONZE AGE...EGYPT... HAMMURABI... SYRIA...
OW!
SORRY, MA'AM
THAT'S ALL I CAN DO...
I WAS GOING ALONG REAL GOOD WHEN ALL OF A SUDDEN, I PULLED A MUSCLE IN MY HEAD!
SCHULZ

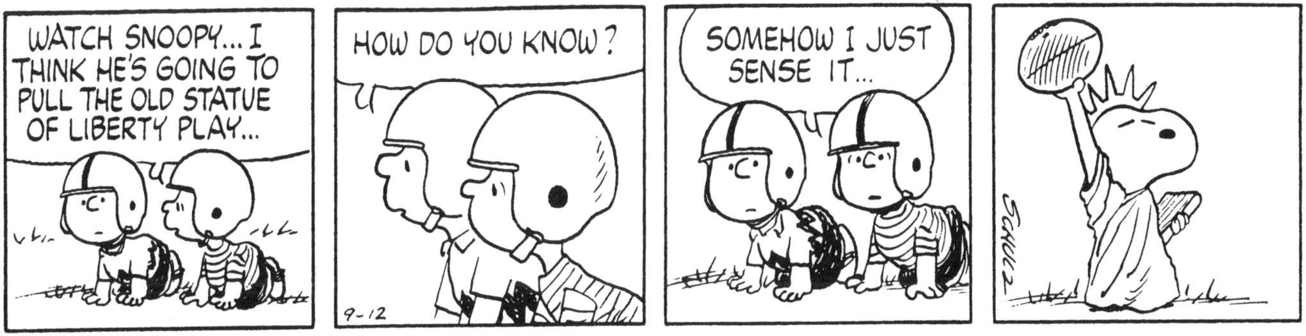
WATCH SNOOPY... I THINK HE'S GOING TO PULL THE OLD STATUE OF LIBERTY PLAY...
HOW DO YOU KNOW?
9-12
SOMEHOW I JUST SENSE IT...

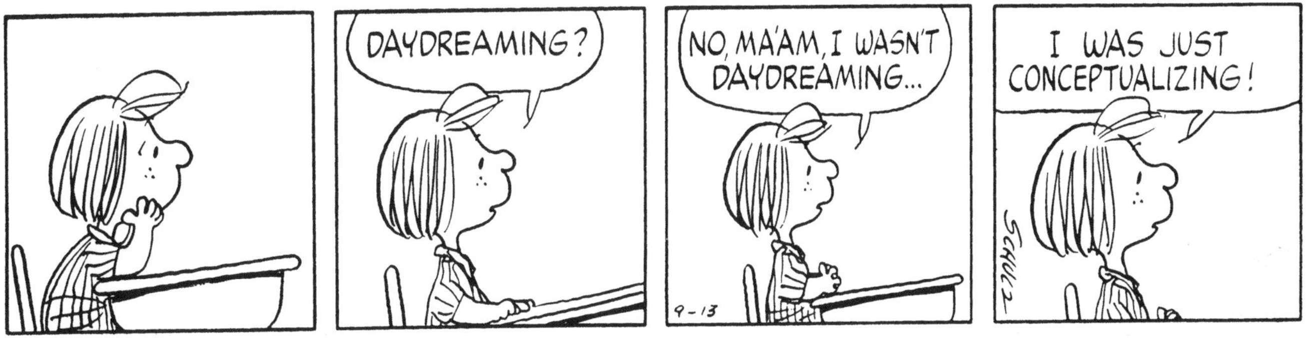
DAYDREAMING?
NO, MA'AM, I WASN'T DAYDREAMING...
9-13
I WAS JUST CONCEPTUALIZING!

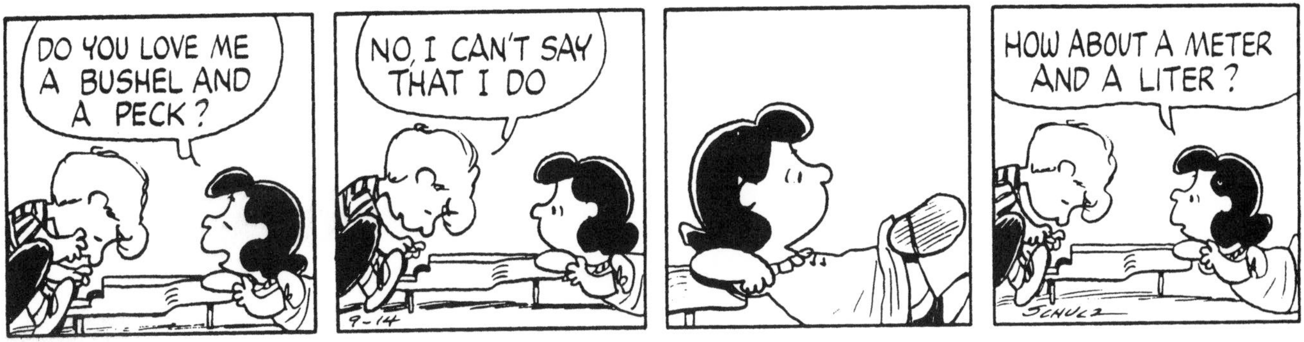
DO YOU LOVE ME A BUSHEL AND A PECK?
NO, I CAN'T SAY THAT I DO
9-14
HOW ABOUT A METER AND A LITER?

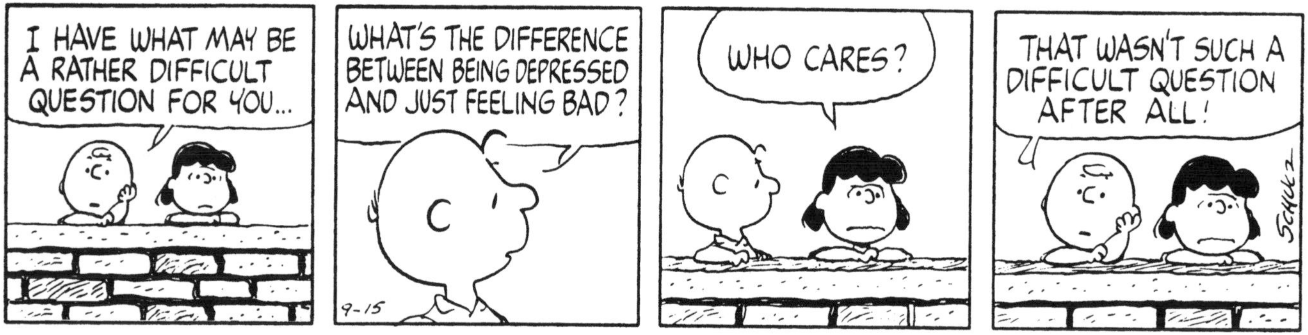
I HAVE WHAT MAY BE A RATHER DIFFICULT QUESTION FOR YOU...
WHAT'S THE DIFFERENCE BETWEEN BEING DEPRESSED AND JUST FEELING BAD?
9-15
WHO CARES?
THAT WASN'T SUCH A DIFFICULT QUESTION AFTER ALL!
SCHULZ

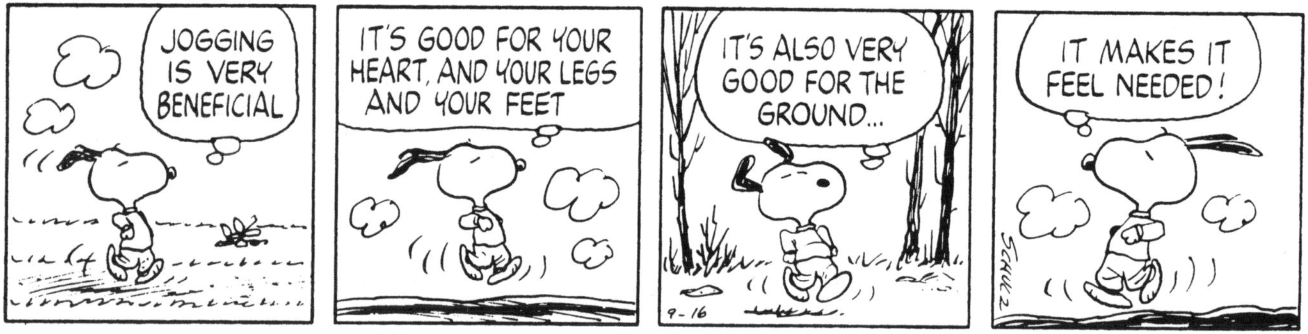
JOGGING IS VERY BENEFICIAL
IT'S GOOD FOR YOUR HEART, AND YOUR LEGS AND YOUR FEET
IT'S ALSO VERY GOOD FOR THE GROUND...
9-16
IT MAKES IT FEEL NEEDED!
SCHULZ

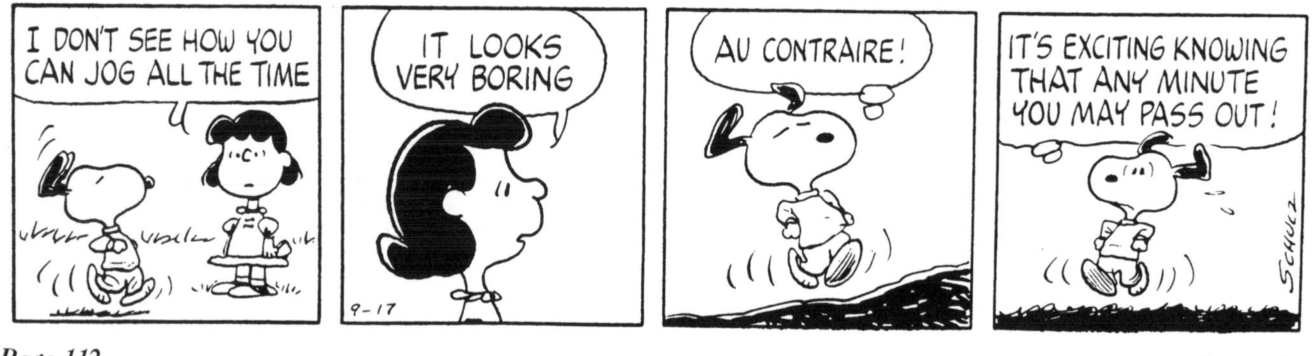
I DON'T SEE HOW YOU CAN JOG ALL THE TIME
IT LOOKS VERY BORING
9-17
AU CONTRAIRE!
IT'S EXCITING KNOWING THAT ANY MINUTE YOU MAY PASS OUT!
SCHULZ

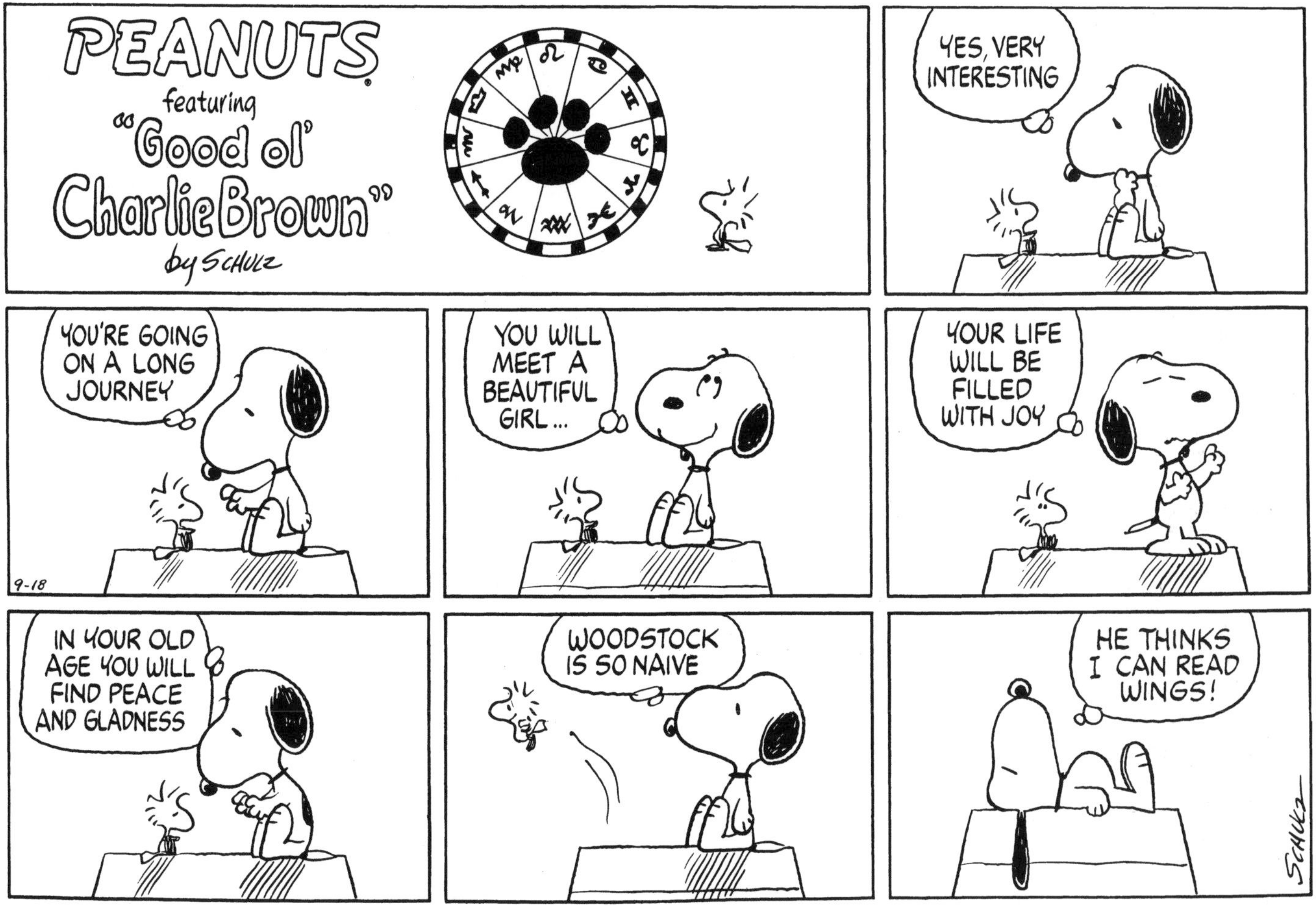
PEANUTS
featuring
"Good ol' Charlie Brown"
by SCHULZ
YES, VERY INTERESTING
YOU'RE GOING ON A LONG JOURNEY
9-18
YOU WILL MEET A BEAUTIFUL GIRL...
YOUR LIFE WILL BE FILLED WITH JOY
IN YOUR OLD AGE YOU WILL FIND PEACE AND GLADNESS
WOODSTOCK IS SO NAIVE
HE THINKS I CAN READ WINGS!
SCHULZ

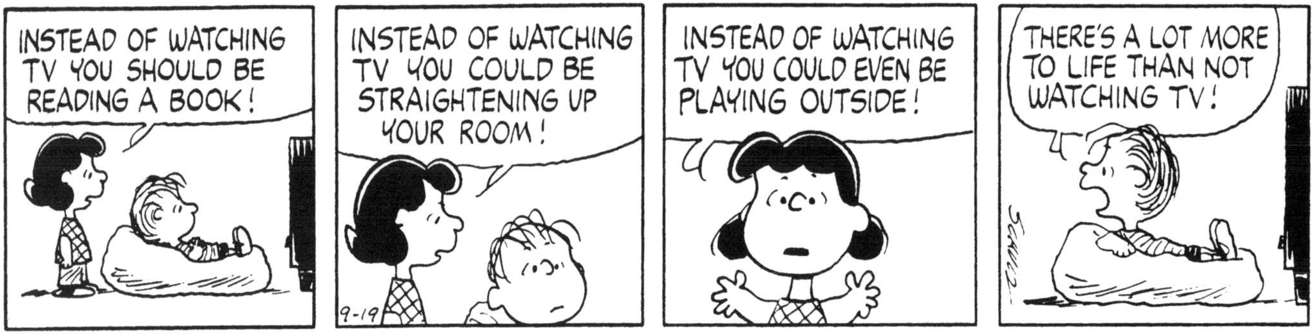
INSTEAD OF WATCHING TV YOU SHOULD BE READING A BOOK!
INSTEAD OF WATCHING TV YOU COULD BE STRAIGHTENING UP YOUR ROOM!
9-19
INSTEAD OF WATCHING TV YOU COULD EVEN BE PLAYING OUTSIDE!
THERE'S A LOT MORE TO LIFE THAN NOT WATCHING TV!
SCHULZ

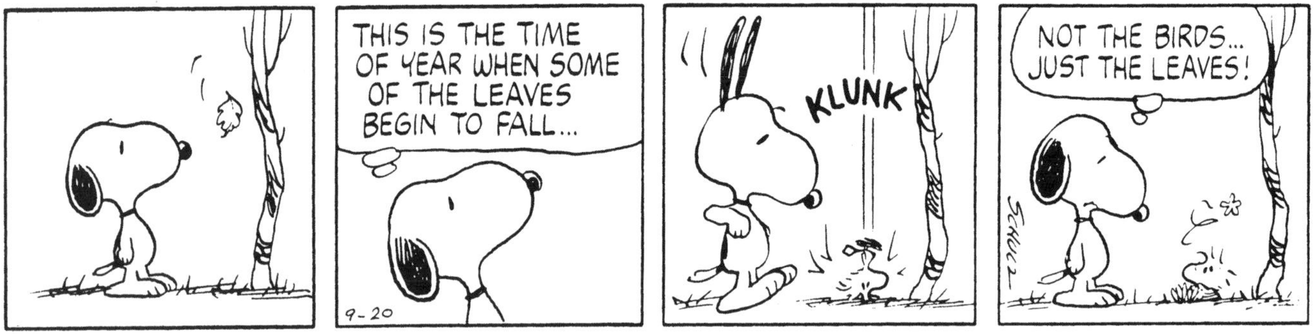
THIS IS THE TIME OF YEAR WHEN SOME OF THE LEAVES BEGIN TO FALL...
9-20
KLUNK
NOT THE BIRDS... JUST THE LEAVES!
SCHULZ

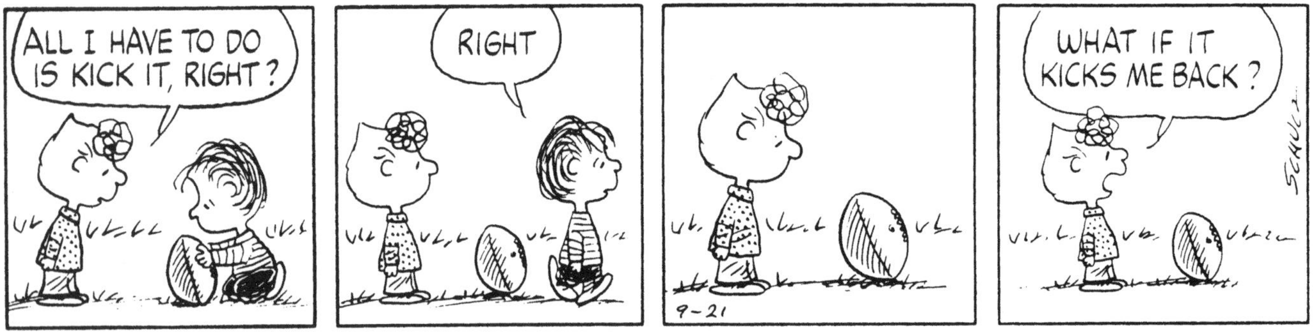
ALL I HAVE TO DO IS KICK IT, RIGHT?
RIGHT
9-21
WHAT IF IT KICKS ME BACK?
SCHULZ

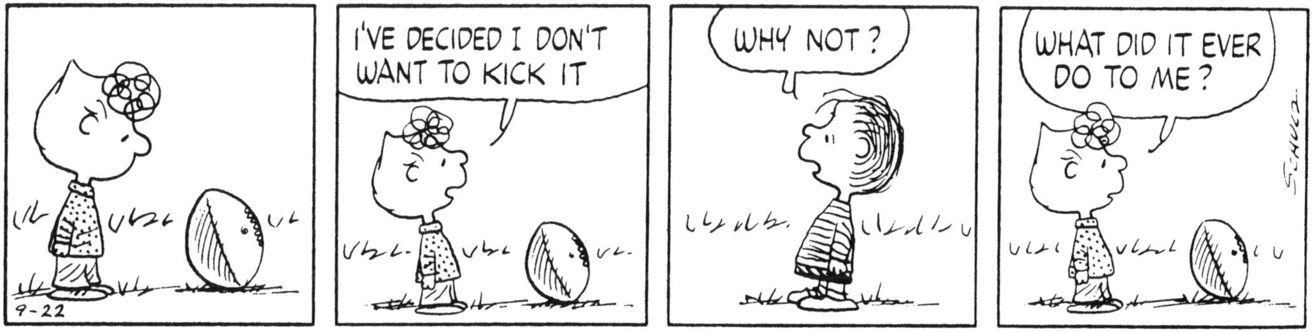
9-22
I'VE DECIDED I DON'T WANT TO KICK IT
WHY NOT?
WHAT DID IT EVER DO TO ME?
SCHULZ

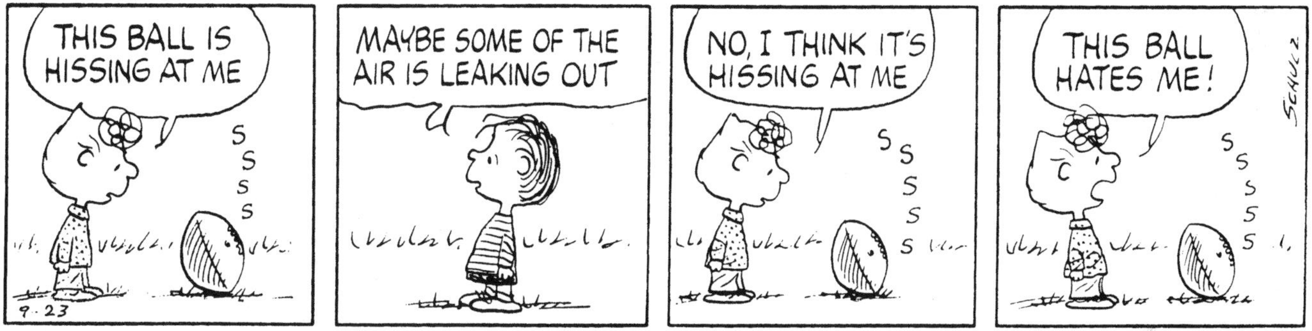
THIS BALL IS HISSING AT ME
SSSS
9-23
MAYBE SOME OF THE AIR IS LEAKING OUT
NO, I THINK IT'S HISSING AT ME
SSSSS
THIS BALL HATES ME!
SSSSS
SCHULZ

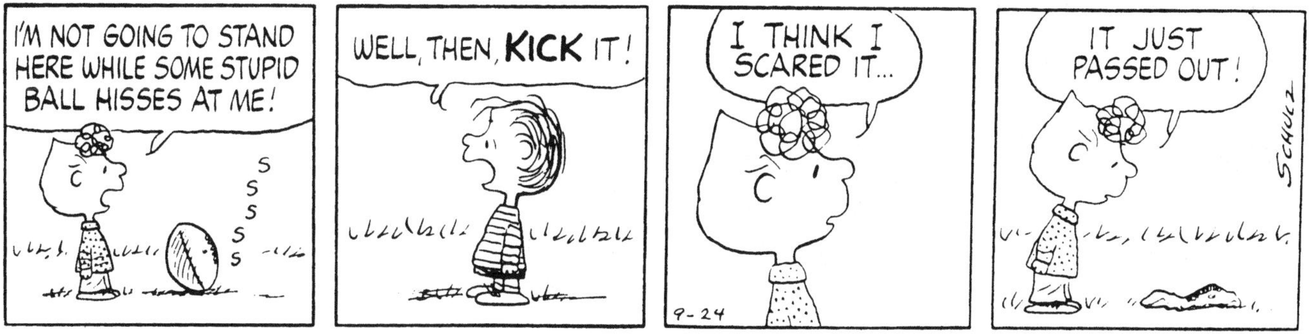
I'M NOT GOING TO STAND HERE WHILE SOME STUPID BALL HISSES AT ME!
SSSSS
WELL, THEN, **KICK** IT!
I THINK I SCARED IT...
9-24
IT JUST PASSED OUT!
SCHULZ

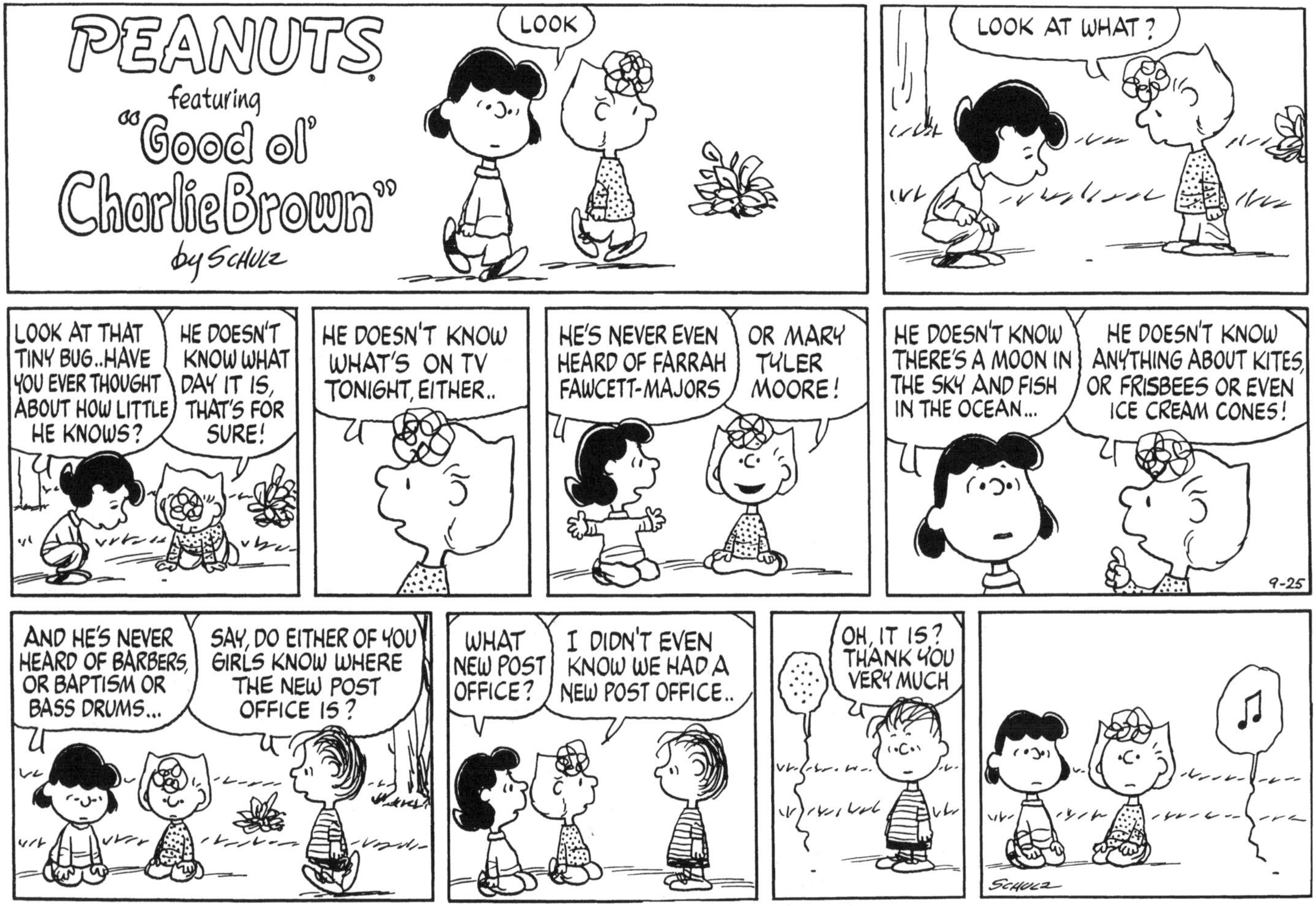
PEANUTS
featuring "Good ol' CharlieBrown"
by SCHULZ
LOOK
LOOK AT WHAT?
LOOK AT THAT TINY BUG..HAVE YOU EVER THOUGHT ABOUT HOW LITTLE HE KNOWS?
HE DOESN'T KNOW WHAT DAY IT IS, THAT'S FOR SURE!
HE DOESN'T KNOW WHAT'S ON TV TONIGHT, EITHER..
HE'S NEVER EVEN HEARD OF FARRAH FAWCETT-MAJORS
OR MARY TYLER MOORE!
HE DOESN'T KNOW THERE'S A MOON IN THE SKY AND FISH IN THE OCEAN...
HE DOESN'T KNOW ANYTHING ABOUT KITES, OR FRISBEES OR EVEN ICE CREAM CONES!
9-25
AND HE'S NEVER HEARD OF BARBERS, OR BAPTISM OR BASS DRUMS...
SAY, DO EITHER OF YOU GIRLS KNOW WHERE THE NEW POST OFFICE IS?
WHAT NEW POST OFFICE?
I DIDN'T EVEN KNOW WE HAD A NEW POST OFFICE..
OH, IT IS? THANK YOU VERY MUCH
♫
SCHULZ

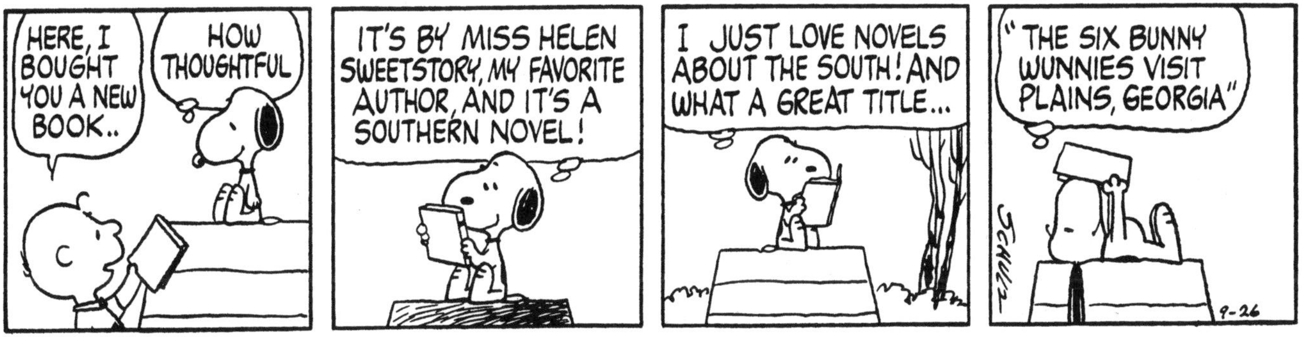
HERE, I BOUGHT YOU A NEW BOOK..
HOW THOUGHTFUL
IT'S BY MISS HELEN SWEETSTORY, MY FAVORITE AUTHOR, AND IT'S A SOUTHERN NOVEL!
I JUST LOVE NOVELS ABOUT THE SOUTH! AND WHAT A GREAT TITLE...
"THE SIX BUNNY WUNNIES VISIT PLAINS, GEORGIA"
9-26

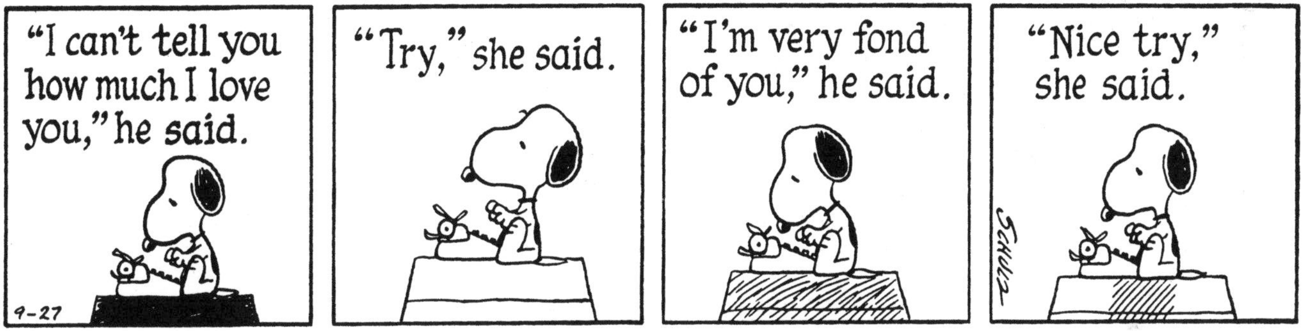
"I can't tell you how much I love you," he said.
9-27
"Try," she said.
"I'm very fond of you," he said.
"Nice try," she said.

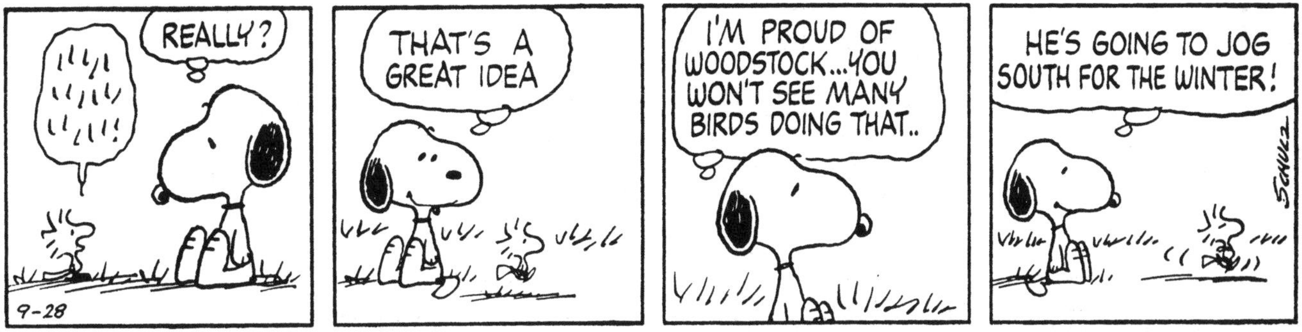
REALLY?
9-28
THAT'S A GREAT IDEA
I'M PROUD OF WOODSTOCK...YOU WON'T SEE MANY BIRDS DOING THAT..
HE'S GOING TO JOG SOUTH FOR THE WINTER!

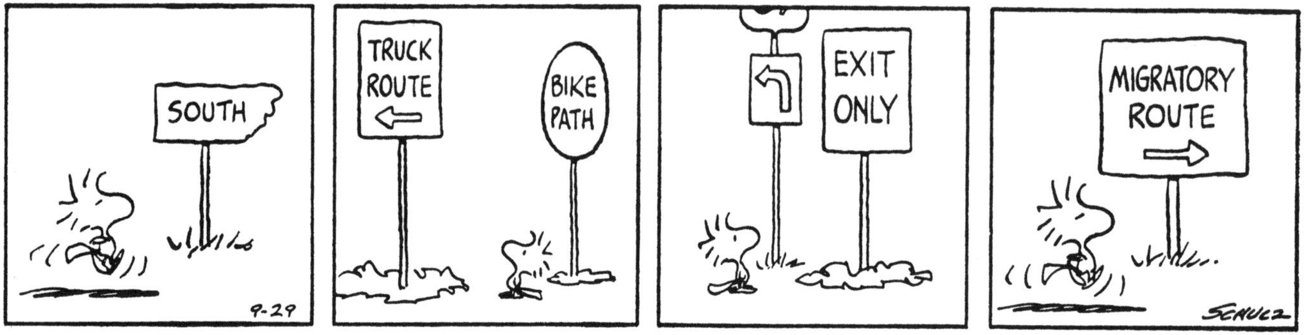
SOUTH
TRUCK ROUTE
BIKE PATH
EXIT ONLY
MIGRATORY ROUTE
9-29
SCHULZ

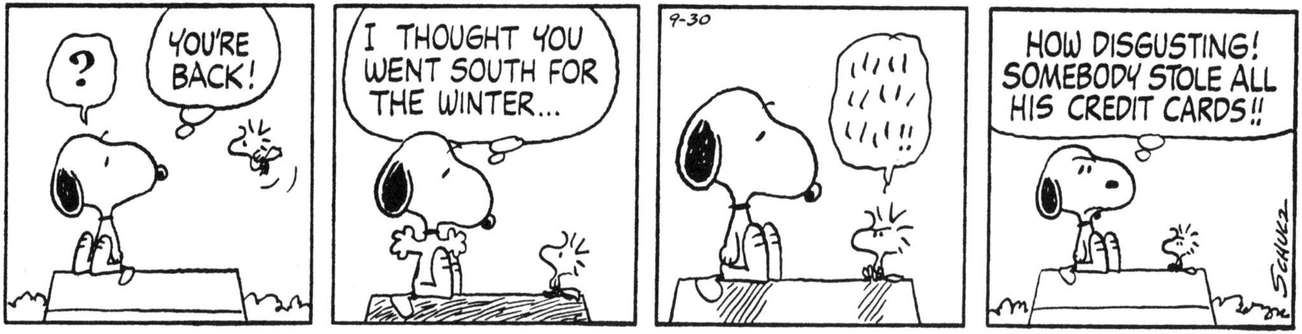
?
YOU'RE BACK!
I THOUGHT YOU WENT SOUTH FOR THE WINTER...
9-30
HOW DISGUSTING! SOMEBODY STOLE ALL HIS CREDIT CARDS!!
SCHULZ

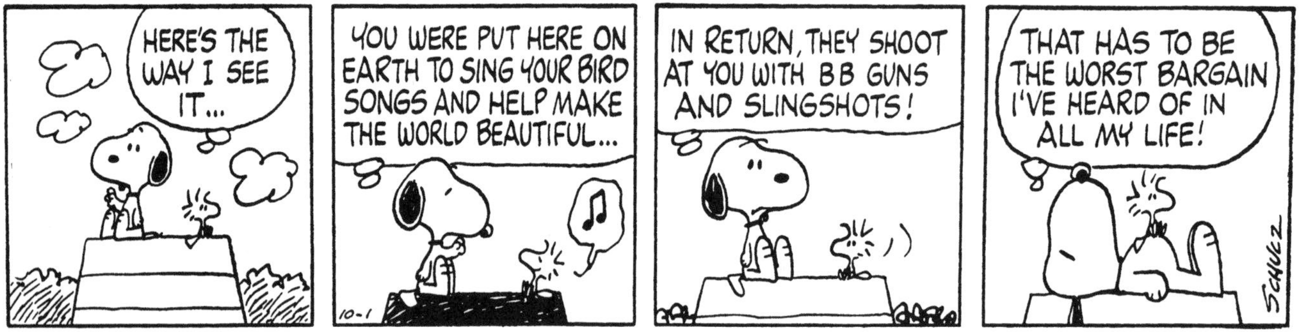
HERE'S THE WAY I SEE IT...
YOU WERE PUT HERE ON EARTH TO SING YOUR BIRD SONGS AND HELP MAKE THE WORLD BEAUTIFUL...
♪
10-1
IN RETURN, THEY SHOOT AT YOU WITH BB GUNS AND SLINGSHOTS!
THAT HAS TO BE THE WORST BARGAIN I'VE HEARD OF IN ALL MY LIFE!
SCHULZ

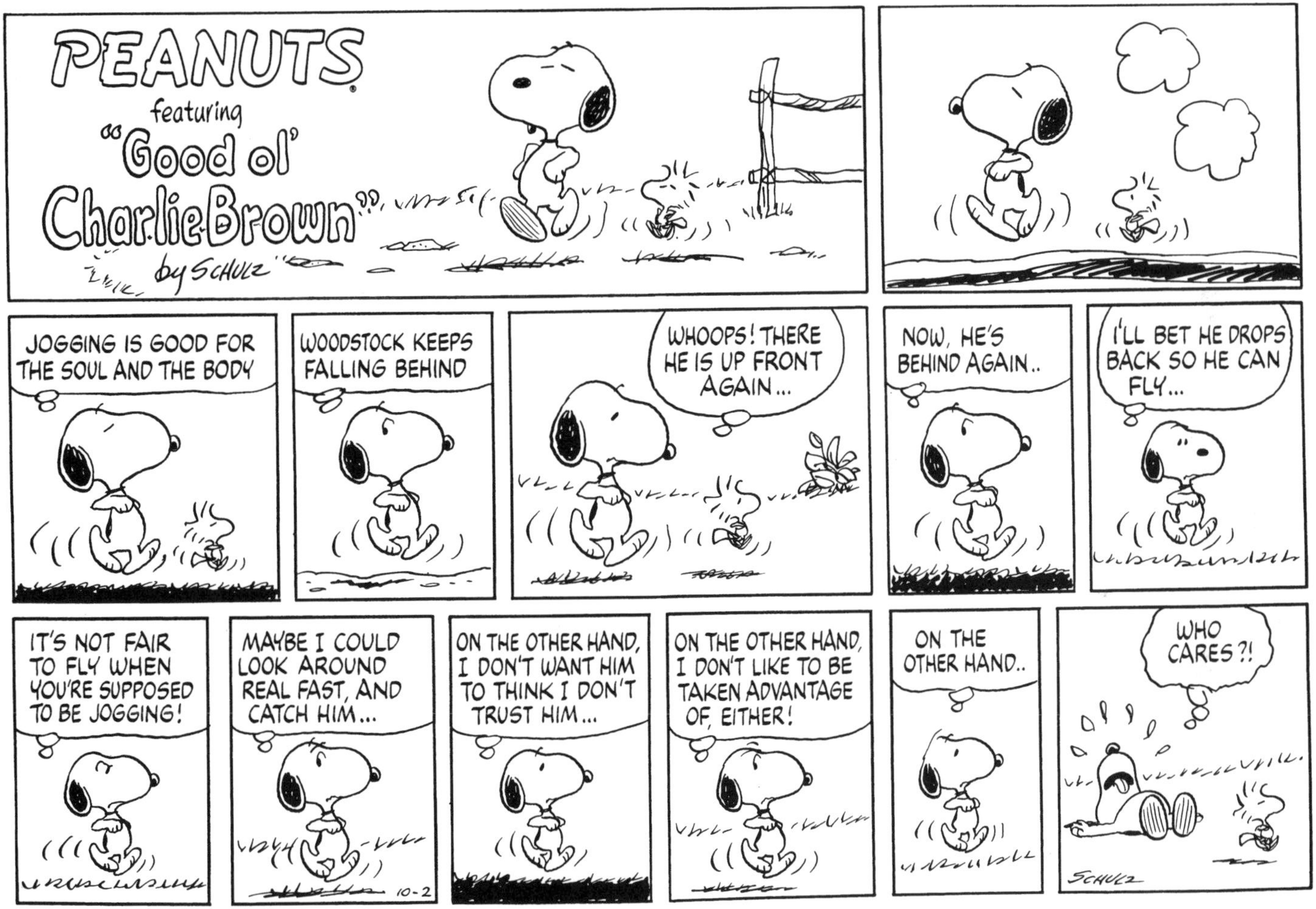
PEANUTS
featuring
"Good ol' Charlie Brown"
by SCHULZ
JOGGING IS GOOD FOR THE SOUL AND THE BODY
WOODSTOCK KEEPS FALLING BEHIND
WHOOPS! THERE HE IS UP FRONT AGAIN...
NOW, HE'S BEHIND AGAIN..
I'LL BET HE DROPS BACK SO HE CAN FLY...
IT'S NOT FAIR TO FLY WHEN YOU'RE SUPPOSED TO BE JOGGING!
MAYBE I COULD LOOK AROUND REAL FAST, AND CATCH HIM...
10-2
ON THE OTHER HAND, I DON'T WANT HIM TO THINK I DON'T TRUST HIM...
ON THE OTHER HAND, I DON'T LIKE TO BE TAKEN ADVANTAGE OF, EITHER!
ON THE OTHER HAND..
WHO CARES?!
SCHULZ

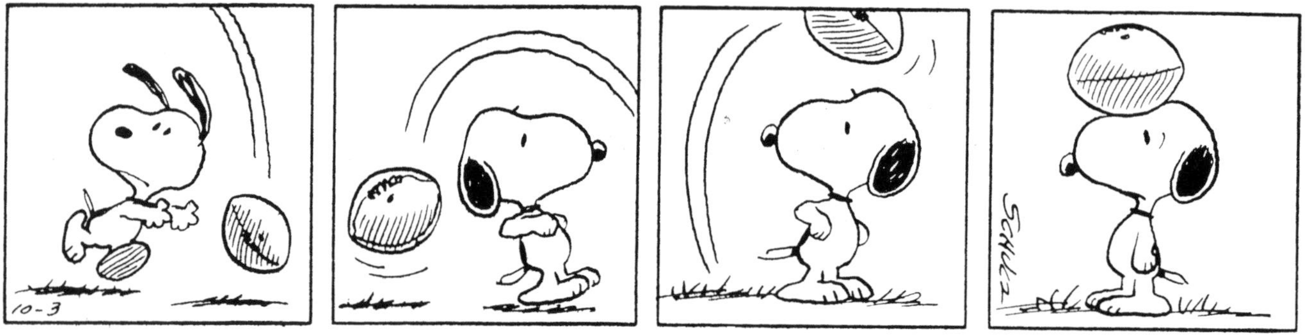

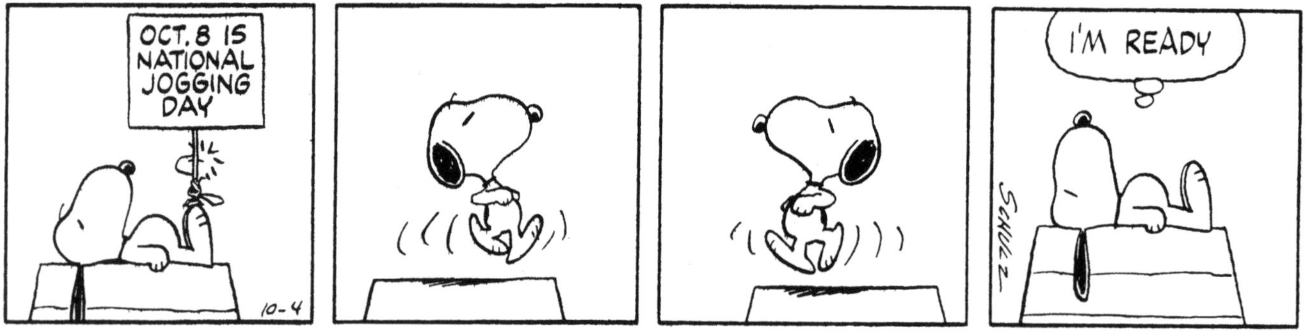
OCT. 8 IS NATIONAL JOGGING DAY
I'M READY

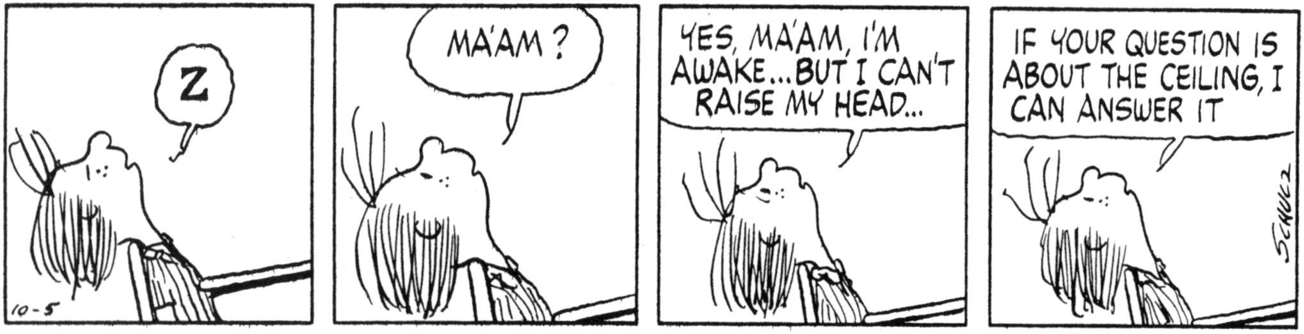
Z
MA'AM ?
YES, MA'AM, I'M AWAKE...BUT I CAN'T RAISE MY HEAD...
IF YOUR QUESTION IS ABOUT THE CEILING, I CAN ANSWER IT

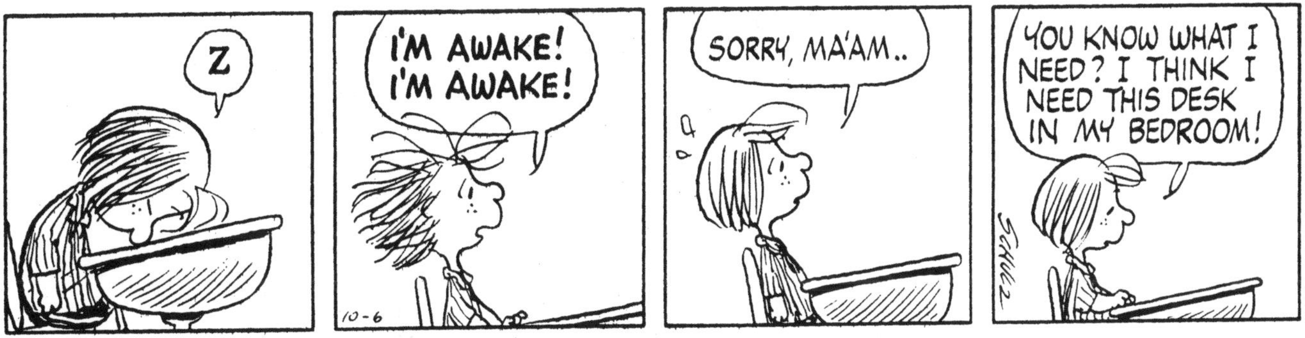
Z
I'M AWAKE! I'M AWAKE!
10-6
SORRY, MA'AM..
YOU KNOW WHAT I NEED? I THINK I NEED THIS DESK IN MY BEDROOM!
SCHULZ

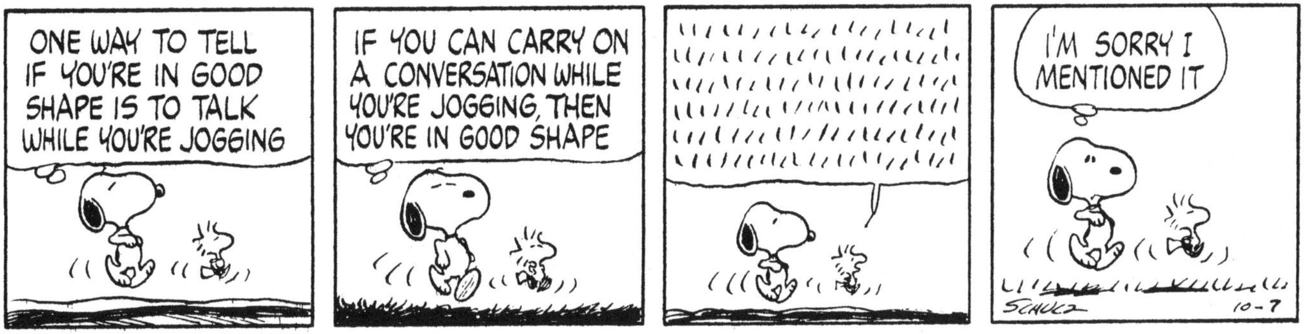
ONE WAY TO TELL IF YOU'RE IN GOOD SHAPE IS TO TALK WHILE YOU'RE JOGGING
IF YOU CAN CARRY ON A CONVERSATION WHILE YOU'RE JOGGING, THEN YOU'RE IN GOOD SHAPE
I'M SORRY I MENTIONED IT
SCHULZ
10-7

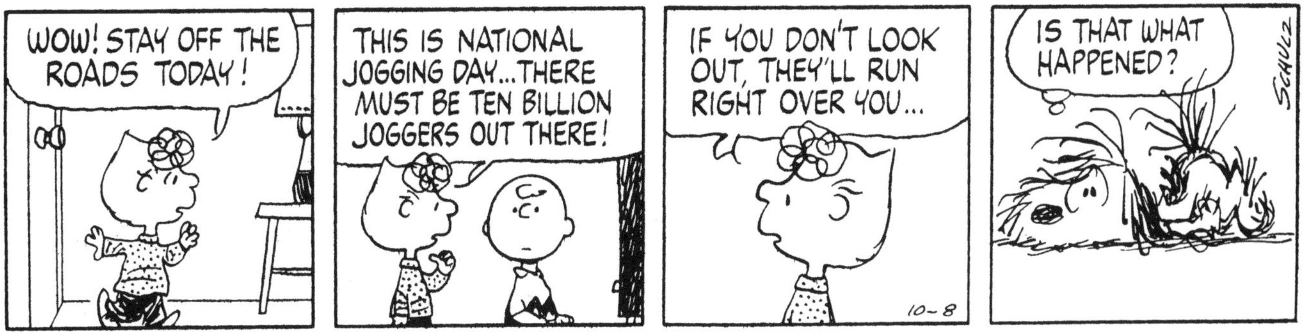
WOW! STAY OFF THE ROADS TODAY!
THIS IS NATIONAL JOGGING DAY...THERE MUST BE TEN BILLION JOGGERS OUT THERE!
IF YOU DON'T LOOK OUT, THEY'LL RUN RIGHT OVER YOU...
10-8
IS THAT WHAT HAPPENED?
SCHULZ

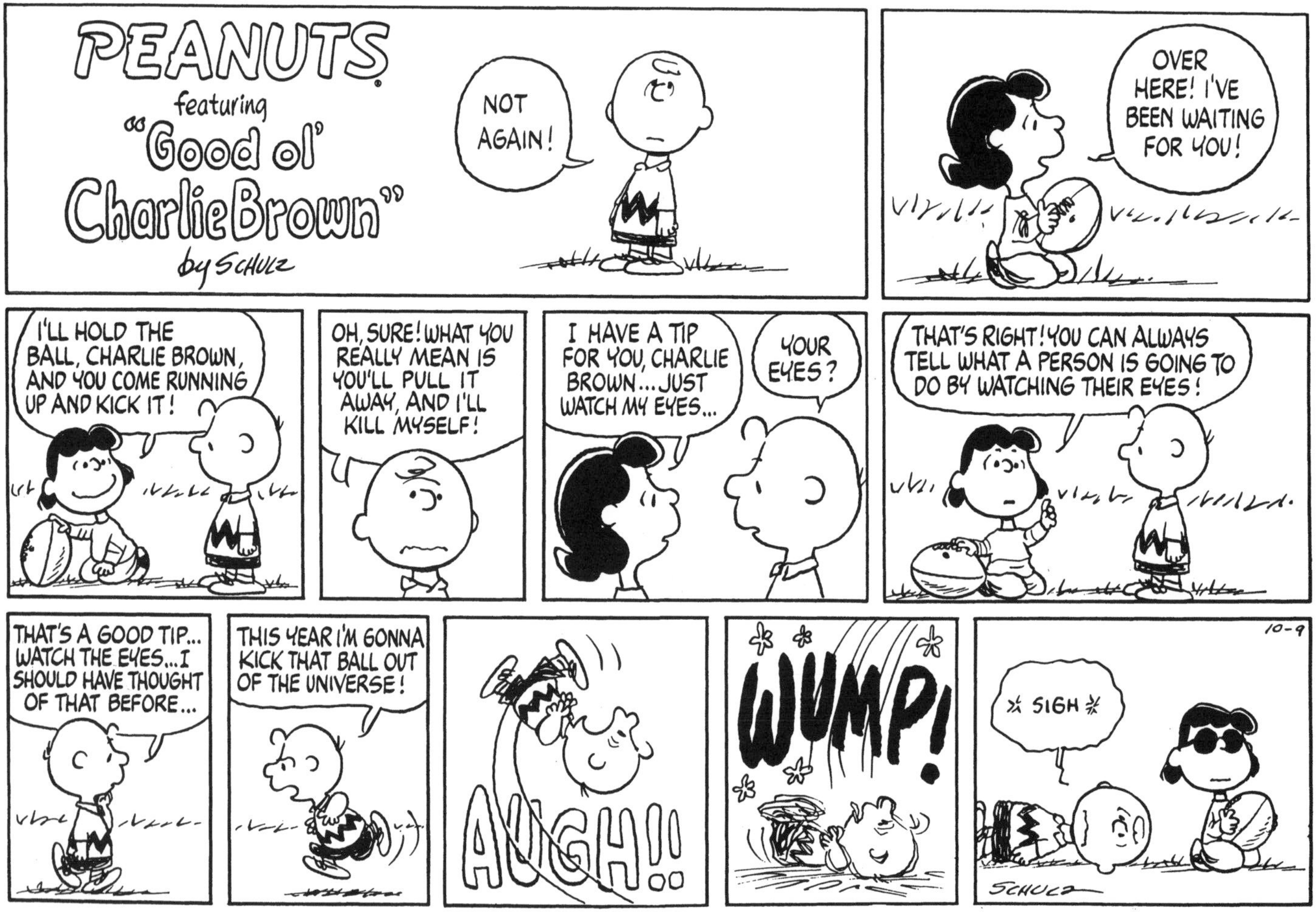
PEANUTS
featuring "Good ol' Charlie Brown"
by SCHULZ
NOT AGAIN!
OVER HERE! I'VE BEEN WAITING FOR YOU!
I'LL HOLD THE BALL, CHARLIE BROWN, AND YOU COME RUNNING UP AND KICK IT!
OH, SURE! WHAT YOU REALLY MEAN IS YOU'LL PULL IT AWAY, AND I'LL KILL MYSELF!
I HAVE A TIP FOR YOU, CHARLIE BROWN...JUST WATCH MY EYES...
YOUR EYES?
THAT'S RIGHT! YOU CAN ALWAYS TELL WHAT A PERSON IS GOING TO DO BY WATCHING THEIR EYES!
THAT'S A GOOD TIP... WATCH THE EYES...I SHOULD HAVE THOUGHT OF THAT BEFORE...
THIS YEAR I'M GONNA KICK THAT BALL OUT OF THE UNIVERSE!
AUGH!!
WUMP!
10-9
☼ SIGH ☼
SCHULZ

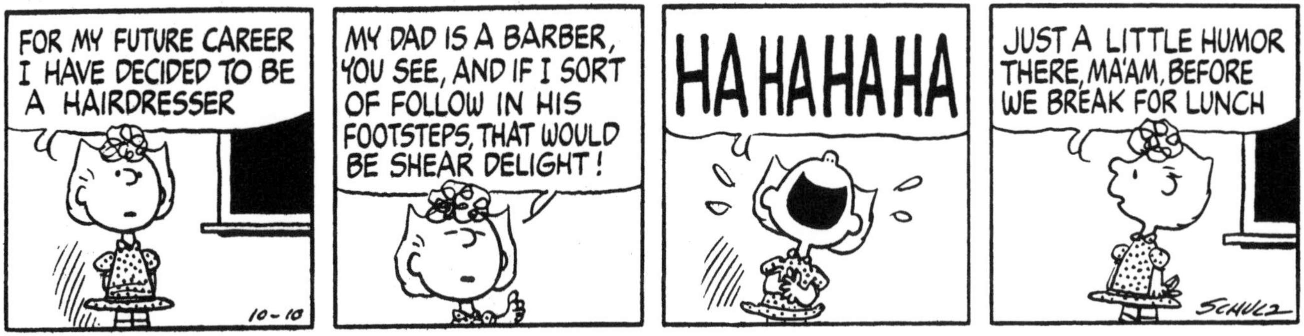
FOR MY FUTURE CAREER I HAVE DECIDED TO BE A HAIRDRESSER
10-10
MY DAD IS A BARBER, YOU SEE, AND IF I SORT OF FOLLOW IN HIS FOOTSTEPS, THAT WOULD BE SHEAR DELIGHT!
HAHAHAHA
JUST A LITTLE HUMOR THERE, MA'AM, BEFORE WE BREAK FOR LUNCH
SCHULZ

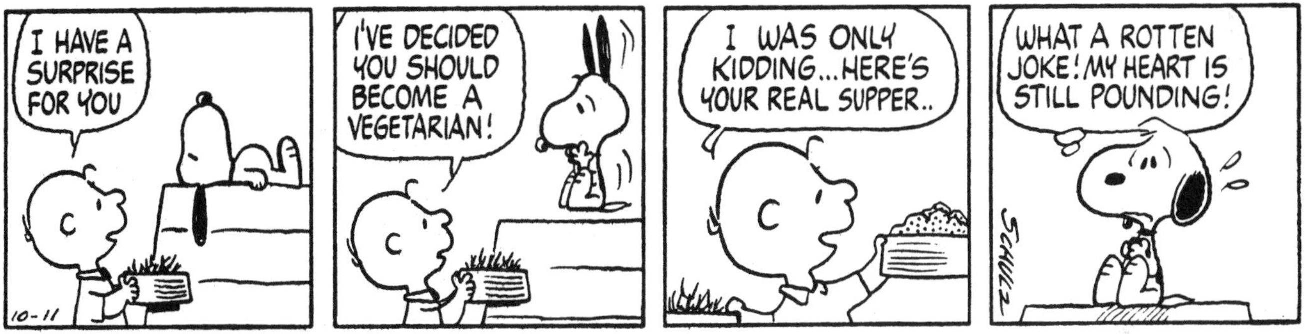
I HAVE A SURPRISE FOR YOU
10-11
I'VE DECIDED YOU SHOULD BECOME A VEGETARIAN!
I WAS ONLY KIDDING...HERE'S YOUR REAL SUPPER..
WHAT A ROTTEN JOKE! MY HEART IS STILL POUNDING!
SCHULZ

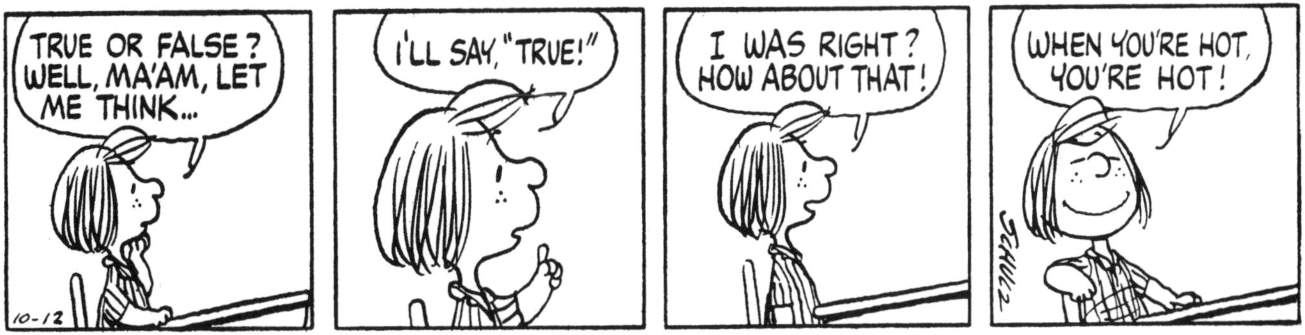
TRUE OR FALSE? WELL, MA'AM, LET ME THINK...
10-12
I'LL SAY, "TRUE!"
I WAS RIGHT? HOW ABOUT THAT!
WHEN YOU'RE HOT, YOU'RE HOT!
SCHULZ

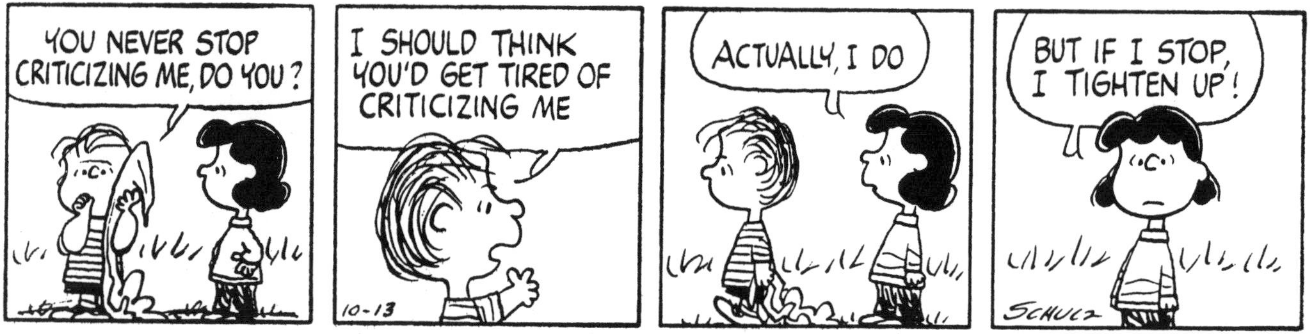
YOU NEVER STOP CRITICIZING ME, DO YOU?
I SHOULD THINK YOU'D GET TIRED OF CRITICIZING ME
10-13
ACTUALLY, I DO
BUT IF I STOP, I TIGHTEN UP!
SCHULZ

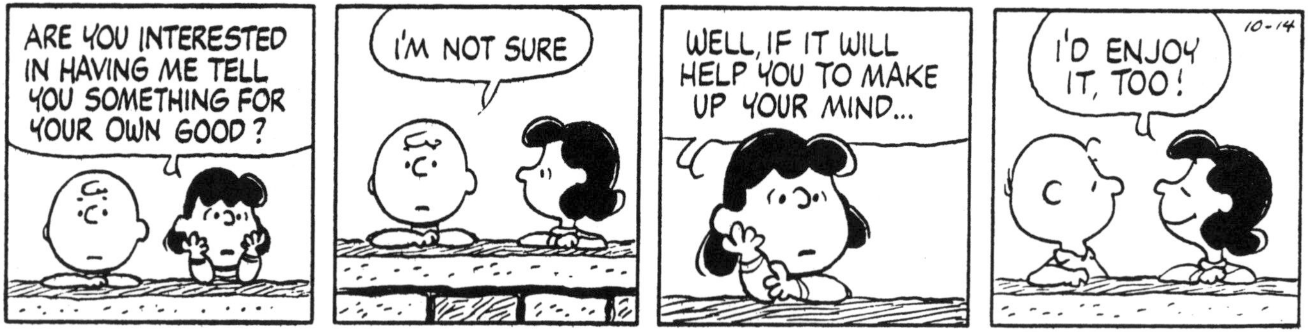
ARE YOU INTERESTED IN HAVING ME TELL YOU SOMETHING FOR YOUR OWN GOOD?
I'M NOT SURE
WELL, IF IT WILL HELP YOU TO MAKE UP YOUR MIND...
10-14
I'D ENJOY IT, TOO!

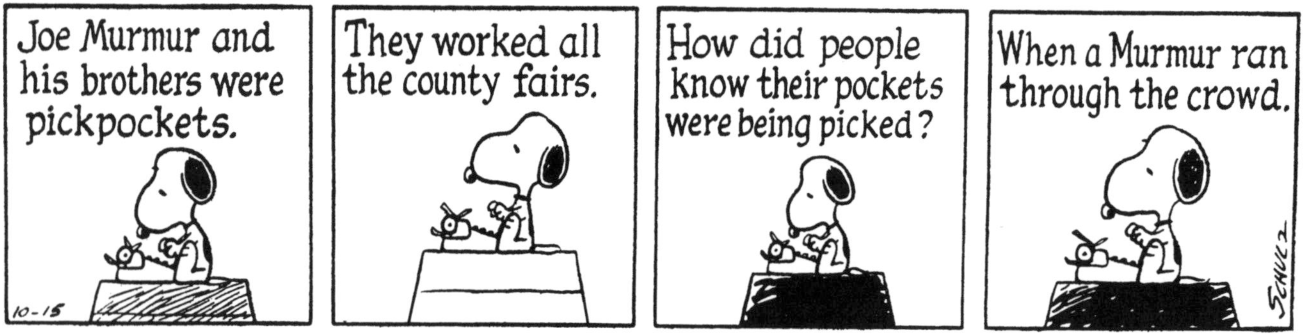
Joe Murmur and his brothers were pickpockets.
10-15
They worked all the county fairs.
How did people know their pockets were being picked?
When a Murmur ran through the crowd.
SCHULZ

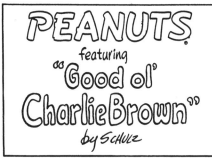

PEANUTS featuring "Good ol' CharlieBrown" *by SCHULZ*

OKAY, THIS IS WHAT WE'LL DO...

YOU GO DOWN TO THE END OF THE FIELD, AND I'LL KICK THE BALL TO YOU

I'LL BE ALL ALONE DOWN THERE...

YOU WON'T BE ALONE..THE BALL WILL BE WITH YOU!

WHAT IF IT DOESN'T SHOW UP?

IT'LL BE THERE... I'M GOING TO KICK IT TO YOU

WHAT IF I GO ALL THE WAY DOWN THERE, AND I GET MUGGED?

HOW CAN YOU GET MUGGED? WE'RE THE ONLY ONES AROUND HERE!

THAT'S WHAT YOU SAY!

10-16

ANOTHER THING...SO I WALK ALL THE WAY DOWN THERE... HOW DO I KNOW YOU WON'T RUN OFF AND LEAVE ME?

OKAY, FORGET IT!

NO, THAT'S ALL RIGHT... I'LL DO IT

MY MOTHER WARNED ME THAT FOOTBALL WAS A RISKY GAME

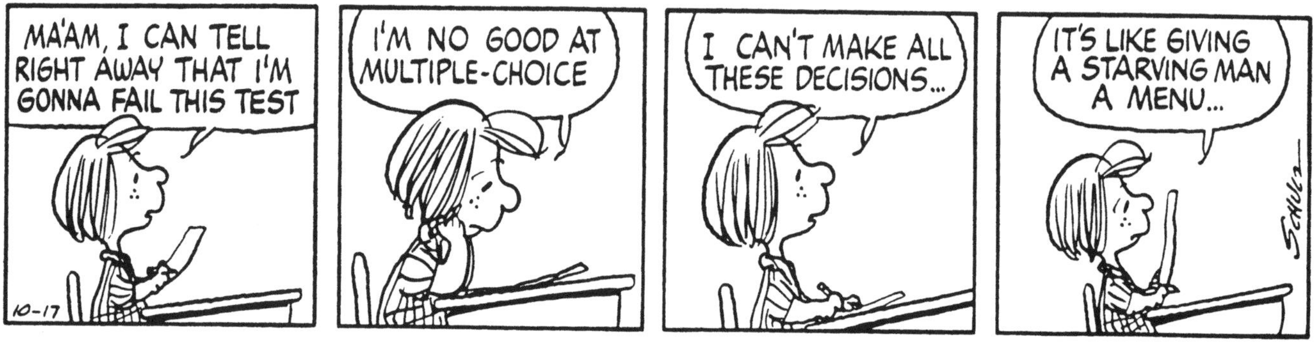
MA'AM, I CAN TELL RIGHT AWAY THAT I'M GONNA FAIL THIS TEST
10-17
I'M NO GOOD AT MULTIPLE-CHOICE
I CAN'T MAKE ALL THESE DECISIONS...
IT'S LIKE GIVING A STARVING MAN A MENU...
SCHULZ

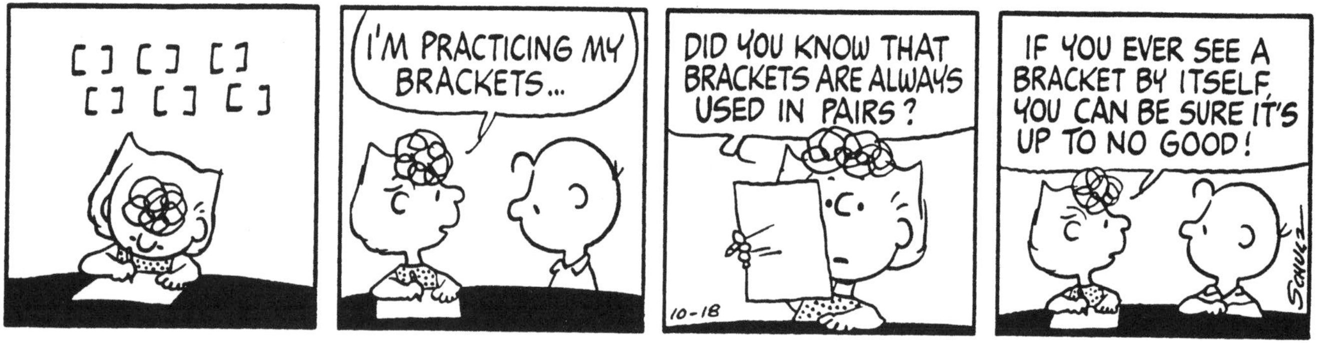
[ ] [ ] [ ]
[ ] [ ] [ ]
I'M PRACTICING MY BRACKETS...
DID YOU KNOW THAT BRACKETS ARE ALWAYS USED IN PAIRS?
10-18
IF YOU EVER SEE A BRACKET BY ITSELF, YOU CAN BE SURE IT'S UP TO NO GOOD!
SCHULZ

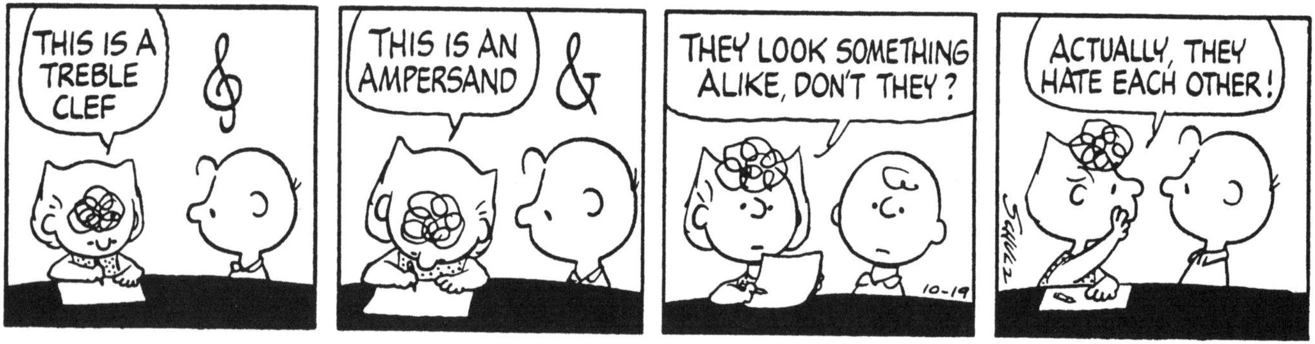
THIS IS A TREBLE CLEF
THIS IS AN AMPERSAND
&
THEY LOOK SOMETHING ALIKE, DON'T THEY?
10-19
ACTUALLY, THEY HATE EACH OTHER!
SCHULZ

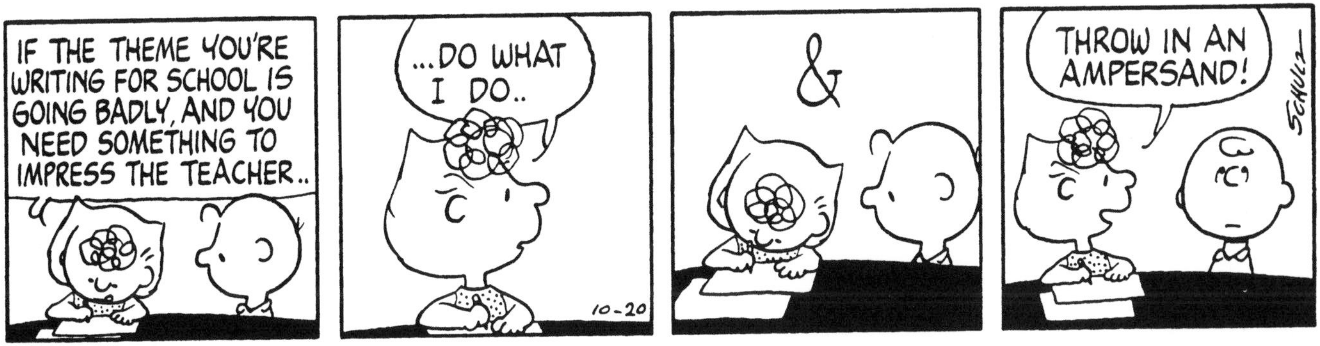
IF THE THEME YOU'RE WRITING FOR SCHOOL IS GOING BADLY, AND YOU NEED SOMETHING TO IMPRESS THE TEACHER..
...DO WHAT I DO..
10-20
&
THROW IN AN AMPERSAND!
SCHULZ

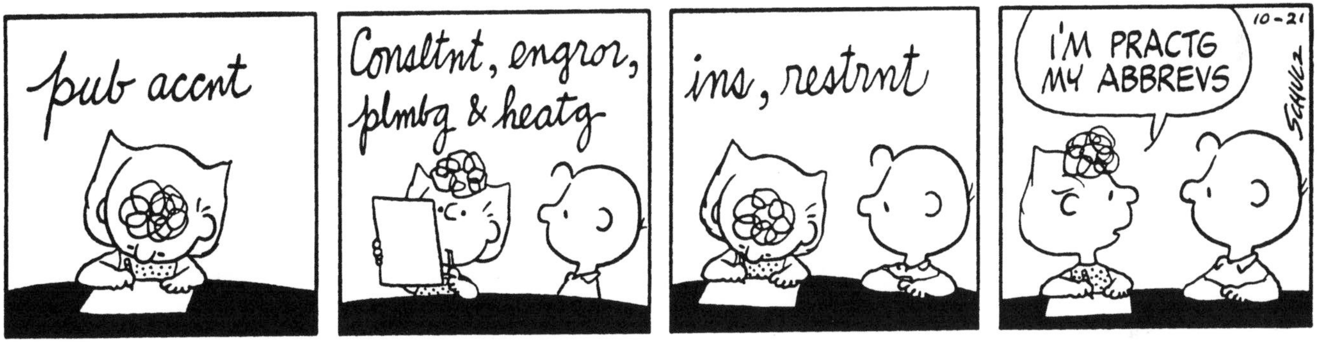
pub accnt
Consltnt, engror, plmbg & heatg
ins, restrnt
10-21
I'M PRACTG MY ABBREVS
SCHULZ

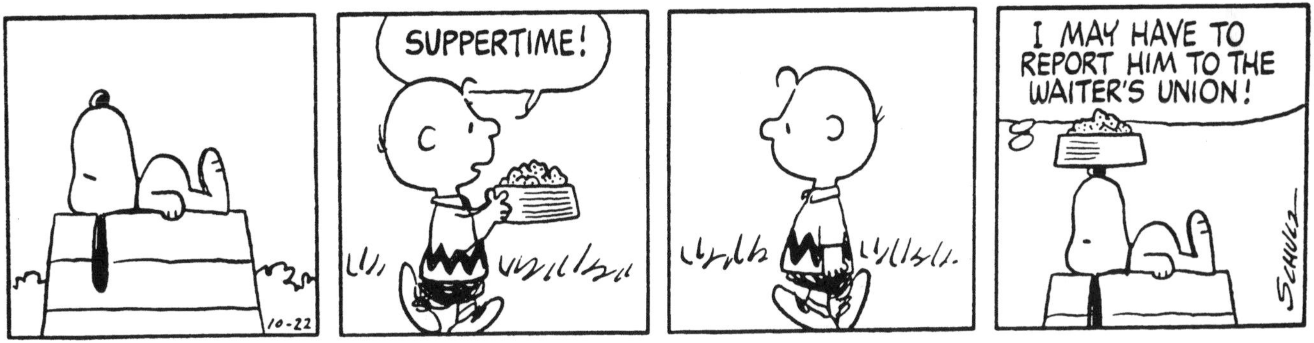
10-22
SUPPERTIME!
I MAY HAVE TO REPORT HIM TO THE WAITER'S UNION!
SCHULZ

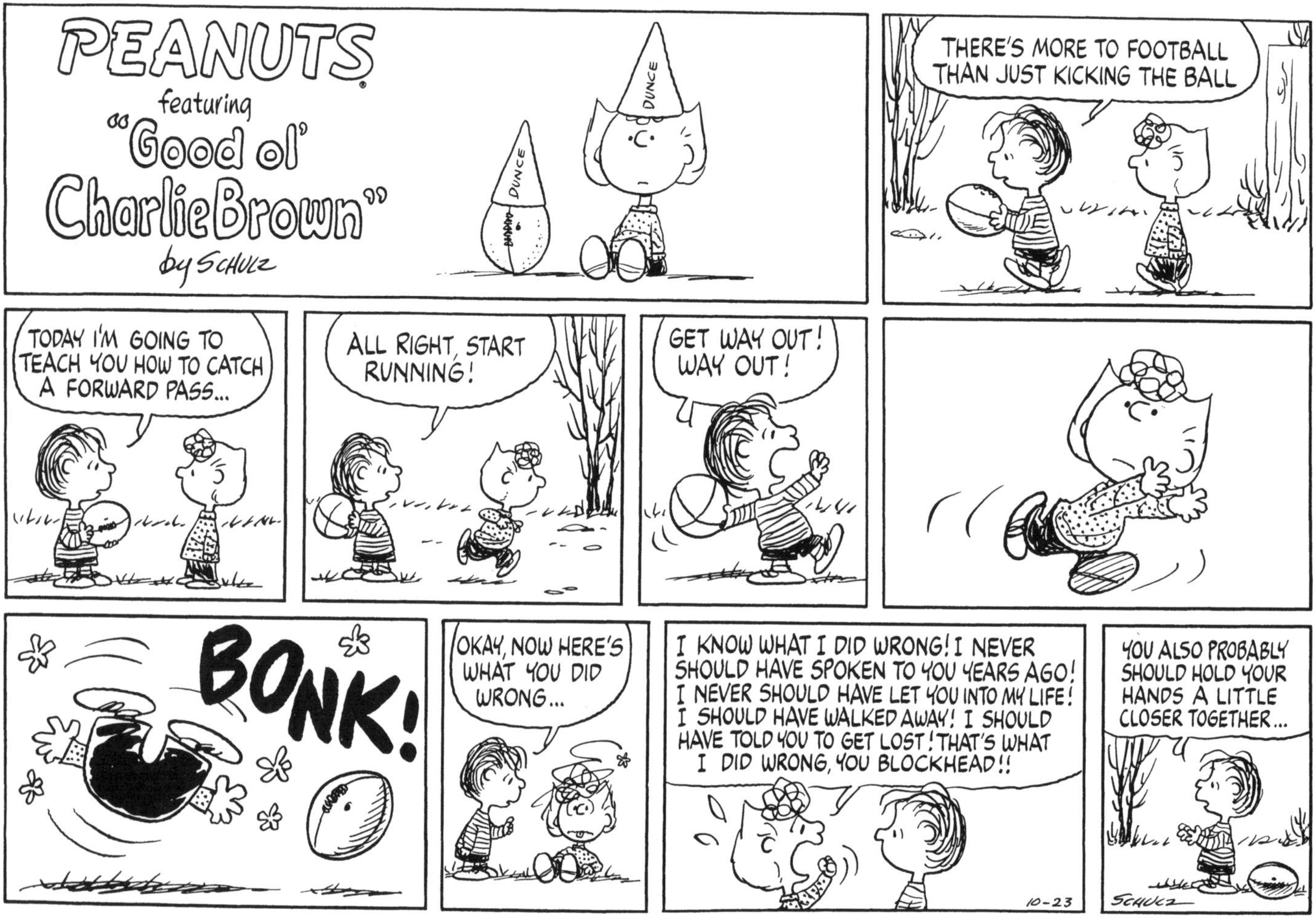
PEANUTS®
featuring
"Good ol' Charlie Brown"
by SCHULZ
DUNCE
DUNCE
THERE'S MORE TO FOOTBALL THAN JUST KICKING THE BALL
TODAY I'M GOING TO TEACH YOU HOW TO CATCH A FORWARD PASS...
ALL RIGHT, START RUNNING!
GET WAY OUT! WAY OUT!
BONK!
OKAY, NOW HERE'S WHAT YOU DID WRONG...
I KNOW WHAT I DID WRONG! I NEVER SHOULD HAVE SPOKEN TO YOU YEARS AGO! I NEVER SHOULD HAVE LET YOU INTO MY LIFE! I SHOULD HAVE WALKED AWAY! I SHOULD HAVE TOLD YOU TO GET LOST! THAT'S WHAT I DID WRONG, YOU BLOCKHEAD!!
10-23
YOU ALSO PROBABLY SHOULD HOLD YOUR HANDS A LITTLE CLOSER TOGETHER...
SCHULZ

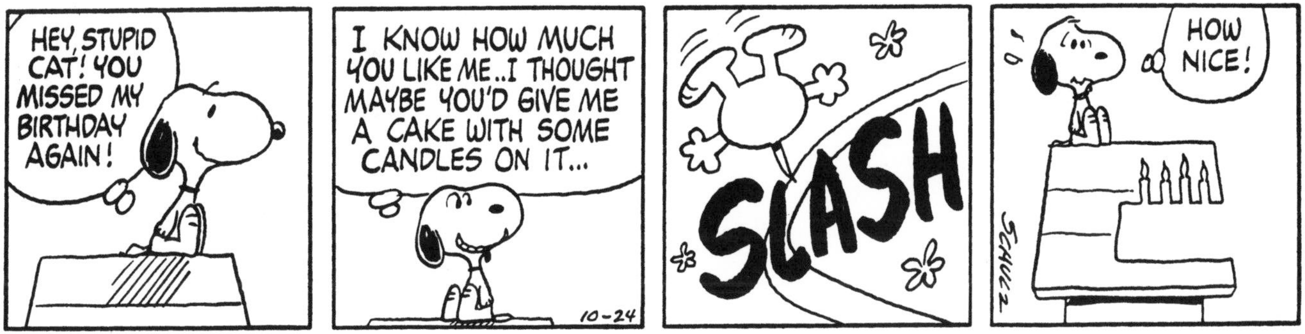
HEY, STUPID CAT! YOU MISSED MY BIRTHDAY AGAIN!
I KNOW HOW MUCH YOU LIKE ME..I THOUGHT MAYBE YOU'D GIVE ME A CAKE WITH SOME CANDLES ON IT...
10-24
SLASH
HOW NICE!
SCHULZ

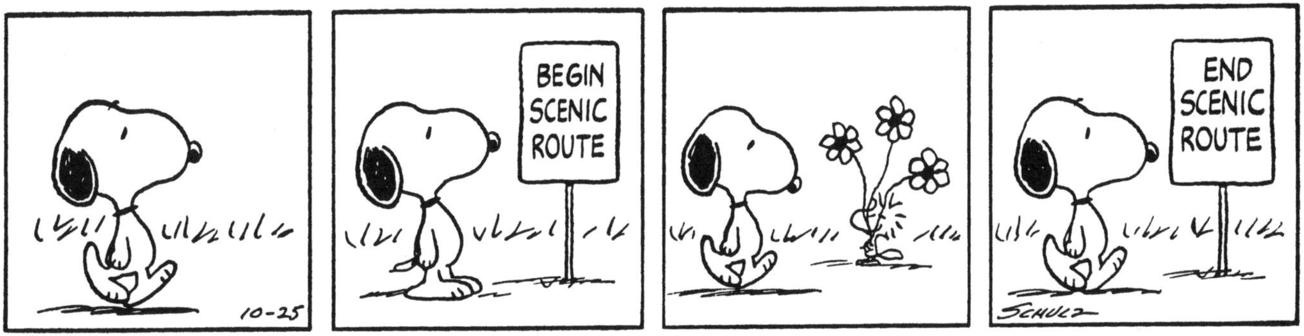
10-25
BEGIN SCENIC ROUTE
END SCENIC ROUTE
SCHULZ

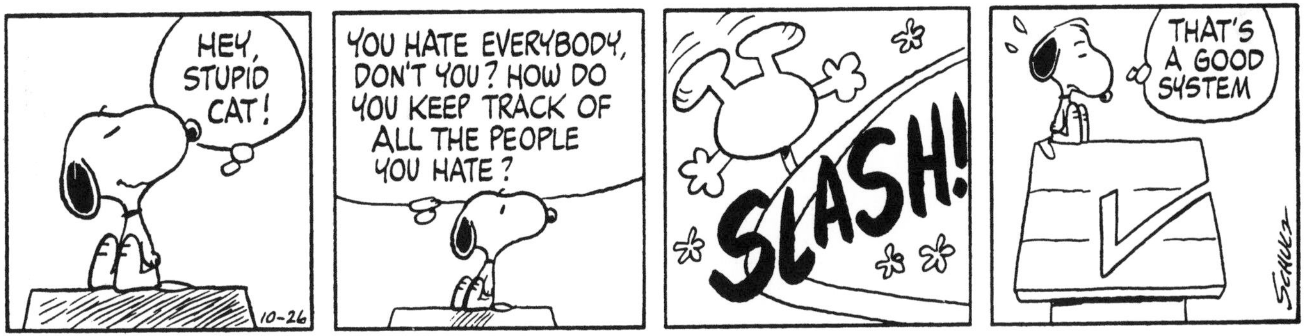
HEY, STUPID CAT!
10-26
YOU HATE EVERYBODY, DON'T YOU? HOW DO YOU KEEP TRACK OF ALL THE PEOPLE YOU HATE?
SLASH!
THAT'S A GOOD SYSTEM
SCHULZ

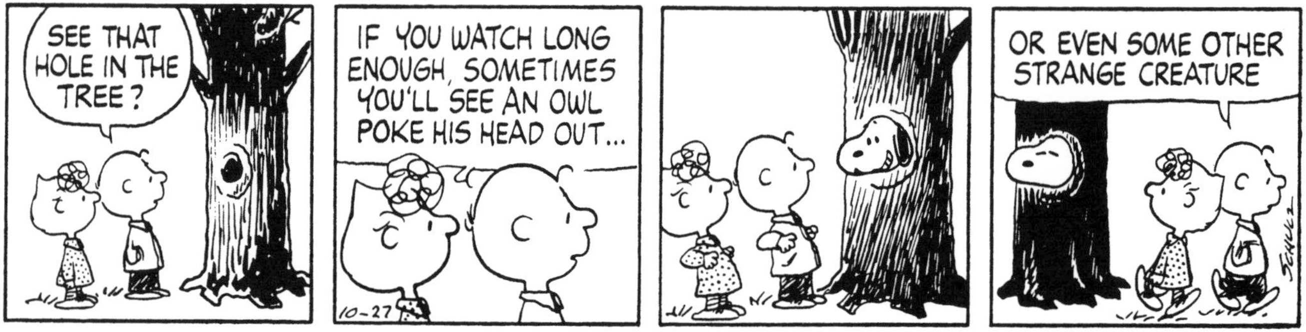
SEE THAT HOLE IN THE TREE?
IF YOU WATCH LONG ENOUGH, SOMETIMES YOU'LL SEE AN OWL POKE HIS HEAD OUT...
OR EVEN SOME OTHER STRANGE CREATURE

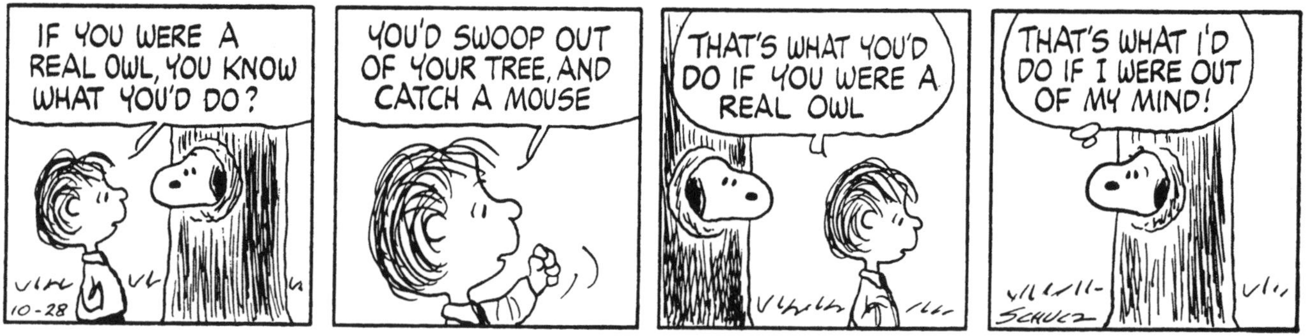
IF YOU WERE A REAL OWL, YOU KNOW WHAT YOU'D DO?
YOU'D SWOOP OUT OF YOUR TREE, AND CATCH A MOUSE
THAT'S WHAT YOU'D DO IF YOU WERE A REAL OWL
THAT'S WHAT I'D DO IF I WERE OUT OF MY MIND!

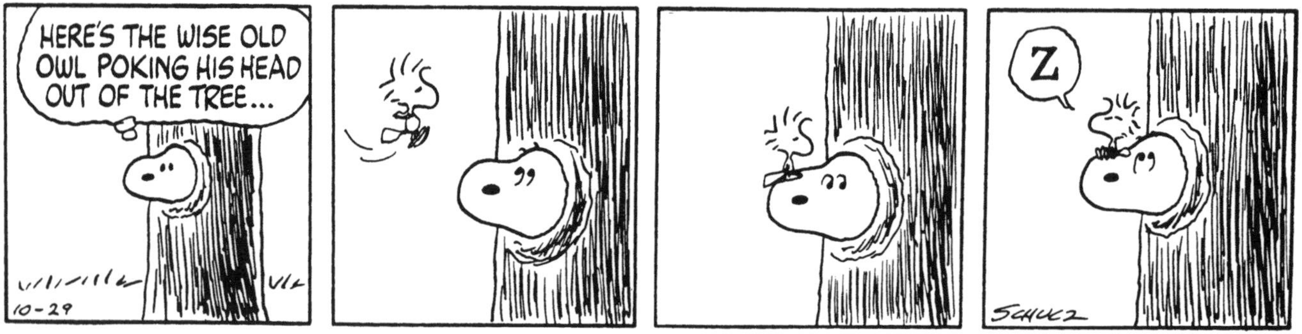
HERE'S THE WISE OLD OWL POKING HIS HEAD OUT OF THE TREE...
Z

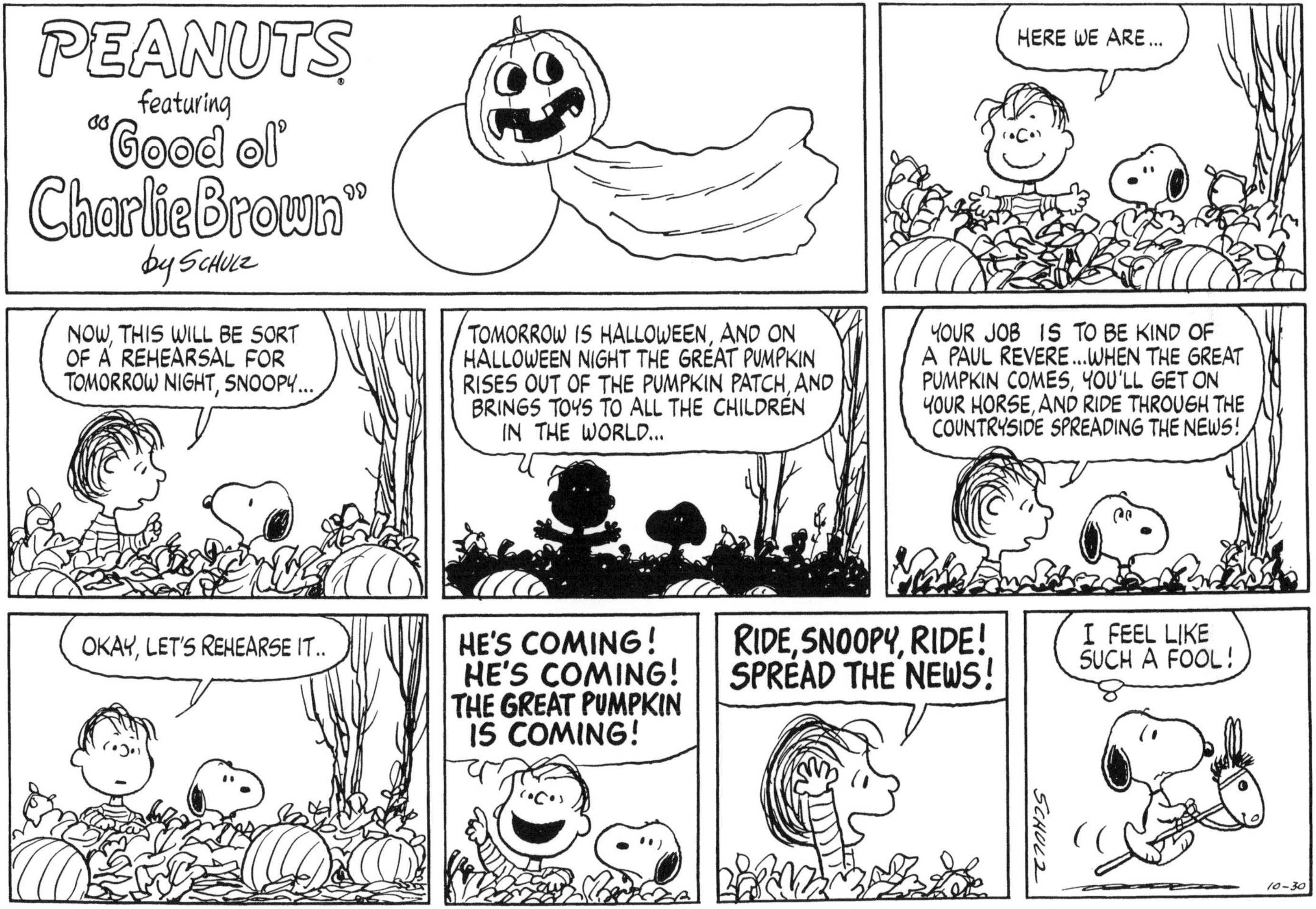
PEANUTS
featuring
"Good ol' CharlieBrown"
by SCHULZ
HERE WE ARE...
NOW, THIS WILL BE SORT OF A REHEARSAL FOR TOMORROW NIGHT, SNOOPY...
TOMORROW IS HALLOWEEN, AND ON HALLOWEEN NIGHT THE GREAT PUMPKIN RISES OUT OF THE PUMPKIN PATCH, AND BRINGS TOYS TO ALL THE CHILDREN IN THE WORLD...
YOUR JOB IS TO BE KIND OF A PAUL REVERE...WHEN THE GREAT PUMPKIN COMES, YOU'LL GET ON YOUR HORSE, AND RIDE THROUGH THE COUNTRYSIDE SPREADING THE NEWS!
OKAY, LET'S REHEARSE IT..
HE'S COMING! HE'S COMING! THE GREAT PUMPKIN IS COMING!
RIDE, SNOOPY, RIDE! SPREAD THE NEWS!
SCHULZ
I FEEL LIKE SUCH A FOOL!
10-30

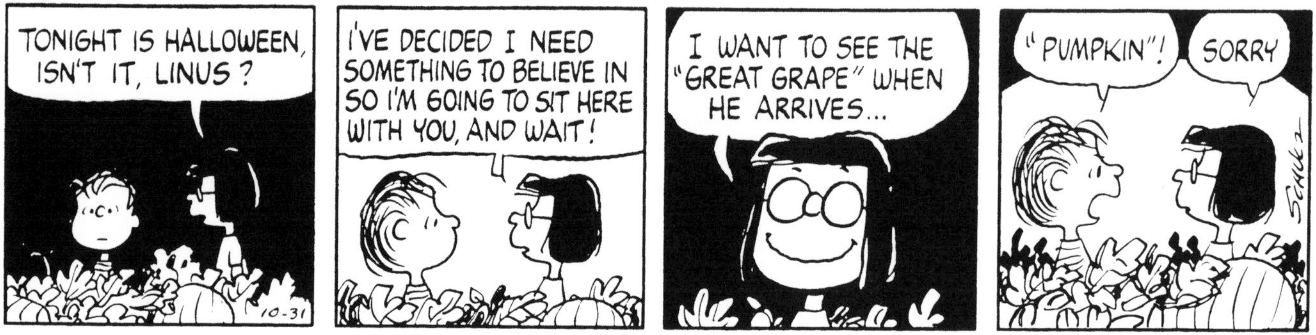
TONIGHT IS HALLOWEEN, ISN'T IT, LINUS ?
10-31
I'VE DECIDED I NEED SOMETHING TO BELIEVE IN SO I'M GOING TO SIT HERE WITH YOU, AND WAIT !
I WANT TO SEE THE "GREAT GRAPE" WHEN HE ARRIVES...
"PUMPKIN"!
SORRY
SCHULZ

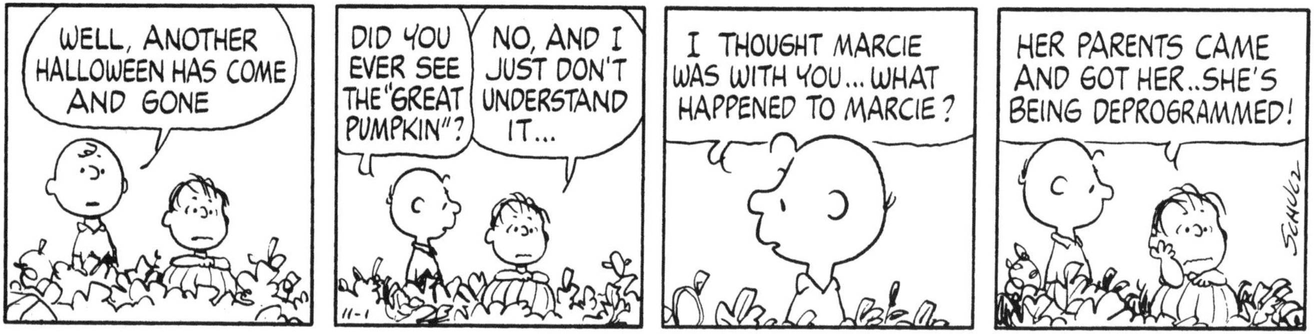
WELL, ANOTHER HALLOWEEN HAS COME AND GONE
DID YOU EVER SEE THE "GREAT PUMPKIN"?
NO, AND I JUST DON'T UNDERSTAND IT...
11-1
I THOUGHT MARCIE WAS WITH YOU... WHAT HAPPENED TO MARCIE ?
HER PARENTS CAME AND GOT HER..SHE'S BEING DEPROGRAMMED!
SCHULZ

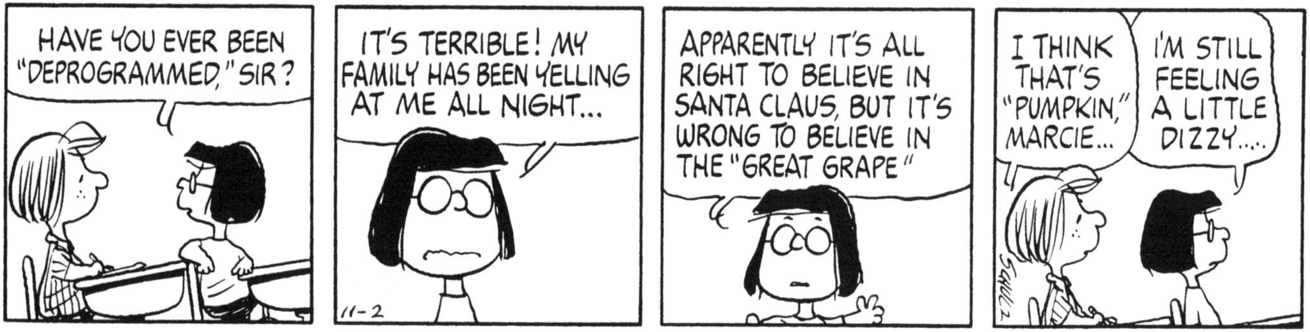
HAVE YOU EVER BEEN "DEPROGRAMMED," SIR ?
IT'S TERRIBLE! MY FAMILY HAS BEEN YELLING AT ME ALL NIGHT...
11-2
APPARENTLY IT'S ALL RIGHT TO BELIEVE IN SANTA CLAUS, BUT IT'S WRONG TO BELIEVE IN THE "GREAT GRAPE"
I THINK THAT'S "PUMPKIN," MARCIE...
I'M STILL FEELING A LITTLE DIZZY.....
SCHULZ

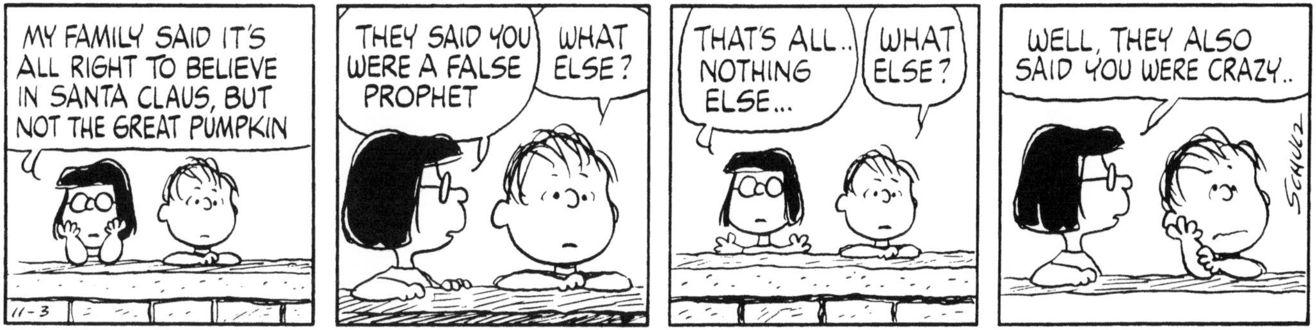
MY FAMILY SAID IT'S ALL RIGHT TO BELIEVE IN SANTA CLAUS, BUT NOT THE GREAT PUMPKIN
11-3
THEY SAID YOU WERE A FALSE PROPHET
WHAT ELSE?
THAT'S ALL.. NOTHING ELSE...
WHAT ELSE?
WELL, THEY ALSO SAID YOU WERE CRAZY..
SCHULZ

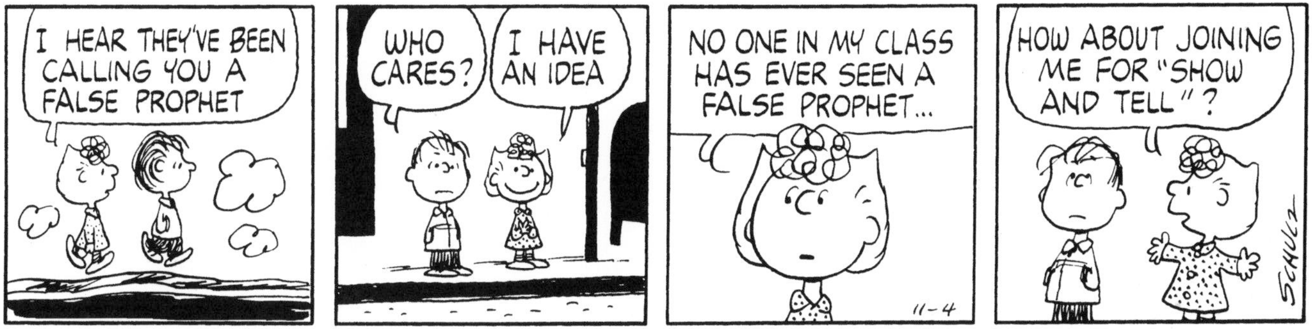
I HEAR THEY'VE BEEN CALLING YOU A FALSE PROPHET
WHO CARES?
I HAVE AN IDEA
NO ONE IN MY CLASS HAS EVER SEEN A FALSE PROPHET...
11-4
HOW ABOUT JOINING ME FOR "SHOW AND TELL"?
SCHULZ

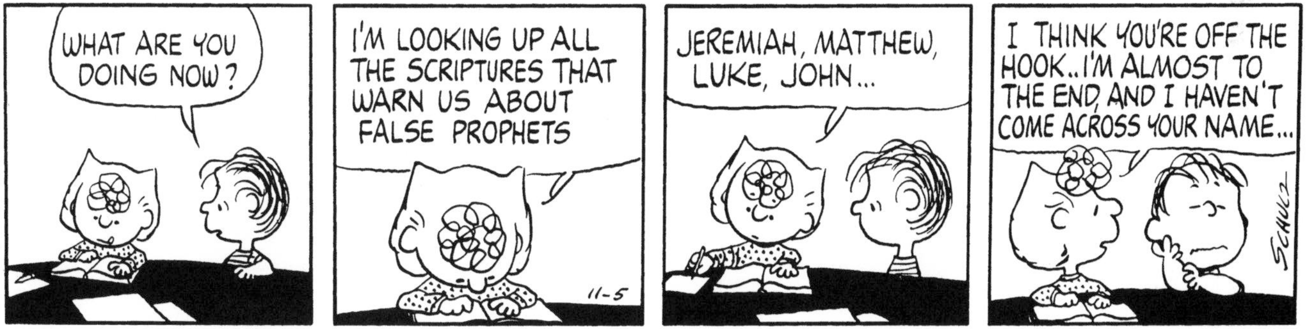
WHAT ARE YOU DOING NOW?
I'M LOOKING UP ALL THE SCRIPTURES THAT WARN US ABOUT FALSE PROPHETS
11-5
JEREMIAH, MATTHEW, LUKE, JOHN...
I THINK YOU'RE OFF THE HOOK..I'M ALMOST TO THE END, AND I HAVEN'T COME ACROSS YOUR NAME...
SCHULZ

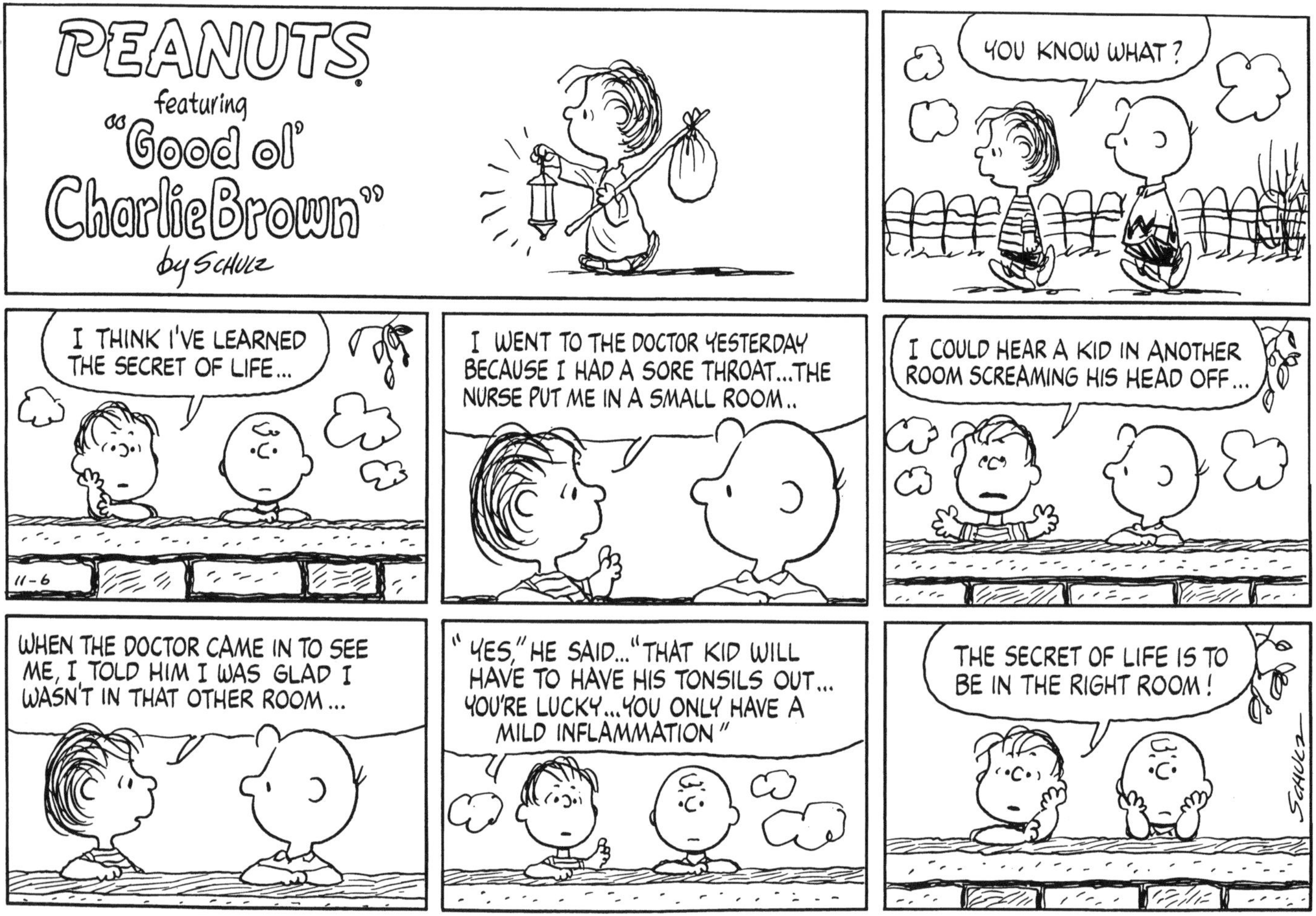
PEANUTS
featuring
"Good ol' Charlie Brown"
by SCHULZ
YOU KNOW WHAT?
I THINK I'VE LEARNED THE SECRET OF LIFE...
11-6
I WENT TO THE DOCTOR YESTERDAY BECAUSE I HAD A SORE THROAT...THE NURSE PUT ME IN A SMALL ROOM..
I COULD HEAR A KID IN ANOTHER ROOM SCREAMING HIS HEAD OFF...
WHEN THE DOCTOR CAME IN TO SEE ME, I TOLD HIM I WAS GLAD I WASN'T IN THAT OTHER ROOM...
"YES," HE SAID..."THAT KID WILL HAVE TO HAVE HIS TONSILS OUT... YOU'RE LUCKY...YOU ONLY HAVE A MILD INFLAMMATION"
THE SECRET OF LIFE IS TO BE IN THE RIGHT ROOM!
SCHULZ

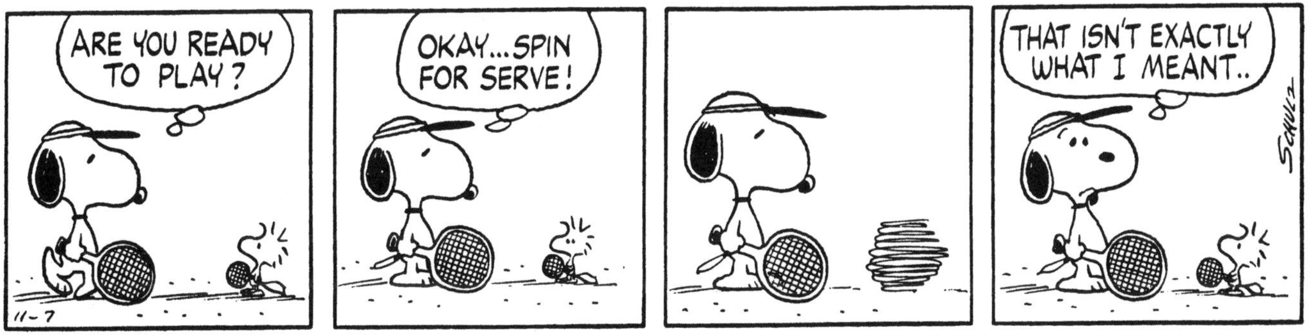
ARE YOU READY TO PLAY?
OKAY...SPIN FOR SERVE!
THAT ISN'T EXACTLY WHAT I MEANT..

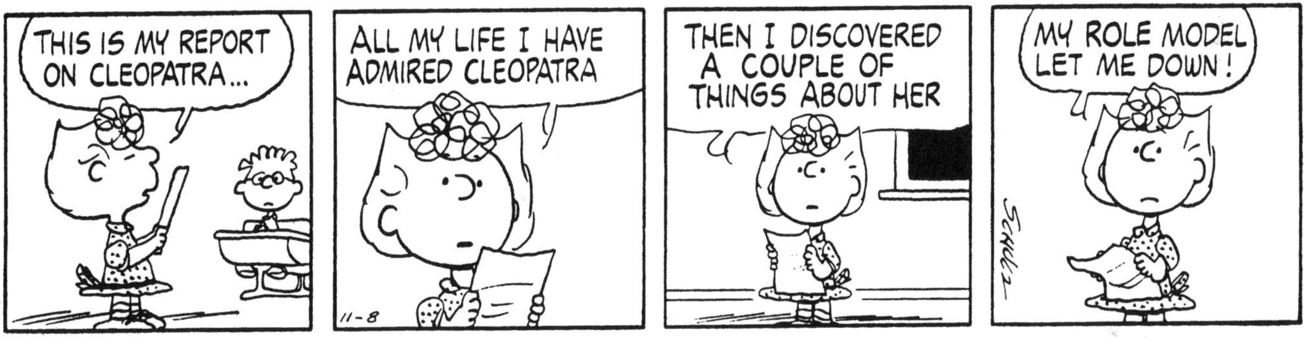
THIS IS MY REPORT ON CLEOPATRA...
ALL MY LIFE I HAVE ADMIRED CLEOPATRA
THEN I DISCOVERED A COUPLE OF THINGS ABOUT HER
MY ROLE MODEL LET ME DOWN!

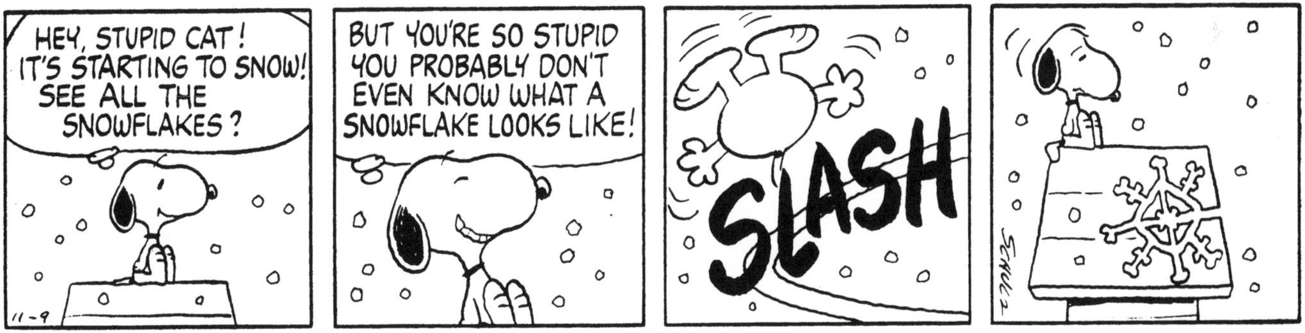
HEY, STUPID CAT! IT'S STARTING TO SNOW! SEE ALL THE SNOWFLAKES?
BUT YOU'RE SO STUPID YOU PROBABLY DON'T EVEN KNOW WHAT A SNOWFLAKE LOOKS LIKE!
SLASH

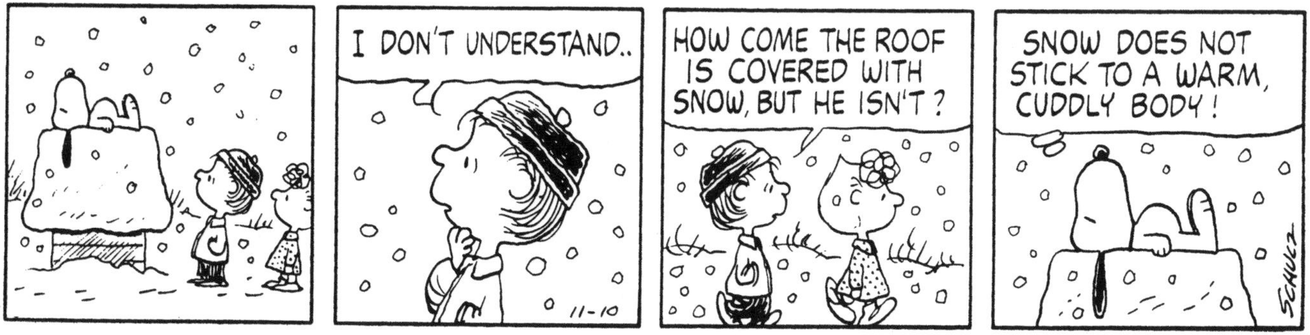
I DON'T UNDERSTAND..
11-10
HOW COME THE ROOF IS COVERED WITH SNOW, BUT HE ISN'T ?
SNOW DOES NOT STICK TO A WARM, CUDDLY BODY !
SCHULZ

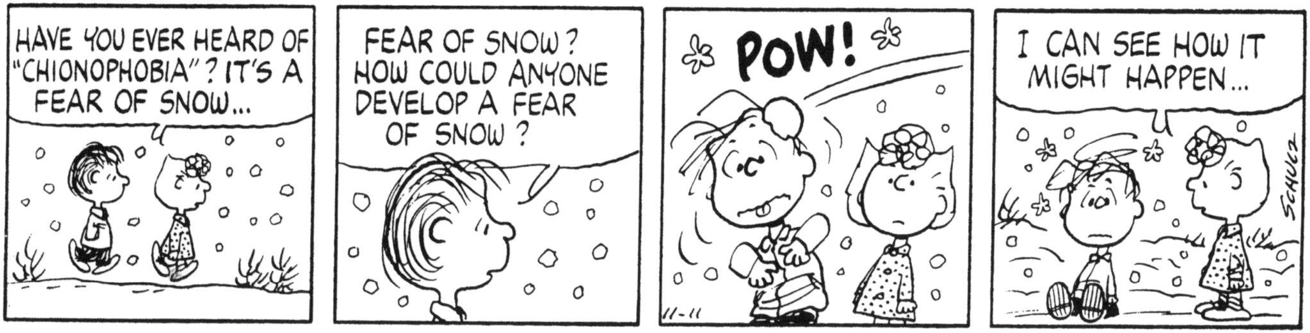
HAVE YOU EVER HEARD OF "CHIONOPHOBIA"? IT'S A FEAR OF SNOW...
FEAR OF SNOW? HOW COULD ANYONE DEVELOP A FEAR OF SNOW ?
POW!
11-11
I CAN SEE HOW IT MIGHT HAPPEN...
SCHULZ

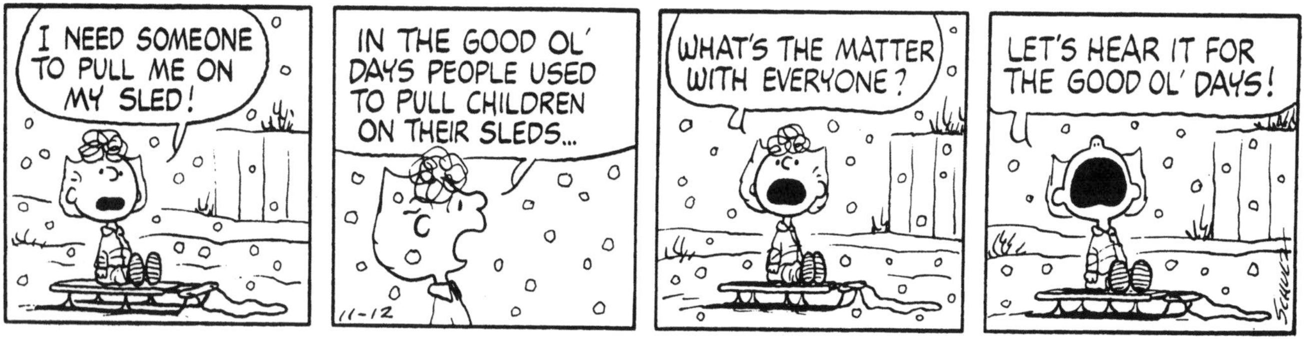
I NEED SOMEONE TO PULL ME ON MY SLED!
IN THE GOOD OL' DAYS PEOPLE USED TO PULL CHILDREN ON THEIR SLEDS...
11-12
WHAT'S THE MATTER WITH EVERYONE?
LET'S HEAR IT FOR THE GOOD OL' DAYS!
SCHULZ

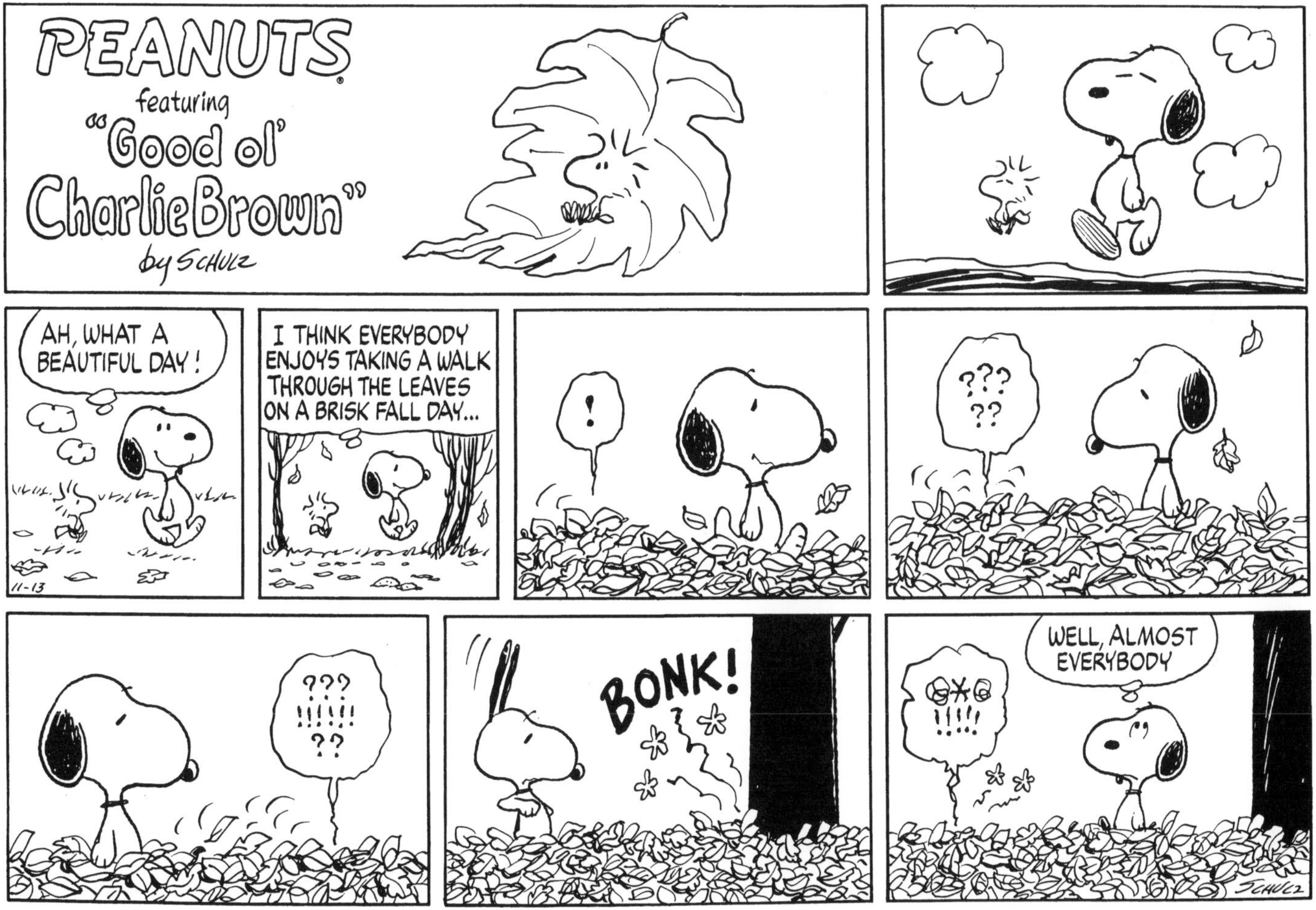
PEANUTS
featuring
"Good ol' Charlie Brown"
by SCHULZ
AH, WHAT A BEAUTIFUL DAY!
11-13
I THINK EVERYBODY ENJOYS TAKING A WALK THROUGH THE LEAVES ON A BRISK FALL DAY...
!
???
??
???
!!!!!!
??
BONK!
!!!!!
WELL, ALMOST EVERYBODY
SCHULZ

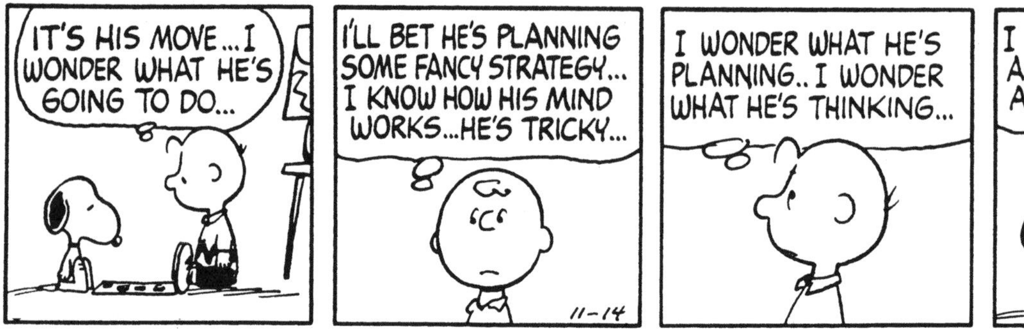
IT'S HIS MOVE...I WONDER WHAT HE'S GOING TO DO...
I'LL BET HE'S PLANNING SOME FANCY STRATEGY... I KNOW HOW HIS MIND WORKS...HE'S TRICKY...
11-14
I WONDER WHAT HE'S PLANNING.. I WONDER WHAT HE'S THINKING...
I NEVER CAN REMEMBER.. AM I THE RED, OR AM I THE BLACK?
SCHULZ

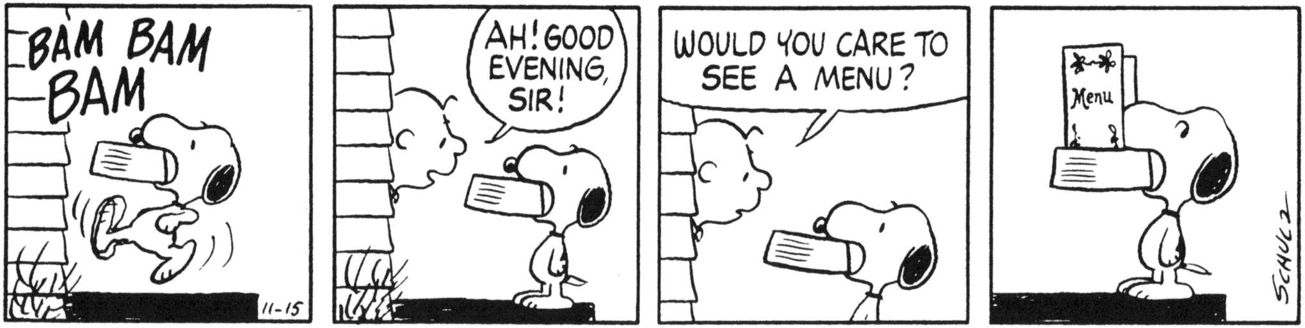
BAM BAM BAM BAM
11-15
AH! GOOD EVENING, SIR!
WOULD YOU CARE TO SEE A MENU?
Menu
SCHULZ

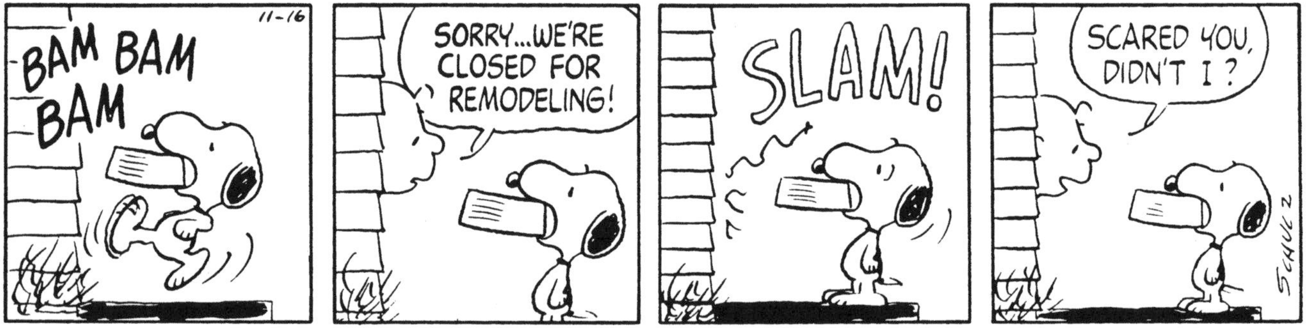
11-16
BAM BAM BAM BAM
SORRY...WE'RE CLOSED FOR REMODELING!
SLAM!
SCARED YOU, DIDN'T I?
SCHULZ

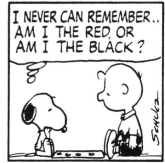

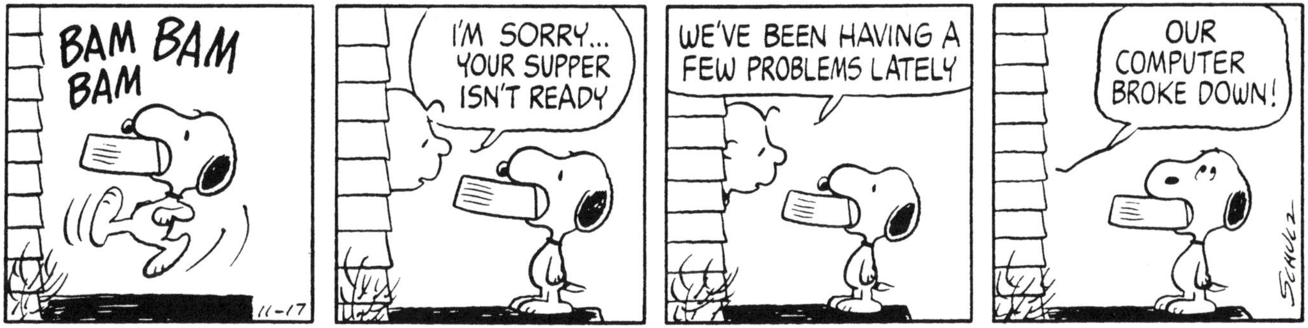
BAM BAM
BAM
11-17
I'M SORRY... YOUR SUPPER ISN'T READY
WE'VE BEEN HAVING A FEW PROBLEMS LATELY
OUR COMPUTER BROKE DOWN!

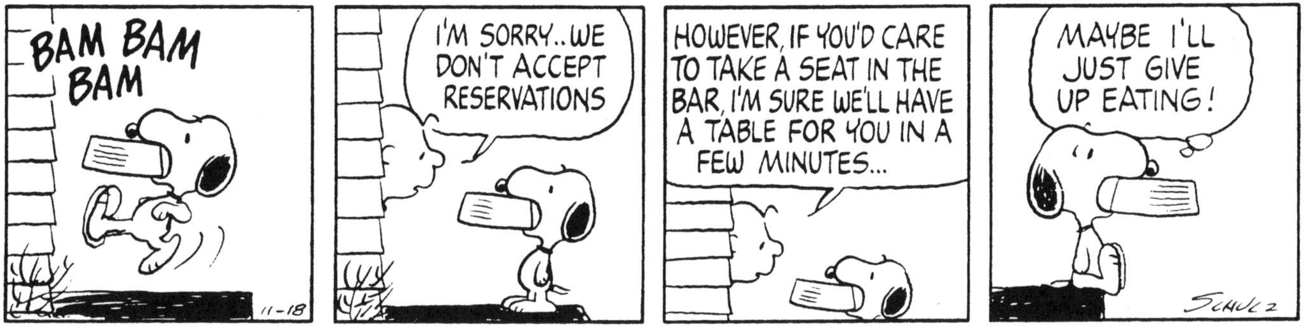
BAM BAM
BAM
11-18
I'M SORRY..WE DON'T ACCEPT RESERVATIONS
HOWEVER, IF YOU'D CARE TO TAKE A SEAT IN THE BAR, I'M SURE WE'LL HAVE A TABLE FOR YOU IN A FEW MINUTES...
MAYBE I'LL JUST GIVE UP EATING!

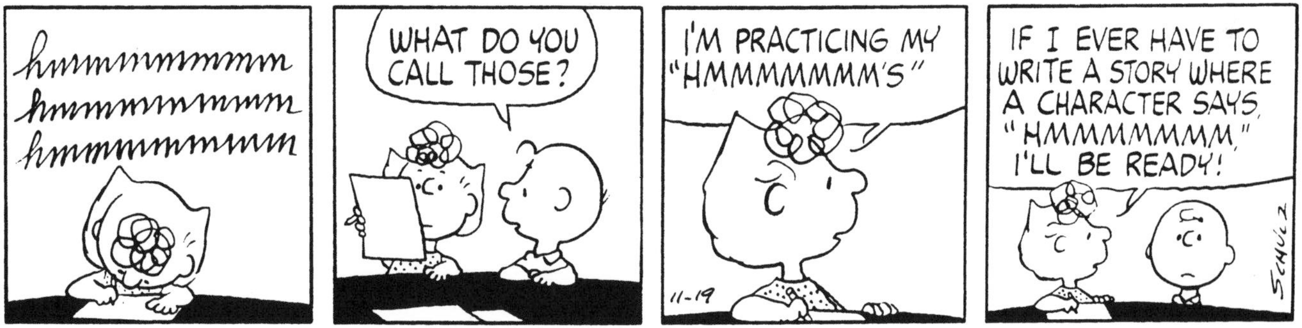
hmmmmmmmm
hmmmmmmmm
hmmmmmmmm
WHAT DO YOU CALL THOSE?
I'M PRACTICING MY "HMMMMMMM'S"
11-19
IF I EVER HAVE TO WRITE A STORY WHERE A CHARACTER SAYS, "HMMMMMMM," I'LL BE READY!

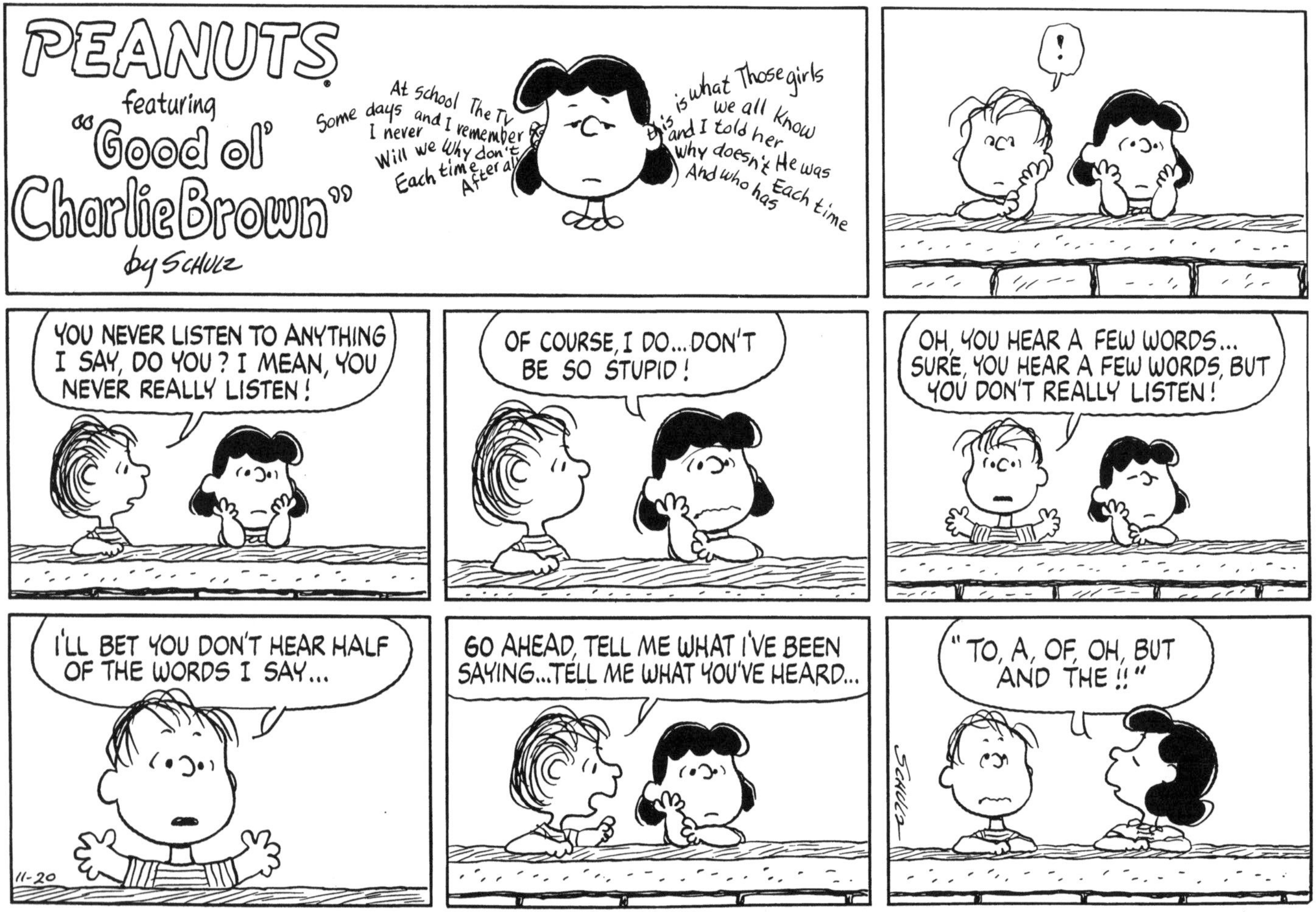
PEANUTS
featuring
"Good ol' Charlie Brown"
by SCHULZ
At school The TV
Some days and I remember
I never
Will we Why don't
Each time After all
this is what Those girls
we all Know
and I told her
Why doesn't He was
And who has Each time
!
YOU NEVER LISTEN TO ANYTHING I SAY, DO YOU? I MEAN, YOU NEVER REALLY LISTEN!
OF COURSE, I DO...DON'T BE SO STUPID!
OH, YOU HEAR A FEW WORDS... SURE, YOU HEAR A FEW WORDS, BUT YOU DON'T REALLY LISTEN!
I'LL BET YOU DON'T HEAR HALF OF THE WORDS I SAY...
11-20
GO AHEAD, TELL ME WHAT I'VE BEEN SAYING...TELL ME WHAT YOU'VE HEARD...
SCHULZ
"TO, A, OF, OH, BUT AND THE!!"

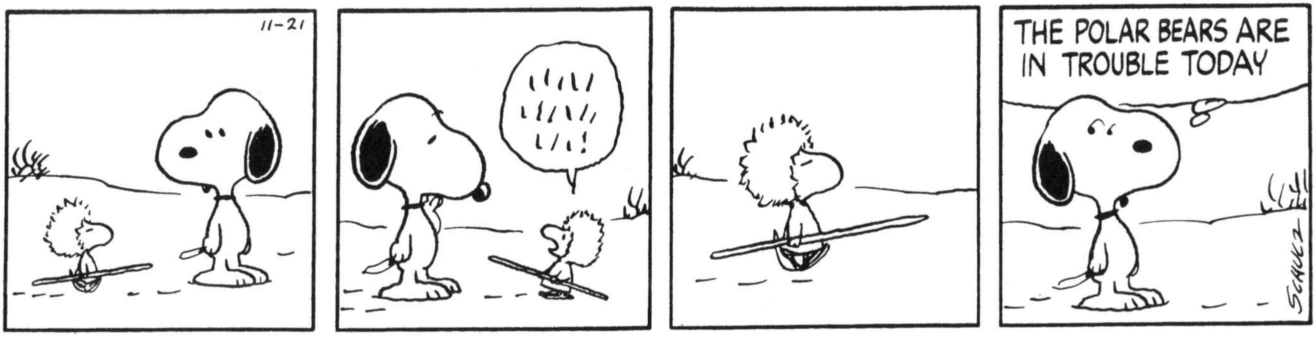
11-21
THE POLAR BEARS ARE IN TROUBLE TODAY

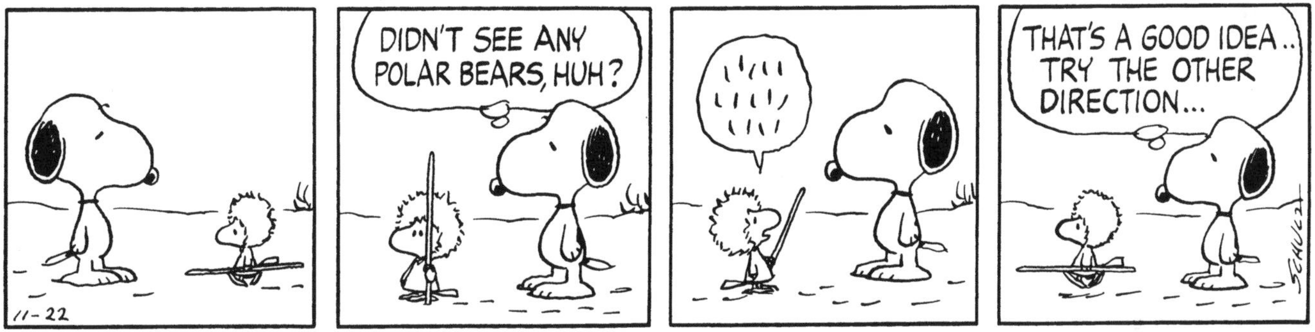
11-22
DIDN'T SEE ANY POLAR BEARS, HUH?
THAT'S A GOOD IDEA.. TRY THE OTHER DIRECTION...

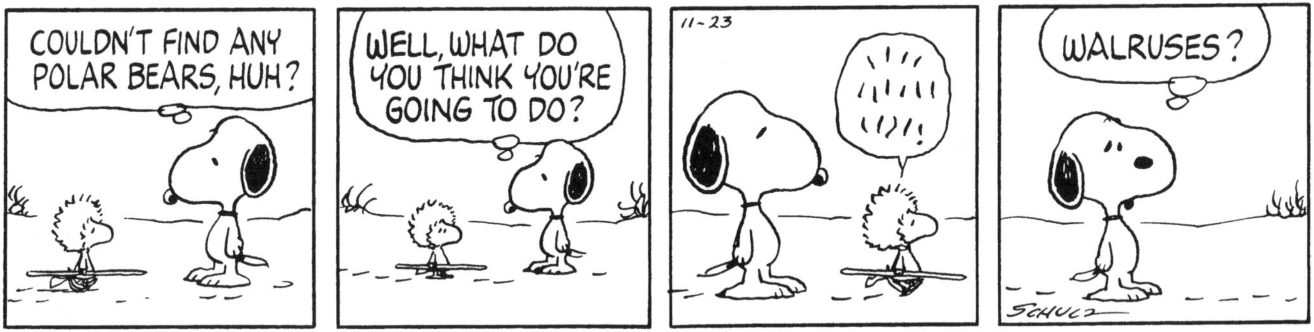
COULDN'T FIND ANY POLAR BEARS, HUH?
WELL, WHAT DO YOU THINK YOU'RE GOING TO DO?
11-23
WALRUSES?

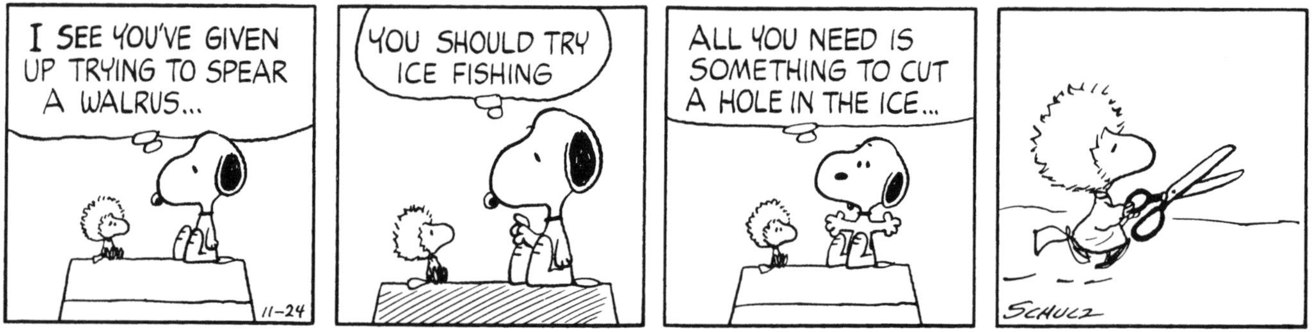
I SEE YOU'VE GIVEN UP TRYING TO SPEAR A WALRUS...
11-24
YOU SHOULD TRY ICE FISHING
ALL YOU NEED IS SOMETHING TO CUT A HOLE IN THE ICE...
SCHULZ

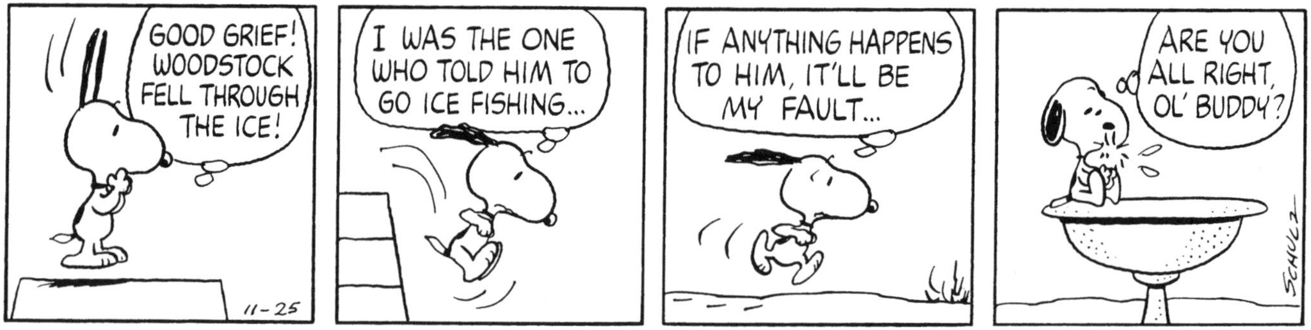
GOOD GRIEF! WOODSTOCK FELL THROUGH THE ICE!
11-25
I WAS THE ONE WHO TOLD HIM TO GO ICE FISHING...
IF ANYTHING HAPPENS TO HIM, IT'LL BE MY FAULT...
ARE YOU ALL RIGHT, OL' BUDDY?
SCHULZ

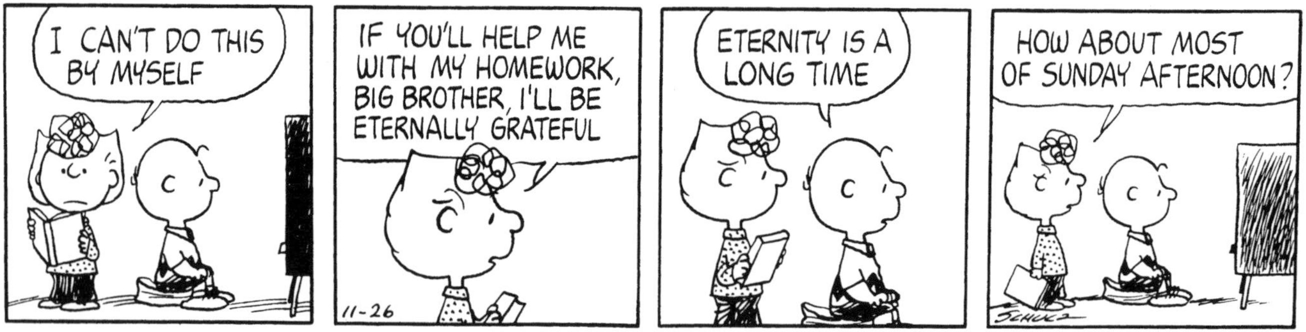
I CAN'T DO THIS BY MYSELF
IF YOU'LL HELP ME WITH MY HOMEWORK, BIG BROTHER, I'LL BE ETERNALLY GRATEFUL
11-26
ETERNITY IS A LONG TIME
HOW ABOUT MOST OF SUNDAY AFTERNOON?
SCHULZ

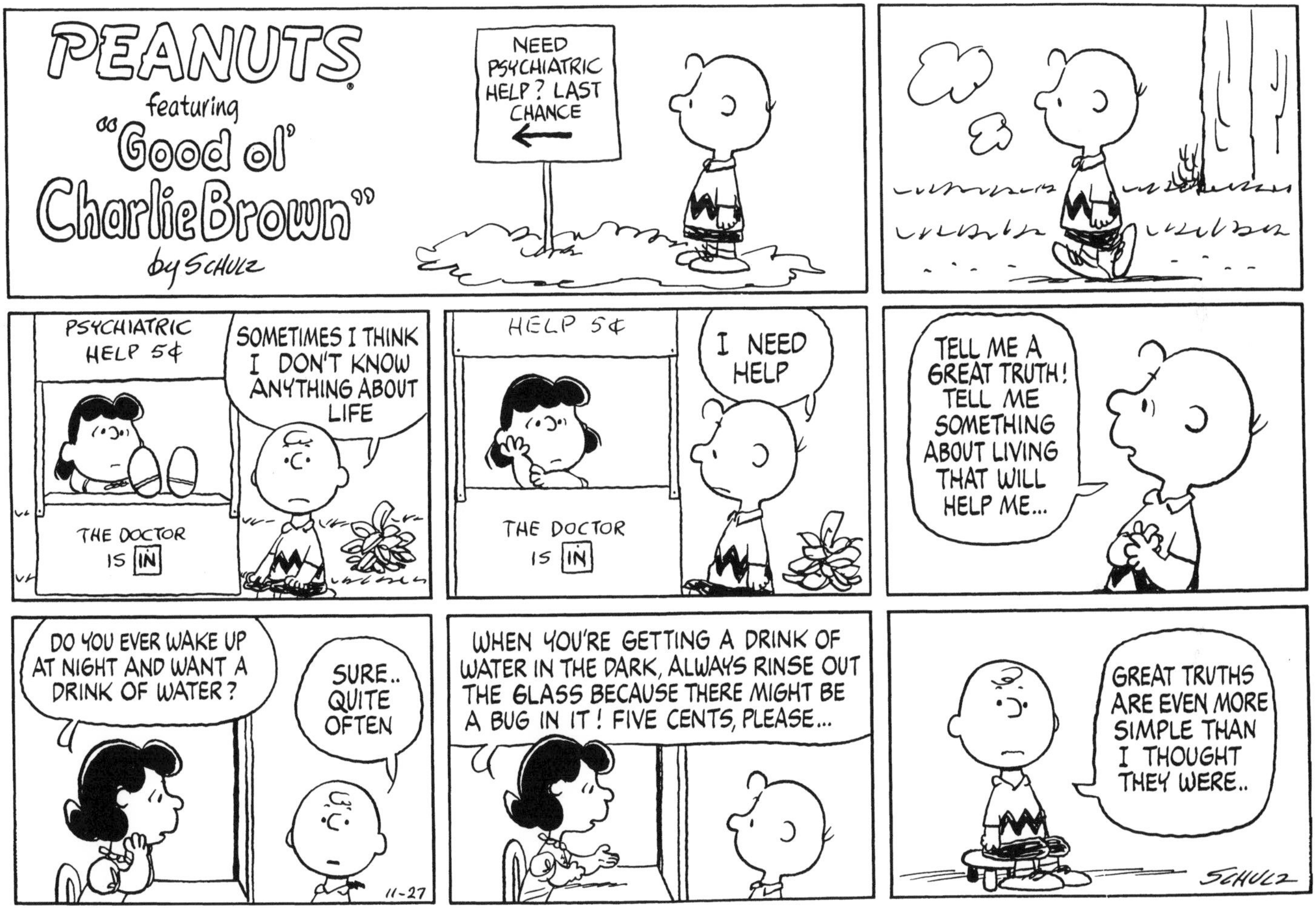
PEANUTS
featuring "Good ol' Charlie Brown" by SCHULZ
NEED PSYCHIATRIC HELP? LAST CHANCE
PSYCHIATRIC HELP 5¢
THE DOCTOR IS IN
SOMETIMES I THINK I DON'T KNOW ANYTHING ABOUT LIFE
HELP 5¢
THE DOCTOR IS IN
I NEED HELP
TELL ME A GREAT TRUTH! TELL ME SOMETHING ABOUT LIVING THAT WILL HELP ME...
DO YOU EVER WAKE UP AT NIGHT AND WANT A DRINK OF WATER?
SURE.. QUITE OFTEN
11-27
WHEN YOU'RE GETTING A DRINK OF WATER IN THE DARK, ALWAYS RINSE OUT THE GLASS BECAUSE THERE MIGHT BE A BUG IN IT! FIVE CENTS, PLEASE...
GREAT TRUTHS ARE EVEN MORE SIMPLE THAN I THOUGHT THEY WERE..
SCHULZ

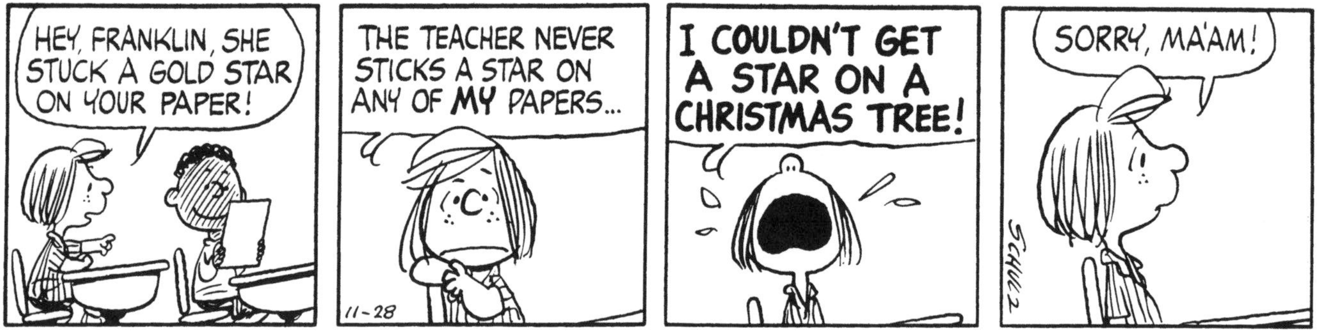
HEY, FRANKLIN, SHE STUCK A GOLD STAR ON YOUR PAPER!
THE TEACHER NEVER STICKS A STAR ON ANY OF MY PAPERS...
11-28
I COULDN'T GET A STAR ON A CHRISTMAS TREE!
SORRY, MA'AM!
SCHULZ

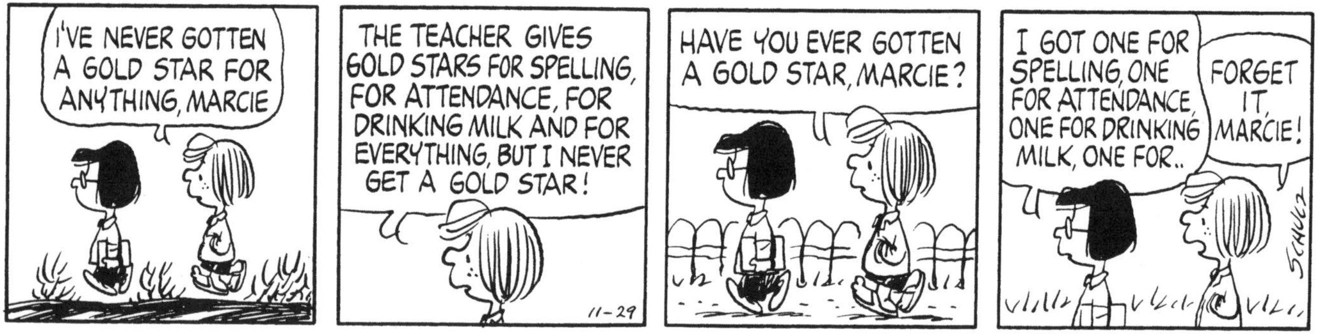
I'VE NEVER GOTTEN A GOLD STAR FOR ANYTHING, MARCIE
THE TEACHER GIVES GOLD STARS FOR SPELLING, FOR ATTENDANCE, FOR DRINKING MILK AND FOR EVERYTHING, BUT I NEVER GET A GOLD STAR!
11-29
HAVE YOU EVER GOTTEN A GOLD STAR, MARCIE?
I GOT ONE FOR SPELLING, ONE FOR ATTENDANCE, ONE FOR DRINKING MILK, ONE FOR..
FORGET IT, MARCIE!
SCHULZ

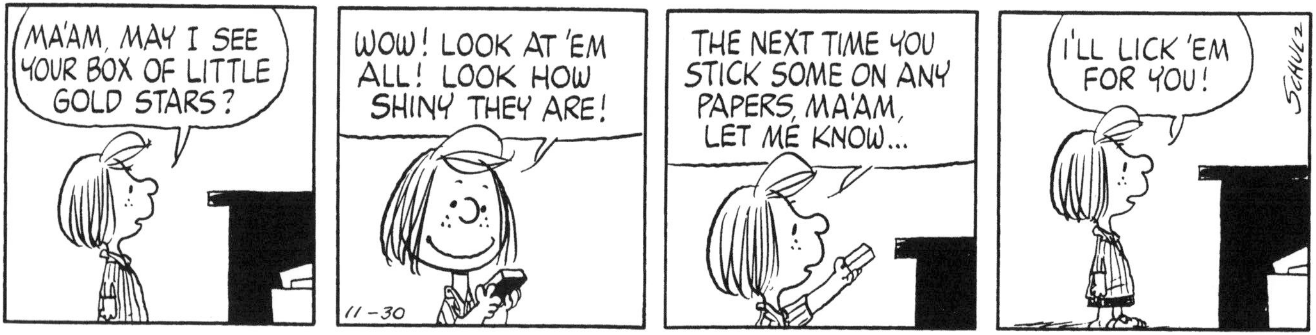
MA'AM, MAY I SEE YOUR BOX OF LITTLE GOLD STARS?
WOW! LOOK AT 'EM ALL! LOOK HOW SHINY THEY ARE!
11-30
THE NEXT TIME YOU STICK SOME ON ANY PAPERS, MA'AM, LET ME KNOW...
I'LL LICK 'EM FOR YOU!
SCHULZ

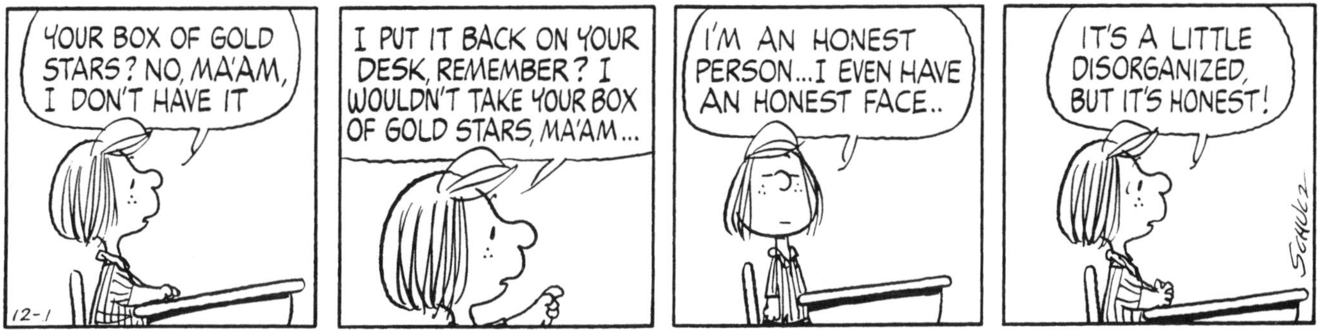
YOUR BOX OF GOLD STARS? NO, MA'AM, I DON'T HAVE IT
12-1
I PUT IT BACK ON YOUR DESK, REMEMBER? I WOULDN'T TAKE YOUR BOX OF GOLD STARS, MA'AM...
I'M AN HONEST PERSON...I EVEN HAVE AN HONEST FACE..
IT'S A LITTLE DISORGANIZED, BUT IT'S HONEST!

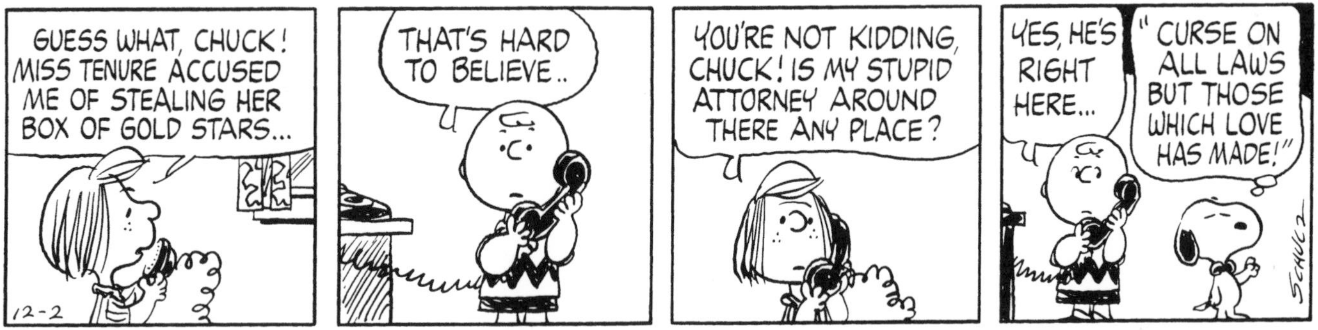
GUESS WHAT, CHUCK! MISS TENURE ACCUSED ME OF STEALING HER BOX OF GOLD STARS...
12-2
THAT'S HARD TO BELIEVE..
YOU'RE NOT KIDDING, CHUCK! IS MY STUPID ATTORNEY AROUND THERE ANY PLACE?
YES, HE'S RIGHT HERE...
" CURSE ON ALL LAWS BUT THOSE WHICH LOVE HAS MADE!"

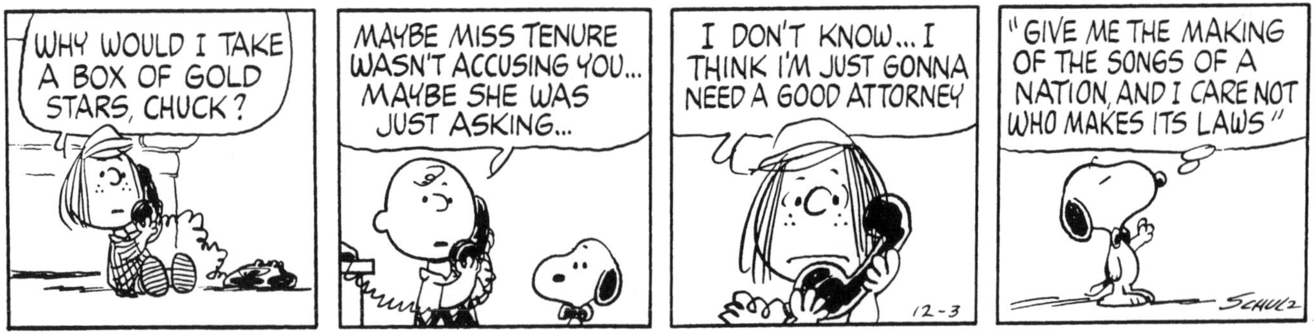
WHY WOULD I TAKE A BOX OF GOLD STARS, CHUCK?
MAYBE MISS TENURE WASN'T ACCUSING YOU... MAYBE SHE WAS JUST ASKING...
I DON'T KNOW... I THINK I'M JUST GONNA NEED A GOOD ATTORNEY
12-3
" GIVE ME THE MAKING OF THE SONGS OF A NATION, AND I CARE NOT WHO MAKES ITS LAWS "

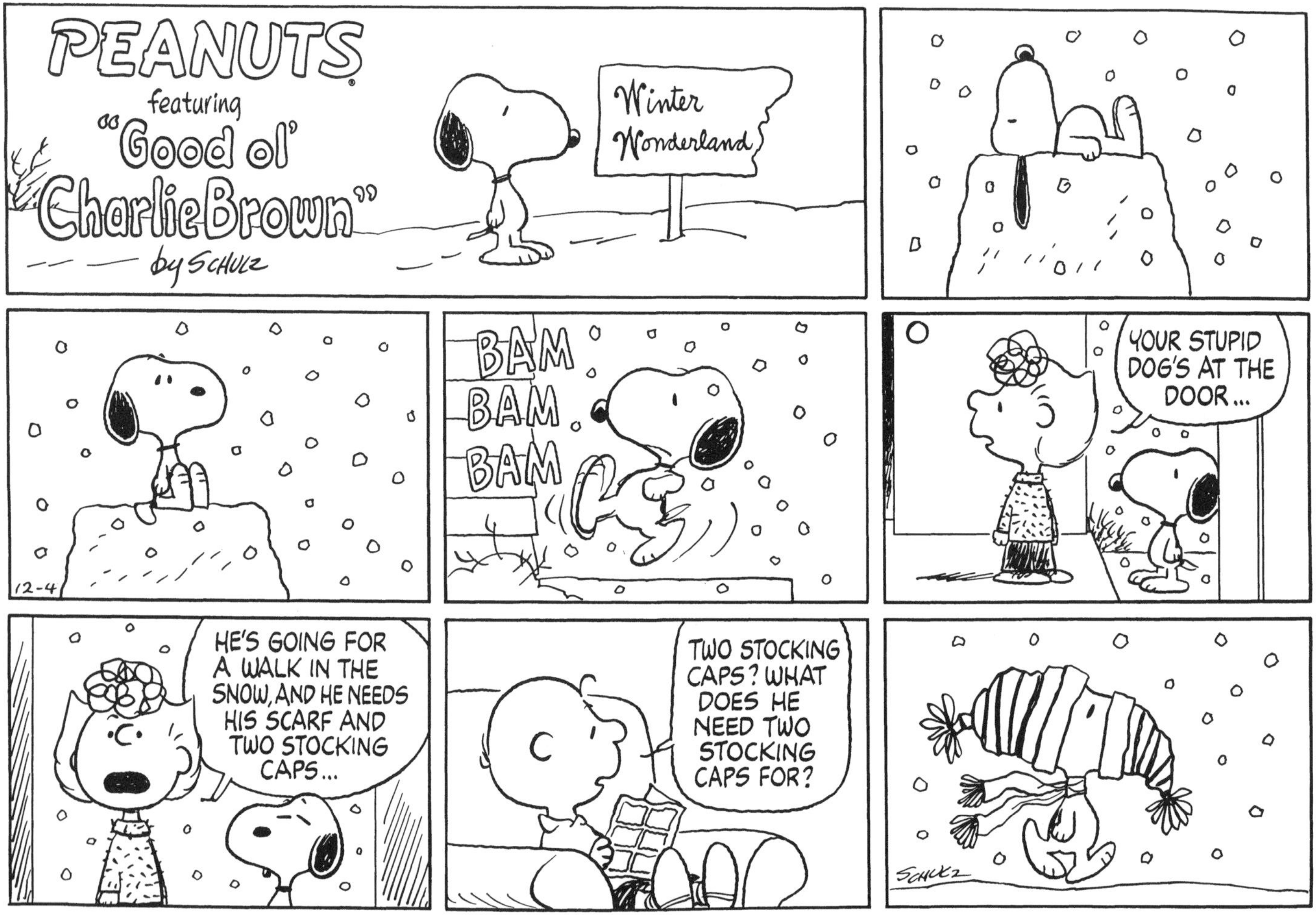
PEANUTS
featuring
"Good ol' Charlie Brown"
by SCHULZ
Winter Wonderland
12-4
BAM
BAM
BAM
YOUR STUPID DOG'S AT THE DOOR...
HE'S GOING FOR A WALK IN THE SNOW, AND HE NEEDS HIS SCARF AND TWO STOCKING CAPS...
TWO STOCKING CAPS? WHAT DOES HE NEED TWO STOCKING CAPS FOR?
SCHULZ

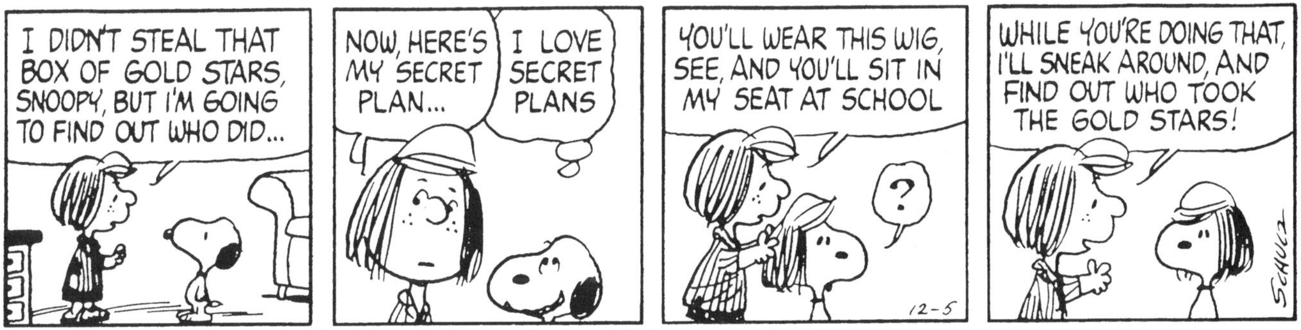
I DIDN'T STEAL THAT BOX OF GOLD STARS, SNOOPY, BUT I'M GOING TO FIND OUT WHO DID...
NOW, HERE'S MY SECRET PLAN...
I LOVE SECRET PLANS
YOU'LL WEAR THIS WIG, SEE, AND YOU'LL SIT IN MY SEAT AT SCHOOL
?
12-5
WHILE YOU'RE DOING THAT, I'LL SNEAK AROUND, AND FIND OUT WHO TOOK THE GOLD STARS!
SCHULZ

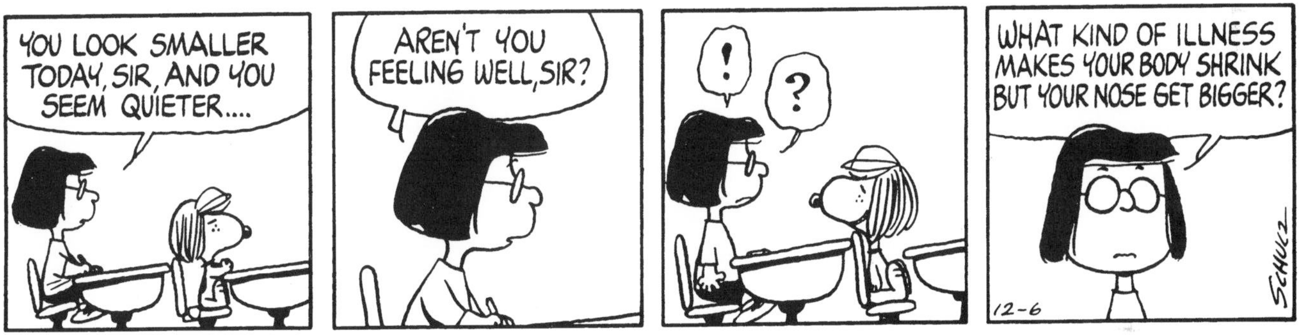
YOU LOOK SMALLER TODAY, SIR, AND YOU SEEM QUIETER....
AREN'T YOU FEELING WELL, SIR?
!
?
WHAT KIND OF ILLNESS MAKES YOUR BODY SHRINK BUT YOUR NOSE GET BIGGER?
SCHULZ
12-6

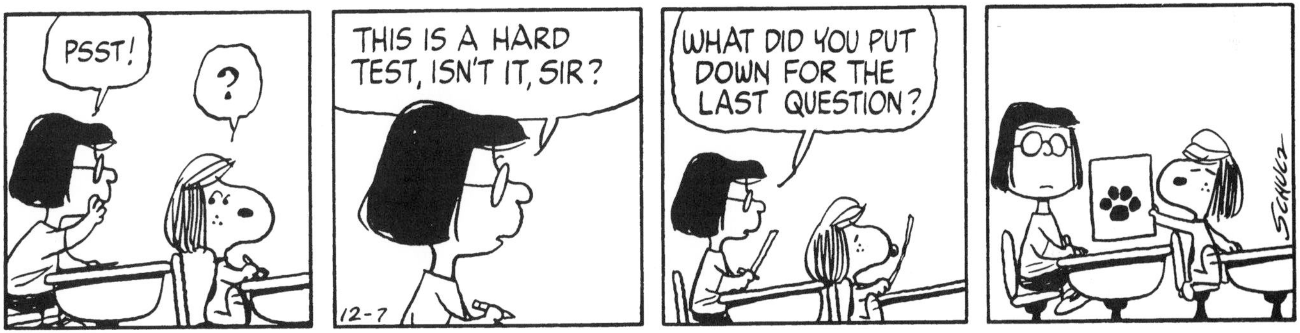
PSST!
?
THIS IS A HARD TEST, ISN'T IT, SIR?
12-7
WHAT DID YOU PUT DOWN FOR THE LAST QUESTION?
SCHULZ

Panel 1:
Marcie: SIR, WHAT ARE YOU DOING OUT HERE IN THE HALLWAY?
Peppermint Patty: QUIET, MARCIE

Panel 2:
Peppermint Patty: I'M IN DISGUISE! I'M TRYING TO FIND OUT WHO TOOK THE BOX OF GOLD STARS...

12-8

Panel 3:
Marcie: BUT I JUST SAW YOU SITTING AT YOUR DESK...
Peppermint Patty: THAT'S MY ATTORNEY... HE'S ALSO IN DISGUISE...

Panel 4:
"I BEFORE E EXCEPT AFTER C"

Panel 5:
Peppermint Patty: YES, MA'AM..I'M HANS HANSEN, THE NEW CUSTODIAN...

12-9

Panel 6:
Peppermint Patty: JUST GO ON WITH YOUR TEACHING, MA'AM..I'LL SWEEP UP A BIT AND EMPTY THE WASTEBASKETS...

Panel 7:
Peppermint Patty: OH, I'M DREAMING OF MY SWEETHEART IN MINNEAPOLIS AND MY MOTHER IN ST. PAUL!

Panel 8:
Peppermint Patty: SORRY, MA'AM..I CAN'T HELP SINGING WHILE I SWEEP...

Panel 9:
Peppermint Patty: LOOK WHAT I FOUND IN YOUR WASTEBASKET, MISS TENURE... YOUR BOX OF GOLD STARS!

12-10

Panel 10:
Peppermint Patty: I'LL BET YOU THOUGHT ONE OF YOUR PUPILS STOLE IT, DIDN'T YOU?

Panel 11:
Peppermint Patty: THEY WOULDN'T DO ANYTHING LIKE THAT... ESPECIALLY THAT CUTE ONE WITH THE BEAUTIFUL HAIR AND THE FRECKLES..

Page 148   *December*

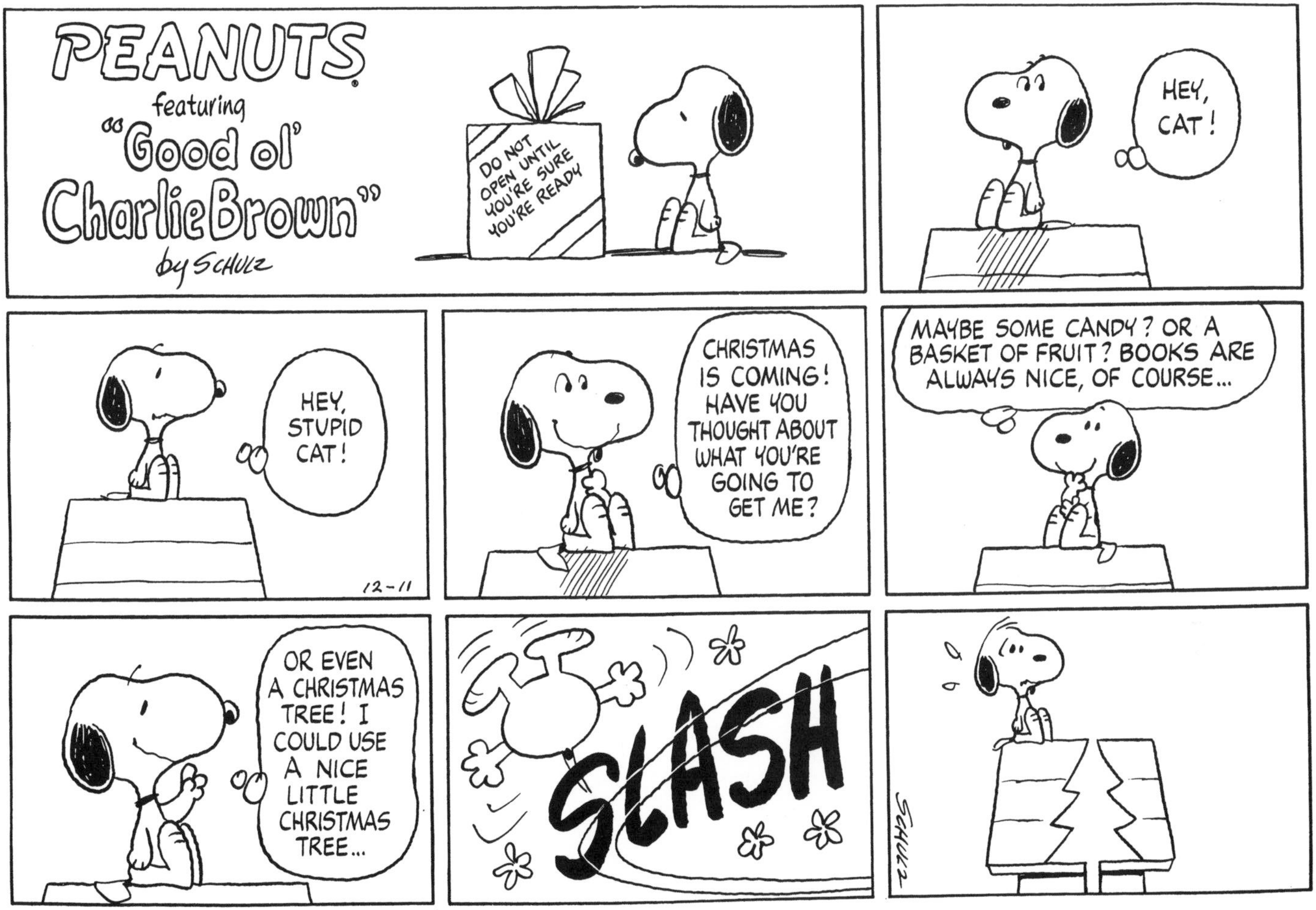
PEANUTS
featuring "Good ol' CharlieBrown"
by SCHULZ
DO NOT OPEN UNTIL YOU'RE SURE YOU'RE READY
HEY, CAT!
HEY, STUPID CAT!
12-11
CHRISTMAS IS COMING! HAVE YOU THOUGHT ABOUT WHAT YOU'RE GOING TO GET ME?
MAYBE SOME CANDY? OR A BASKET OF FRUIT? BOOKS ARE ALWAYS NICE, OF COURSE...
OR EVEN A CHRISTMAS TREE! I COULD USE A NICE LITTLE CHRISTMAS TREE...
SLASH
SCHULZ

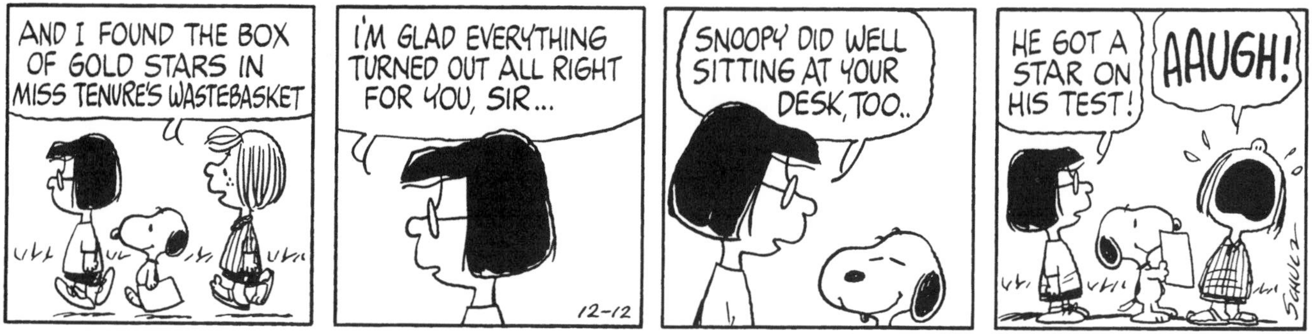
AND I FOUND THE BOX OF GOLD STARS IN MISS TENURE'S WASTEBASKET
I'M GLAD EVERYTHING TURNED OUT ALL RIGHT FOR YOU, SIR...
12-12
SNOOPY DID WELL SITTING AT YOUR DESK, TOO..
HE GOT A STAR ON HIS TEST!
AAUGH!
SCHULZ

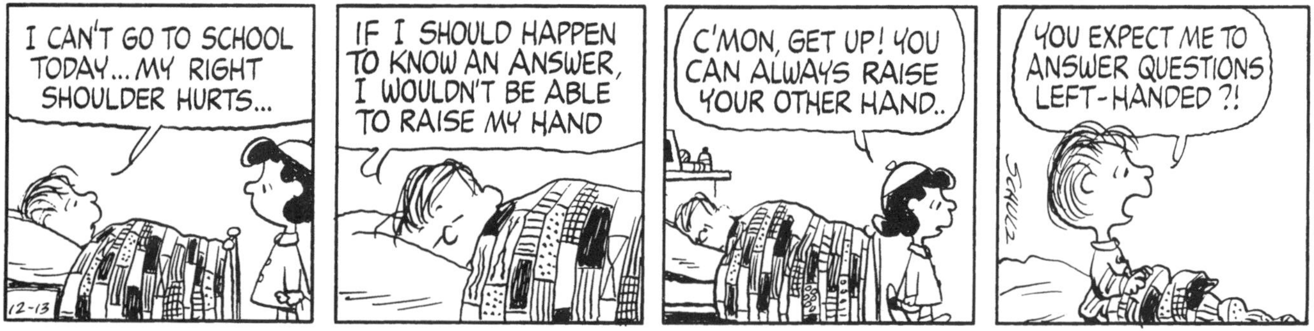
I CAN'T GO TO SCHOOL TODAY... MY RIGHT SHOULDER HURTS...
12-13
IF I SHOULD HAPPEN TO KNOW AN ANSWER, I WOULDN'T BE ABLE TO RAISE MY HAND
C'MON, GET UP! YOU CAN ALWAYS RAISE YOUR OTHER HAND..
SCHULZ
YOU EXPECT ME TO ANSWER QUESTIONS LEFT-HANDED?!

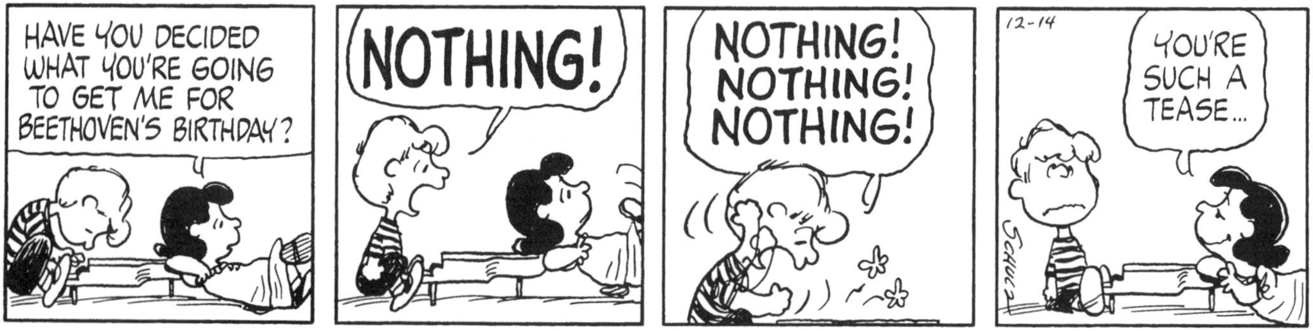
HAVE YOU DECIDED WHAT YOU'RE GOING TO GET ME FOR BEETHOVEN'S BIRTHDAY?
NOTHING!
NOTHING! NOTHING! NOTHING!
12-14
YOU'RE SUCH A TEASE...
SCHULZ

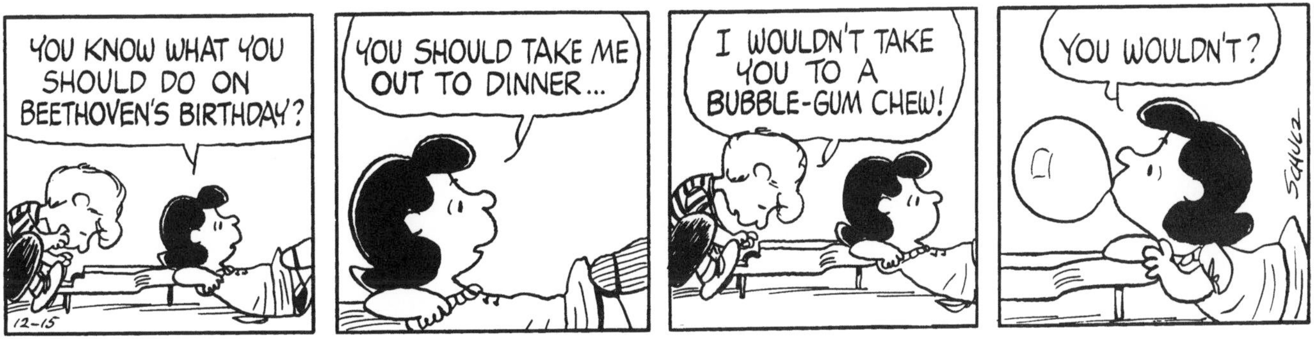
YOU KNOW WHAT YOU SHOULD DO ON BEETHOVEN'S BIRTHDAY?
YOU SHOULD TAKE ME OUT TO DINNER...
I WOULDN'T TAKE YOU TO A BUBBLE-GUM CHEW!
YOU WOULDN'T?

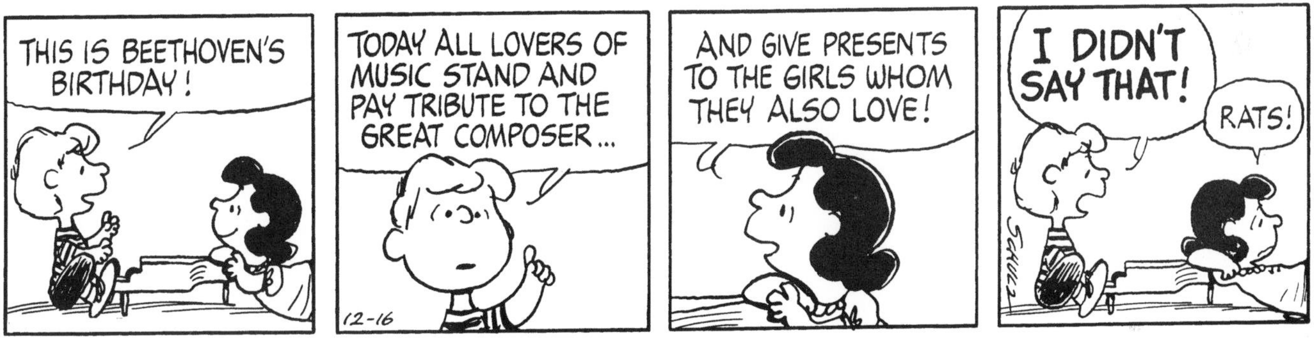
THIS IS BEETHOVEN'S BIRTHDAY!
TODAY ALL LOVERS OF MUSIC STAND AND PAY TRIBUTE TO THE GREAT COMPOSER...
AND GIVE PRESENTS TO THE GIRLS WHOM THEY ALSO LOVE!
I DIDN'T SAY THAT!
RATS!

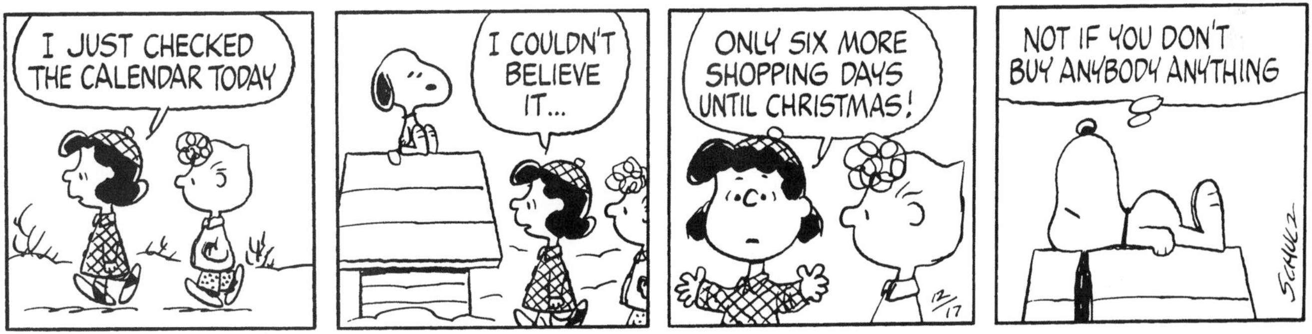
I JUST CHECKED THE CALENDAR TODAY
I COULDN'T BELIEVE IT...
ONLY SIX MORE SHOPPING DAYS UNTIL CHRISTMAS!
NOT IF YOU DON'T BUY ANYBODY ANYTHING

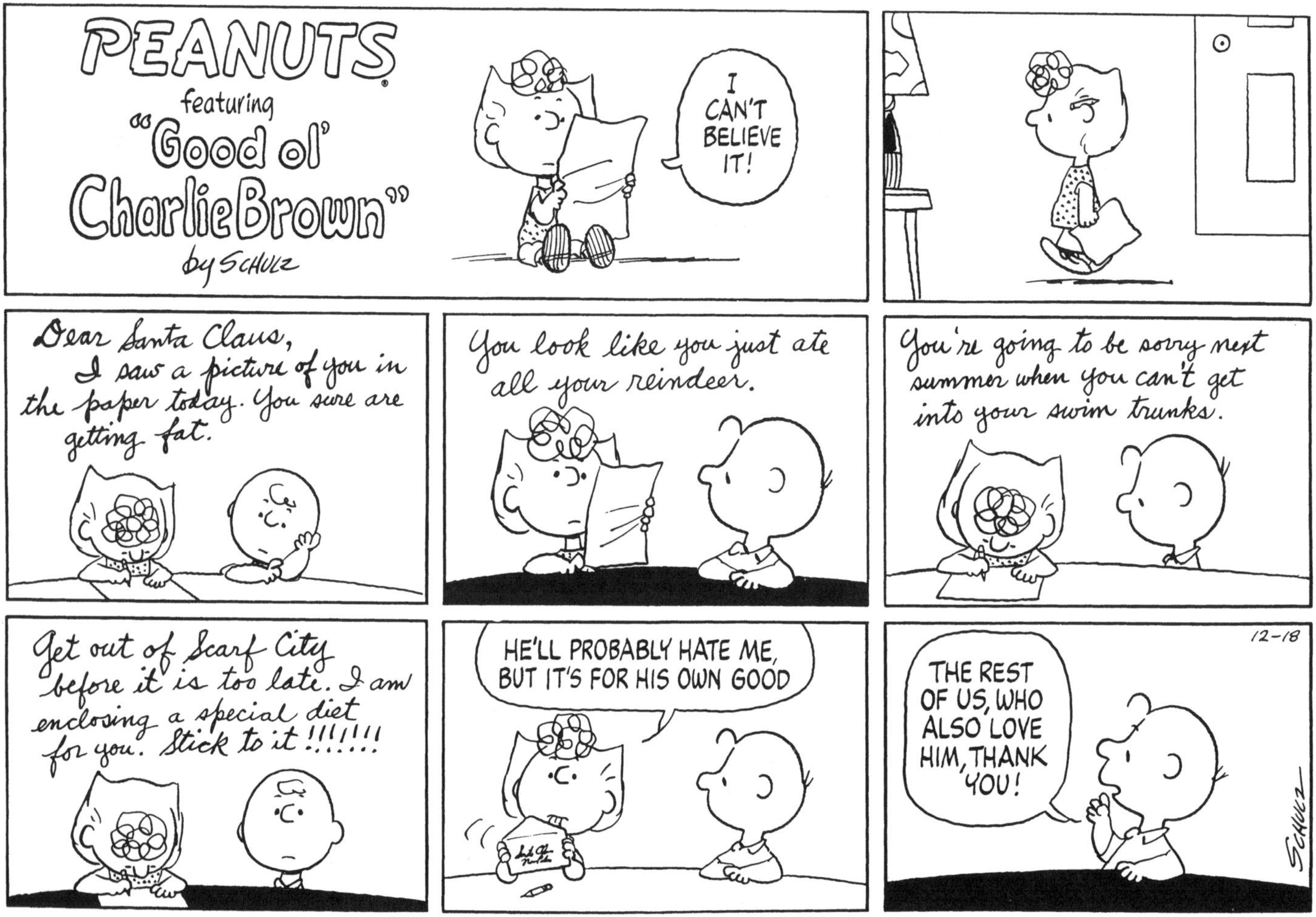
PEANUTS
featuring
"Good ol' CharlieBrown"
by SCHULZ
I CAN'T BELIEVE IT!
Dear Santa Claus,
I saw a picture of you in the paper today. You sure are getting fat.
You look like you just ate all your reindeer.
You're going to be sorry next summer when you can't get into your swim trunks.
Get out of Scarf City before it is too late. I am enclosing a special diet for you. Stick to it !!!!!!!
HE'LL PROBABLY HATE ME, BUT IT'S FOR HIS OWN GOOD
12-18
THE REST OF US, WHO ALSO LOVE HIM, THANK YOU!
SCHULZ

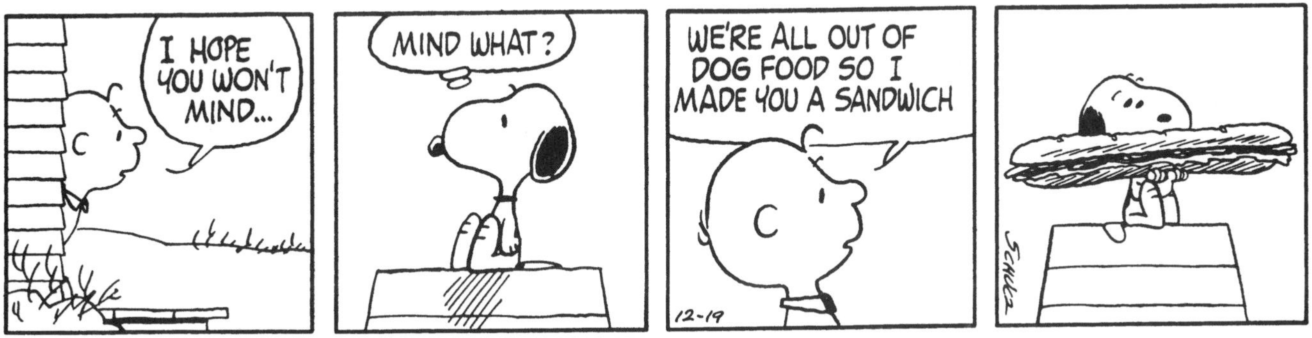
I HOPE YOU WON'T MIND...
MIND WHAT?
WE'RE ALL OUT OF DOG FOOD SO I MADE YOU A SANDWICH
12-19
SCHULZ

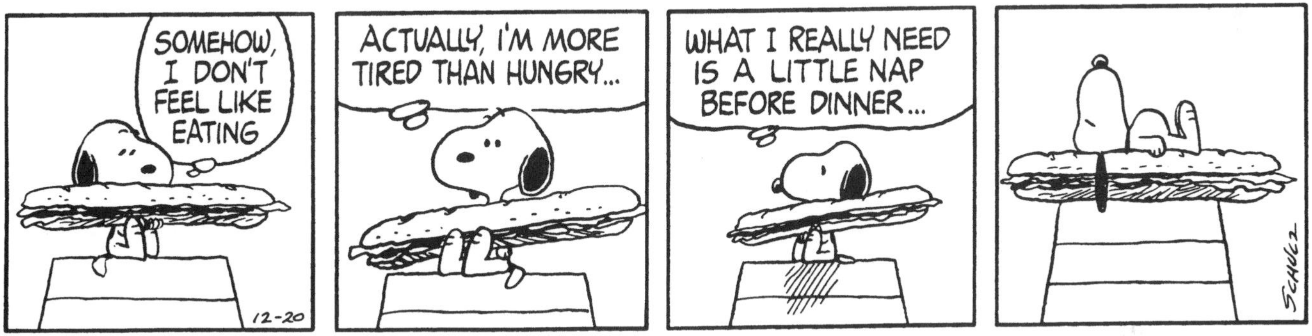
SOMEHOW, I DON'T FEEL LIKE EATING
12-20
ACTUALLY, I'M MORE TIRED THAN HUNGRY...
WHAT I REALLY NEED IS A LITTLE NAP BEFORE DINNER...
SCHULZ

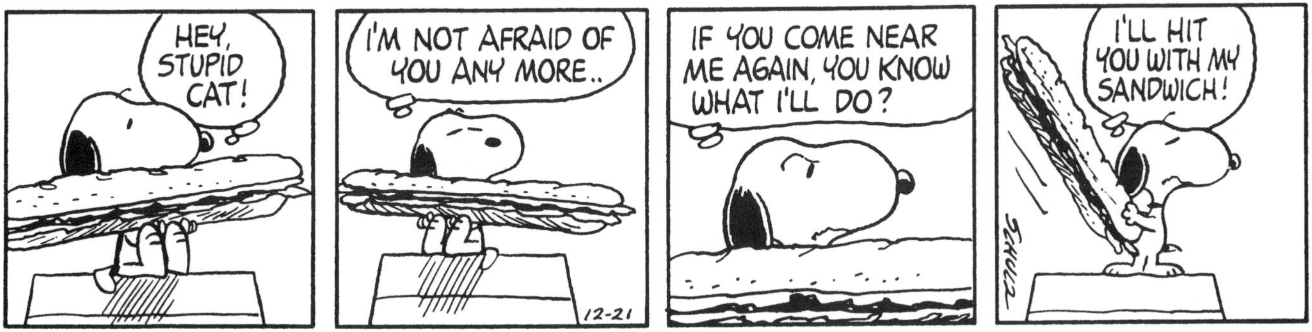
HEY, STUPID CAT!
I'M NOT AFRAID OF YOU ANY MORE..
12-21
IF YOU COME NEAR ME AGAIN, YOU KNOW WHAT I'LL DO?
I'LL HIT YOU WITH MY SANDWICH!
SCHULZ

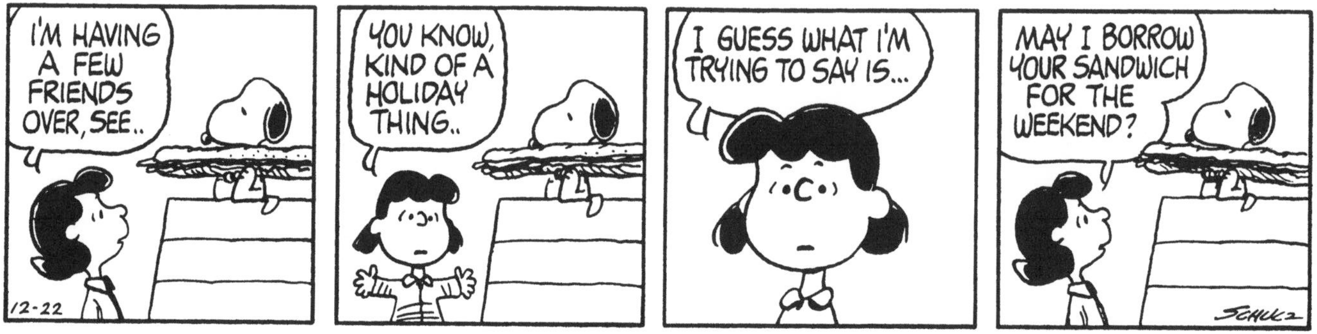
I'M HAVING A FEW FRIENDS OVER, SEE..
12-22
YOU KNOW, KIND OF A HOLIDAY THING..
I GUESS WHAT I'M TRYING TO SAY IS...
MAY I BORROW YOUR SANDWICH FOR THE WEEKEND?
SCHULZ

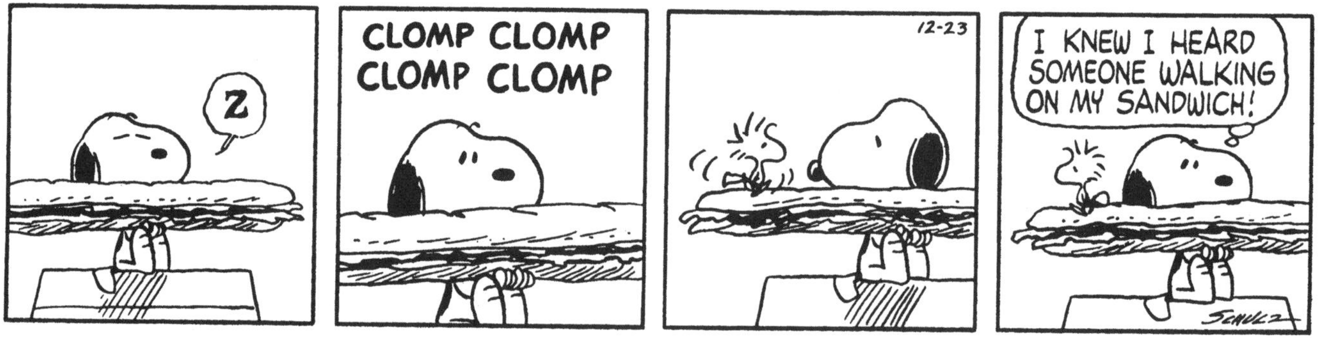
Z
CLOMP CLOMP CLOMP CLOMP
12-23
I KNEW I HEARD SOMEONE WALKING ON MY SANDWICH!
SCHULZ

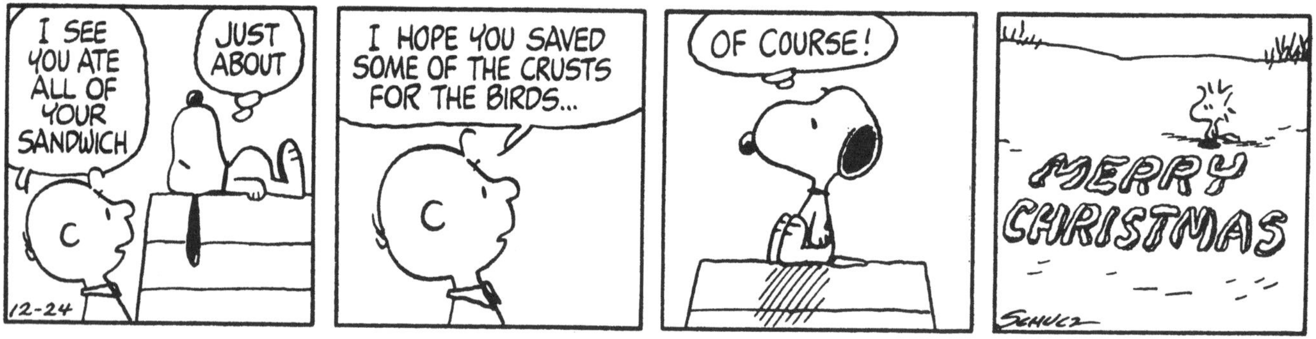
I SEE YOU ATE ALL OF YOUR SANDWICH
JUST ABOUT
12-24
I HOPE YOU SAVED SOME OF THE CRUSTS FOR THE BIRDS...
OF COURSE!
MERRY CHRISTMAS
SCHULZ

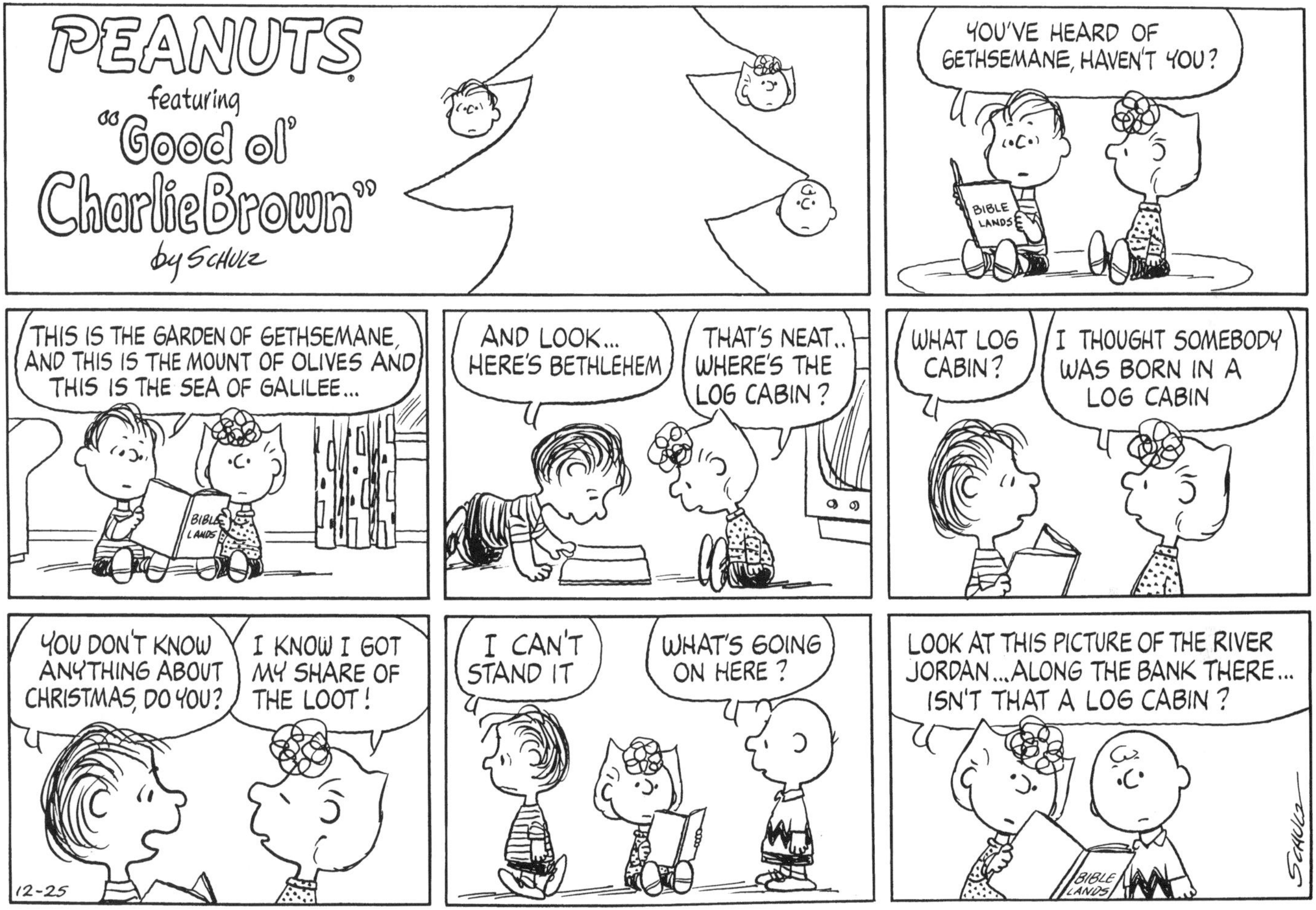
PEANUTS
featuring
"Good ol' Charlie Brown"
by SCHULZ
YOU'VE HEARD OF GETHSEMANE, HAVEN'T YOU?
BIBLE LANDS
THIS IS THE GARDEN OF GETHSEMANE, AND THIS IS THE MOUNT OF OLIVES AND THIS IS THE SEA OF GALILEE...
BIBLE LANDS
AND LOOK... HERE'S BETHLEHEM
THAT'S NEAT.. WHERE'S THE LOG CABIN?
WHAT LOG CABIN?
I THOUGHT SOMEBODY WAS BORN IN A LOG CABIN
YOU DON'T KNOW ANYTHING ABOUT CHRISTMAS, DO YOU?
I KNOW I GOT MY SHARE OF THE LOOT!
12-25
I CAN'T STAND IT
WHAT'S GOING ON HERE?
LOOK AT THIS PICTURE OF THE RIVER JORDAN...ALONG THE BANK THERE... ISN'T THAT A LOG CABIN?
BIBLE LANDS
SCHULZ

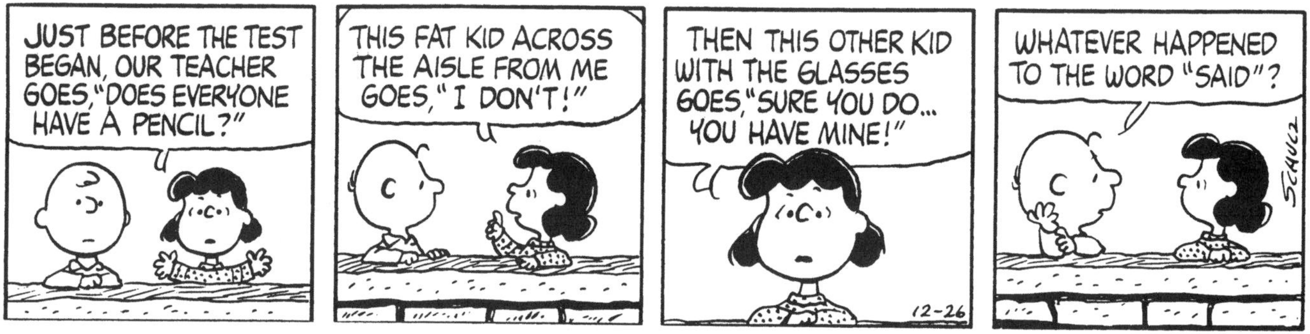
JUST BEFORE THE TEST BEGAN, OUR TEACHER GOES, "DOES EVERYONE HAVE A PENCIL?"
THIS FAT KID ACROSS THE AISLE FROM ME GOES, "I DON'T!"
THEN THIS OTHER KID WITH THE GLASSES GOES, "SURE YOU DO... YOU HAVE MINE!"
12-26
WHATEVER HAPPENED TO THE WORD "SAID"?
SCHULZ

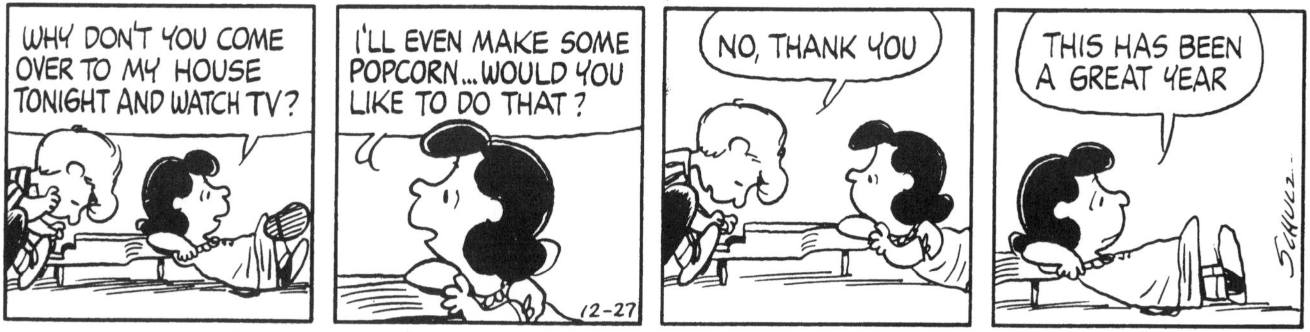
WHY DON'T YOU COME OVER TO MY HOUSE TONIGHT AND WATCH TV?
I'LL EVEN MAKE SOME POPCORN...WOULD YOU LIKE TO DO THAT?
12-27
NO, THANK YOU
THIS HAS BEEN A GREAT YEAR
SCHULZ

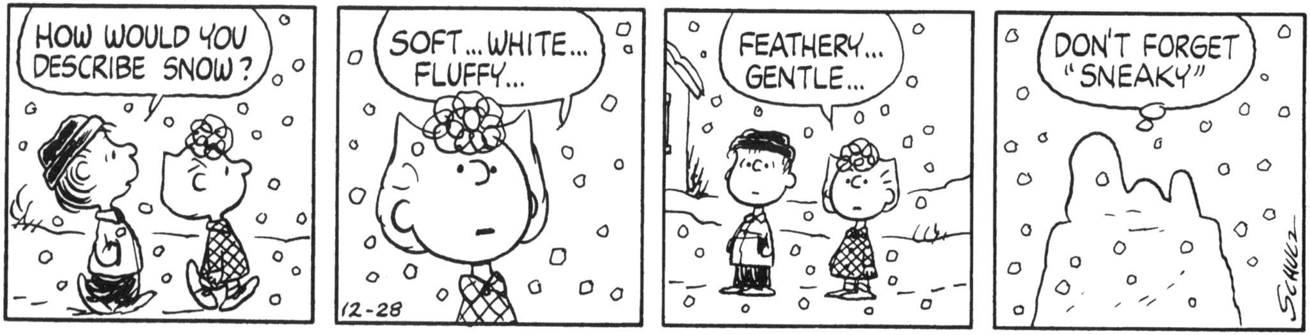
HOW WOULD YOU DESCRIBE SNOW?
SOFT...WHITE... FLUFFY...
12-28
FEATHERY... GENTLE...
DON'T FORGET "SNEAKY"
SCHULZ

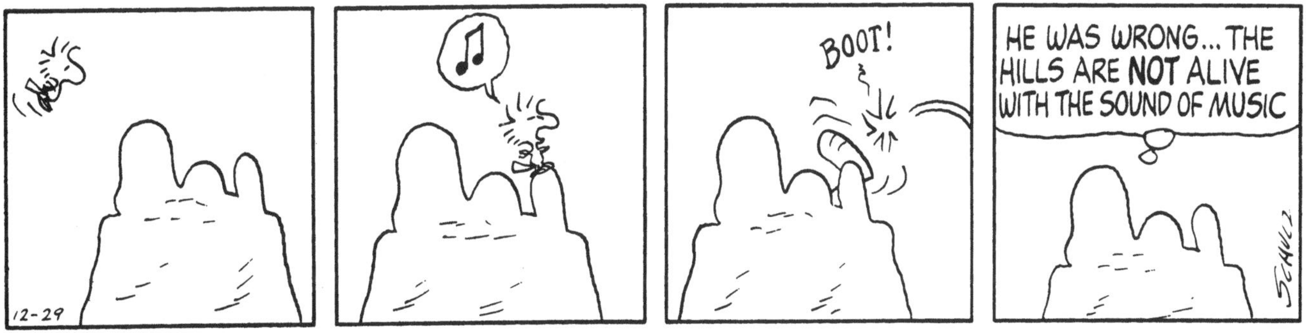
12-29
BOOT!
HE WAS WRONG... THE HILLS ARE **NOT** ALIVE WITH THE SOUND OF MUSIC
SCHULZ

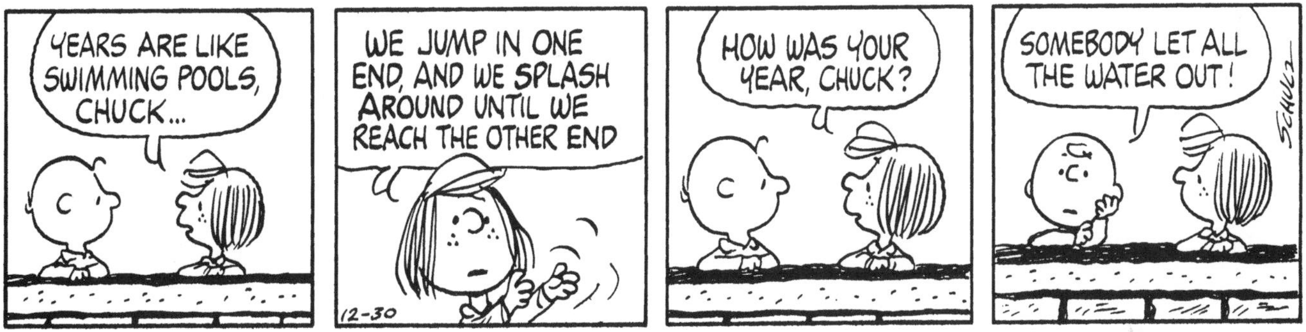
YEARS ARE LIKE SWIMMING POOLS, CHUCK...
WE JUMP IN ONE END, AND WE SPLASH AROUND UNTIL WE REACH THE OTHER END
12-30
HOW WAS YOUR YEAR, CHUCK?
SOMEBODY LET ALL THE WATER OUT!
SCHULZ

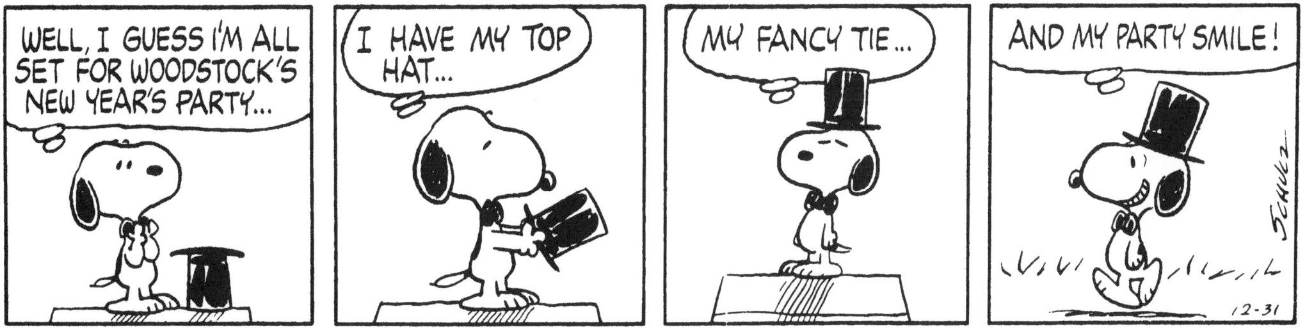
WELL, I GUESS I'M ALL SET FOR WOODSTOCK'S NEW YEAR'S PARTY...
I HAVE MY TOP HAT...
MY FANCY TIE...
AND MY PARTY SMILE!
SCHULZ
12-31

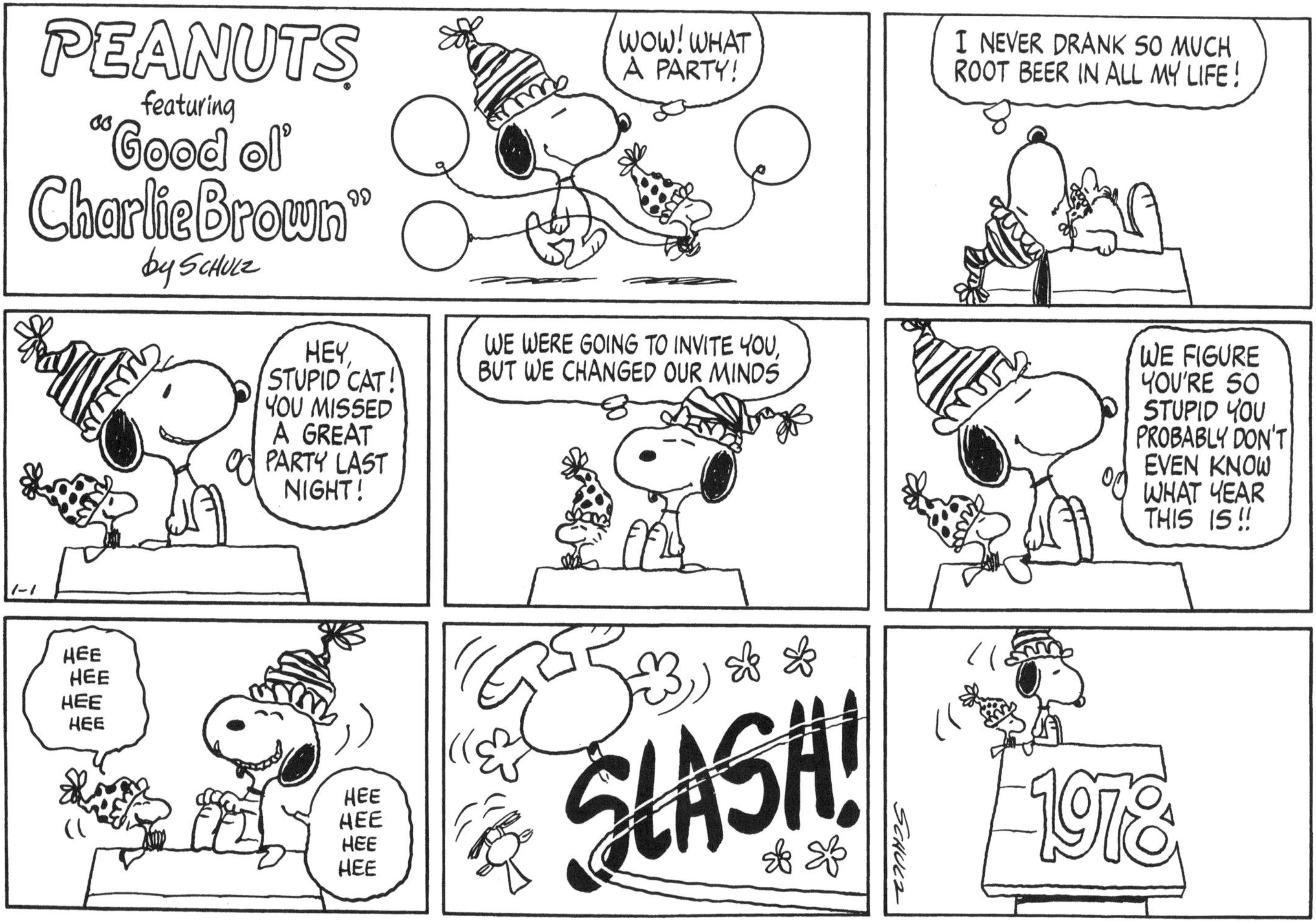
PEANUTS
featuring "Good ol' CharlieBrown"
by SCHULZ
WOW! WHAT A PARTY!
I NEVER DRANK SO MUCH ROOT BEER IN ALL MY LIFE!
HEY, STUPID CAT! YOU MISSED A GREAT PARTY LAST NIGHT!
1-1
WE WERE GOING TO INVITE YOU, BUT WE CHANGED OUR MINDS
WE FIGURE YOU'RE SO STUPID YOU PROBABLY DON'T EVEN KNOW WHAT YEAR THIS IS!!
HEE HEE HEE HEE
HEE HEE HEE HEE
SLASH!
SCHULZ
1978

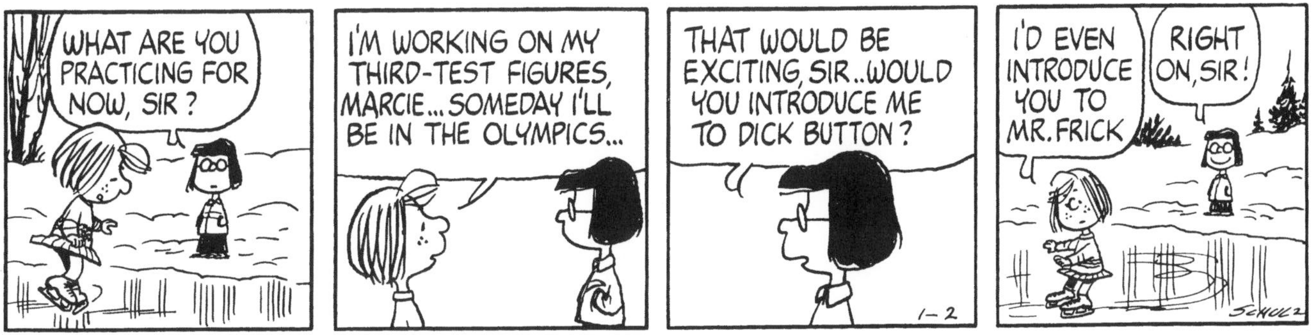
WHAT ARE YOU PRACTICING FOR NOW, SIR?
I'M WORKING ON MY THIRD-TEST FIGURES, MARCIE... SOMEDAY I'LL BE IN THE OLYMPICS...
THAT WOULD BE EXCITING, SIR..WOULD YOU INTRODUCE ME TO DICK BUTTON?
I'D EVEN INTRODUCE YOU TO MR. FRICK
RIGHT ON, SIR!
1-2
SCHULZ

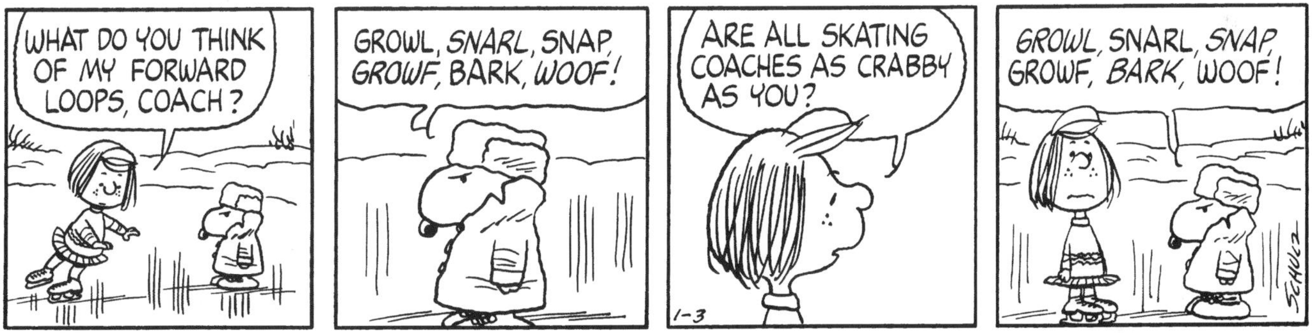
WHAT DO YOU THINK OF MY FORWARD LOOPS, COACH?
GROWL, SNARL, SNAP, GROWF, BARK, WOOF!
ARE ALL SKATING COACHES AS CRABBY AS YOU?
1-3
GROWL, SNARL, SNAP, GROWF, BARK, WOOF!
SCHULZ

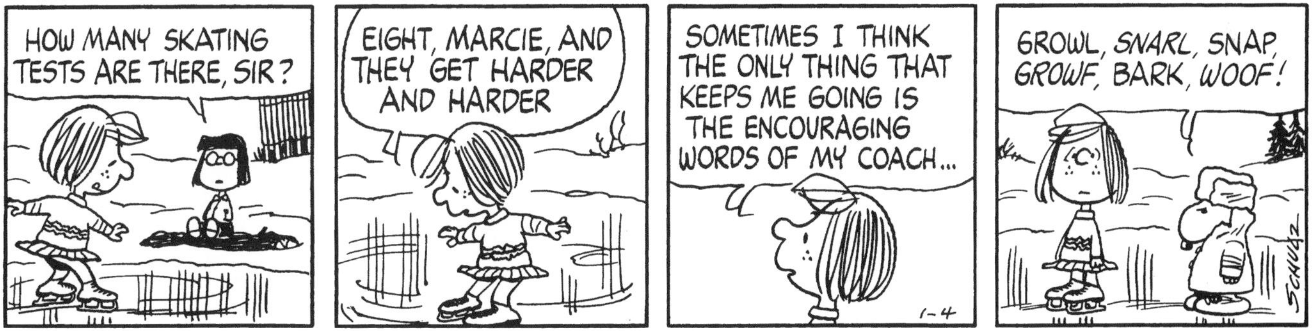
HOW MANY SKATING TESTS ARE THERE, SIR?
EIGHT, MARCIE, AND THEY GET HARDER AND HARDER
SOMETIMES I THINK THE ONLY THING THAT KEEPS ME GOING IS THE ENCOURAGING WORDS OF MY COACH...
1-4
GROWL, SNARL, SNAP, GROWF, BARK, WOOF!
SCHULZ

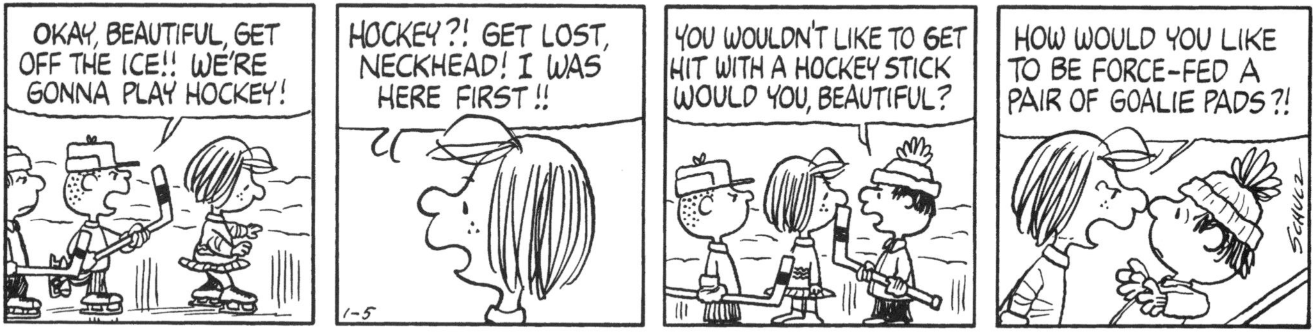
OKAY, BEAUTIFUL, GET OFF THE ICE!! WE'RE GONNA PLAY HOCKEY!
HOCKEY?! GET LOST, NECKHEAD! I WAS HERE FIRST!!
1-5
YOU WOULDN'T LIKE TO GET HIT WITH A HOCKEY STICK WOULD YOU, BEAUTIFUL?
HOW WOULD YOU LIKE TO BE FORCE-FED A PAIR OF GOALIE PADS?!
SCHULZ

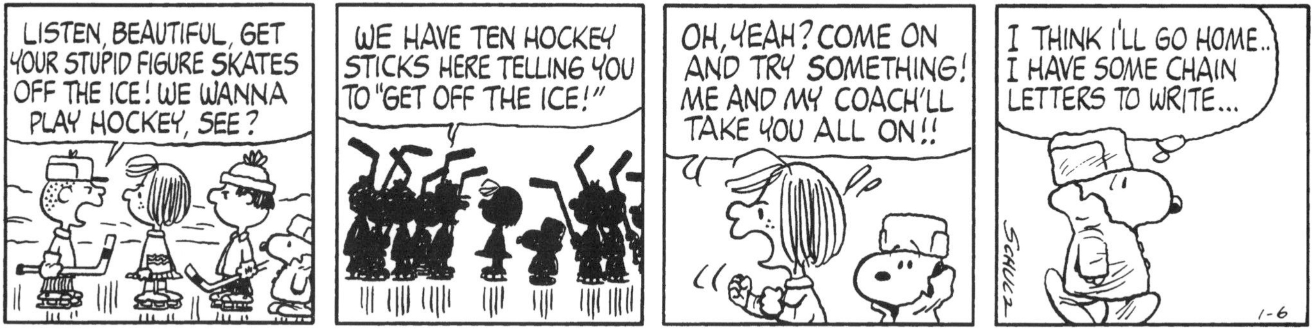
LISTEN, BEAUTIFUL, GET YOUR STUPID FIGURE SKATES OFF THE ICE! WE WANNA PLAY HOCKEY, SEE?
WE HAVE TEN HOCKEY STICKS HERE TELLING YOU TO "GET OFF THE ICE!"
OH, YEAH? COME ON AND TRY SOMETHING! ME AND MY COACH'LL TAKE YOU ALL ON!!
I THINK I'LL GO HOME.. I HAVE SOME CHAIN LETTERS TO WRITE...
SCHULZ
1-6

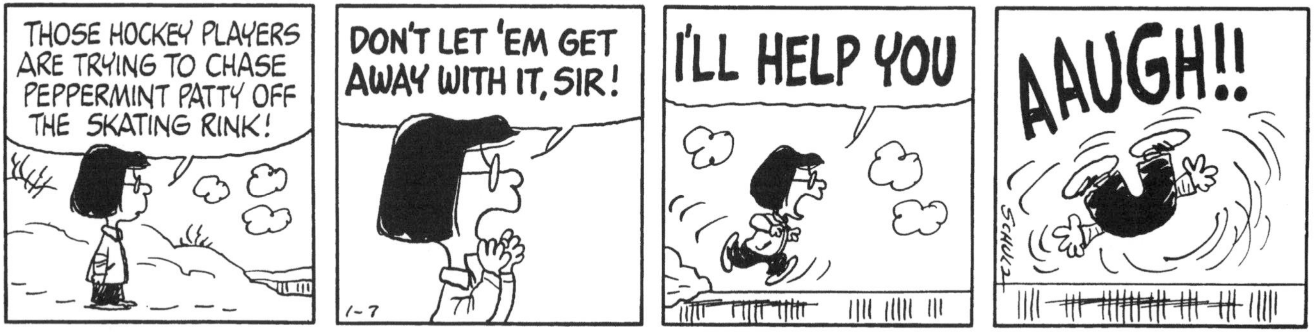
THOSE HOCKEY PLAYERS ARE TRYING TO CHASE PEPPERMINT PATTY OFF THE SKATING RINK!
DON'T LET 'EM GET AWAY WITH IT, SIR!
1-7
I'LL HELP YOU
AAUGH!!
SCHULZ

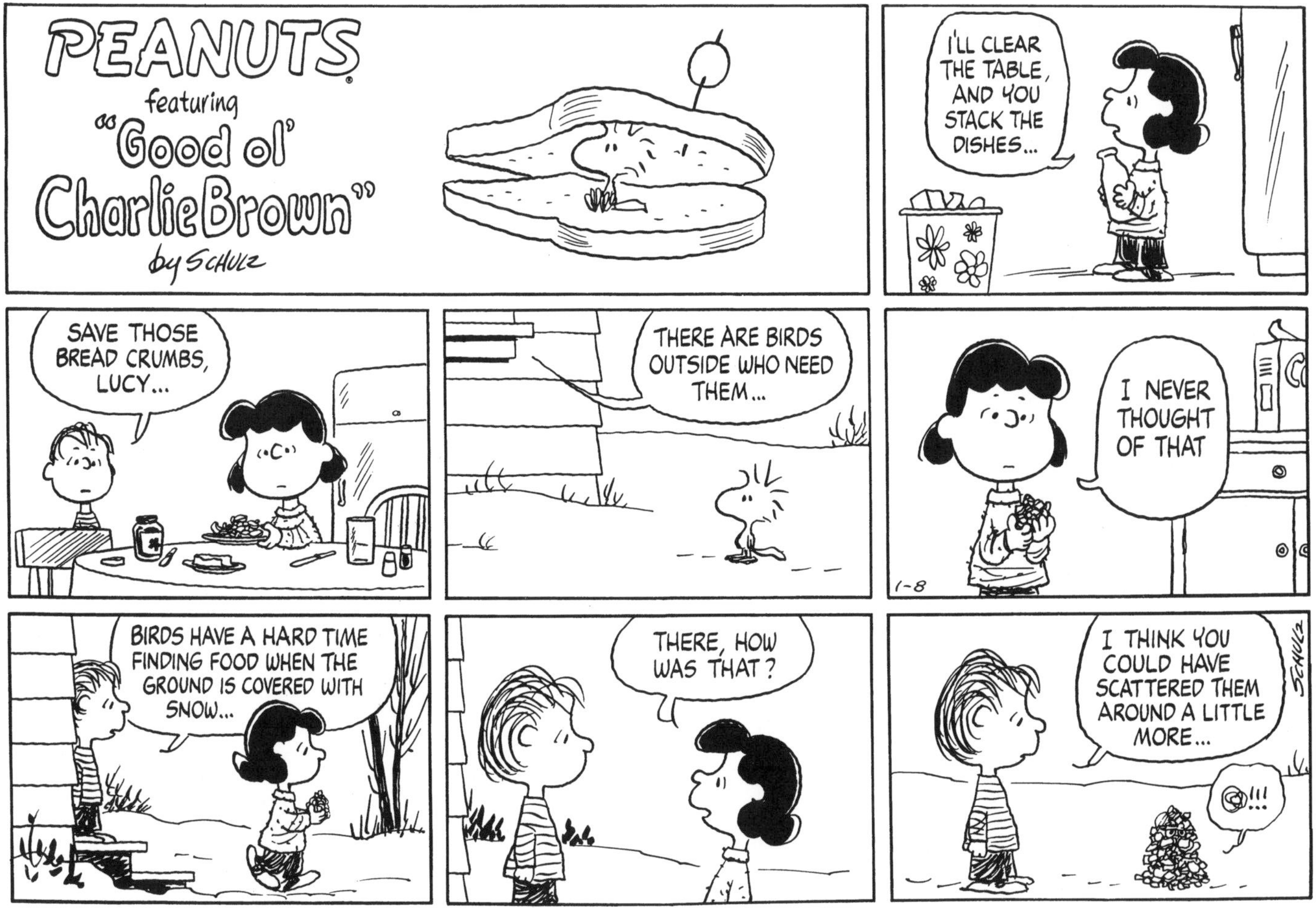
PEANUTS
featuring "Good ol' Charlie Brown"
by SCHULZ
I'LL CLEAR THE TABLE, AND YOU STACK THE DISHES...
SAVE THOSE BREAD CRUMBS, LUCY...
THERE ARE BIRDS OUTSIDE WHO NEED THEM...
I NEVER THOUGHT OF THAT
1-8
BIRDS HAVE A HARD TIME FINDING FOOD WHEN THE GROUND IS COVERED WITH SNOW...
THERE, HOW WAS THAT?
I THINK YOU COULD HAVE SCATTERED THEM AROUND A LITTLE MORE...
!!!
SCHULZ

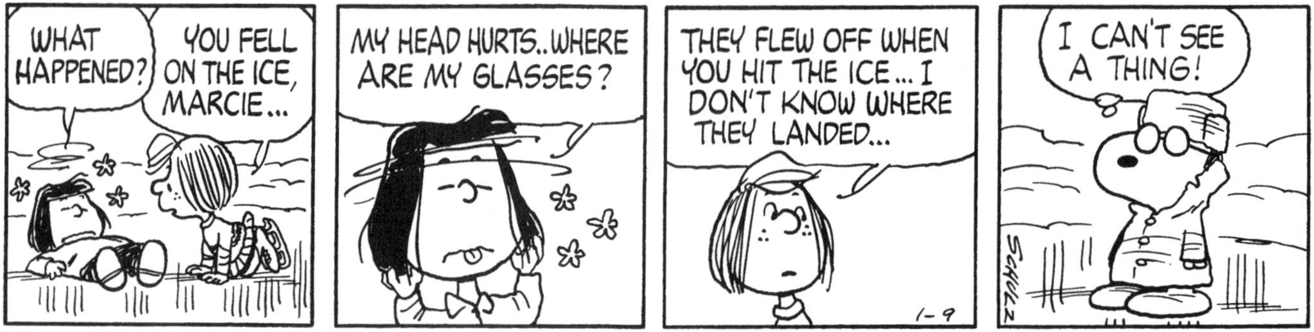
WHAT HAPPENED?
YOU FELL ON THE ICE, MARCIE...
MY HEAD HURTS..WHERE ARE MY GLASSES?
THEY FLEW OFF WHEN YOU HIT THE ICE... I DON'T KNOW WHERE THEY LANDED...
1-9
I CAN'T SEE A THING!
SCHULZ

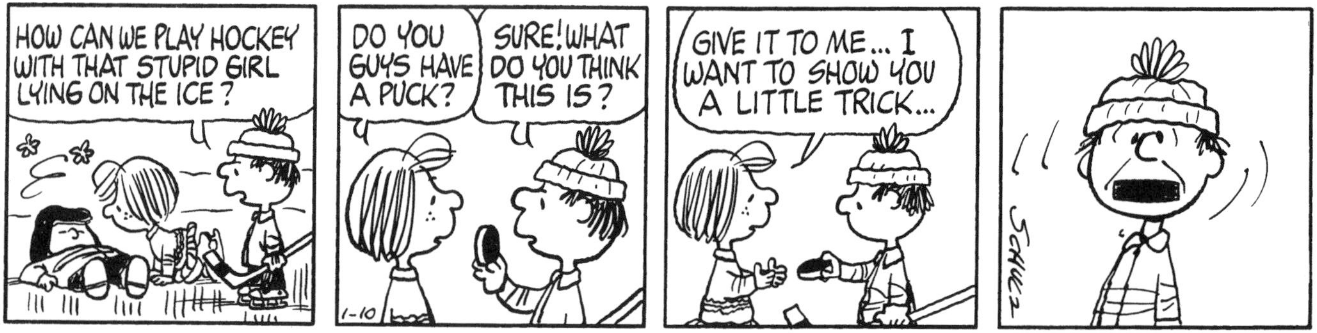
HOW CAN WE PLAY HOCKEY WITH THAT STUPID GIRL LYING ON THE ICE?
DO YOU GUYS HAVE A PUCK?
SURE! WHAT DO YOU THINK THIS IS?
1-10
GIVE IT TO ME... I WANT TO SHOW YOU A LITTLE TRICK...
SCHULZ

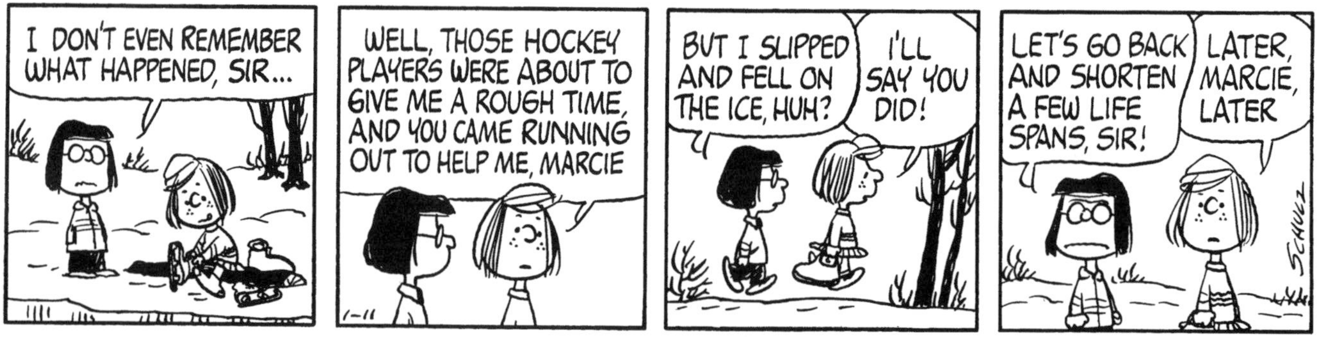
I DON'T EVEN REMEMBER WHAT HAPPENED, SIR...
WELL, THOSE HOCKEY PLAYERS WERE ABOUT TO GIVE ME A ROUGH TIME, AND YOU CAME RUNNING OUT TO HELP ME, MARCIE
1-11
BUT I SLIPPED AND FELL ON THE ICE, HUH?
I'LL SAY YOU DID!
LET'S GO BACK AND SHORTEN A FEW LIFE SPANS, SIR!
LATER, MARCIE, LATER
SCHULZ

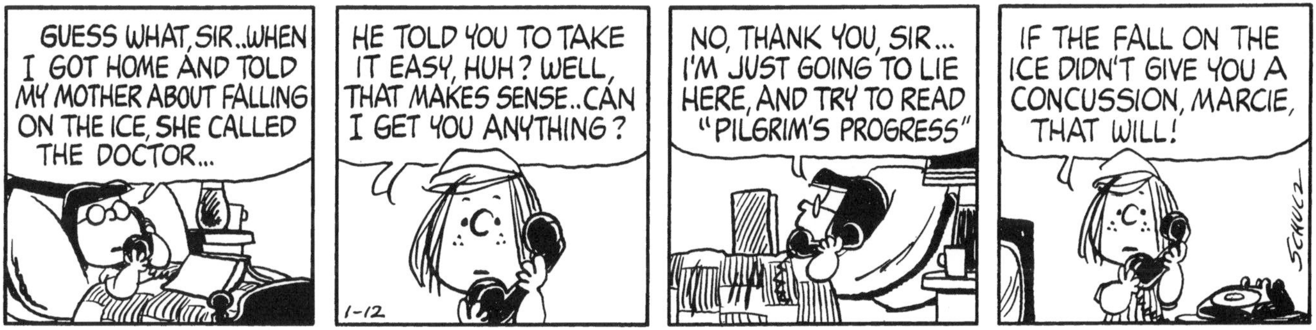
GUESS WHAT, SIR..WHEN I GOT HOME AND TOLD MY MOTHER ABOUT FALLING ON THE ICE, SHE CALLED THE DOCTOR...
HE TOLD YOU TO TAKE IT EASY, HUH? WELL, THAT MAKES SENSE..CAN I GET YOU ANYTHING?
NO, THANK YOU, SIR... I'M JUST GOING TO LIE HERE, AND TRY TO READ "PILGRIM'S PROGRESS"
IF THE FALL ON THE ICE DIDN'T GIVE YOU A CONCUSSION, MARCIE, THAT WILL!

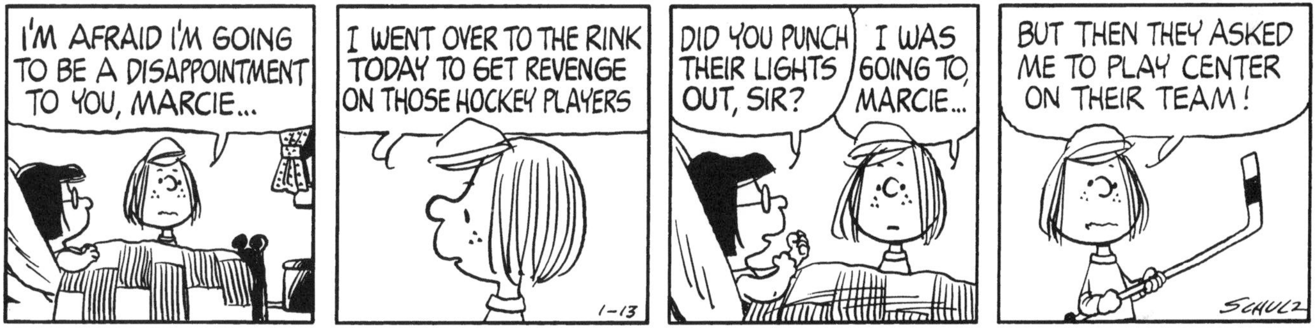
I'M AFRAID I'M GOING TO BE A DISAPPOINTMENT TO YOU, MARCIE...
I WENT OVER TO THE RINK TODAY TO GET REVENGE ON THOSE HOCKEY PLAYERS
DID YOU PUNCH THEIR LIGHTS OUT, SIR?
I WAS GOING TO, MARCIE...
BUT THEN THEY ASKED ME TO PLAY CENTER ON THEIR TEAM!

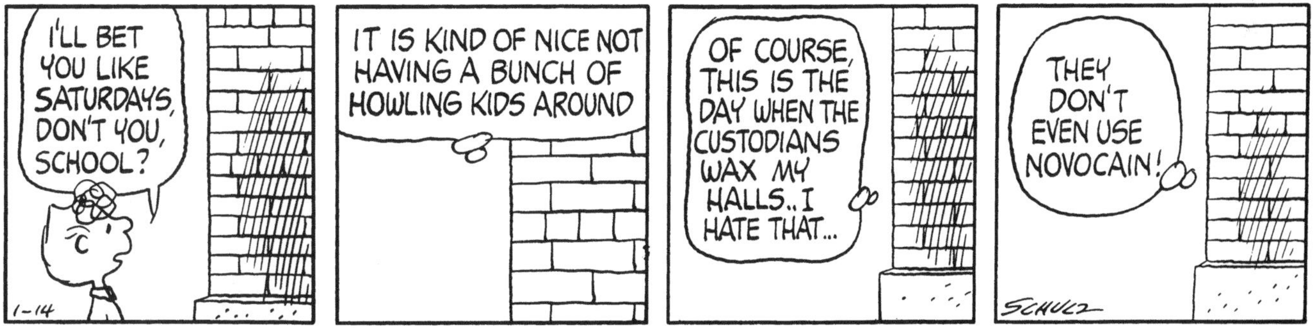
I'LL BET YOU LIKE SATURDAYS, DON'T YOU, SCHOOL?
IT IS KIND OF NICE NOT HAVING A BUNCH OF HOWLING KIDS AROUND
OF COURSE, THIS IS THE DAY WHEN THE CUSTODIANS WAX MY HALLS..I HATE THAT...
THEY DON'T EVEN USE NOVOCAIN!

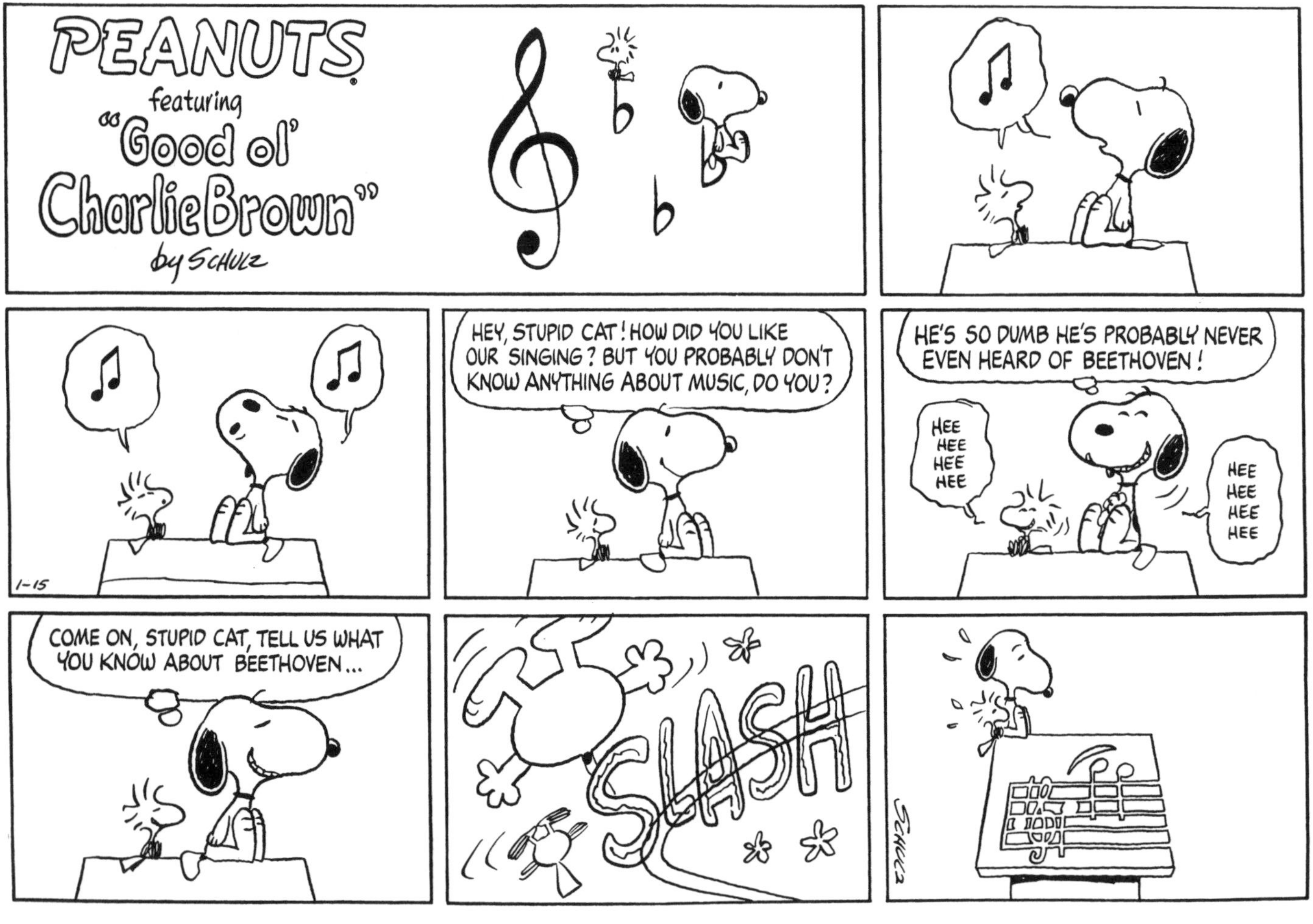
PEANUTS
featuring "Good ol' Charlie Brown"
by SCHULZ
1-15
HEY, STUPID CAT! HOW DID YOU LIKE OUR SINGING? BUT YOU PROBABLY DON'T KNOW ANYTHING ABOUT MUSIC, DO YOU?
HE'S SO DUMB HE'S PROBABLY NEVER EVEN HEARD OF BEETHOVEN!
HEE HEE HEE HEE
HEE HEE HEE HEE
COME ON, STUPID CAT, TELL US WHAT YOU KNOW ABOUT BEETHOVEN...
SLASH
SCHULZ

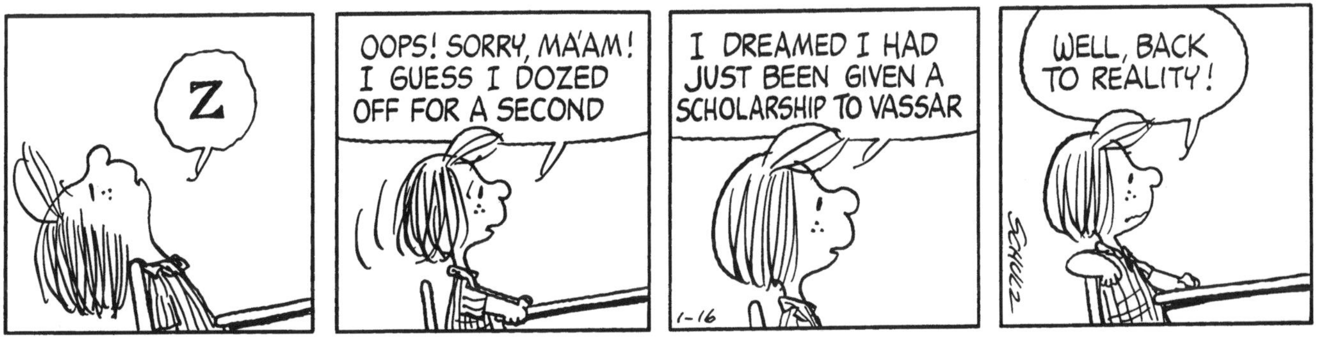
Z
OOPS! SORRY, MA'AM! I GUESS I DOZED OFF FOR A SECOND
I DREAMED I HAD JUST BEEN GIVEN A SCHOLARSHIP TO VASSAR
1-16
WELL, BACK TO REALITY!
SCHULZ

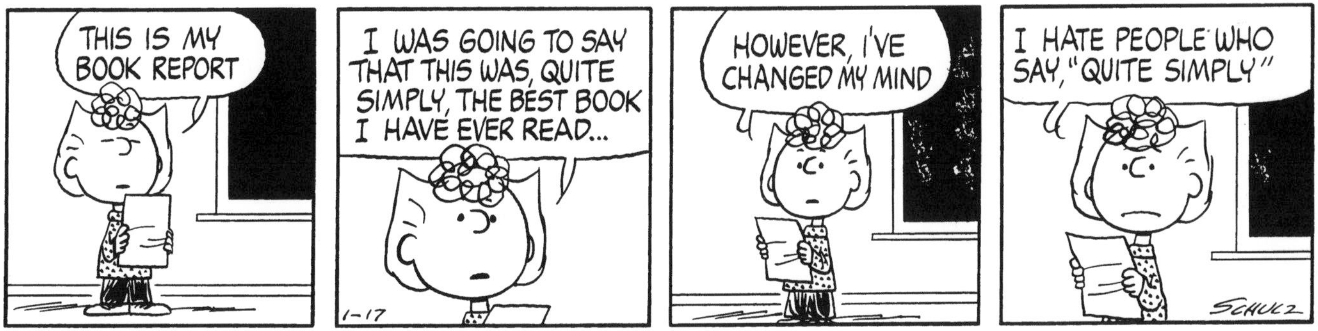
THIS IS MY BOOK REPORT
I WAS GOING TO SAY THAT THIS WAS, QUITE SIMPLY, THE BEST BOOK I HAVE EVER READ...
1-17
HOWEVER, I'VE CHANGED MY MIND
I HATE PEOPLE WHO SAY, "QUITE SIMPLY"
SCHULZ

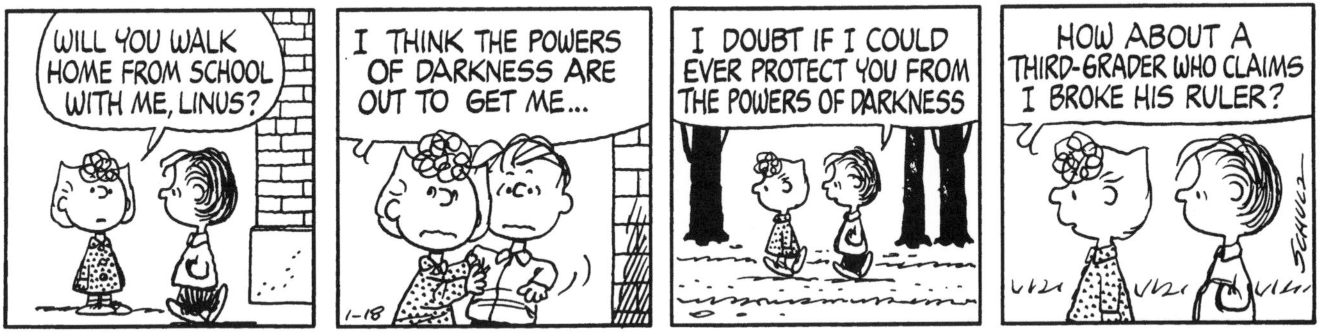
WILL YOU WALK HOME FROM SCHOOL WITH ME, LINUS?
I THINK THE POWERS OF DARKNESS ARE OUT TO GET ME...
1-18
I DOUBT IF I COULD EVER PROTECT YOU FROM THE POWERS OF DARKNESS
HOW ABOUT A THIRD-GRADER WHO CLAIMS I BROKE HIS RULER?
SCHULZ

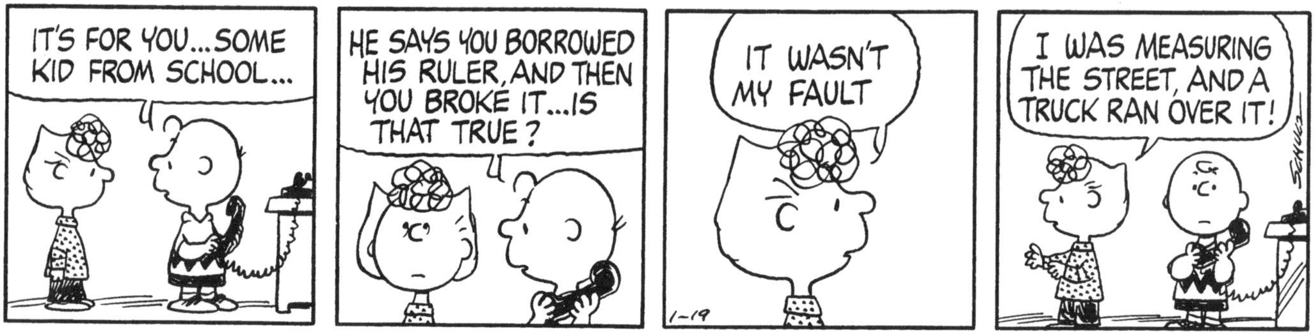
IT'S FOR YOU...SOME KID FROM SCHOOL...
HE SAYS YOU BORROWED HIS RULER, AND THEN YOU BROKE IT...IS THAT TRUE?
IT WASN'T MY FAULT
1-19
I WAS MEASURING THE STREET, AND A TRUCK RAN OVER IT!

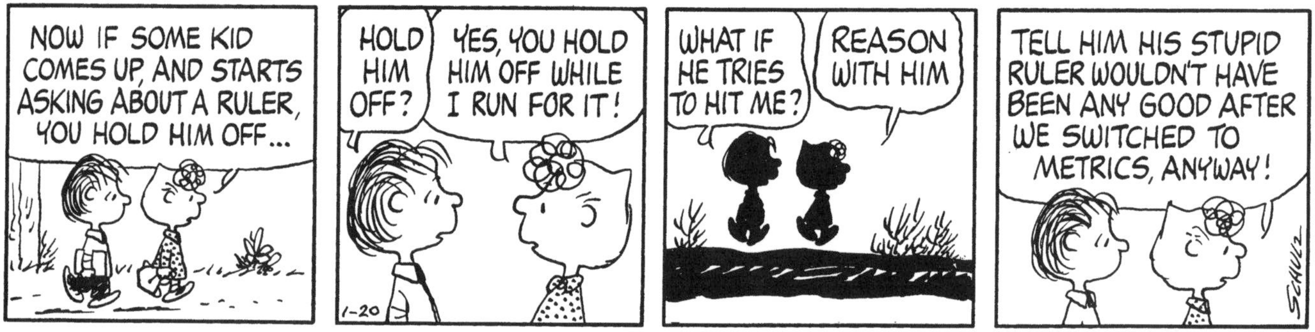
NOW IF SOME KID COMES UP, AND STARTS ASKING ABOUT A RULER, YOU HOLD HIM OFF...
HOLD HIM OFF?
YES, YOU HOLD HIM OFF WHILE I RUN FOR IT!
1-20
WHAT IF HE TRIES TO HIT ME?
REASON WITH HIM
TELL HIM HIS STUPID RULER WOULDN'T HAVE BEEN ANY GOOD AFTER WE SWITCHED TO METRICS, ANYWAY!

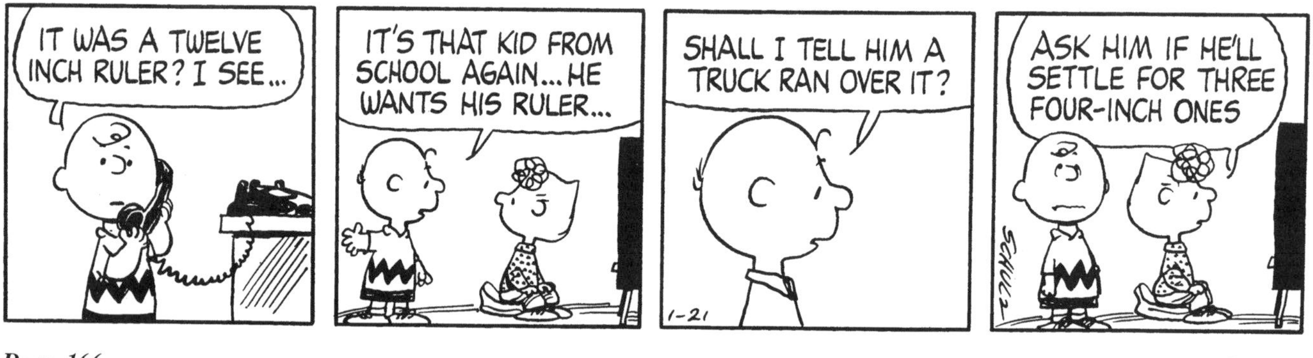
IT WAS A TWELVE INCH RULER? I SEE...
IT'S THAT KID FROM SCHOOL AGAIN...HE WANTS HIS RULER...
SHALL I TELL HIM A TRUCK RAN OVER IT?
1-21
ASK HIM IF HE'LL SETTLE FOR THREE FOUR-INCH ONES

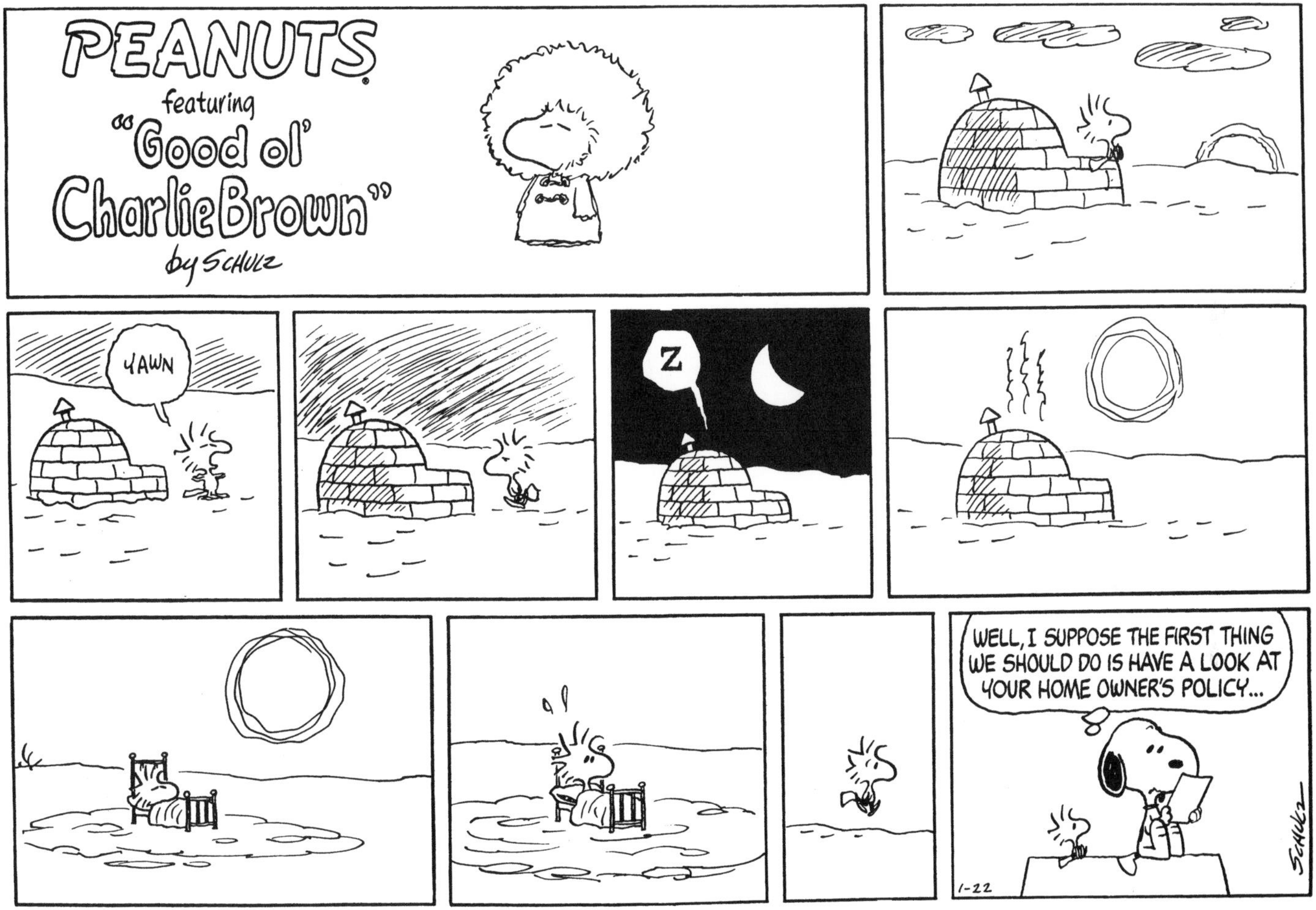
PEANUTS
featuring
"Good ol' CharlieBrown"
by SCHULZ
YAWN
Z
WELL, I SUPPOSE THE FIRST THING WE SHOULD DO IS HAVE A LOOK AT YOUR HOME OWNER'S POLICY...
1-22
SCHULZ

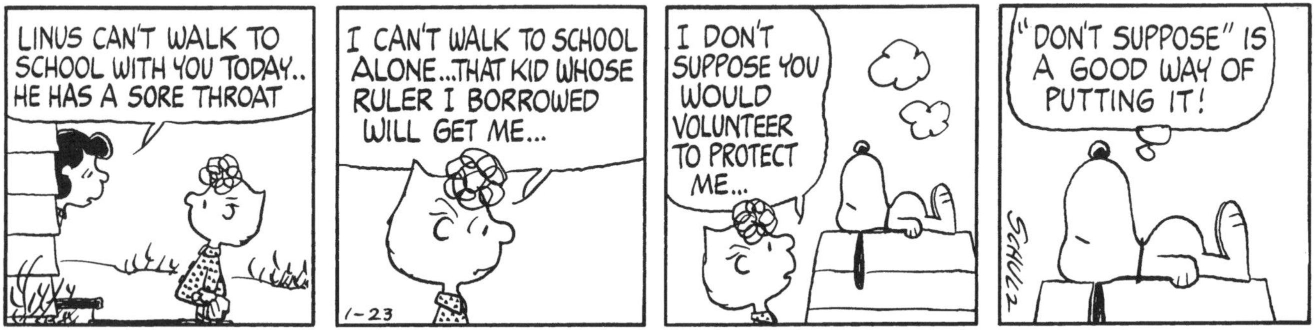
LINUS CAN'T WALK TO SCHOOL WITH YOU TODAY.. HE HAS A SORE THROAT
I CAN'T WALK TO SCHOOL ALONE...THAT KID WHOSE RULER I BORROWED WILL GET ME...
1-23
I DON'T SUPPOSE YOU WOULD VOLUNTEER TO PROTECT ME...
"DON'T SUPPOSE" IS A GOOD WAY OF PUTTING IT!
SCHULZ

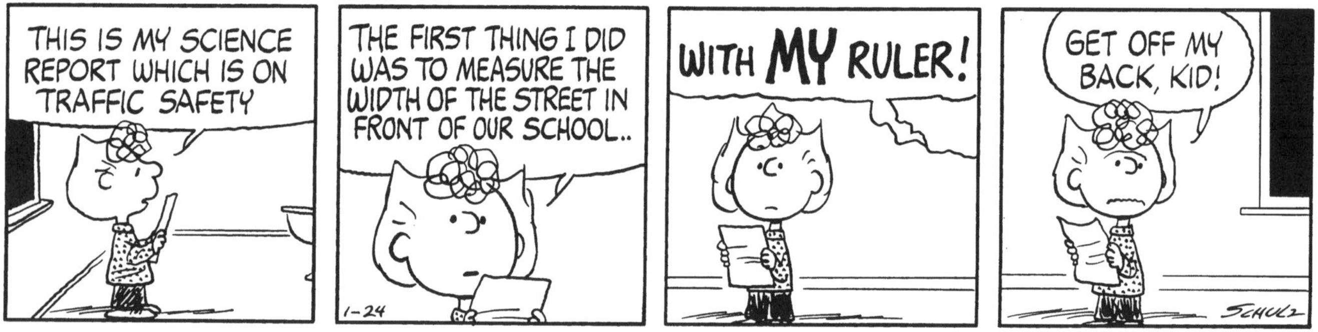
THIS IS MY SCIENCE REPORT WHICH IS ON TRAFFIC SAFETY
THE FIRST THING I DID WAS TO MEASURE THE WIDTH OF THE STREET IN FRONT OF OUR SCHOOL..
1-24
WITH MY RULER!
GET OFF MY BACK, KID!
SCHULZ

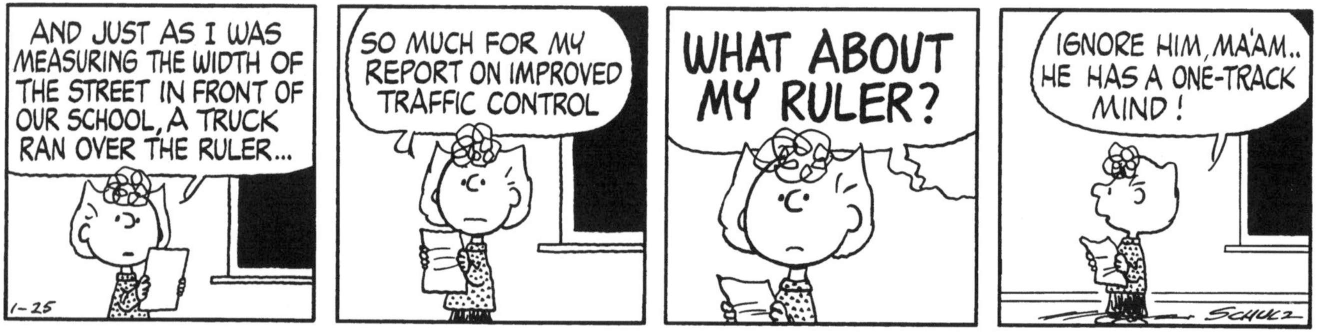
AND JUST AS I WAS MEASURING THE WIDTH OF THE STREET IN FRONT OF OUR SCHOOL, A TRUCK RAN OVER THE RULER...
1-25
SO MUCH FOR MY REPORT ON IMPROVED TRAFFIC CONTROL
WHAT ABOUT MY RULER?
IGNORE HIM, MA'AM.. HE HAS A ONE-TRACK MIND!
SCHULZ

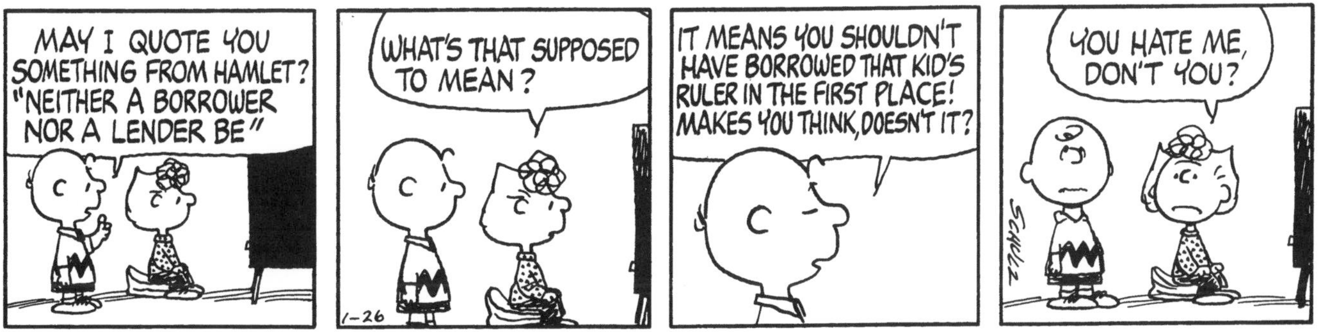

MAY I QUOTE YOU SOMETHING FROM HAMLET? "NEITHER A BORROWER NOR A LENDER BE"
WHAT'S THAT SUPPOSED TO MEAN?
1-26
IT MEANS YOU SHOULDN'T HAVE BORROWED THAT KID'S RULER IN THE FIRST PLACE! MAKES YOU THINK, DOESN'T IT?
YOU HATE ME, DON'T YOU?
SCHULZ

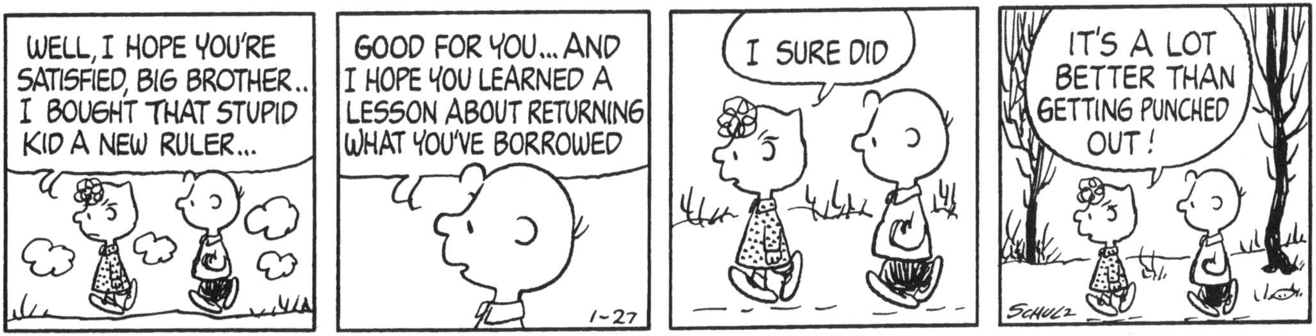

WELL, I HOPE YOU'RE SATISFIED, BIG BROTHER.. I BOUGHT THAT STUPID KID A NEW RULER...
GOOD FOR YOU... AND I HOPE YOU LEARNED A LESSON ABOUT RETURNING WHAT YOU'VE BORROWED
1-27
I SURE DID
IT'S A LOT BETTER THAN GETTING PUNCHED OUT!
SCHULZ

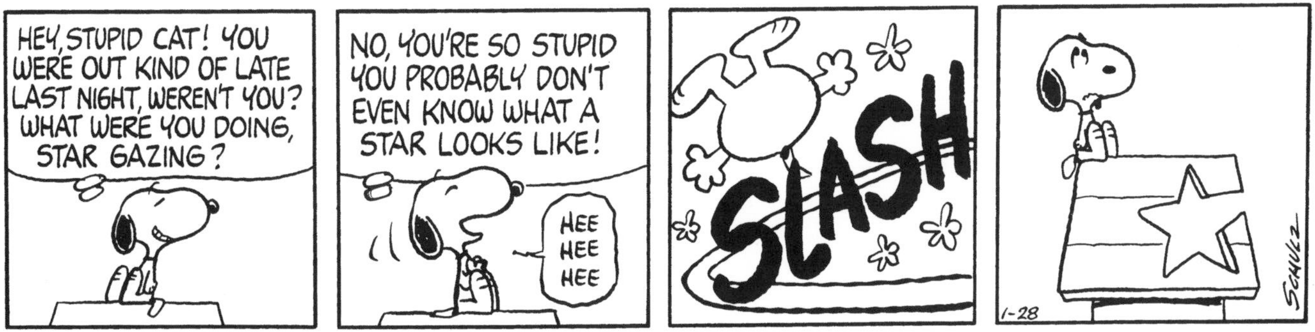

HEY, STUPID CAT! YOU WERE OUT KIND OF LATE LAST NIGHT, WEREN'T YOU? WHAT WERE YOU DOING, STAR GAZING?
NO, YOU'RE SO STUPID YOU PROBABLY DON'T EVEN KNOW WHAT A STAR LOOKS LIKE!
HEE HEE HEE
SLASH
1-28
SCHULZ

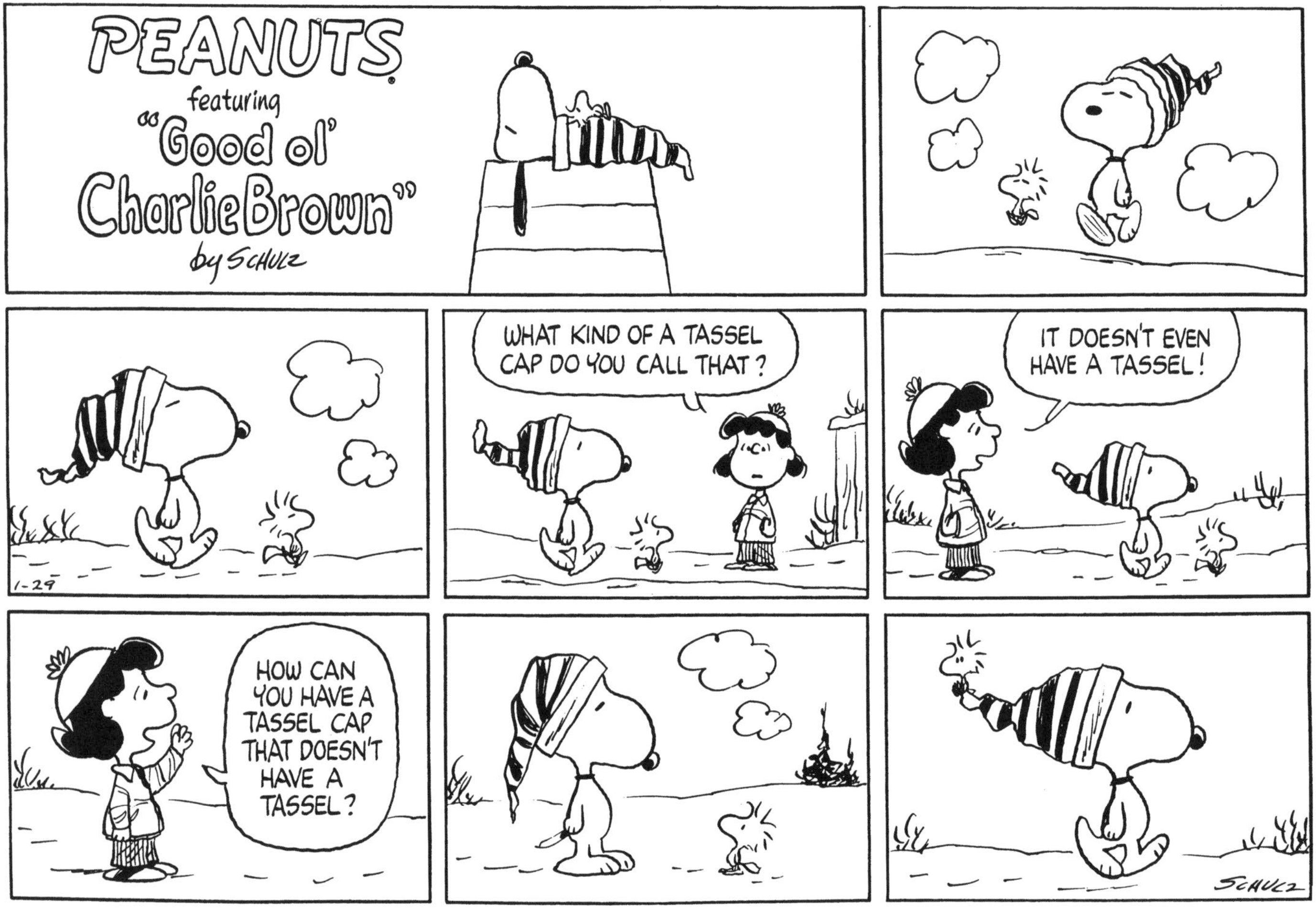
PEANUTS
featuring
"Good ol' Charlie Brown"
by SCHULZ
1-29
WHAT KIND OF A TASSEL CAP DO YOU CALL THAT?
IT DOESN'T EVEN HAVE A TASSEL!
HOW CAN YOU HAVE A TASSEL CAP THAT DOESN'T HAVE A TASSEL?
SCHULZ

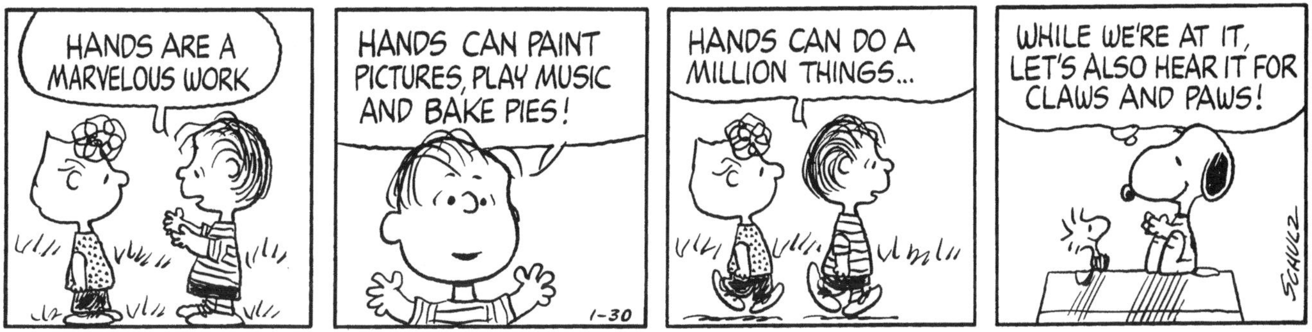
HANDS ARE A MARVELOUS WORK
HANDS CAN PAINT PICTURES, PLAY MUSIC AND BAKE PIES!
1-30
HANDS CAN DO A MILLION THINGS...
WHILE WE'RE AT IT, LET'S ALSO HEAR IT FOR CLAWS AND PAWS!
SCHULZ

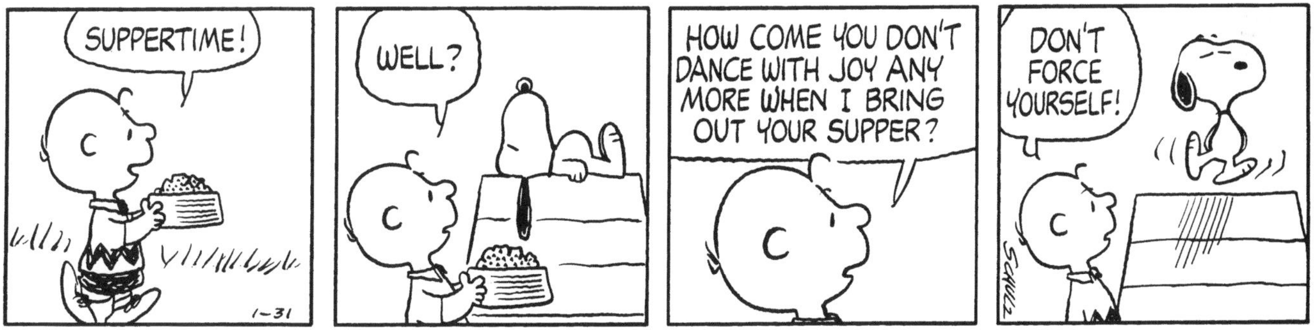
SUPPERTIME!
1-31
WELL?
HOW COME YOU DON'T DANCE WITH JOY ANY MORE WHEN I BRING OUT YOUR SUPPER?
DON'T FORCE YOURSELF!
SCHULZ

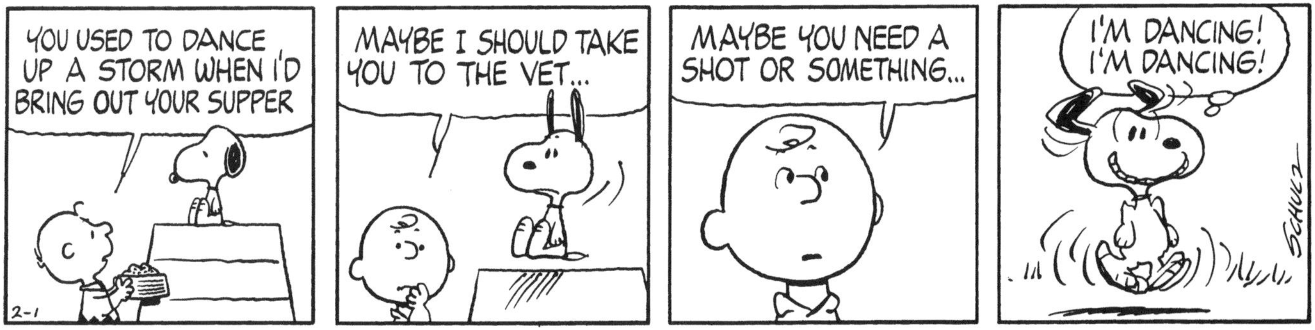
YOU USED TO DANCE UP A STORM WHEN I'D BRING OUT YOUR SUPPER
2-1
MAYBE I SHOULD TAKE YOU TO THE VET...
MAYBE YOU NEED A SHOT OR SOMETHING...
I'M DANCING! I'M DANCING!
SCHULZ

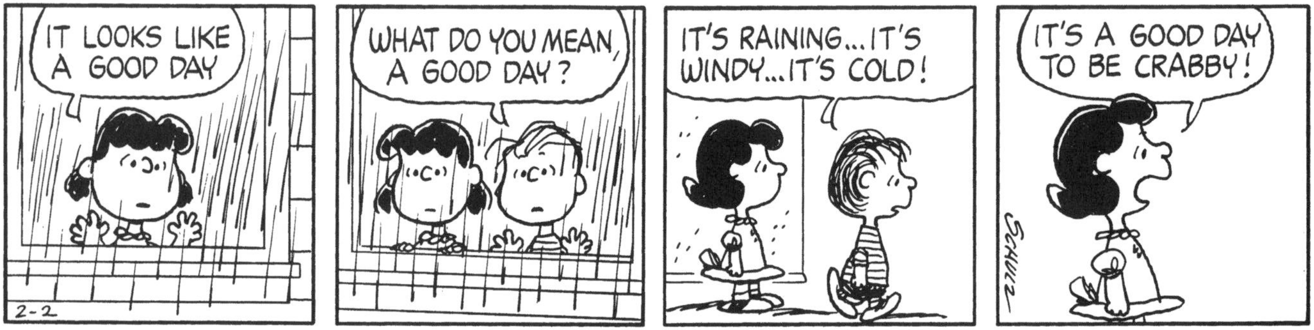
IT LOOKS LIKE A GOOD DAY
WHAT DO YOU MEAN, A GOOD DAY?
IT'S RAINING...IT'S WINDY...IT'S COLD!
IT'S A GOOD DAY TO BE CRABBY!

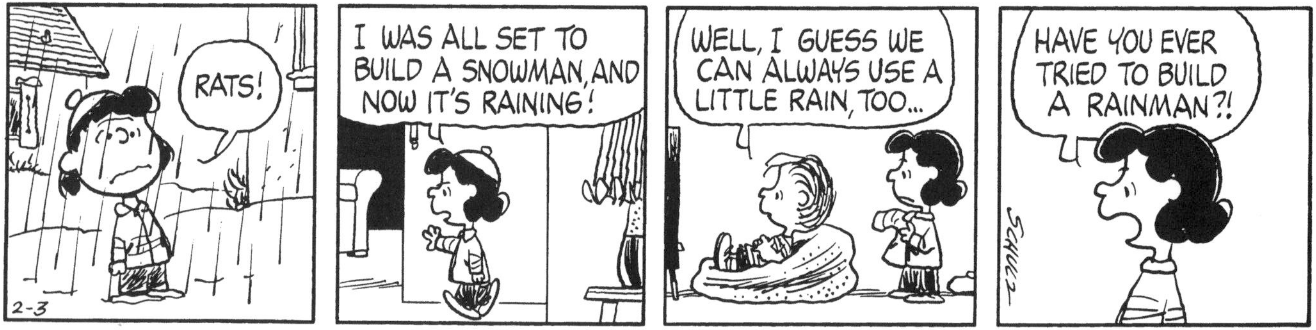
RATS!
I WAS ALL SET TO BUILD A SNOWMAN, AND NOW IT'S RAINING!
WELL, I GUESS WE CAN ALWAYS USE A LITTLE RAIN, TOO...
HAVE YOU EVER TRIED TO BUILD A RAINMAN?!

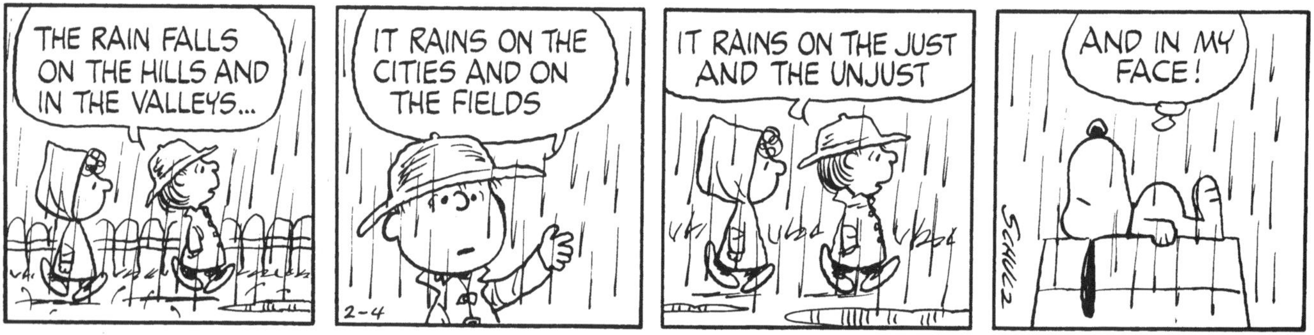
THE RAIN FALLS ON THE HILLS AND IN THE VALLEYS...
IT RAINS ON THE CITIES AND ON THE FIELDS
IT RAINS ON THE JUST AND THE UNJUST
AND IN MY FACE!

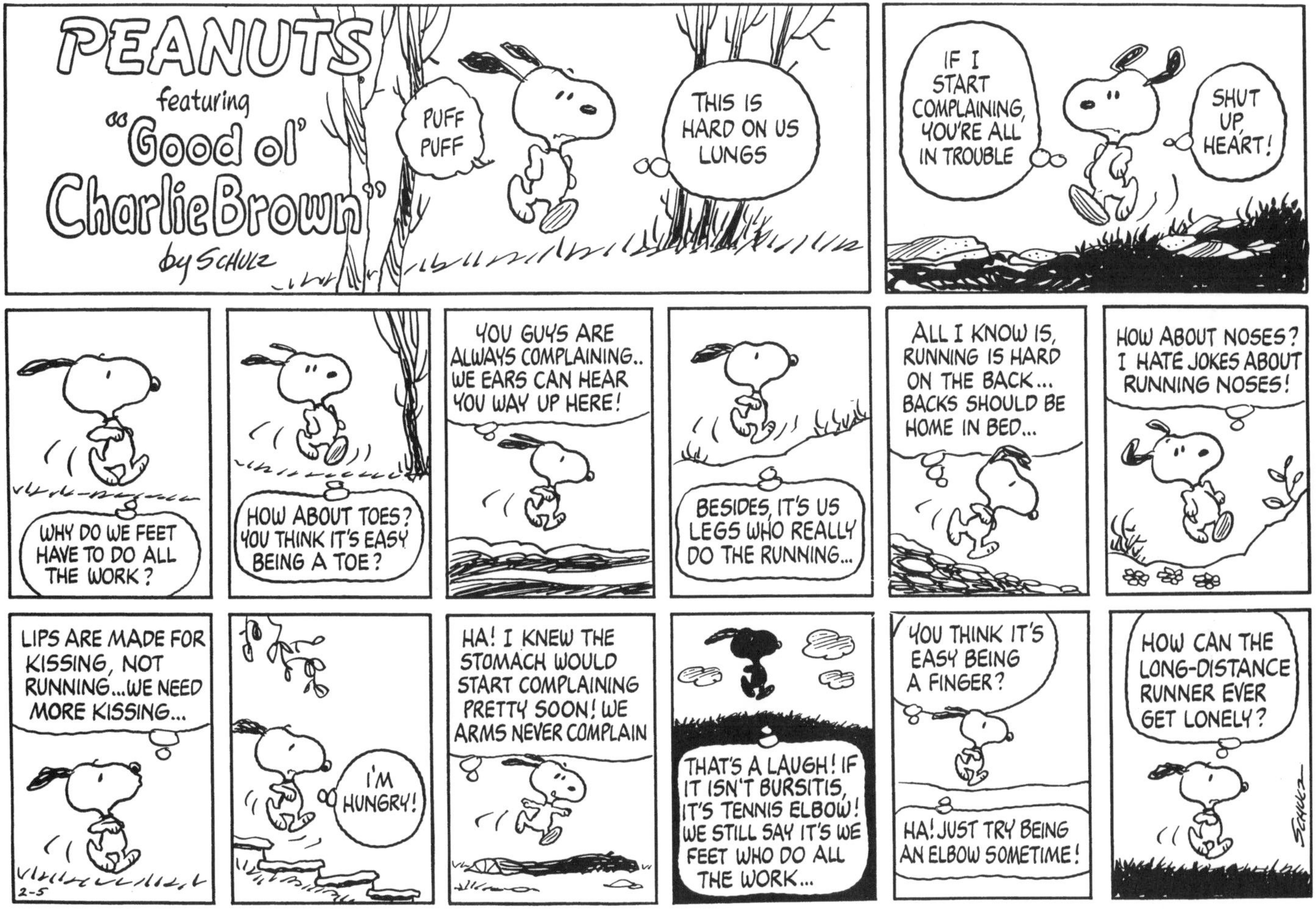

PEANUTS
featuring "Good ol' Charlie Brown"
by SCHULZ
PUFF PUFF
THIS IS HARD ON US LUNGS
IF I START COMPLAINING, YOU'RE ALL IN TROUBLE
SHUT UP, HEART!
WHY DO WE FEET HAVE TO DO ALL THE WORK?
HOW ABOUT TOES? YOU THINK IT'S EASY BEING A TOE?
YOU GUYS ARE ALWAYS COMPLAINING.. WE EARS CAN HEAR YOU WAY UP HERE!
BESIDES, IT'S US LEGS WHO REALLY DO THE RUNNING...
ALL I KNOW IS, RUNNING IS HARD ON THE BACK... BACKS SHOULD BE HOME IN BED...
HOW ABOUT NOSES? I HATE JOKES ABOUT RUNNING NOSES!
LIPS ARE MADE FOR KISSING, NOT RUNNING...WE NEED MORE KISSING...
2-5
I'M HUNGRY!
HA! I KNEW THE STOMACH WOULD START COMPLAINING PRETTY SOON! WE ARMS NEVER COMPLAIN
THAT'S A LAUGH! IF IT ISN'T BURSITIS, IT'S TENNIS ELBOW! WE STILL SAY IT'S WE FEET WHO DO ALL THE WORK...
YOU THINK IT'S EASY BEING A FINGER?
HA! JUST TRY BEING AN ELBOW SOMETIME!
HOW CAN THE LONG-DISTANCE RUNNER EVER GET LONELY?
SCHULZ

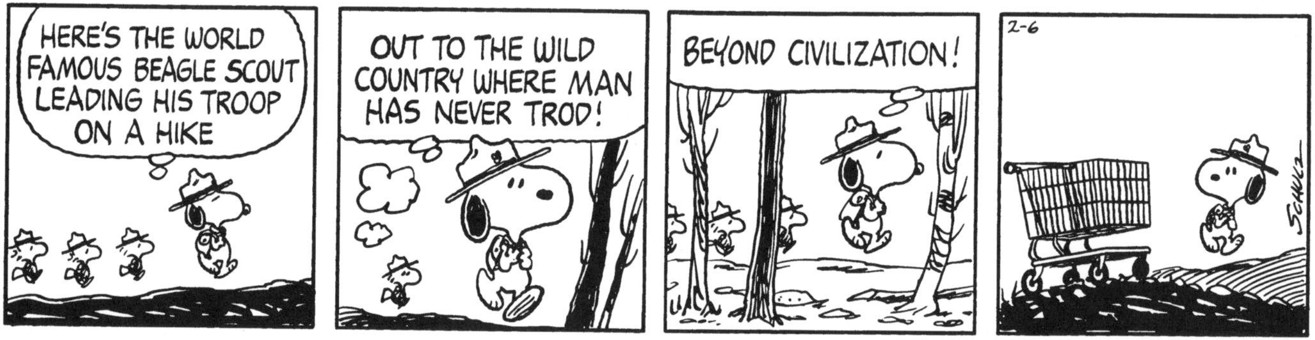
HERE'S THE WORLD FAMOUS BEAGLE SCOUT LEADING HIS TROOP ON A HIKE
OUT TO THE WILD COUNTRY WHERE MAN HAS NEVER TROD!
BEYOND CIVILIZATION!
2-6
SCHULZ

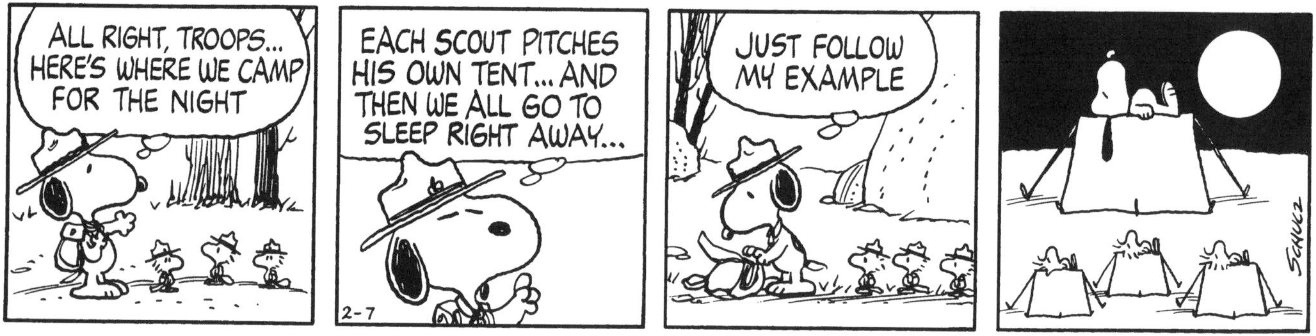
ALL RIGHT, TROOPS... HERE'S WHERE WE CAMP FOR THE NIGHT
EACH SCOUT PITCHES HIS OWN TENT... AND THEN WE ALL GO TO SLEEP RIGHT AWAY...
2-7
JUST FOLLOW MY EXAMPLE
SCHULZ

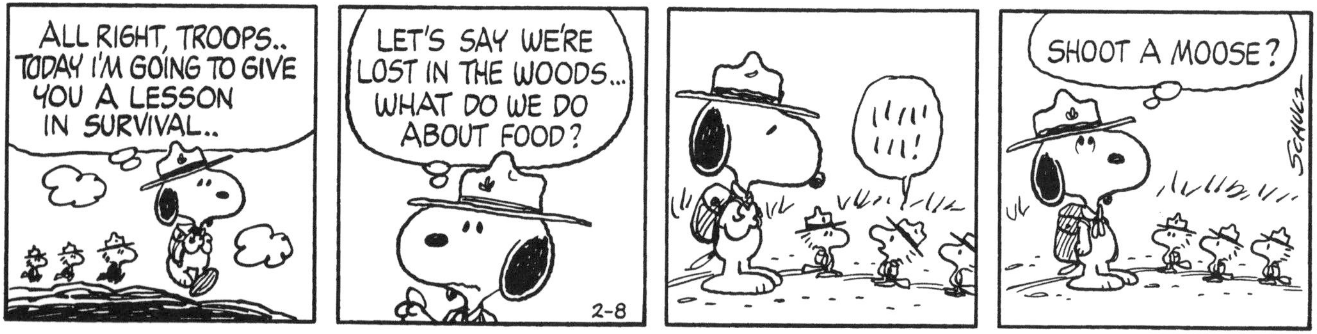
ALL RIGHT, TROOPS.. TODAY I'M GOING TO GIVE YOU A LESSON IN SURVIVAL..
LET'S SAY WE'RE LOST IN THE WOODS... WHAT DO WE DO ABOUT FOOD?
2-8
SHOOT A MOOSE?
SCHULZ

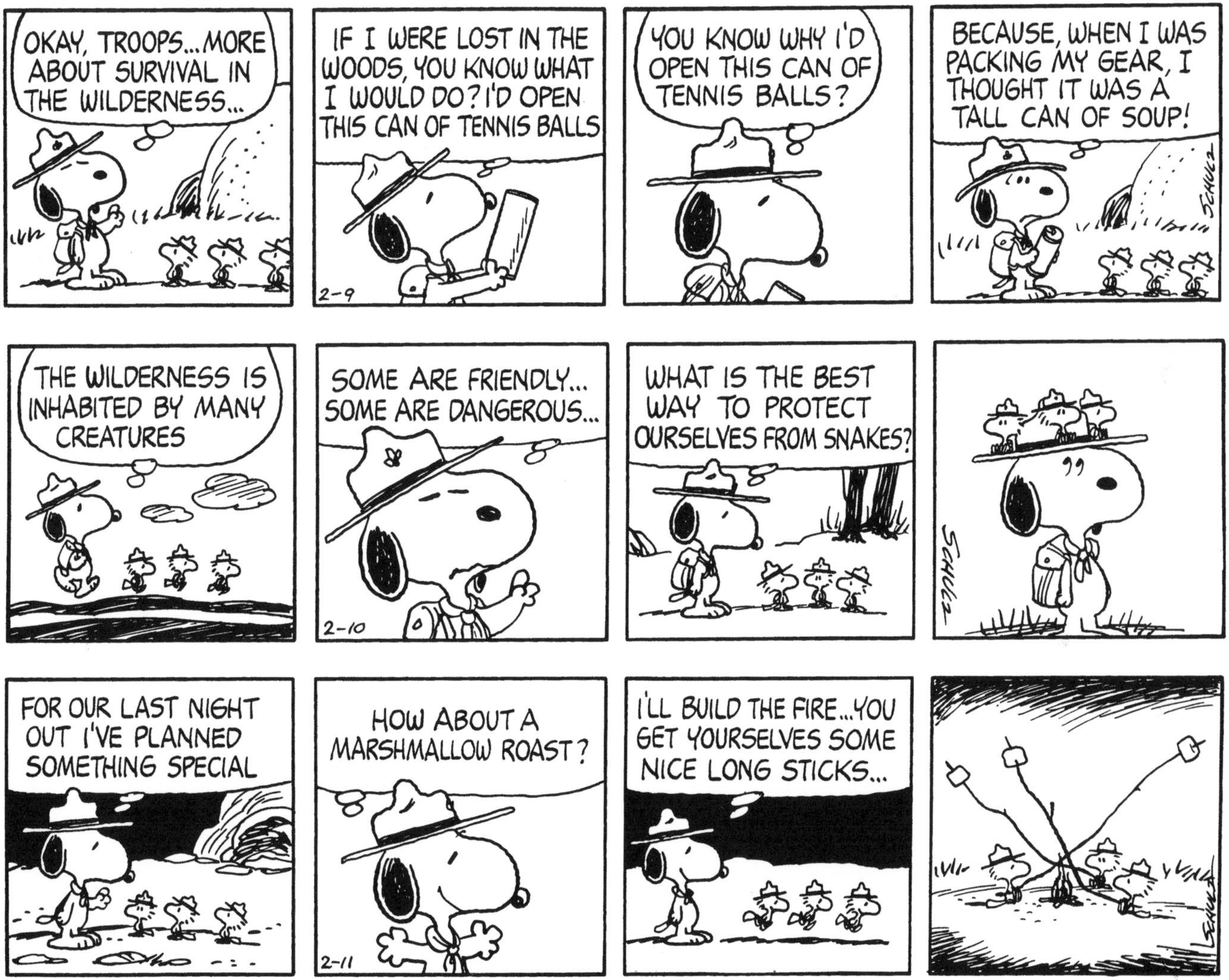
OKAY, TROOPS...MORE ABOUT SURVIVAL IN THE WILDERNESS...
IF I WERE LOST IN THE WOODS, YOU KNOW WHAT I WOULD DO? I'D OPEN THIS CAN OF TENNIS BALLS
2-9
YOU KNOW WHY I'D OPEN THIS CAN OF TENNIS BALLS?
BECAUSE, WHEN I WAS PACKING MY GEAR, I THOUGHT IT WAS A TALL CAN OF SOUP!
SCHULZ
THE WILDERNESS IS INHABITED BY MANY CREATURES
SOME ARE FRIENDLY... SOME ARE DANGEROUS...
2-10
WHAT IS THE BEST WAY TO PROTECT OURSELVES FROM SNAKES?
SCHULZ
FOR OUR LAST NIGHT OUT I'VE PLANNED SOMETHING SPECIAL
HOW ABOUT A MARSHMALLOW ROAST?
2-11
I'LL BUILD THE FIRE...YOU GET YOURSELVES SOME NICE LONG STICKS...
SCHULZ

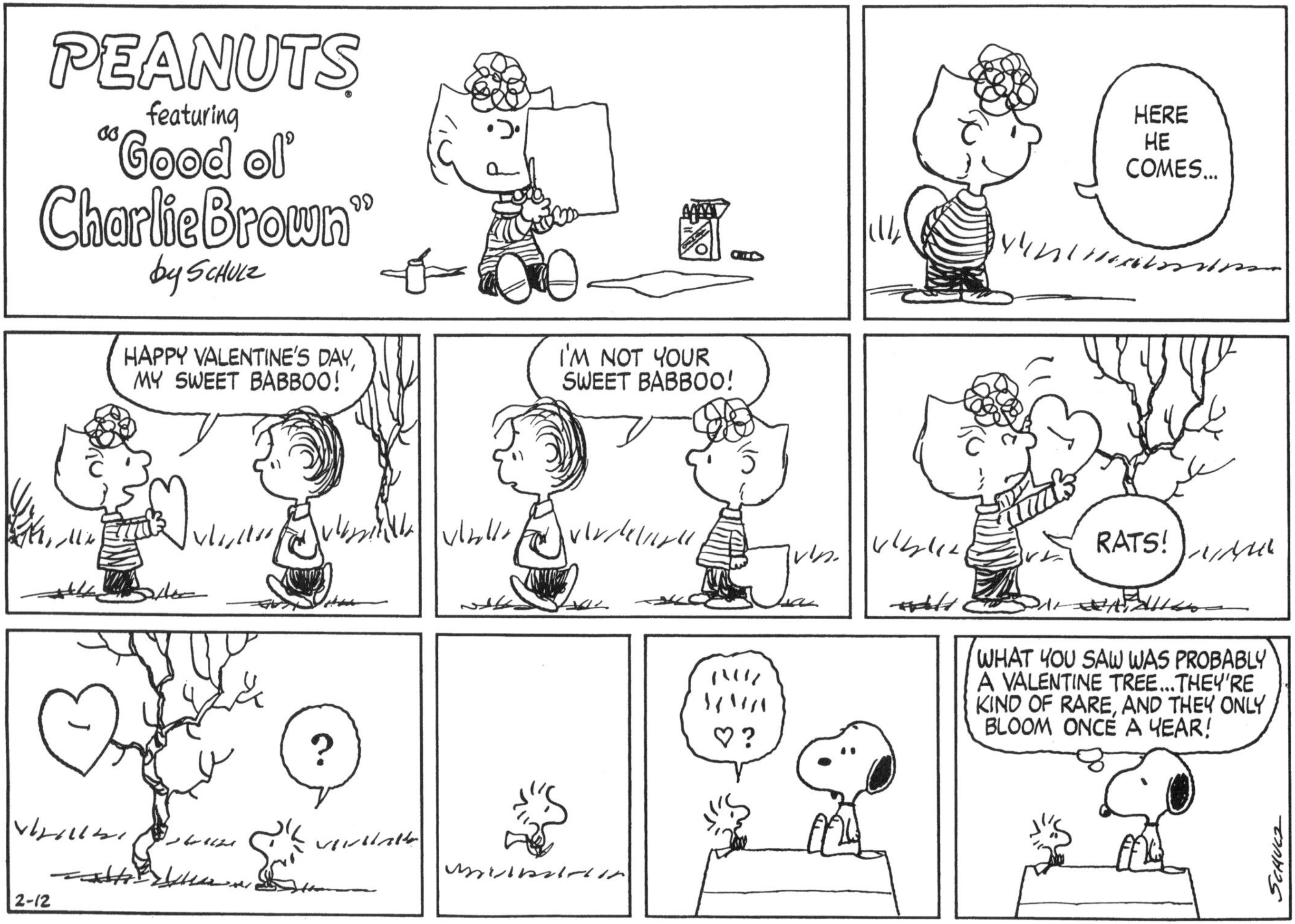
PEANUTS
featuring
"Good ol' CharlieBrown"
by SCHULZ
HERE HE COMES...
HAPPY VALENTINE'S DAY, MY SWEET BABBOO!
I'M NOT YOUR SWEET BABBOO!
RATS!
?
2-12
♡ ?
WHAT YOU SAW WAS PROBABLY A VALENTINE TREE...THEY'RE KIND OF RARE, AND THEY ONLY BLOOM ONCE A YEAR!
SCHULZ

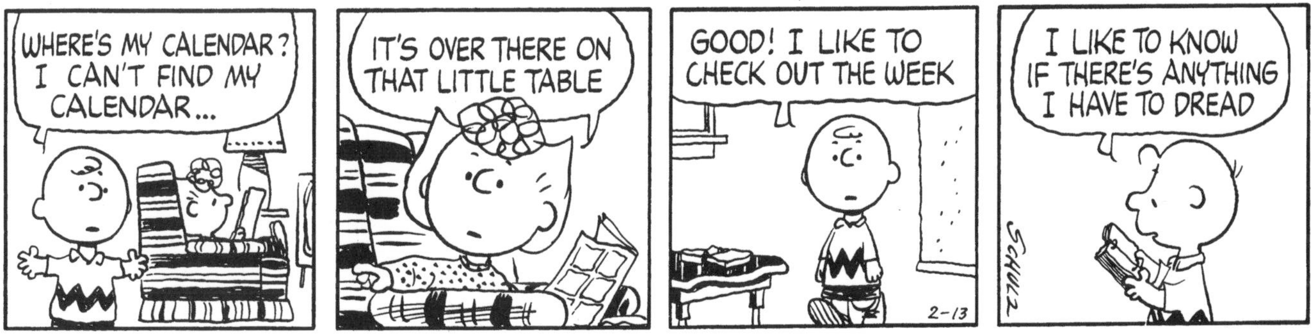
WHERE'S MY CALENDAR? I CAN'T FIND MY CALENDAR...
IT'S OVER THERE ON THAT LITTLE TABLE
GOOD! I LIKE TO CHECK OUT THE WEEK
2-13
I LIKE TO KNOW IF THERE'S ANYTHING I HAVE TO DREAD
SCHULZ

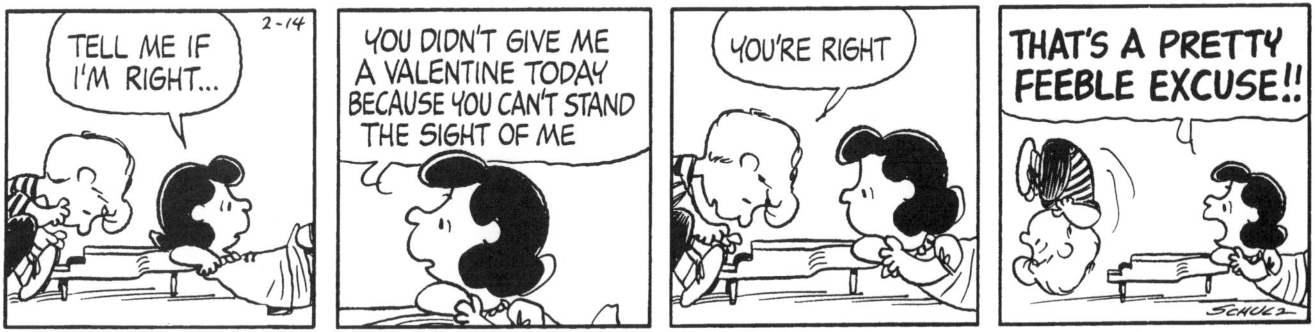
TELL ME IF I'M RIGHT...
2-14
YOU DIDN'T GIVE ME A VALENTINE TODAY BECAUSE YOU CAN'T STAND THE SIGHT OF ME
YOU'RE RIGHT
THAT'S A PRETTY FEEBLE EXCUSE!!
SCHULZ

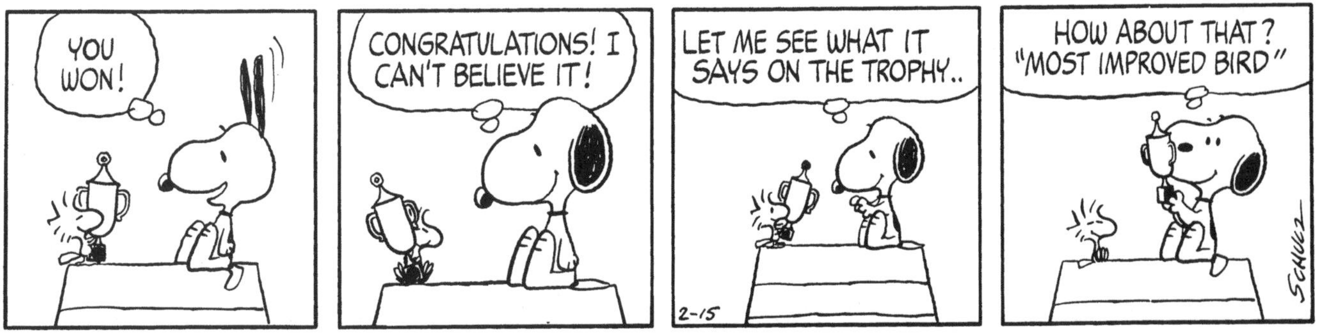
YOU WON!
CONGRATULATIONS! I CAN'T BELIEVE IT!
LET ME SEE WHAT IT SAYS ON THE TROPHY..
2-15
HOW ABOUT THAT? "MOST IMPROVED BIRD"
SCHULZ

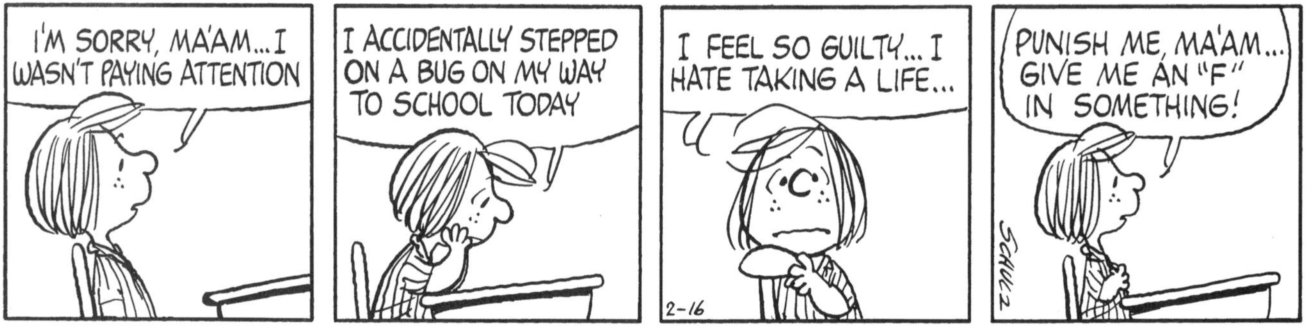
I'M SORRY, MA'AM...I WASN'T PAYING ATTENTION
I ACCIDENTALLY STEPPED ON A BUG ON MY WAY TO SCHOOL TODAY
I FEEL SO GUILTY...I HATE TAKING A LIFE...
PUNISH ME, MA'AM...GIVE ME AN "F" IN SOMETHING!

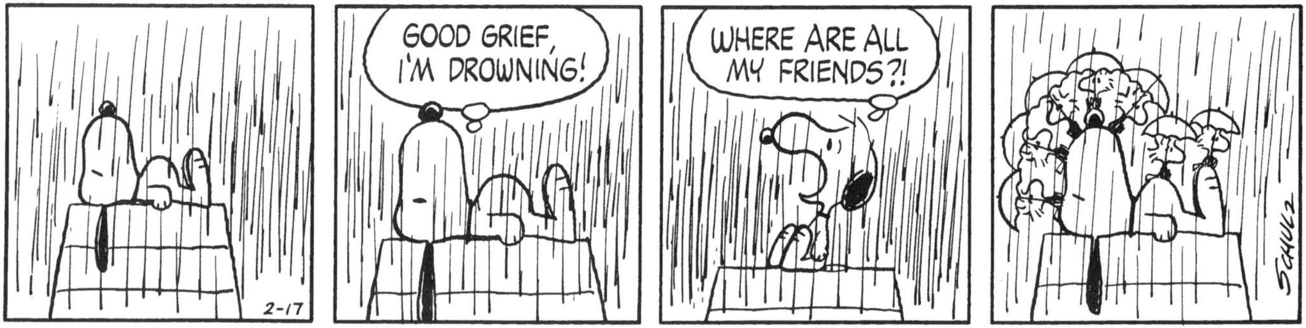
GOOD GRIEF, I'M DROWNING!
WHERE ARE ALL MY FRIENDS?!

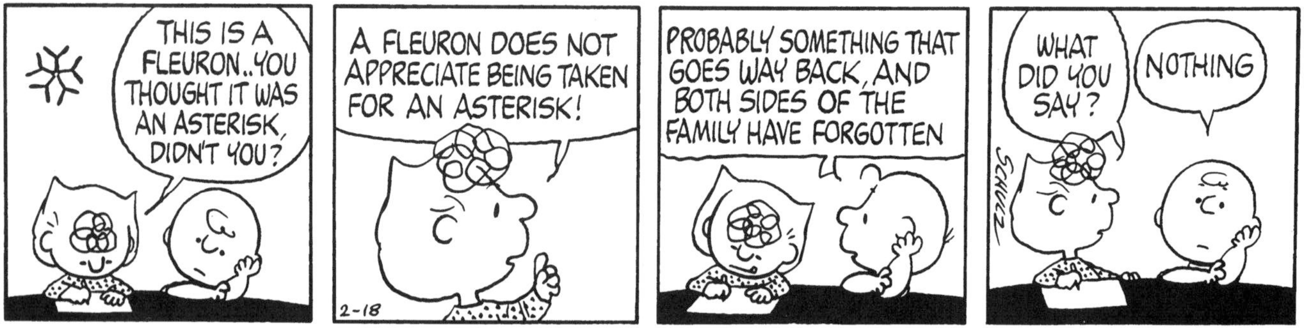
THIS IS A FLEURON..YOU THOUGHT IT WAS AN ASTERISK, DIDN'T YOU?
A FLEURON DOES NOT APPRECIATE BEING TAKEN FOR AN ASTERISK!
PROBABLY SOMETHING THAT GOES WAY BACK, AND BOTH SIDES OF THE FAMILY HAVE FORGOTTEN
WHAT DID YOU SAY?
NOTHING

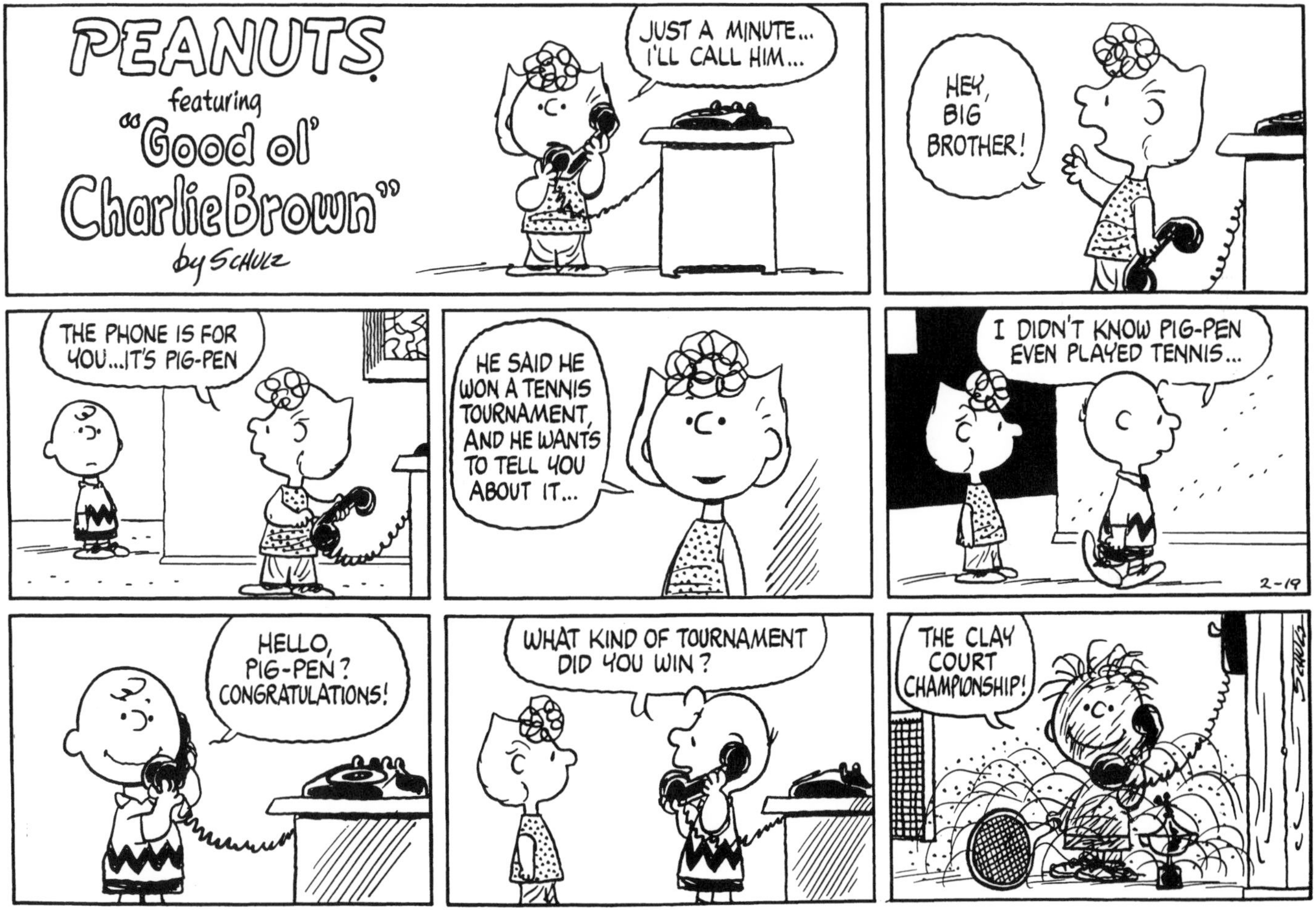
PEANUTS
featuring "Good ol' Charlie Brown"
by SCHULZ
JUST A MINUTE... I'LL CALL HIM...
HEY, BIG BROTHER!
THE PHONE IS FOR YOU...IT'S PIG-PEN
HE SAID HE WON A TENNIS TOURNAMENT, AND HE WANTS TO TELL YOU ABOUT IT...
I DIDN'T KNOW PIG-PEN EVEN PLAYED TENNIS...
2-19
HELLO, PIG-PEN? CONGRATULATIONS!
WHAT KIND OF TOURNAMENT DID YOU WIN?
THE CLAY COURT CHAMPIONSHIP!
SCHULZ

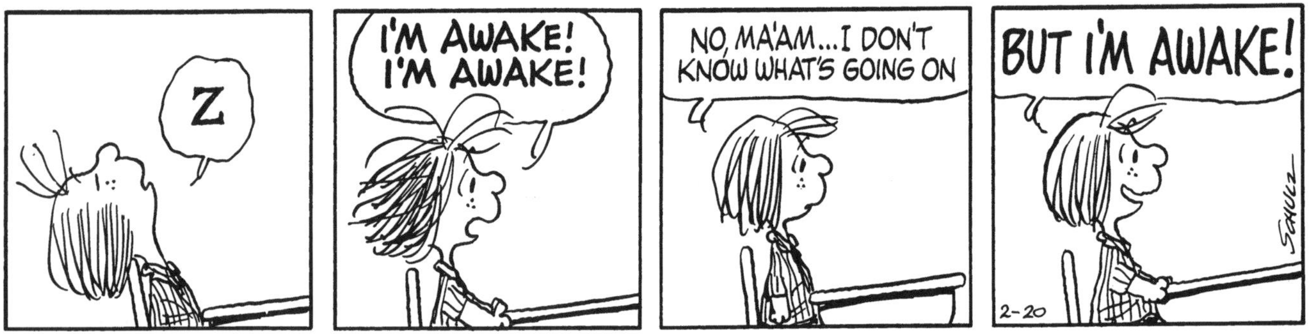
Z
I'M AWAKE! I'M AWAKE!
NO, MA'AM...I DON'T KNOW WHAT'S GOING ON
BUT I'M AWAKE!
2-20
SCHULZ

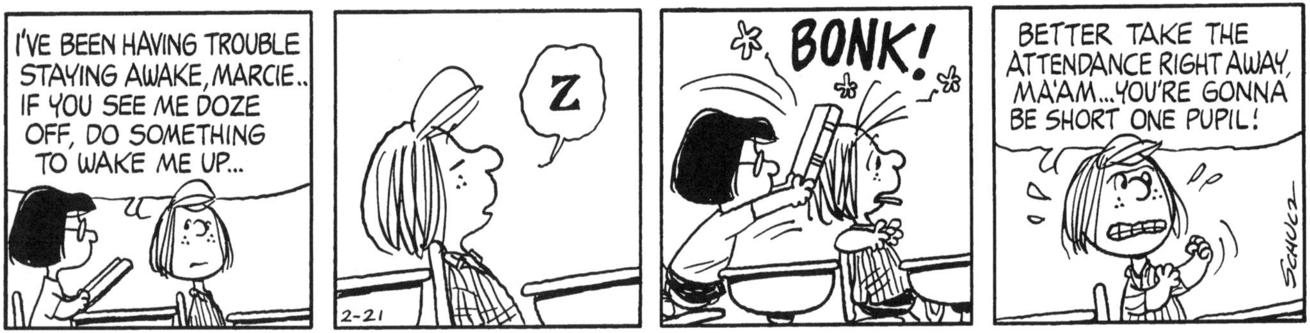
I'VE BEEN HAVING TROUBLE STAYING AWAKE, MARCIE.. IF YOU SEE ME DOZE OFF, DO SOMETHING TO WAKE ME UP...
Z
2-21
BONK!
BETTER TAKE THE ATTENDANCE RIGHT AWAY, MA'AM...YOU'RE GONNA BE SHORT ONE PUPIL!
SCHULZ

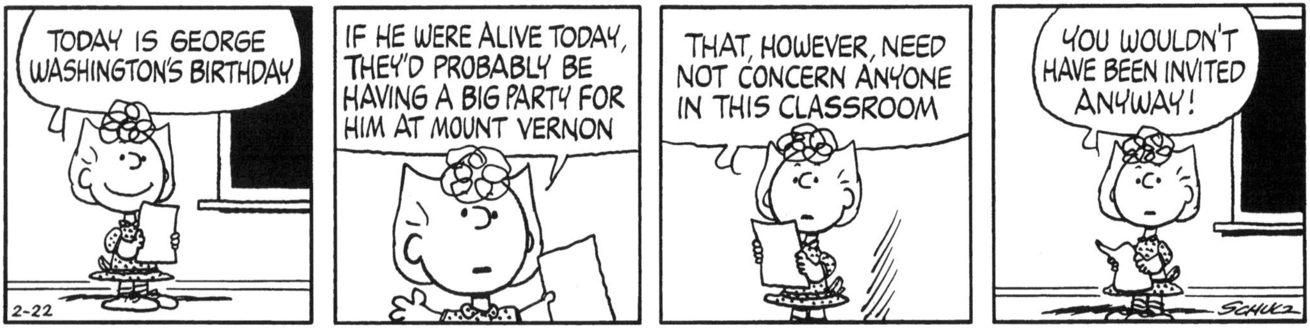
TODAY IS GEORGE WASHINGTON'S BIRTHDAY
2-22
IF HE WERE ALIVE TODAY, THEY'D PROBABLY BE HAVING A BIG PARTY FOR HIM AT MOUNT VERNON
THAT, HOWEVER, NEED NOT CONCERN ANYONE IN THIS CLASSROOM
YOU WOULDN'T HAVE BEEN INVITED ANYWAY!
SCHULZ

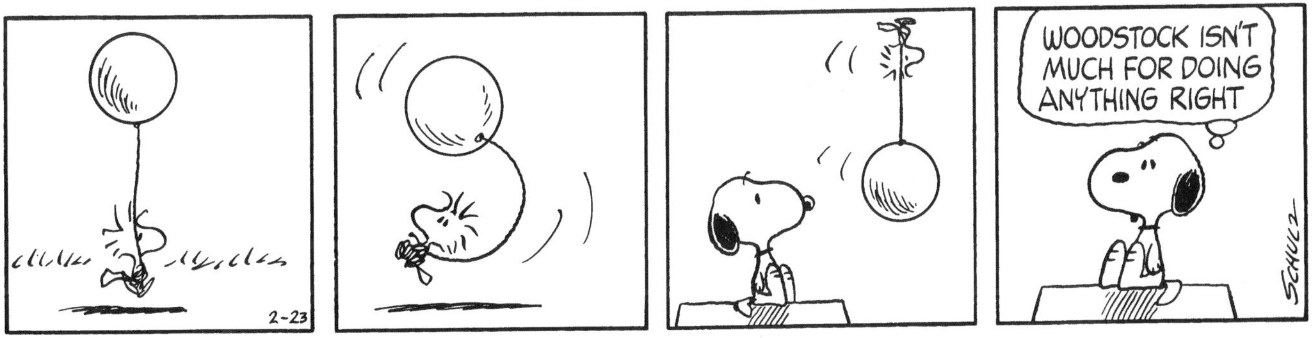
2-23
WOODSTOCK ISN'T MUCH FOR DOING ANYTHING RIGHT
SCHULZ

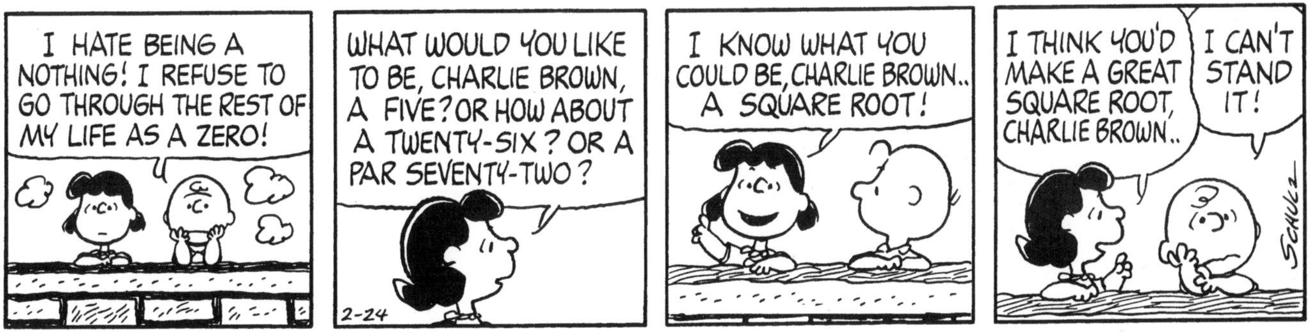
I HATE BEING A NOTHING! I REFUSE TO GO THROUGH THE REST OF MY LIFE AS A ZERO!
WHAT WOULD YOU LIKE TO BE, CHARLIE BROWN, A FIVE? OR HOW ABOUT A TWENTY-SIX? OR A PAR SEVENTY-TWO?
2-24
I KNOW WHAT YOU COULD BE, CHARLIE BROWN.. A SQUARE ROOT!
I THINK YOU'D MAKE A GREAT SQUARE ROOT, CHARLIE BROWN..
I CAN'T STAND IT!
SCHULZ

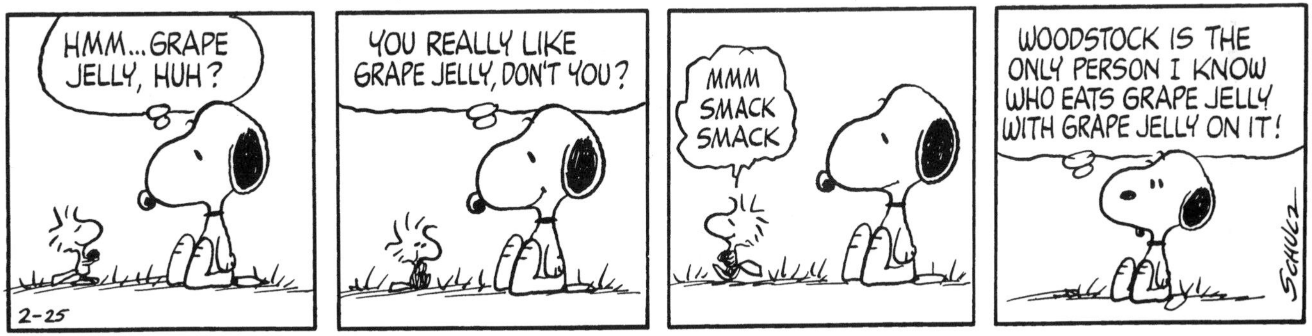
HMM...GRAPE JELLY, HUH?
2-25
YOU REALLY LIKE GRAPE JELLY, DON'T YOU?
MMM SMACK SMACK
WOODSTOCK IS THE ONLY PERSON I KNOW WHO EATS GRAPE JELLY WITH GRAPE JELLY ON IT!
SCHULZ

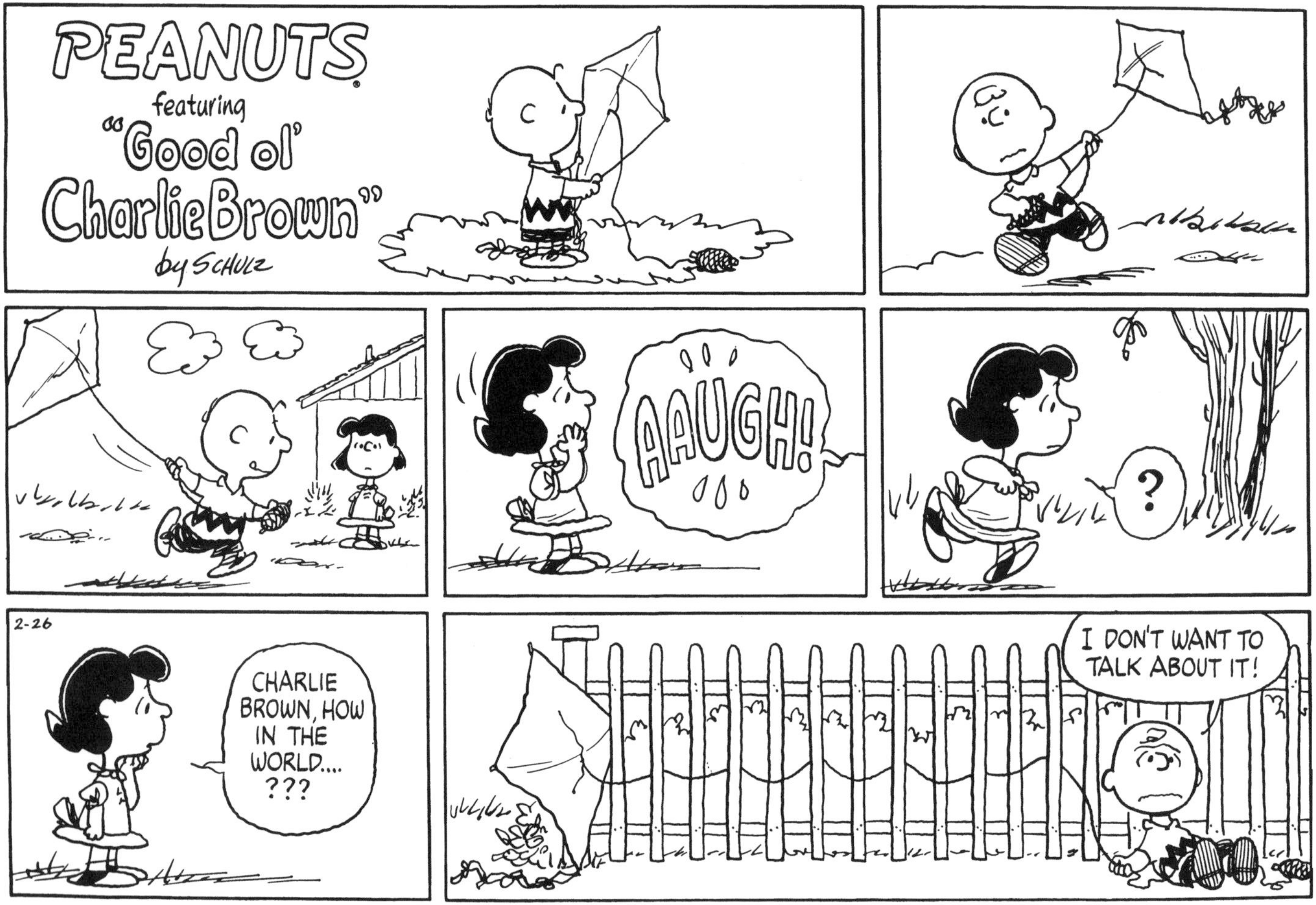
PEANUTS
featuring
"Good ol' Charlie Brown"
by SCHULZ
AAUGH!
?
2-26
CHARLIE BROWN, HOW IN THE WORLD.... ???
I DON'T WANT TO TALK ABOUT IT!

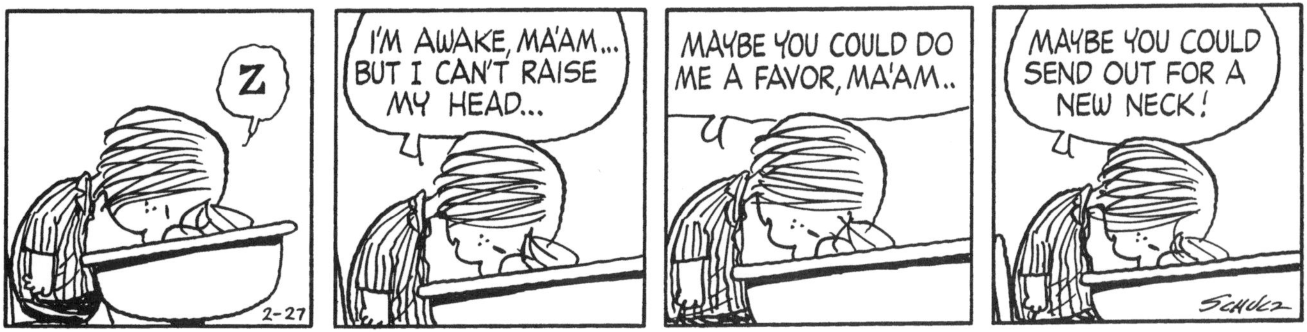
Z
I'M AWAKE, MA'AM... BUT I CAN'T RAISE MY HEAD...
MAYBE YOU COULD DO ME A FAVOR, MA'AM..
MAYBE YOU COULD SEND OUT FOR A NEW NECK!
2-27
SCHULZ

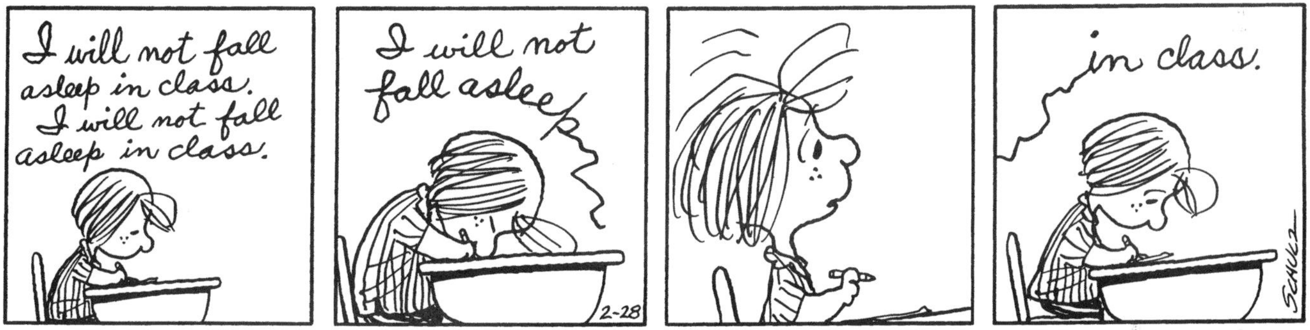
I will not fall asleep in class. I will not fall asleep in class.
I will not fall asleep
in class.
2-28
SCHULZ

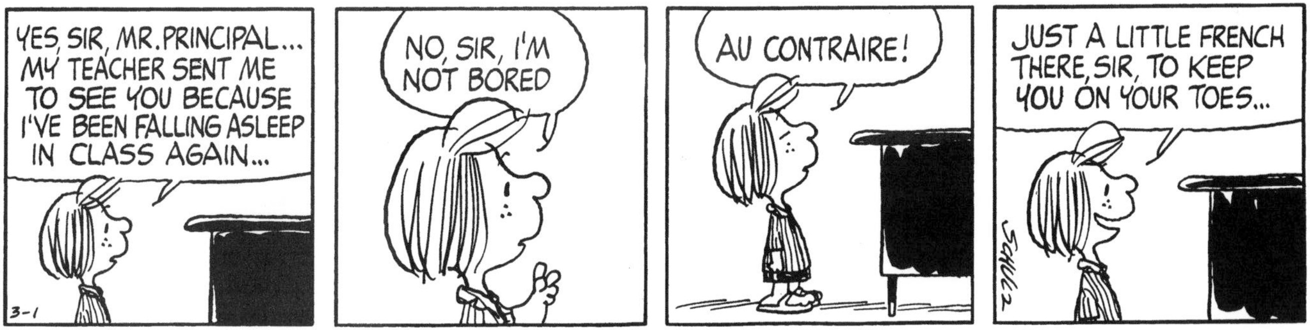
YES, SIR, MR. PRINCIPAL... MY TEACHER SENT ME TO SEE YOU BECAUSE I'VE BEEN FALLING ASLEEP IN CLASS AGAIN...
NO, SIR, I'M NOT BORED
AU CONTRAIRE!
JUST A LITTLE FRENCH THERE, SIR, TO KEEP YOU ON YOUR TOES...
3-1
SCHULZ

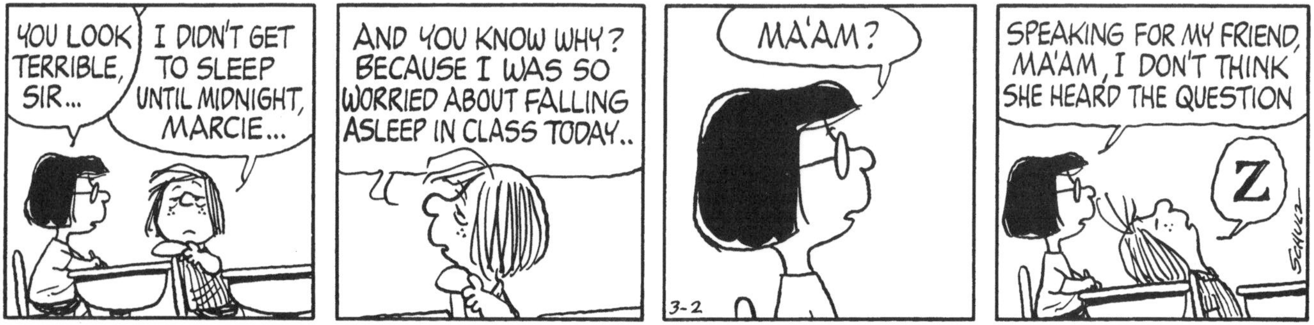
YOU LOOK TERRIBLE, SIR...
I DIDN'T GET TO SLEEP UNTIL MIDNIGHT, MARCIE...
AND YOU KNOW WHY? BECAUSE I WAS SO WORRIED ABOUT FALLING ASLEEP IN CLASS TODAY..
MA'AM?
3-2
SPEAKING FOR MY FRIEND, MA'AM, I DON'T THINK SHE HEARD THE QUESTION
Z

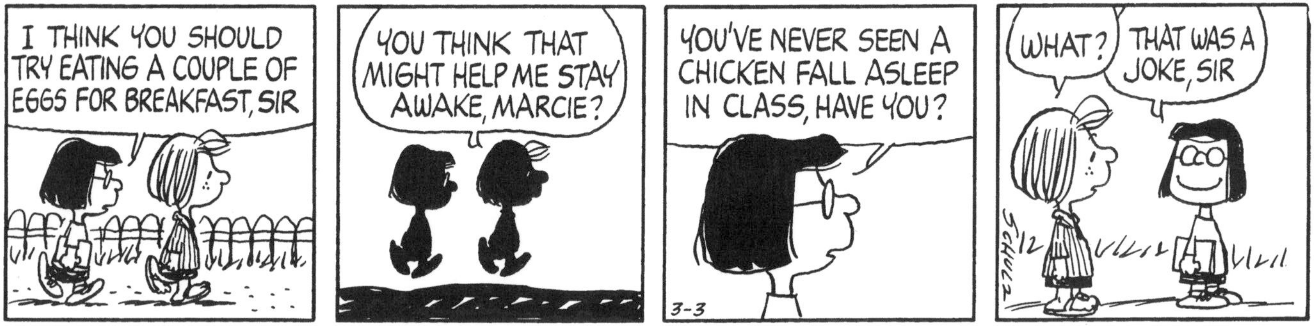
I THINK YOU SHOULD TRY EATING A COUPLE OF EGGS FOR BREAKFAST, SIR
YOU THINK THAT MIGHT HELP ME STAY AWAKE, MARCIE?
YOU'VE NEVER SEEN A CHICKEN FALL ASLEEP IN CLASS, HAVE YOU?
3-3
WHAT?
THAT WAS A JOKE, SIR

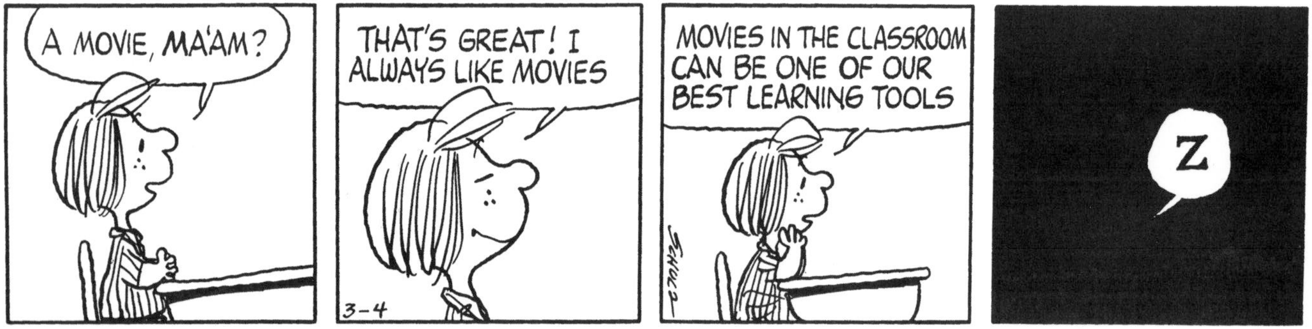
A MOVIE, MA'AM?
THAT'S GREAT! I ALWAYS LIKE MOVIES
3-4
MOVIES IN THE CLASSROOM CAN BE ONE OF OUR BEST LEARNING TOOLS
Z

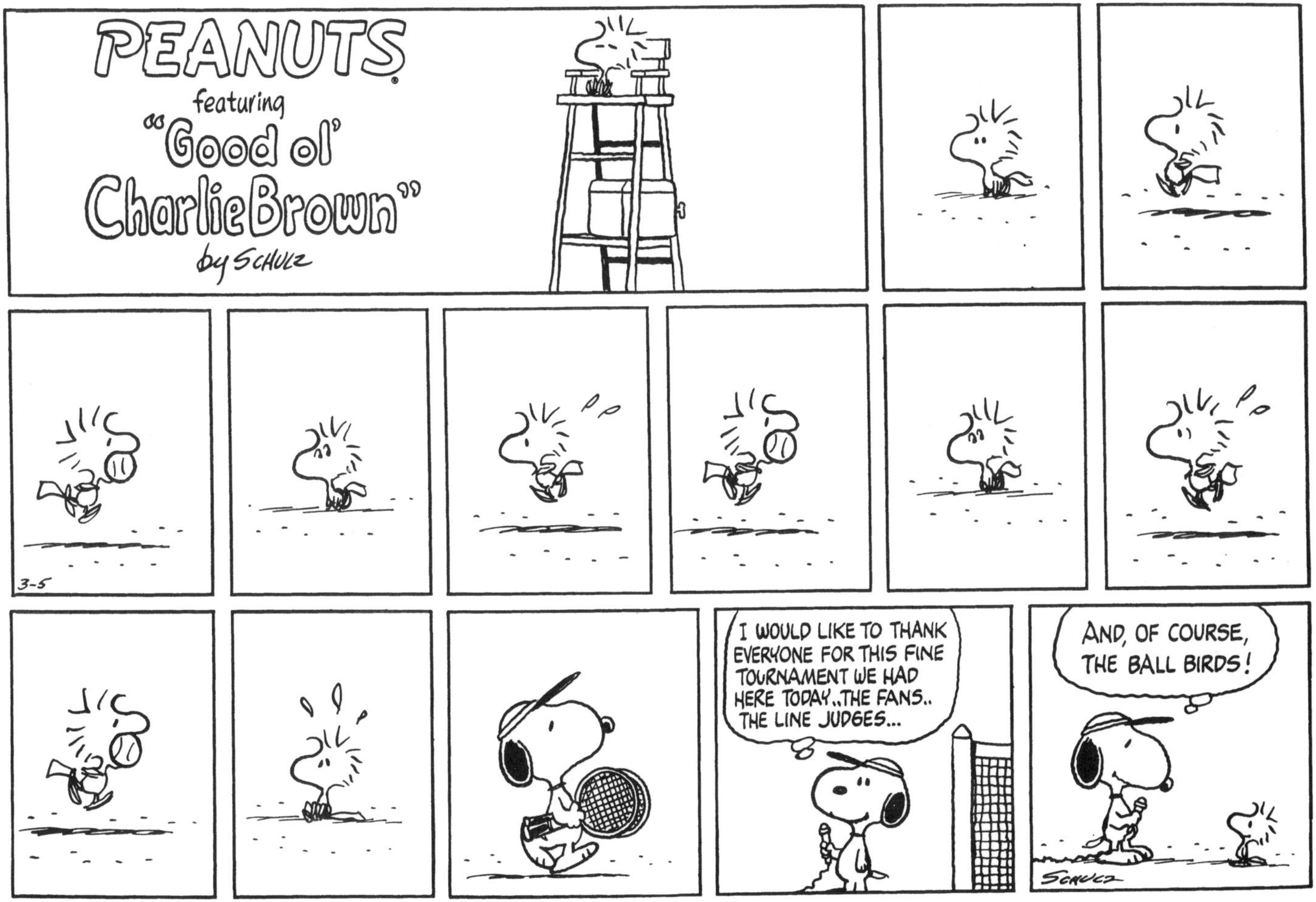
PEANUTS
featuring
"Good ol' Charlie Brown"
by SCHULZ
3-5
I WOULD LIKE TO THANK EVERYONE FOR THIS FINE TOURNAMENT WE HAD HERE TODAY..THE FANS.. THE LINE JUDGES...
AND, OF COURSE, THE BALL BIRDS!
SCHULZ

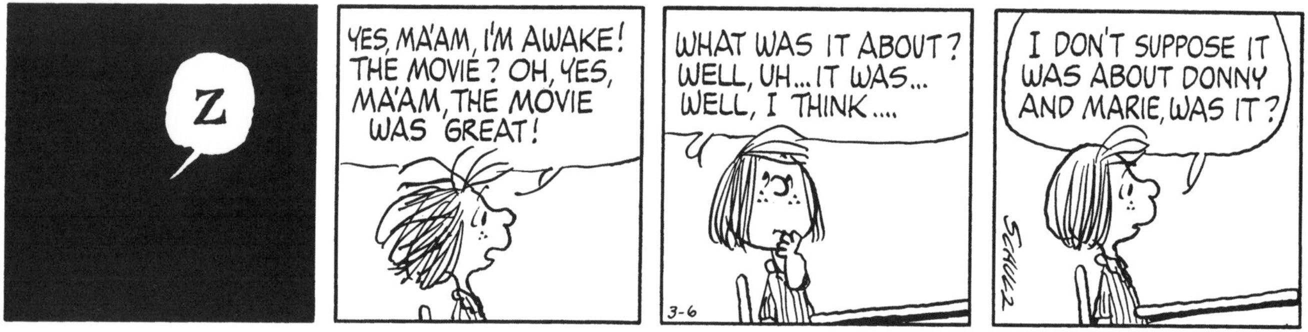
Z
YES, MA'AM, I'M AWAKE! THE MOVIE? OH, YES, MA'AM, THE MOVIE WAS GREAT!
WHAT WAS IT ABOUT? WELL, UH... IT WAS... WELL, I THINK....
3-6
I DON'T SUPPOSE IT WAS ABOUT DONNY AND MARIE, WAS IT?
SCHULZ

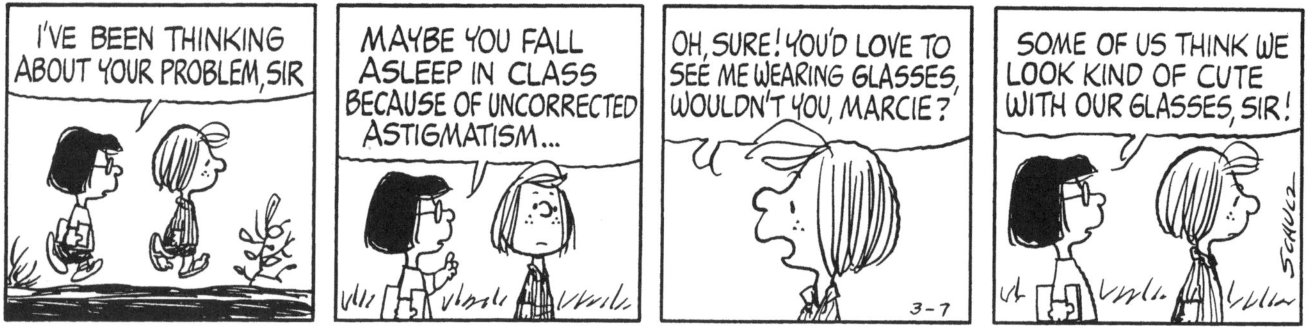
I'VE BEEN THINKING ABOUT YOUR PROBLEM, SIR
MAYBE YOU FALL ASLEEP IN CLASS BECAUSE OF UNCORRECTED ASTIGMATISM...
OH, SURE! YOU'D LOVE TO SEE ME WEARING GLASSES, WOULDN'T YOU, MARCIE?
3-7
SOME OF US THINK WE LOOK KIND OF CUTE WITH OUR GLASSES, SIR!
SCHULZ

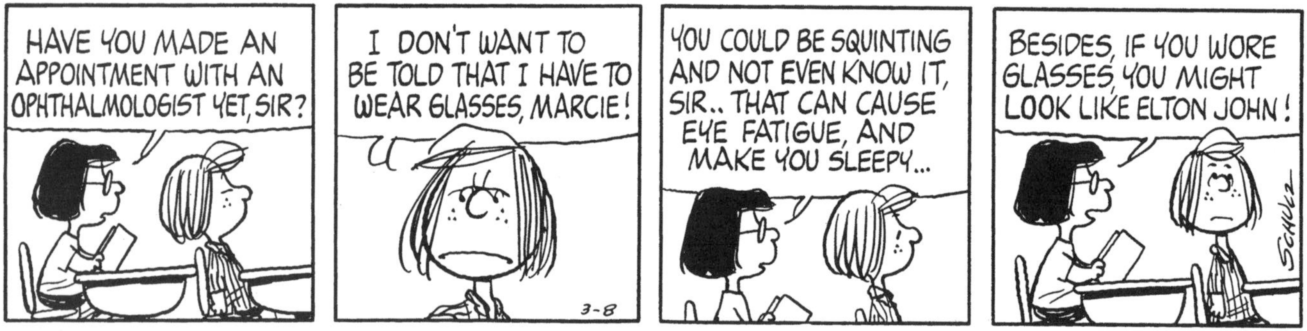
HAVE YOU MADE AN APPOINTMENT WITH AN OPHTHALMOLOGIST YET, SIR?
I DON'T WANT TO BE TOLD THAT I HAVE TO WEAR GLASSES, MARCIE!
3-8
YOU COULD BE SQUINTING AND NOT EVEN KNOW IT, SIR.. THAT CAN CAUSE EYE FATIGUE, AND MAKE YOU SLEEPY...
BESIDES, IF YOU WORE GLASSES, YOU MIGHT LOOK LIKE ELTON JOHN!
SCHULZ

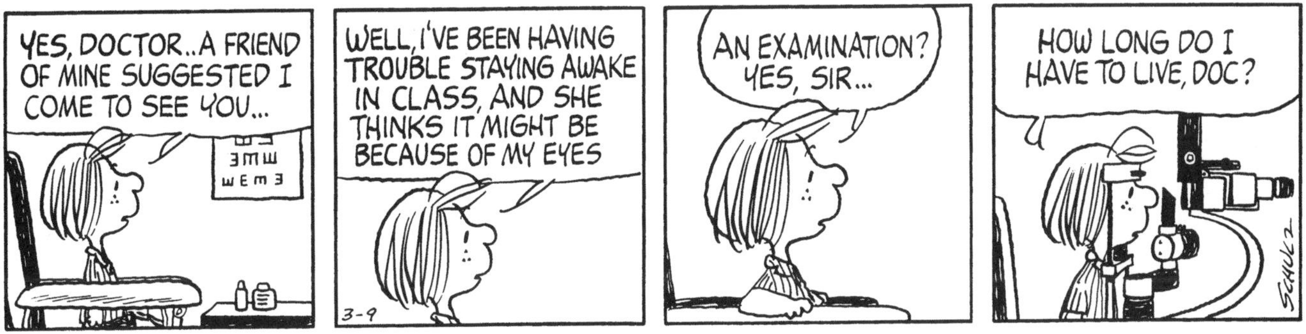
YES, DOCTOR...A FRIEND OF MINE SUGGESTED I COME TO SEE YOU...
WELL, I'VE BEEN HAVING TROUBLE STAYING AWAKE IN CLASS, AND SHE THINKS IT MIGHT BE BECAUSE OF MY EYES
3-9
AN EXAMINATION? YES, SIR...
HOW LONG DO I HAVE TO LIVE, DOC?
SCHULZ

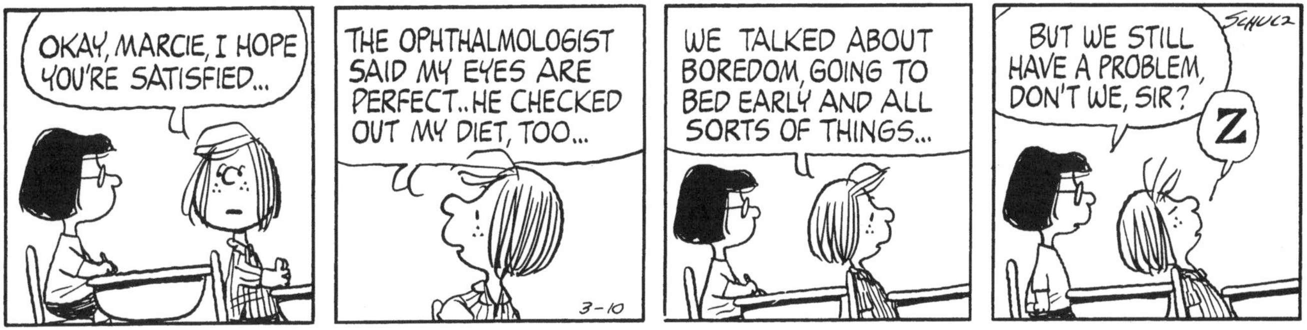
OKAY, MARCIE, I HOPE YOU'RE SATISFIED...
THE OPHTHALMOLOGIST SAID MY EYES ARE PERFECT..HE CHECKED OUT MY DIET, TOO...
3-10
WE TALKED ABOUT BOREDOM, GOING TO BED EARLY AND ALL SORTS OF THINGS...
SCHULZ
BUT WE STILL HAVE A PROBLEM, DON'T WE, SIR?
Z

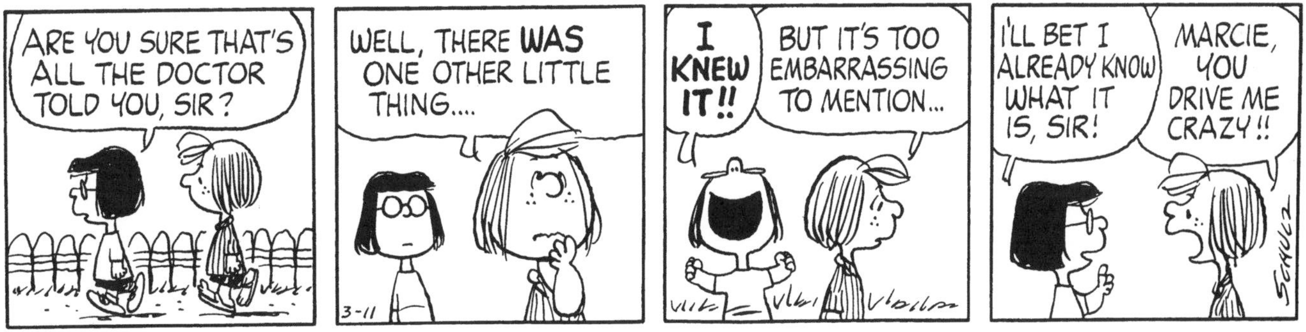
ARE YOU SURE THAT'S ALL THE DOCTOR TOLD YOU, SIR?
WELL, THERE **WAS** ONE OTHER LITTLE THING....
3-11
I KNEW IT!!
BUT IT'S TOO EMBARRASSING TO MENTION...
I'LL BET I ALREADY KNOW WHAT IT IS, SIR!
MARCIE, YOU DRIVE ME CRAZY!!
SCHULZ

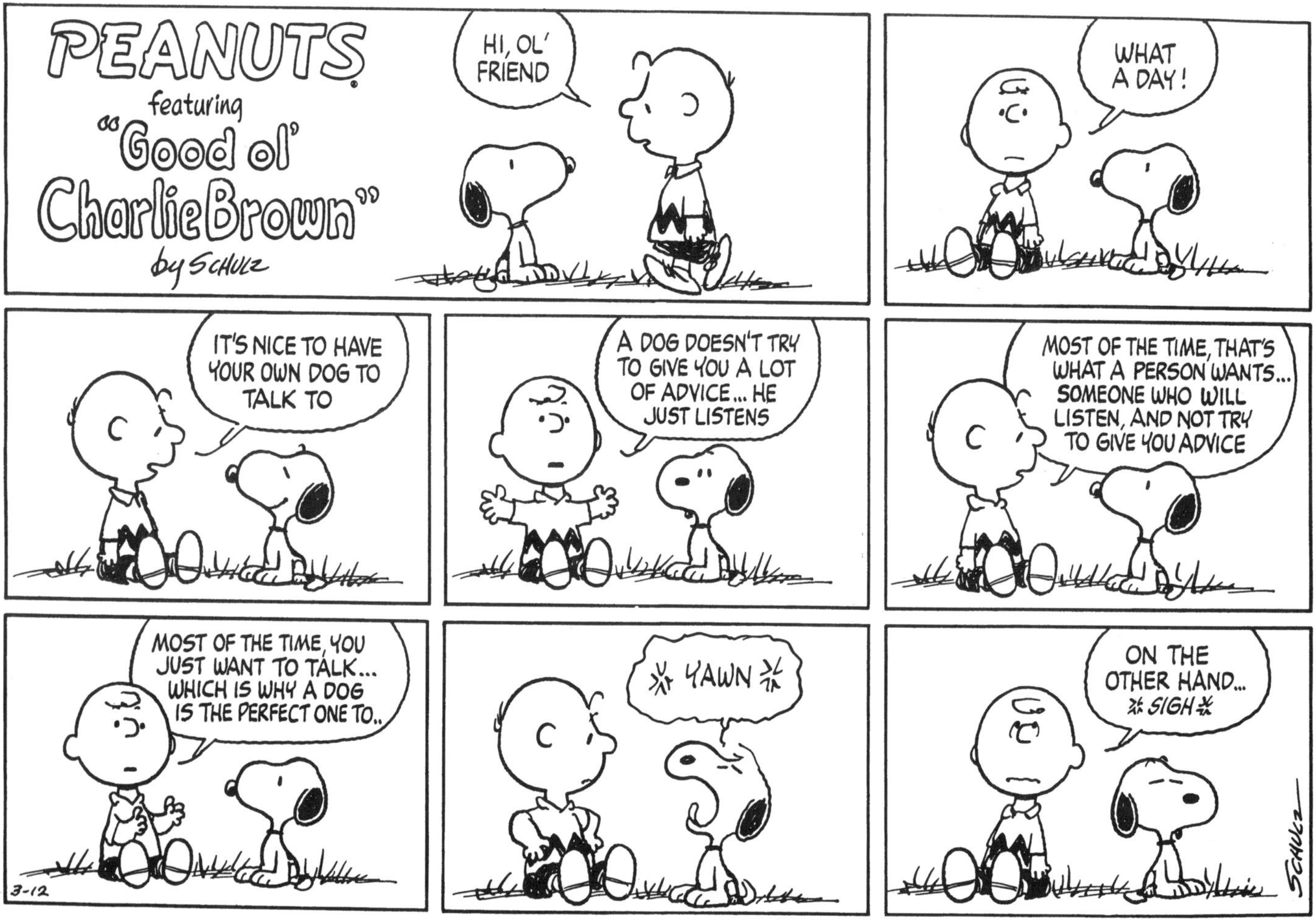
PEANUTS
featuring
"Good ol' Charlie Brown"
by SCHULZ
HI, OL' FRIEND
WHAT A DAY!
IT'S NICE TO HAVE YOUR OWN DOG TO TALK TO
A DOG DOESN'T TRY TO GIVE YOU A LOT OF ADVICE... HE JUST LISTENS
MOST OF THE TIME, THAT'S WHAT A PERSON WANTS... SOMEONE WHO WILL LISTEN, AND NOT TRY TO GIVE YOU ADVICE
MOST OF THE TIME, YOU JUST WANT TO TALK... WHICH IS WHY A DOG IS THE PERFECT ONE TO..
3-12
YAWN
ON THE OTHER HAND... SIGH
SCHULZ

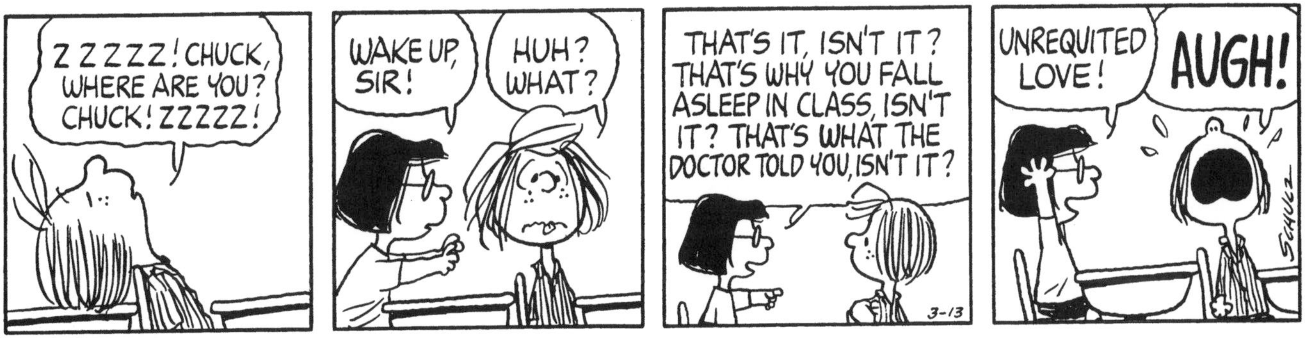
Z Z Z Z Z! CHUCK, WHERE ARE YOU? CHUCK! ZZZZZ!
WAKE UP, SIR!
HUH? WHAT?
THAT'S IT, ISN'T IT? THAT'S WHY YOU FALL ASLEEP IN CLASS, ISN'T IT? THAT'S WHAT THE DOCTOR TOLD YOU, ISN'T IT?
3-13
UNREQUITED LOVE!
AUGH!
SCHULZ

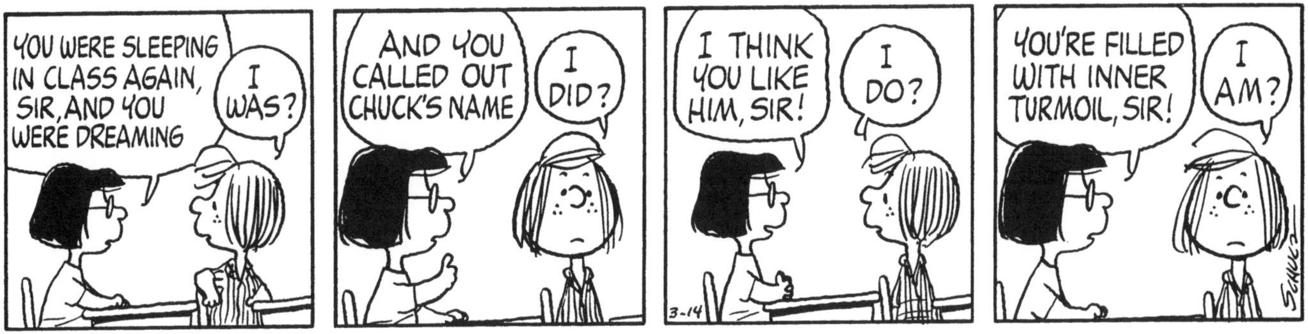
YOU WERE SLEEPING IN CLASS AGAIN, SIR, AND YOU WERE DREAMING
I WAS?
AND YOU CALLED OUT CHUCK'S NAME
I DID?
I THINK YOU LIKE HIM, SIR!
I DO?
3-14
YOU'RE FILLED WITH INNER TURMOIL, SIR!
I AM?
SCHULZ

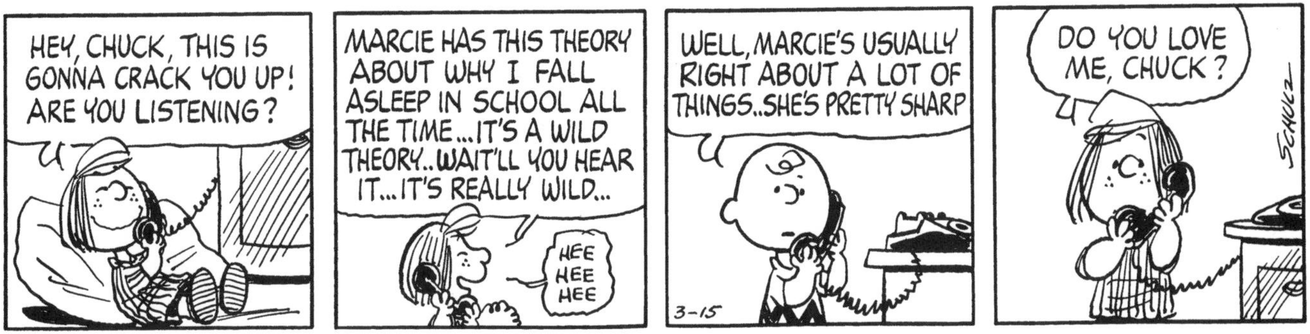
HEY, CHUCK, THIS IS GONNA CRACK YOU UP! ARE YOU LISTENING?
MARCIE HAS THIS THEORY ABOUT WHY I FALL ASLEEP IN SCHOOL ALL THE TIME... IT'S A WILD THEORY.. WAIT'LL YOU HEAR IT... IT'S REALLY WILD...
HEE HEE HEE
WELL, MARCIE'S USUALLY RIGHT ABOUT A LOT OF THINGS.. SHE'S PRETTY SHARP
3-15
DO YOU LOVE ME, CHUCK?
SCHULZ

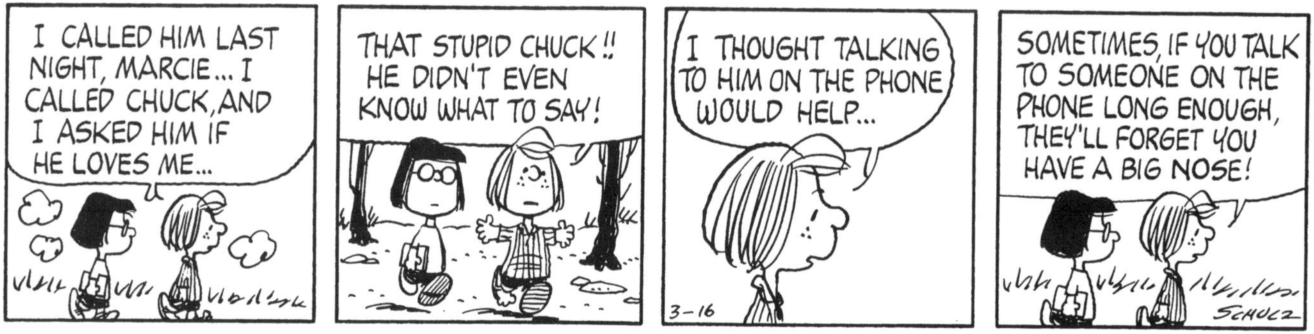
I CALLED HIM LAST NIGHT, MARCIE... I CALLED CHUCK, AND I ASKED HIM IF HE LOVES ME...
THAT STUPID CHUCK!! HE DIDN'T EVEN KNOW WHAT TO SAY!
I THOUGHT TALKING TO HIM ON THE PHONE WOULD HELP...
3-16
SOMETIMES, IF YOU TALK TO SOMEONE ON THE PHONE LONG ENOUGH, THEY'LL FORGET YOU HAVE A BIG NOSE!
SCHULZ

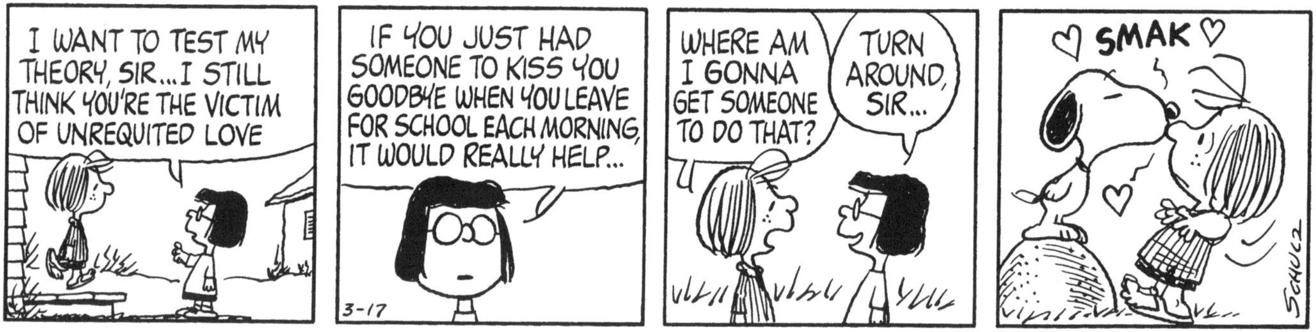
I WANT TO TEST MY THEORY, SIR... I STILL THINK YOU'RE THE VICTIM OF UNREQUITED LOVE
IF YOU JUST HAD SOMEONE TO KISS YOU GOODBYE WHEN YOU LEAVE FOR SCHOOL EACH MORNING, IT WOULD REALLY HELP...
3-17
WHERE AM I GONNA GET SOMEONE TO DO THAT?
TURN AROUND, SIR...
SMAK
SCHULZ

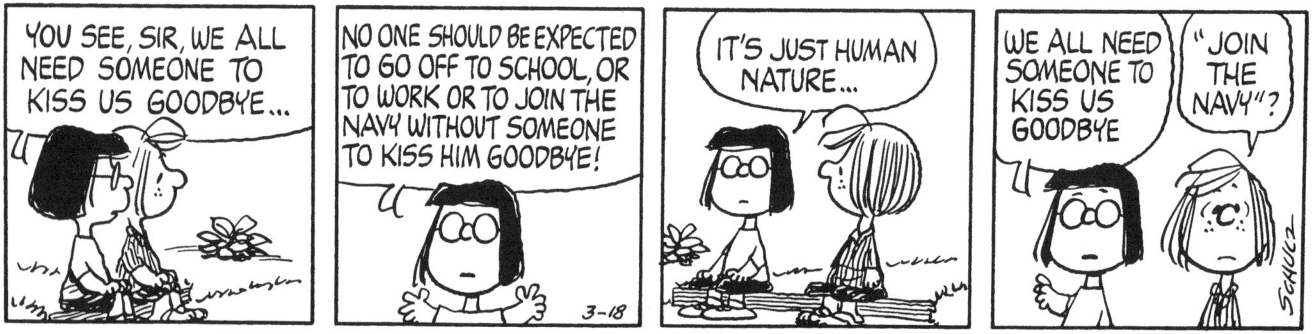
YOU SEE, SIR, WE ALL NEED SOMEONE TO KISS US GOODBYE...
NO ONE SHOULD BE EXPECTED TO GO OFF TO SCHOOL, OR TO WORK OR TO JOIN THE NAVY WITHOUT SOMEONE TO KISS HIM GOODBYE!
3-18
IT'S JUST HUMAN NATURE...
WE ALL NEED SOMEONE TO KISS US GOODBYE
"JOIN THE NAVY"?
SCHULZ

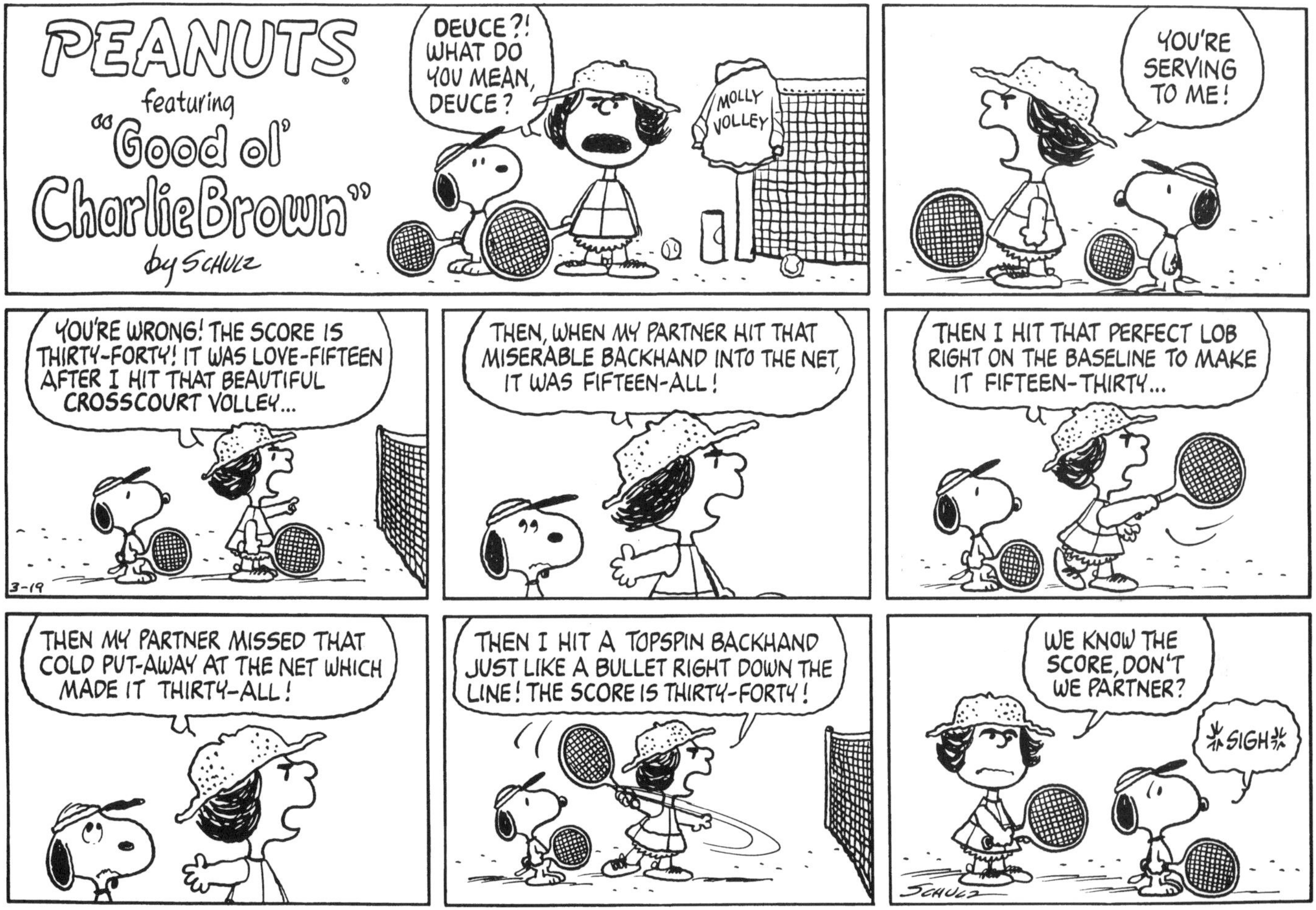
PEANUTS
featuring
"Good ol' Charlie Brown"
by SCHULZ
DEUCE?! WHAT DO YOU MEAN, DEUCE?
MOLLY VOLLEY
YOU'RE SERVING TO ME!
YOU'RE WRONG! THE SCORE IS THIRTY-FORTY! IT WAS LOVE-FIFTEEN AFTER I HIT THAT BEAUTIFUL CROSSCOURT VOLLEY...
3-19
THEN, WHEN MY PARTNER HIT THAT MISERABLE BACKHAND INTO THE NET, IT WAS FIFTEEN-ALL!
THEN I HIT THAT PERFECT LOB RIGHT ON THE BASELINE TO MAKE IT FIFTEEN-THIRTY...
THEN MY PARTNER MISSED THAT COLD PUT-AWAY AT THE NET WHICH MADE IT THIRTY-ALL!
THEN I HIT A TOPSPIN BACKHAND JUST LIKE A BULLET RIGHT DOWN THE LINE! THE SCORE IS THIRTY-FORTY!
WE KNOW THE SCORE, DON'T WE PARTNER?
SIGH
SCHULZ

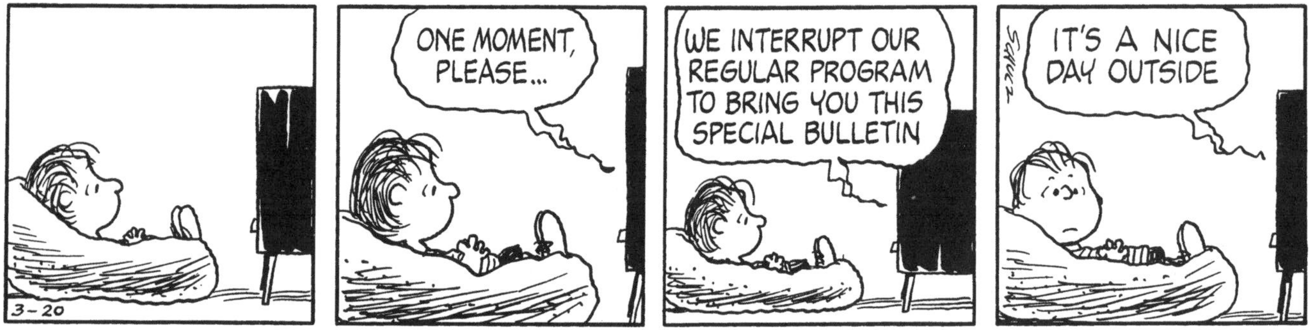
3-20
ONE MOMENT, PLEASE...
WE INTERRUPT OUR REGULAR PROGRAM TO BRING YOU THIS SPECIAL BULLETIN
SCHULZ
IT'S A NICE DAY OUTSIDE

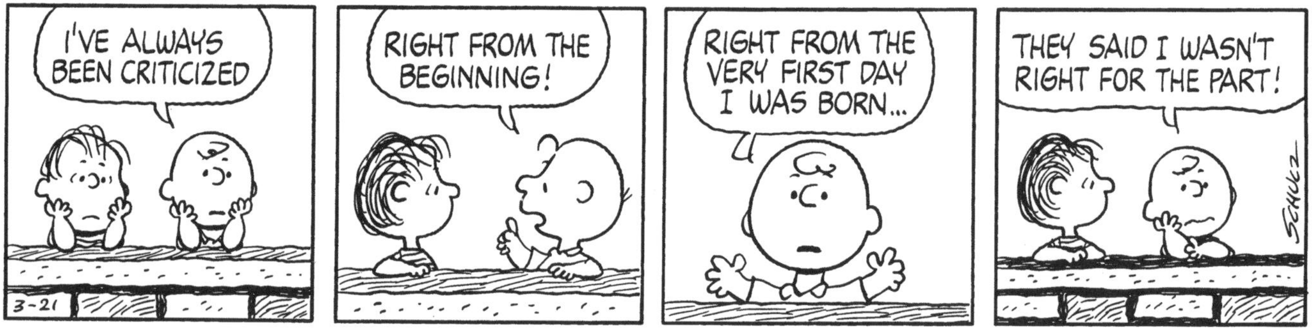
I'VE ALWAYS BEEN CRITICIZED
3-21
RIGHT FROM THE BEGINNING!
RIGHT FROM THE VERY FIRST DAY I WAS BORN...
THEY SAID I WASN'T RIGHT FOR THE PART!
SCHULZ

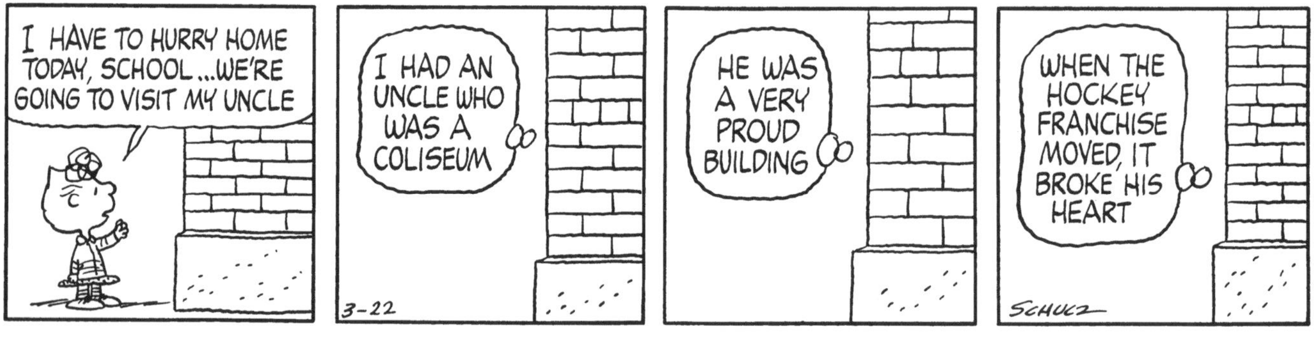
I HAVE TO HURRY HOME TODAY, SCHOOL...WE'RE GOING TO VISIT MY UNCLE
I HAD AN UNCLE WHO WAS A COLISEUM
3-22
HE WAS A VERY PROUD BUILDING
WHEN THE HOCKEY FRANCHISE MOVED, IT BROKE HIS HEART
SCHULZ

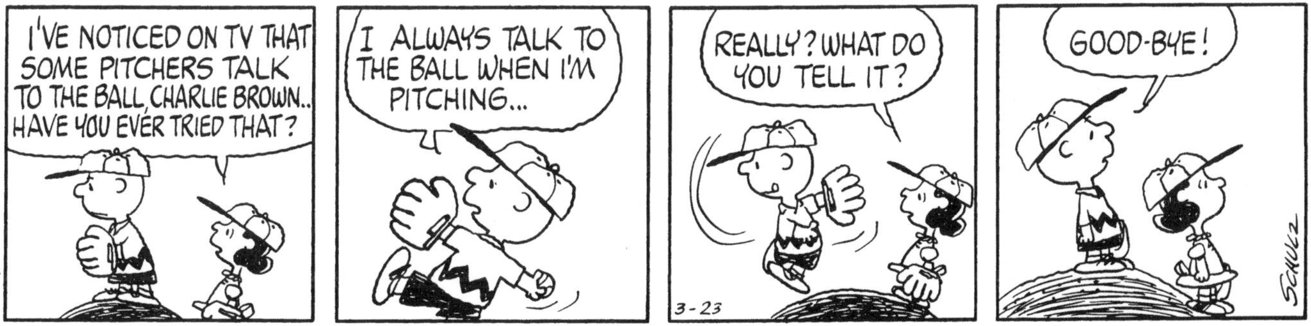
I'VE NOTICED ON TV THAT SOME PITCHERS TALK TO THE BALL, CHARLIE BROWN.. HAVE YOU EVER TRIED THAT?
I ALWAYS TALK TO THE BALL WHEN I'M PITCHING...
REALLY? WHAT DO YOU TELL IT?
3-23
GOOD-BYE!
SCHULZ

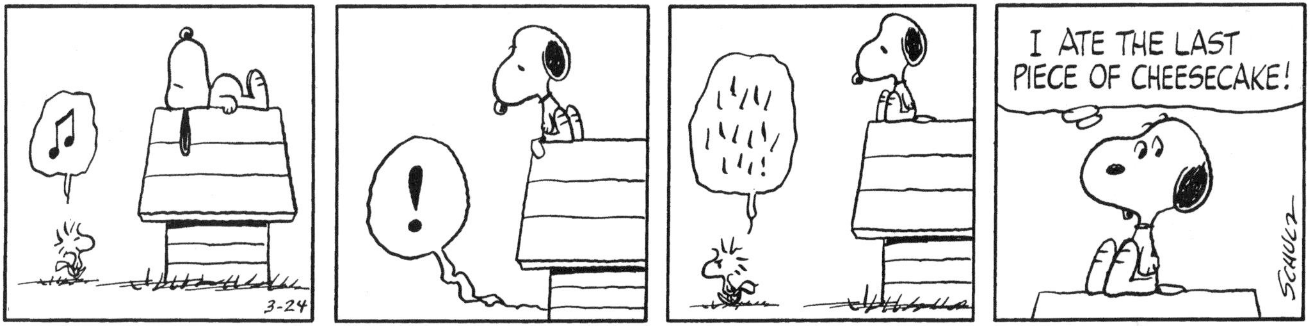
3-24
!
I ATE THE LAST PIECE OF CHEESECAKE!
SCHULZ

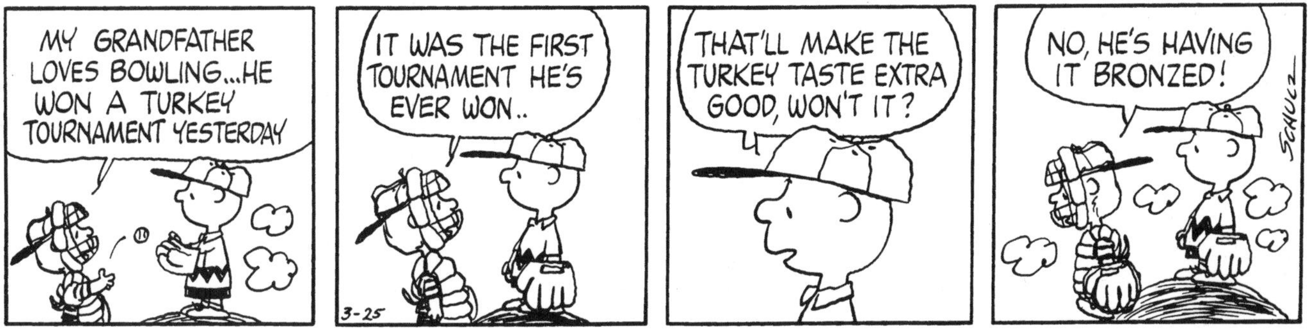
MY GRANDFATHER LOVES BOWLING...HE WON A TURKEY TOURNAMENT YESTERDAY
IT WAS THE FIRST TOURNAMENT HE'S EVER WON..
3-25
THAT'LL MAKE THE TURKEY TASTE EXTRA GOOD, WON'T IT?
NO, HE'S HAVING IT BRONZED!
SCHULZ

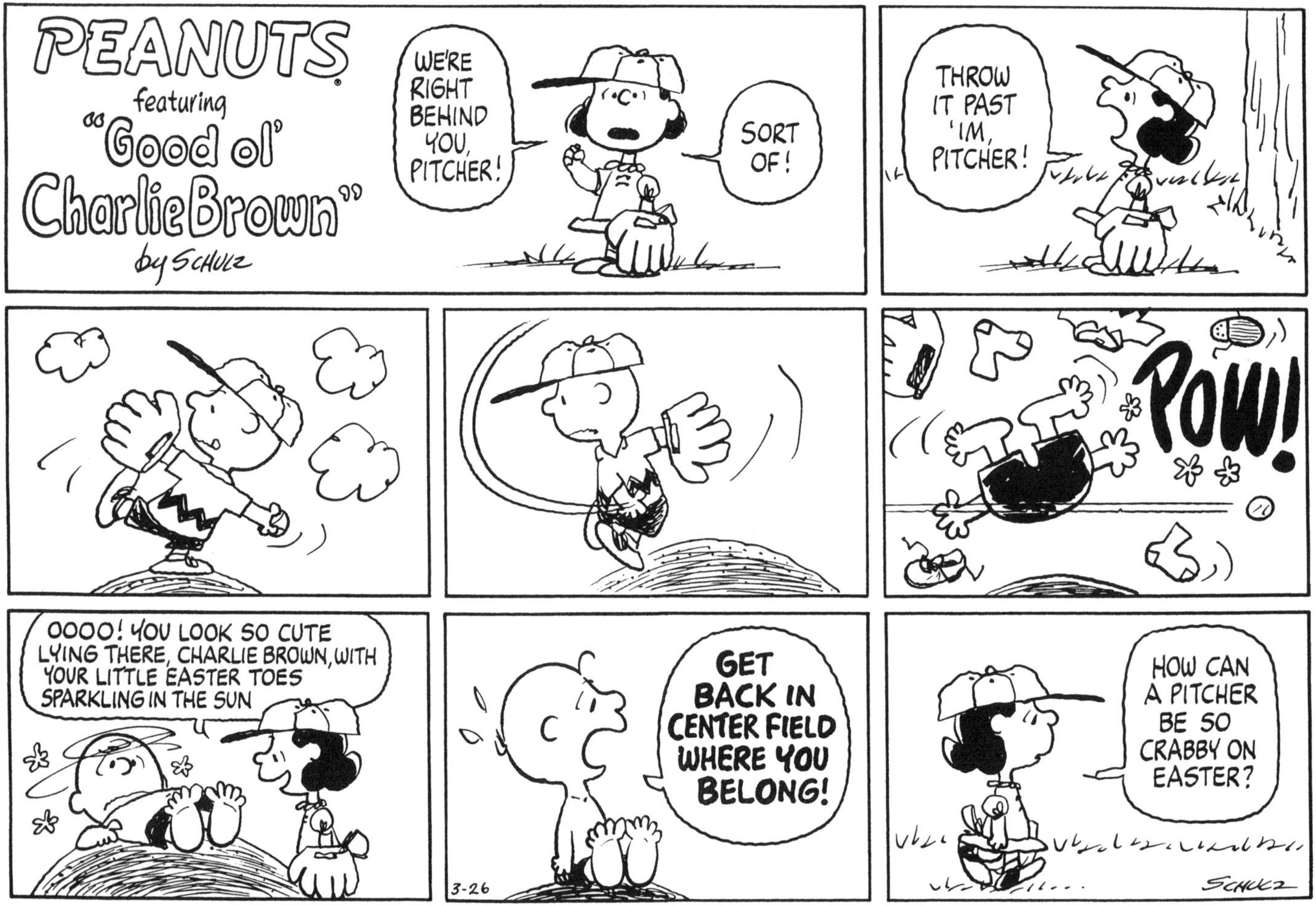
PEANUTS
featuring "Good ol' CharlieBrown"
by SCHULZ
WE'RE RIGHT BEHIND YOU, PITCHER!
SORT OF!
THROW IT PAST 'IM, PITCHER!
POW!
OOOO! YOU LOOK SO CUTE LYING THERE, CHARLIE BROWN, WITH YOUR LITTLE EASTER TOES SPARKLING IN THE SUN
GET BACK IN CENTER FIELD WHERE YOU BELONG!
3-26
HOW CAN A PITCHER BE SO CRABBY ON EASTER?
SCHULZ

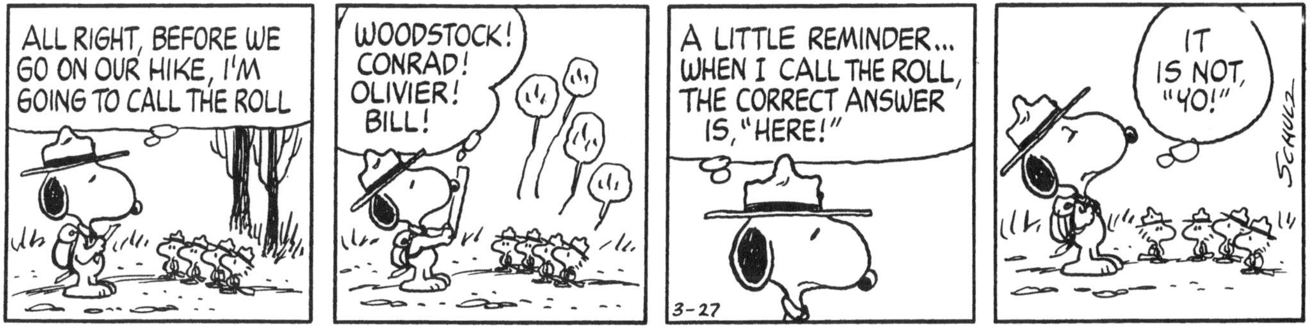
ALL RIGHT, BEFORE WE GO ON OUR HIKE, I'M GOING TO CALL THE ROLL
WOODSTOCK! CONRAD! OLIVIER! BILL!
A LITTLE REMINDER... WHEN I CALL THE ROLL, THE CORRECT ANSWER IS, "HERE!"
3-27
IT IS NOT, "YO!"
SCHULZ

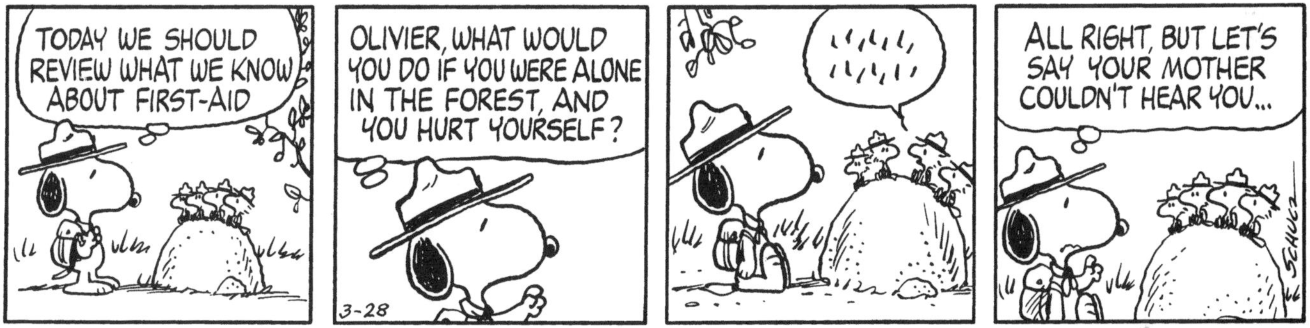
TODAY WE SHOULD REVIEW WHAT WE KNOW ABOUT FIRST-AID
OLIVIER, WHAT WOULD YOU DO IF YOU WERE ALONE IN THE FOREST, AND YOU HURT YOURSELF?
3-28
ALL RIGHT, BUT LET'S SAY YOUR MOTHER COULDN'T HEAR YOU...
SCHULZ

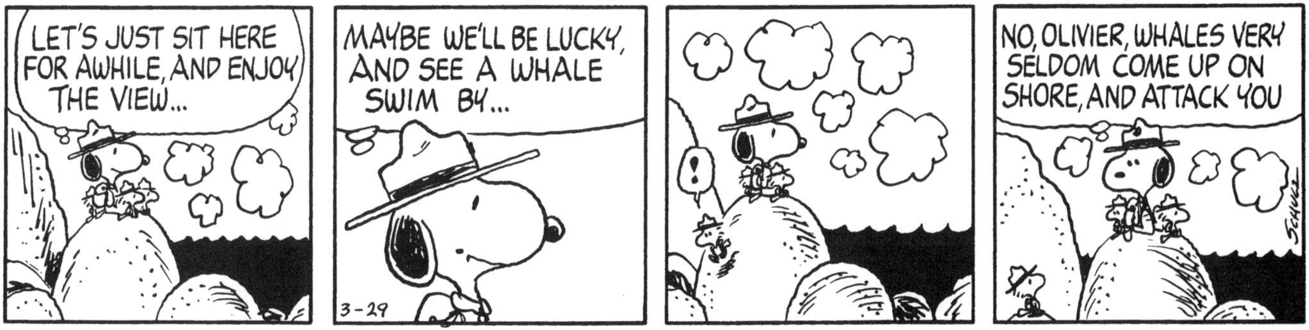
LET'S JUST SIT HERE FOR AWHILE, AND ENJOY THE VIEW...
MAYBE WE'LL BE LUCKY, AND SEE A WHALE SWIM BY...
3-29
!
NO, OLIVIER, WHALES VERY SELDOM COME UP ON SHORE, AND ATTACK YOU
SCHULZ

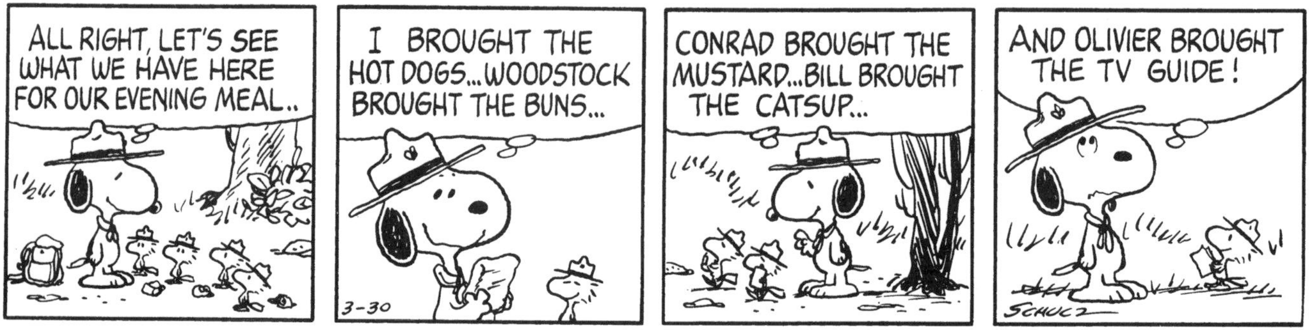
ALL RIGHT, LET'S SEE WHAT WE HAVE HERE FOR OUR EVENING MEAL..
I BROUGHT THE HOT DOGS...WOODSTOCK BROUGHT THE BUNS...
3-30
CONRAD BROUGHT THE MUSTARD...BILL BROUGHT THE CATSUP...
AND OLIVIER BROUGHT THE TV GUIDE!

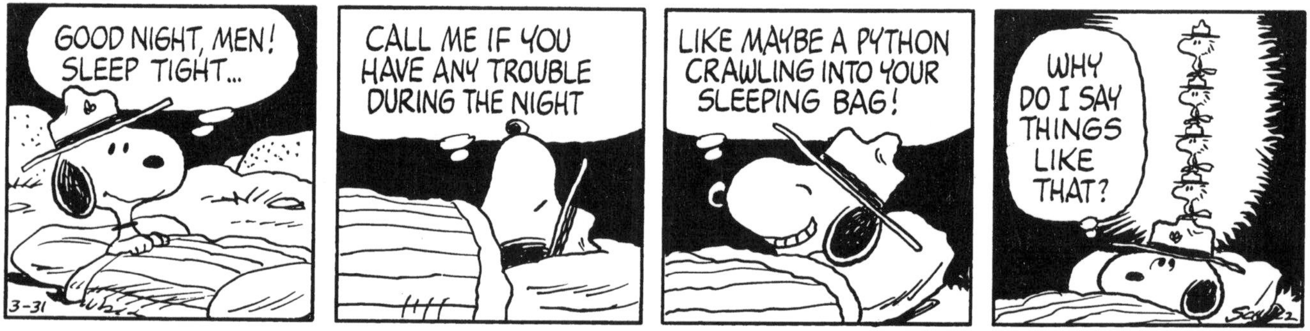
GOOD NIGHT, MEN! SLEEP TIGHT...
3-31
CALL ME IF YOU HAVE ANY TROUBLE DURING THE NIGHT
LIKE MAYBE A PYTHON CRAWLING INTO YOUR SLEEPING BAG!
WHY DO I SAY THINGS LIKE THAT?

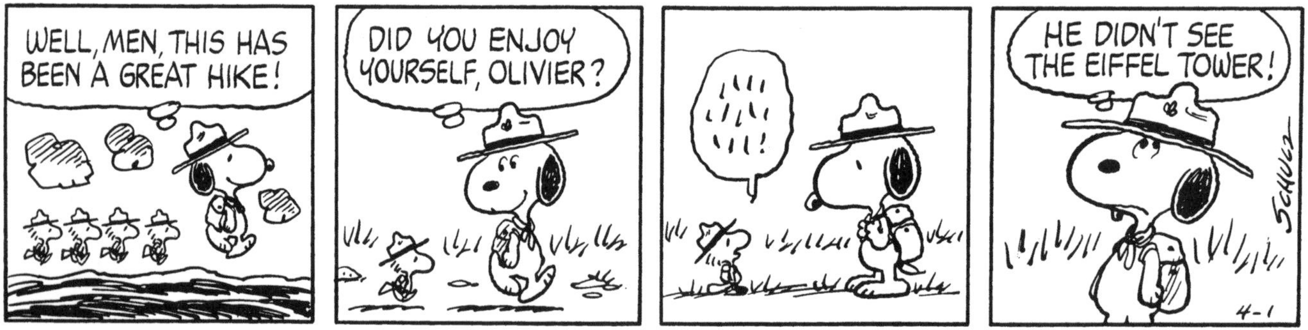
WELL, MEN, THIS HAS BEEN A GREAT HIKE!
DID YOU ENJOY YOURSELF, OLIVIER?
HE DIDN'T SEE THE EIFFEL TOWER!
4-1

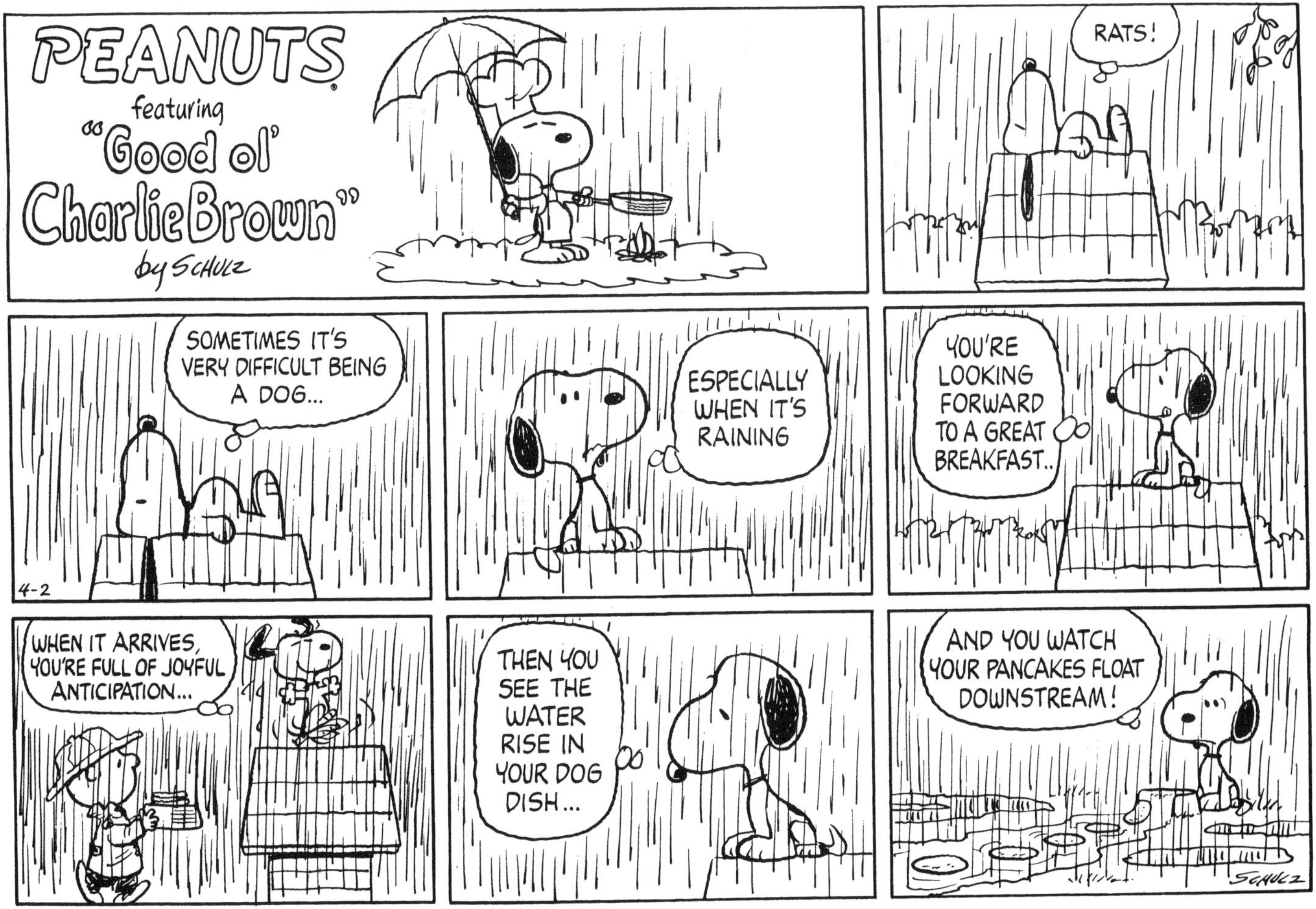
PEANUTS
featuring
"Good ol' Charlie Brown"
by SCHULZ
RATS!
SOMETIMES IT'S VERY DIFFICULT BEING A DOG...
4-2
ESPECIALLY WHEN IT'S RAINING
YOU'RE LOOKING FORWARD TO A GREAT BREAKFAST..
WHEN IT ARRIVES, YOU'RE FULL OF JOYFUL ANTICIPATION...
THEN YOU SEE THE WATER RISE IN YOUR DOG DISH...
AND YOU WATCH YOUR PANCAKES FLOAT DOWNSTREAM!
SCHULZ

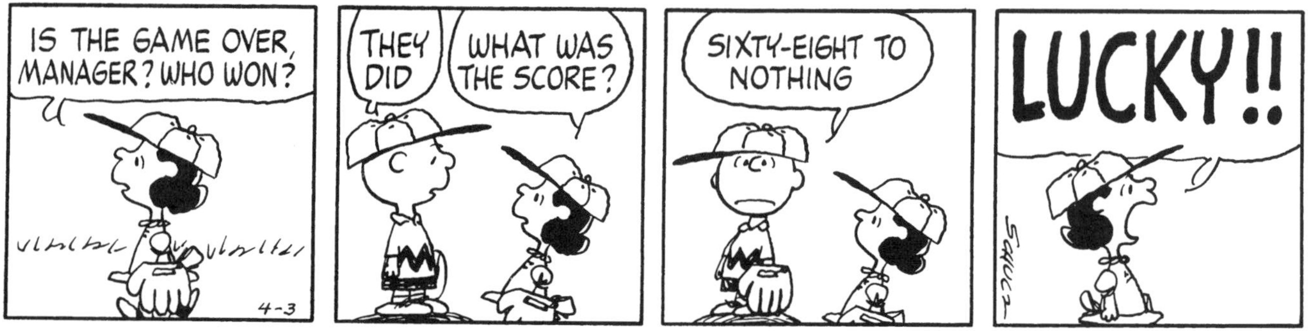
IS THE GAME OVER, MANAGER? WHO WON?
THEY DID
WHAT WAS THE SCORE?
SIXTY-EIGHT TO NOTHING
LUCKY!!
4-3

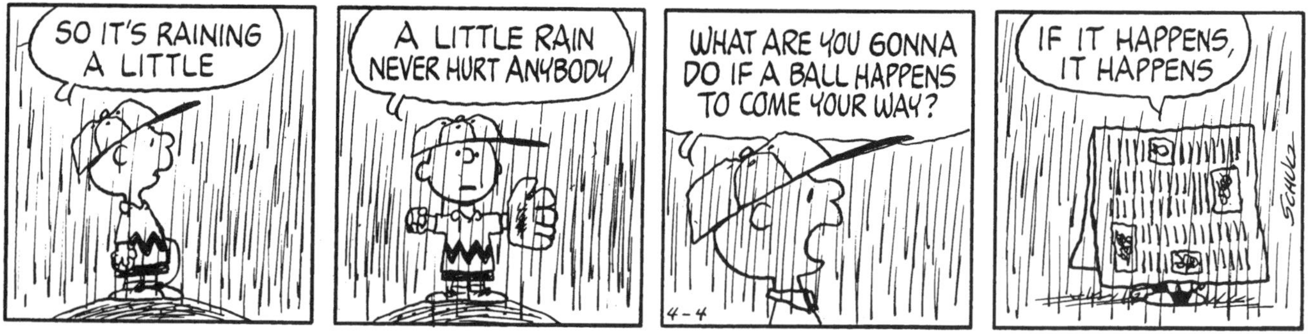
SO IT'S RAINING A LITTLE
A LITTLE RAIN NEVER HURT ANYBODY
WHAT ARE YOU GONNA DO IF A BALL HAPPENS TO COME YOUR WAY?
IF IT HAPPENS, IT HAPPENS
4-4

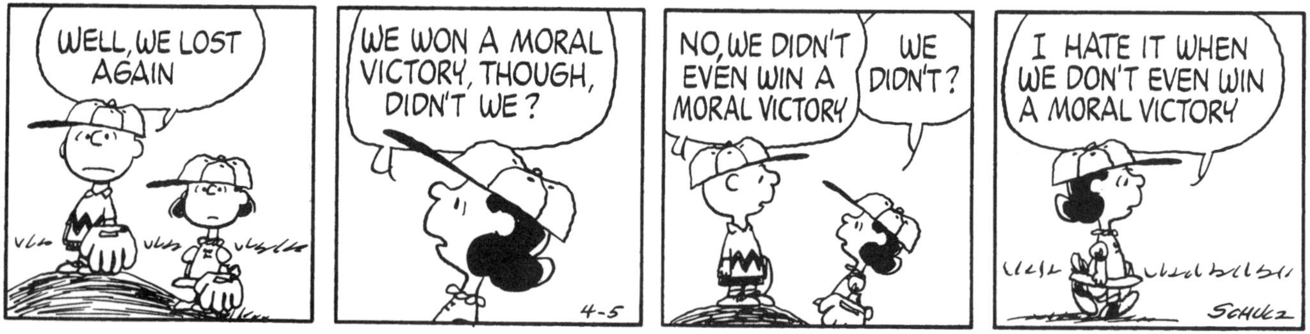
WELL, WE LOST AGAIN
WE WON A MORAL VICTORY, THOUGH, DIDN'T WE?
NO, WE DIDN'T EVEN WIN A MORAL VICTORY
WE DIDN'T?
I HATE IT WHEN WE DON'T EVEN WIN A MORAL VICTORY
4-5

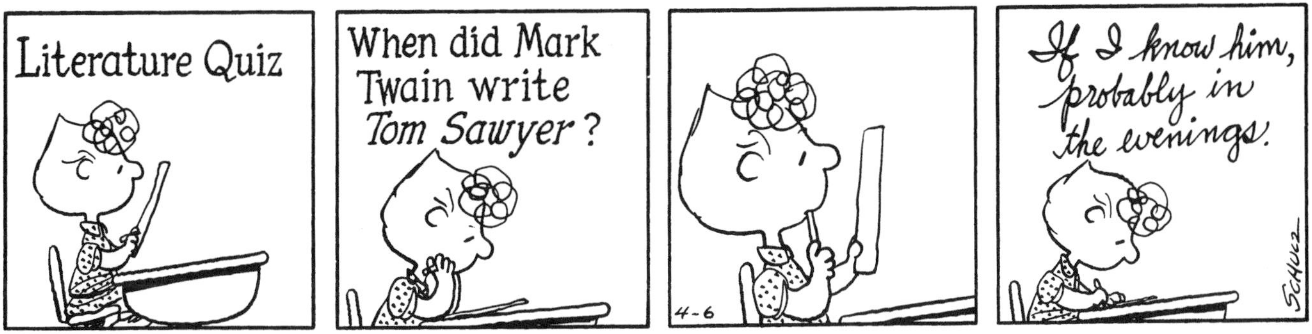
Literature Quiz
When did Mark Twain write *Tom Sawyer* ?
4-6
If I know him, probably in the evenings.
SCHULZ

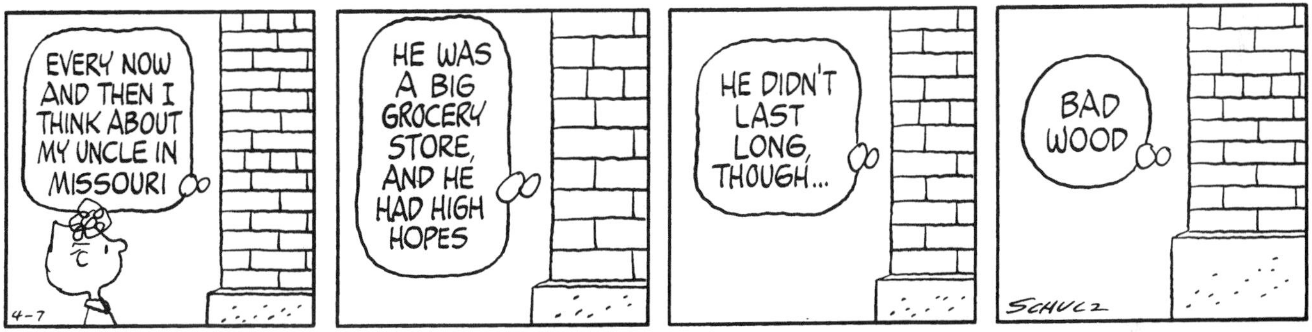
EVERY NOW AND THEN I THINK ABOUT MY UNCLE IN MISSOURI
4-7
HE WAS A BIG GROCERY STORE, AND HE HAD HIGH HOPES
HE DIDN'T LAST LONG, THOUGH...
BAD WOOD
SCHULZ

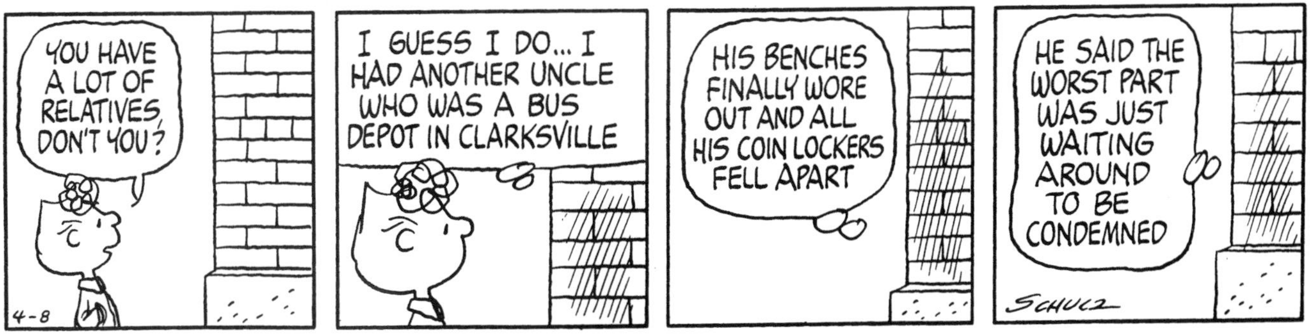
YOU HAVE A LOT OF RELATIVES, DON'T YOU?
4-8
I GUESS I DO... I HAD ANOTHER UNCLE WHO WAS A BUS DEPOT IN CLARKSVILLE
HIS BENCHES FINALLY WORE OUT AND ALL HIS COIN LOCKERS FELL APART
HE SAID THE WORST PART WAS JUST WAITING AROUND TO BE CONDEMNED
SCHULZ

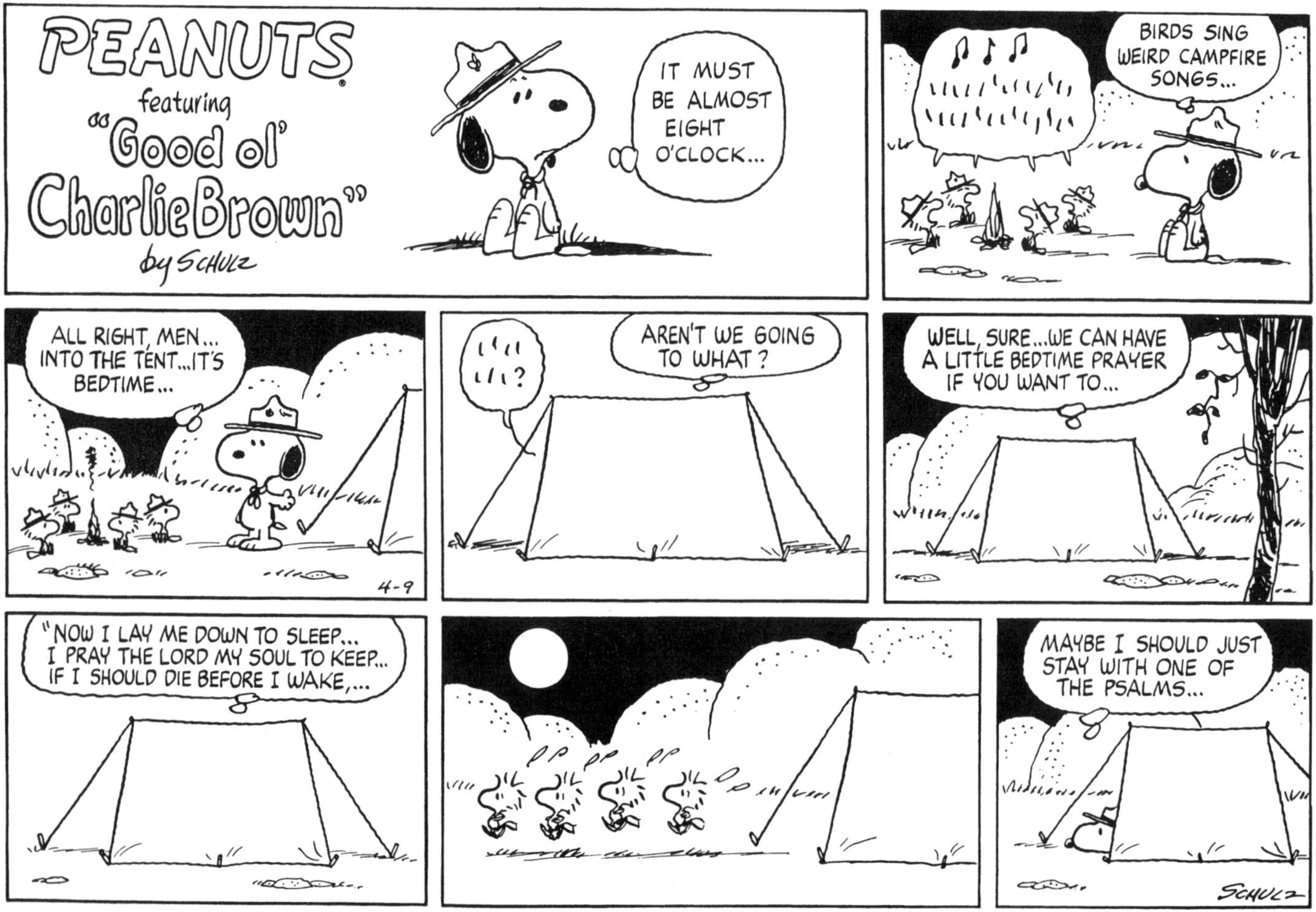
PEANUTS
featuring
"Good ol' Charlie Brown"
by SCHULZ
IT MUST BE ALMOST EIGHT O'CLOCK...
BIRDS SING WEIRD CAMPFIRE SONGS...
ALL RIGHT, MEN... INTO THE TENT...IT'S BEDTIME...
4-9
?
AREN'T WE GOING TO WHAT?
WELL, SURE...WE CAN HAVE A LITTLE BEDTIME PRAYER IF YOU WANT TO...
"NOW I LAY ME DOWN TO SLEEP... I PRAY THE LORD MY SOUL TO KEEP... IF I SHOULD DIE BEFORE I WAKE,...
MAYBE I SHOULD JUST STAY WITH ONE OF THE PSALMS...
SCHULZ

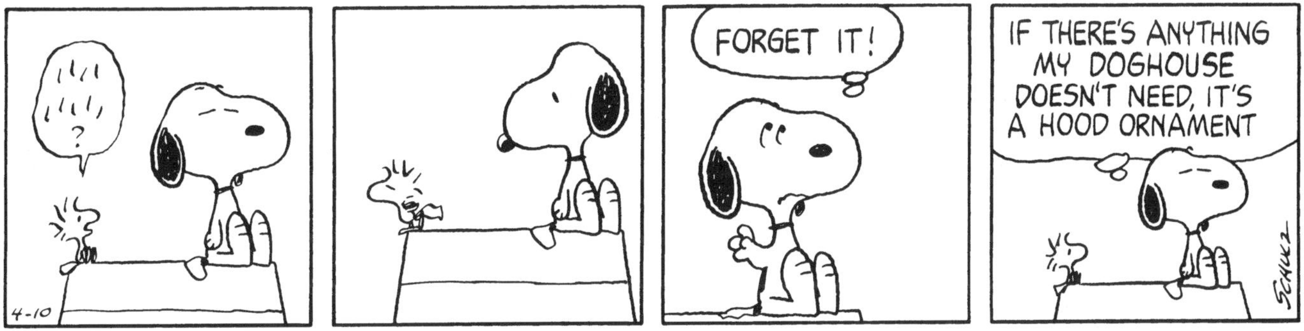
?
FORGET IT!
IF THERE'S ANYTHING MY DOGHOUSE DOESN'T NEED, IT'S A HOOD ORNAMENT
4-10
SCHULZ

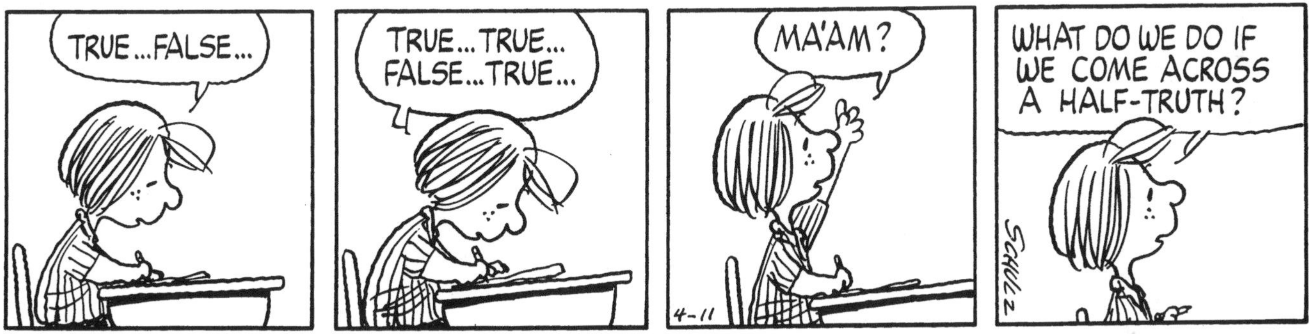
TRUE...FALSE...
TRUE...TRUE... FALSE...TRUE...
MA'AM?
WHAT DO WE DO IF WE COME ACROSS A HALF-TRUTH?
4-11
SCHULZ

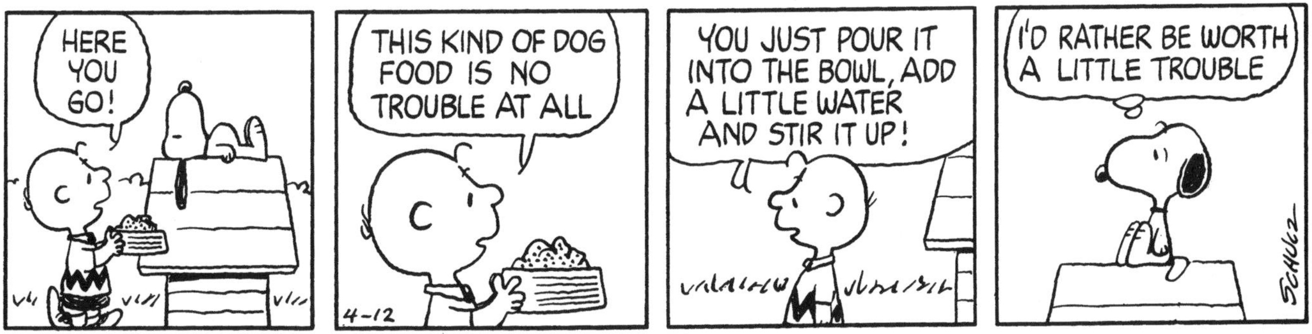
HERE YOU GO!
THIS KIND OF DOG FOOD IS NO TROUBLE AT ALL
YOU JUST POUR IT INTO THE BOWL, ADD A LITTLE WATER AND STIR IT UP!
I'D RATHER BE WORTH A LITTLE TROUBLE
4-12
SCHULZ

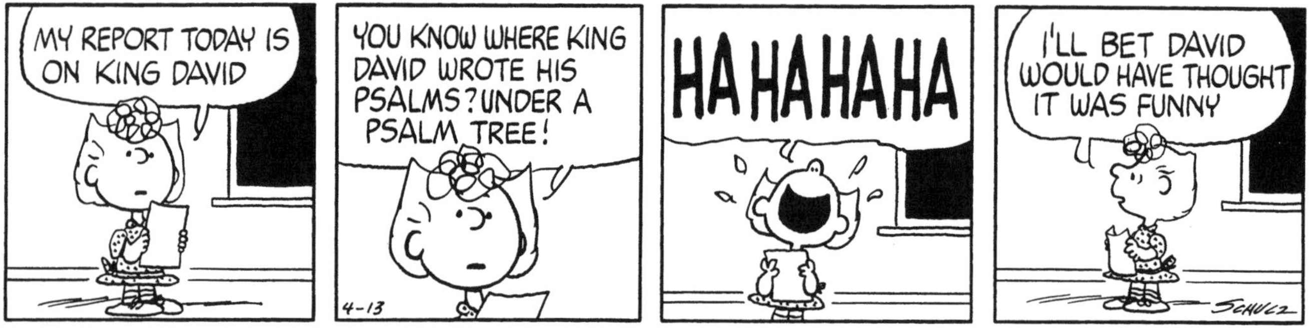
MY REPORT TODAY IS ON KING DAVID
YOU KNOW WHERE KING DAVID WROTE HIS PSALMS? UNDER A PSALM TREE!
4-13
HA HA HA HA
I'LL BET DAVID WOULD HAVE THOUGHT IT WAS FUNNY
SCHULZ

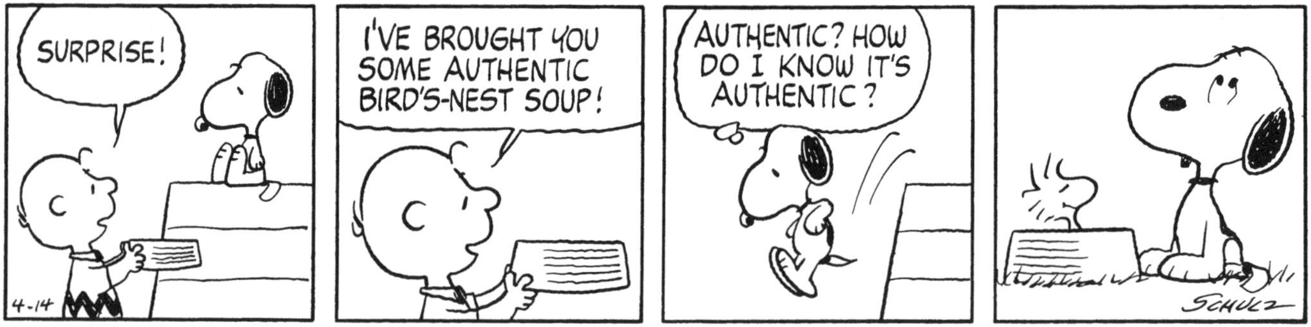
SURPRISE!
4-14
I'VE BROUGHT YOU SOME AUTHENTIC BIRD'S-NEST SOUP!
AUTHENTIC? HOW DO I KNOW IT'S AUTHENTIC?
SCHULZ

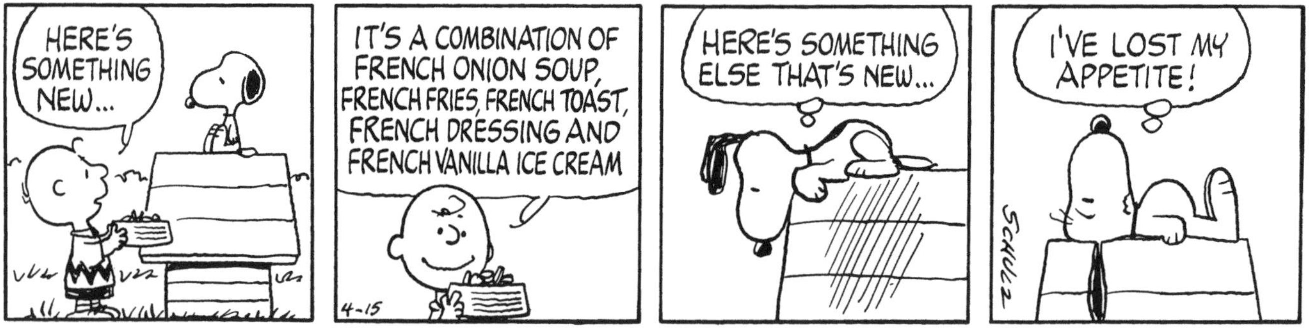
HERE'S SOMETHING NEW...
IT'S A COMBINATION OF FRENCH ONION SOUP, FRENCH FRIES, FRENCH TOAST, FRENCH DRESSING AND FRENCH VANILLA ICE CREAM
4-15
HERE'S SOMETHING ELSE THAT'S NEW...
SCHULZ
I'VE LOST MY APPETITE!

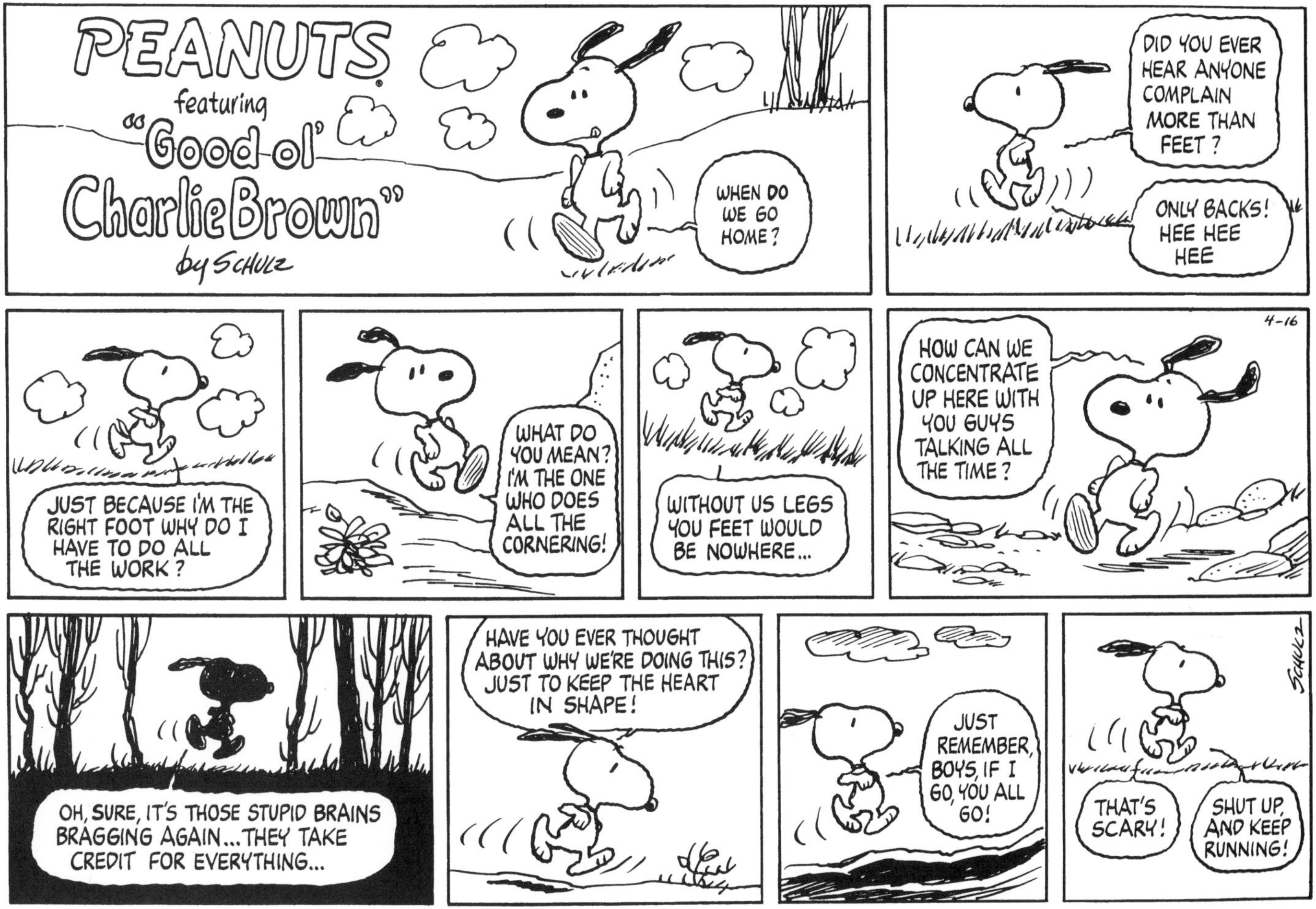
PEANUTS
featuring
"Good ol' Charlie Brown"
by SCHULZ
WHEN DO WE GO HOME?
DID YOU EVER HEAR ANYONE COMPLAIN MORE THAN FEET?
ONLY BACKS! HEE HEE HEE
JUST BECAUSE I'M THE RIGHT FOOT WHY DO I HAVE TO DO ALL THE WORK?
WHAT DO YOU MEAN? I'M THE ONE WHO DOES ALL THE CORNERING!
WITHOUT US LEGS YOU FEET WOULD BE NOWHERE...
4-16
HOW CAN WE CONCENTRATE UP HERE WITH YOU GUYS TALKING ALL THE TIME?
OH, SURE, IT'S THOSE STUPID BRAINS BRAGGING AGAIN...THEY TAKE CREDIT FOR EVERYTHING...
HAVE YOU EVER THOUGHT ABOUT WHY WE'RE DOING THIS? JUST TO KEEP THE HEART IN SHAPE!
JUST REMEMBER, BOYS, IF I GO, YOU ALL GO!
SCHULZ
THAT'S SCARY!
SHUT UP, AND KEEP RUNNING!

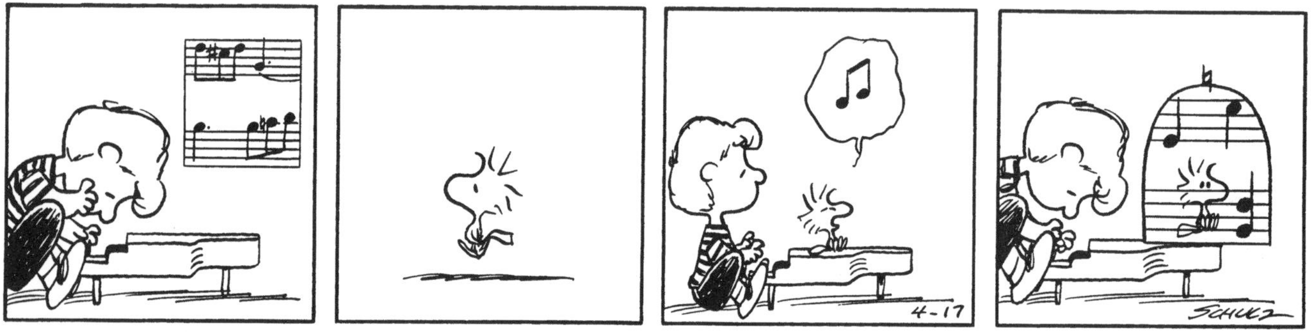

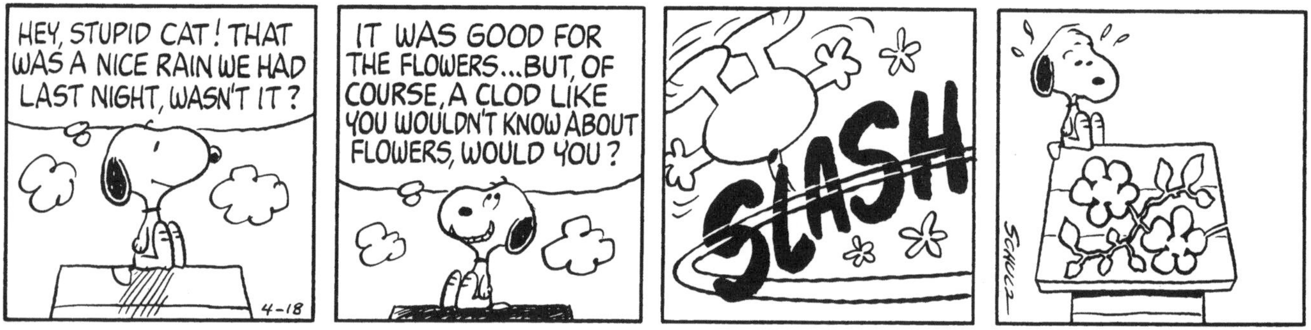
HEY, STUPID CAT! THAT WAS A NICE RAIN WE HAD LAST NIGHT, WASN'T IT?
IT WAS GOOD FOR THE FLOWERS...BUT, OF COURSE, A CLOD LIKE YOU WOULDN'T KNOW ABOUT FLOWERS, WOULD YOU?
SLASH

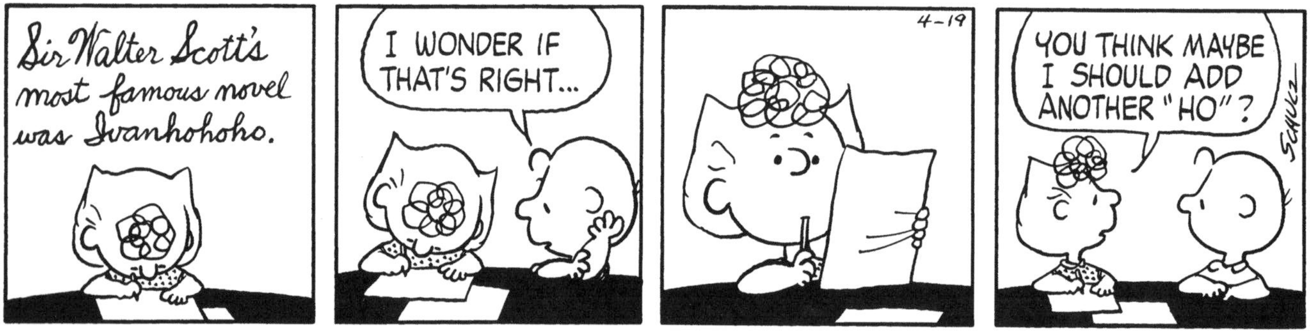
Sir Walter Scott's most famous novel was Ivanhohoho.
I WONDER IF THAT'S RIGHT...
YOU THINK MAYBE I SHOULD ADD ANOTHER "HO"?

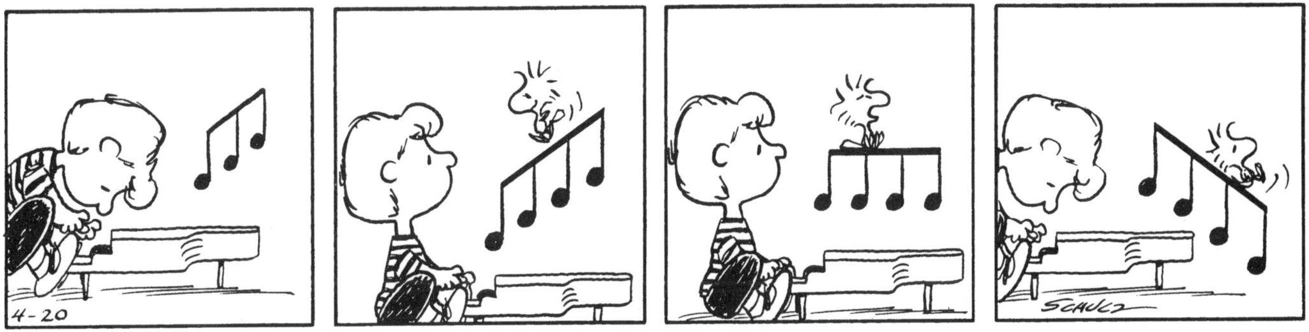
4-20
SCHULZ

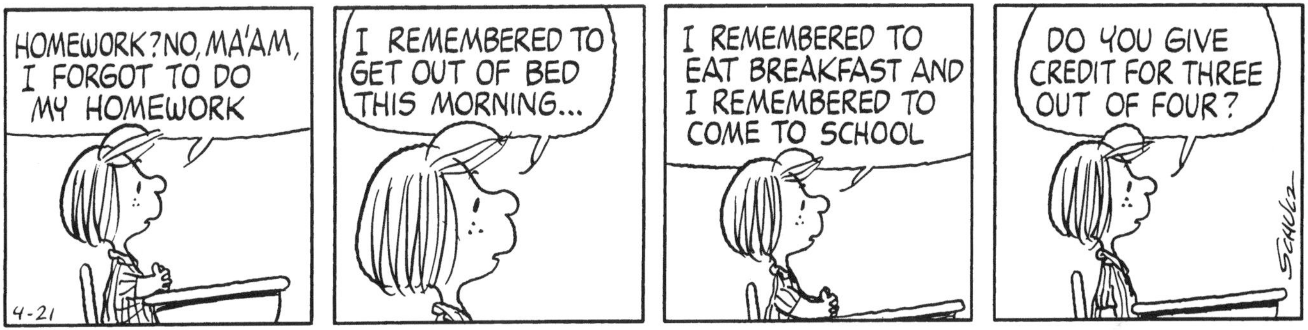
HOMEWORK? NO, MA'AM, I FORGOT TO DO MY HOMEWORK
4-21
I REMEMBERED TO GET OUT OF BED THIS MORNING...
I REMEMBERED TO EAT BREAKFAST AND I REMEMBERED TO COME TO SCHOOL
DO YOU GIVE CREDIT FOR THREE OUT OF FOUR?
SCHULZ

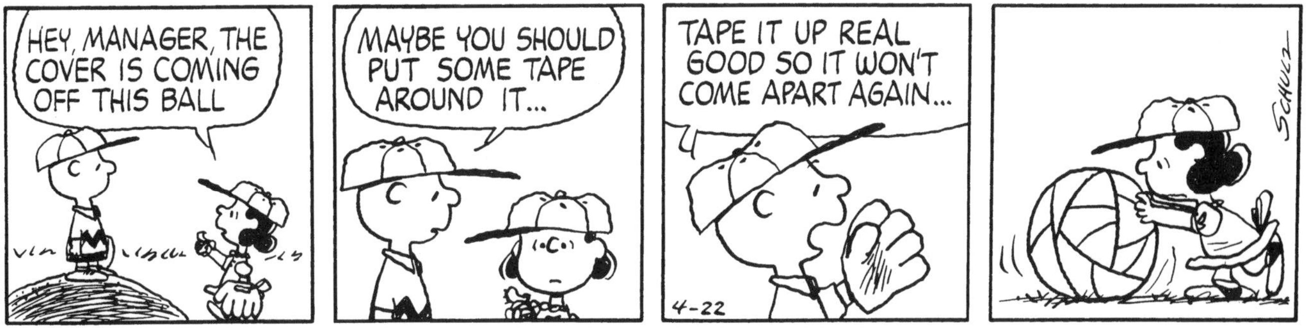
HEY, MANAGER, THE COVER IS COMING OFF THIS BALL
MAYBE YOU SHOULD PUT SOME TAPE AROUND IT...
TAPE IT UP REAL GOOD SO IT WON'T COME APART AGAIN...
4-22
SCHULZ

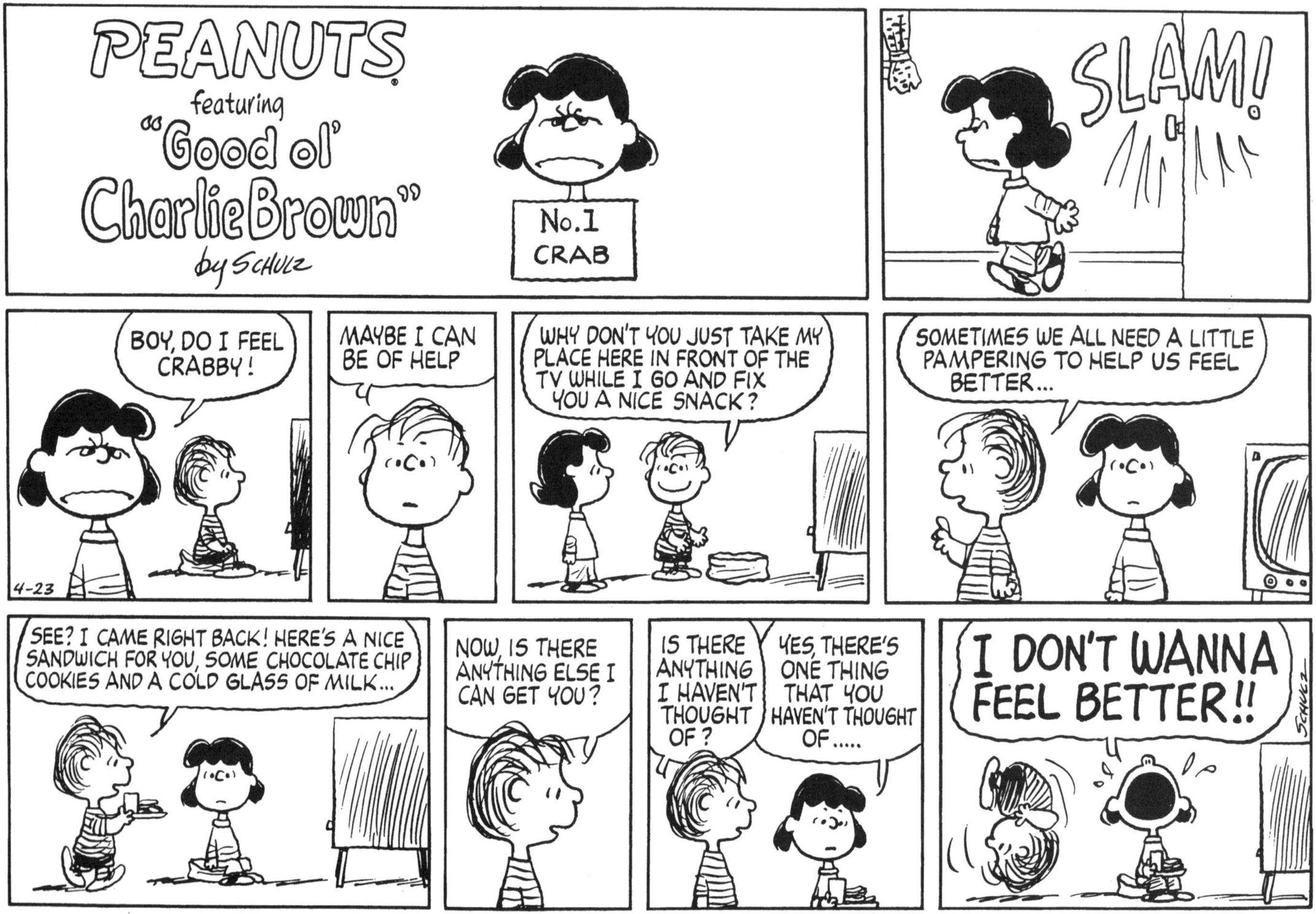
PEANUTS
featuring
"Good ol' Charlie Brown"
by SCHULZ
No.1
CRAB
SLAM!
BOY, DO I FEEL CRABBY!
4-23
MAYBE I CAN BE OF HELP
WHY DON'T YOU JUST TAKE MY PLACE HERE IN FRONT OF THE TV WHILE I GO AND FIX YOU A NICE SNACK?
SOMETIMES WE ALL NEED A LITTLE PAMPERING TO HELP US FEEL BETTER...
SEE? I CAME RIGHT BACK! HERE'S A NICE SANDWICH FOR YOU, SOME CHOCOLATE CHIP COOKIES AND A COLD GLASS OF MILK...
NOW, IS THERE ANYTHING ELSE I CAN GET YOU?
IS THERE ANYTHING I HAVEN'T THOUGHT OF?
YES, THERE'S ONE THING THAT YOU HAVEN'T THOUGHT OF.....
I DON'T WANNA FEEL BETTER!!
SCHULZ

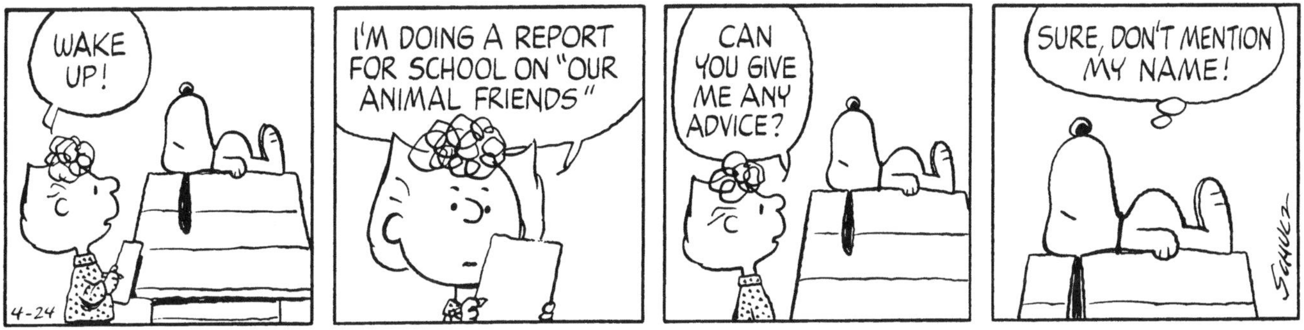
WAKE UP!
I'M DOING A REPORT FOR SCHOOL ON "OUR ANIMAL FRIENDS"
CAN YOU GIVE ME ANY ADVICE?
SURE, DON'T MENTION MY NAME!
4-24
SCHULZ

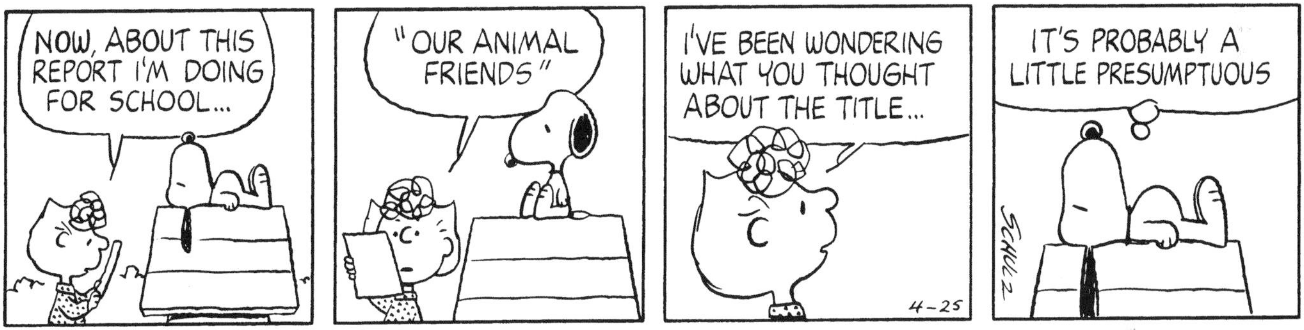
NOW, ABOUT THIS REPORT I'M DOING FOR SCHOOL...
"OUR ANIMAL FRIENDS"
I'VE BEEN WONDERING WHAT YOU THOUGHT ABOUT THE TITLE...
IT'S PROBABLY A LITTLE PRESUMPTUOUS
4-25
SCHULZ

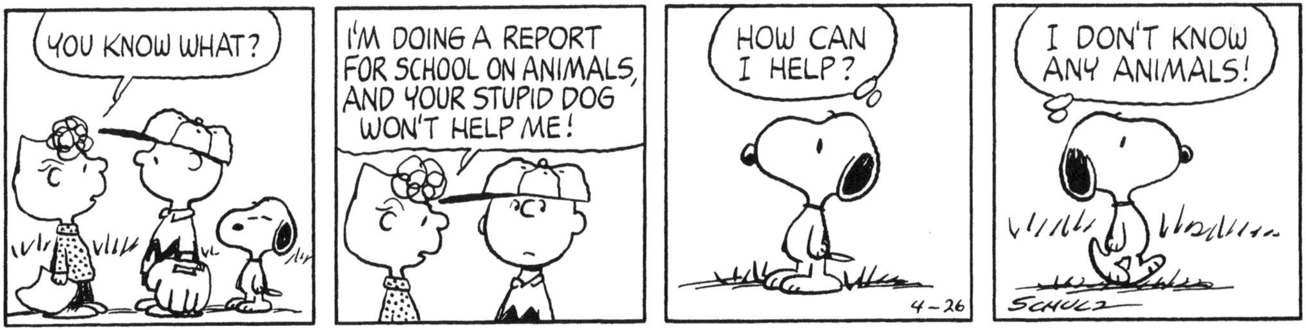
YOU KNOW WHAT?
I'M DOING A REPORT FOR SCHOOL ON ANIMALS, AND YOUR STUPID DOG WON'T HELP ME!
HOW CAN I HELP?
I DON'T KNOW ANY ANIMALS!
4-26
SCHULZ

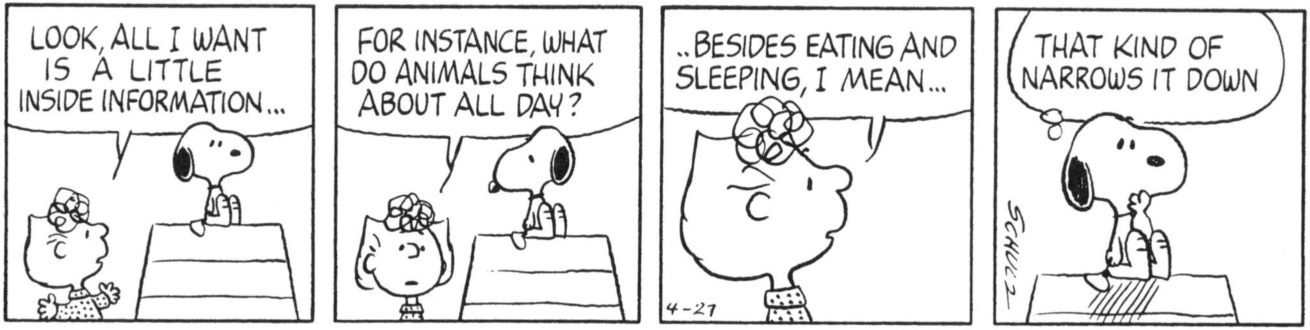
LOOK, ALL I WANT IS A LITTLE INSIDE INFORMATION...
FOR INSTANCE, WHAT DO ANIMALS THINK ABOUT ALL DAY?
..BESIDES EATING AND SLEEPING, I MEAN...
THAT KIND OF NARROWS IT DOWN

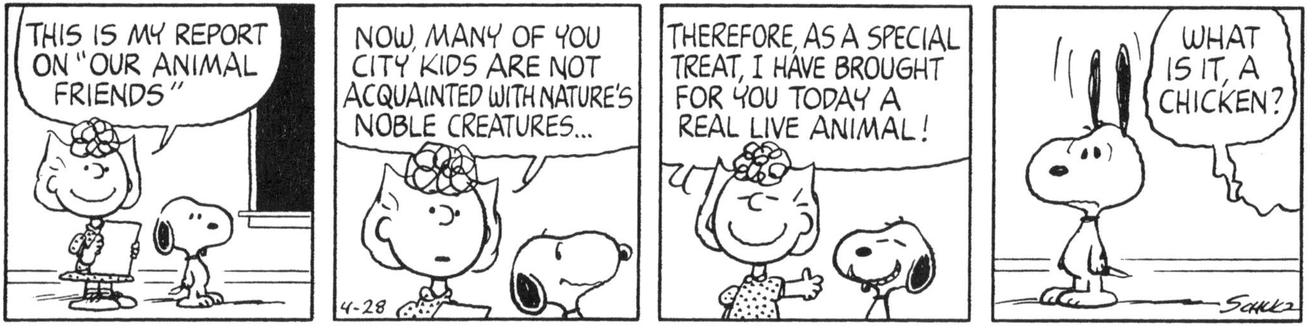
THIS IS MY REPORT ON "OUR ANIMAL FRIENDS"
NOW, MANY OF YOU CITY KIDS ARE NOT ACQUAINTED WITH NATURE'S NOBLE CREATURES...
THEREFORE, AS A SPECIAL TREAT, I HAVE BROUGHT FOR YOU TODAY A REAL LIVE ANIMAL!
WHAT IS IT, A CHICKEN?

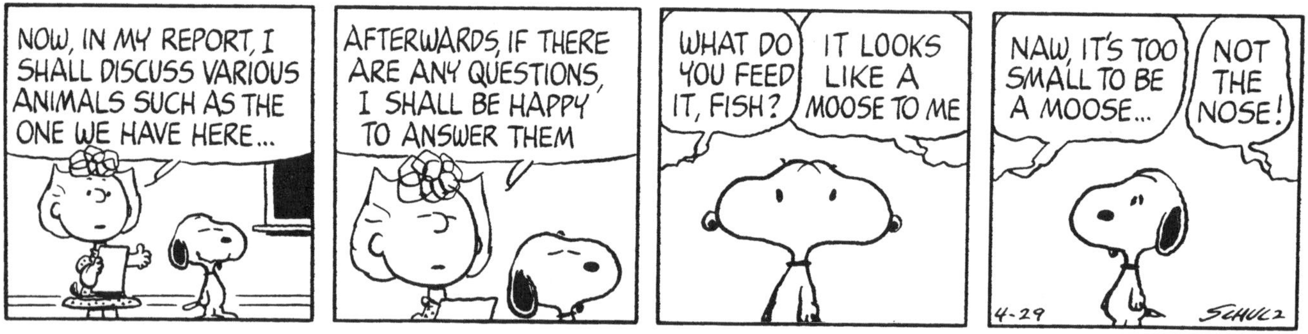
NOW, IN MY REPORT, I SHALL DISCUSS VARIOUS ANIMALS SUCH AS THE ONE WE HAVE HERE...
AFTERWARDS, IF THERE ARE ANY QUESTIONS, I SHALL BE HAPPY TO ANSWER THEM
WHAT DO YOU FEED IT, FISH?
IT LOOKS LIKE A MOOSE TO ME
NAW, IT'S TOO SMALL TO BE A MOOSE...
NOT THE NOSE!

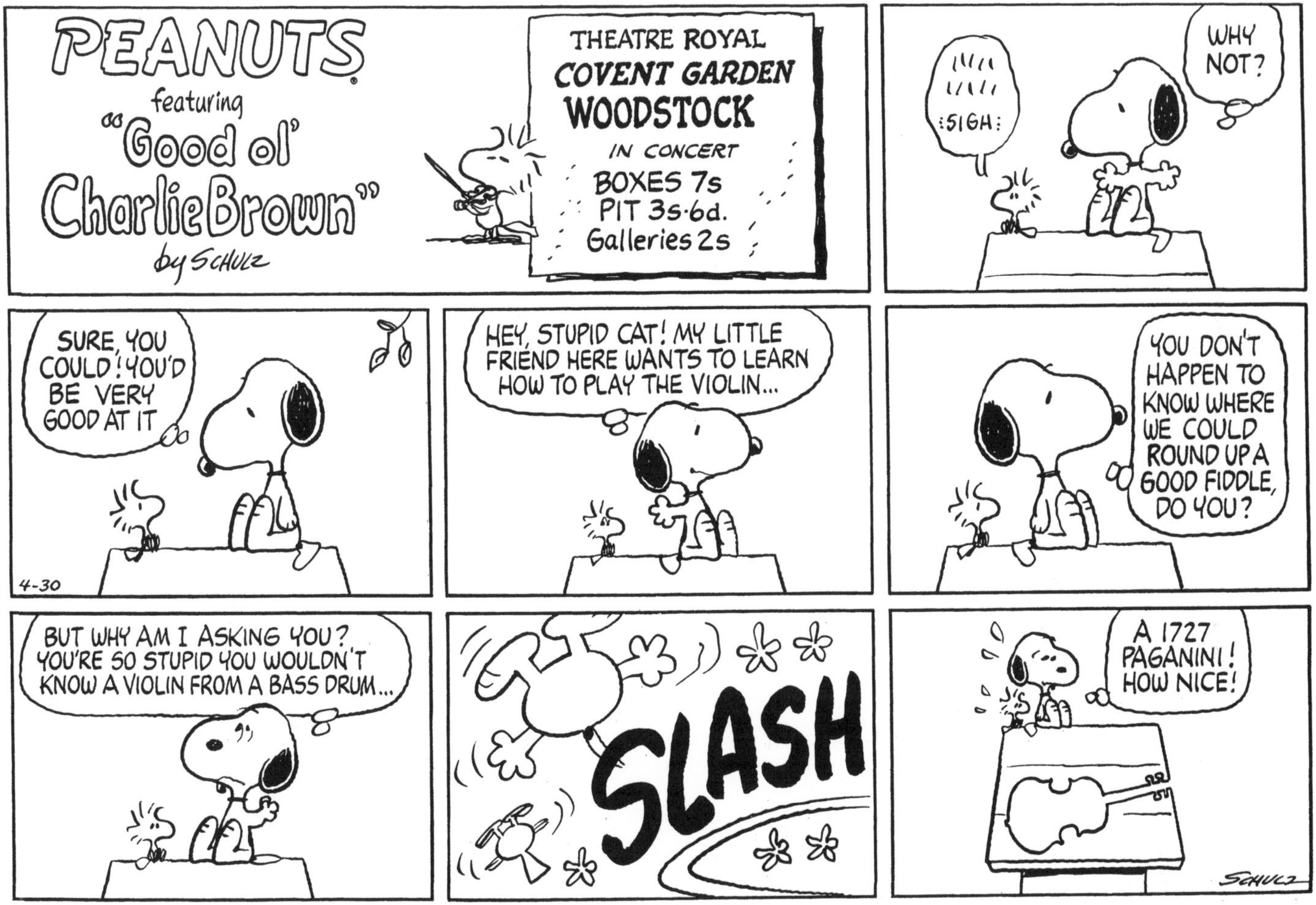
PEANUTS
featuring
"Good ol' Charlie Brown"
by SCHULZ
THEATRE ROYAL
COVENT GARDEN
WOODSTOCK
IN CONCERT
BOXES 7s
PIT 3s·6d.
Galleries 2s
SIGH
WHY NOT?
SURE, YOU COULD! YOU'D BE VERY GOOD AT IT
4-30
HEY, STUPID CAT! MY LITTLE FRIEND HERE WANTS TO LEARN HOW TO PLAY THE VIOLIN...
YOU DON'T HAPPEN TO KNOW WHERE WE COULD ROUND UP A GOOD FIDDLE, DO YOU?
BUT WHY AM I ASKING YOU? YOU'RE SO STUPID YOU WOULDN'T KNOW A VIOLIN FROM A BASS DRUM...
SLASH
A 1727 PAGANINI! HOW NICE!
SCHULZ

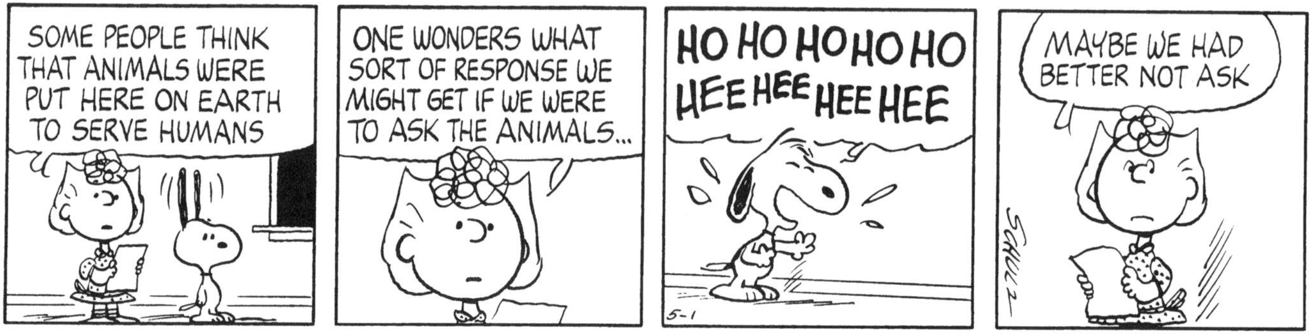
SOME PEOPLE THINK THAT ANIMALS WERE PUT HERE ON EARTH TO SERVE HUMANS
ONE WONDERS WHAT SORT OF RESPONSE WE MIGHT GET IF WE WERE TO ASK THE ANIMALS...
HO HO HO HO HO HO
HEE HEE HEE HEE
5-1
MAYBE WE HAD BETTER NOT ASK
SCHULZ

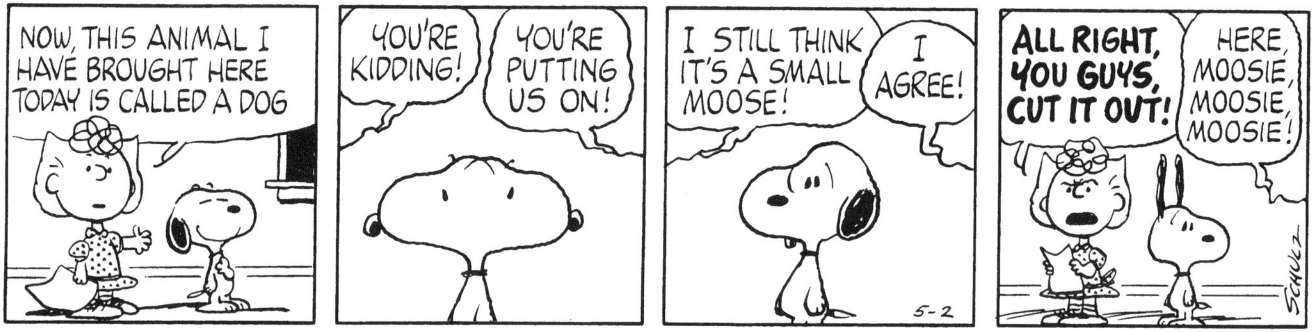
NOW, THIS ANIMAL I HAVE BROUGHT HERE TODAY IS CALLED A DOG
YOU'RE KIDDING!
YOU'RE PUTTING US ON!
I STILL THINK IT'S A SMALL MOOSE!
I AGREE!
5-2
ALL RIGHT, YOU GUYS, CUT IT OUT!
HERE, MOOSIE, MOOSIE, MOOSIE, MOOSIE!
SCHULZ

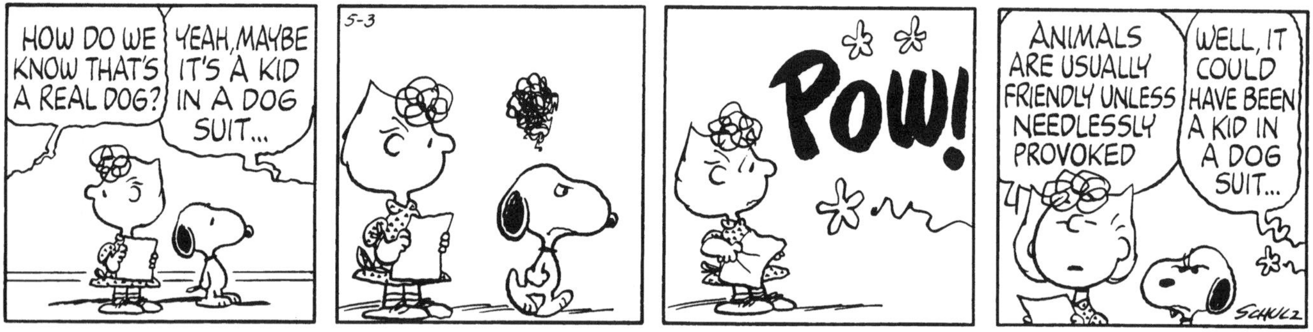
HOW DO WE KNOW THAT'S A REAL DOG?
YEAH, MAYBE IT'S A KID IN A DOG SUIT...
5-3
POW!
ANIMALS ARE USUALLY FRIENDLY UNLESS NEEDLESSLY PROVOKED
WELL, IT COULD HAVE BEEN A KID IN A DOG SUIT...
SCHULZ

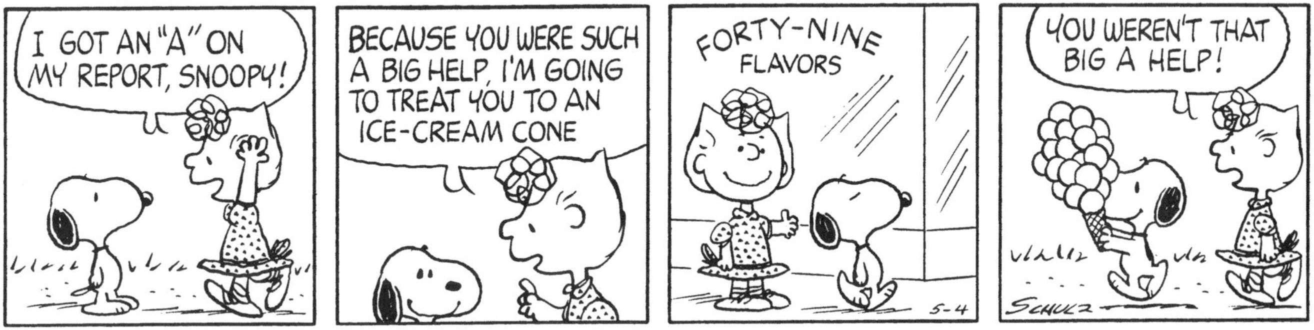
I GOT AN "A" ON MY REPORT, SNOOPY!
BECAUSE YOU WERE SUCH A BIG HELP, I'M GOING TO TREAT YOU TO AN ICE-CREAM CONE
FORTY-NINE FLAVORS
5-4
YOU WEREN'T THAT BIG A HELP!
SCHULZ

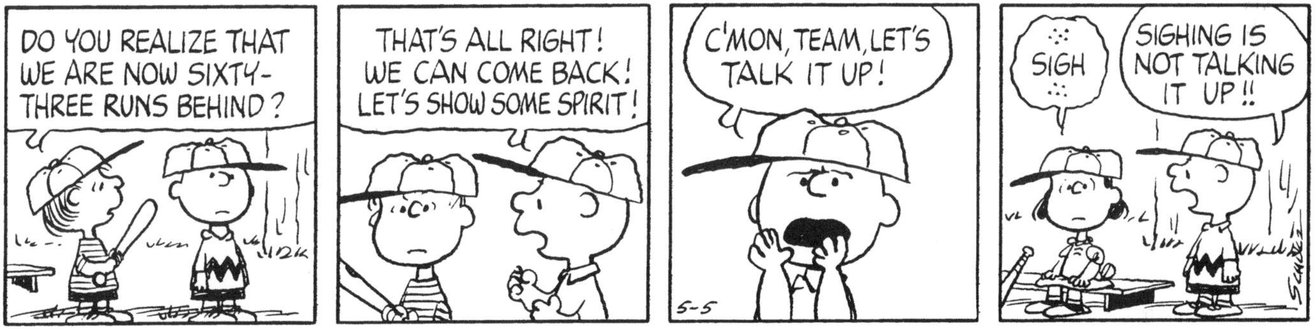
DO YOU REALIZE THAT WE ARE NOW SIXTY-THREE RUNS BEHIND?
THAT'S ALL RIGHT! WE CAN COME BACK! LET'S SHOW SOME SPIRIT!
C'MON, TEAM, LET'S TALK IT UP!
5-5
SIGH
SIGHING IS NOT TALKING IT UP!!
SCHULZ

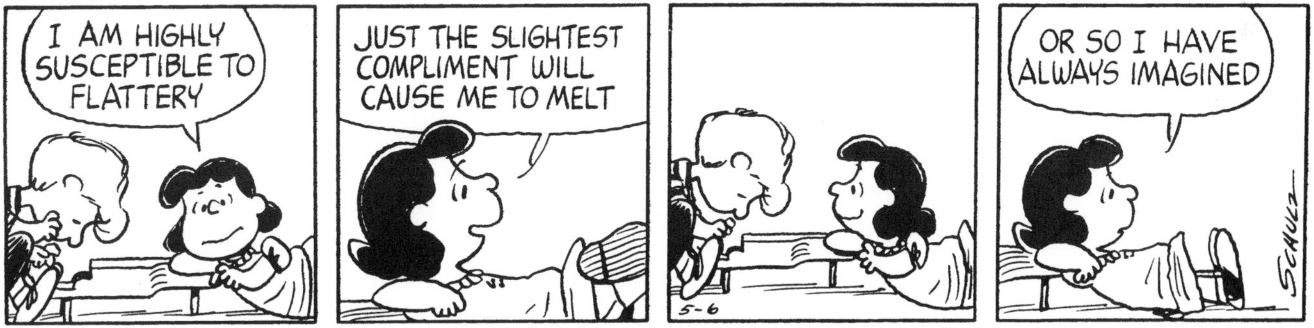
I AM HIGHLY SUSCEPTIBLE TO FLATTERY
JUST THE SLIGHTEST COMPLIMENT WILL CAUSE ME TO MELT
5-6
OR SO I HAVE ALWAYS IMAGINED
SCHULZ

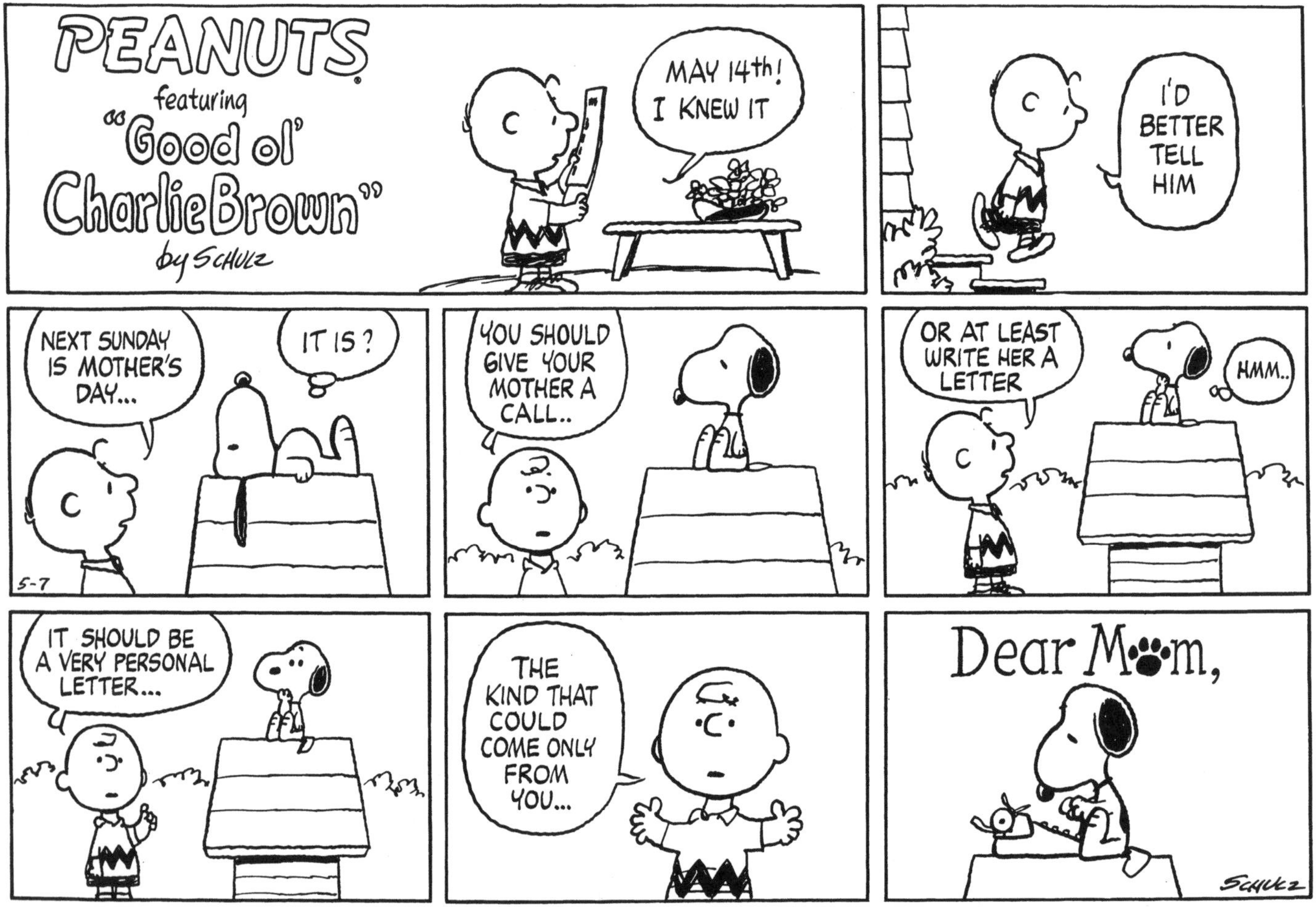
PEANUTS
featuring "Good ol' Charlie Brown"
by SCHULZ
MAY 14th! I KNEW IT
I'D BETTER TELL HIM
NEXT SUNDAY IS MOTHER'S DAY...
IT IS?
5-7
YOU SHOULD GIVE YOUR MOTHER A CALL..
OR AT LEAST WRITE HER A LETTER
HMM..
IT SHOULD BE A VERY PERSONAL LETTER...
THE KIND THAT COULD COME ONLY FROM YOU...
Dear Mom,
SCHULZ

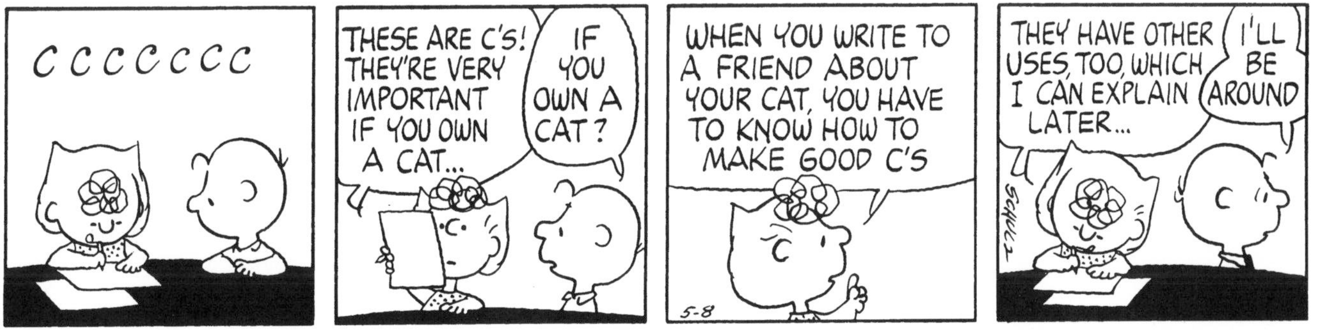
CCCCCCC
THESE ARE C'S! THEY'RE VERY IMPORTANT IF YOU OWN A CAT...
IF YOU OWN A CAT?
WHEN YOU WRITE TO A FRIEND ABOUT YOUR CAT, YOU HAVE TO KNOW HOW TO MAKE GOOD C'S
THEY HAVE OTHER USES, TOO, WHICH I CAN EXPLAIN LATER...
I'LL BE AROUND

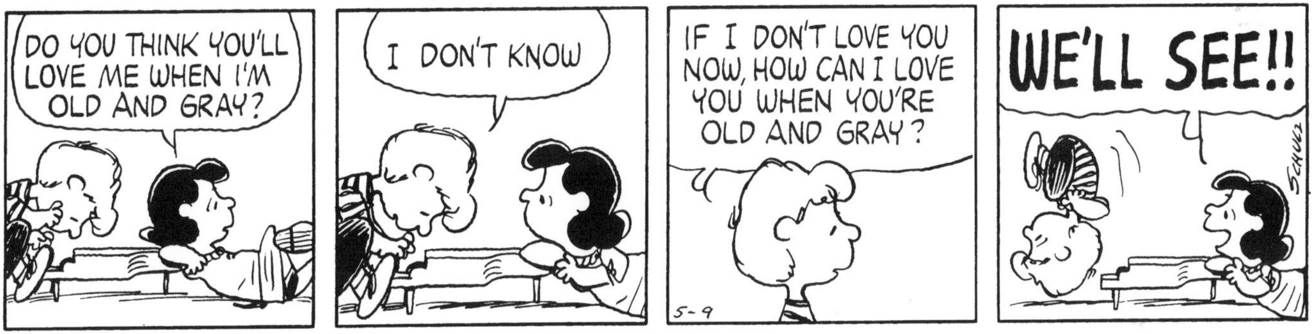
DO YOU THINK YOU'LL LOVE ME WHEN I'M OLD AND GRAY?
I DON'T KNOW
IF I DON'T LOVE YOU NOW, HOW CAN I LOVE YOU WHEN YOU'RE OLD AND GRAY?
WE'LL SEE!!

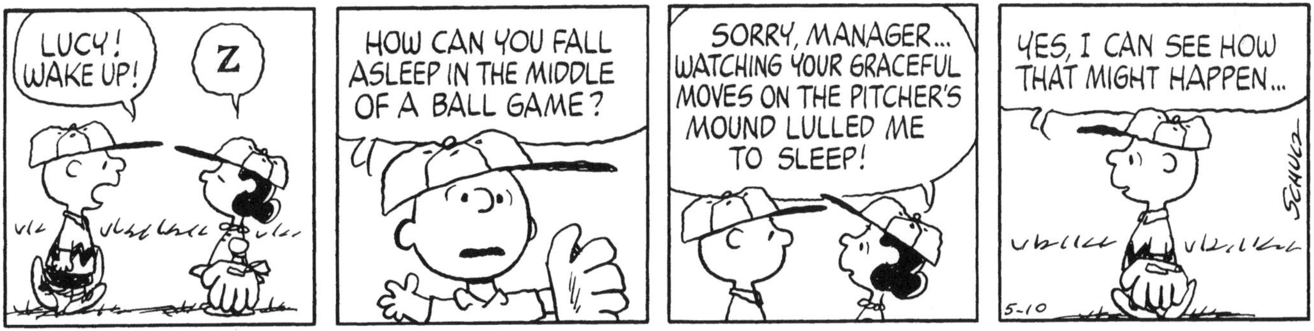
LUCY! WAKE UP!
Z
HOW CAN YOU FALL ASLEEP IN THE MIDDLE OF A BALL GAME?
SORRY, MANAGER... WATCHING YOUR GRACEFUL MOVES ON THE PITCHER'S MOUND LULLED ME TO SLEEP!
YES, I CAN SEE HOW THAT MIGHT HAPPEN...

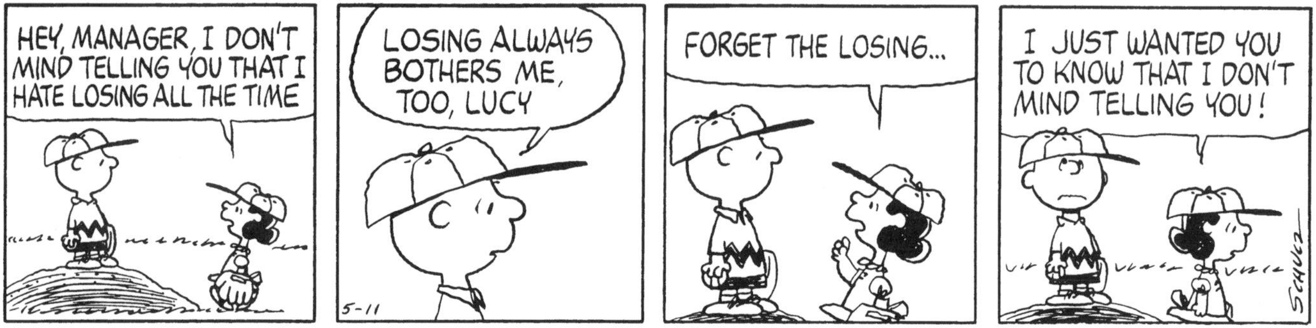
HEY, MANAGER, I DON'T MIND TELLING YOU THAT I HATE LOSING ALL THE TIME
LOSING ALWAYS BOTHERS ME, TOO, LUCY
FORGET THE LOSING...
I JUST WANTED YOU TO KNOW THAT I DON'T MIND TELLING YOU!

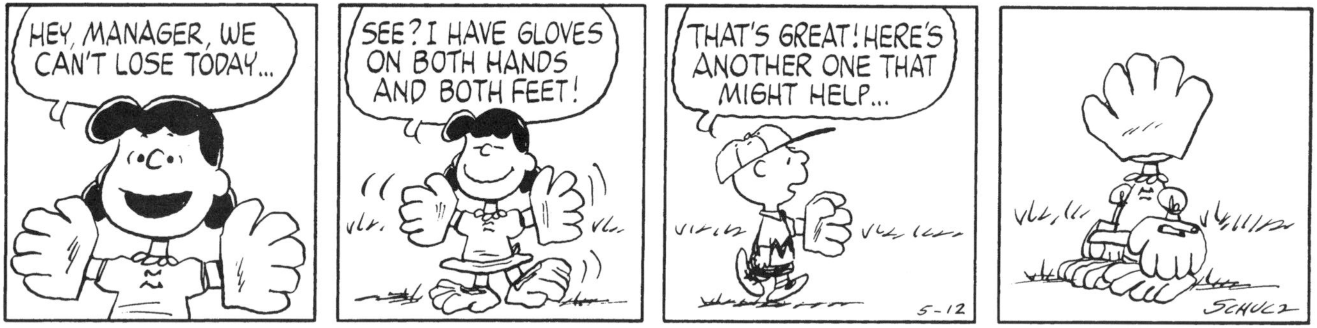
HEY, MANAGER, WE CAN'T LOSE TODAY...
SEE? I HAVE GLOVES ON BOTH HANDS AND BOTH FEET!
THAT'S GREAT! HERE'S ANOTHER ONE THAT MIGHT HELP...

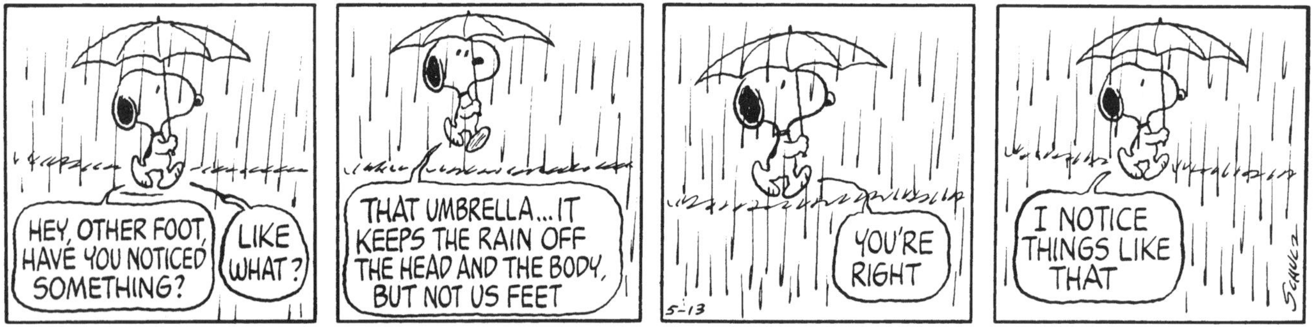
HEY, OTHER FOOT, HAVE YOU NOTICED SOMETHING?
LIKE WHAT?
THAT UMBRELLA...IT KEEPS THE RAIN OFF THE HEAD AND THE BODY, BUT NOT US FEET
YOU'RE RIGHT
I NOTICE THINGS LIKE THAT

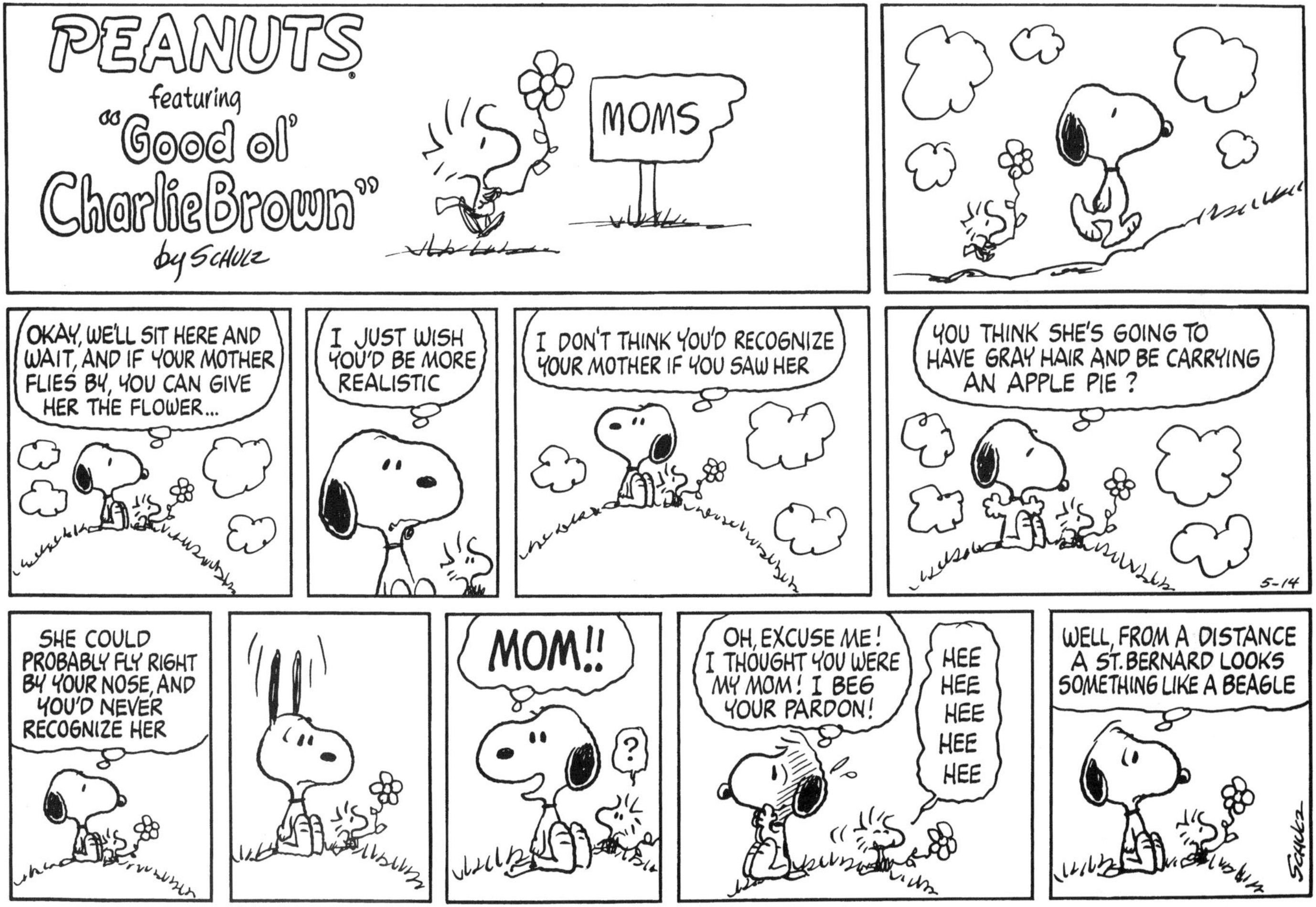
PEANUTS
featuring
"Good ol' CharlieBrown"
by SCHULZ
MOMS
OKAY, WE'LL SIT HERE AND WAIT, AND IF YOUR MOTHER FLIES BY, YOU CAN GIVE HER THE FLOWER...
I JUST WISH YOU'D BE MORE REALISTIC
I DON'T THINK YOU'D RECOGNIZE YOUR MOTHER IF YOU SAW HER
YOU THINK SHE'S GOING TO HAVE GRAY HAIR AND BE CARRYING AN APPLE PIE ?
5-14
SHE COULD PROBABLY FLY RIGHT BY YOUR NOSE, AND YOU'D NEVER RECOGNIZE HER
MOM!!
?
OH, EXCUSE ME! I THOUGHT YOU WERE MY MOM! I BEG YOUR PARDON!
HEE HEE HEE HEE HEE
WELL, FROM A DISTANCE A ST. BERNARD LOOKS SOMETHING LIKE A BEAGLE
SCHULZ

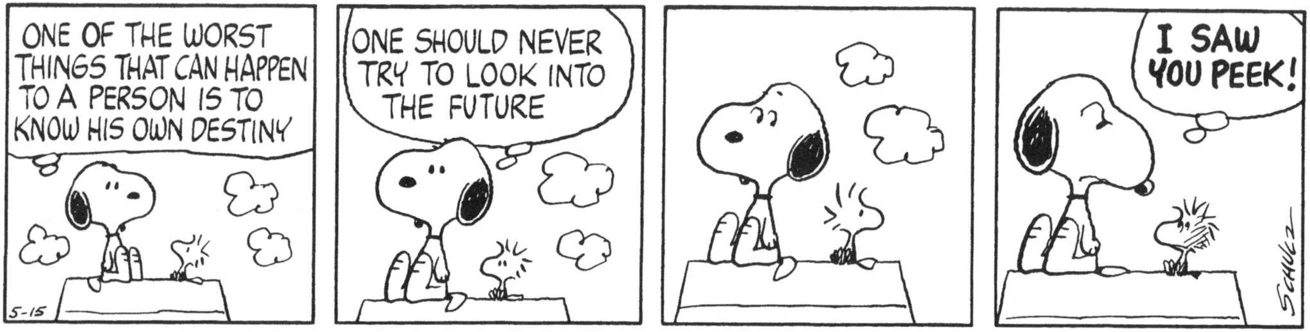
ONE OF THE WORST THINGS THAT CAN HAPPEN TO A PERSON IS TO KNOW HIS OWN DESTINY
5-15
ONE SHOULD NEVER TRY TO LOOK INTO THE FUTURE
I SAW YOU PEEK!
SCHULZ

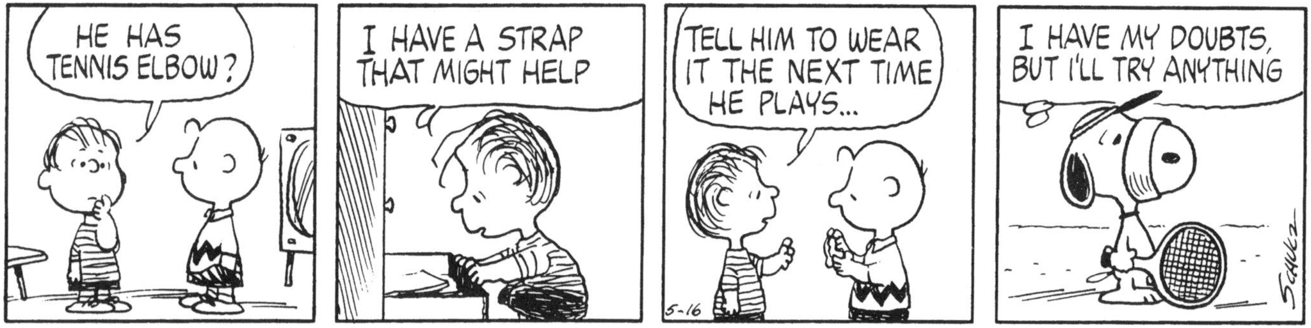
HE HAS TENNIS ELBOW?
I HAVE A STRAP THAT MIGHT HELP
TELL HIM TO WEAR IT THE NEXT TIME HE PLAYS...
5-16
I HAVE MY DOUBTS, BUT I'LL TRY ANYTHING
SCHULZ

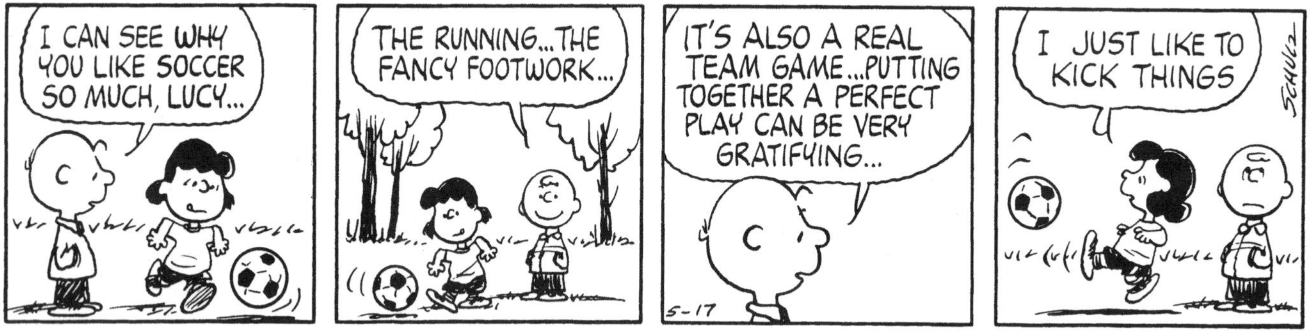
I CAN SEE WHY YOU LIKE SOCCER SO MUCH, LUCY...
THE RUNNING...THE FANCY FOOTWORK...
IT'S ALSO A REAL TEAM GAME...PUTTING TOGETHER A PERFECT PLAY CAN BE VERY GRATIFYING...
5-17
I JUST LIKE TO KICK THINGS
SCHULZ

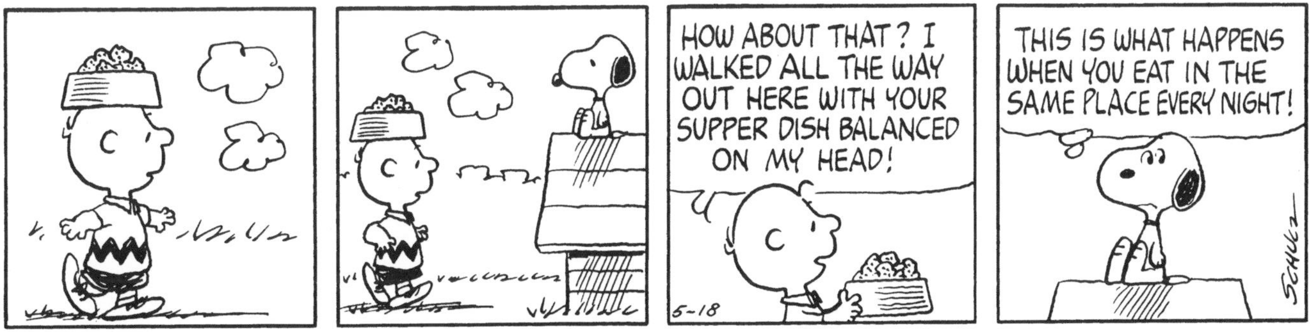
HOW ABOUT THAT? I WALKED ALL THE WAY OUT HERE WITH YOUR SUPPER DISH BALANCED ON MY HEAD!
5-18
THIS IS WHAT HAPPENS WHEN YOU EAT IN THE SAME PLACE EVERY NIGHT!
SCHULZ

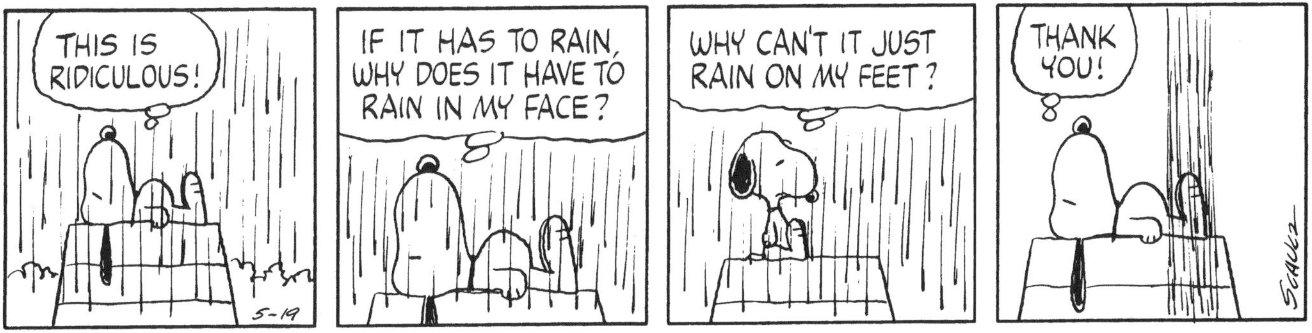
THIS IS RIDICULOUS!
5-19
IF IT HAS TO RAIN, WHY DOES IT HAVE TO RAIN IN MY FACE?
WHY CAN'T IT JUST RAIN ON MY FEET?
THANK YOU!
SCHULZ

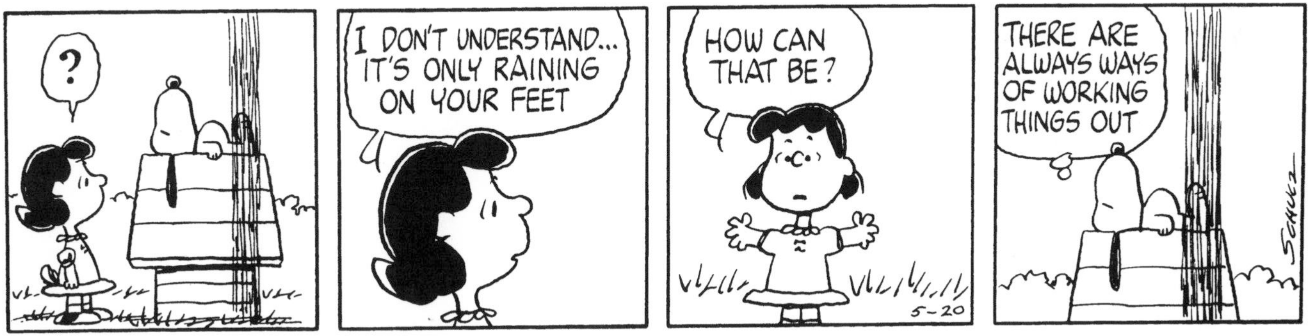
?
I DON'T UNDERSTAND... IT'S ONLY RAINING ON YOUR FEET
HOW CAN THAT BE?
5-20
THERE ARE ALWAYS WAYS OF WORKING THINGS OUT
SCHULZ

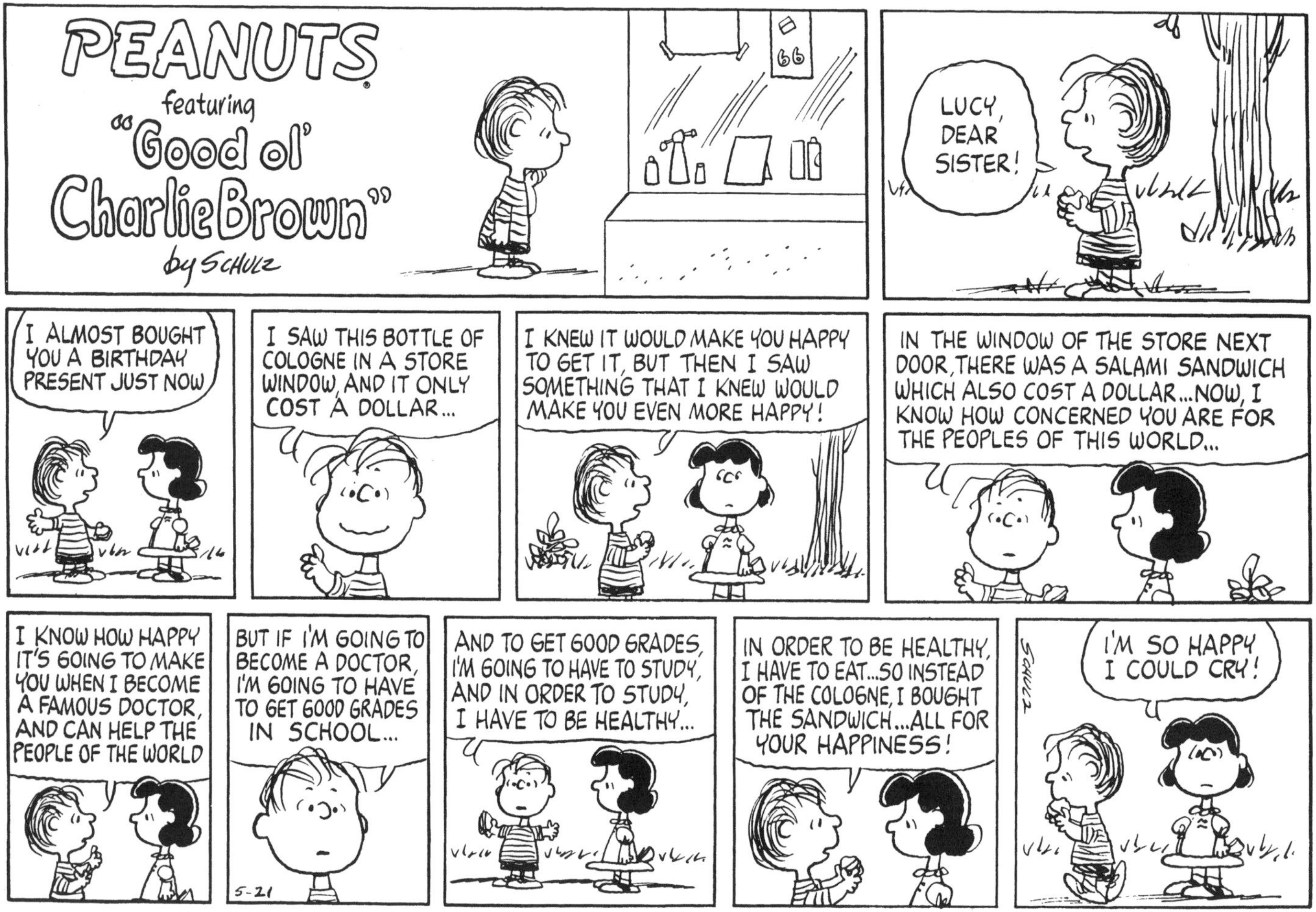
PEANUTS
featuring
"Good ol' Charlie Brown"
by SCHULZ
LUCY, DEAR SISTER!
I ALMOST BOUGHT YOU A BIRTHDAY PRESENT JUST NOW
I SAW THIS BOTTLE OF COLOGNE IN A STORE WINDOW, AND IT ONLY COST A DOLLAR...
I KNEW IT WOULD MAKE YOU HAPPY TO GET IT, BUT THEN I SAW SOMETHING THAT I KNEW WOULD MAKE YOU EVEN MORE HAPPY!
IN THE WINDOW OF THE STORE NEXT DOOR, THERE WAS A SALAMI SANDWICH WHICH ALSO COST A DOLLAR...NOW, I KNOW HOW CONCERNED YOU ARE FOR THE PEOPLES OF THIS WORLD...
I KNOW HOW HAPPY IT'S GOING TO MAKE YOU WHEN I BECOME A FAMOUS DOCTOR, AND CAN HELP THE PEOPLE OF THE WORLD
BUT IF I'M GOING TO BECOME A DOCTOR, I'M GOING TO HAVE TO GET GOOD GRADES IN SCHOOL...
5-21
AND TO GET GOOD GRADES, I'M GOING TO HAVE TO STUDY, AND IN ORDER TO STUDY, I HAVE TO BE HEALTHY...
IN ORDER TO BE HEALTHY, I HAVE TO EAT...SO INSTEAD OF THE COLOGNE, I BOUGHT THE SANDWICH...ALL FOR YOUR HAPPINESS!
SCHULZ
I'M SO HAPPY I COULD CRY!

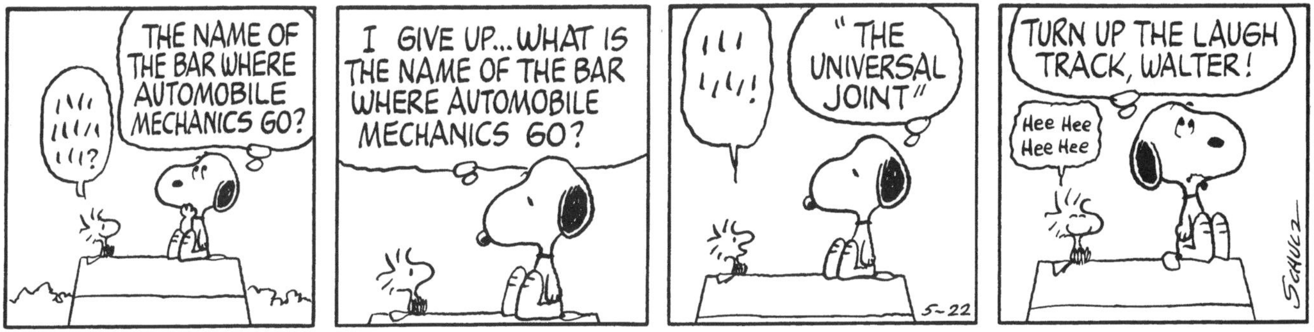
THE NAME OF THE BAR WHERE AUTOMOBILE MECHANICS GO?
I GIVE UP...WHAT IS THE NAME OF THE BAR WHERE AUTOMOBILE MECHANICS GO?
"THE UNIVERSAL JOINT"
TURN UP THE LAUGH TRACK, WALTER!
Hee Hee Hee Hee
5-22
SCHULZ

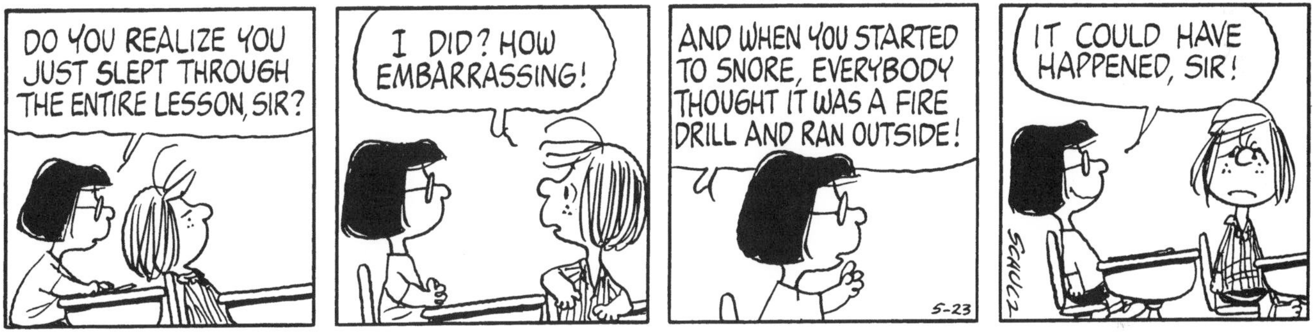
DO YOU REALIZE YOU JUST SLEPT THROUGH THE ENTIRE LESSON, SIR?
I DID? HOW EMBARRASSING!
AND WHEN YOU STARTED TO SNORE, EVERYBODY THOUGHT IT WAS A FIRE DRILL AND RAN OUTSIDE!
5-23
IT COULD HAVE HAPPENED, SIR!
SCHULZ

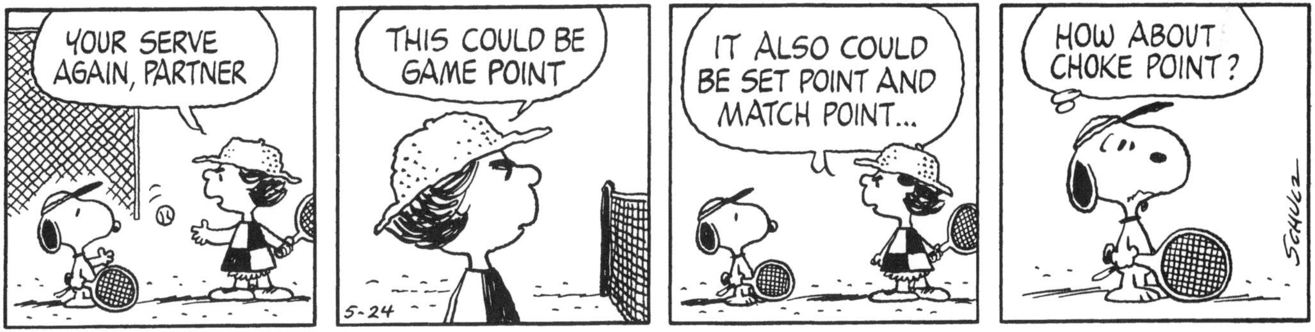
YOUR SERVE AGAIN, PARTNER
THIS COULD BE GAME POINT
5-24
IT ALSO COULD BE SET POINT AND MATCH POINT...
HOW ABOUT CHOKE POINT?
SCHULZ

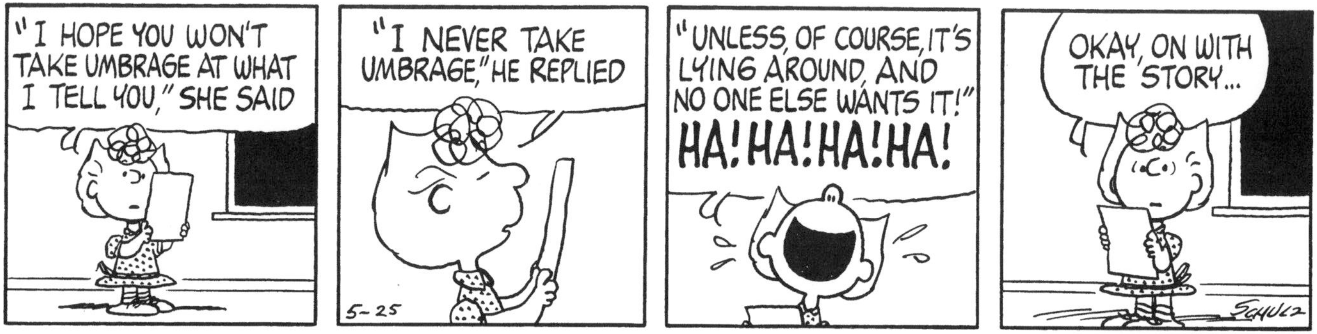
"I HOPE YOU WON'T TAKE UMBRAGE AT WHAT I TELL YOU," SHE SAID
"I NEVER TAKE UMBRAGE," HE REPLIED
5-25
"UNLESS, OF COURSE, IT'S LYING AROUND, AND NO ONE ELSE WANTS IT!"
HA! HA! HA! HA!
OKAY, ON WITH THE STORY...
SCHULZ

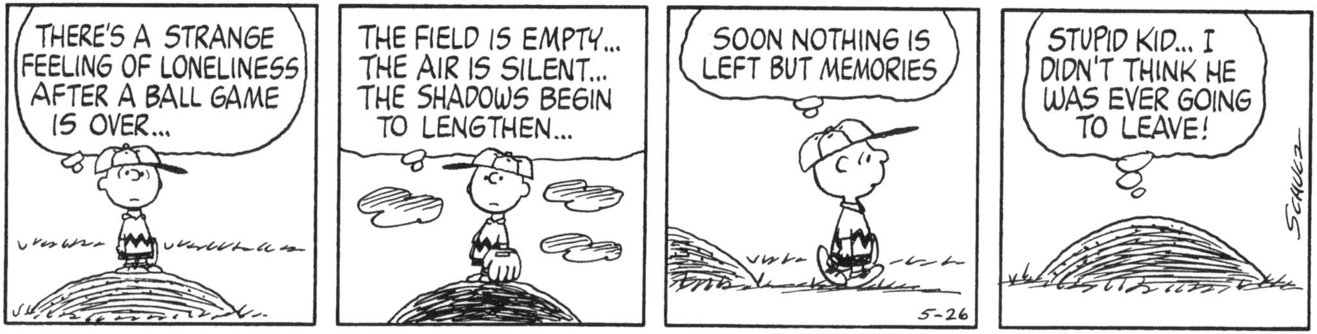
THERE'S A STRANGE FEELING OF LONELINESS AFTER A BALL GAME IS OVER...
THE FIELD IS EMPTY... THE AIR IS SILENT... THE SHADOWS BEGIN TO LENGTHEN...
SOON NOTHING IS LEFT BUT MEMORIES
5-26
STUPID KID... I DIDN'T THINK HE WAS EVER GOING TO LEAVE!
SCHULZ

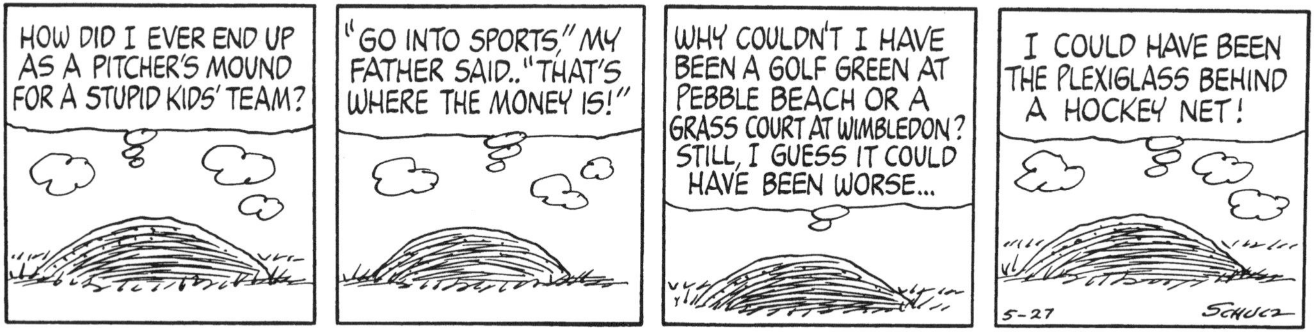
HOW DID I EVER END UP AS A PITCHER'S MOUND FOR A STUPID KIDS' TEAM?
"GO INTO SPORTS," MY FATHER SAID.. "THAT'S WHERE THE MONEY IS!"
WHY COULDN'T I HAVE BEEN A GOLF GREEN AT PEBBLE BEACH OR A GRASS COURT AT WIMBLEDON? STILL, I GUESS IT COULD HAVE BEEN WORSE...
I COULD HAVE BEEN THE PLEXIGLASS BEHIND A HOCKEY NET!
5-27
SCHULZ

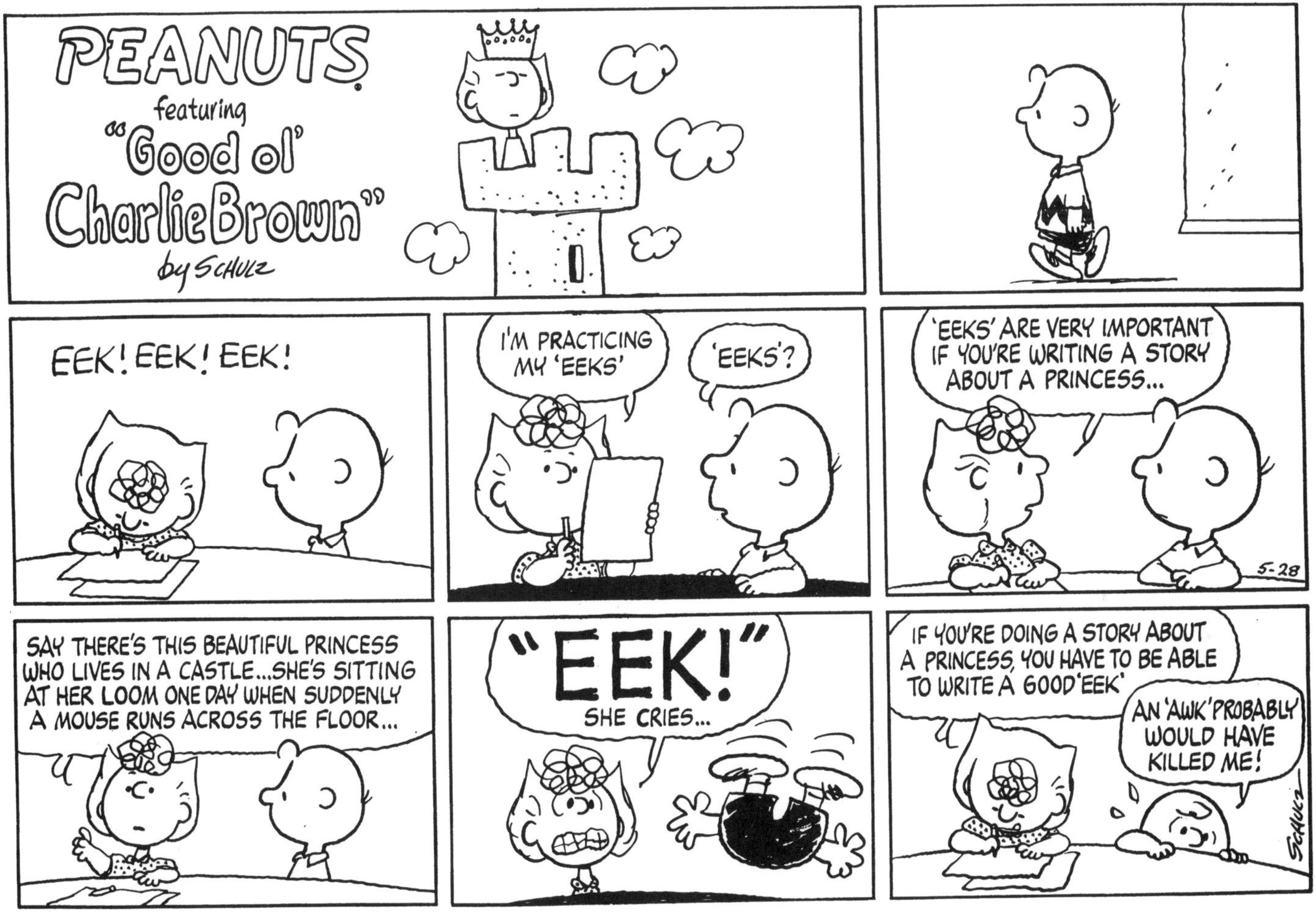
PEANUTS
featuring
"Good ol' Charlie Brown"
by SCHULZ
EEK! EEK! EEK!
I'M PRACTICING MY 'EEKS'
'EEKS'?
'EEKS' ARE VERY IMPORTANT IF YOU'RE WRITING A STORY ABOUT A PRINCESS...
5-28
SAY THERE'S THIS BEAUTIFUL PRINCESS WHO LIVES IN A CASTLE...SHE'S SITTING AT HER LOOM ONE DAY WHEN SUDDENLY A MOUSE RUNS ACROSS THE FLOOR...
"EEK!" SHE CRIES...
IF YOU'RE DOING A STORY ABOUT A PRINCESS, YOU HAVE TO BE ABLE TO WRITE A GOOD 'EEK'
AN 'AWK' PROBABLY WOULD HAVE KILLED ME!
SCHULZ

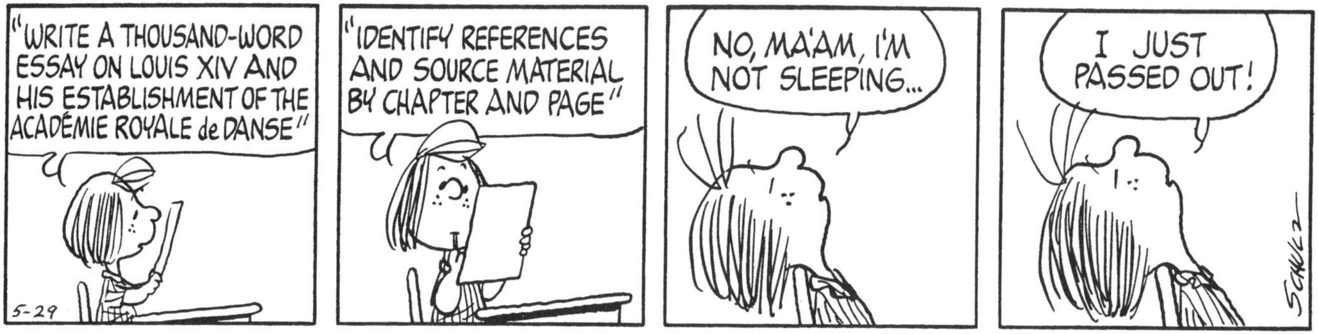
"WRITE A THOUSAND-WORD ESSAY ON LOUIS XIV AND HIS ESTABLISHMENT OF THE ACADÉMIE ROYALE de DANSE"
5-29
"IDENTIFY REFERENCES AND SOURCE MATERIAL BY CHAPTER AND PAGE"
NO, MA'AM, I'M NOT SLEEPING...
I JUST PASSED OUT!
SCHULZ

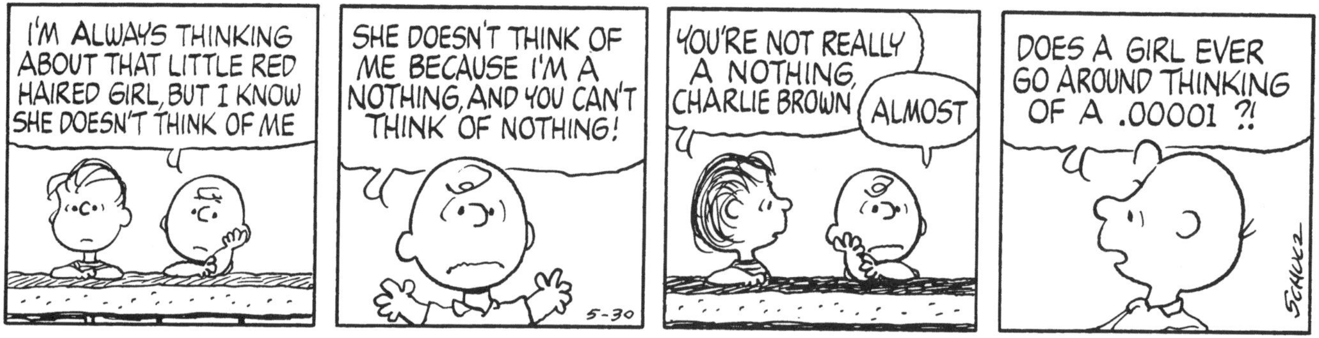
I'M ALWAYS THINKING ABOUT THAT LITTLE RED HAIRED GIRL, BUT I KNOW SHE DOESN'T THINK OF ME
SHE DOESN'T THINK OF ME BECAUSE I'M A NOTHING, AND YOU CAN'T THINK OF NOTHING!
5-30
YOU'RE NOT REALLY A NOTHING, CHARLIE BROWN
ALMOST
DOES A GIRL EVER GO AROUND THINKING OF A .00001 ?!
SCHULZ

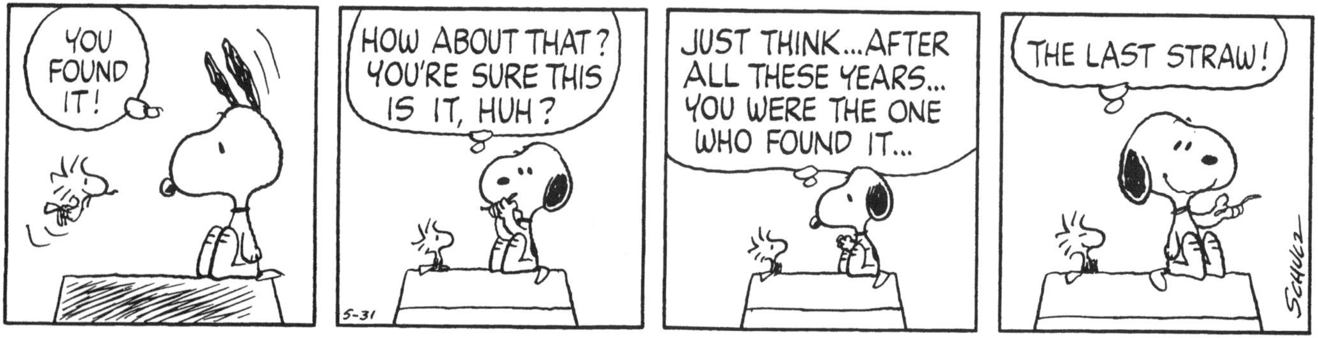
YOU FOUND IT!
HOW ABOUT THAT? YOU'RE SURE THIS IS IT, HUH?
5-31
JUST THINK...AFTER ALL THESE YEARS... YOU WERE THE ONE WHO FOUND IT...
THE LAST STRAW!
SCHULZ

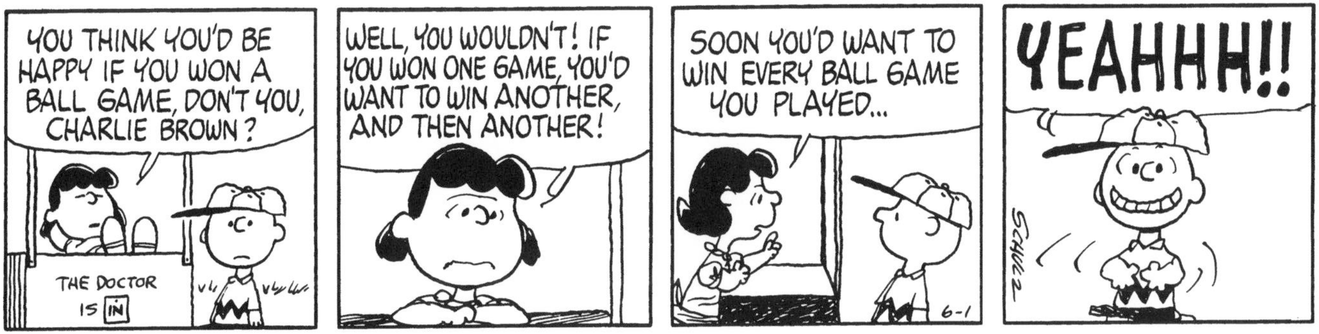
YOU THINK YOU'D BE HAPPY IF YOU WON A BALL GAME, DON'T YOU, CHARLIE BROWN?
THE DOCTOR IS IN
WELL, YOU WOULDN'T! IF YOU WON ONE GAME, YOU'D WANT TO WIN ANOTHER, AND THEN ANOTHER!
SOON YOU'D WANT TO WIN EVERY BALL GAME YOU PLAYED...
6-1
YEAHHH!!
SCHULZ

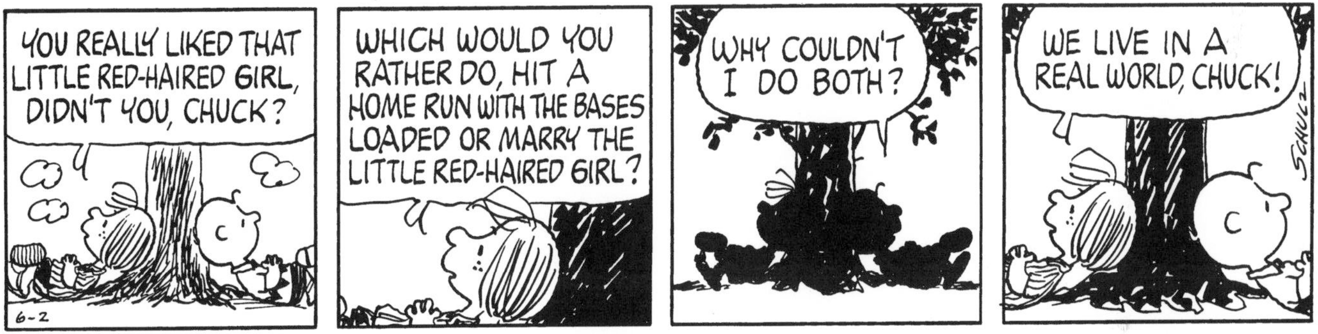
YOU REALLY LIKED THAT LITTLE RED-HAIRED GIRL, DIDN'T YOU, CHUCK?
6-2
WHICH WOULD YOU RATHER DO, HIT A HOME RUN WITH THE BASES LOADED OR MARRY THE LITTLE RED-HAIRED GIRL?
WHY COULDN'T I DO BOTH?
WE LIVE IN A REAL WORLD, CHUCK!
SCHULZ

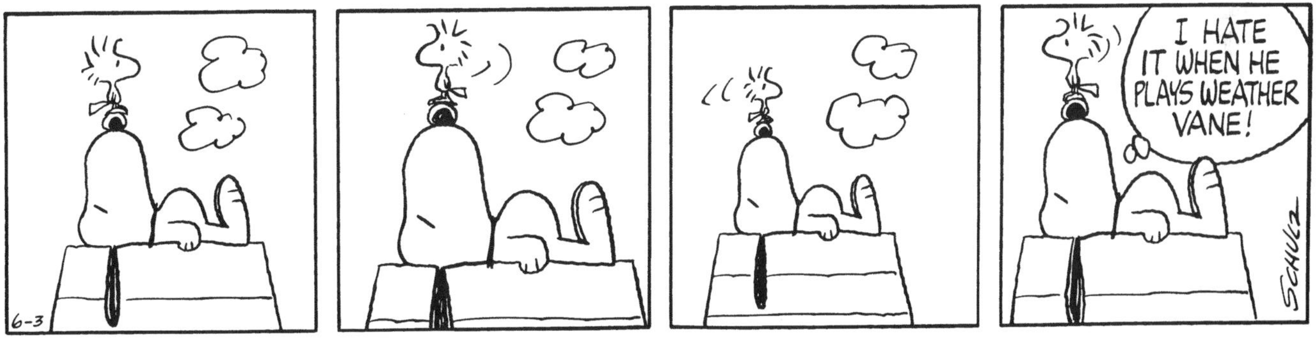
6-3
I HATE IT WHEN HE PLAYS WEATHER VANE!
SCHULZ

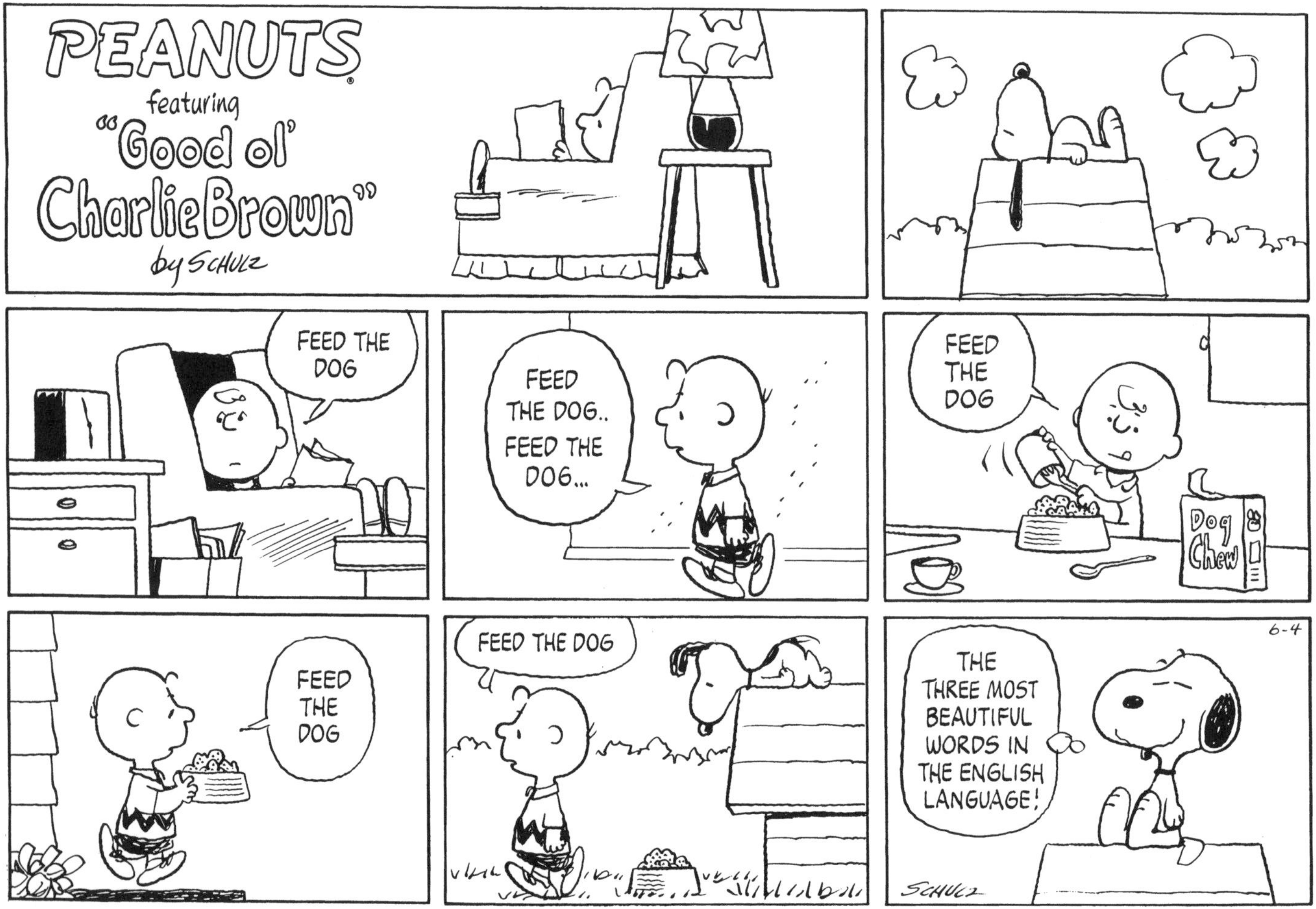
PEANUTS®
featuring "Good ol' Charlie Brown"
by SCHULZ
FEED THE DOG
FEED THE DOG.. FEED THE DOG...
FEED THE DOG
Dog Chew
FEED THE DOG
FEED THE DOG
6-4
THE THREE MOST BEAUTIFUL WORDS IN THE ENGLISH LANGUAGE!
SCHULZ

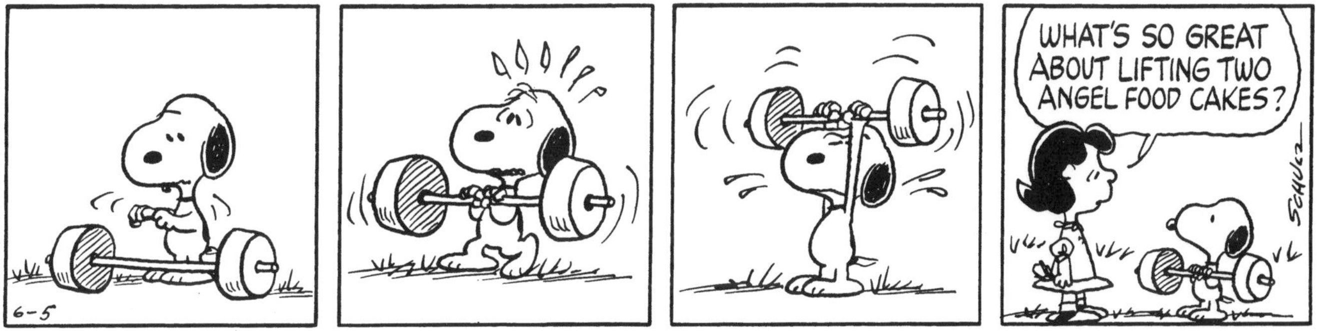
6-5
WHAT'S SO GREAT ABOUT LIFTING TWO ANGEL FOOD CAKES?
SCHULZ

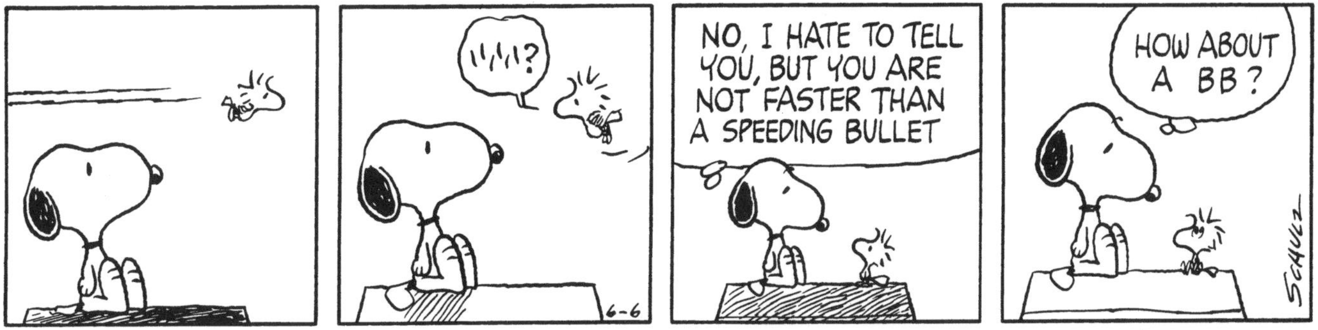
NO, I HATE TO TELL YOU, BUT YOU ARE NOT FASTER THAN A SPEEDING BULLET
6-6
HOW ABOUT A BB?
SCHULZ

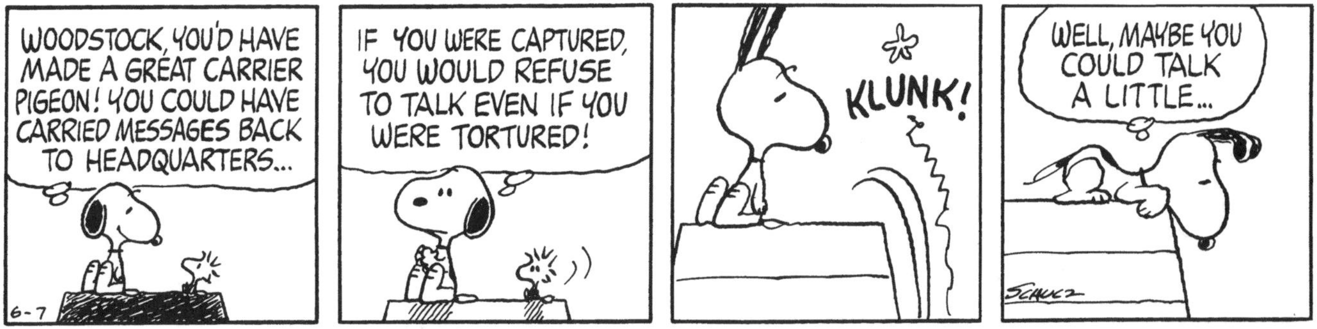
WOODSTOCK, YOU'D HAVE MADE A GREAT CARRIER PIGEON! YOU COULD HAVE CARRIED MESSAGES BACK TO HEADQUARTERS...
6-7
IF YOU WERE CAPTURED, YOU WOULD REFUSE TO TALK EVEN IF YOU WERE TORTURED!
KLUNK!
WELL, MAYBE YOU COULD TALK A LITTLE...
SCHULZ

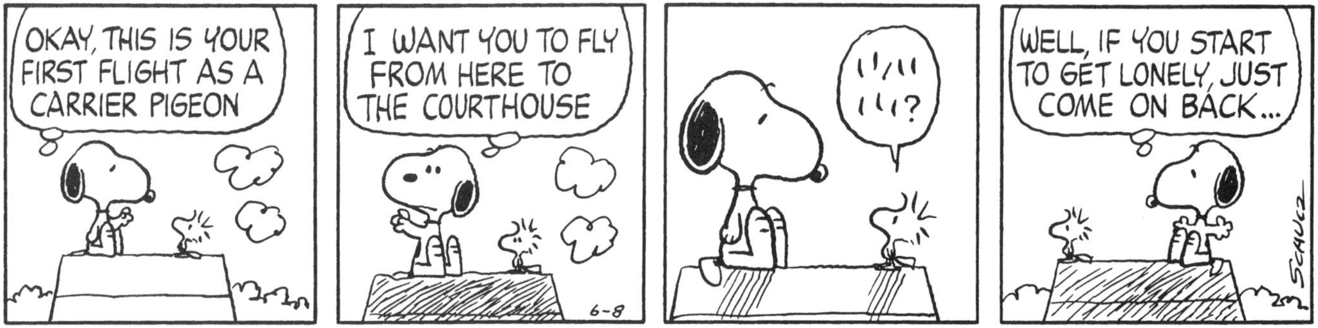
OKAY, THIS IS YOUR FIRST FLIGHT AS A CARRIER PIGEON
I WANT YOU TO FLY FROM HERE TO THE COURTHOUSE
6-8
WELL, IF YOU START TO GET LONELY, JUST COME ON BACK...
SCHULZ

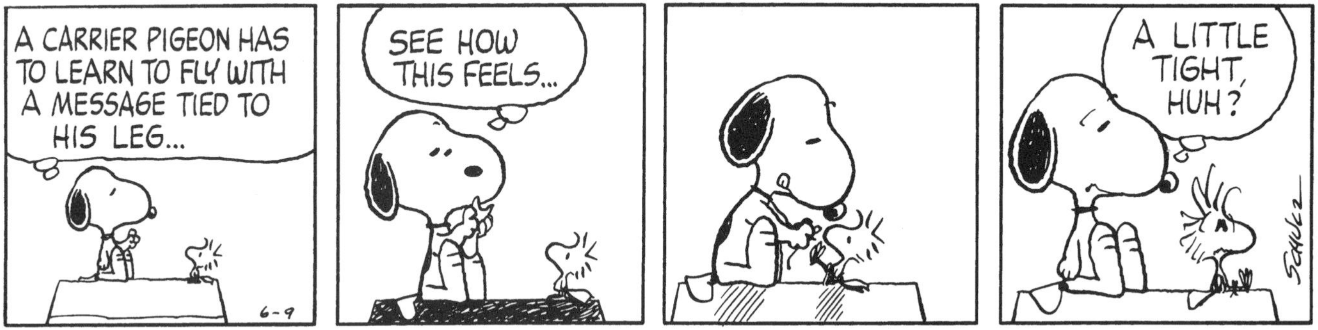
A CARRIER PIGEON HAS TO LEARN TO FLY WITH A MESSAGE TIED TO HIS LEG...
6-9
SEE HOW THIS FEELS...
A LITTLE TIGHT, HUH?
SCHULZ

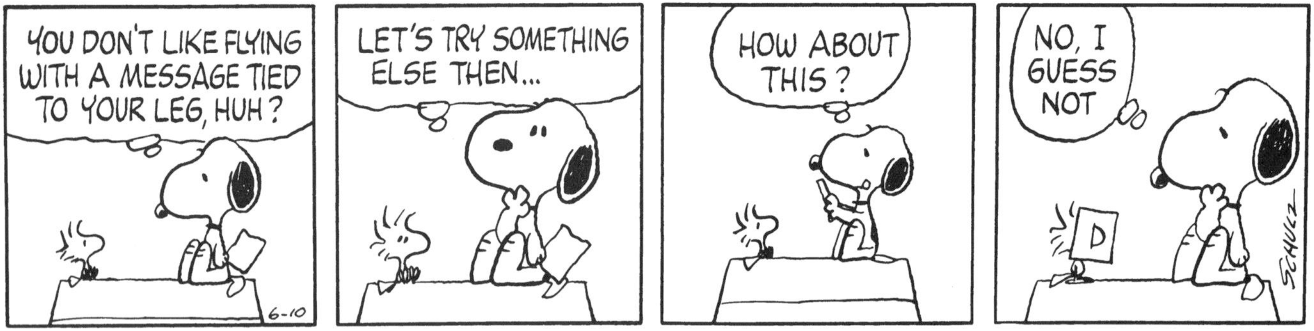
YOU DON'T LIKE FLYING WITH A MESSAGE TIED TO YOUR LEG, HUH?
6-10
LET'S TRY SOMETHING ELSE THEN...
HOW ABOUT THIS?
NO, I GUESS NOT
D
SCHULZ

PEANUTS featuring "Good ol' Charlie Brown" by Schulz

Deer

6-11

THAT SHOULD BE "DEAR"

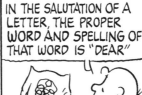
IN THE SALUTATION OF A LETTER, THE PROPER WORD AND SPELLING OF THAT WORD IS "DEAR"

Deer are beautiful animals found in most parts of the world.

I'M SORRY... I DIDN'T REALIZE YOU WERE WRITING ABOUT DEER... I APOLOGIZE...

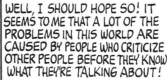

WELL, I SHOULD HOPE SO! IT SEEMS TO ME THAT A LOT OF THE PROBLEMS IN THIS WORLD ARE CAUSED BY PEOPLE WHO CRITICIZE OTHER PEOPLE BEFORE THEY KNOW WHAT THEY'RE TALKING ABOUT!

Dear Grandma,

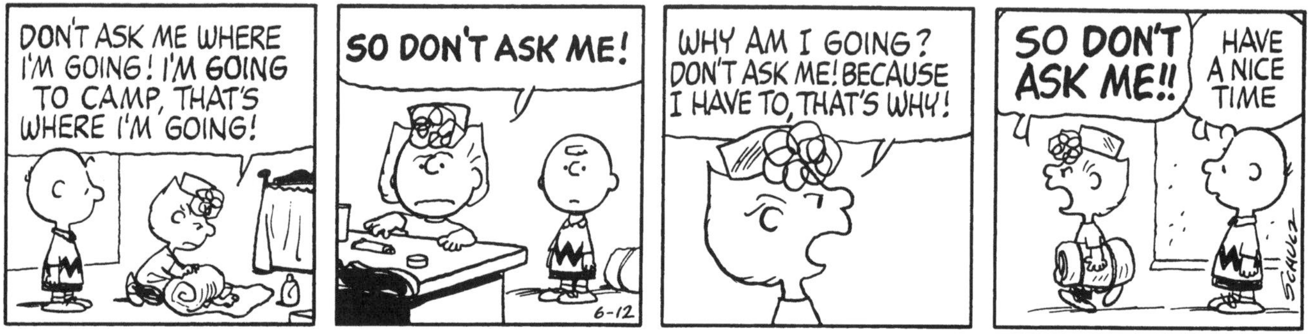
DON'T ASK ME WHERE I'M GOING! I'M GOING TO CAMP, THAT'S WHERE I'M GOING!
SO DON'T ASK ME!
6-12
WHY AM I GOING? DON'T ASK ME! BECAUSE I HAVE TO, THAT'S WHY!
SO DON'T ASK ME!!
HAVE A NICE TIME
SCHULZ

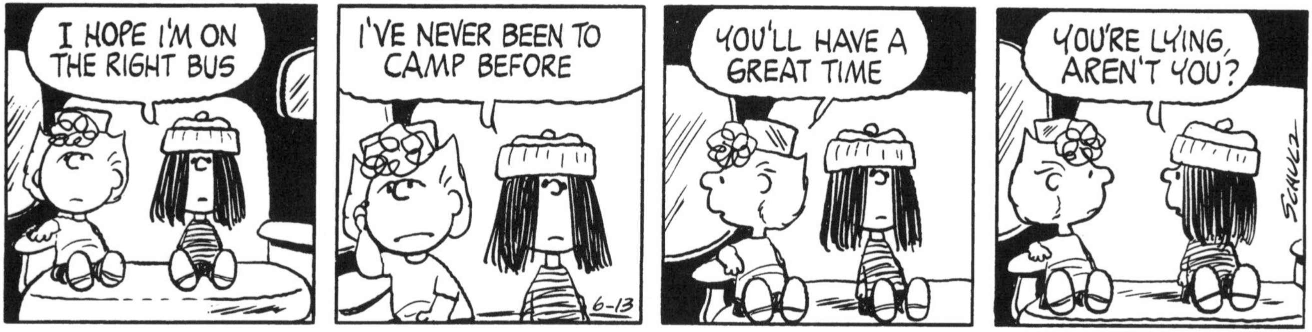
I HOPE I'M ON THE RIGHT BUS
I'VE NEVER BEEN TO CAMP BEFORE
6-13
YOU'LL HAVE A GREAT TIME
YOU'RE LYING, AREN'T YOU?
SCHULZ

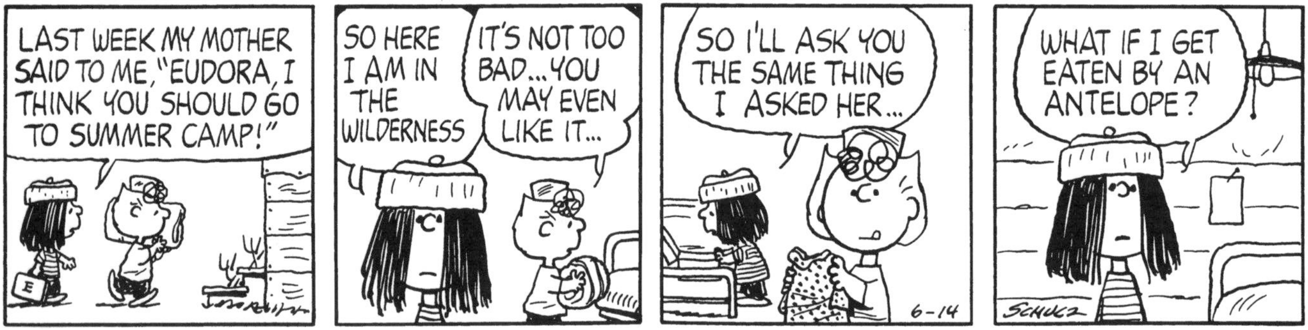
LAST WEEK MY MOTHER SAID TO ME, "EUDORA, I THINK YOU SHOULD GO TO SUMMER CAMP!"
E
SO HERE I AM IN THE WILDERNESS
IT'S NOT TOO BAD...YOU MAY EVEN LIKE IT...
SO I'LL ASK YOU THE SAME THING I ASKED HER...
6-14
WHAT IF I GET EATEN BY AN ANTELOPE?
SCHULZ

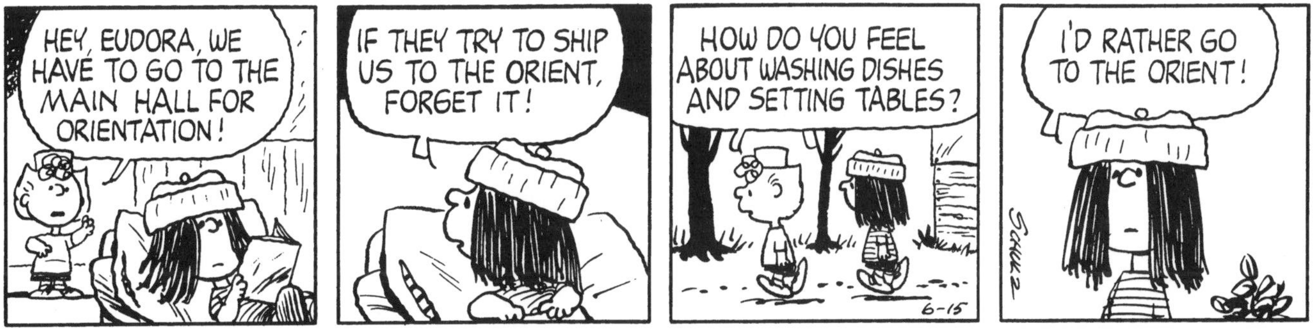
HEY, EUDORA, WE HAVE TO GO TO THE MAIN HALL FOR ORIENTATION!
IF THEY TRY TO SHIP US TO THE ORIENT, FORGET IT!
HOW DO YOU FEEL ABOUT WASHING DISHES AND SETTING TABLES?
6-15
I'D RATHER GO TO THE ORIENT!
SCHULZ

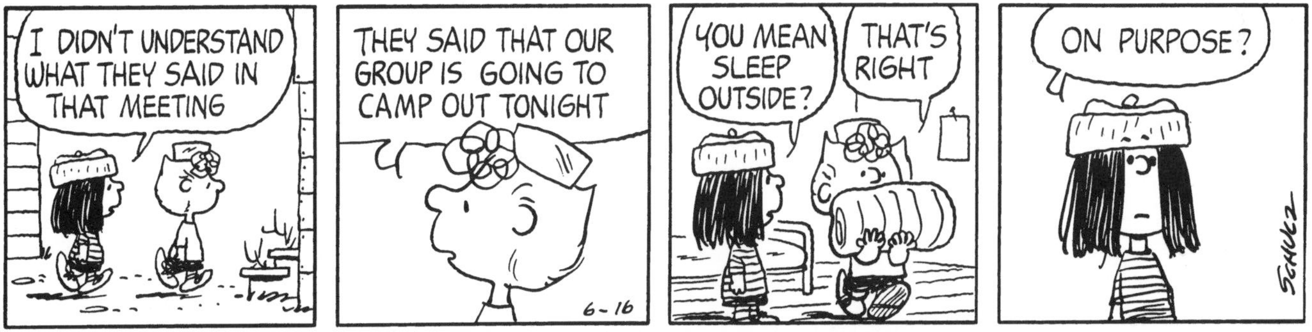
I DIDN'T UNDERSTAND WHAT THEY SAID IN THAT MEETING
THEY SAID THAT OUR GROUP IS GOING TO CAMP OUT TONIGHT
6-16
YOU MEAN SLEEP OUTSIDE?
THAT'S RIGHT
ON PURPOSE?
SCHULZ

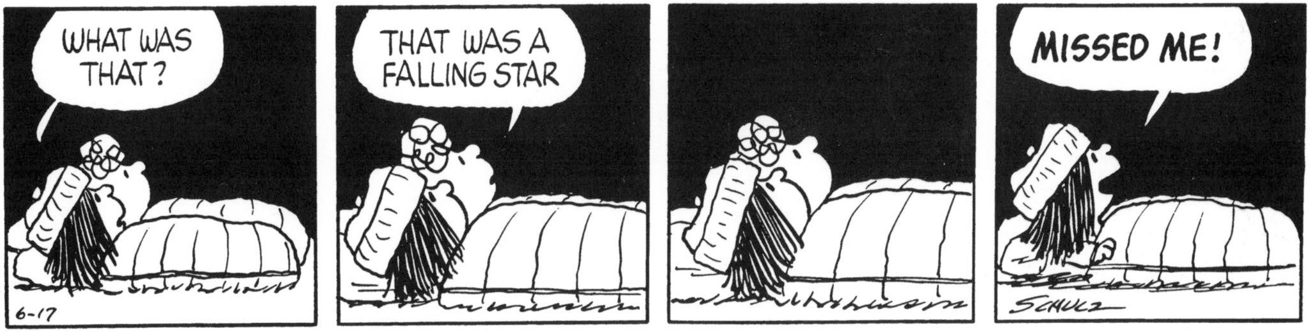
WHAT WAS THAT?
6-17
THAT WAS A FALLING STAR
MISSED ME!
SCHULZ

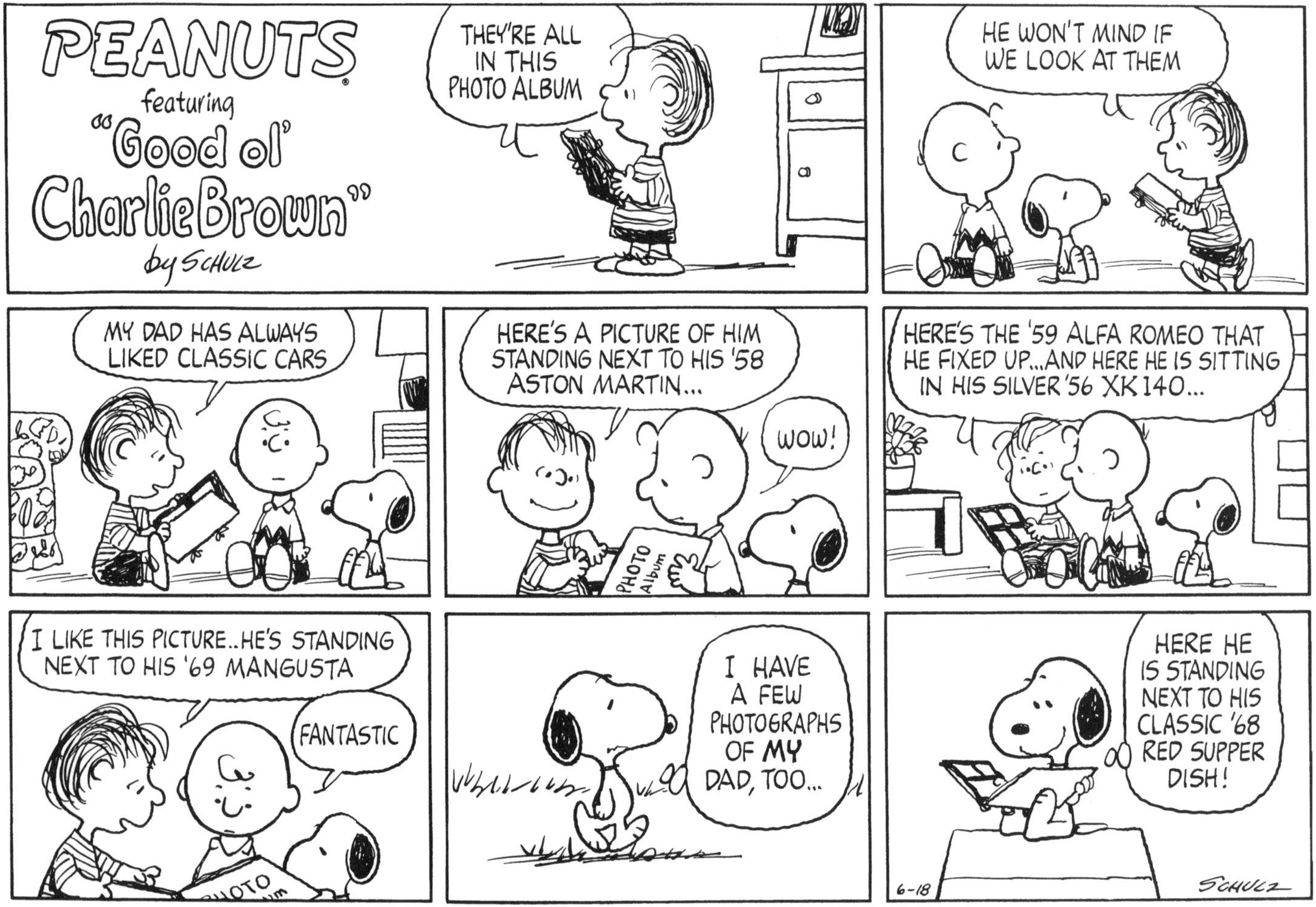
PEANUTS
featuring
"Good ol' Charlie Brown"
by SCHULZ
THEY'RE ALL IN THIS PHOTO ALBUM
HE WON'T MIND IF WE LOOK AT THEM
MY DAD HAS ALWAYS LIKED CLASSIC CARS
HERE'S A PICTURE OF HIM STANDING NEXT TO HIS '58 ASTON MARTIN...
WOW!
PHOTO Album
HERE'S THE '59 ALFA ROMEO THAT HE FIXED UP...AND HERE HE IS SITTING IN HIS SILVER '56 XK140...
I LIKE THIS PICTURE..HE'S STANDING NEXT TO HIS '69 MANGUSTA
FANTASTIC
I HAVE A FEW PHOTOGRAPHS OF MY DAD, TOO...
HERE HE IS STANDING NEXT TO HIS CLASSIC '68 RED SUPPER DISH!
6-18
SCHULZ

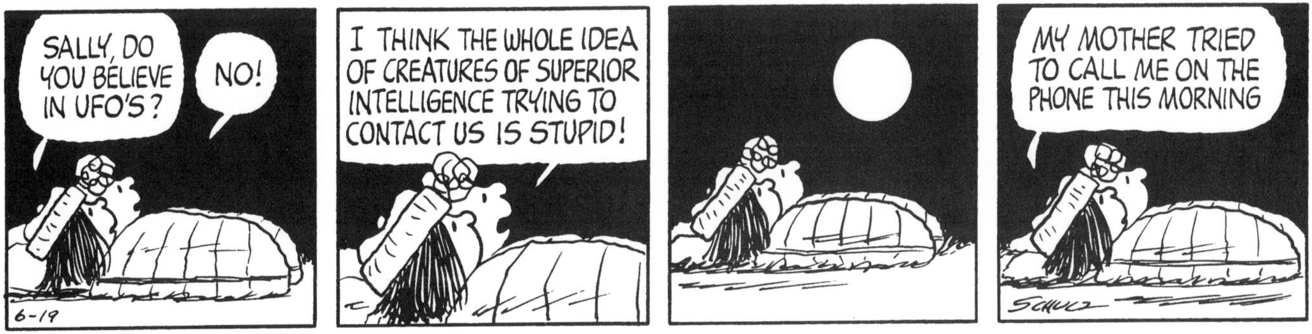
SALLY, DO YOU BELIEVE IN UFO'S?
NO!
I THINK THE WHOLE IDEA OF CREATURES OF SUPERIOR INTELLIGENCE TRYING TO CONTACT US IS STUPID!
MY MOTHER TRIED TO CALL ME ON THE PHONE THIS MORNING
6-19
SCHULZ

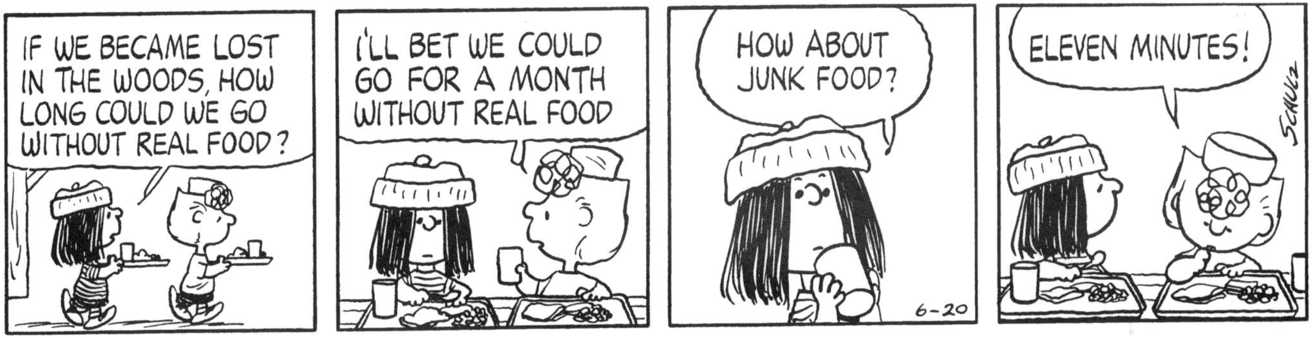
IF WE BECAME LOST IN THE WOODS, HOW LONG COULD WE GO WITHOUT REAL FOOD?
I'LL BET WE COULD GO FOR A MONTH WITHOUT REAL FOOD
HOW ABOUT JUNK FOOD?
ELEVEN MINUTES!
6-20
SCHULZ

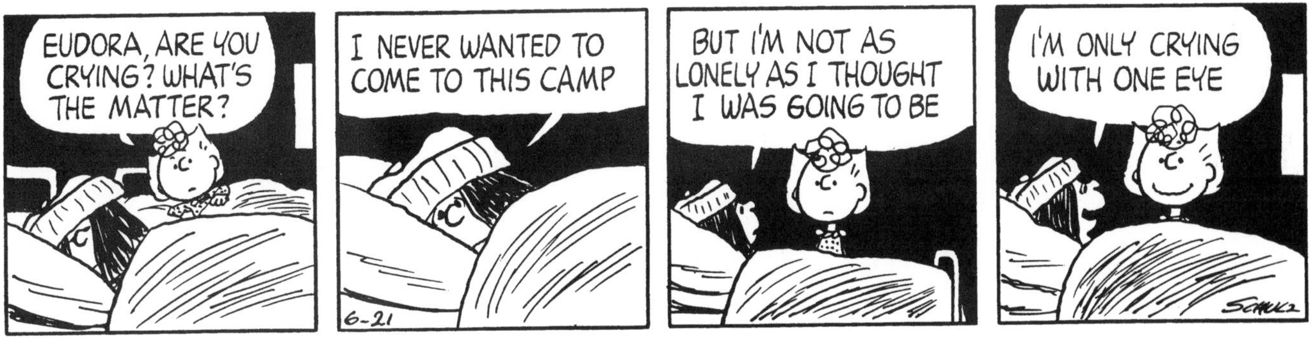
EUDORA, ARE YOU CRYING? WHAT'S THE MATTER?
I NEVER WANTED TO COME TO THIS CAMP
BUT I'M NOT AS LONELY AS I THOUGHT I WAS GOING TO BE
I'M ONLY CRYING WITH ONE EYE
6-21
SCHULZ

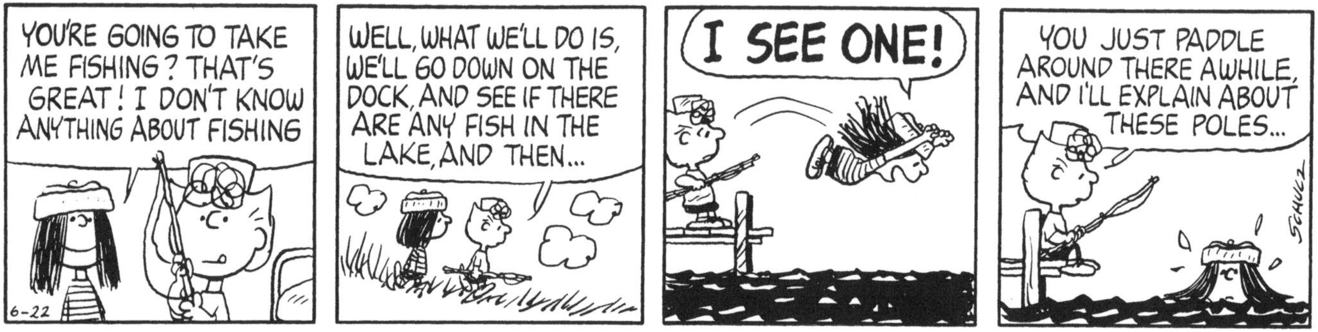
YOU'RE GOING TO TAKE ME FISHING? THAT'S GREAT! I DON'T KNOW ANYTHING ABOUT FISHING
6-22
WELL, WHAT WE'LL DO IS, WE'LL GO DOWN ON THE DOCK, AND SEE IF THERE ARE ANY FISH IN THE LAKE, AND THEN...
I SEE ONE!
YOU JUST PADDLE AROUND THERE AWHILE, AND I'LL EXPLAIN ABOUT THESE POLES...
SCHULZ

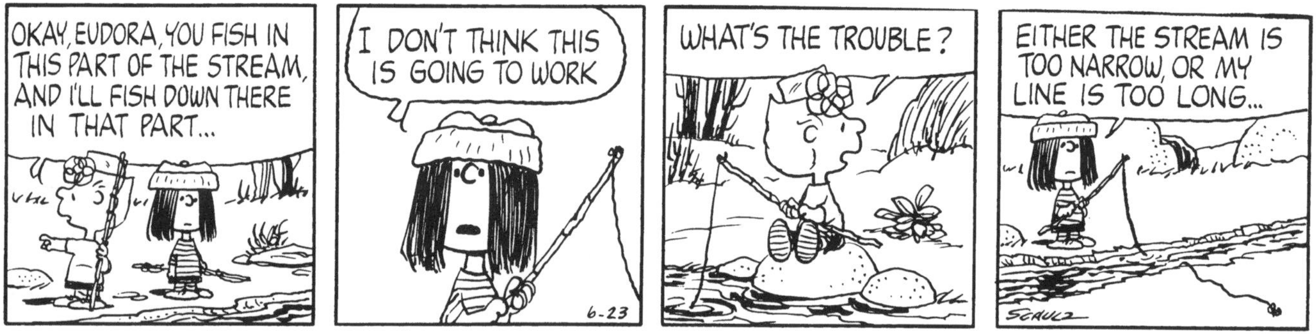
OKAY, EUDORA, YOU FISH IN THIS PART OF THE STREAM, AND I'LL FISH DOWN THERE IN THAT PART...
I DON'T THINK THIS IS GOING TO WORK
6-23
WHAT'S THE TROUBLE?
EITHER THE STREAM IS TOO NARROW, OR MY LINE IS TOO LONG...
SCHULZ

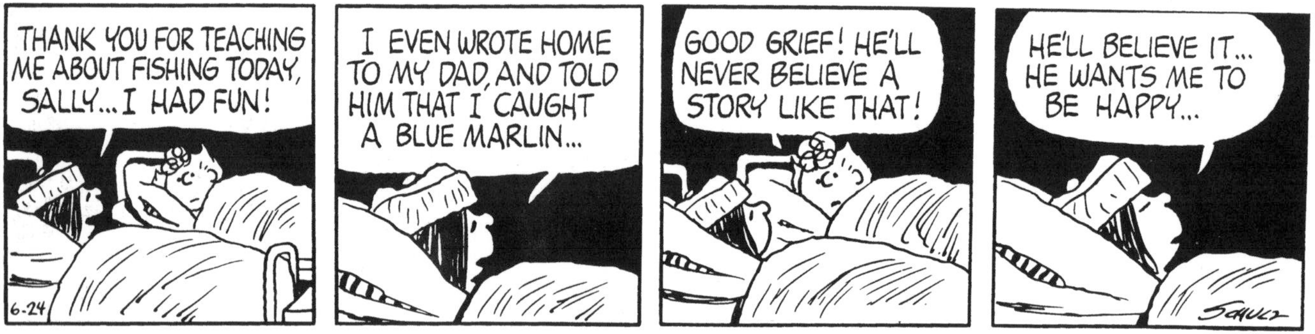
THANK YOU FOR TEACHING ME ABOUT FISHING TODAY, SALLY... I HAD FUN!
6-24
I EVEN WROTE HOME TO MY DAD, AND TOLD HIM THAT I CAUGHT A BLUE MARLIN...
GOOD GRIEF! HE'LL NEVER BELIEVE A STORY LIKE THAT!
HE'LL BELIEVE IT... HE WANTS ME TO BE HAPPY...
SCHULZ

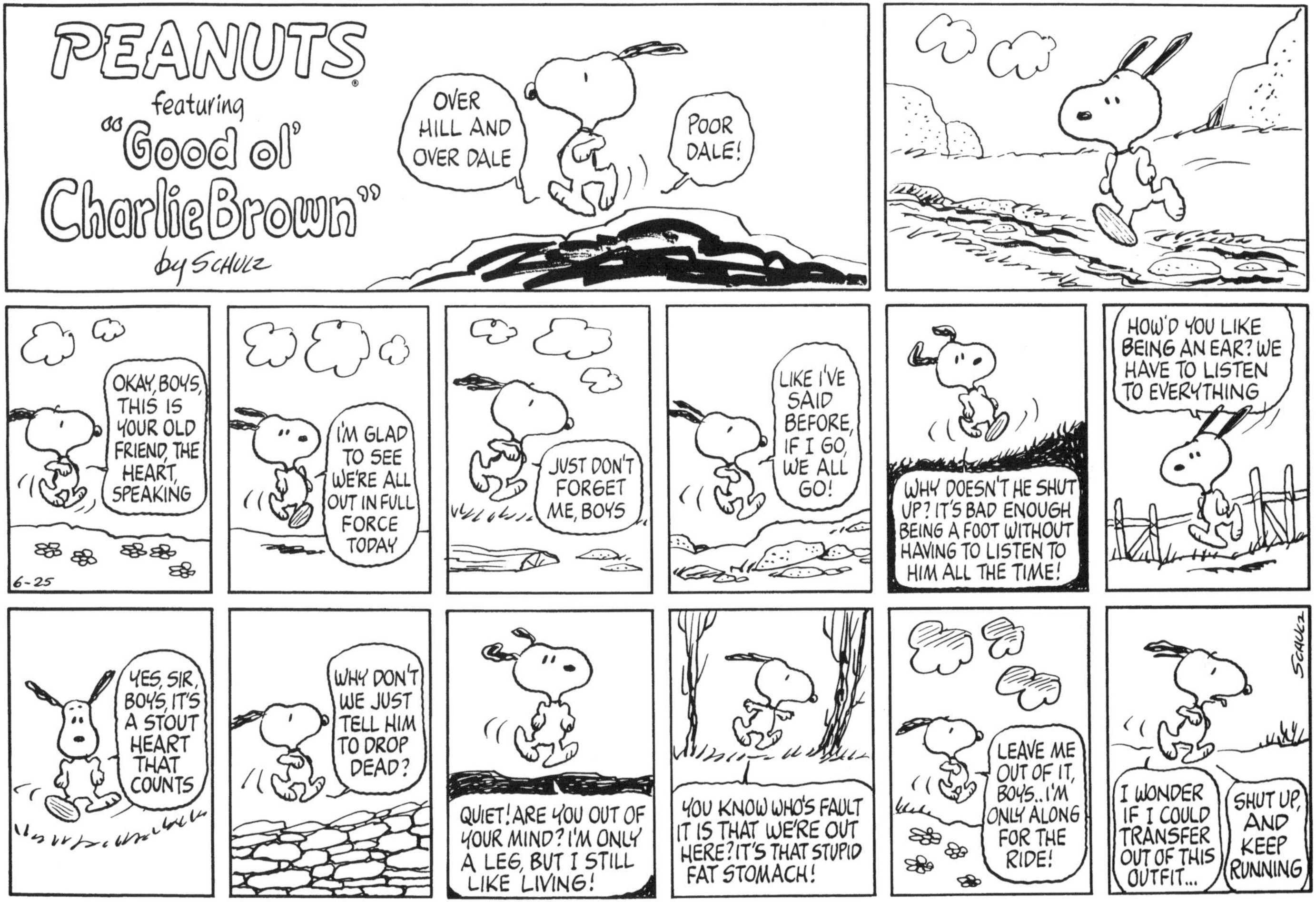
PEANUTS
featuring "Good ol' Charlie Brown"
by SCHULZ
OVER HILL AND OVER DALE
POOR DALE!
OKAY, BOYS, THIS IS YOUR OLD FRIEND, THE HEART, SPEAKING
6-25
I'M GLAD TO SEE WE'RE ALL OUT IN FULL FORCE TODAY
JUST DON'T FORGET ME, BOYS
LIKE I'VE SAID BEFORE, IF I GO, WE ALL GO!
WHY DOESN'T HE SHUT UP? IT'S BAD ENOUGH BEING A FOOT WITHOUT HAVING TO LISTEN TO HIM ALL THE TIME!
HOW'D YOU LIKE BEING AN EAR? WE HAVE TO LISTEN TO EVERYTHING
YES, SIR, BOYS, IT'S A STOUT HEART THAT COUNTS
WHY DON'T WE JUST TELL HIM TO DROP DEAD?
QUIET! ARE YOU OUT OF YOUR MIND? I'M ONLY A LEG, BUT I STILL LIKE LIVING!
YOU KNOW WHO'S FAULT IT IS THAT WE'RE OUT HERE? IT'S THAT STUPID FAT STOMACH!
LEAVE ME OUT OF IT, BOYS.. I'M ONLY ALONG FOR THE RIDE!
SCHULZ
I WONDER IF I COULD TRANSFER OUT OF THIS OUTFIT...
SHUT UP, AND KEEP RUNNING

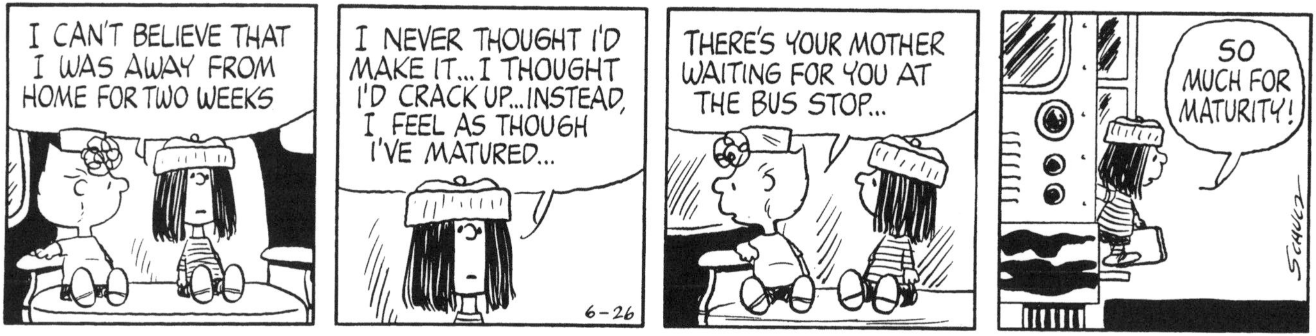
I CAN'T BELIEVE THAT I WAS AWAY FROM HOME FOR TWO WEEKS
I NEVER THOUGHT I'D MAKE IT...I THOUGHT I'D CRACK UP...INSTEAD, I FEEL AS THOUGH I'VE MATURED...
6-26
THERE'S YOUR MOTHER WAITING FOR YOU AT THE BUS STOP...
SO MUCH FOR MATURITY!
SCHULZ

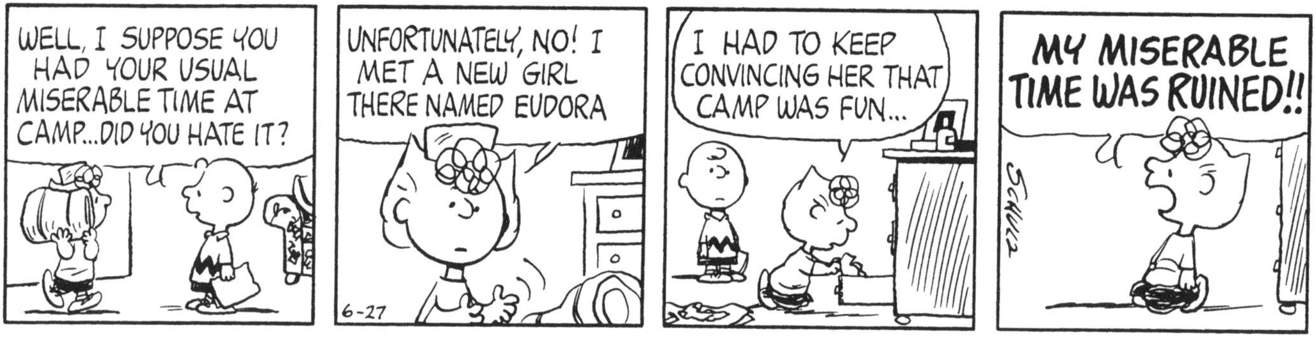
WELL, I SUPPOSE YOU HAD YOUR USUAL MISERABLE TIME AT CAMP...DID YOU HATE IT?
UNFORTUNATELY, NO! I MET A NEW GIRL THERE NAMED EUDORA
6-27
I HAD TO KEEP CONVINCING HER THAT CAMP WAS FUN...
MY MISERABLE TIME WAS RUINED!!
SCHULZ

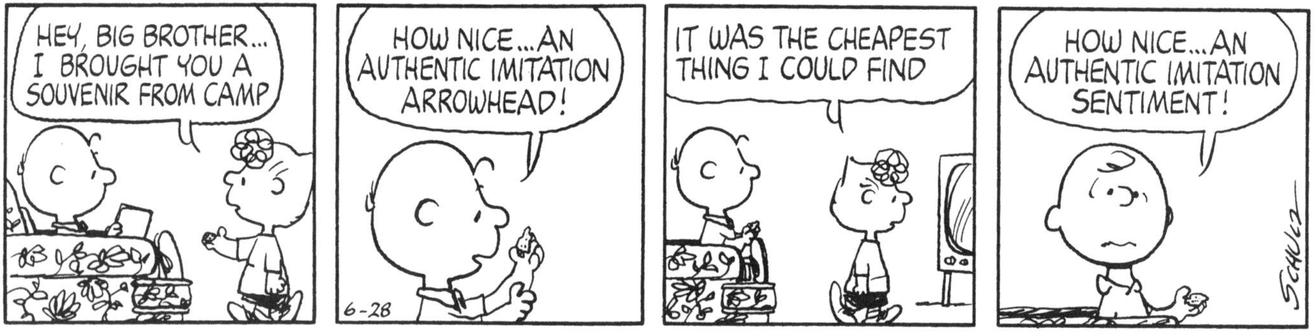
HEY, BIG BROTHER... I BROUGHT YOU A SOUVENIR FROM CAMP
HOW NICE...AN AUTHENTIC IMITATION ARROWHEAD!
6-28
IT WAS THE CHEAPEST THING I COULD FIND
HOW NICE...AN AUTHENTIC IMITATION SENTIMENT!
SCHULZ

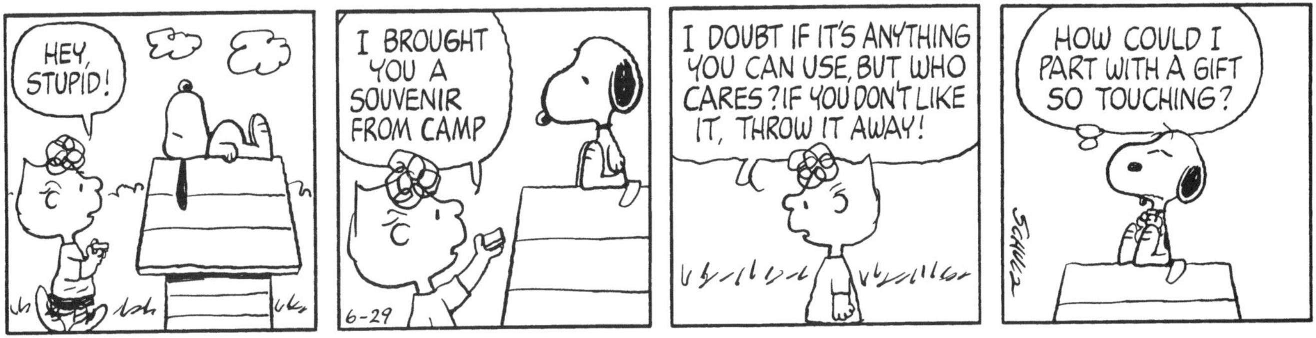
HEY, STUPID!
I BROUGHT YOU A SOUVENIR FROM CAMP
6-29
I DOUBT IF IT'S ANYTHING YOU CAN USE, BUT WHO CARES? IF YOU DON'T LIKE IT, THROW IT AWAY!
HOW COULD I PART WITH A GIFT SO TOUCHING?
SCHULZ

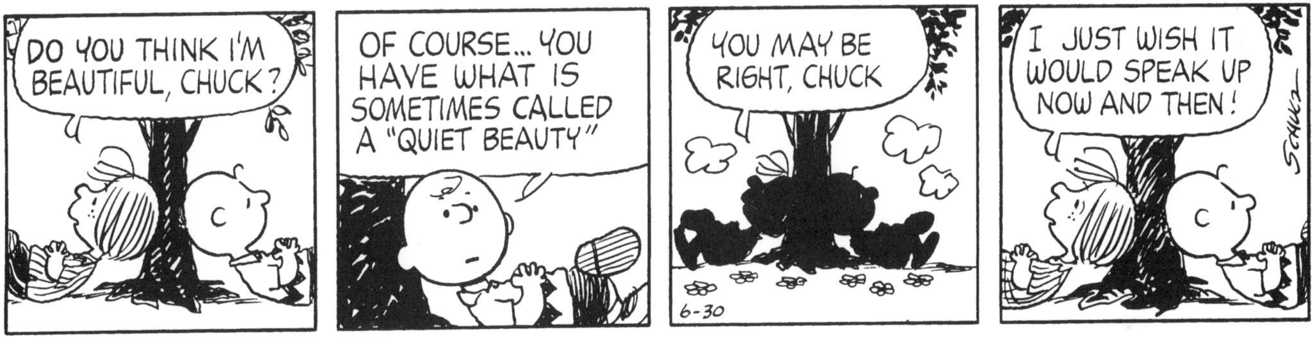
DO YOU THINK I'M BEAUTIFUL, CHUCK?
OF COURSE... YOU HAVE WHAT IS SOMETIMES CALLED A "QUIET BEAUTY"
YOU MAY BE RIGHT, CHUCK
6-30
I JUST WISH IT WOULD SPEAK UP NOW AND THEN!
SCHULZ

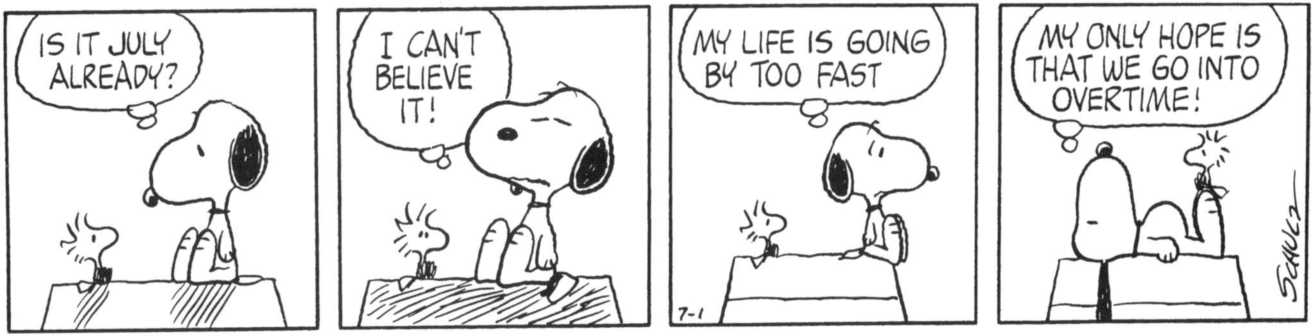
IS IT JULY ALREADY?
I CAN'T BELIEVE IT!
MY LIFE IS GOING BY TOO FAST
7-1
MY ONLY HOPE IS THAT WE GO INTO OVERTIME!
SCHULZ

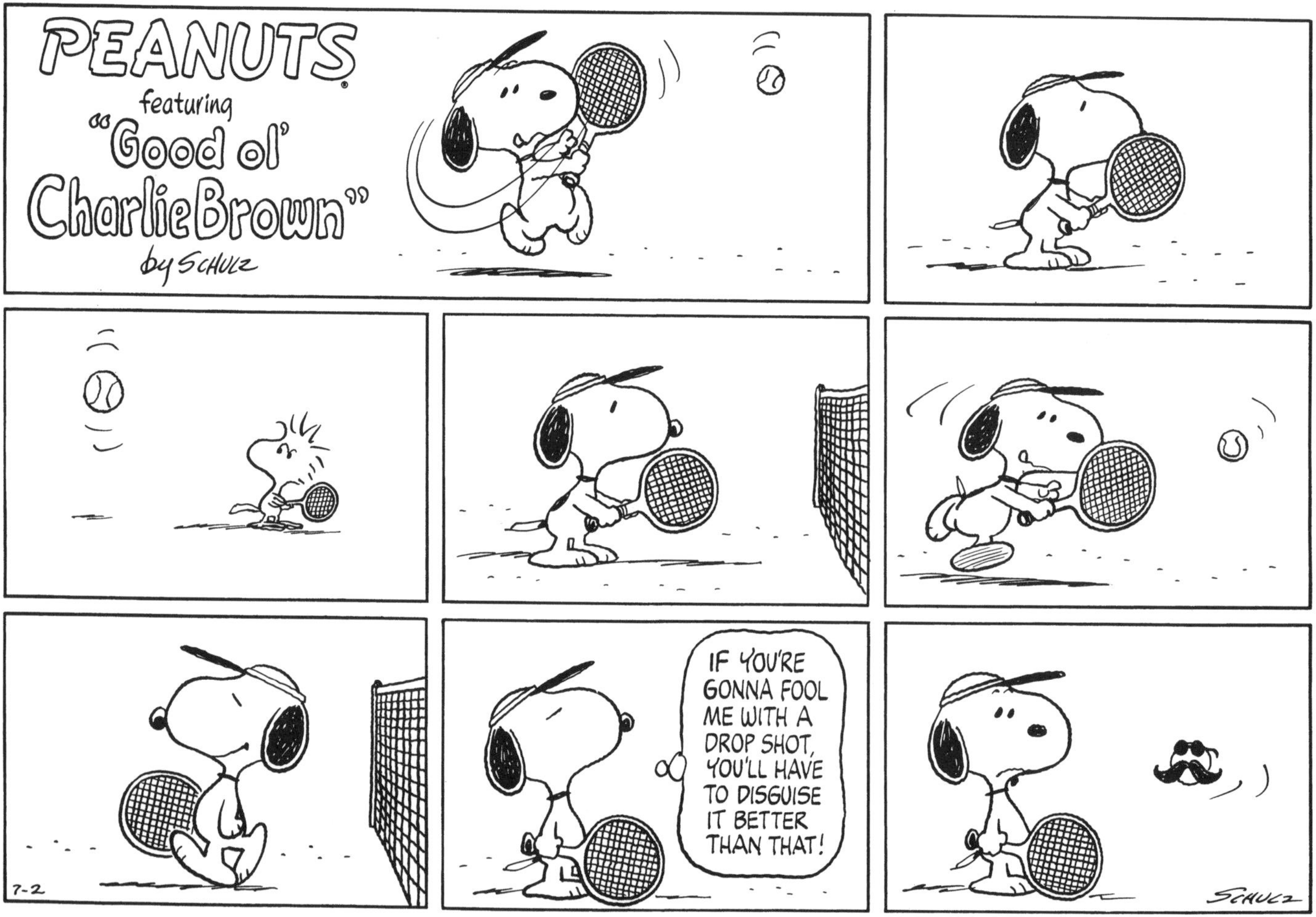
PEANUTS
featuring
"Good ol' Charlie Brown"
by SCHULZ
7-2
IF YOU'RE GONNA FOOL ME WITH A DROP SHOT, YOU'LL HAVE TO DISGUISE IT BETTER THAN THAT!
SCHULZ

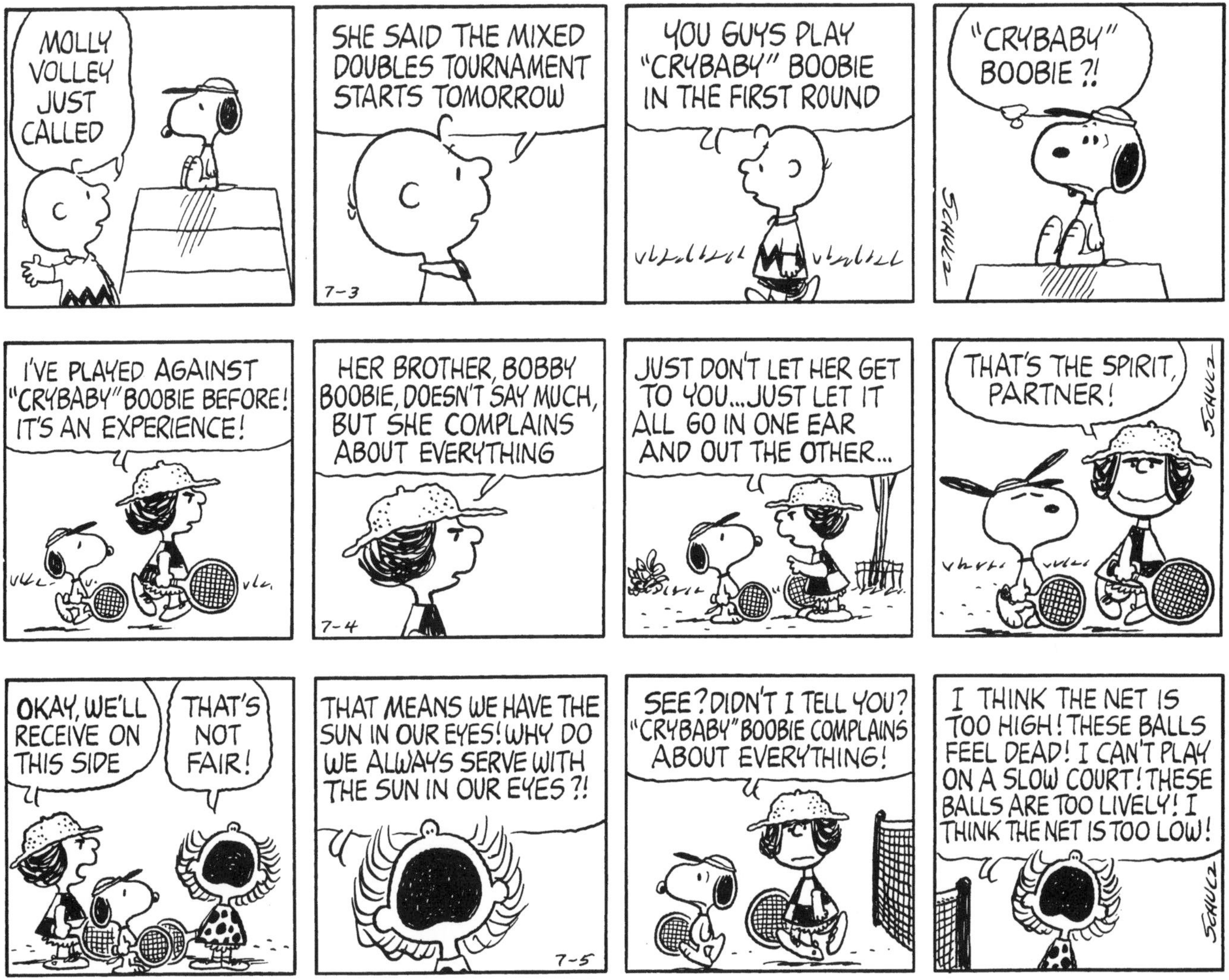
MOLLY VOLLEY JUST CALLED
SHE SAID THE MIXED DOUBLES TOURNAMENT STARTS TOMORROW
YOU GUYS PLAY "CRYBABY" BOOBIE IN THE FIRST ROUND
"CRYBABY" BOOBIE ?!
SCHULZ
7-3
I'VE PLAYED AGAINST "CRYBABY" BOOBIE BEFORE! IT'S AN EXPERIENCE!
HER BROTHER, BOBBY BOOBIE, DOESN'T SAY MUCH, BUT SHE COMPLAINS ABOUT EVERYTHING
JUST DON'T LET HER GET TO YOU...JUST LET IT ALL GO IN ONE EAR AND OUT THE OTHER...
THAT'S THE SPIRIT, PARTNER!
SCHULZ
7-4
OKAY, WE'LL RECEIVE ON THIS SIDE
THAT'S NOT FAIR!
THAT MEANS WE HAVE THE SUN IN OUR EYES! WHY DO WE ALWAYS SERVE WITH THE SUN IN OUR EYES?!
SEE? DIDN'T I TELL YOU? "CRYBABY" BOOBIE COMPLAINS ABOUT EVERYTHING!
I THINK THE NET IS TOO HIGH! THESE BALLS FEEL DEAD! I CAN'T PLAY ON A SLOW COURT! THESE BALLS ARE TOO LIVELY! I THINK THE NET IS TOO LOW!
SCHULZ
7-5

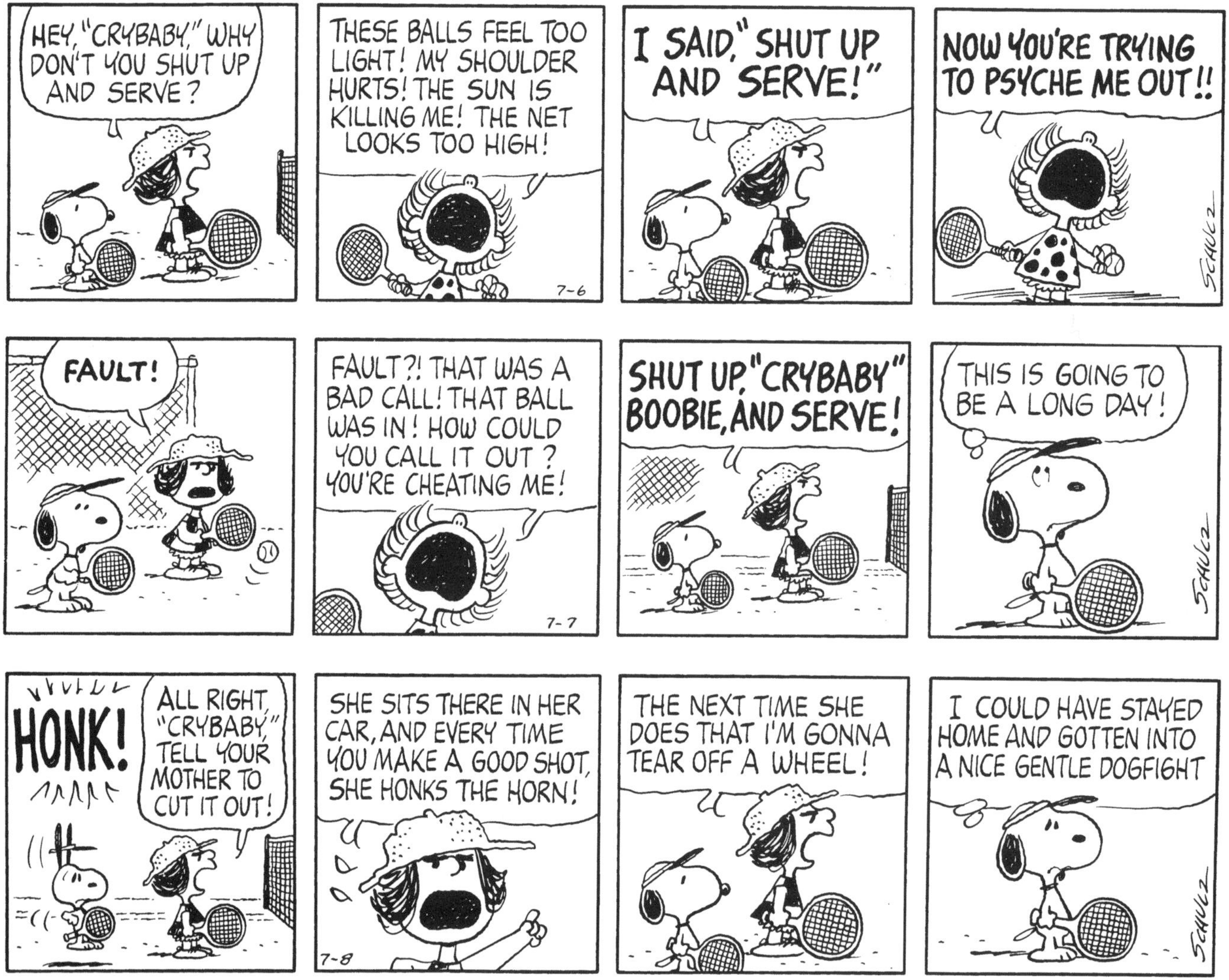
HEY, "CRYBABY," WHY DON'T YOU SHUT UP AND SERVE?
THESE BALLS FEEL TOO LIGHT! MY SHOULDER HURTS! THE SUN IS KILLING ME! THE NET LOOKS TOO HIGH!
7-6
I SAID, "SHUT UP AND SERVE!"
NOW YOU'RE TRYING TO PSYCHE ME OUT!!
SCHULZ
FAULT!
FAULT?! THAT WAS A BAD CALL! THAT BALL WAS IN! HOW COULD YOU CALL IT OUT? YOU'RE CHEATING ME!
7-7
SHUT UP, "CRYBABY" BOOBIE, AND SERVE!
THIS IS GOING TO BE A LONG DAY!
SCHULZ
HONK!
ALL RIGHT, "CRYBABY," TELL YOUR MOTHER TO CUT IT OUT!
SHE SITS THERE IN HER CAR, AND EVERY TIME YOU MAKE A GOOD SHOT, SHE HONKS THE HORN!
7-8
THE NEXT TIME SHE DOES THAT I'M GONNA TEAR OFF A WHEEL!
I COULD HAVE STAYED HOME AND GOTTEN INTO A NICE GENTLE DOGFIGHT
SCHULZ

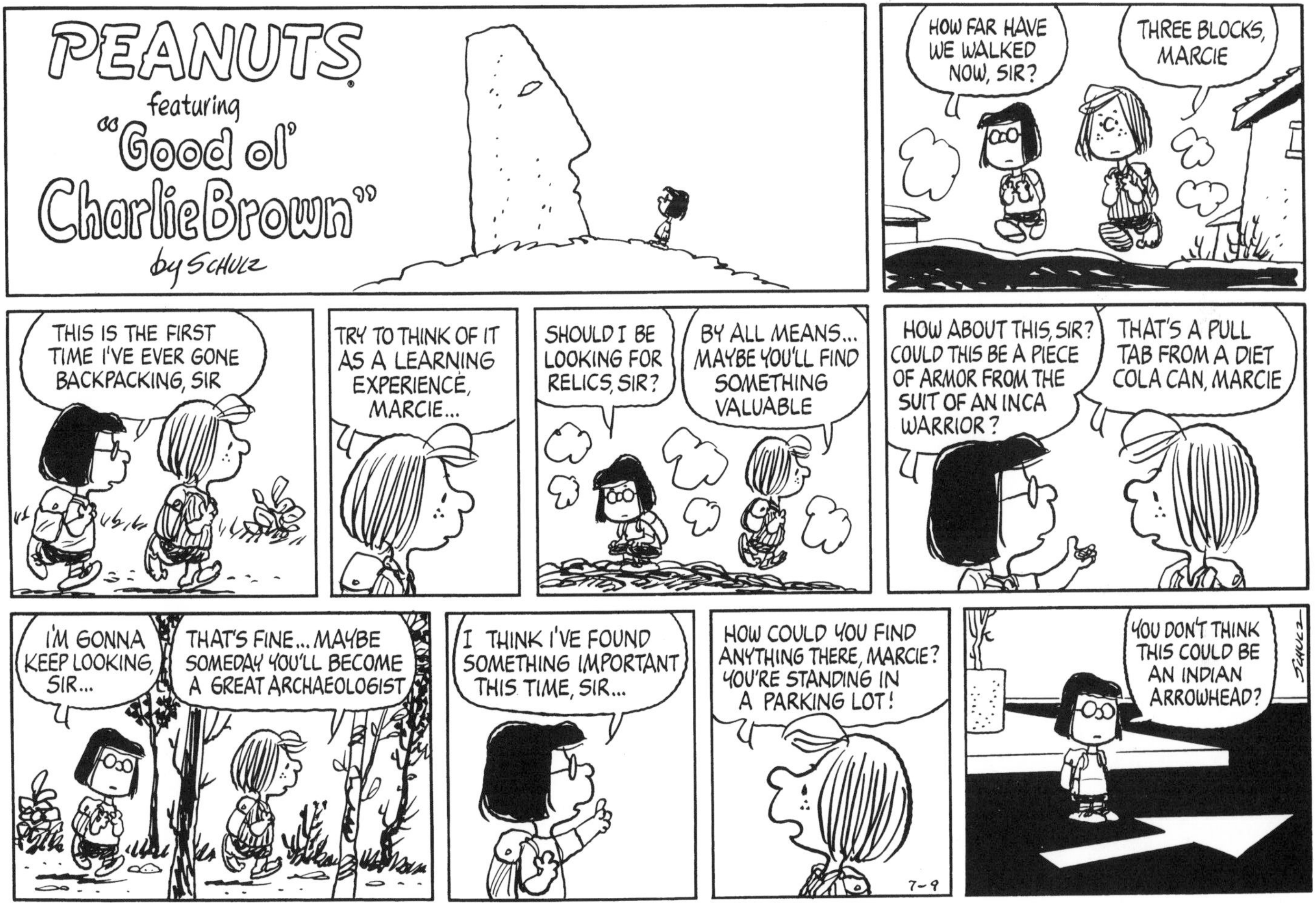
PEANUTS
featuring
"Good ol' CharlieBrown"
by SCHULZ
HOW FAR HAVE WE WALKED NOW, SIR?
THREE BLOCKS, MARCIE
THIS IS THE FIRST TIME I'VE EVER GONE BACKPACKING, SIR
TRY TO THINK OF IT AS A LEARNING EXPERIENCE, MARCIE...
SHOULD I BE LOOKING FOR RELICS, SIR?
BY ALL MEANS... MAYBE YOU'LL FIND SOMETHING VALUABLE
HOW ABOUT THIS, SIR? COULD THIS BE A PIECE OF ARMOR FROM THE SUIT OF AN INCA WARRIOR?
THAT'S A PULL TAB FROM A DIET COLA CAN, MARCIE
I'M GONNA KEEP LOOKING, SIR...
THAT'S FINE... MAYBE SOMEDAY YOU'LL BECOME A GREAT ARCHAEOLOGIST
I THINK I'VE FOUND SOMETHING IMPORTANT THIS TIME, SIR...
HOW COULD YOU FIND ANYTHING THERE, MARCIE? YOU'RE STANDING IN A PARKING LOT!
7-9
YOU DON'T THINK THIS COULD BE AN INDIAN ARROWHEAD?
SCHULZ

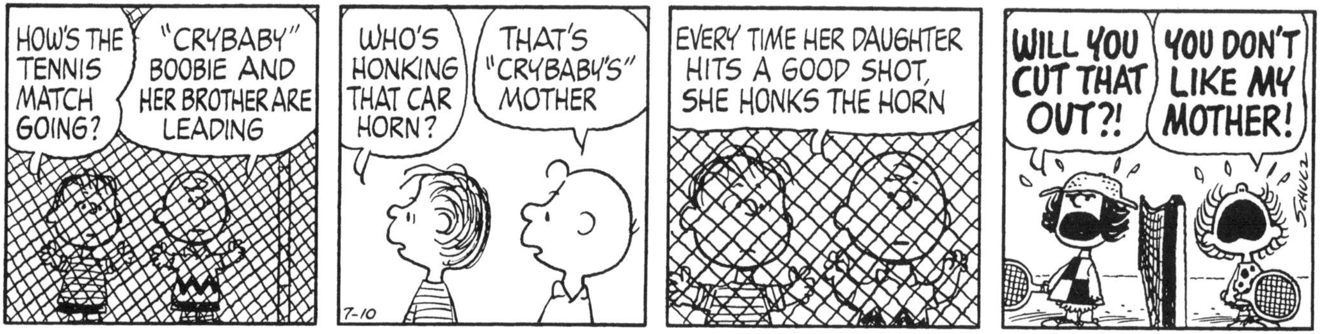
HOW'S THE TENNIS MATCH GOING?
"CRYBABY" BOOBIE AND HER BROTHER ARE LEADING
WHO'S HONKING THAT CAR HORN?
THAT'S "CRYBABY'S" MOTHER
EVERY TIME HER DAUGHTER HITS A GOOD SHOT, SHE HONKS THE HORN
WILL YOU CUT THAT OUT?!
YOU DON'T LIKE MY MOTHER!

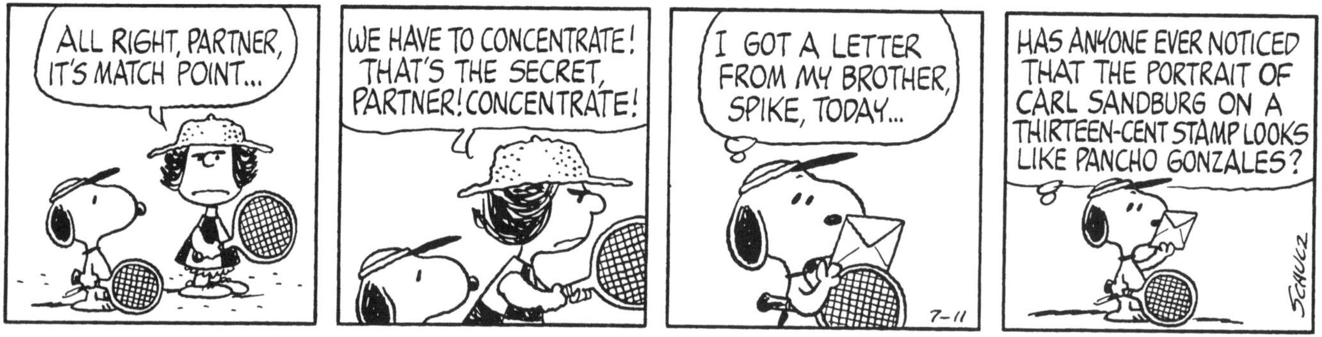
ALL RIGHT, PARTNER, IT'S MATCH POINT...
WE HAVE TO CONCENTRATE! THAT'S THE SECRET, PARTNER! CONCENTRATE!
I GOT A LETTER FROM MY BROTHER, SPIKE, TODAY...
HAS ANYONE EVER NOTICED THAT THE PORTRAIT OF CARL SANDBURG ON A THIRTEEN-CENT STAMP LOOKS LIKE PANCHO GONZALES?

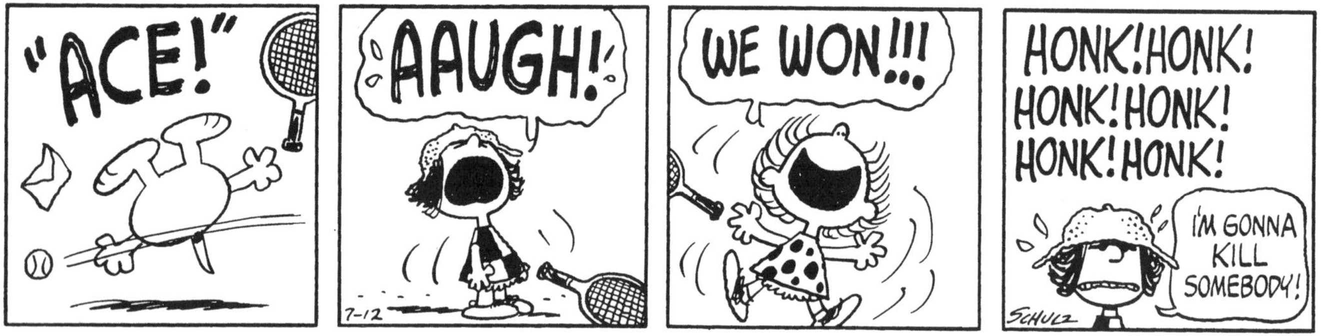
"ACE!"
AAUGH!
WE WON!!!
HONK! HONK! HONK! HONK! HONK! HONK!
I'M GONNA KILL SOMEBODY!

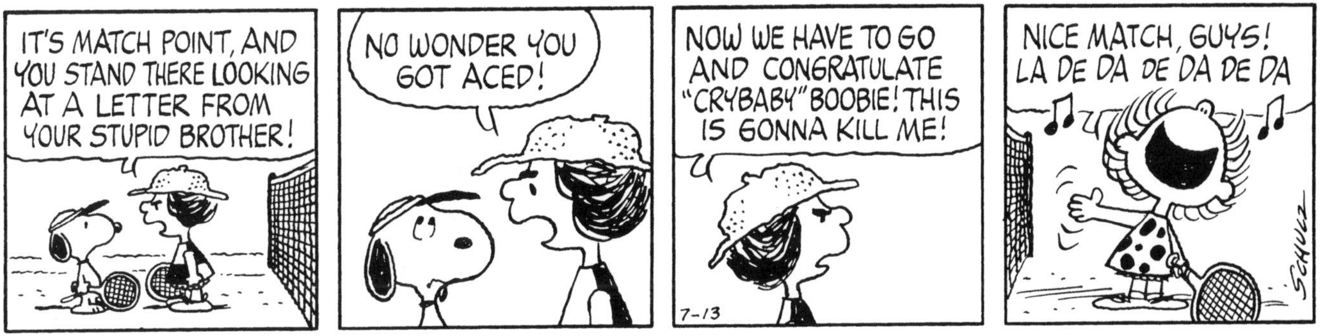
IT'S MATCH POINT, AND YOU STAND THERE LOOKING AT A LETTER FROM YOUR STUPID BROTHER!
NO WONDER YOU GOT ACED!
NOW WE HAVE TO GO AND CONGRATULATE "CRYBABY" BOOBIE! THIS IS GONNA KILL ME!
7-13
NICE MATCH, GUYS! LA DE DA DE DA DE DA
SCHULZ

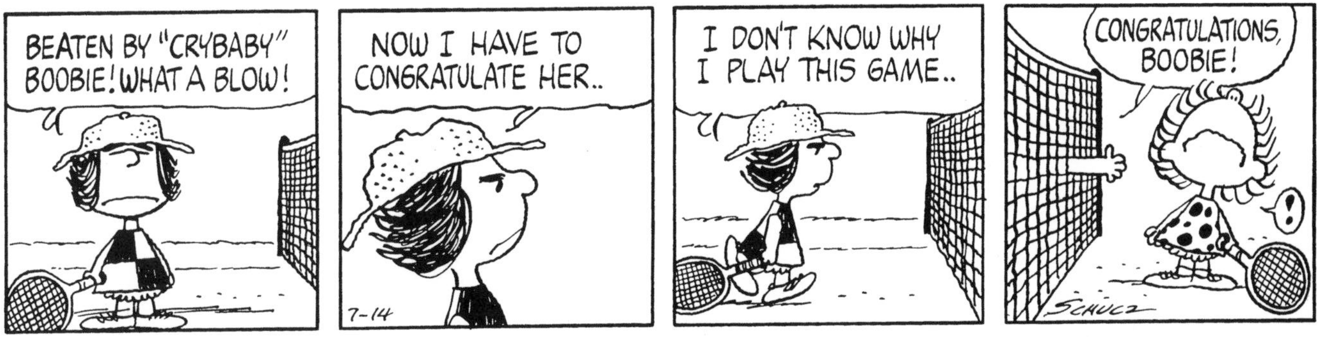
BEATEN BY "CRYBABY" BOOBIE! WHAT A BLOW!
NOW I HAVE TO CONGRATULATE HER..
7-14
I DON'T KNOW WHY I PLAY THIS GAME..
CONGRATULATIONS, BOOBIE!
!
SCHULZ

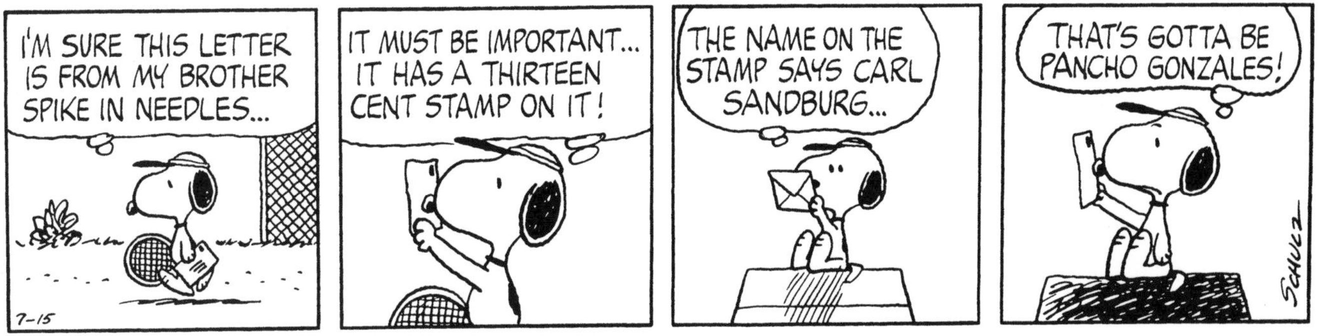
I'M SURE THIS LETTER IS FROM MY BROTHER SPIKE IN NEEDLES...
7-15
IT MUST BE IMPORTANT... IT HAS A THIRTEEN CENT STAMP ON IT!
THE NAME ON THE STAMP SAYS CARL SANDBURG...
THAT'S GOTTA BE PANCHO GONZALES!
SCHULZ

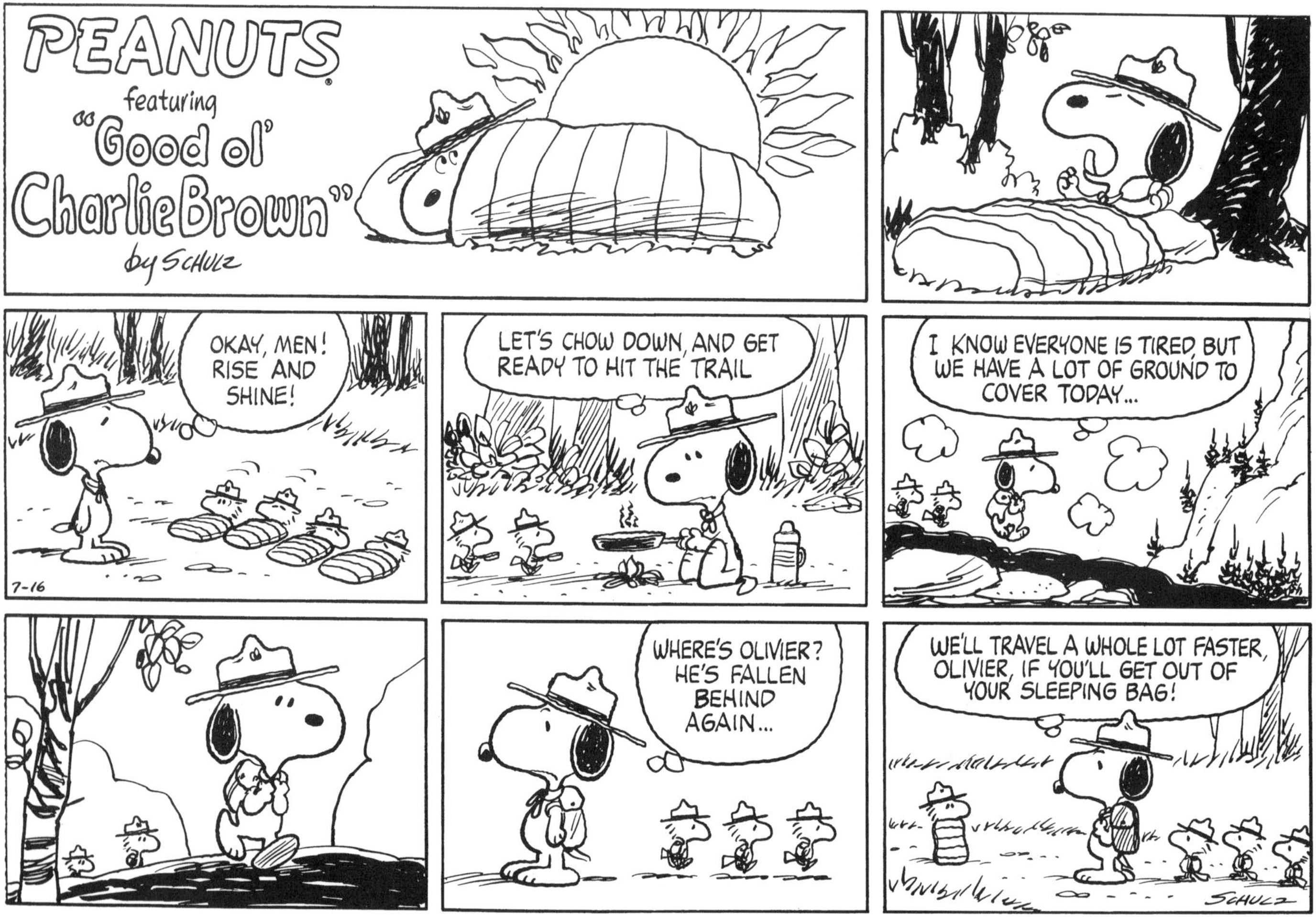
PEANUTS
featuring "Good ol' Charlie Brown"
by SCHULZ
OKAY, MEN! RISE AND SHINE!
7-16
LET'S CHOW DOWN, AND GET READY TO HIT THE TRAIL
I KNOW EVERYONE IS TIRED, BUT WE HAVE A LOT OF GROUND TO COVER TODAY...
WHERE'S OLIVIER? HE'S FALLEN BEHIND AGAIN...
WE'LL TRAVEL A WHOLE LOT FASTER, OLIVIER, IF YOU'LL GET OUT OF YOUR SLEEPING BAG!
SCHULZ

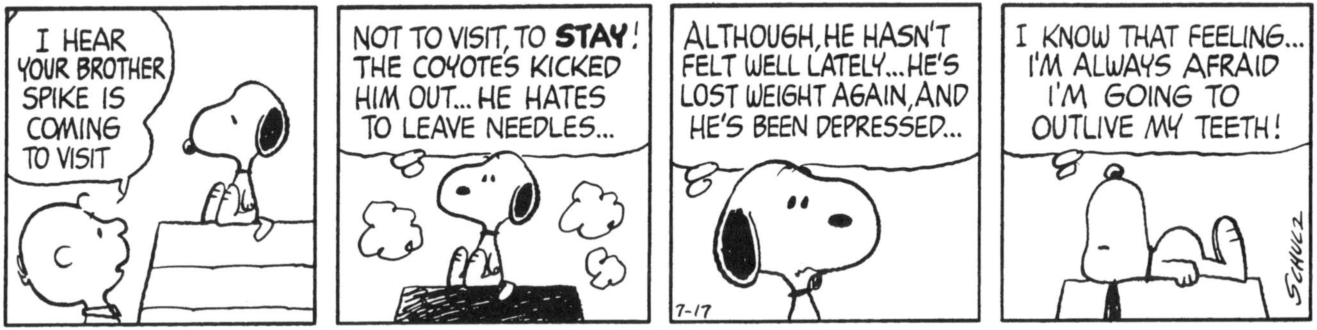
I HEAR YOUR BROTHER SPIKE IS COMING TO VISIT
NOT TO VISIT, TO **STAY**! THE COYOTES KICKED HIM OUT... HE HATES TO LEAVE NEEDLES...
ALTHOUGH, HE HASN'T FELT WELL LATELY...HE'S LOST WEIGHT AGAIN, AND HE'S BEEN DEPRESSED...
7-17
I KNOW THAT FEELING... I'M ALWAYS AFRAID I'M GOING TO OUTLIVE MY TEETH!
SCHULZ

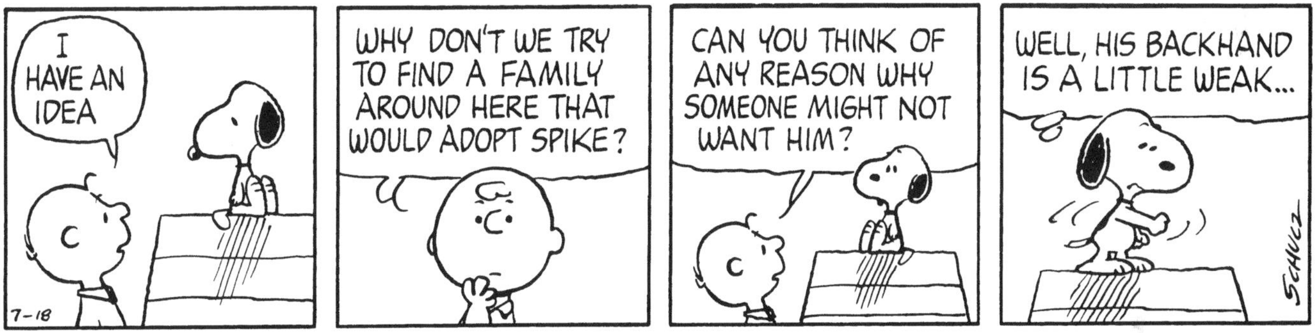
I HAVE AN IDEA
7-18
WHY DON'T WE TRY TO FIND A FAMILY AROUND HERE THAT WOULD ADOPT SPIKE?
CAN YOU THINK OF ANY REASON WHY SOMEONE MIGHT NOT WANT HIM?
WELL, HIS BACKHAND IS A LITTLE WEAK...
SCHULZ

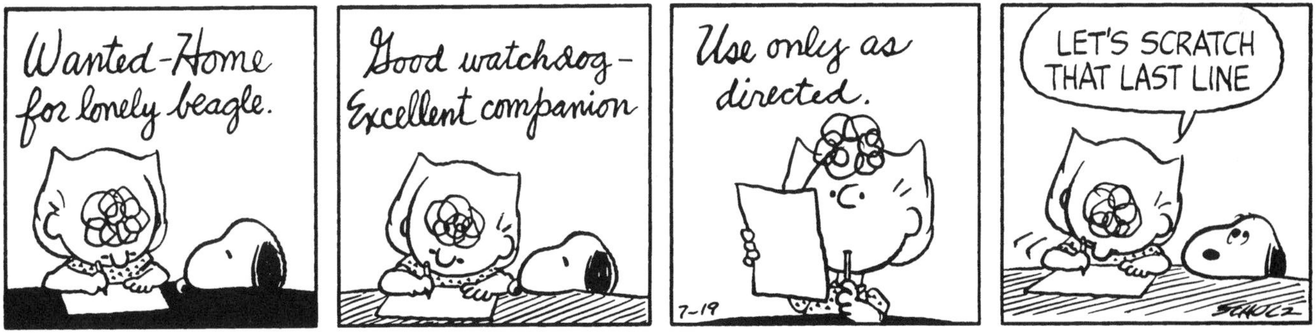
Wanted-Home for lonely beagle.
Good watchdog - Excellent companion
Use only as directed.
7-19
LET'S SCRATCH THAT LAST LINE
SCHULZ

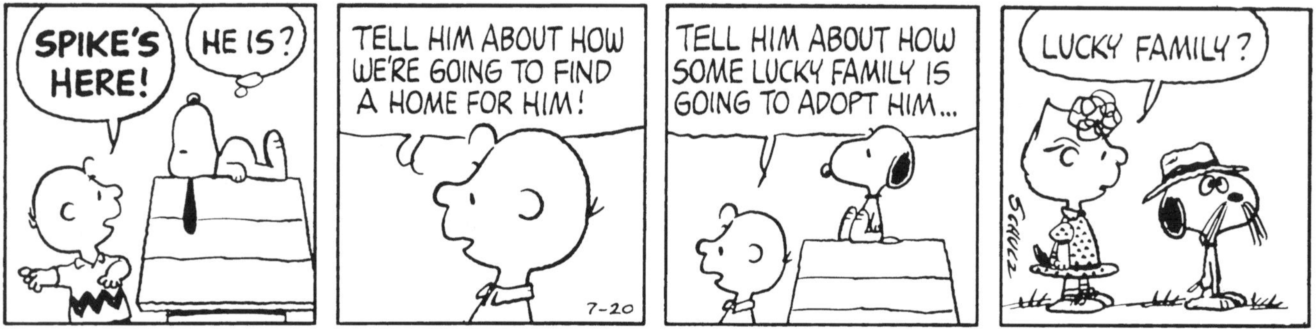
SPIKE'S HERE!
HE IS?
TELL HIM ABOUT HOW WE'RE GOING TO FIND A HOME FOR HIM!
7-20
TELL HIM ABOUT HOW SOME LUCKY FAMILY IS GOING TO ADOPT HIM...
LUCKY FAMILY?

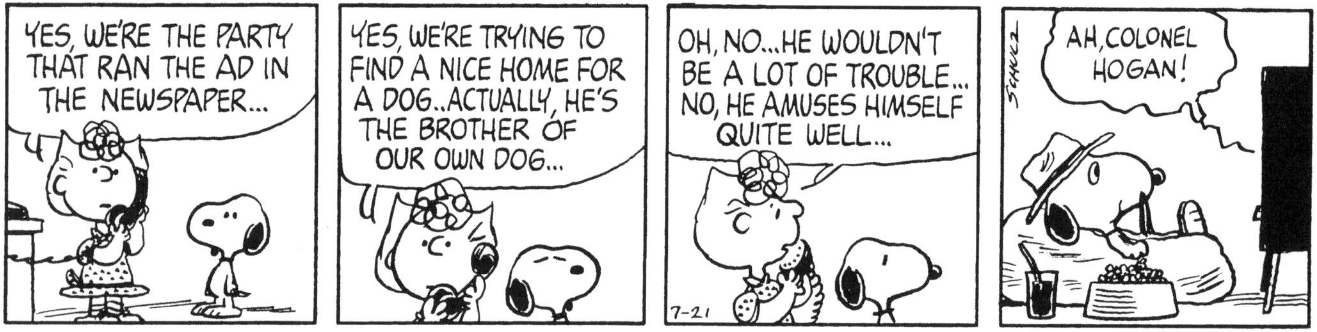
YES, WE'RE THE PARTY THAT RAN THE AD IN THE NEWSPAPER...
YES, WE'RE TRYING TO FIND A NICE HOME FOR A DOG..ACTUALLY, HE'S THE BROTHER OF OUR OWN DOG...
OH, NO...HE WOULDN'T BE A LOT OF TROUBLE... NO, HE AMUSES HIMSELF QUITE WELL...
7-21
AH, COLONEL HOGAN!

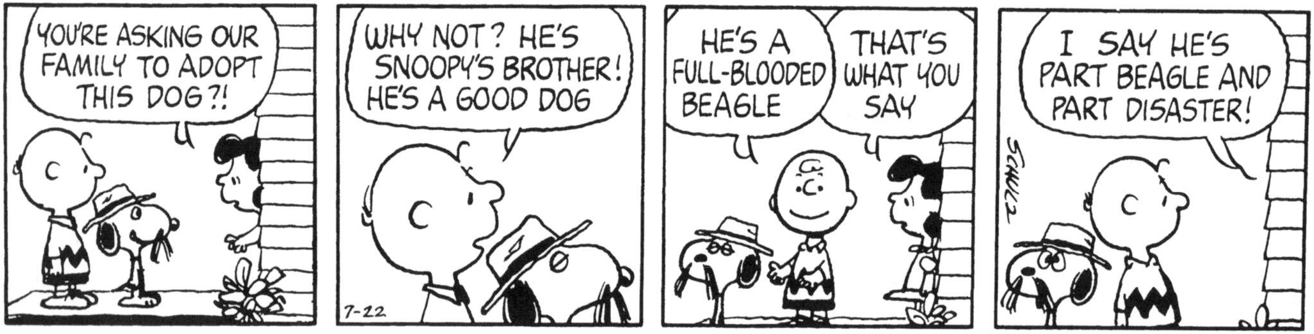
YOU'RE ASKING OUR FAMILY TO ADOPT THIS DOG?!
WHY NOT? HE'S SNOOPY'S BROTHER! HE'S A GOOD DOG
7-22
HE'S A FULL-BLOODED BEAGLE
THAT'S WHAT YOU SAY
I SAY HE'S PART BEAGLE AND PART DISASTER!

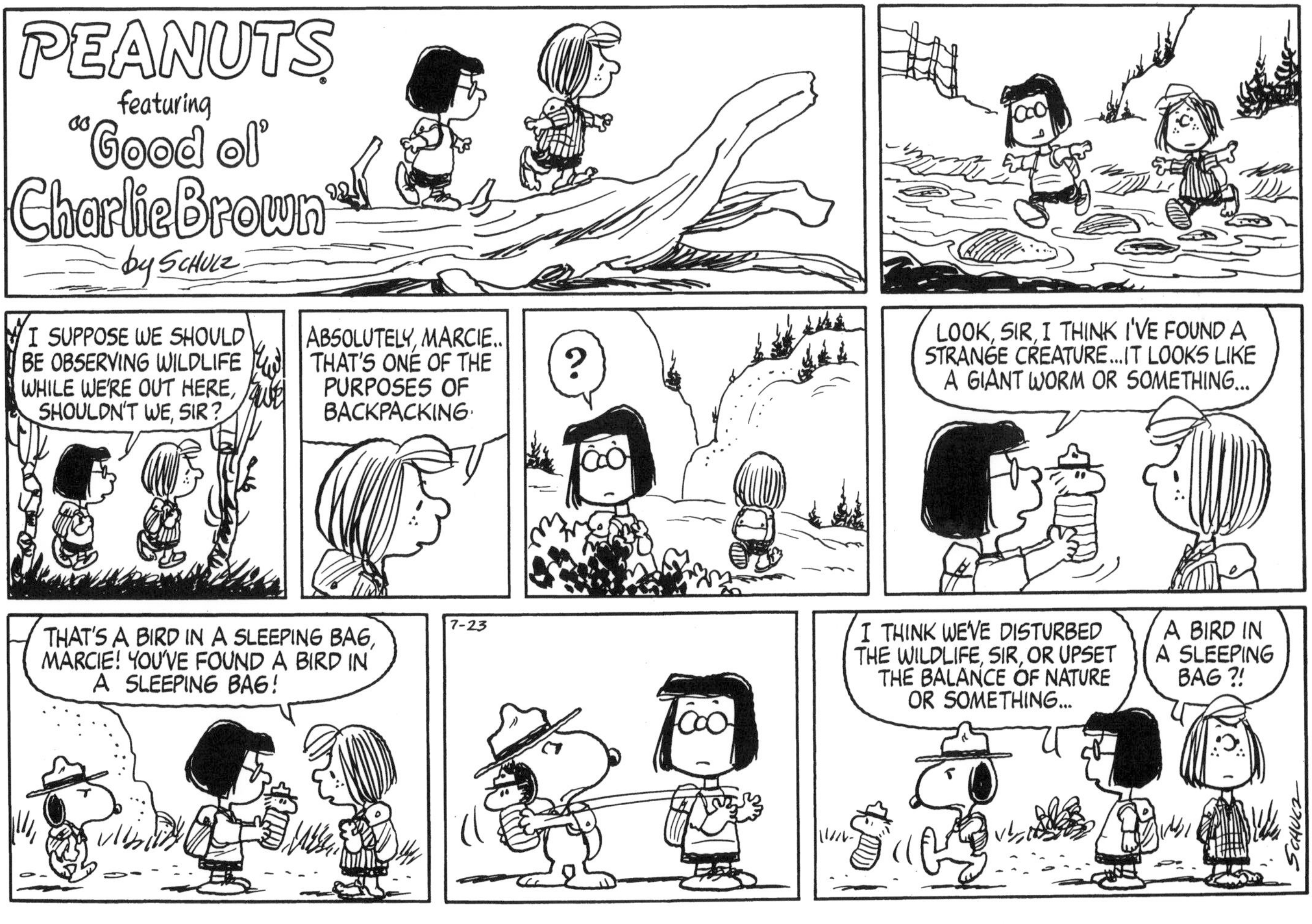
PEANUTS
featuring "Good ol' Charlie Brown"
by SCHULZ
I SUPPOSE WE SHOULD BE OBSERVING WILDLIFE WHILE WE'RE OUT HERE, SHOULDN'T WE, SIR?
ABSOLUTELY, MARCIE.. THAT'S ONE OF THE PURPOSES OF BACKPACKING.
?
LOOK, SIR, I THINK I'VE FOUND A STRANGE CREATURE...IT LOOKS LIKE A GIANT WORM OR SOMETHING...
THAT'S A BIRD IN A SLEEPING BAG, MARCIE! YOU'VE FOUND A BIRD IN A SLEEPING BAG!
7-23
I THINK WE'VE DISTURBED THE WILDLIFE, SIR, OR UPSET THE BALANCE OF NATURE OR SOMETHING...
A BIRD IN A SLEEPING BAG?!
SCHULZ

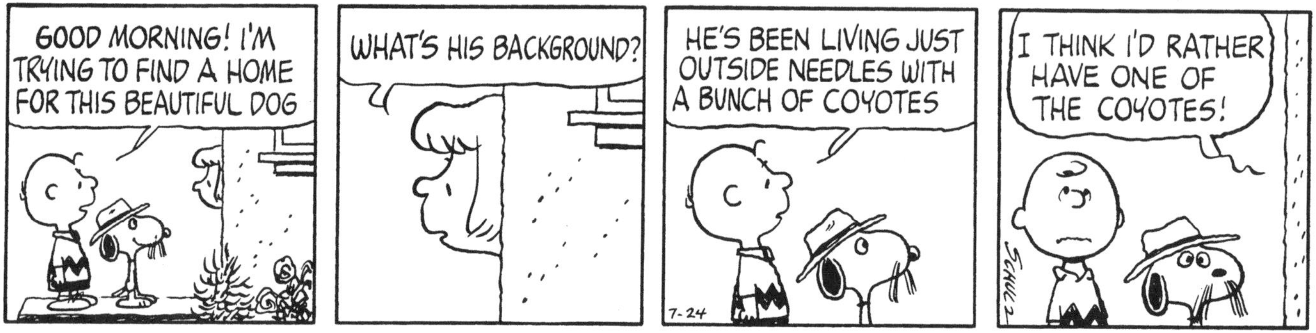
GOOD MORNING! I'M TRYING TO FIND A HOME FOR THIS BEAUTIFUL DOG
WHAT'S HIS BACKGROUND?
HE'S BEEN LIVING JUST OUTSIDE NEEDLES WITH A BUNCH OF COYOTES
7-24
I THINK I'D RATHER HAVE ONE OF THE COYOTES!
SCHULZ

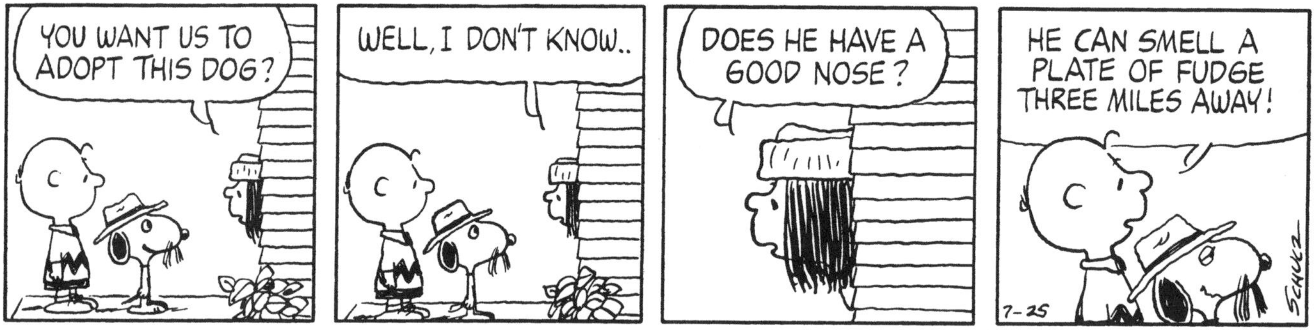
YOU WANT US TO ADOPT THIS DOG?
WELL, I DON'T KNOW..
DOES HE HAVE A GOOD NOSE?
HE CAN SMELL A PLATE OF FUDGE THREE MILES AWAY!
7-25
SCHULZ

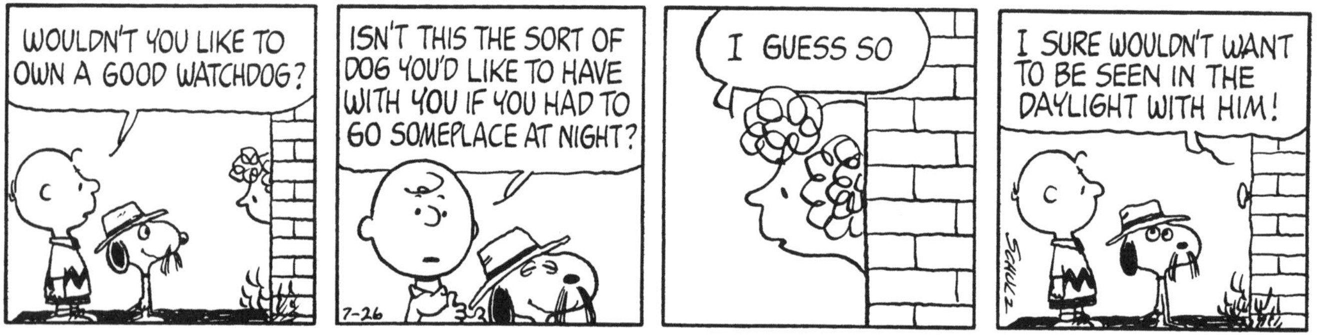
WOULDN'T YOU LIKE TO OWN A GOOD WATCHDOG?
ISN'T THIS THE SORT OF DOG YOU'D LIKE TO HAVE WITH YOU IF YOU HAD TO GO SOMEPLACE AT NIGHT?
7-26
I GUESS SO
I SURE WOULDN'T WANT TO BE SEEN IN THE DAYLIGHT WITH HIM!
SCHULZ

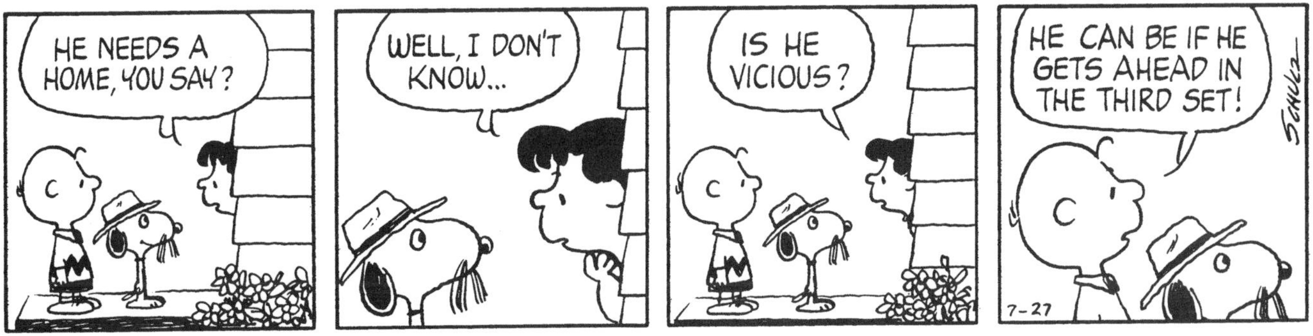
HE NEEDS A HOME, YOU SAY?
WELL, I DON'T KNOW...
IS HE VICIOUS?
HE CAN BE IF HE GETS AHEAD IN THE THIRD SET!
SCHULZ
7-27

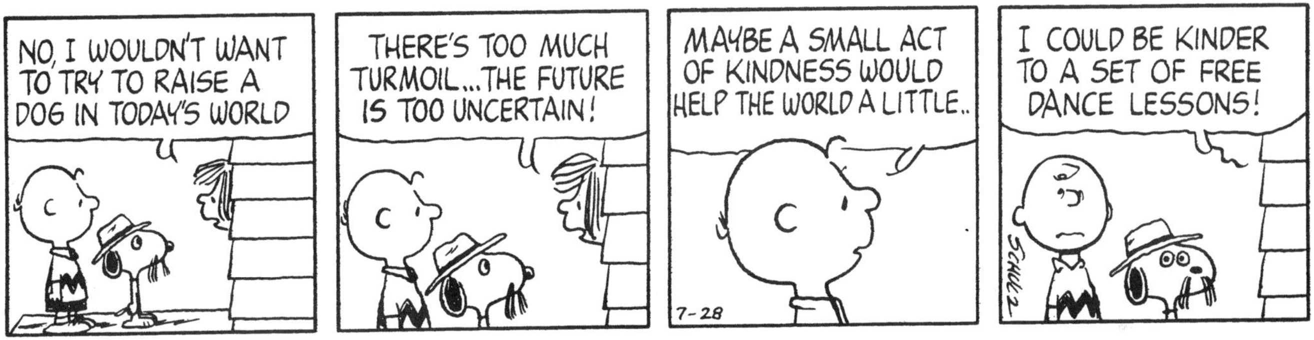
NO, I WOULDN'T WANT TO TRY TO RAISE A DOG IN TODAY'S WORLD
THERE'S TOO MUCH TURMOIL...THE FUTURE IS TOO UNCERTAIN!
MAYBE A SMALL ACT OF KINDNESS WOULD HELP THE WORLD A LITTLE..
7-28
I COULD BE KINDER TO A SET OF FREE DANCE LESSONS!
SCHULZ

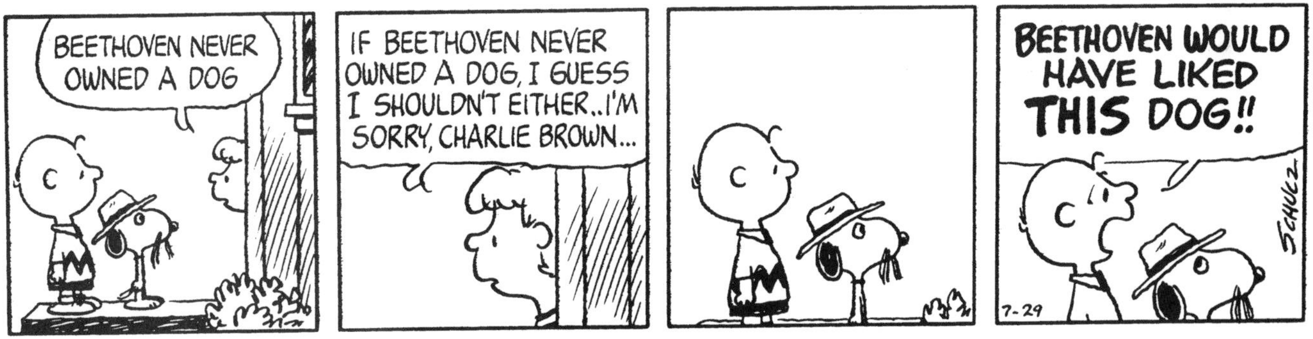
BEETHOVEN NEVER OWNED A DOG
IF BEETHOVEN NEVER OWNED A DOG, I GUESS I SHOULDN'T EITHER..I'M SORRY, CHARLIE BROWN...
BEETHOVEN WOULD HAVE LIKED THIS DOG!!
SCHULZ
7-29

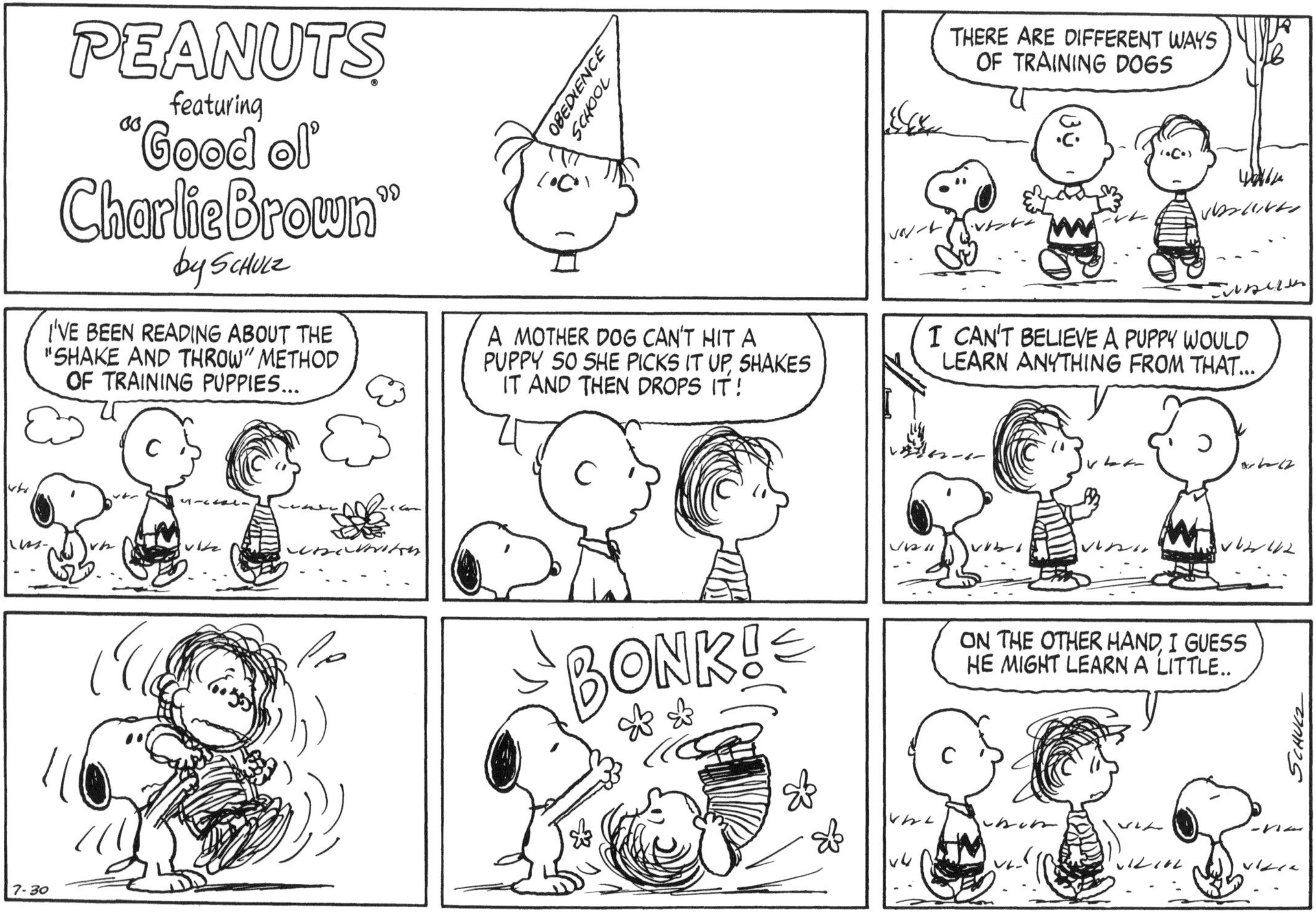
PEANUTS
featuring
"Good ol' Charlie Brown"
by SCHULZ
OBEDIENCE SCHOOL
THERE ARE DIFFERENT WAYS OF TRAINING DOGS
I'VE BEEN READING ABOUT THE "SHAKE AND THROW" METHOD OF TRAINING PUPPIES...
A MOTHER DOG CAN'T HIT A PUPPY SO SHE PICKS IT UP, SHAKES IT AND THEN DROPS IT!
I CAN'T BELIEVE A PUPPY WOULD LEARN ANYTHING FROM THAT...
7-30
BONK!
ON THE OTHER HAND, I GUESS HE MIGHT LEARN A LITTLE..
SCHULZ

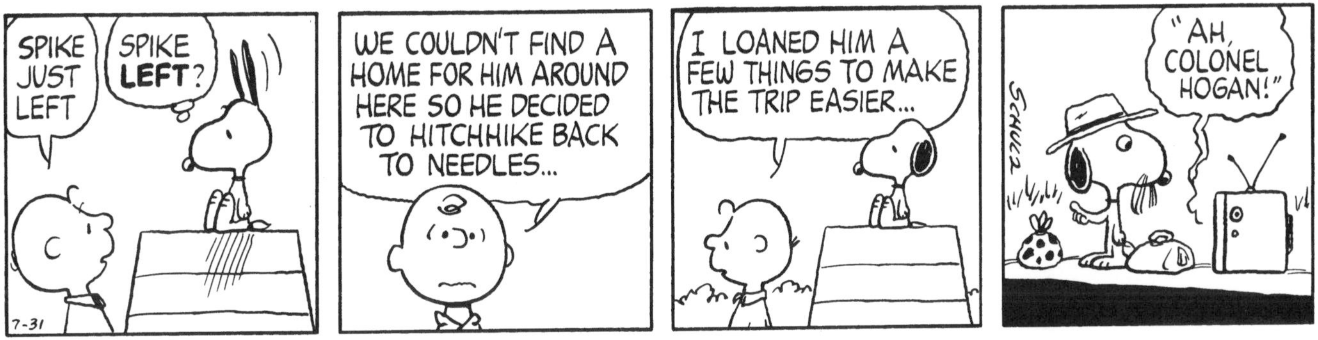
SPIKE JUST LEFT
SPIKE LEFT?
7-31
WE COULDN'T FIND A HOME FOR HIM AROUND HERE SO HE DECIDED TO HITCHHIKE BACK TO NEEDLES...
I LOANED HIM A FEW THINGS TO MAKE THE TRIP EASIER...
SCHULZ
"AH, COLONEL HOGAN!"

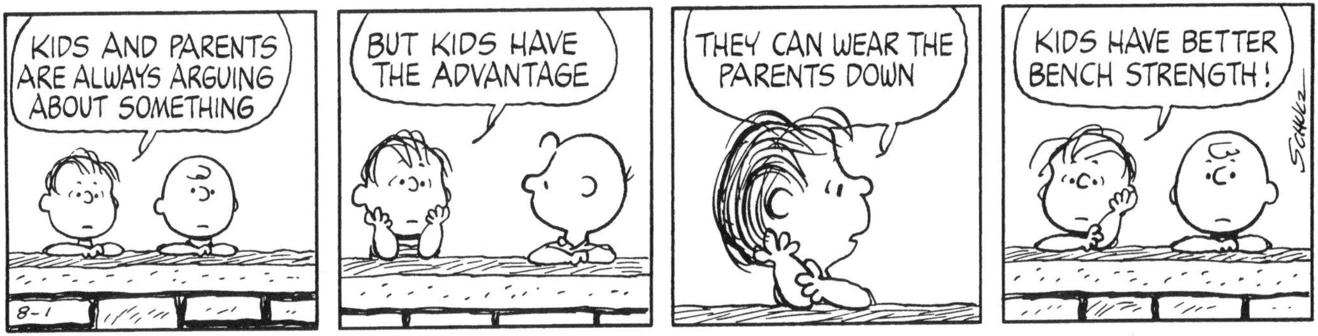
KIDS AND PARENTS ARE ALWAYS ARGUING ABOUT SOMETHING
8-1
BUT KIDS HAVE THE ADVANTAGE
THEY CAN WEAR THE PARENTS DOWN
KIDS HAVE BETTER BENCH STRENGTH!
SCHULZ

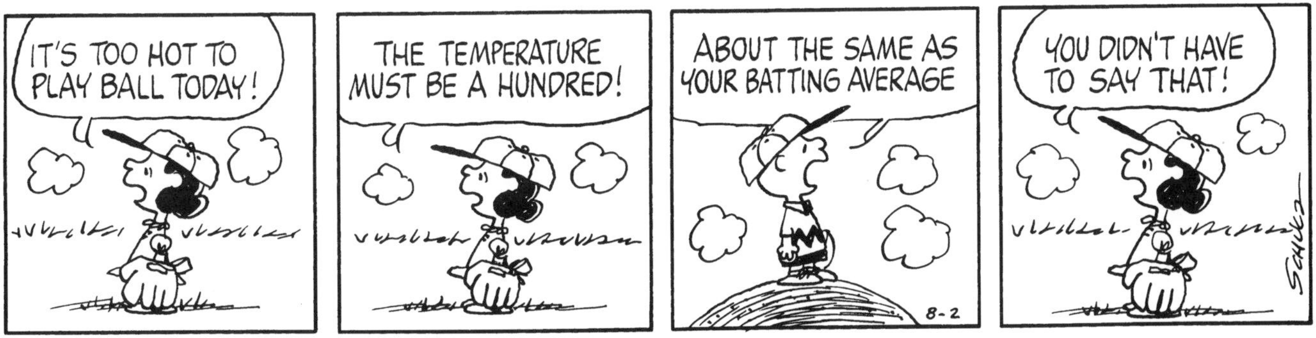
IT'S TOO HOT TO PLAY BALL TODAY!
THE TEMPERATURE MUST BE A HUNDRED!
ABOUT THE SAME AS YOUR BATTING AVERAGE
8-2
YOU DIDN'T HAVE TO SAY THAT!
SCHULZ

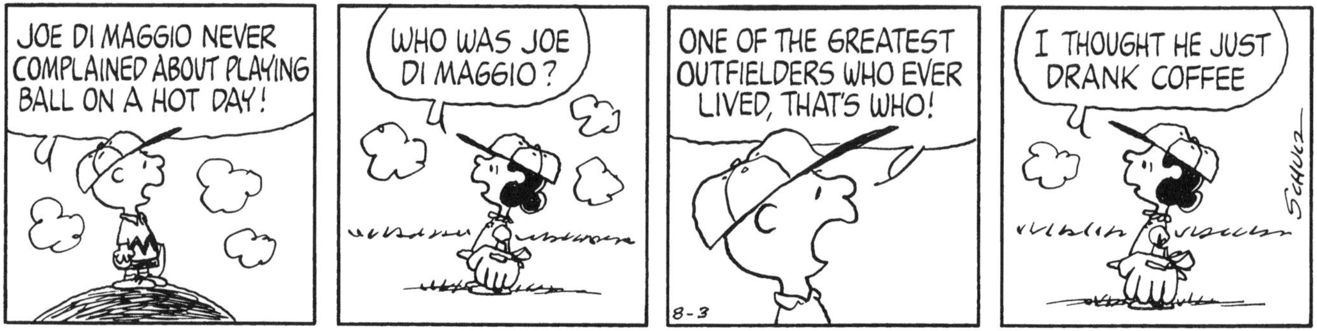
JOE DI MAGGIO NEVER COMPLAINED ABOUT PLAYING BALL ON A HOT DAY!
WHO WAS JOE DI MAGGIO?
ONE OF THE GREATEST OUTFIELDERS WHO EVER LIVED, THAT'S WHO!
8-3
I THOUGHT HE JUST DRANK COFFEE
SCHULZ

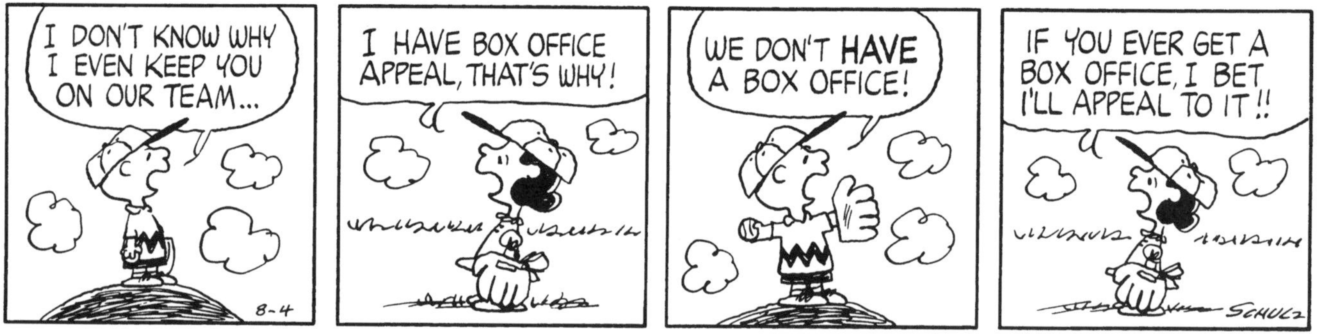
I DON'T KNOW WHY I EVEN KEEP YOU ON OUR TEAM...
8-4
I HAVE BOX OFFICE APPEAL, THAT'S WHY!
WE DON'T **HAVE** A BOX OFFICE!
IF YOU EVER GET A BOX OFFICE, I BET I'LL APPEAL TO IT!!
SCHULZ

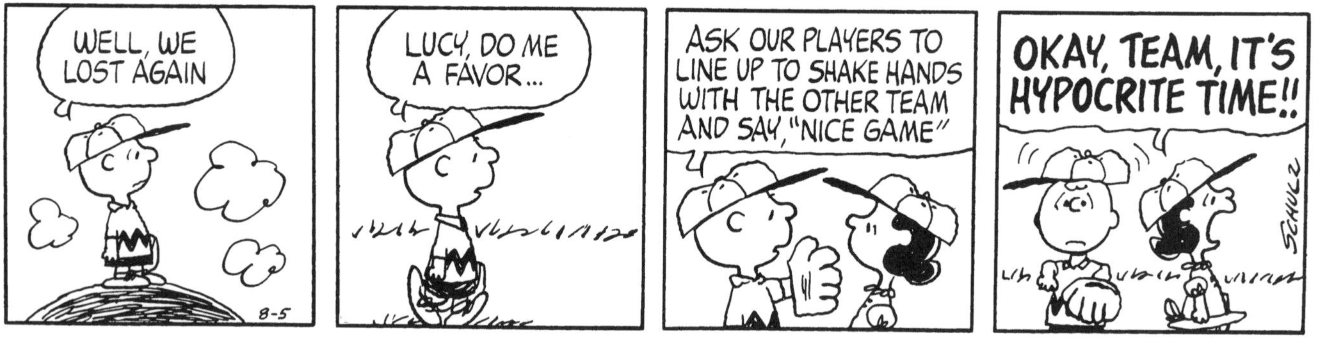
WELL, WE LOST AGAIN
8-5
LUCY, DO ME A FAVOR...
ASK OUR PLAYERS TO LINE UP TO SHAKE HANDS WITH THE OTHER TEAM AND SAY, "NICE GAME"
OKAY, TEAM, IT'S HYPOCRITE TIME!!
SCHULZ

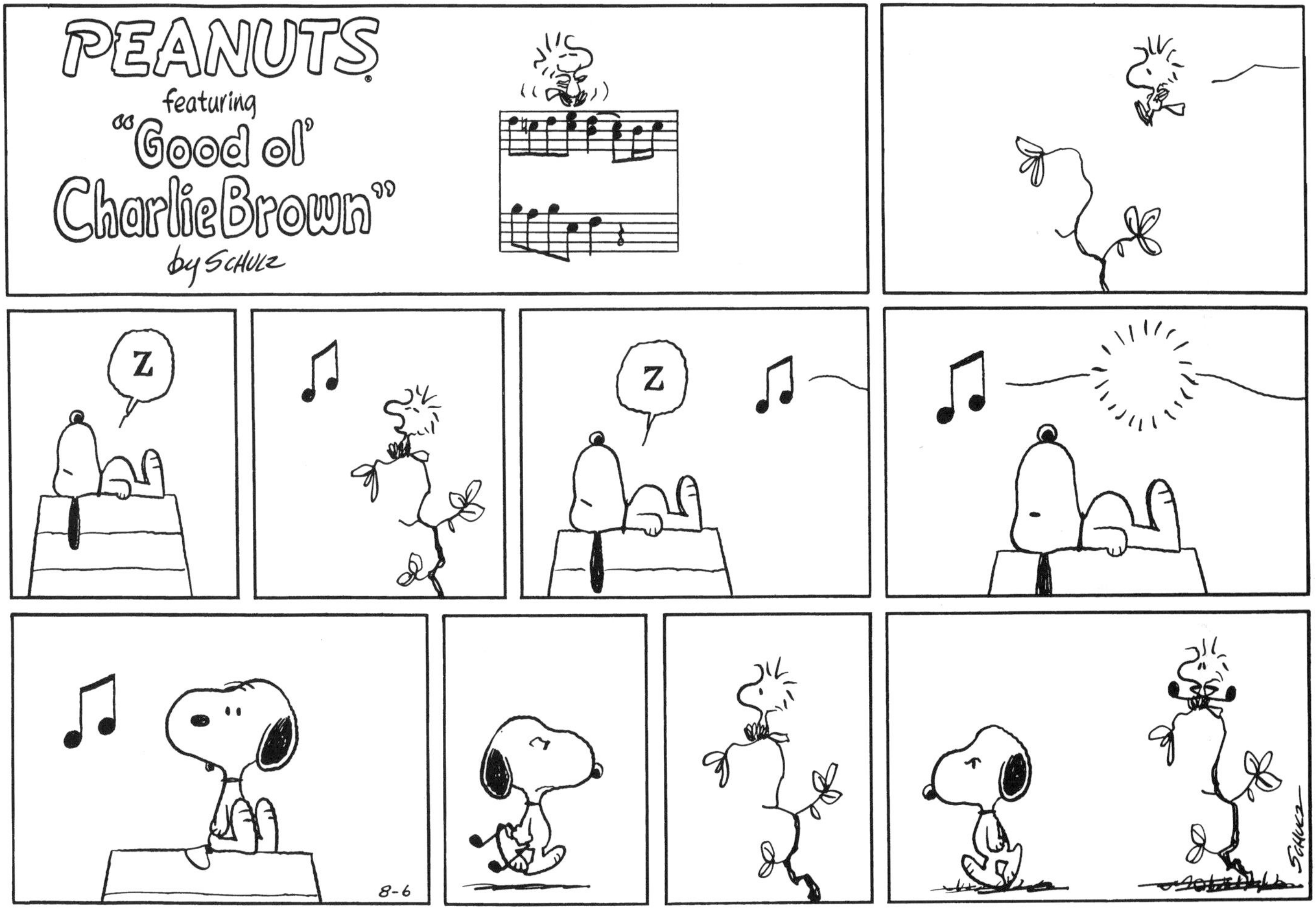
PEANUTS
featuring
"Good ol' Charlie Brown"
by SCHULZ
Z
Z
8-6
SCHULZ

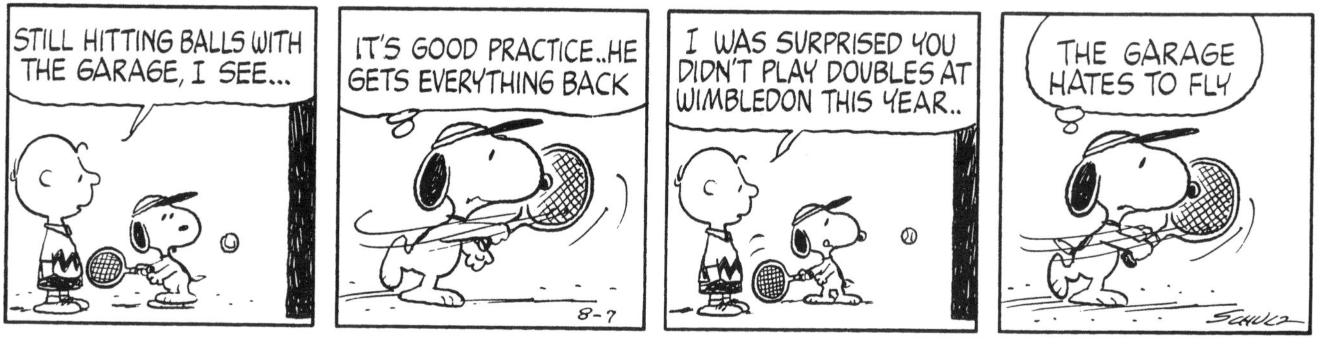
STILL HITTING BALLS WITH THE GARAGE, I SEE...
IT'S GOOD PRACTICE..HE GETS EVERYTHING BACK
8-7
I WAS SURPRISED YOU DIDN'T PLAY DOUBLES AT WIMBLEDON THIS YEAR..
THE GARAGE HATES TO FLY
SCHULZ

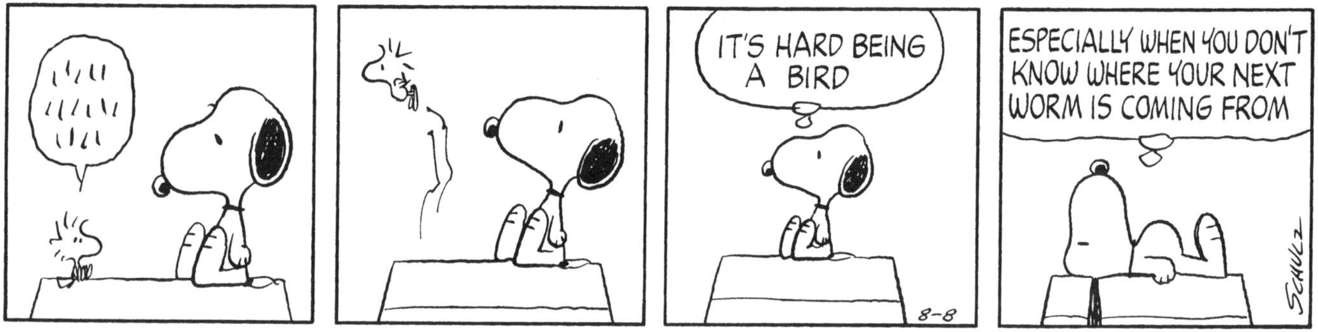
IT'S HARD BEING A BIRD
8-8
ESPECIALLY WHEN YOU DON'T KNOW WHERE YOUR NEXT WORM IS COMING FROM
SCHULZ

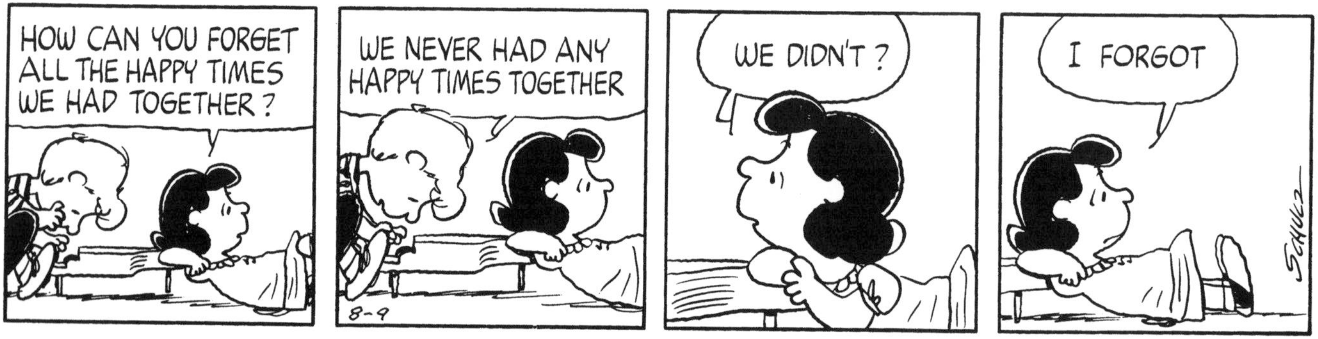
HOW CAN YOU FORGET ALL THE HAPPY TIMES WE HAD TOGETHER ?
WE NEVER HAD ANY HAPPY TIMES TOGETHER
8-9
WE DIDN'T ?
I FORGOT
SCHULZ

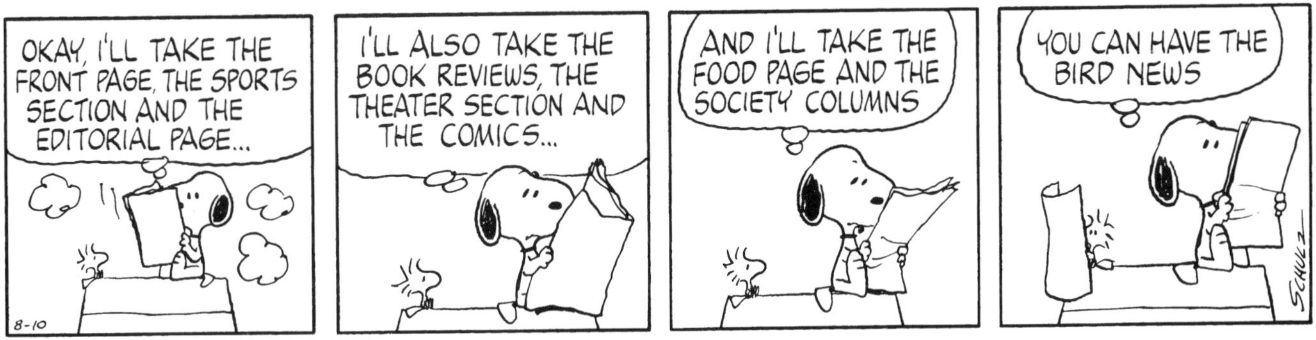
OKAY, I'LL TAKE THE FRONT PAGE, THE SPORTS SECTION AND THE EDITORIAL PAGE...
I'LL ALSO TAKE THE BOOK REVIEWS, THE THEATER SECTION AND THE COMICS...
AND I'LL TAKE THE FOOD PAGE AND THE SOCIETY COLUMNS
YOU CAN HAVE THE BIRD NEWS

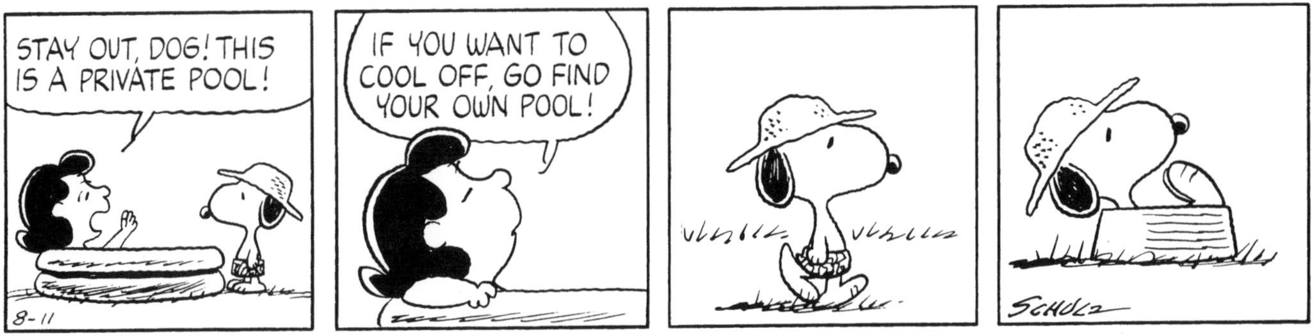
STAY OUT, DOG! THIS IS A PRIVATE POOL!
IF YOU WANT TO COOL OFF, GO FIND YOUR OWN POOL!

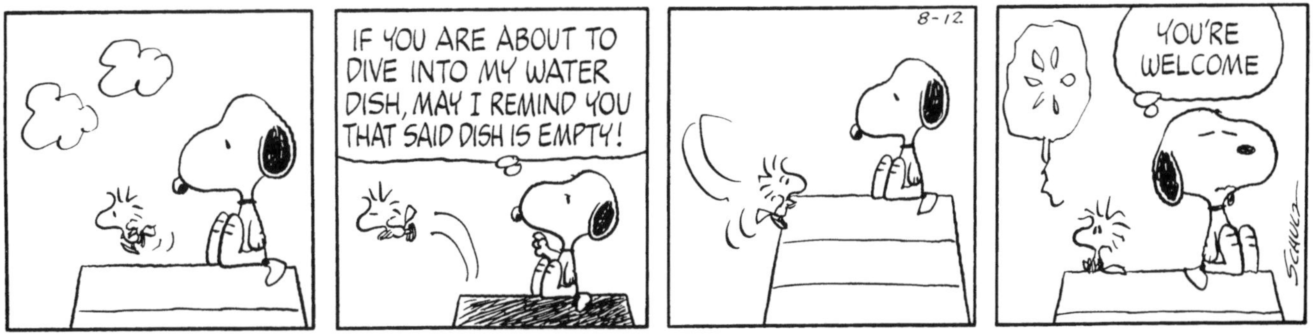
IF YOU ARE ABOUT TO DIVE INTO MY WATER DISH, MAY I REMIND YOU THAT SAID DISH IS EMPTY!
YOU'RE WELCOME

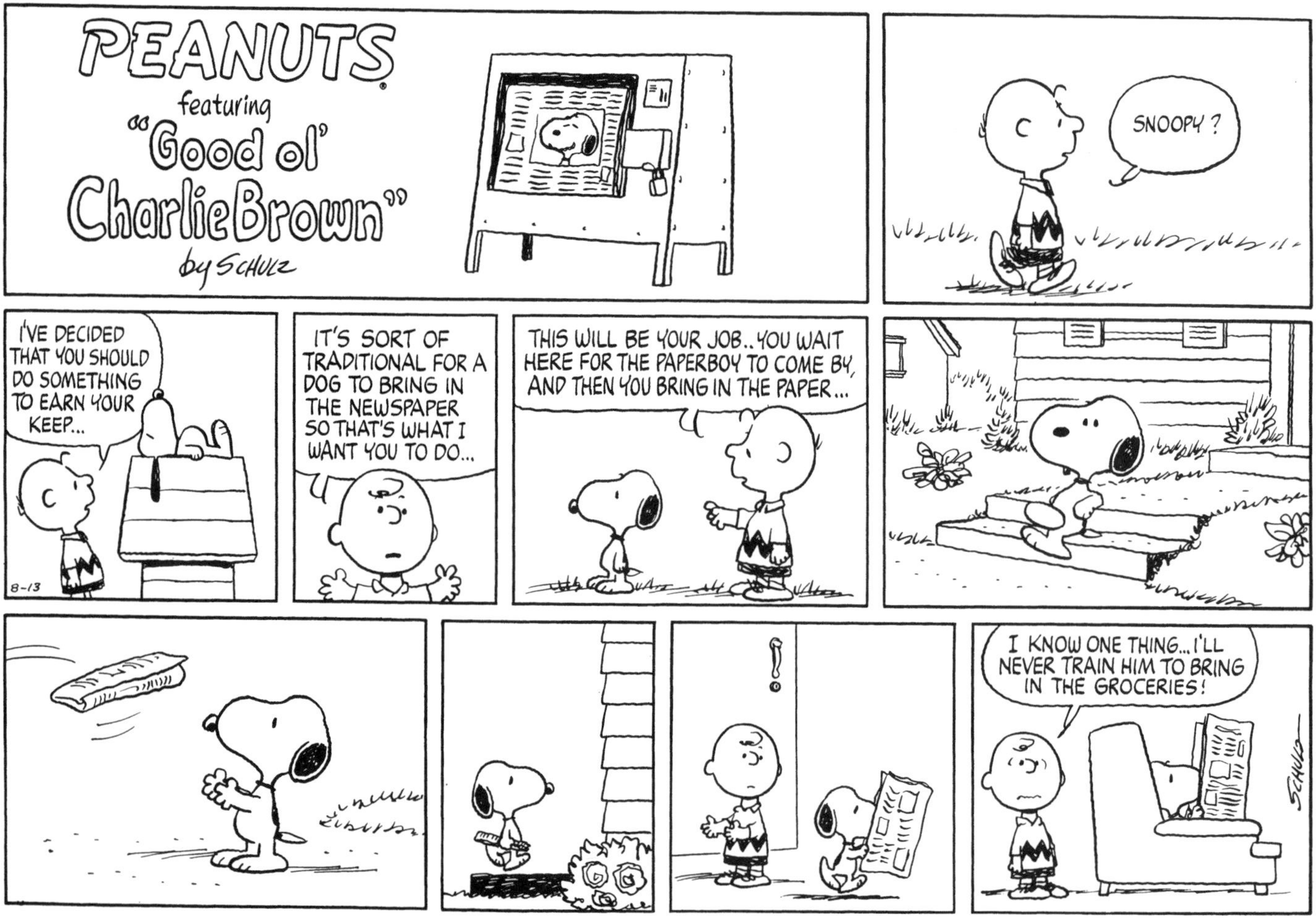
PEANUTS
featuring
"Good ol' Charlie Brown"
by SCHULZ
SNOOPY ?
I'VE DECIDED THAT YOU SHOULD DO SOMETHING TO EARN YOUR KEEP...
8-13
IT'S SORT OF TRADITIONAL FOR A DOG TO BRING IN THE NEWSPAPER SO THAT'S WHAT I WANT YOU TO DO...
THIS WILL BE YOUR JOB..YOU WAIT HERE FOR THE PAPERBOY TO COME BY, AND THEN YOU BRING IN THE PAPER...
!
I KNOW ONE THING...I'LL NEVER TRAIN HIM TO BRING IN THE GROCERIES!
SCHULZ

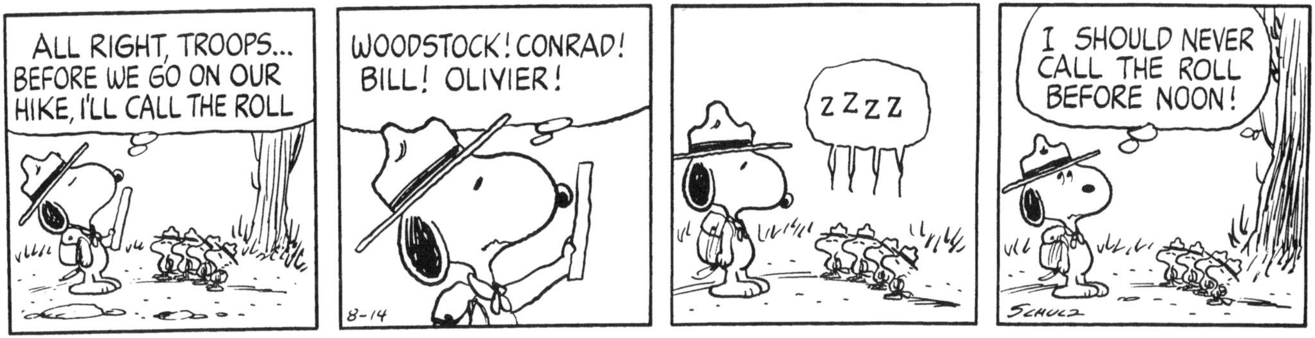
ALL RIGHT, TROOPS... BEFORE WE GO ON OUR HIKE, I'LL CALL THE ROLL
WOODSTOCK! CONRAD! BILL! OLIVIER!
8-14
Z Z Z Z
I SHOULD NEVER CALL THE ROLL BEFORE NOON!
SCHULZ

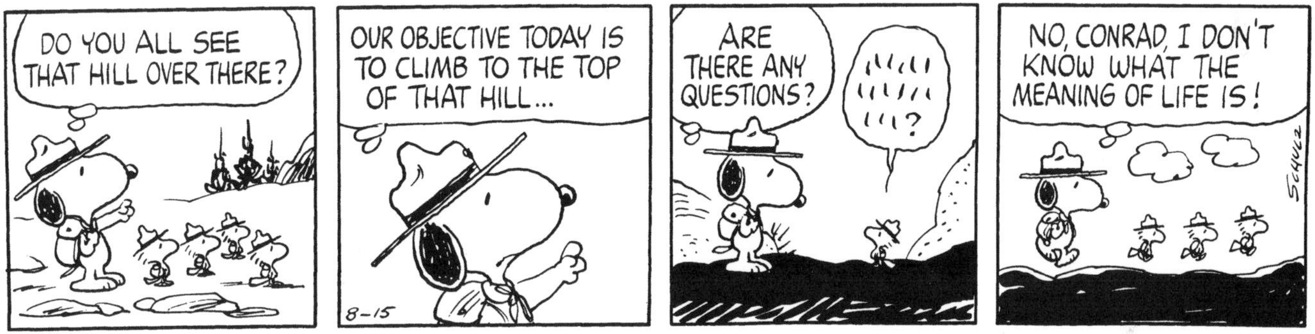
DO YOU ALL SEE THAT HILL OVER THERE?
OUR OBJECTIVE TODAY IS TO CLIMB TO THE TOP OF THAT HILL...
8-15
ARE THERE ANY QUESTIONS?
?
NO, CONRAD, I DON'T KNOW WHAT THE MEANING OF LIFE IS!
SCHULZ

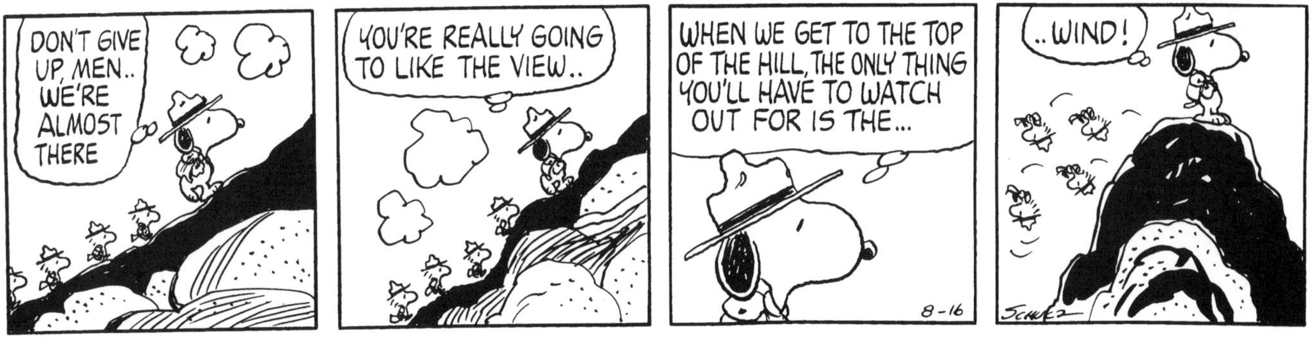
DON'T GIVE UP, MEN.. WE'RE ALMOST THERE
YOU'RE REALLY GOING TO LIKE THE VIEW..
WHEN WE GET TO THE TOP OF THE HILL, THE ONLY THING YOU'LL HAVE TO WATCH OUT FOR IS THE...
8-16
..WIND!
SCHULZ

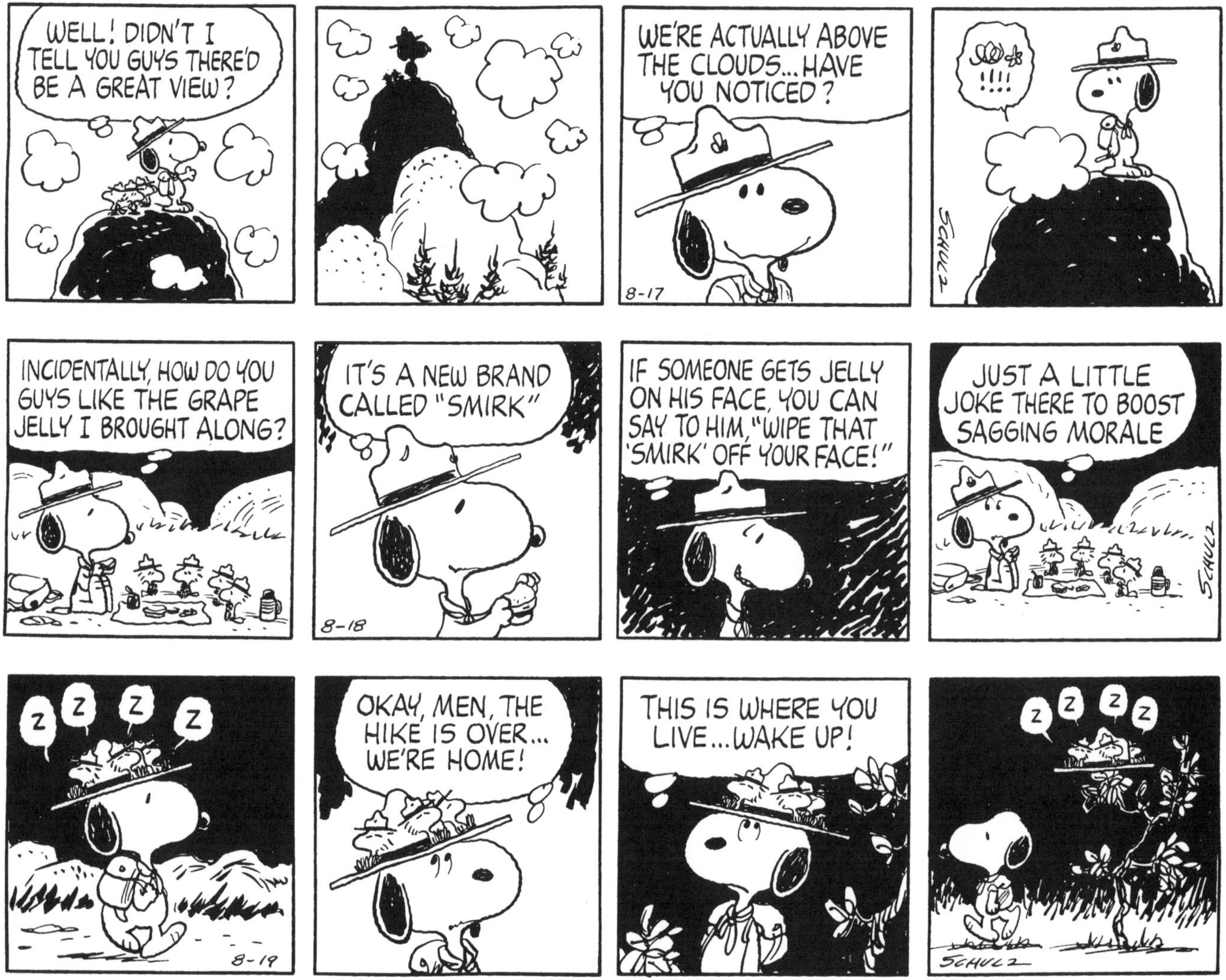
WELL! DIDN'T I TELL YOU GUYS THERE'D BE A GREAT VIEW?
WE'RE ACTUALLY ABOVE THE CLOUDS...HAVE YOU NOTICED?
8-17
!!!!
SCHULZ
INCIDENTALLY, HOW DO YOU GUYS LIKE THE GRAPE JELLY I BROUGHT ALONG?
IT'S A NEW BRAND CALLED "SMIRK"
8-18
IF SOMEONE GETS JELLY ON HIS FACE, YOU CAN SAY TO HIM, "WIPE THAT 'SMIRK' OFF YOUR FACE!"
JUST A LITTLE JOKE THERE TO BOOST SAGGING MORALE
SCHULZ
Z Z Z Z
8-19
OKAY, MEN, THE HIKE IS OVER... WE'RE HOME!
THIS IS WHERE YOU LIVE...WAKE UP!
Z Z Z Z
SCHULZ

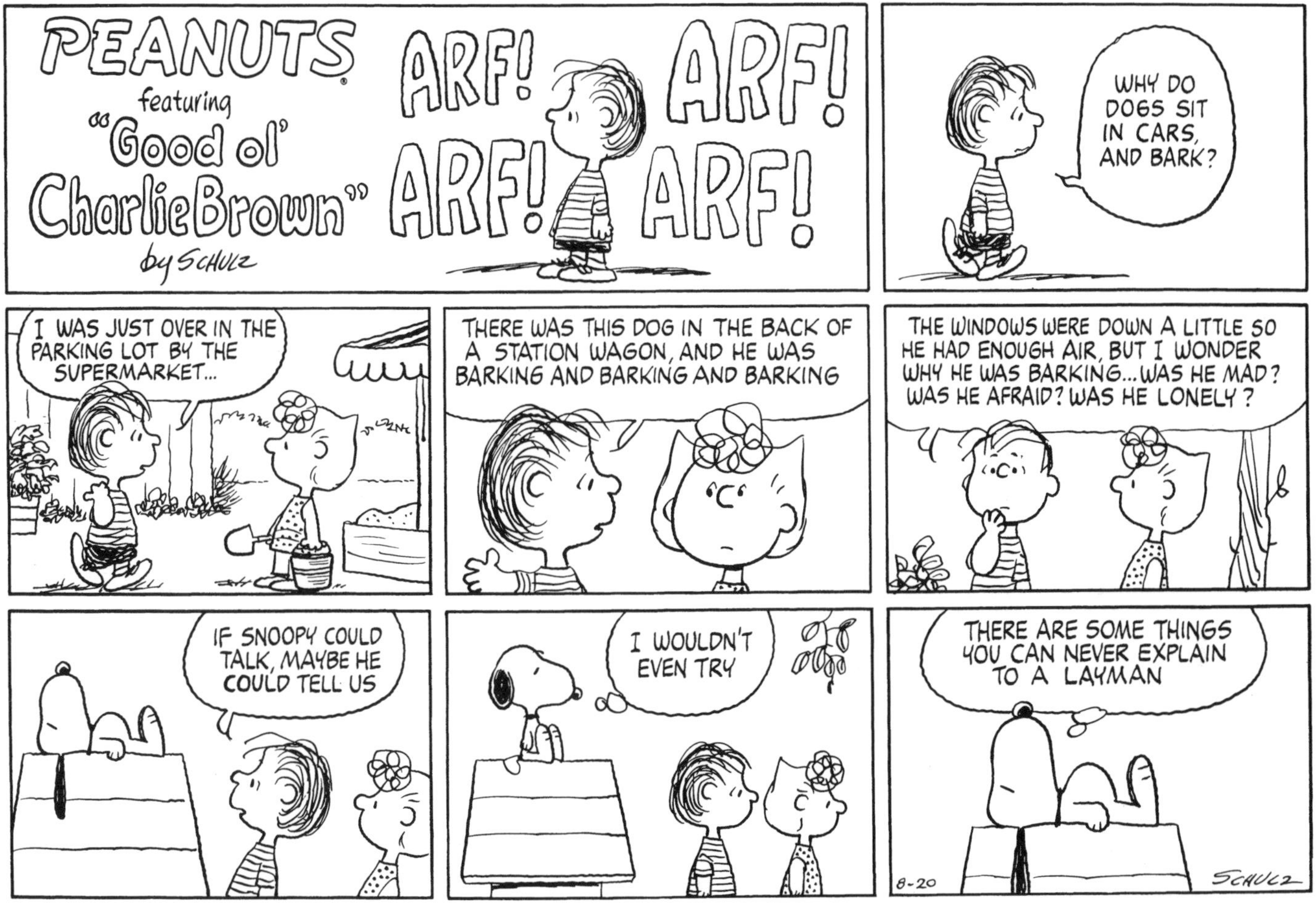
PEANUTS
featuring "Good ol' Charlie Brown"
by SCHULZ
ARF! ARF! ARF! ARF!
WHY DO DOGS SIT IN CARS, AND BARK?
I WAS JUST OVER IN THE PARKING LOT BY THE SUPERMARKET...
THERE WAS THIS DOG IN THE BACK OF A STATION WAGON, AND HE WAS BARKING AND BARKING AND BARKING
THE WINDOWS WERE DOWN A LITTLE SO HE HAD ENOUGH AIR, BUT I WONDER WHY HE WAS BARKING...WAS HE MAD? WAS HE AFRAID? WAS HE LONELY?
IF SNOOPY COULD TALK, MAYBE HE COULD TELL US
I WOULDN'T EVEN TRY
THERE ARE SOME THINGS YOU CAN NEVER EXPLAIN TO A LAYMAN
8-20
SCHULZ

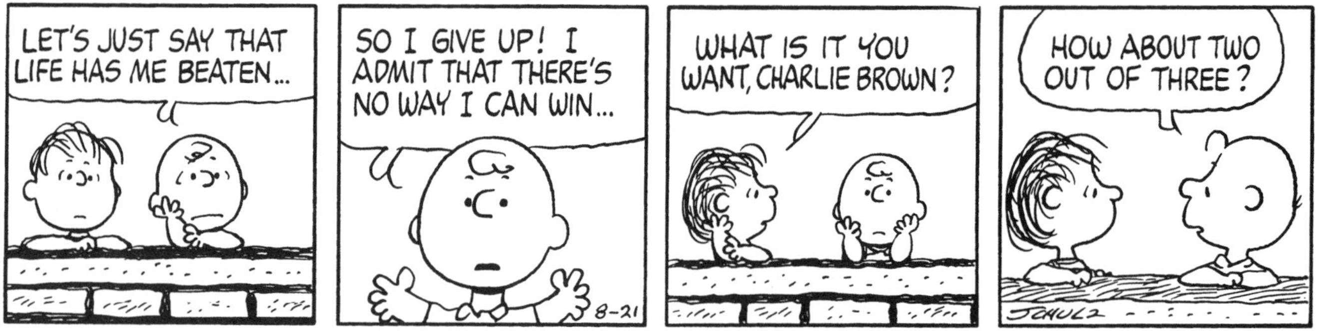
LET'S JUST SAY THAT LIFE HAS ME BEATEN...
SO I GIVE UP! I ADMIT THAT THERE'S NO WAY I CAN WIN...
8-21
WHAT IS IT YOU WANT, CHARLIE BROWN?
HOW ABOUT TWO OUT OF THREE?
SCHULZ

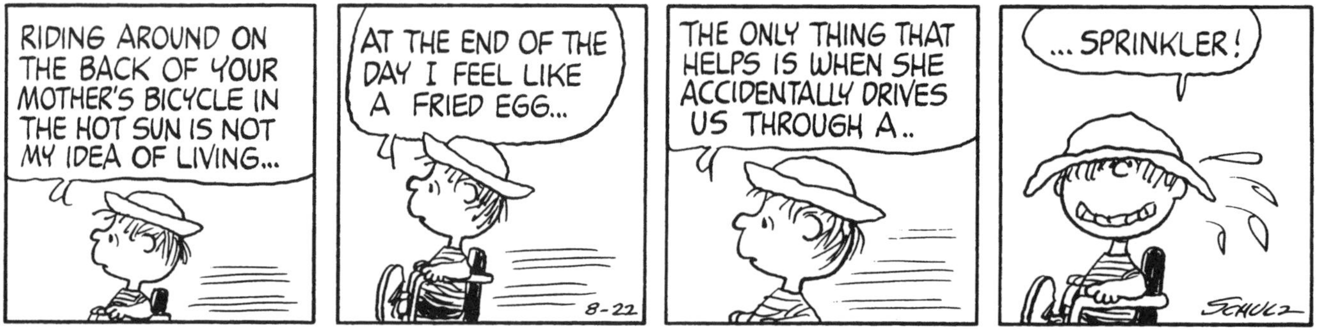
RIDING AROUND ON THE BACK OF YOUR MOTHER'S BICYCLE IN THE HOT SUN IS NOT MY IDEA OF LIVING...
AT THE END OF THE DAY I FEEL LIKE A FRIED EGG...
8-22
THE ONLY THING THAT HELPS IS WHEN SHE ACCIDENTALLY DRIVES US THROUGH A..
...SPRINKLER!
SCHULZ

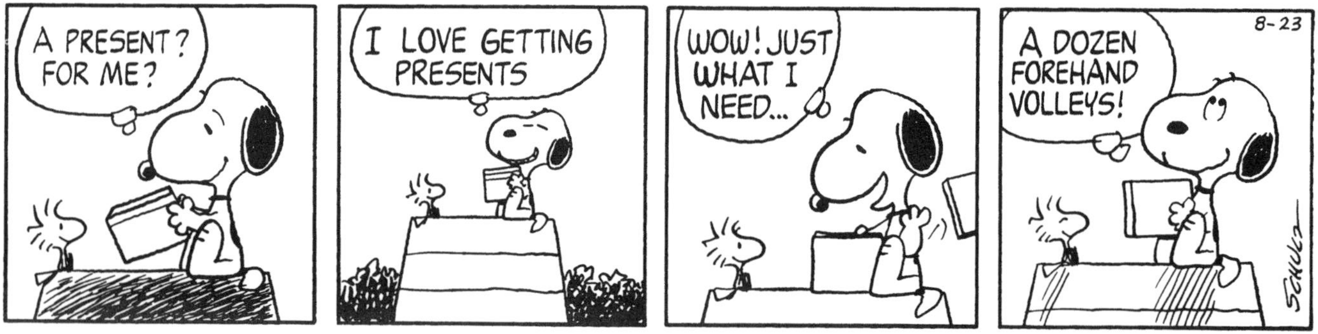
A PRESENT? FOR ME?
I LOVE GETTING PRESENTS
WOW! JUST WHAT I NEED...
8-23
A DOZEN FOREHAND VOLLEYS!
SCHULZ

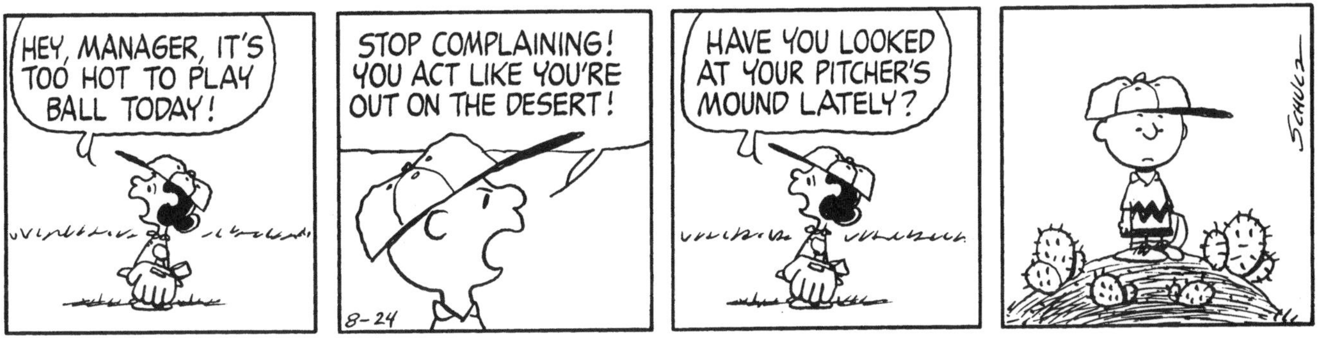
HEY, MANAGER, IT'S TOO HOT TO PLAY BALL TODAY!
STOP COMPLAINING! YOU ACT LIKE YOU'RE OUT ON THE DESERT!
8-24
HAVE YOU LOOKED AT YOUR PITCHER'S MOUND LATELY?
SCHULZ

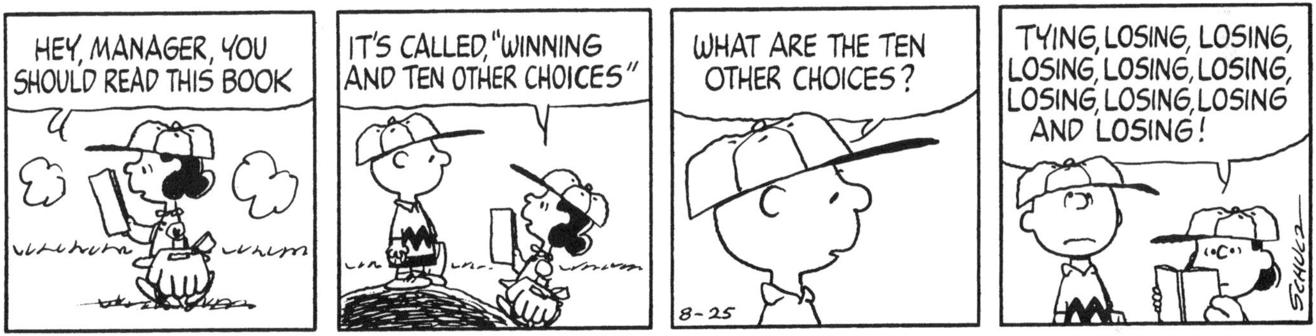
HEY, MANAGER, YOU SHOULD READ THIS BOOK
IT'S CALLED, "WINNING AND TEN OTHER CHOICES"
WHAT ARE THE TEN OTHER CHOICES?
8-25
TYING, LOSING, LOSING, LOSING, LOSING, LOSING, LOSING, LOSING, LOSING AND LOSING!
SCHULZ

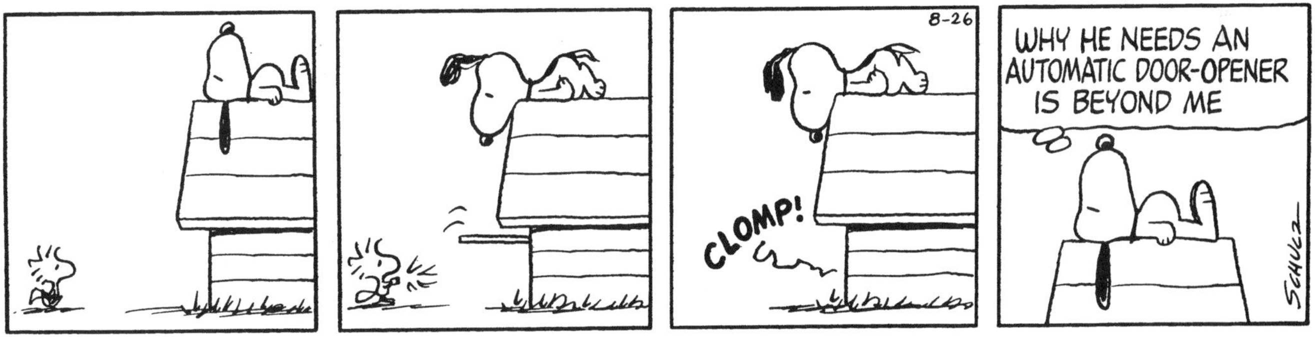
8-26
CLOMP!
WHY HE NEEDS AN AUTOMATIC DOOR-OPENER IS BEYOND ME
SCHULZ

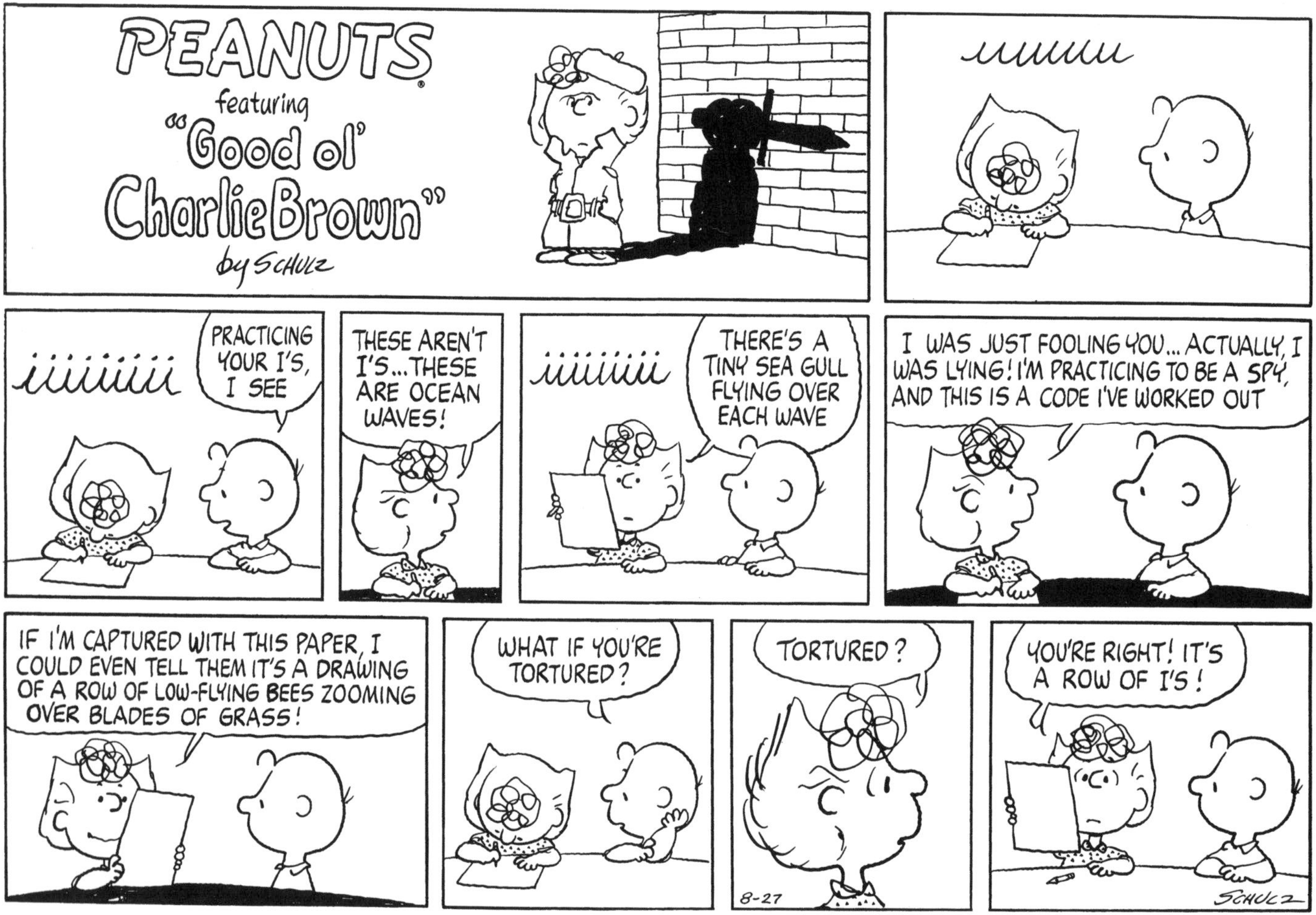
PEANUTS
featuring "Good ol' Charlie Brown"
by SCHULZ
iiiiiii
iiiiiiiii
PRACTICING YOUR I'S, I SEE
THESE AREN'T I'S...THESE ARE OCEAN WAVES!
iiiiiiiii
THERE'S A TINY SEA GULL FLYING OVER EACH WAVE
I WAS JUST FOOLING YOU... ACTUALLY, I WAS LYING! I'M PRACTICING TO BE A SPY, AND THIS IS A CODE I'VE WORKED OUT
IF I'M CAPTURED WITH THIS PAPER, I COULD EVEN TELL THEM IT'S A DRAWING OF A ROW OF LOW-FLYING BEES ZOOMING OVER BLADES OF GRASS!
WHAT IF YOU'RE TORTURED?
TORTURED?
YOU'RE RIGHT! IT'S A ROW OF I'S!
8-27
SCHULZ

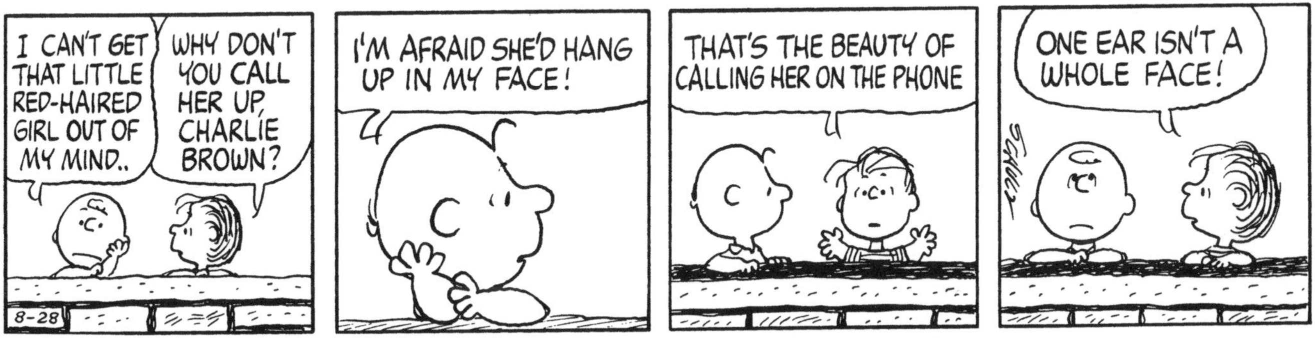
I CAN'T GET THAT LITTLE RED-HAIRED GIRL OUT OF MY MIND..
WHY DON'T YOU CALL HER UP, CHARLIE BROWN?
8-28
I'M AFRAID SHE'D HANG UP IN MY FACE!
THAT'S THE BEAUTY OF CALLING HER ON THE PHONE
ONE EAR ISN'T A WHOLE FACE!
SCHULZ

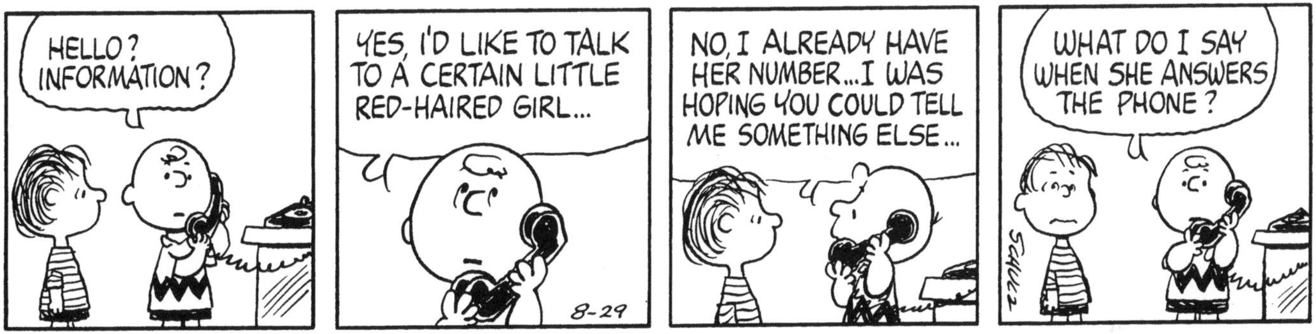
HELLO? INFORMATION?
YES, I'D LIKE TO TALK TO A CERTAIN LITTLE RED-HAIRED GIRL...
8-29
NO, I ALREADY HAVE HER NUMBER...I WAS HOPING YOU COULD TELL ME SOMETHING ELSE...
WHAT DO I SAY WHEN SHE ANSWERS THE PHONE?
SCHULZ

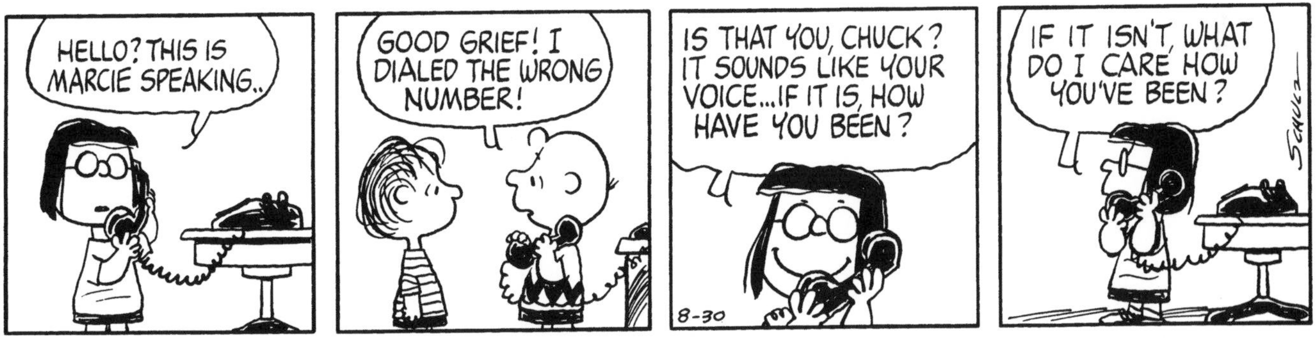
HELLO? THIS IS MARCIE SPEAKING..
GOOD GRIEF! I DIALED THE WRONG NUMBER!
IS THAT YOU, CHUCK? IT SOUNDS LIKE YOUR VOICE...IF IT IS, HOW HAVE YOU BEEN?
8-30
IF IT ISN'T, WHAT DO I CARE HOW YOU'VE BEEN?
SCHULZ

Panel 1: I'LL BET YOU DIALED MY NUMBER BY MISTAKE, DIDN'T YOU, CHUCK? I'LL BET YOU MEANT TO CALL PEPPERMINT PATTY...

8-31

Panel 2: SHE JUST HAPPENS TO BE RIGHT HERE BESIDE ME..I'LL PUT HER ON...

Panel 3: NO! WAIT! I...

Panel 4: HI, CHUCK! FINALLY GOT UP NERVE TO CALL ME, EH?

Panel 5: WHAT DID YOU WANT TO TALK TO ME ABOUT, CHUCK?

Panel 6: IF IT'S ABOUT GOING TO THE SHOW, WHY DON'T WE JUST MEET THERE AROUND ONE? THAT'LL SAVE YOU COMIN' CLEAR OVER HERE!

Panel 7: SEE YOU, CHUCK! GLAD YOU GOT OVER YOUR SHYNESS AND DECIDED TO CALL!

9-1

Panel 8: I CAN'T STAND IT...

Panel 9: WHERE ARE YOU GOING, BIG BROTHER?

9-2

Panel 10: WELL, I FINALLY GOT UP NERVE TO CALL THAT LITTLE RED-HAIRED GIRL, BUT I DIALED MARCIE BY MISTAKE, AND GOT A DATE WITH PEPPERMINT PATTY...

Panel 11: I THINK YOU'RE TOO WISHY-WASHY, BIG BROTHER

Panel 12: IT'S NOT A LOST ART!

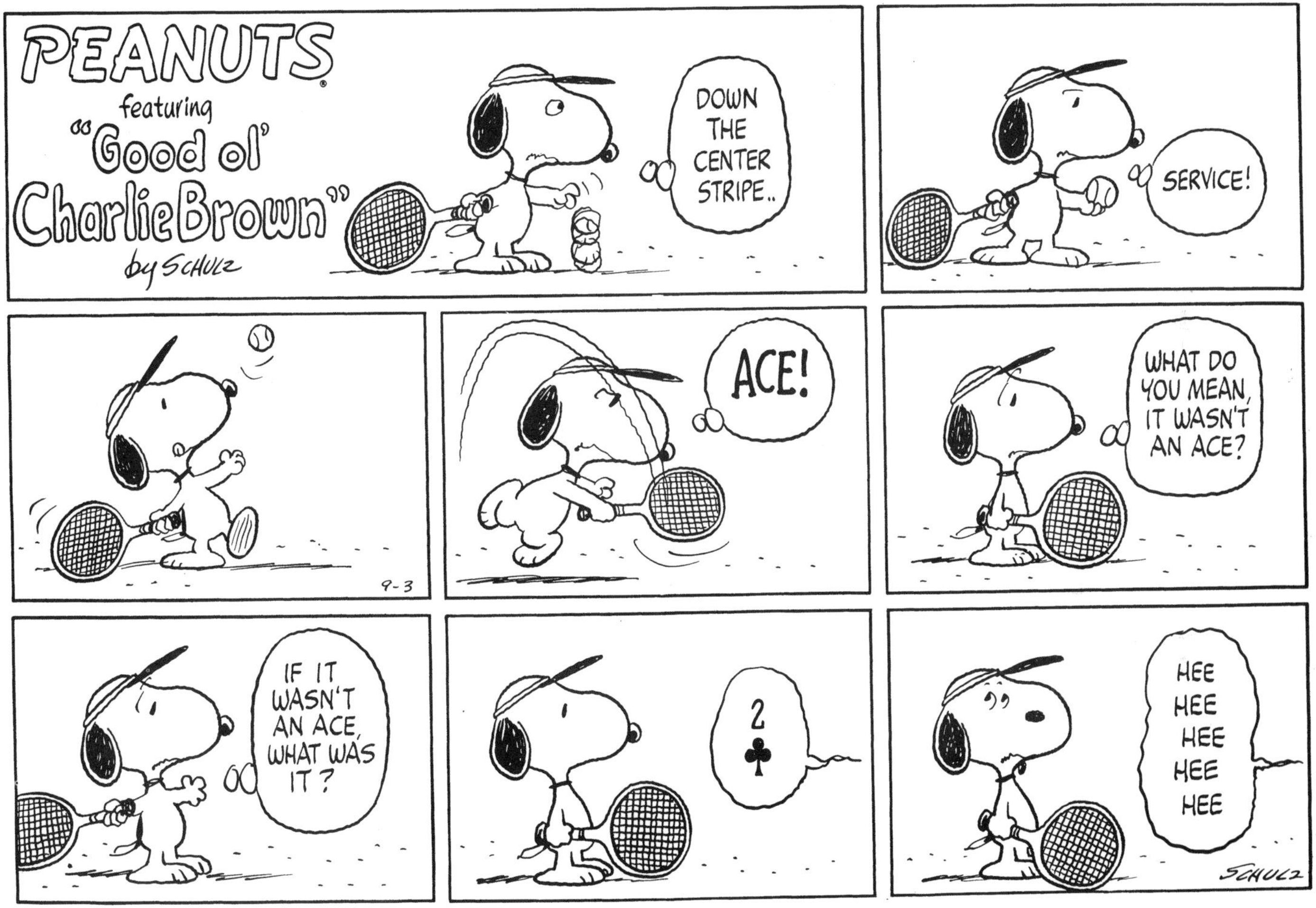
PEANUTS
featuring
"Good ol' Charlie Brown"
by SCHULZ
DOWN THE CENTER STRIPE..
SERVICE!
9-3
ACE!
WHAT DO YOU MEAN, IT WASN'T AN ACE?
IF IT WASN'T AN ACE, WHAT WAS IT?
2 ♣
HEE HEE HEE HEE HEE
SCHULZ

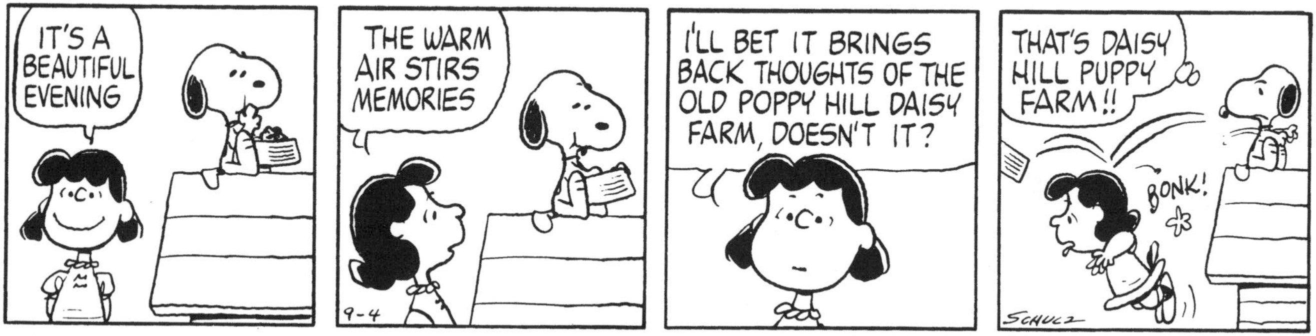
IT'S A BEAUTIFUL EVENING
THE WARM AIR STIRS MEMORIES
I'LL BET IT BRINGS BACK THOUGHTS OF THE OLD POPPY HILL DAISY FARM, DOESN'T IT?
THAT'S DAISY HILL PUPPY FARM!!
BONK!

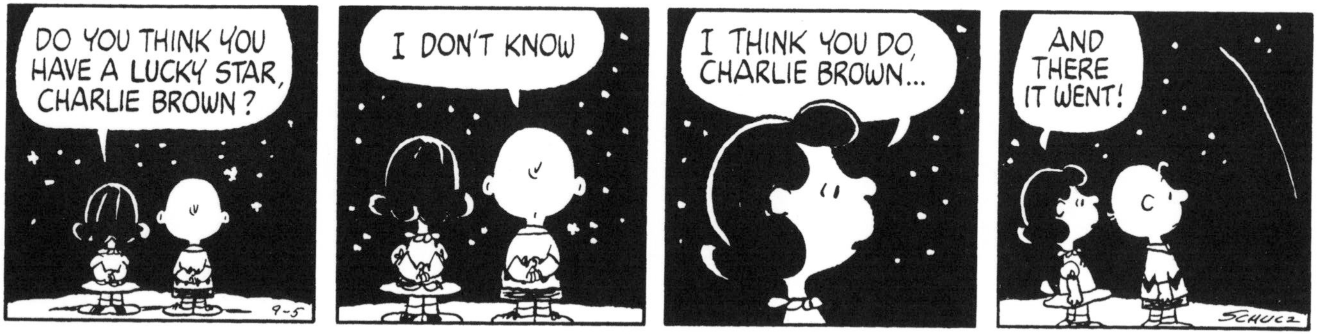
DO YOU THINK YOU HAVE A LUCKY STAR, CHARLIE BROWN?
I DON'T KNOW
I THINK YOU DO, CHARLIE BROWN...
AND THERE IT WENT!

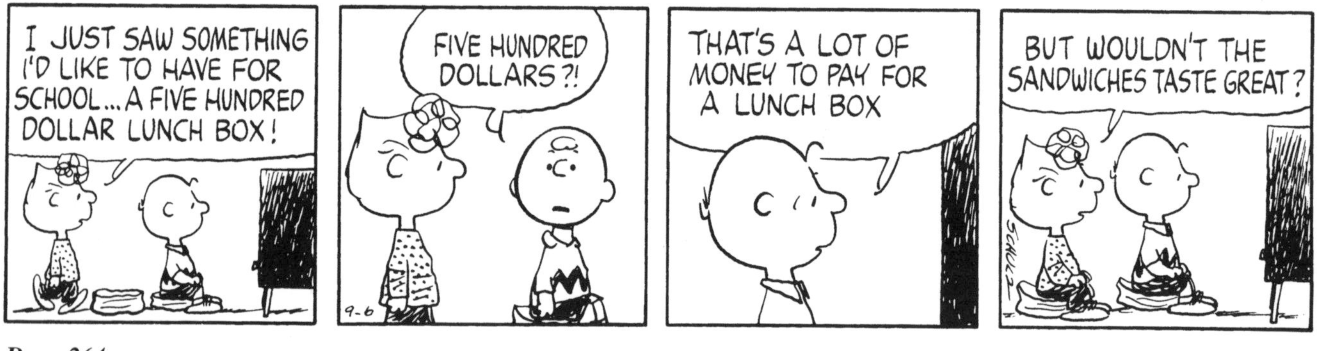
I JUST SAW SOMETHING I'D LIKE TO HAVE FOR SCHOOL... A FIVE HUNDRED DOLLAR LUNCH BOX!
FIVE HUNDRED DOLLARS?!
THAT'S A LOT OF MONEY TO PAY FOR A LUNCH BOX
BUT WOULDN'T THE SANDWICHES TASTE GREAT?

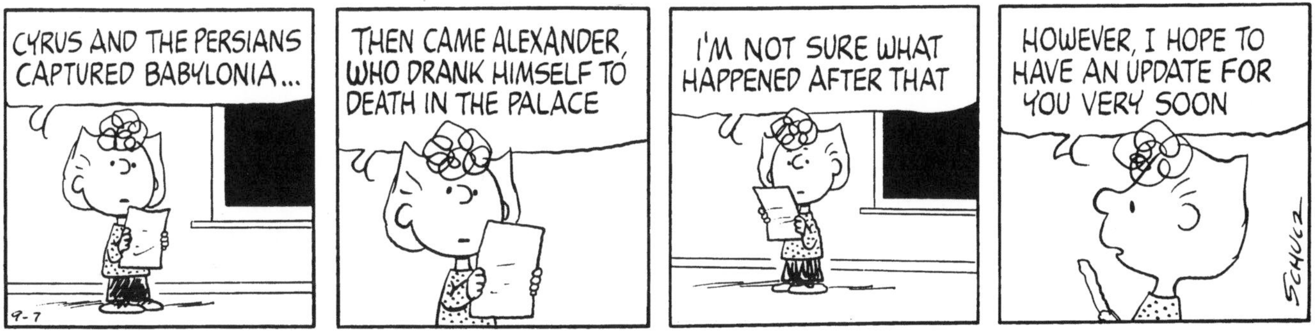
CYRUS AND THE PERSIANS CAPTURED BABYLONIA...
THEN CAME ALEXANDER, WHO DRANK HIMSELF TO DEATH IN THE PALACE
I'M NOT SURE WHAT HAPPENED AFTER THAT
HOWEVER, I HOPE TO HAVE AN UPDATE FOR YOU VERY SOON

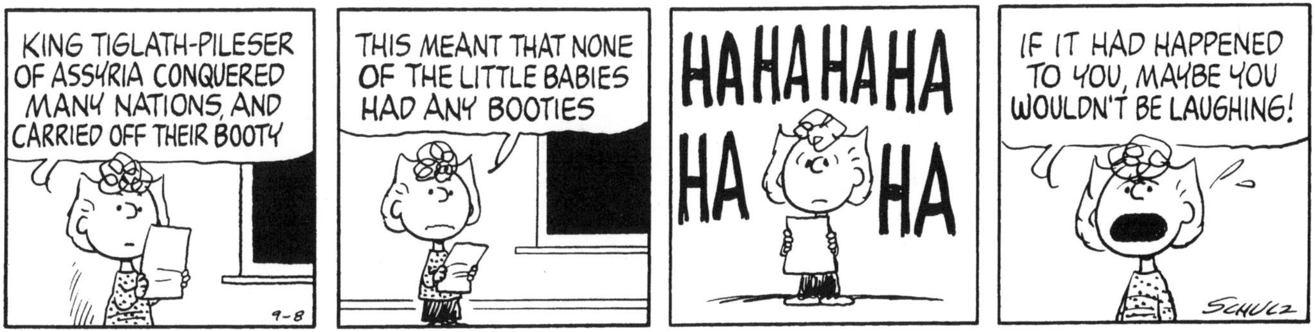
KING TIGLATH-PILESER OF ASSYRIA CONQUERED MANY NATIONS, AND CARRIED OFF THEIR BOOTY
THIS MEANT THAT NONE OF THE LITTLE BABIES HAD ANY BOOTIES
HAHAHAHAHA HA HA
IF IT HAD HAPPENED TO YOU, MAYBE YOU WOULDN'T BE LAUGHING!

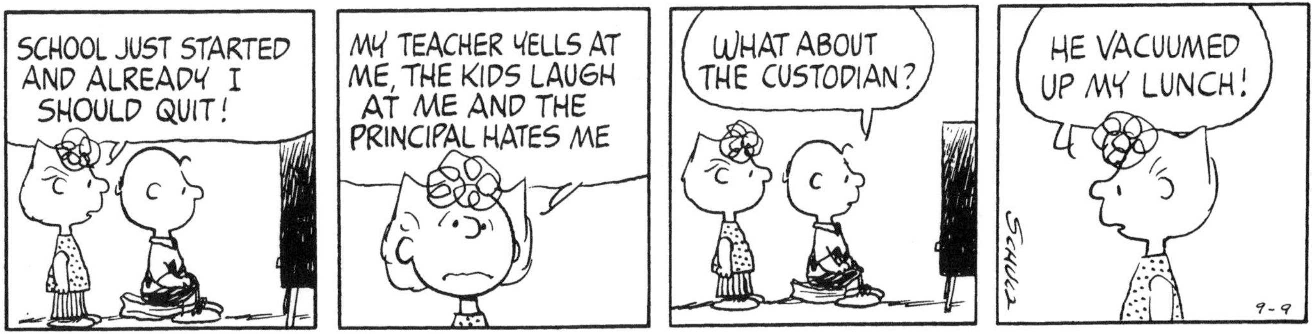
SCHOOL JUST STARTED AND ALREADY I SHOULD QUIT!
MY TEACHER YELLS AT ME, THE KIDS LAUGH AT ME AND THE PRINCIPAL HATES ME
WHAT ABOUT THE CUSTODIAN?
HE VACUUMED UP MY LUNCH!

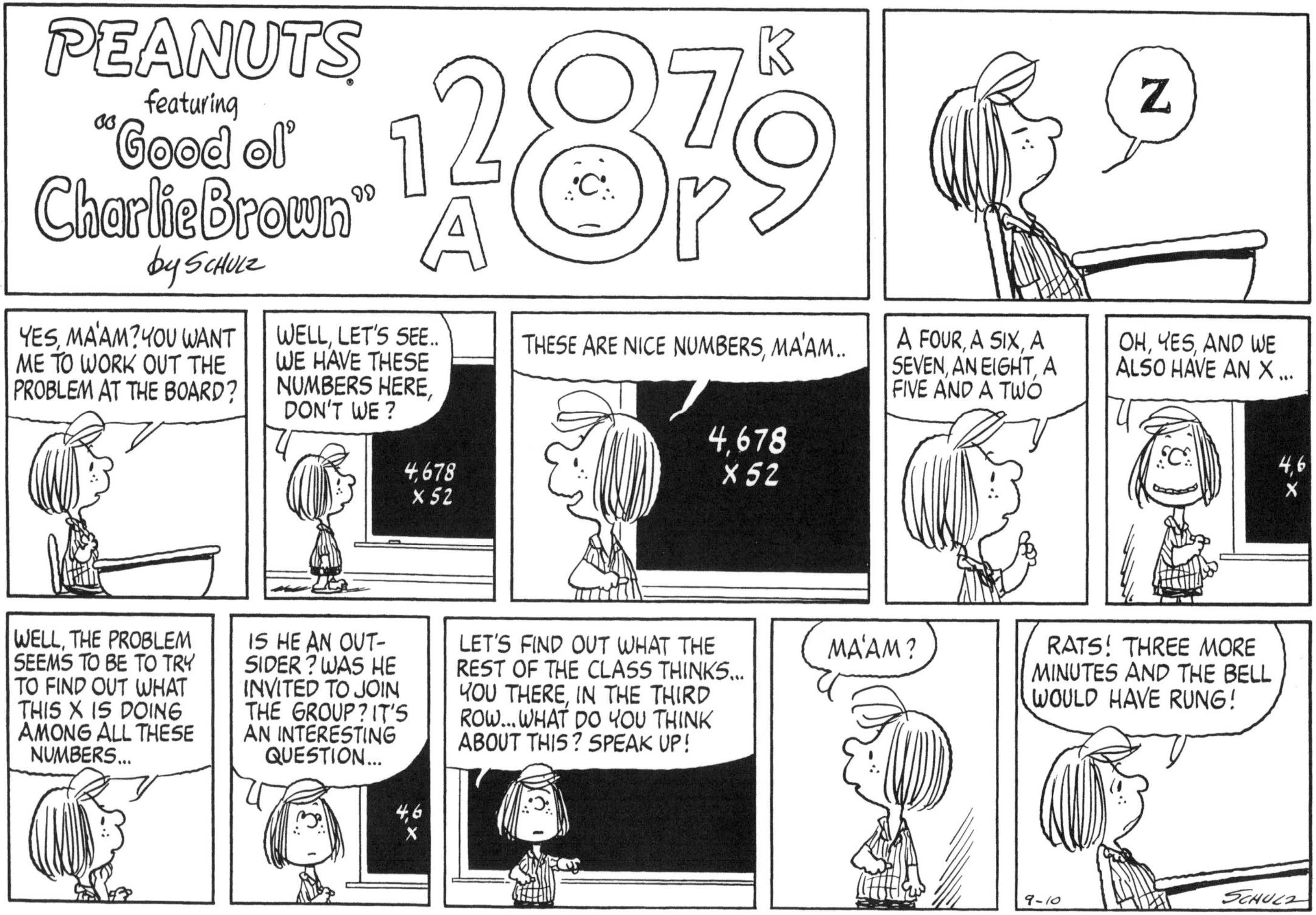
PEANUTS
featuring "Good ol' Charlie Brown"
by SCHULZ
Z
YES, MA'AM? YOU WANT ME TO WORK OUT THE PROBLEM AT THE BOARD?
WELL, LET'S SEE.. WE HAVE THESE NUMBERS HERE, DON'T WE?
4,678
X 52
THESE ARE NICE NUMBERS, MA'AM..
4,678
X 52
A FOUR, A SIX, A SEVEN, AN EIGHT, A FIVE AND A TWO
OH, YES, AND WE ALSO HAVE AN X...
4,6
X
WELL, THE PROBLEM SEEMS TO BE TO TRY TO FIND OUT WHAT THIS X IS DOING AMONG ALL THESE NUMBERS...
IS HE AN OUT-SIDER? WAS HE INVITED TO JOIN THE GROUP? IT'S AN INTERESTING QUESTION...
4,6
X
LET'S FIND OUT WHAT THE REST OF THE CLASS THINKS... YOU THERE, IN THE THIRD ROW...WHAT DO YOU THINK ABOUT THIS? SPEAK UP!
MA'AM?
RATS! THREE MORE MINUTES AND THE BELL WOULD HAVE RUNG!
9-10
SCHULZ

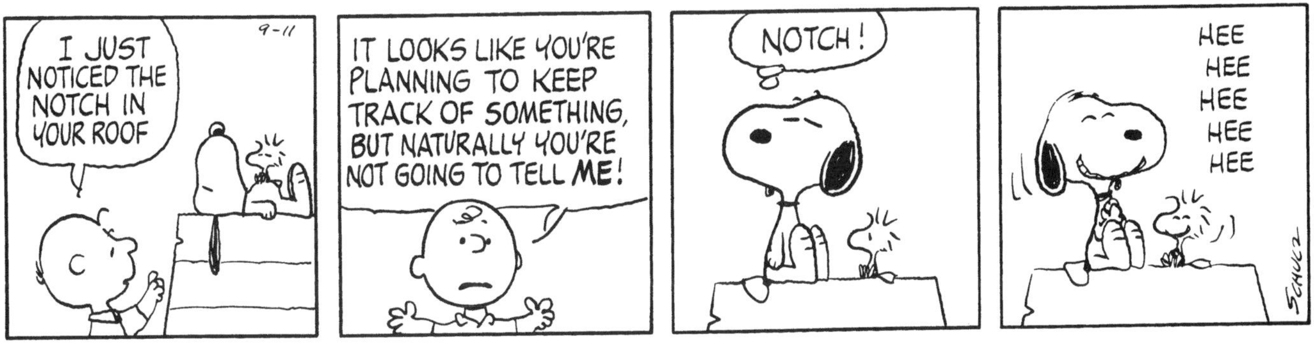

9-11
I JUST NOTICED THE NOTCH IN YOUR ROOF
IT LOOKS LIKE YOU'RE PLANNING TO KEEP TRACK OF SOMETHING, BUT NATURALLY YOU'RE NOT GOING TO TELL ME!
NOTCH!
HEE HEE HEE HEE HEE
SCHULZ

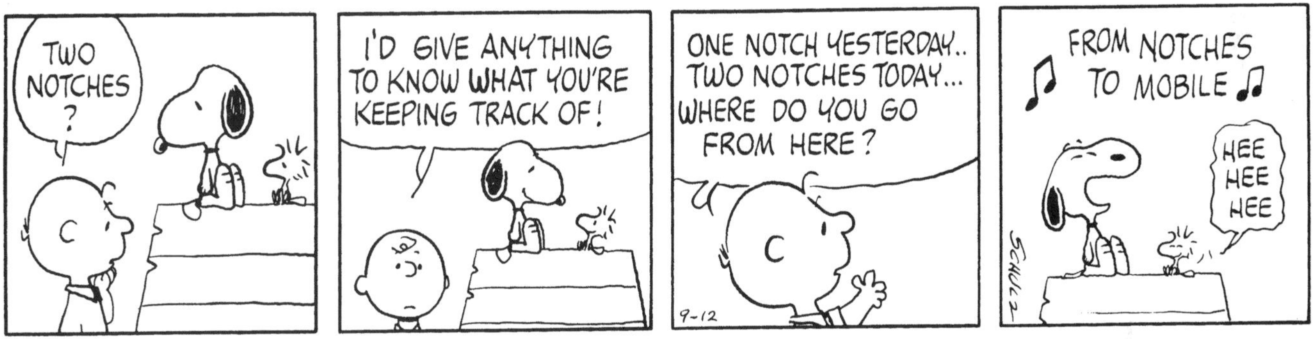

TWO NOTCHES ?
I'D GIVE ANYTHING TO KNOW WHAT YOU'RE KEEPING TRACK OF!
ONE NOTCH YESTERDAY.. TWO NOTCHES TODAY... WHERE DO YOU GO FROM HERE?
9-12
FROM NOTCHES TO MOBILE
HEE HEE HEE
SCHULZ

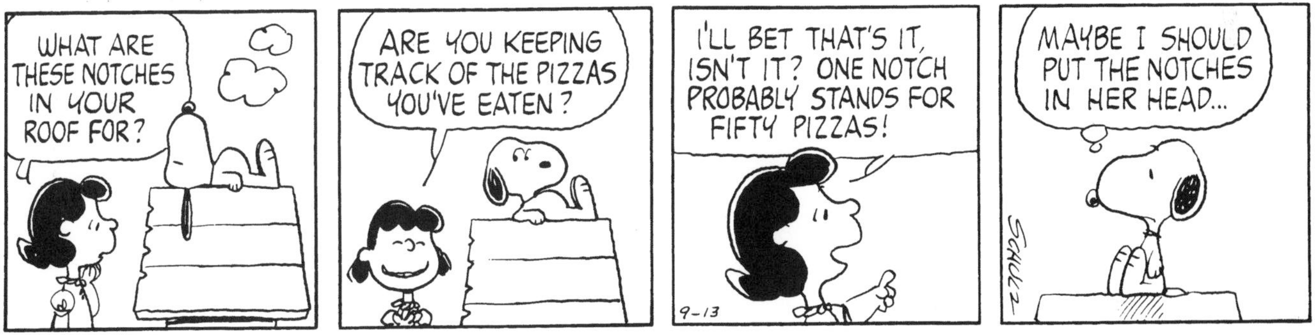

WHAT ARE THESE NOTCHES IN YOUR ROOF FOR?
ARE YOU KEEPING TRACK OF THE PIZZAS YOU'VE EATEN?
I'LL BET THAT'S IT, ISN'T IT? ONE NOTCH PROBABLY STANDS FOR FIFTY PIZZAS!
9-13
SCHULZ
MAYBE I SHOULD PUT THE NOTCHES IN HER HEAD...

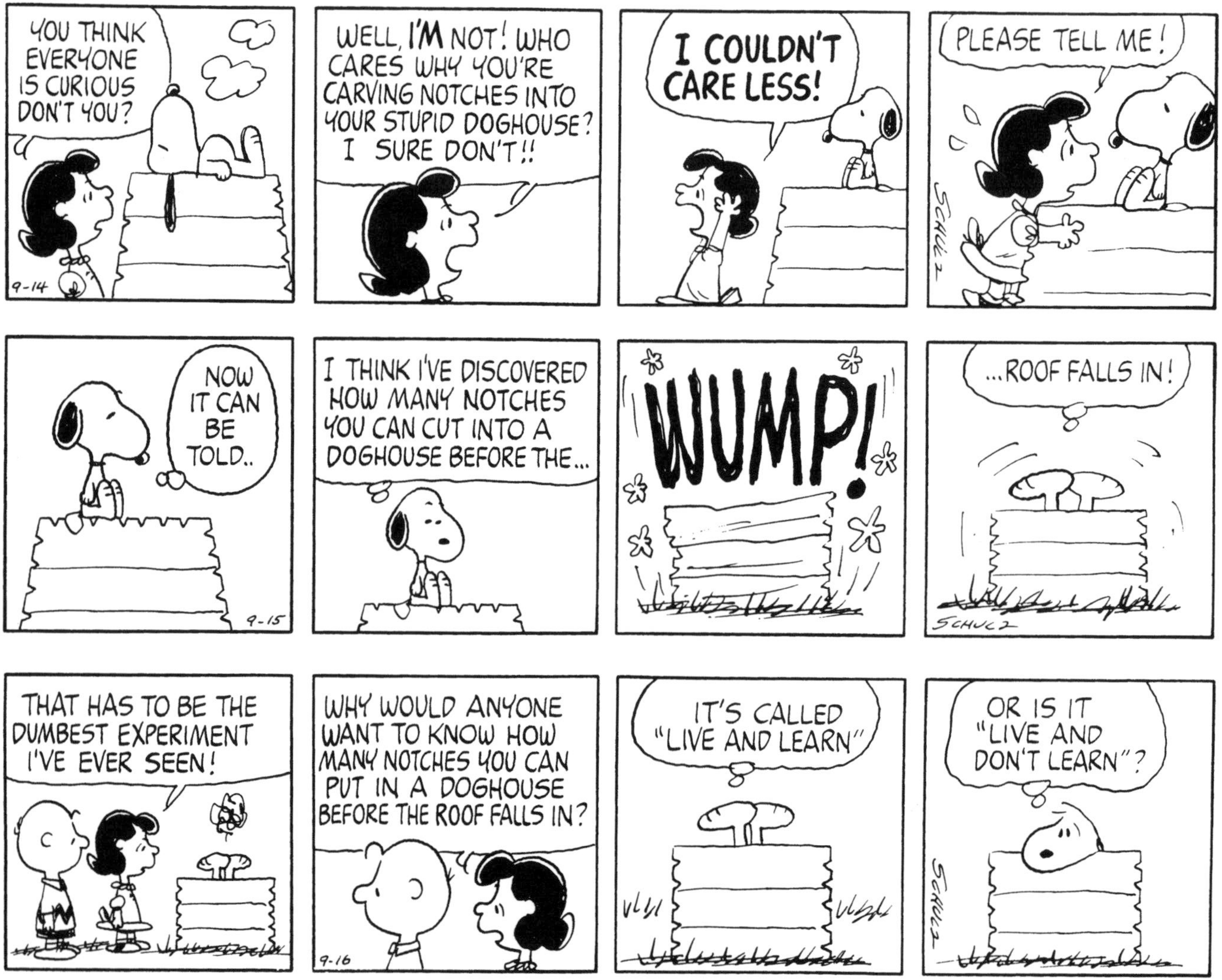
YOU THINK EVERYONE IS CURIOUS DON'T YOU?
9-14
WELL, I'M NOT! WHO CARES WHY YOU'RE CARVING NOTCHES INTO YOUR STUPID DOGHOUSE? I SURE DON'T!!
I COULDN'T CARE LESS!
PLEASE TELL ME!
SCHULZ
NOW IT CAN BE TOLD..
9-15
I THINK I'VE DISCOVERED HOW MANY NOTCHES YOU CAN CUT INTO A DOGHOUSE BEFORE THE...
WUMP!
...ROOF FALLS IN!
SCHULZ
THAT HAS TO BE THE DUMBEST EXPERIMENT I'VE EVER SEEN!
WHY WOULD ANYONE WANT TO KNOW HOW MANY NOTCHES YOU CAN PUT IN A DOGHOUSE BEFORE THE ROOF FALLS IN?
9-16
IT'S CALLED "LIVE AND LEARN"
OR IS IT "LIVE AND DON'T LEARN"?
SCHULZ

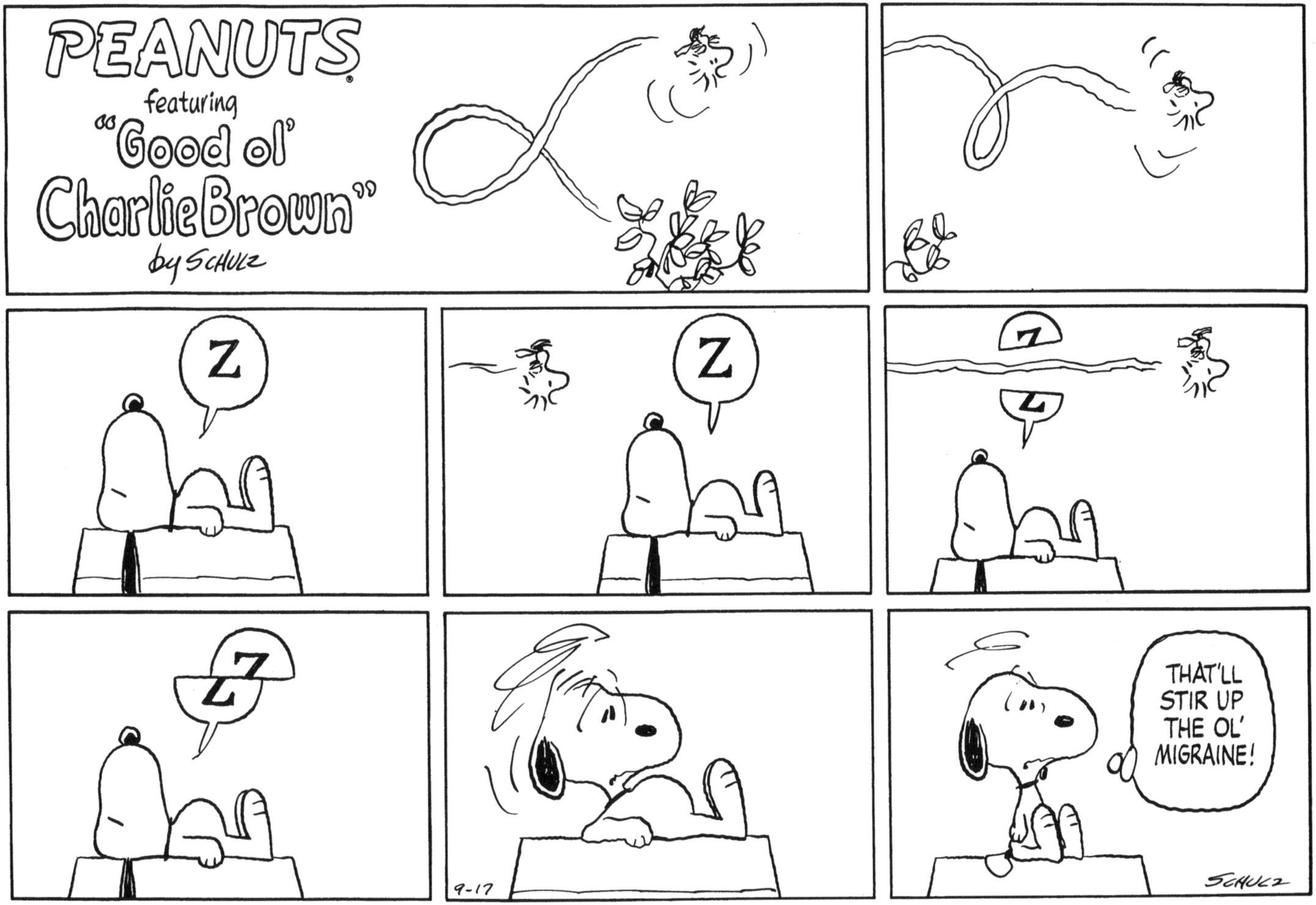
PEANUTS
featuring
"Good ol' Charlie Brown"
by SCHULZ
Z
Z
Z
Z
Z
Z
THAT'LL STIR UP THE OL' MIGRAINE!
9-17
SCHULZ

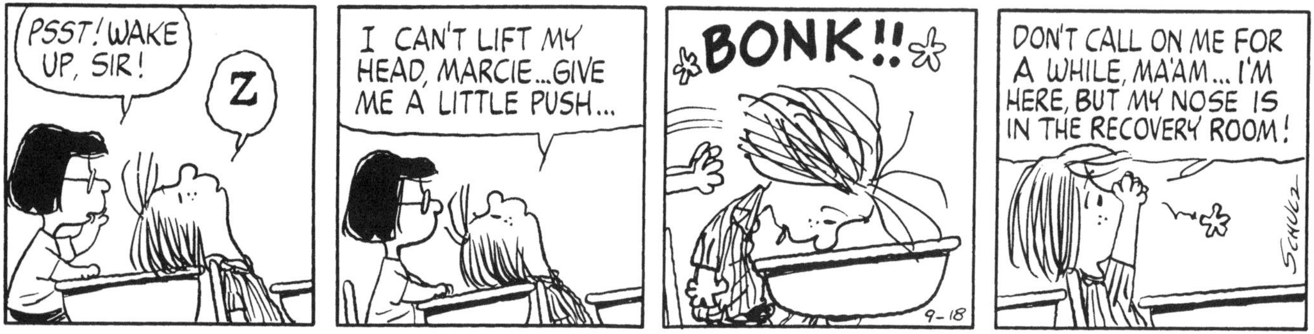
PSST! WAKE UP, SIR!
Z
I CAN'T LIFT MY HEAD, MARCIE...GIVE ME A LITTLE PUSH...
BONK!!
DON'T CALL ON ME FOR A WHILE, MA'AM... I'M HERE, BUT MY NOSE IS IN THE RECOVERY ROOM!
SCHULZ
9-18

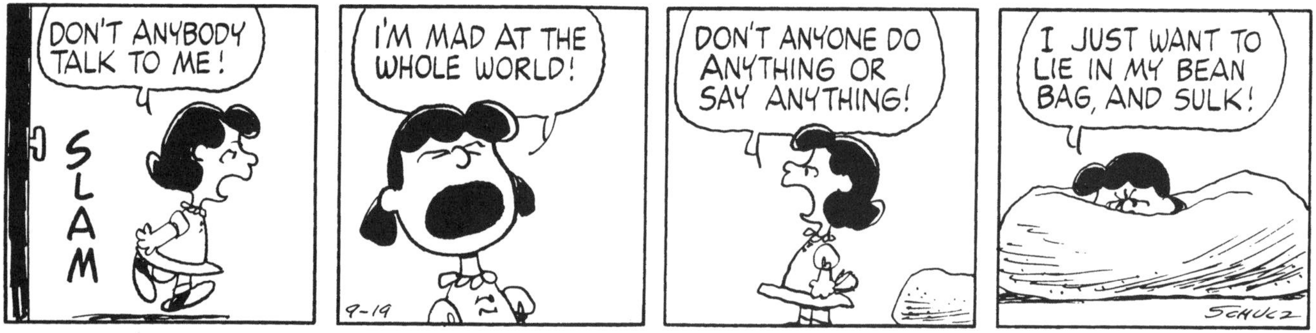
DON'T ANYBODY TALK TO ME!
SLAM
I'M MAD AT THE WHOLE WORLD!
9-19
DON'T ANYONE DO ANYTHING OR SAY ANYTHING!
I JUST WANT TO LIE IN MY BEAN BAG, AND SULK!
SCHULZ

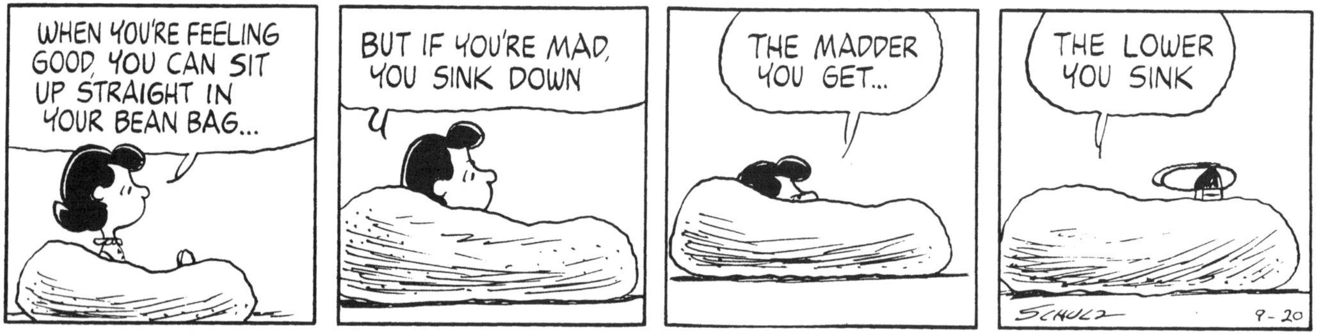
WHEN YOU'RE FEELING GOOD, YOU CAN SIT UP STRAIGHT IN YOUR BEAN BAG...
BUT IF YOU'RE MAD, YOU SINK DOWN
THE MADDER YOU GET...
THE LOWER YOU SINK
SCHULZ
9-20

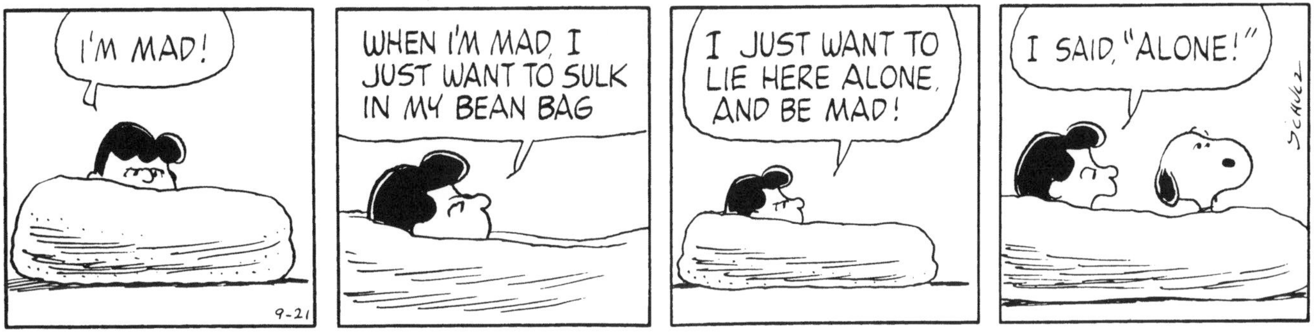
I'M MAD!
WHEN I'M MAD, I JUST WANT TO SULK IN MY BEAN BAG
I JUST WANT TO LIE HERE ALONE, AND BE MAD!
I SAID, "ALONE!"

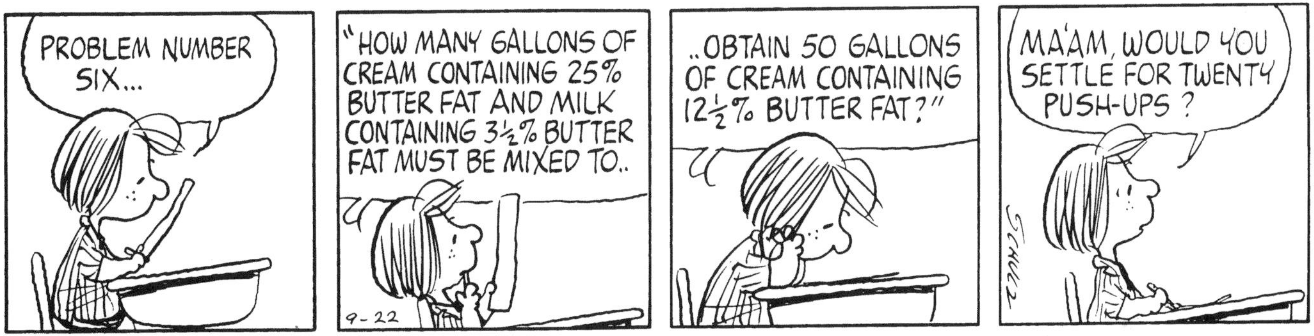
PROBLEM NUMBER SIX...
"HOW MANY GALLONS OF CREAM CONTAINING 25% BUTTER FAT AND MILK CONTAINING 3½% BUTTER FAT MUST BE MIXED TO..
..OBTAIN 50 GALLONS OF CREAM CONTAINING 12½% BUTTER FAT?"
MA'AM, WOULD YOU SETTLE FOR TWENTY PUSH-UPS ?

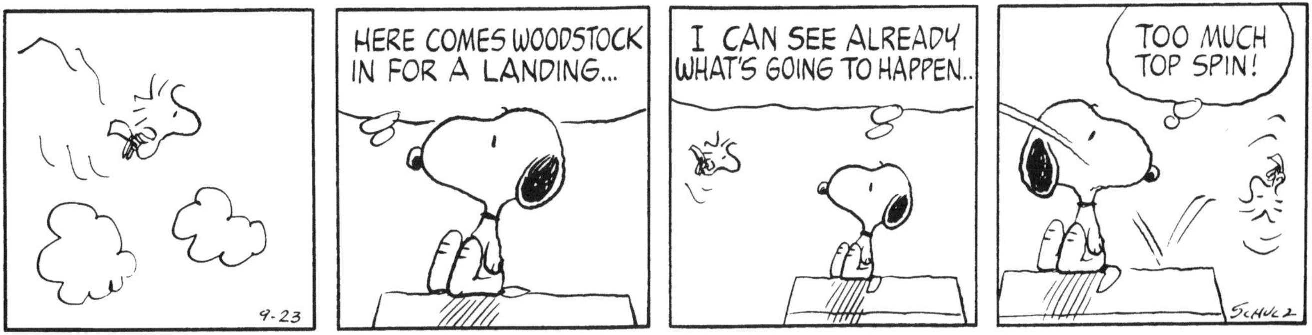
HERE COMES WOODSTOCK IN FOR A LANDING...
I CAN SEE ALREADY WHAT'S GOING TO HAPPEN..
TOO MUCH TOP SPIN!

PEANUTS featuring "*Good ol' Charlie Brown*" by SCHULZ

Dear Grandma, How are you? I am fine.

I have been working hard in school.

WHICH GRANDMA ARE YOU WRITING TO? WE HAVE TWO GRANDMAS, YOU KNOW...

I AM WELL AWARE OF THAT! I AM ALSO AWARE THAT THEY DON'T LIKE EACH OTHER...

AND THAT BRINGS UP A PROBLEM...

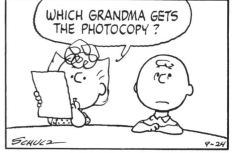

WHICH GRANDMA GETS THE PHOTOCOPY?

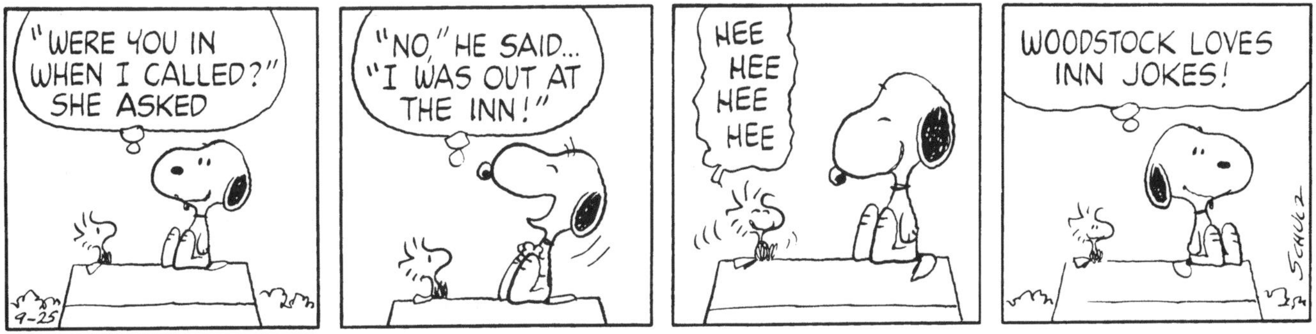
"WERE YOU IN WHEN I CALLED?" SHE ASKED
"NO," HE SAID... "I WAS OUT AT THE INN!"
HEE HEE HEE HEE
WOODSTOCK LOVES INN JOKES!

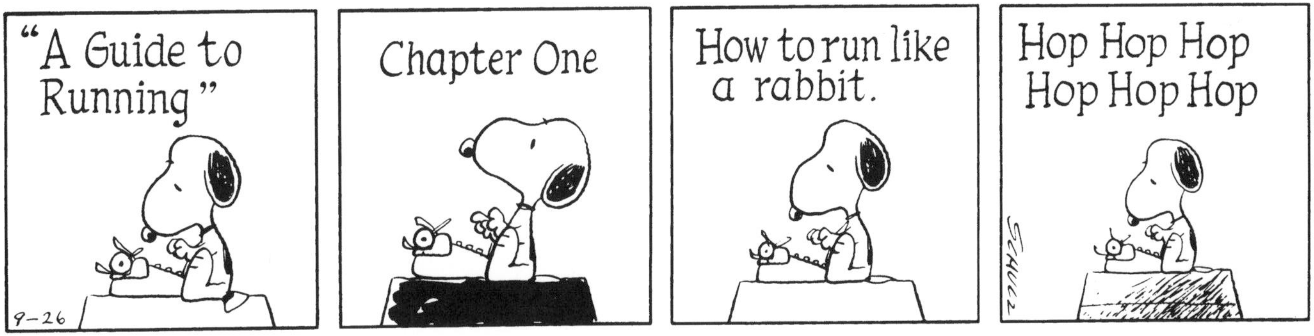
"A Guide to Running"
Chapter One
How to run like a rabbit.
Hop Hop Hop Hop Hop Hop

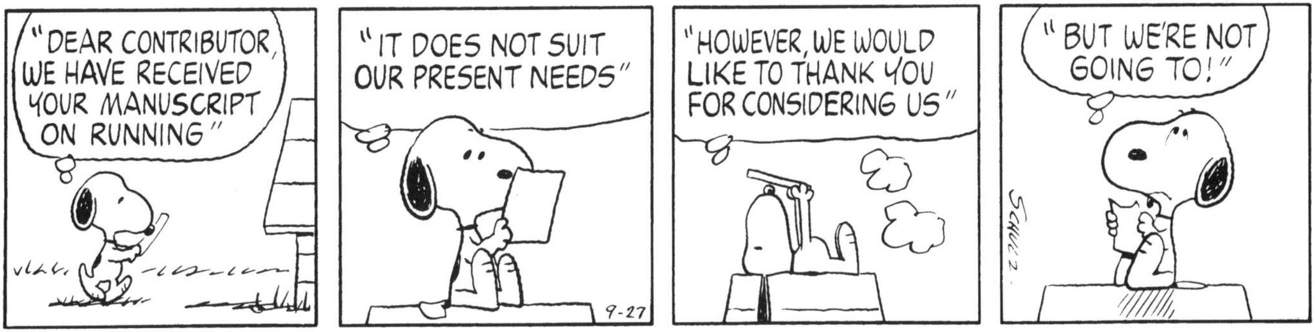
"DEAR CONTRIBUTOR, WE HAVE RECEIVED YOUR MANUSCRIPT ON RUNNING"
"IT DOES NOT SUIT OUR PRESENT NEEDS"
"HOWEVER, WE WOULD LIKE TO THANK YOU FOR CONSIDERING US"
"BUT WE'RE NOT GOING TO!"

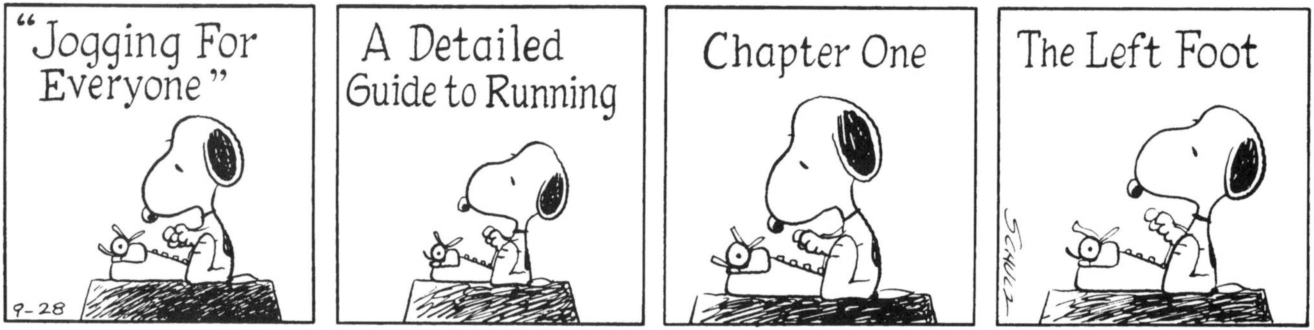
"Jogging For Everyone"
9-28
A Detailed Guide to Running
Chapter One
The Left Foot
SCHULZ

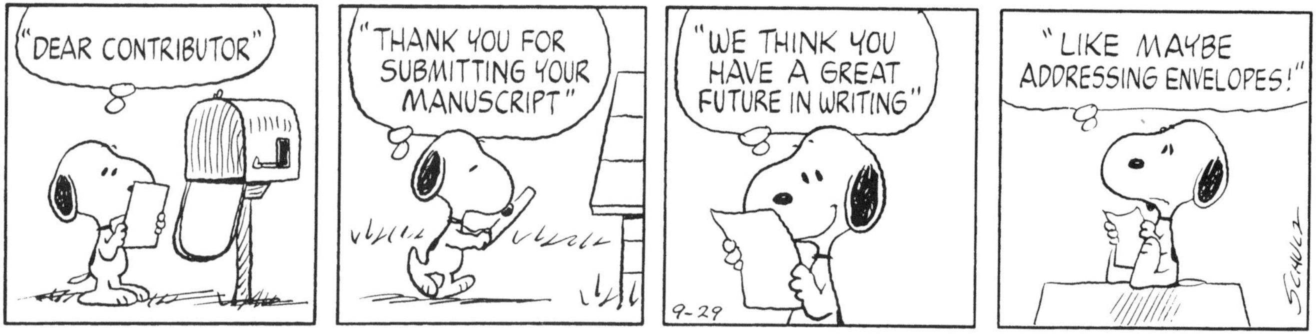
"DEAR CONTRIBUTOR"
"THANK YOU FOR SUBMITTING YOUR MANUSCRIPT"
"WE THINK YOU HAVE A GREAT FUTURE IN WRITING"
9-29
"LIKE MAYBE ADDRESSING ENVELOPES!"
SCHULZ

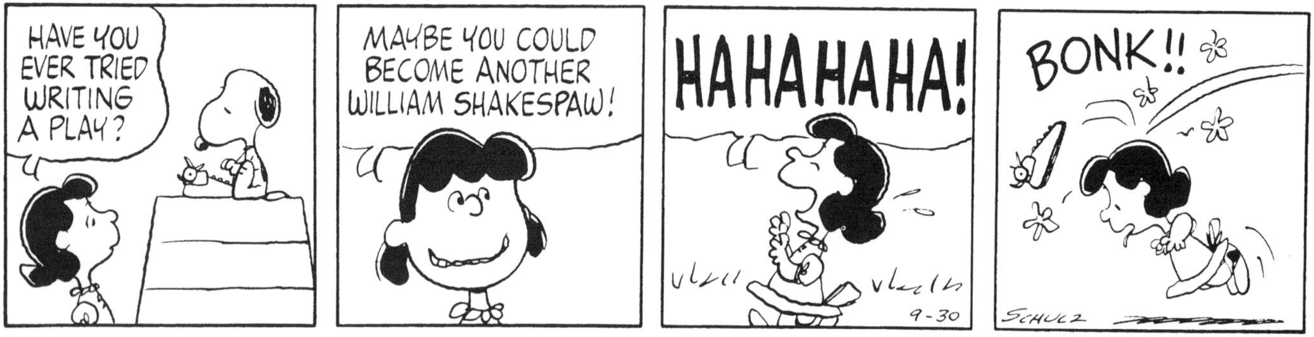
HAVE YOU EVER TRIED WRITING A PLAY?
MAYBE YOU COULD BECOME ANOTHER WILLIAM SHAKESPAW!
HAHAHAHA!
9-30
BONK!!
SCHULZ

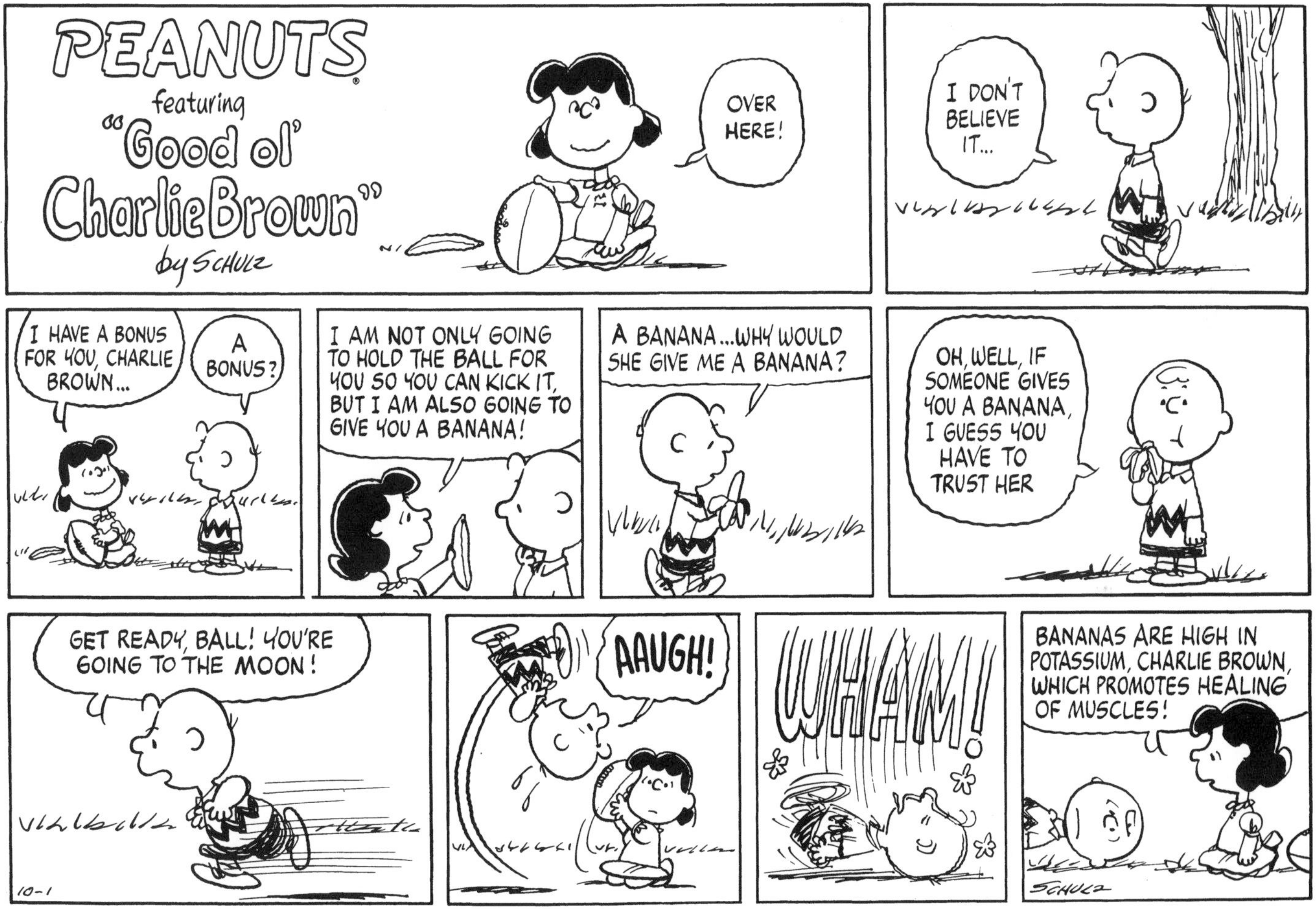
PEANUTS
featuring
"Good ol' Charlie Brown"
by SCHULZ
OVER HERE!
I DON'T BELIEVE IT...
I HAVE A BONUS FOR YOU, CHARLIE BROWN...
A BONUS?
I AM NOT ONLY GOING TO HOLD THE BALL FOR YOU SO YOU CAN KICK IT, BUT I AM ALSO GOING TO GIVE YOU A BANANA!
A BANANA...WHY WOULD SHE GIVE ME A BANANA?
OH, WELL, IF SOMEONE GIVES YOU A BANANA, I GUESS YOU HAVE TO TRUST HER
GET READY, BALL! YOU'RE GOING TO THE MOON!
10-1
AAUGH!
WHAM!
BANANAS ARE HIGH IN POTASSIUM, CHARLIE BROWN, WHICH PROMOTES HEALING OF MUSCLES!
SCHULZ

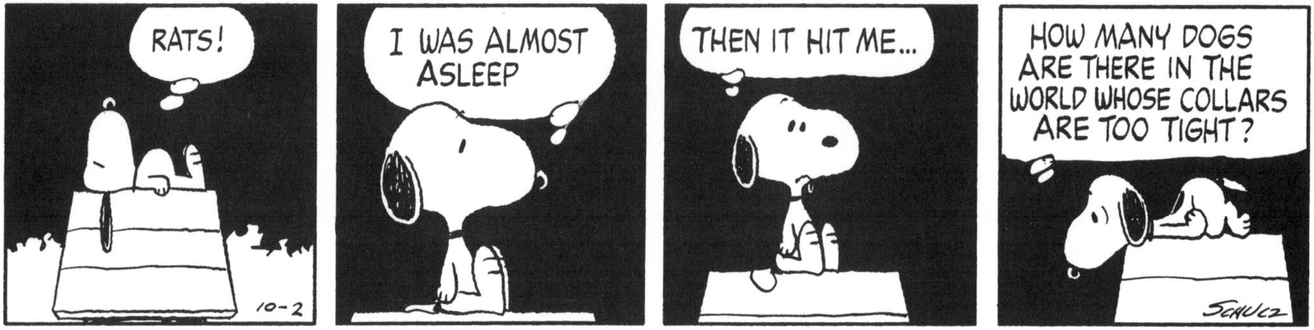
RATS!
I WAS ALMOST ASLEEP
THEN IT HIT ME...
HOW MANY DOGS ARE THERE IN THE WORLD WHOSE COLLARS ARE TOO TIGHT?
10-2
SCHULZ

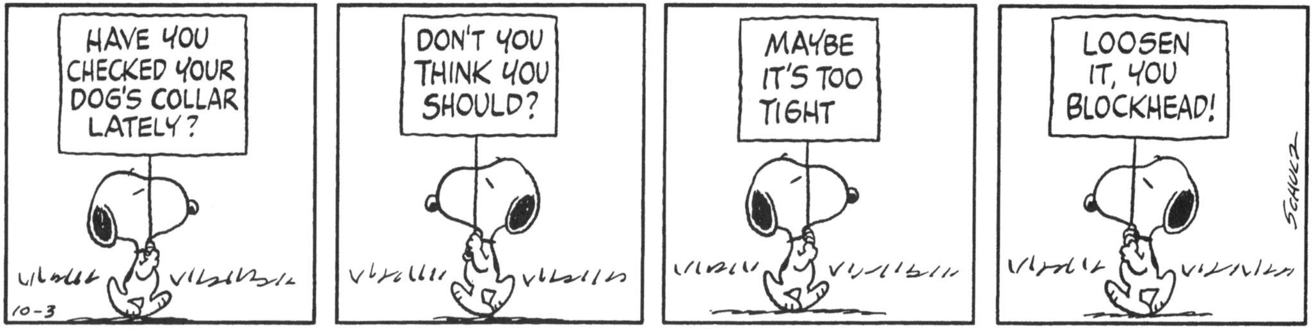
HAVE YOU CHECKED YOUR DOG'S COLLAR LATELY?
DON'T YOU THINK YOU SHOULD?
MAYBE IT'S TOO TIGHT
LOOSEN IT, YOU BLOCKHEAD!
10-3
SCHULZ

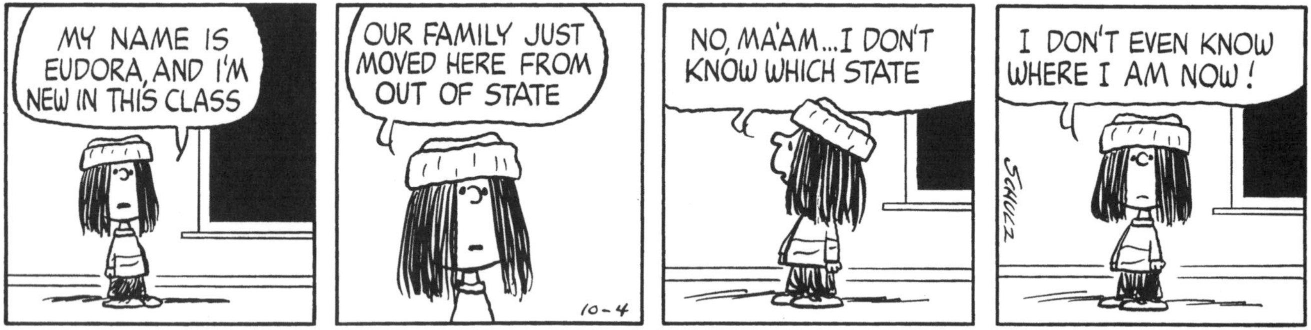
MY NAME IS EUDORA, AND I'M NEW IN THIS CLASS
OUR FAMILY JUST MOVED HERE FROM OUT OF STATE
NO, MA'AM...I DON'T KNOW WHICH STATE
I DON'T EVEN KNOW WHERE I AM NOW!
10-4
SCHULZ

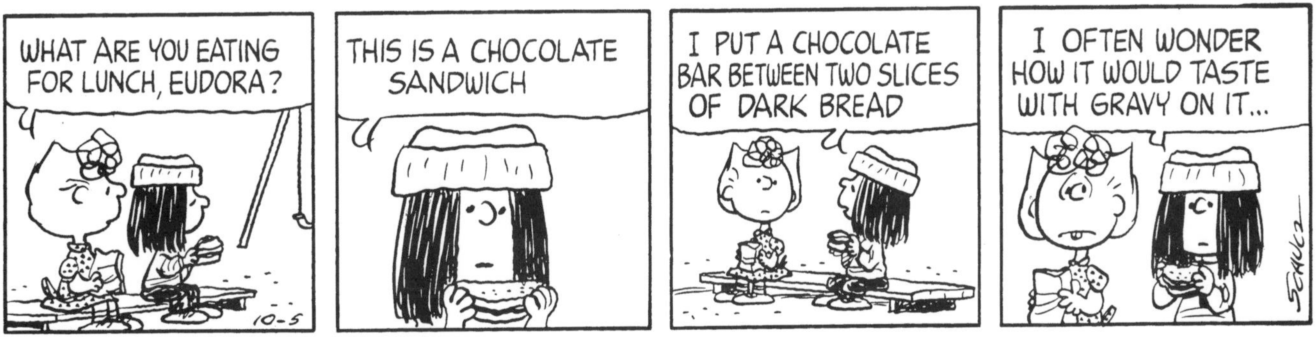
WHAT ARE YOU EATING FOR LUNCH, EUDORA?
10-5
THIS IS A CHOCOLATE SANDWICH
I PUT A CHOCOLATE BAR BETWEEN TWO SLICES OF DARK BREAD
I OFTEN WONDER HOW IT WOULD TASTE WITH GRAVY ON IT...
SCHULZ

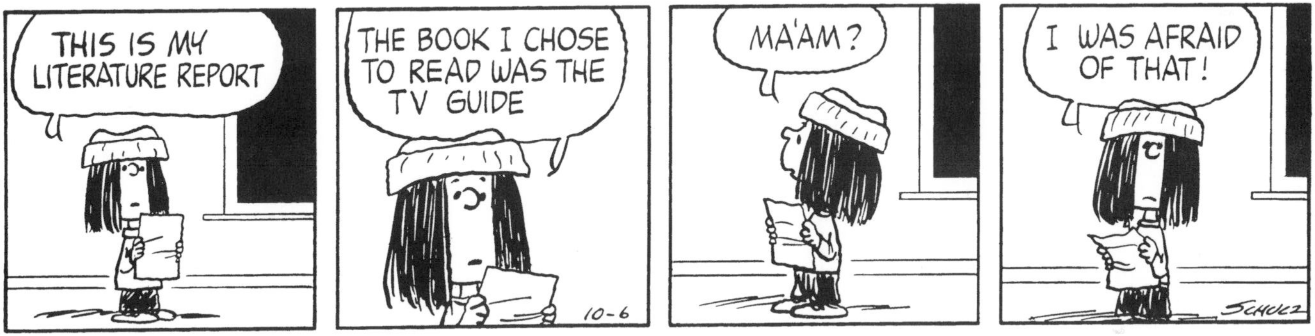
THIS IS MY LITERATURE REPORT
THE BOOK I CHOSE TO READ WAS THE TV GUIDE
10-6
MA'AM?
I WAS AFRAID OF THAT!
SCHULZ

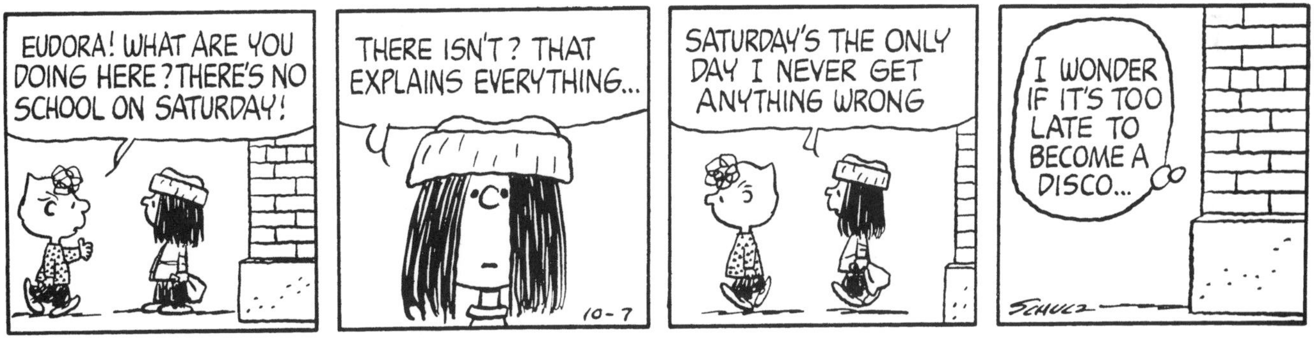
EUDORA! WHAT ARE YOU DOING HERE? THERE'S NO SCHOOL ON SATURDAY!
THERE ISN'T? THAT EXPLAINS EVERYTHING...
10-7
SATURDAY'S THE ONLY DAY I NEVER GET ANYTHING WRONG
I WONDER IF IT'S TOO LATE TO BECOME A DISCO...
SCHULZ

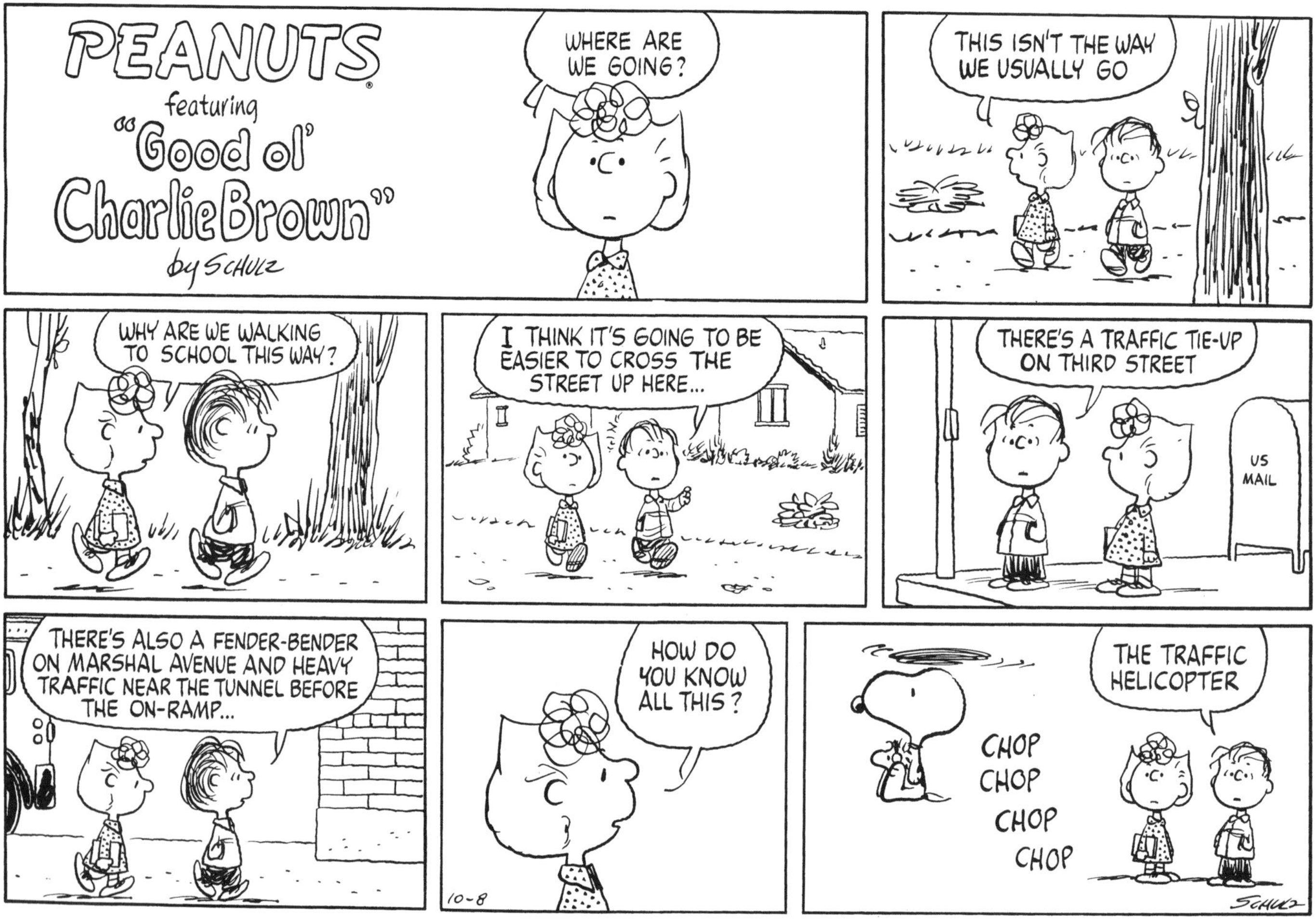
PEANUTS
featuring "Good ol' Charlie Brown"
by SCHULZ
WHERE ARE WE GOING?
THIS ISN'T THE WAY WE USUALLY GO
WHY ARE WE WALKING TO SCHOOL THIS WAY?
I THINK IT'S GOING TO BE EASIER TO CROSS THE STREET UP HERE...
THERE'S A TRAFFIC TIE-UP ON THIRD STREET
US MAIL
THERE'S ALSO A FENDER-BENDER ON MARSHAL AVENUE AND HEAVY TRAFFIC NEAR THE TUNNEL BEFORE THE ON-RAMP...
HOW DO YOU KNOW ALL THIS?
10-8
THE TRAFFIC HELICOPTER
CHOP
CHOP
CHOP
CHOP
SCHULZ

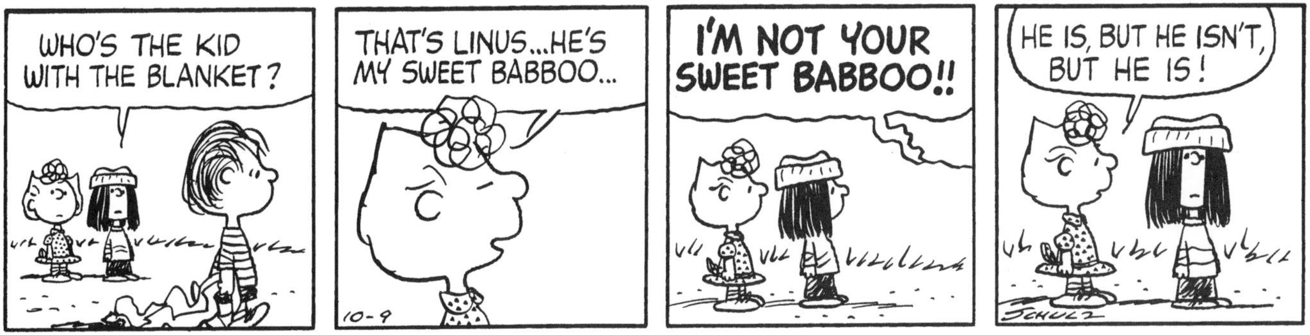
WHO'S THE KID WITH THE BLANKET?
THAT'S LINUS...HE'S MY SWEET BABBOO...
10-9
I'M NOT YOUR SWEET BABBOO!!
HE IS, BUT HE ISN'T, BUT HE IS!
SCHULZ

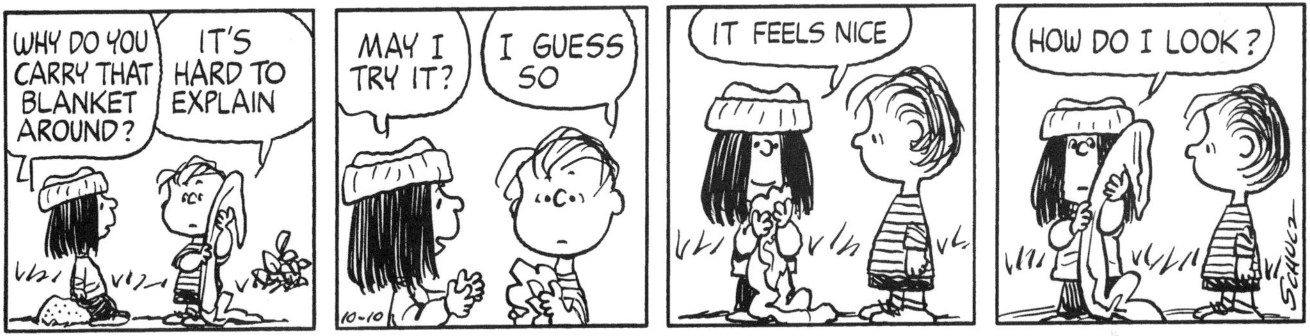
WHY DO YOU CARRY THAT BLANKET AROUND?
IT'S HARD TO EXPLAIN
MAY I TRY IT?
I GUESS SO
10-10
IT FEELS NICE
HOW DO I LOOK?
SCHULZ

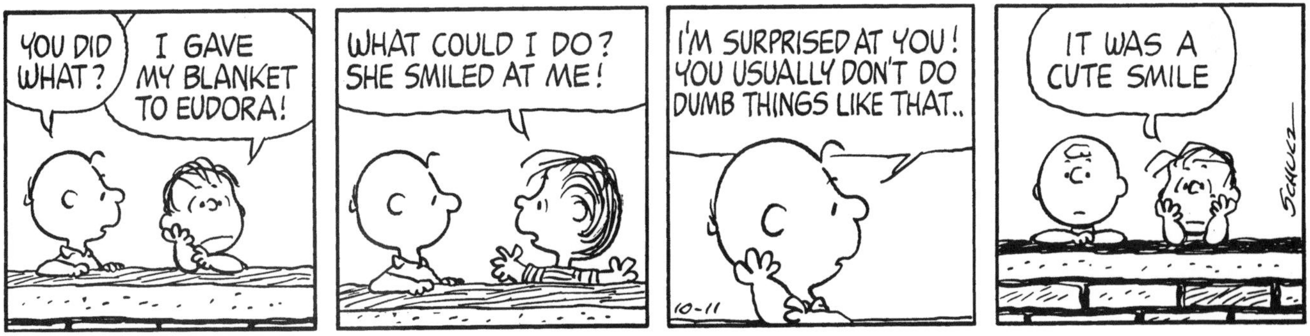
YOU DID WHAT?
I GAVE MY BLANKET TO EUDORA!
WHAT COULD I DO? SHE SMILED AT ME!
I'M SURPRISED AT YOU! YOU USUALLY DON'T DO DUMB THINGS LIKE THAT..
10-11
IT WAS A CUTE SMILE
SCHULZ

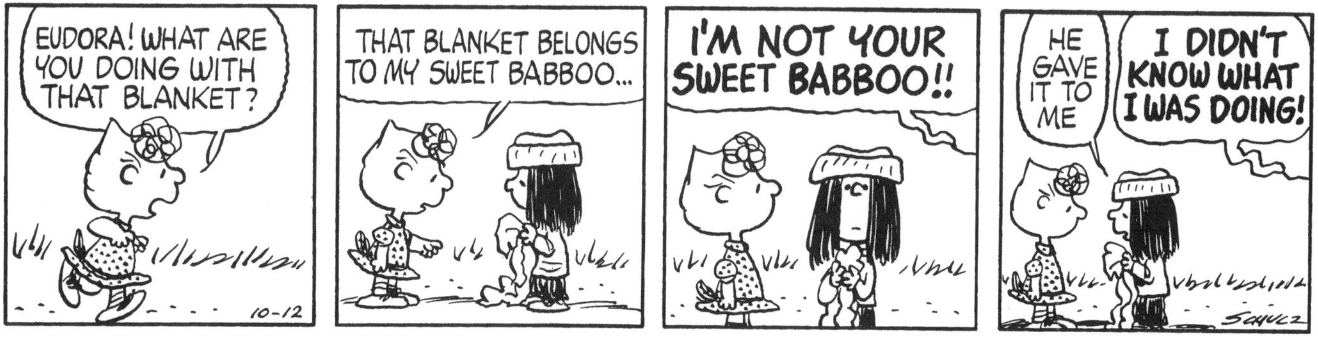
EUDORA! WHAT ARE YOU DOING WITH THAT BLANKET?
THAT BLANKET BELONGS TO MY SWEET BABBOO...
I'M NOT YOUR SWEET BABBOO!!
HE GAVE IT TO ME
I DIDN'T KNOW WHAT I WAS DOING!
10-12
SCHULZ

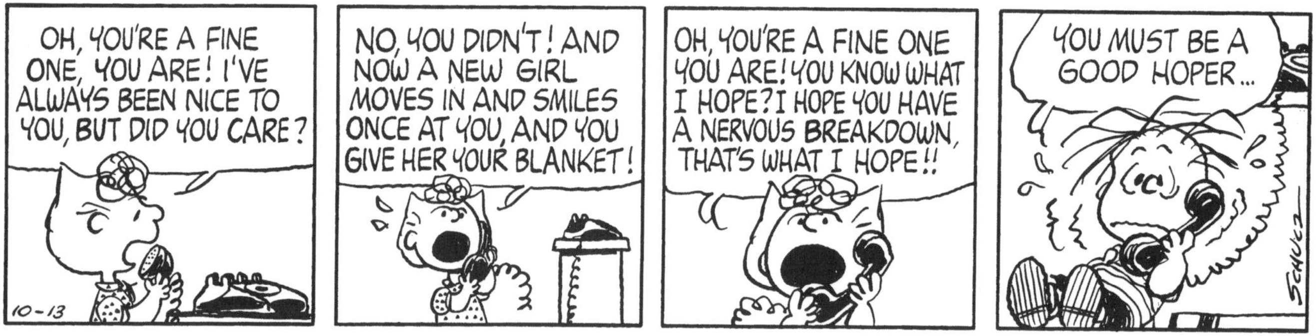
OH, YOU'RE A FINE ONE, YOU ARE! I'VE ALWAYS BEEN NICE TO YOU, BUT DID YOU CARE?
10-13
NO, YOU DIDN'T! AND NOW A NEW GIRL MOVES IN AND SMILES ONCE AT YOU, AND YOU GIVE HER YOUR BLANKET!
OH, YOU'RE A FINE ONE YOU ARE! YOU KNOW WHAT I HOPE? I HOPE YOU HAVE A NERVOUS BREAKDOWN, THAT'S WHAT I HOPE!!
YOU MUST BE A GOOD HOPER...
SCHULZ

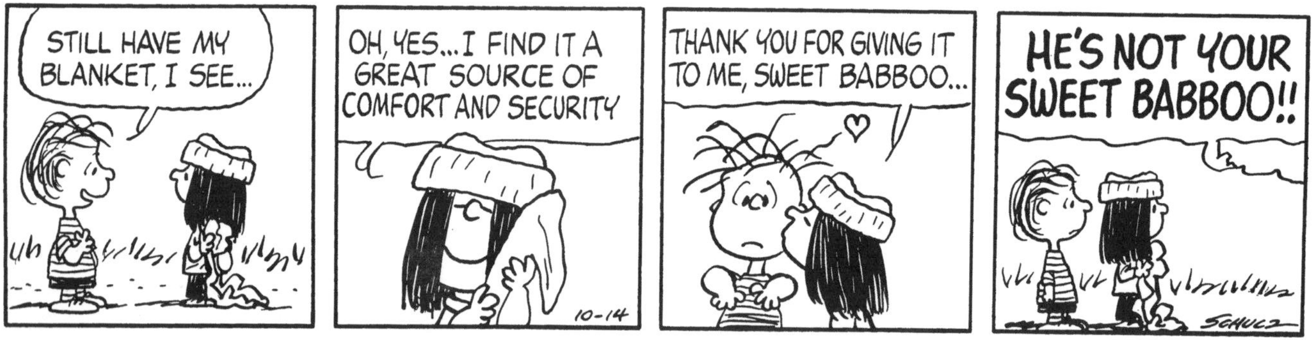
STILL HAVE MY BLANKET, I SEE...
OH, YES...I FIND IT A GREAT SOURCE OF COMFORT AND SECURITY
10-14
THANK YOU FOR GIVING IT TO ME, SWEET BABBOO...
HE'S NOT YOUR SWEET BABBOO!!
SCHULZ

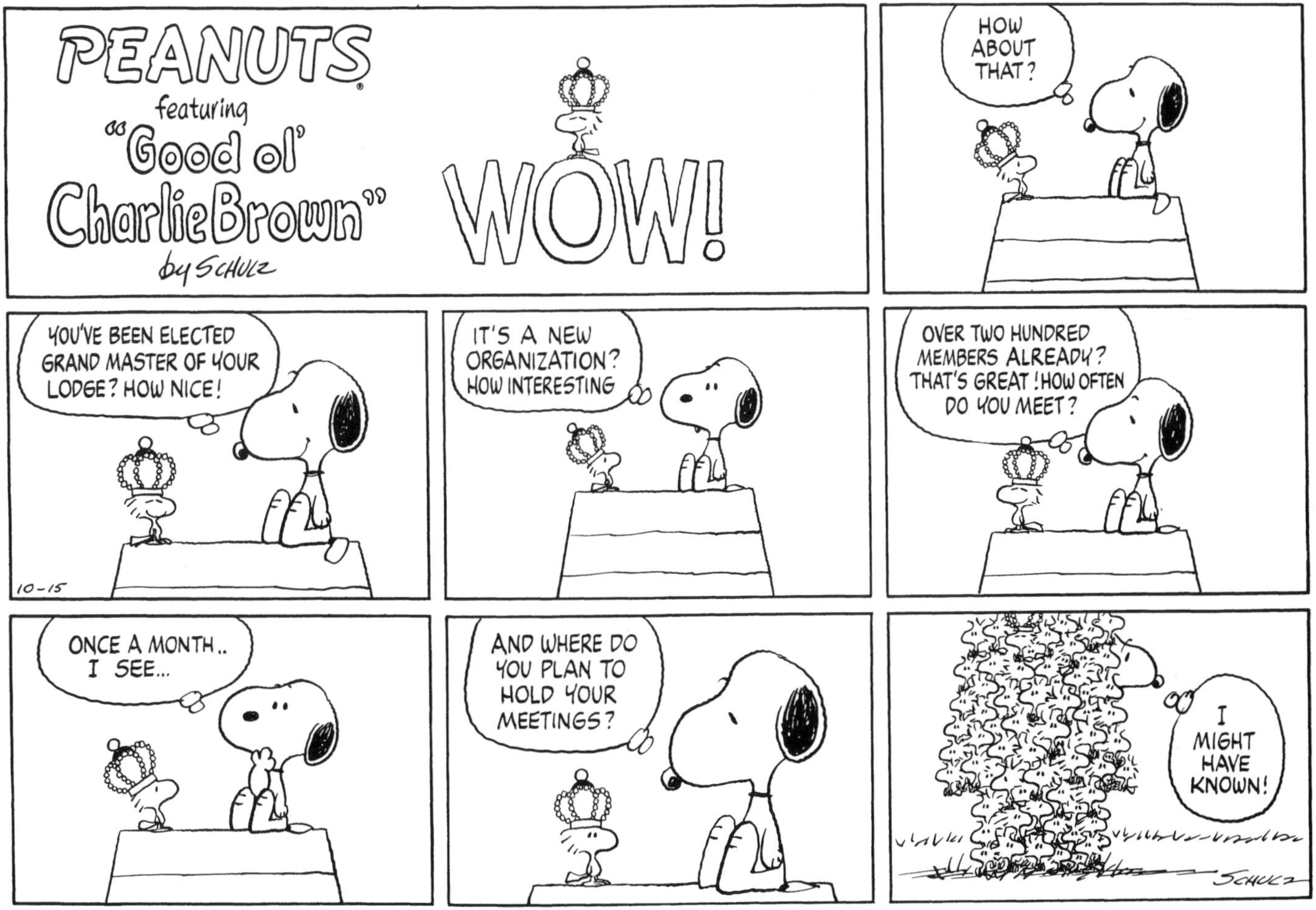
PEANUTS
featuring
"Good ol' Charlie Brown"
by SCHULZ
WOW!
HOW ABOUT THAT?
YOU'VE BEEN ELECTED GRAND MASTER OF YOUR LODGE? HOW NICE!
10-15
IT'S A NEW ORGANIZATION? HOW INTERESTING
OVER TWO HUNDRED MEMBERS ALREADY? THAT'S GREAT! HOW OFTEN DO YOU MEET?
ONCE A MONTH.. I SEE...
AND WHERE DO YOU PLAN TO HOLD YOUR MEETINGS?
I MIGHT HAVE KNOWN!
SCHULZ

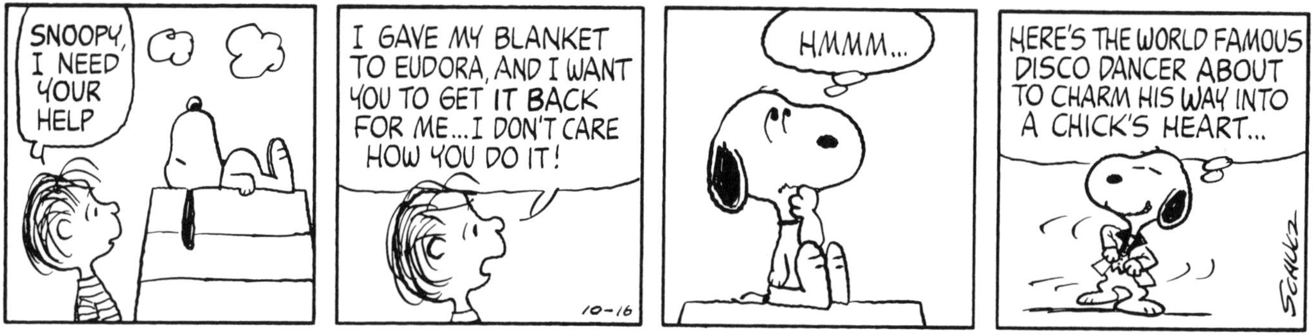
SNOOPY, I NEED YOUR HELP
I GAVE MY BLANKET TO EUDORA, AND I WANT YOU TO GET IT BACK FOR ME...I DON'T CARE HOW YOU DO IT!
10-16
HMMM...
HERE'S THE WORLD FAMOUS DISCO DANCER ABOUT TO CHARM HIS WAY INTO A CHICK'S HEART...
SCHULZ

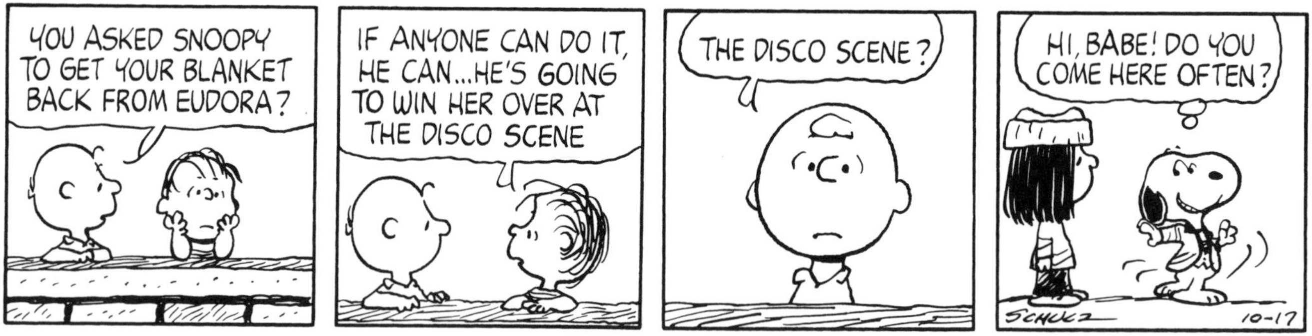
YOU ASKED SNOOPY TO GET YOUR BLANKET BACK FROM EUDORA?
IF ANYONE CAN DO IT, HE CAN...HE'S GOING TO WIN HER OVER AT THE DISCO SCENE
THE DISCO SCENE?
HI, BABE! DO YOU COME HERE OFTEN?
SCHULZ
10-17

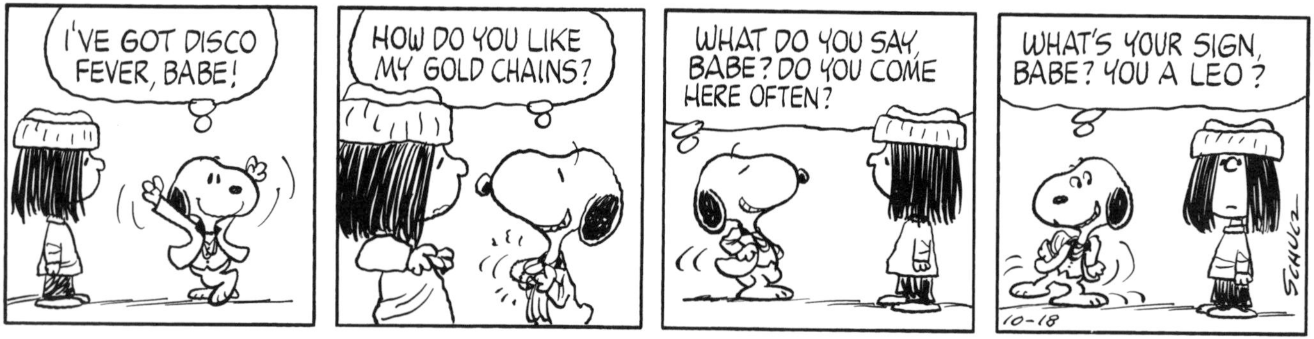
I'VE GOT DISCO FEVER, BABE!
HOW DO YOU LIKE MY GOLD CHAINS?
WHAT DO YOU SAY, BABE? DO YOU COME HERE OFTEN?
WHAT'S YOUR SIGN, BABE? YOU A LEO?
SCHULZ
10-18

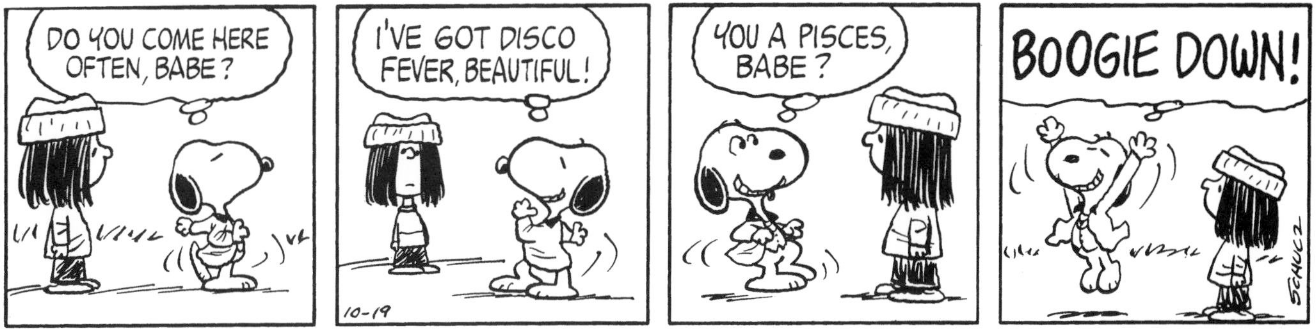
DO YOU COME HERE OFTEN, BABE?
I'VE GOT DISCO FEVER, BEAUTIFUL!
10-19
YOU A PISCES, BABE?
BOOGIE DOWN!
SCHULZ

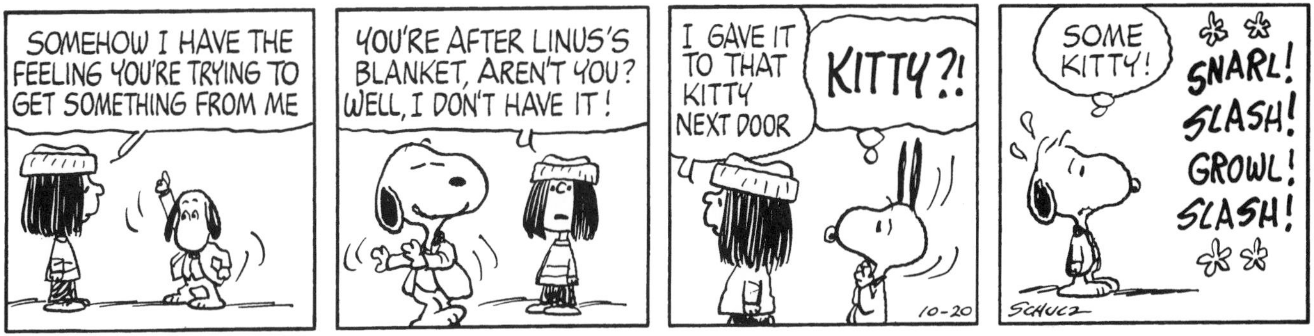
SOMEHOW I HAVE THE FEELING YOU'RE TRYING TO GET SOMETHING FROM ME
YOU'RE AFTER LINUS'S BLANKET, AREN'T YOU? WELL, I DON'T HAVE IT!
I GAVE IT TO THAT KITTY NEXT DOOR
KITTY?!
10-20
SOME KITTY!
SNARL! SLASH! GROWL! SLASH!
SCHULZ

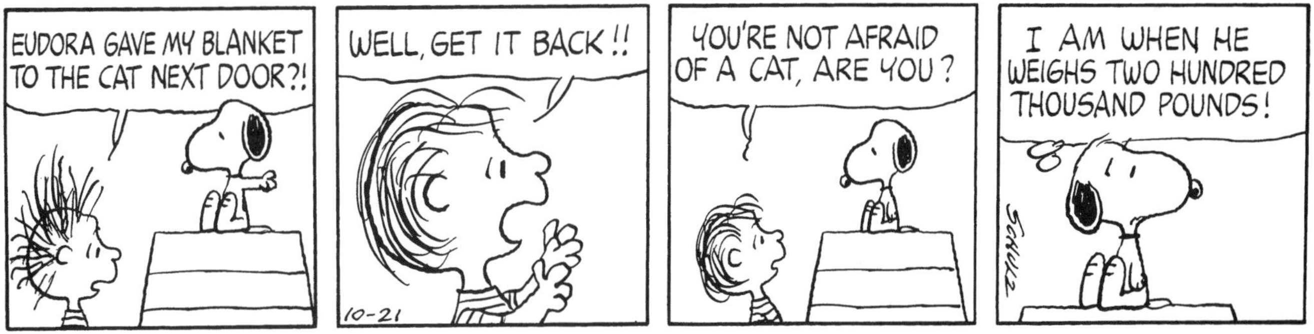
EUDORA GAVE MY BLANKET TO THE CAT NEXT DOOR?!
WELL, GET IT BACK!!
10-21
YOU'RE NOT AFRAID OF A CAT, ARE YOU?
SCHULZ
I AM WHEN HE WEIGHS TWO HUNDRED THOUSAND POUNDS!

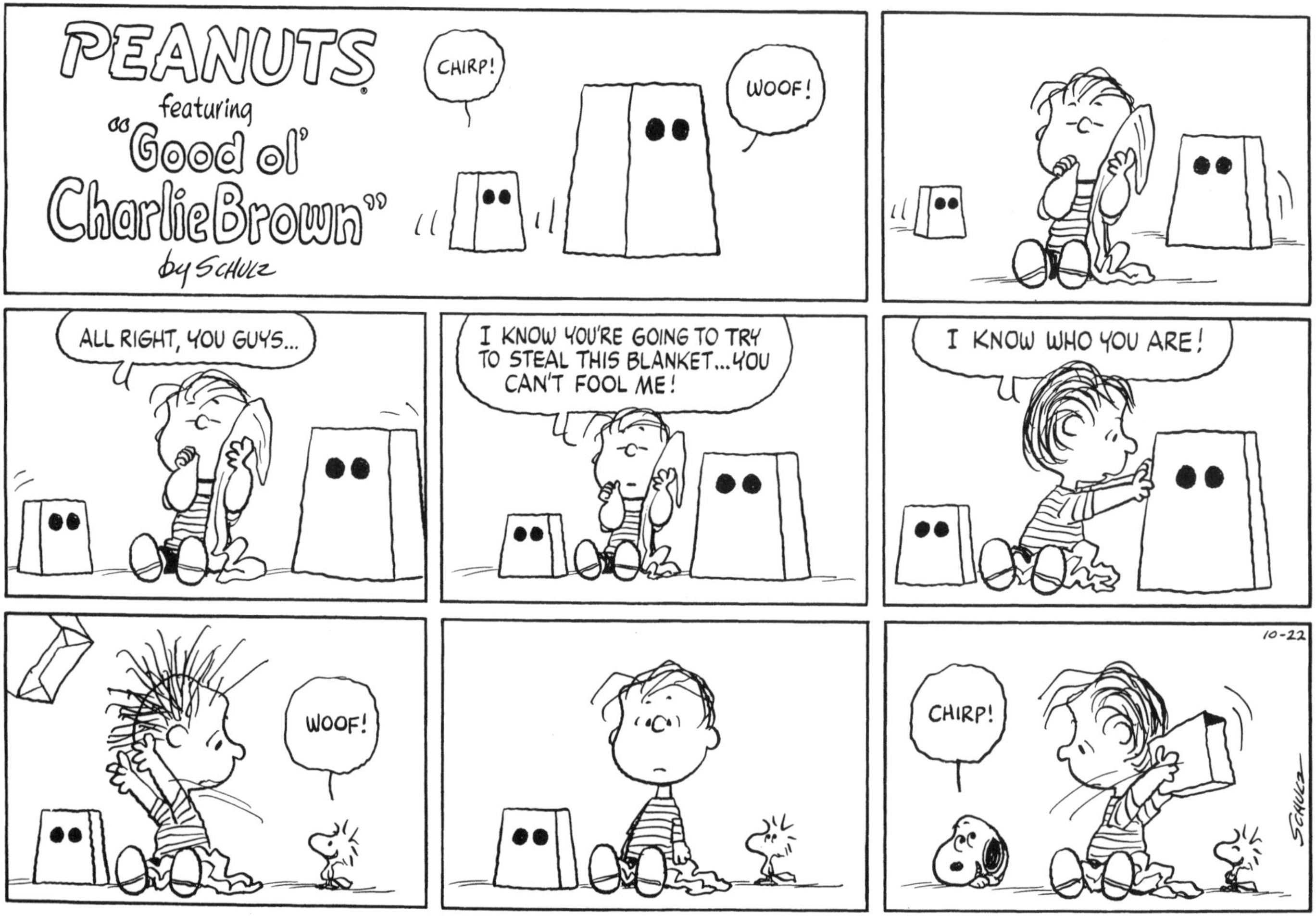
PEANUTS
featuring
"Good ol' Charlie Brown"
by SCHULZ
CHIRP!
WOOF!
ALL RIGHT, YOU GUYS...
I KNOW YOU'RE GOING TO TRY TO STEAL THIS BLANKET...YOU CAN'T FOOL ME!
I KNOW WHO YOU ARE!
WOOF!
10-22
CHIRP!
SCHULZ

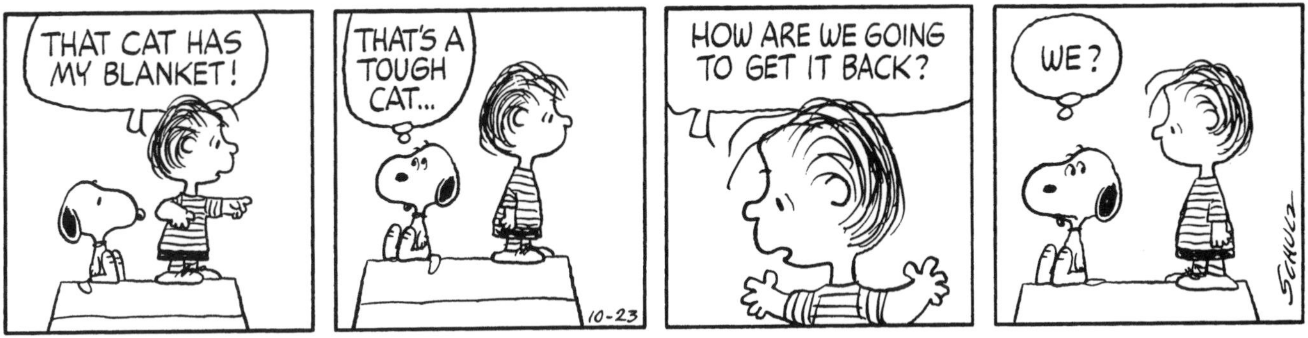
THAT CAT HAS MY BLANKET!
THAT'S A TOUGH CAT...
HOW ARE WE GOING TO GET IT BACK?
WE?
SCHULZ
10-23

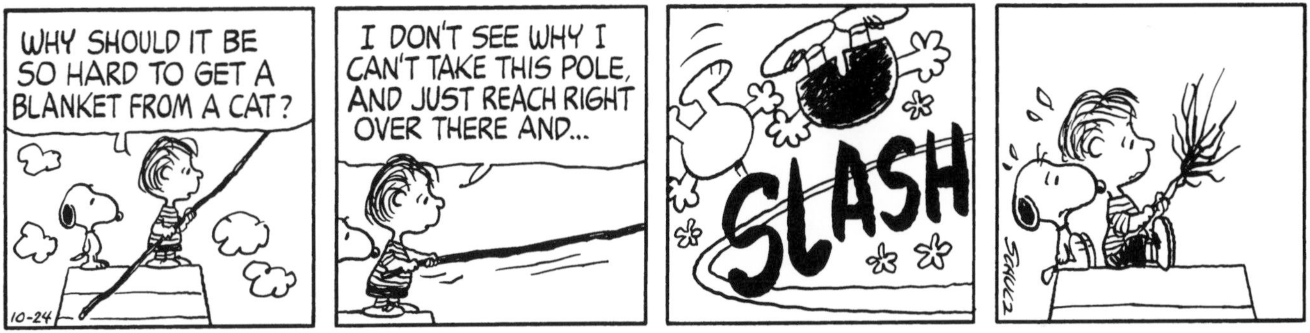
WHY SHOULD IT BE SO HARD TO GET A BLANKET FROM A CAT?
I DON'T SEE WHY I CAN'T TAKE THIS POLE, AND JUST REACH RIGHT OVER THERE AND...
SLASH
SCHULZ
10-24

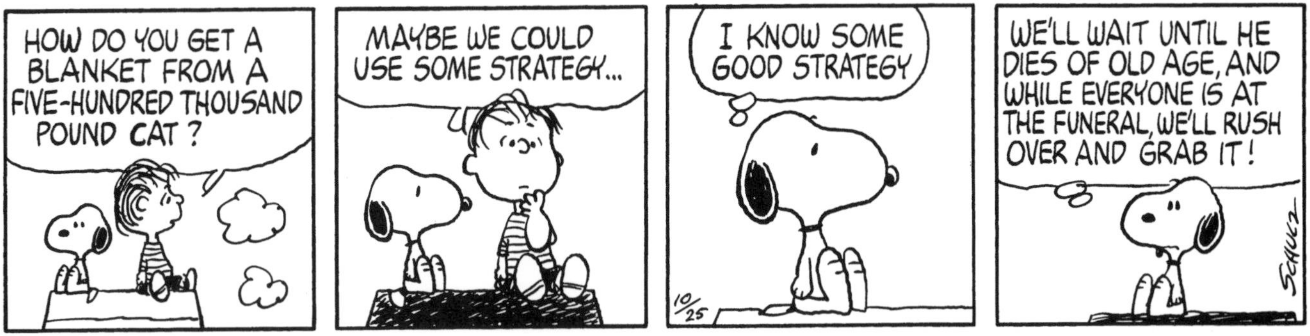
HOW DO YOU GET A BLANKET FROM A FIVE-HUNDRED THOUSAND POUND CAT?
MAYBE WE COULD USE SOME STRATEGY...
I KNOW SOME GOOD STRATEGY
WE'LL WAIT UNTIL HE DIES OF OLD AGE, AND WHILE EVERYONE IS AT THE FUNERAL, WE'LL RUSH OVER AND GRAB IT!
SCHULZ
10/25

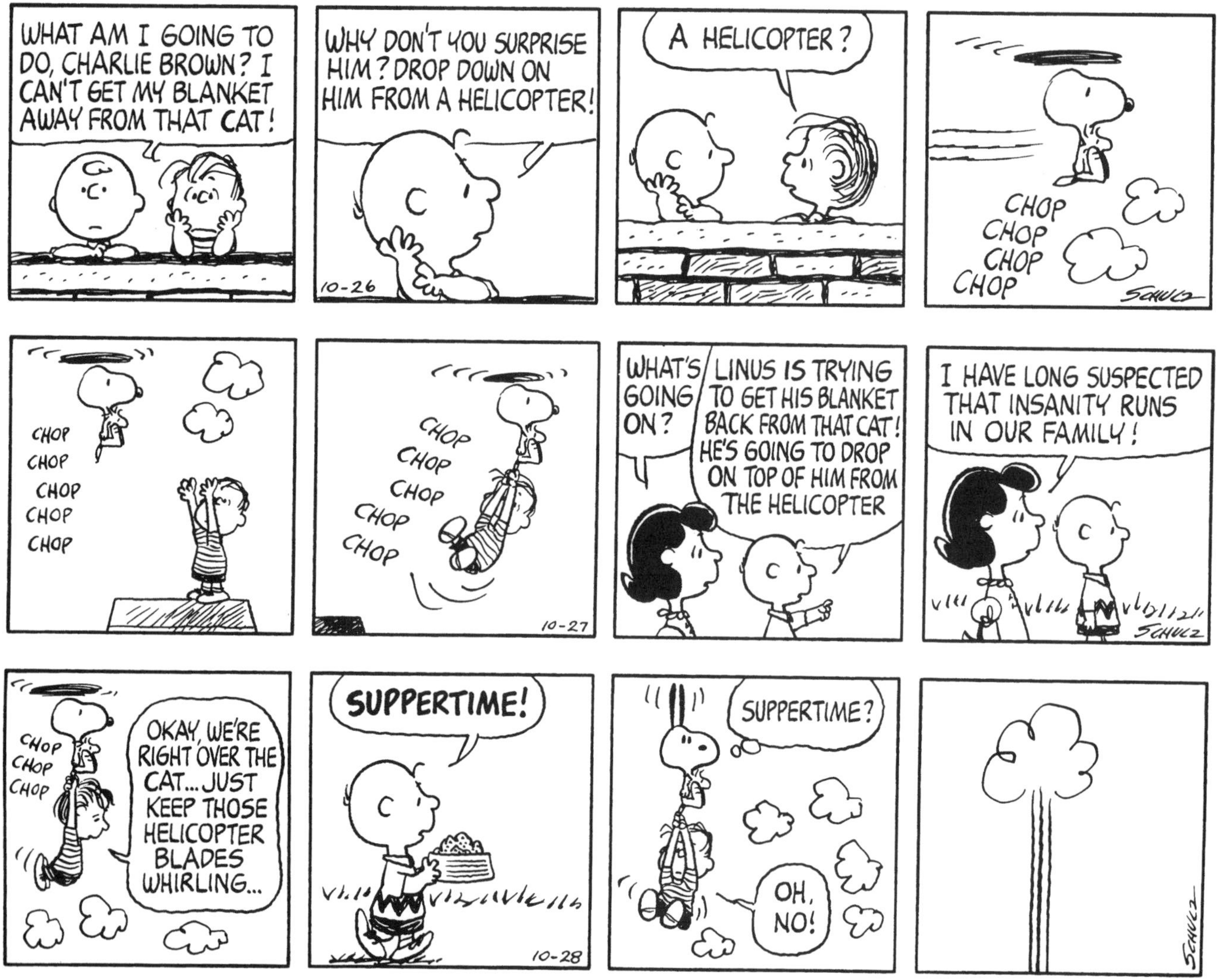

WHAT AM I GOING TO DO, CHARLIE BROWN? I CAN'T GET MY BLANKET AWAY FROM THAT CAT!
WHY DON'T YOU SURPRISE HIM? DROP DOWN ON HIM FROM A HELICOPTER!
10-26
A HELICOPTER?
CHOP CHOP CHOP CHOP
SCHULZ
CHOP CHOP CHOP CHOP CHOP
CHOP CHOP CHOP CHOP CHOP
10-27
WHAT'S GOING ON?
LINUS IS TRYING TO GET HIS BLANKET BACK FROM THAT CAT! HE'S GOING TO DROP ON TOP OF HIM FROM THE HELICOPTER
I HAVE LONG SUSPECTED THAT INSANITY RUNS IN OUR FAMILY!
SCHULZ
CHOP CHOP CHOP
OKAY, WE'RE RIGHT OVER THE CAT... JUST KEEP THOSE HELICOPTER BLADES WHIRLING...
SUPPERTIME!
10-28
SUPPERTIME?
OH, NO!
SCHULZ

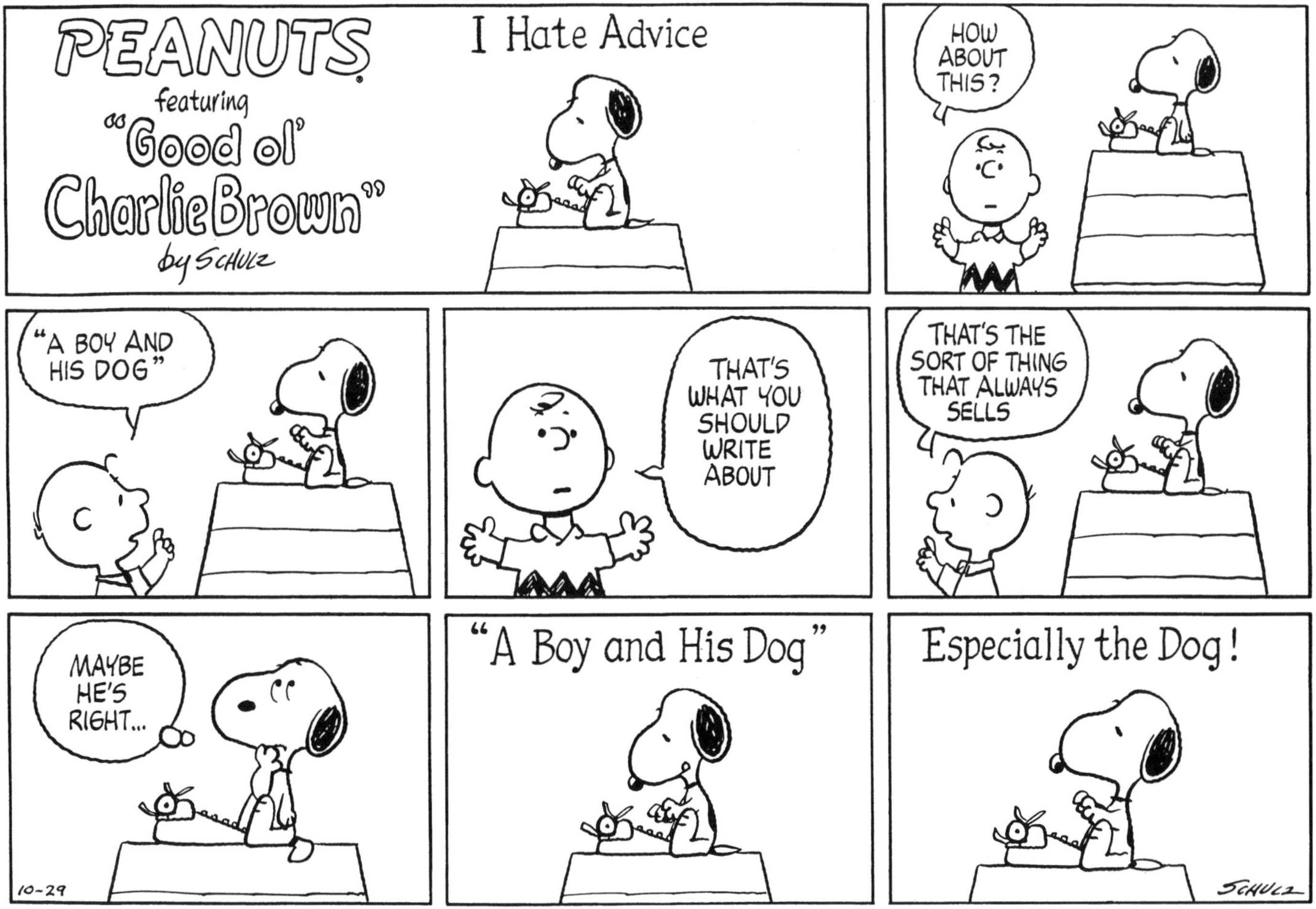
PEANUTS
featuring
"Good ol' Charlie Brown"
by SCHULZ
I Hate Advice
HOW ABOUT THIS?
"A BOY AND HIS DOG"
THAT'S WHAT YOU SHOULD WRITE ABOUT
THAT'S THE SORT OF THING THAT ALWAYS SELLS
MAYBE HE'S RIGHT...
10-29
"A Boy and His Dog"
Especially the Dog!
SCHULZ

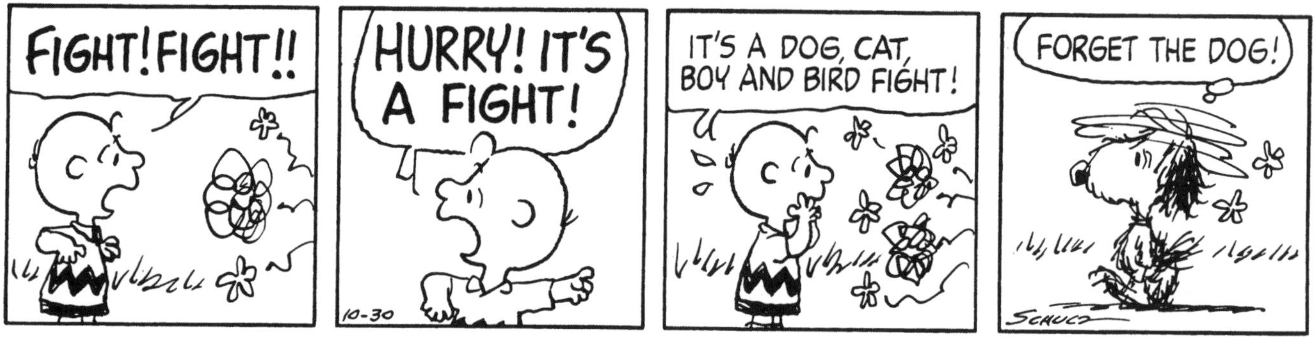
FIGHT! FIGHT!!
HURRY! IT'S A FIGHT!
10-30
IT'S A DOG, CAT, BOY AND BIRD FIGHT!
FORGET THE DOG!

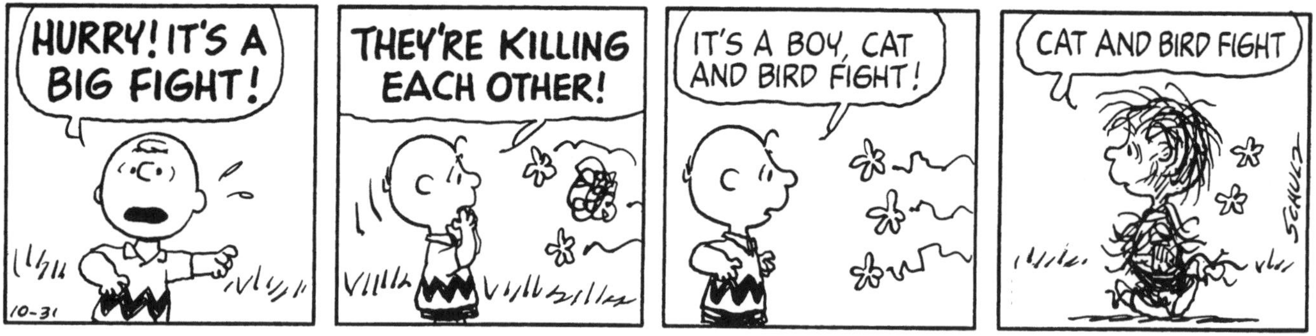
HURRY! IT'S A BIG FIGHT!
10-31
THEY'RE KILLING EACH OTHER!
IT'S A BOY, CAT AND BIRD FIGHT!
CAT AND BIRD FIGHT

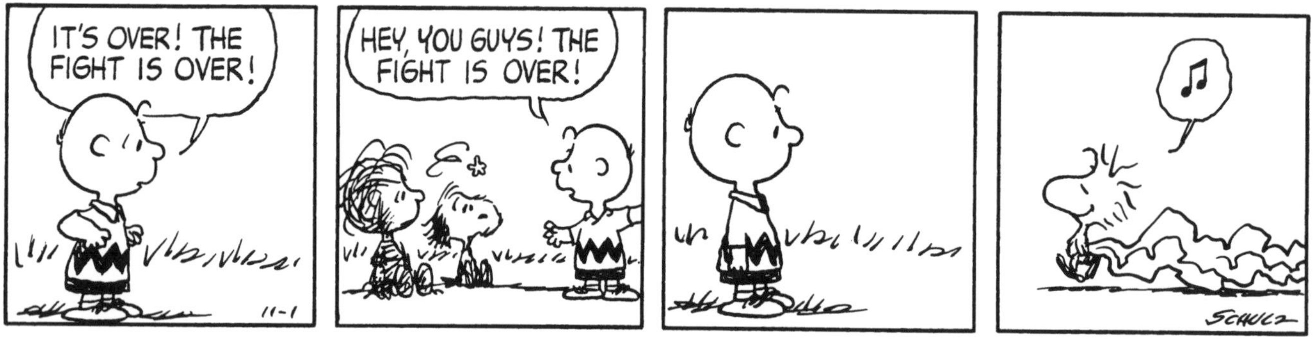
IT'S OVER! THE FIGHT IS OVER!
11-1
HEY, YOU GUYS! THE FIGHT IS OVER!

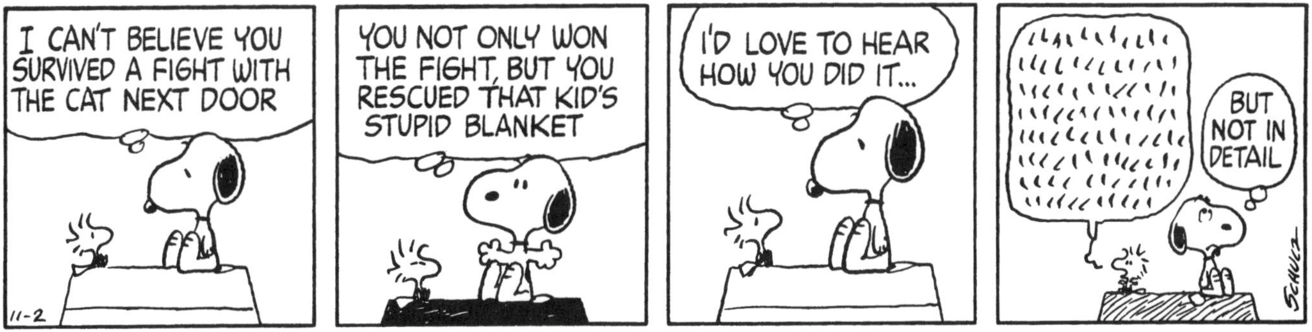
11-2
I CAN'T BELIEVE YOU SURVIVED A FIGHT WITH THE CAT NEXT DOOR
YOU NOT ONLY WON THE FIGHT, BUT YOU RESCUED THAT KID'S STUPID BLANKET
I'D LOVE TO HEAR HOW YOU DID IT...
BUT NOT IN DETAIL
SCHULZ

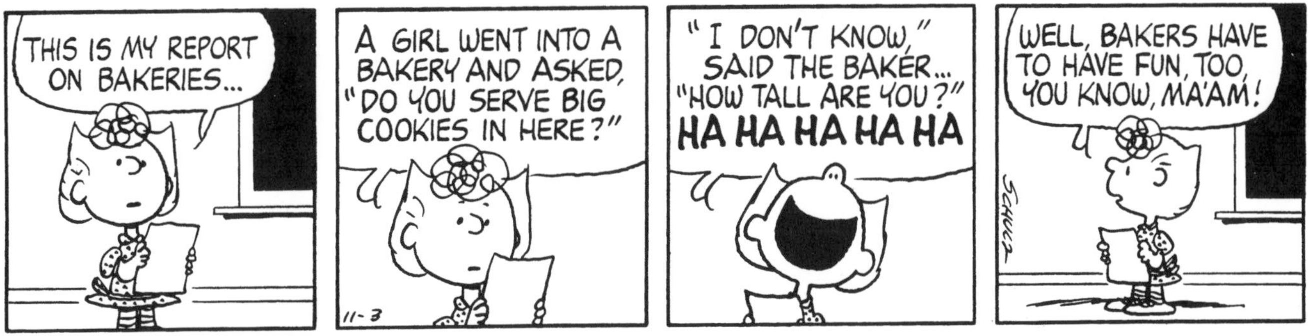
THIS IS MY REPORT ON BAKERIES...
A GIRL WENT INTO A BAKERY AND ASKED, "DO YOU SERVE BIG COOKIES IN HERE?"
11-3
"I DON'T KNOW," SAID THE BAKER... "HOW TALL ARE YOU?" HA HA HA HA HA
WELL, BAKERS HAVE TO HAVE FUN, TOO, YOU KNOW, MA'AM!
SCHULZ

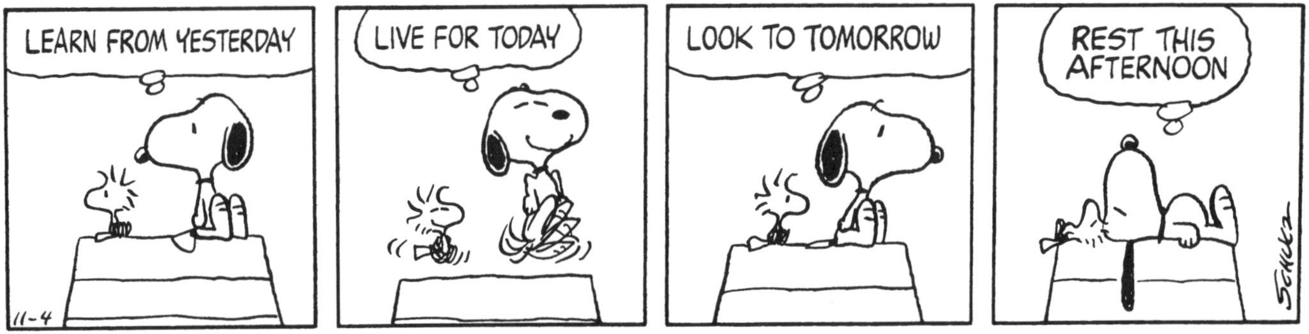
LEARN FROM YESTERDAY
11-4
LIVE FOR TODAY
LOOK TO TOMORROW
REST THIS AFTERNOON
SCHULZ

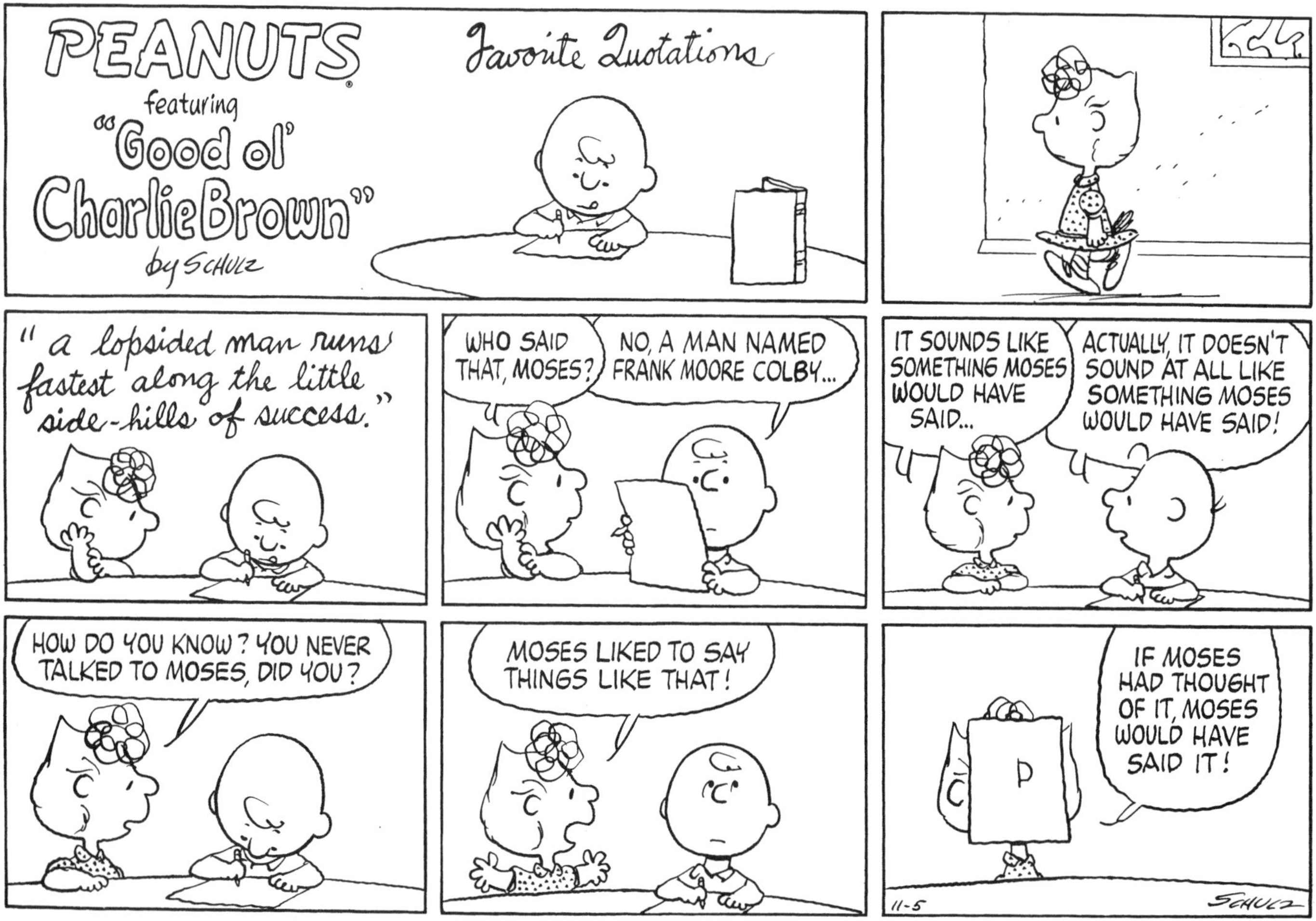
PEANUTS
featuring
"Good ol' CharlieBrown"
by SCHULZ
Favorite Quotations
" a lopsided man runs fastest along the little side-hills of success."
WHO SAID THAT, MOSES?
NO, A MAN NAMED FRANK MOORE COLBY...
IT SOUNDS LIKE SOMETHING MOSES WOULD HAVE SAID...
ACTUALLY, IT DOESN'T SOUND AT ALL LIKE SOMETHING MOSES WOULD HAVE SAID!
HOW DO YOU KNOW? YOU NEVER TALKED TO MOSES, DID YOU?
MOSES LIKED TO SAY THINGS LIKE THAT!
IF MOSES HAD THOUGHT OF IT, MOSES WOULD HAVE SAID IT!
11-5
SCHULZ

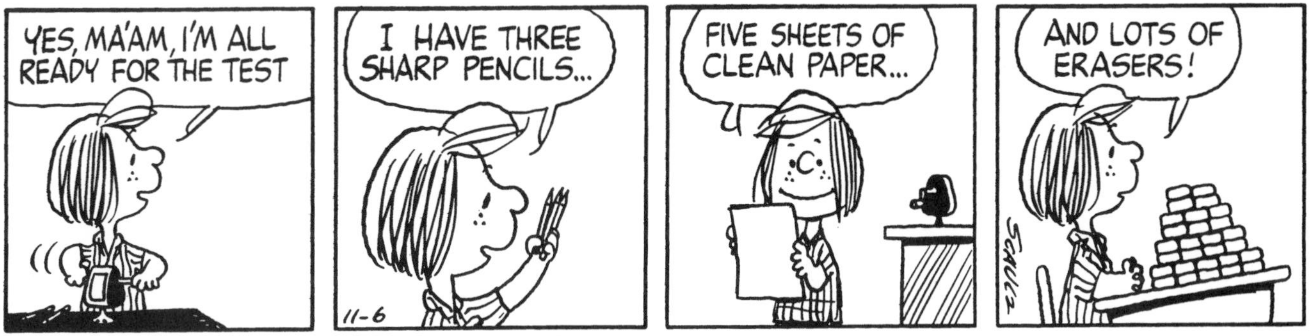
YES, MA'AM, I'M ALL READY FOR THE TEST
I HAVE THREE SHARP PENCILS...
11-6
FIVE SHEETS OF CLEAN PAPER...
AND LOTS OF ERASERS!
SCHULZ

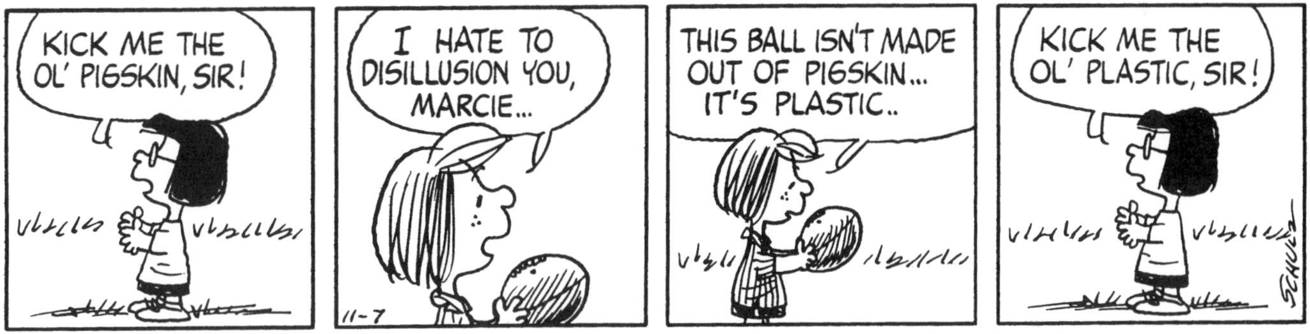
KICK ME THE OL' PIGSKIN, SIR!
I HATE TO DISILLUSION YOU, MARCIE...
11-7
THIS BALL ISN'T MADE OUT OF PIGSKIN... IT'S PLASTIC..
KICK ME THE OL' PLASTIC, SIR!
SCHULZ

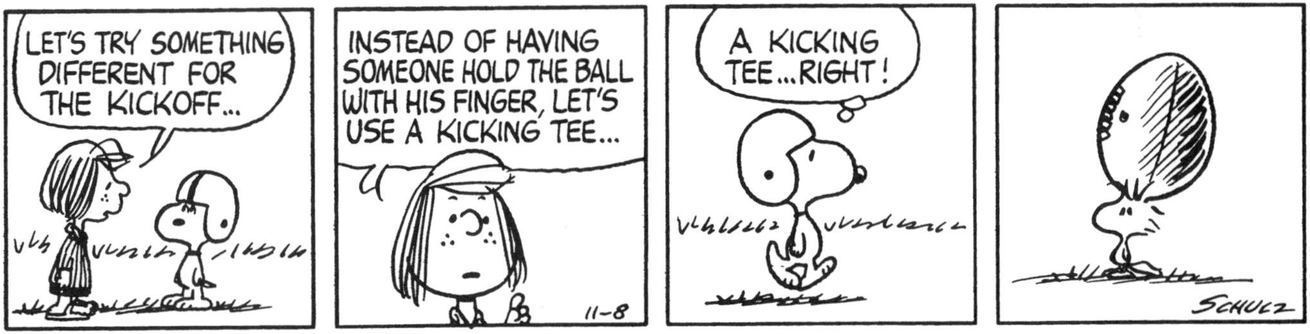
LET'S TRY SOMETHING DIFFERENT FOR THE KICKOFF...
INSTEAD OF HAVING SOMEONE HOLD THE BALL WITH HIS FINGER, LET'S USE A KICKING TEE...
11-8
A KICKING TEE...RIGHT!
SCHULZ

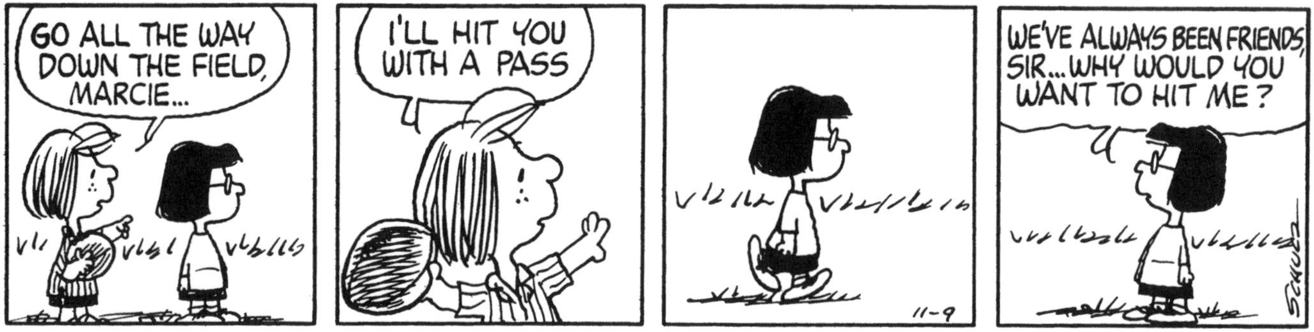
GO ALL THE WAY DOWN THE FIELD, MARCIE...
I'LL HIT YOU WITH A PASS
WE'VE ALWAYS BEEN FRIENDS, SIR...WHY WOULD YOU WANT TO HIT ME?

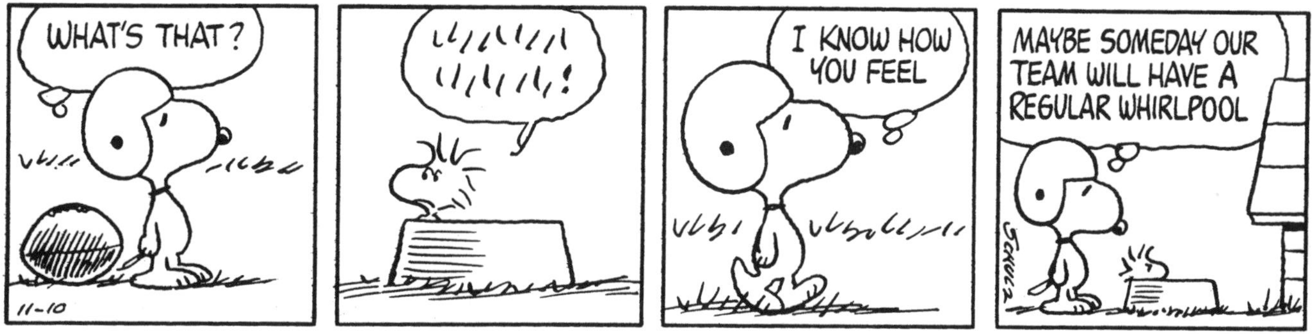
WHAT'S THAT?
I KNOW HOW YOU FEEL
MAYBE SOMEDAY OUR TEAM WILL HAVE A REGULAR WHIRLPOOL

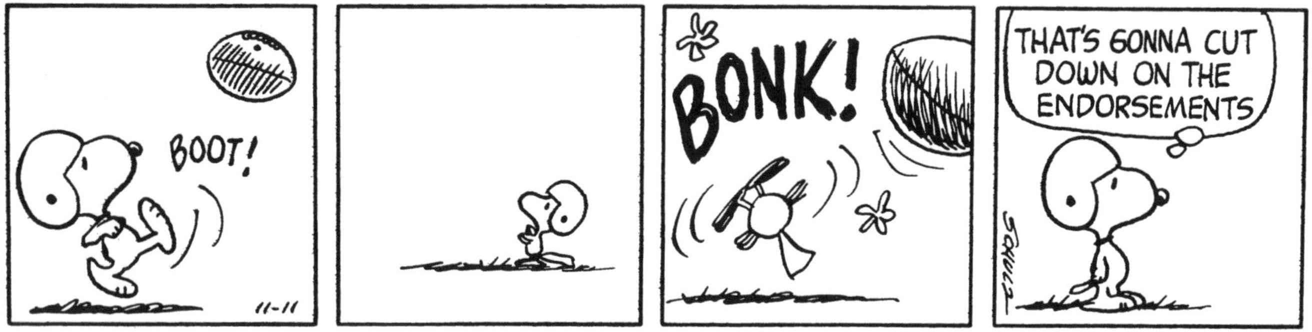
BOOT!
BONK!
THAT'S GONNA CUT DOWN ON THE ENDORSEMENTS

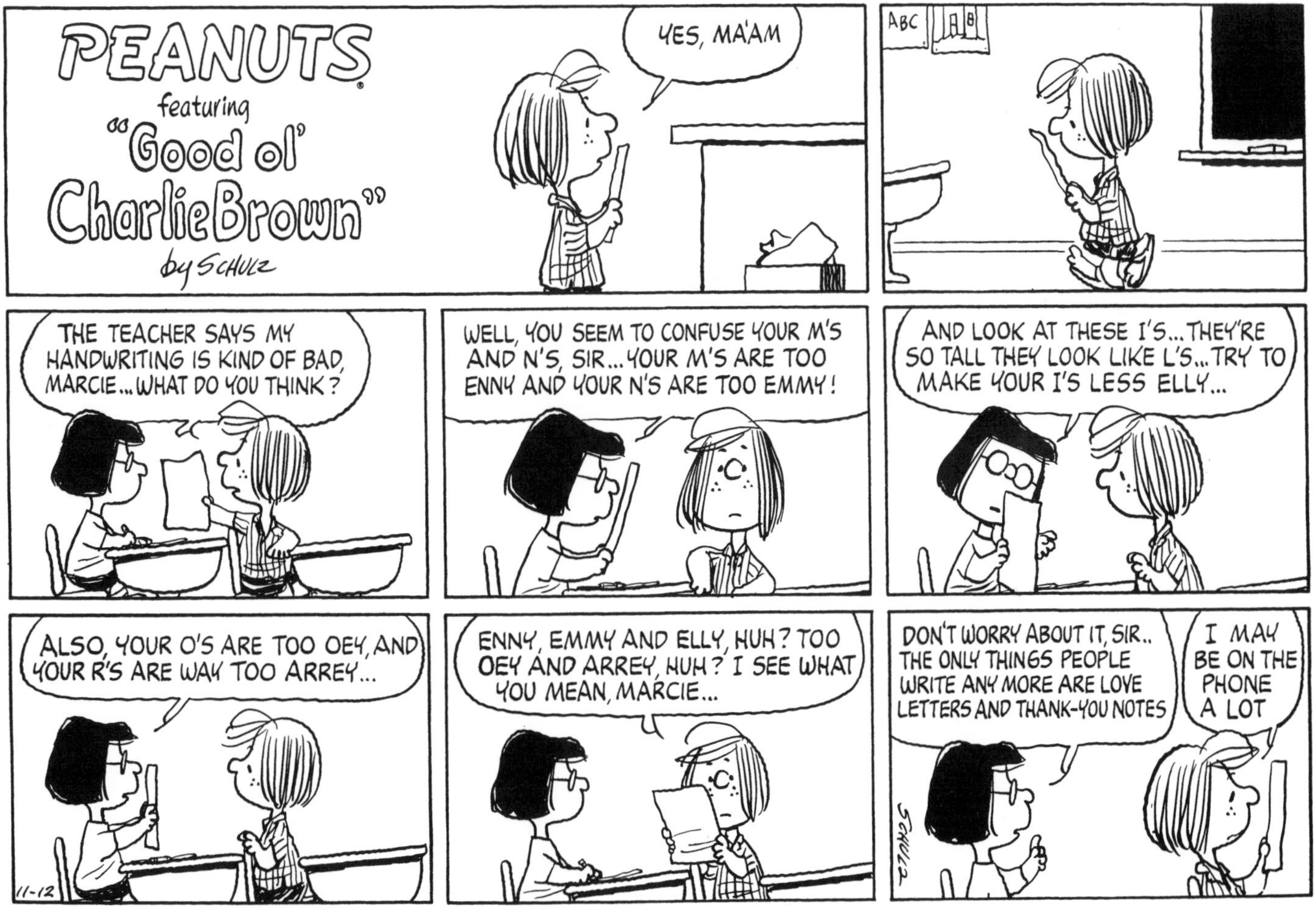
PEANUTS
featuring "Good ol' Charlie Brown"
by SCHULZ
YES, MA'AM
ABC
THE TEACHER SAYS MY HANDWRITING IS KIND OF BAD, MARCIE... WHAT DO YOU THINK?
WELL, YOU SEEM TO CONFUSE YOUR M'S AND N'S, SIR... YOUR M'S ARE TOO ENNY AND YOUR N'S ARE TOO EMMY!
AND LOOK AT THESE I'S... THEY'RE SO TALL THEY LOOK LIKE L'S... TRY TO MAKE YOUR I'S LESS ELLY...
ALSO, YOUR O'S ARE TOO OEY, AND YOUR R'S ARE WAY TOO ARREY...
11-12
ENNY, EMMY AND ELLY, HUH? TOO OEY AND ARREY, HUH? I SEE WHAT YOU MEAN, MARCIE...
DON'T WORRY ABOUT IT, SIR.. THE ONLY THINGS PEOPLE WRITE ANY MORE ARE LOVE LETTERS AND THANK-YOU NOTES
I MAY BE ON THE PHONE A LOT
SCHULZ

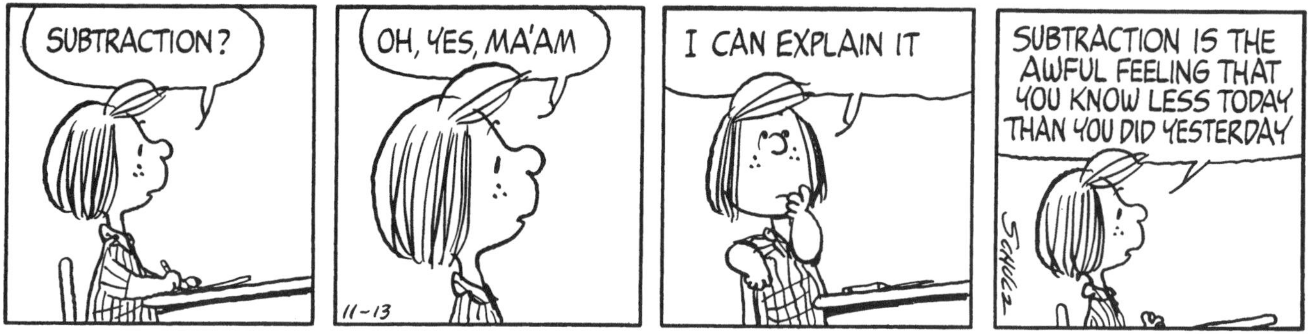
SUBTRACTION?
OH, YES, MA'AM
11-13
I CAN EXPLAIN IT
SUBTRACTION IS THE AWFUL FEELING THAT YOU KNOW LESS TODAY THAN YOU DID YESTERDAY
SCHULZ

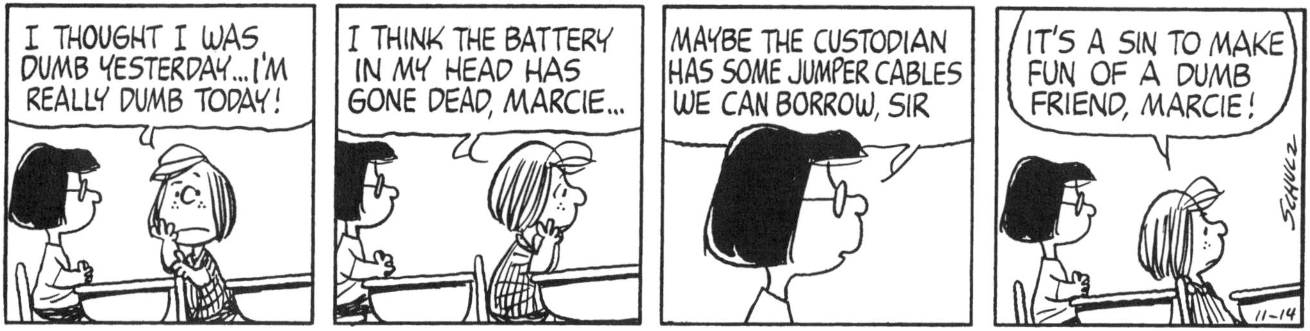
I THOUGHT I WAS DUMB YESTERDAY...I'M REALLY DUMB TODAY!
I THINK THE BATTERY IN MY HEAD HAS GONE DEAD, MARCIE...
MAYBE THE CUSTODIAN HAS SOME JUMPER CABLES WE CAN BORROW, SIR
IT'S A SIN TO MAKE FUN OF A DUMB FRIEND, MARCIE!
SCHULZ
11-14

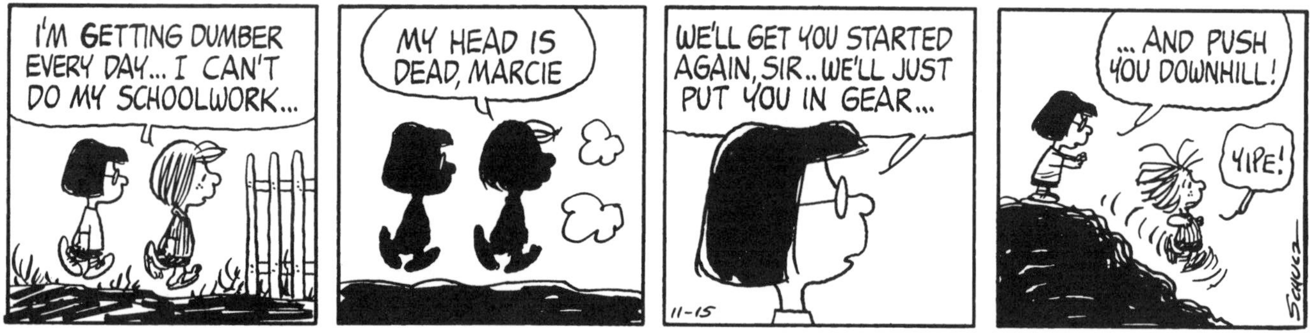
I'M GETTING DUMBER EVERY DAY... I CAN'T DO MY SCHOOLWORK...
MY HEAD IS DEAD, MARCIE
WE'LL GET YOU STARTED AGAIN, SIR.. WE'LL JUST PUT YOU IN GEAR...
11-15
... AND PUSH YOU DOWNHILL!
YIPE!
SCHULZ

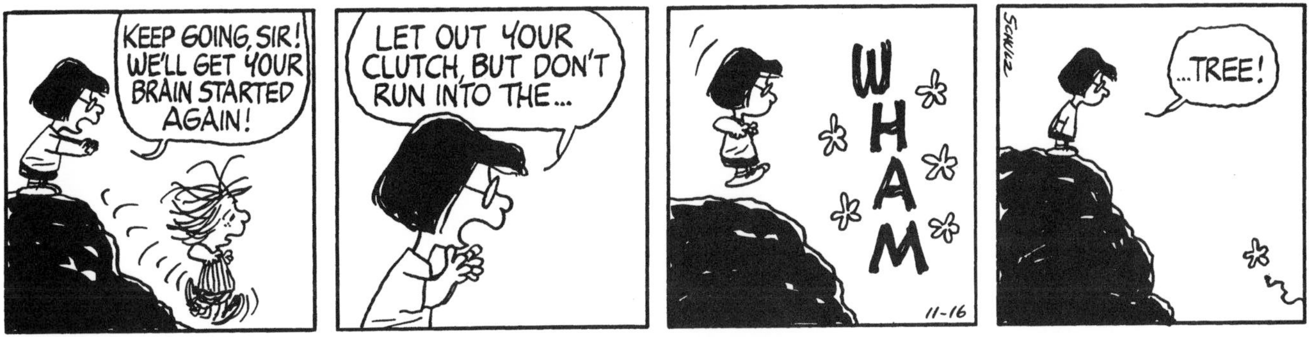
KEEP GOING, SIR! WE'LL GET YOUR BRAIN STARTED AGAIN!
LET OUT YOUR CLUTCH, BUT DON'T RUN INTO THE...
WHAM
...TREE!
SCHULZ
11-16

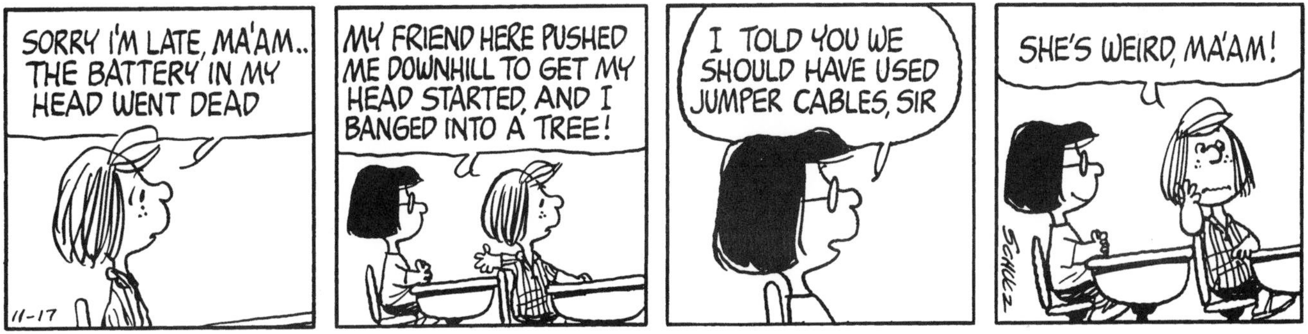
SORRY I'M LATE, MA'AM.. THE BATTERY IN MY HEAD WENT DEAD
11-17
MY FRIEND HERE PUSHED ME DOWNHILL TO GET MY HEAD STARTED, AND I BANGED INTO A TREE!
I TOLD YOU WE SHOULD HAVE USED JUMPER CABLES, SIR
SHE'S WEIRD, MA'AM!
SCHULZ

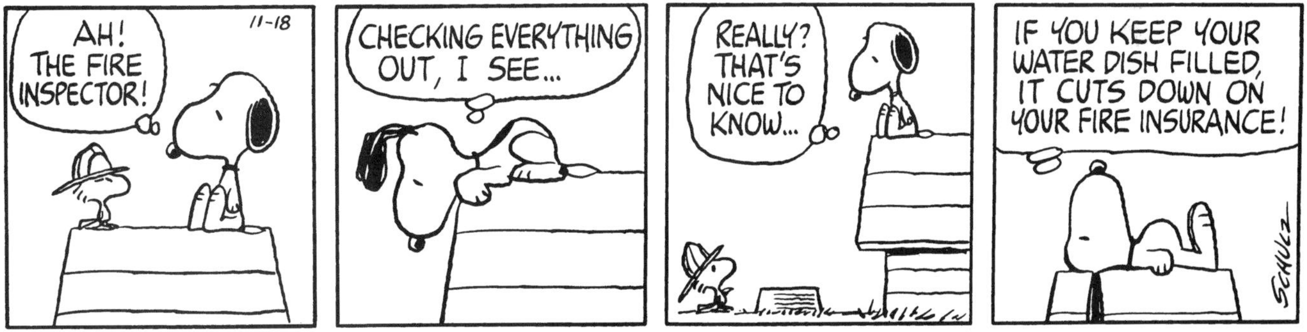
AH! THE FIRE INSPECTOR!
11-18
CHECKING EVERYTHING OUT, I SEE...
REALLY? THAT'S NICE TO KNOW...
IF YOU KEEP YOUR WATER DISH FILLED, IT CUTS DOWN ON YOUR FIRE INSURANCE!
SCHULZ

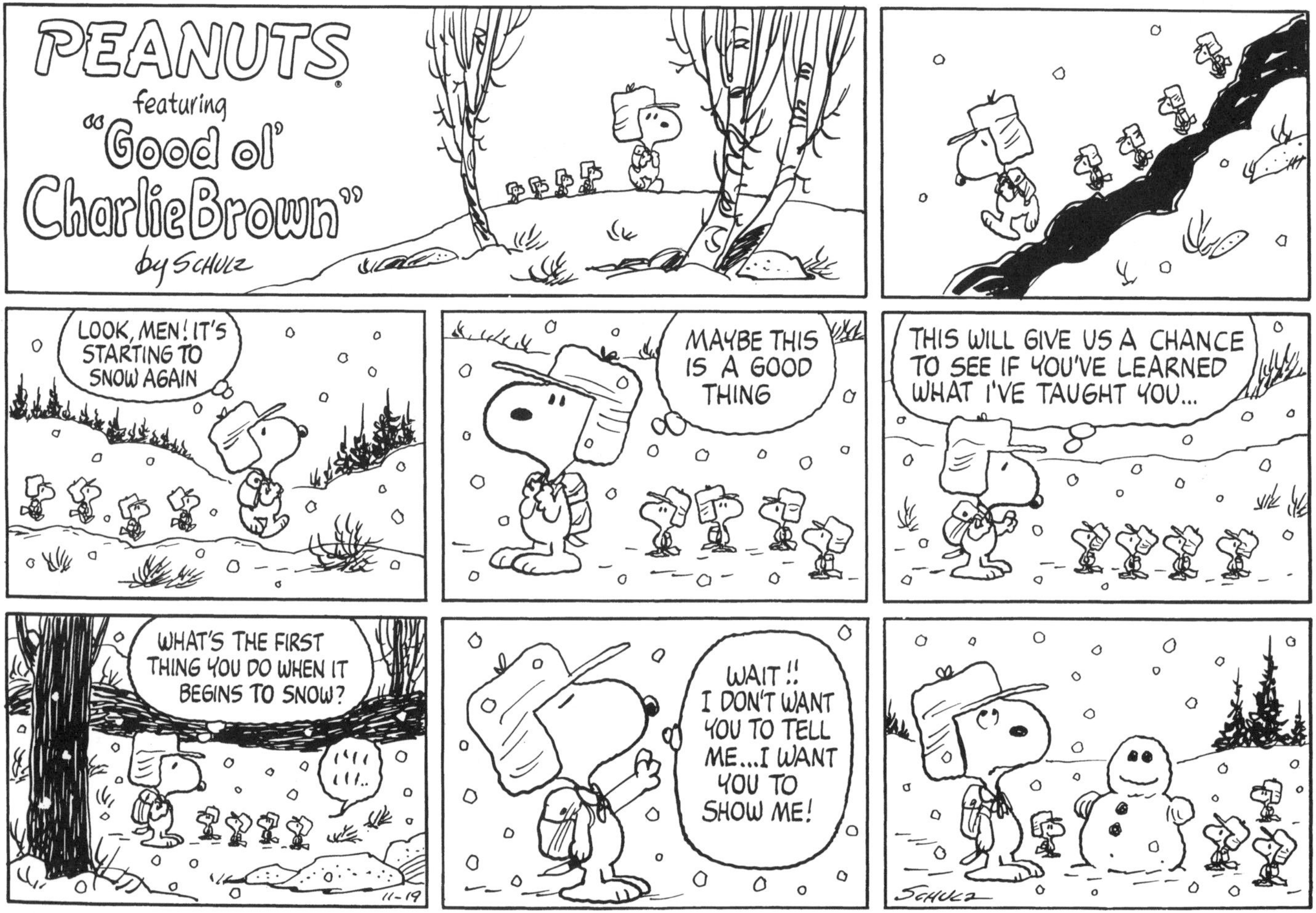
PEANUTS
featuring
"Good ol' Charlie Brown"
by SCHULZ
LOOK, MEN! IT'S STARTING TO SNOW AGAIN
MAYBE THIS IS A GOOD THING
THIS WILL GIVE US A CHANCE TO SEE IF YOU'VE LEARNED WHAT I'VE TAUGHT YOU...
WHAT'S THE FIRST THING YOU DO WHEN IT BEGINS TO SNOW?
11-19
WAIT!! I DON'T WANT YOU TO TELL ME...I WANT YOU TO SHOW ME!
SCHULZ

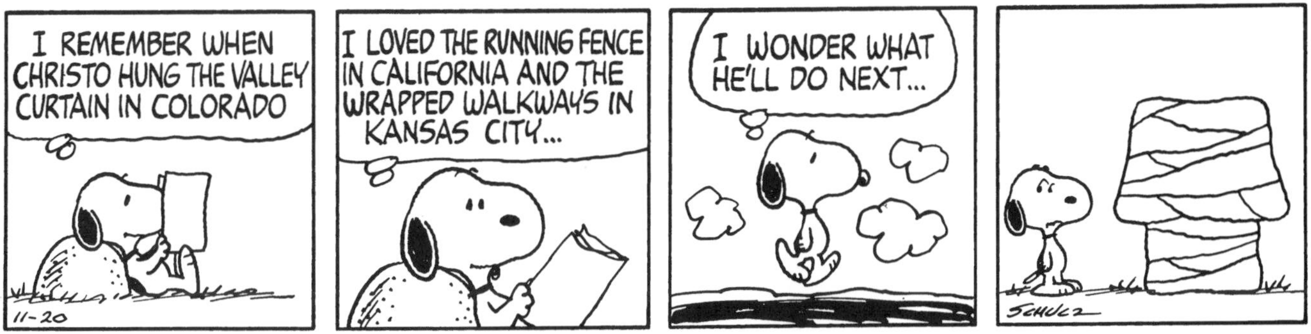
I REMEMBER WHEN CHRISTO HUNG THE VALLEY CURTAIN IN COLORADO
11-20
I LOVED THE RUNNING FENCE IN CALIFORNIA AND THE WRAPPED WALKWAYS IN KANSAS CITY...
I WONDER WHAT HE'LL DO NEXT...
SCHULZ

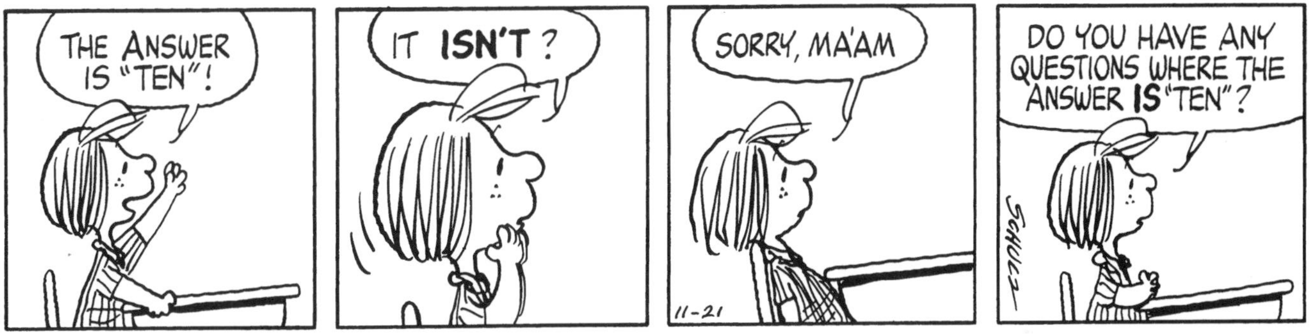
THE ANSWER IS "TEN"!
IT ISN'T ?
SORRY, MA'AM
11-21
DO YOU HAVE ANY QUESTIONS WHERE THE ANSWER IS "TEN"?
SCHULZ

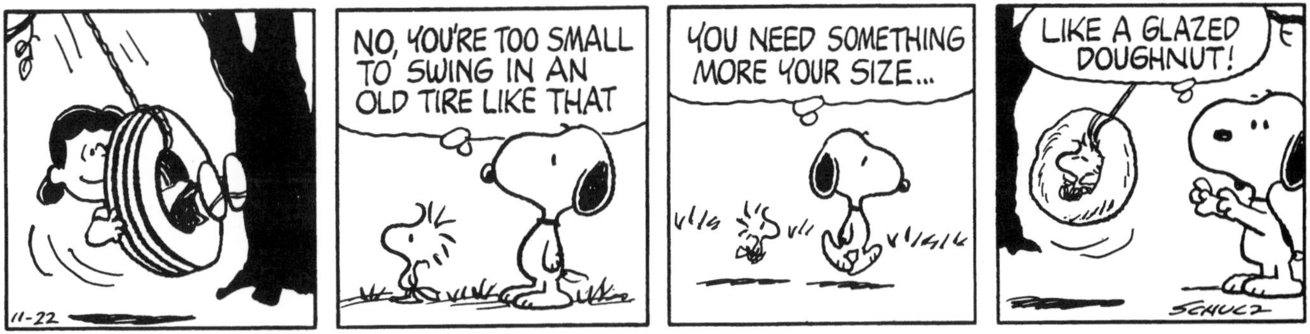
11-22
NO, YOU'RE TOO SMALL TO SWING IN AN OLD TIRE LIKE THAT
YOU NEED SOMETHING MORE YOUR SIZE...
LIKE A GLAZED DOUGHNUT!
SCHULZ

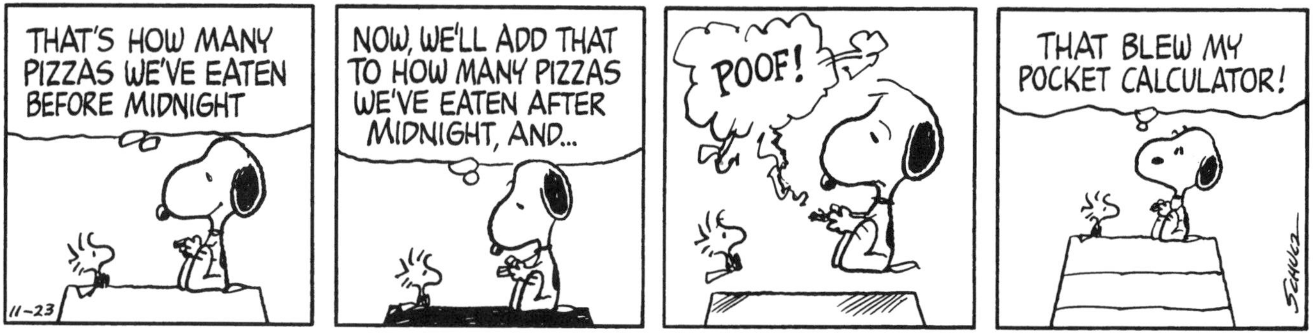
THAT'S HOW MANY PIZZAS WE'VE EATEN BEFORE MIDNIGHT
11-23
NOW, WE'LL ADD THAT TO HOW MANY PIZZAS WE'VE EATEN AFTER MIDNIGHT, AND...
POOF!
THAT BLEW MY POCKET CALCULATOR!
SCHULZ

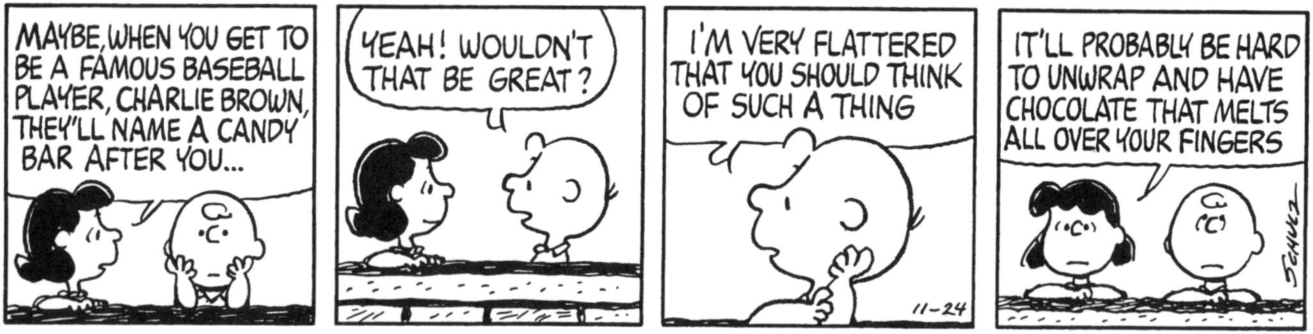
MAYBE, WHEN YOU GET TO BE A FAMOUS BASEBALL PLAYER, CHARLIE BROWN, THEY'LL NAME A CANDY BAR AFTER YOU...
YEAH! WOULDN'T THAT BE GREAT?
I'M VERY FLATTERED THAT YOU SHOULD THINK OF SUCH A THING
11-24
IT'LL PROBABLY BE HARD TO UNWRAP AND HAVE CHOCOLATE THAT MELTS ALL OVER YOUR FINGERS
SCHULZ

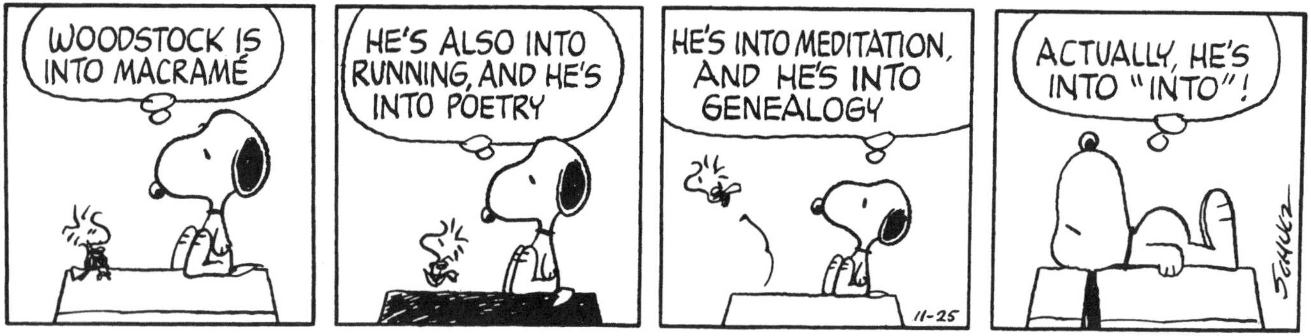
WOODSTOCK IS INTO MACRAMÉ
HE'S ALSO INTO RUNNING, AND HE'S INTO POETRY
HE'S INTO MEDITATION, AND HE'S INTO GENEALOGY
11-25
ACTUALLY, HE'S INTO "INTO"!
SCHULZ

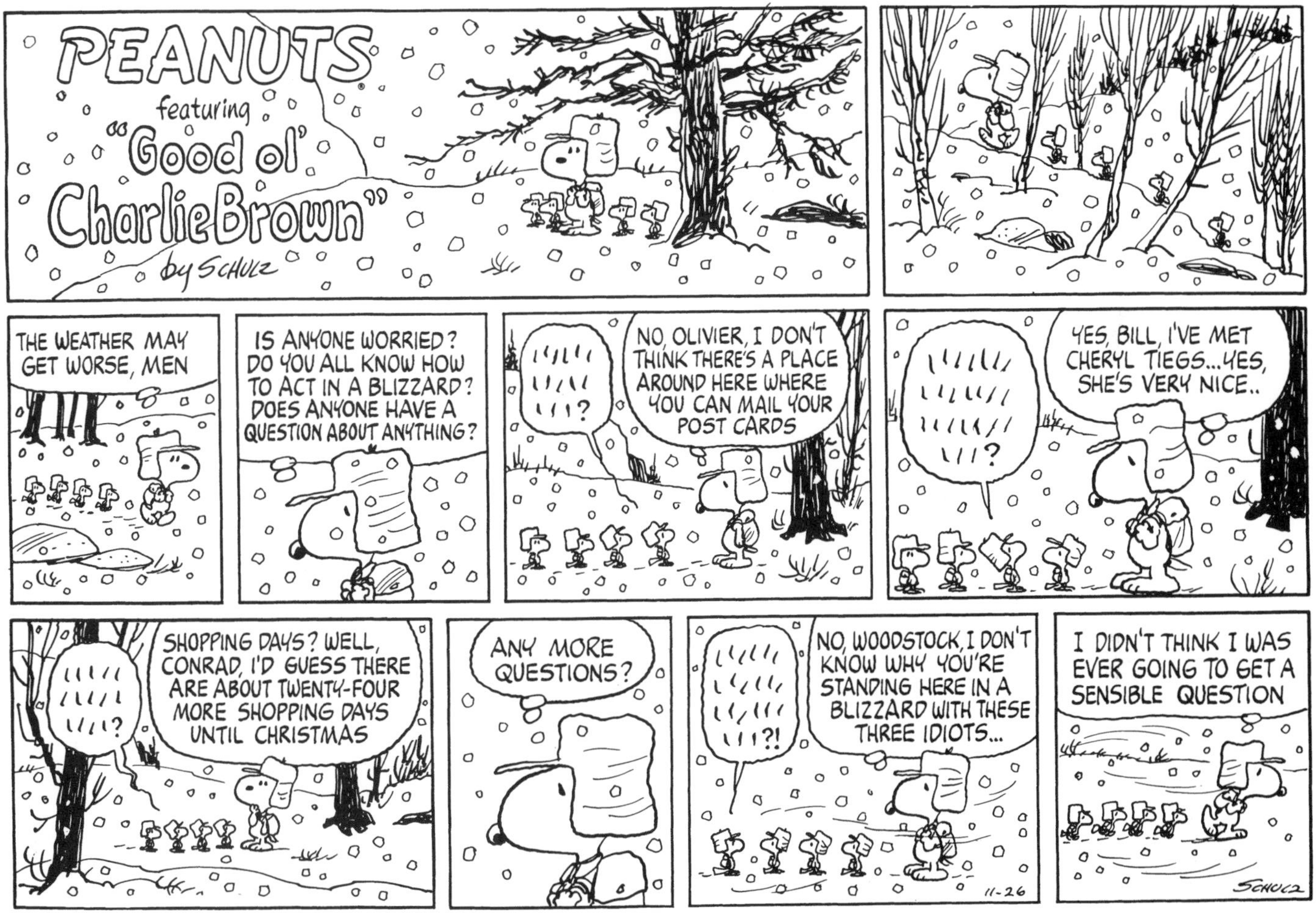
PEANUTS
featuring "Good ol' CharlieBrown"
by SCHULZ
THE WEATHER MAY GET WORSE, MEN
IS ANYONE WORRIED? DO YOU ALL KNOW HOW TO ACT IN A BLIZZARD? DOES ANYONE HAVE A QUESTION ABOUT ANYTHING?
?
NO, OLIVIER, I DON'T THINK THERE'S A PLACE AROUND HERE WHERE YOU CAN MAIL YOUR POST CARDS
?
YES, BILL, I'VE MET CHERYL TIEGS...YES, SHE'S VERY NICE..
?
SHOPPING DAYS? WELL, CONRAD, I'D GUESS THERE ARE ABOUT TWENTY-FOUR MORE SHOPPING DAYS UNTIL CHRISTMAS
ANY MORE QUESTIONS?
?!
NO, WOODSTOCK, I DON'T KNOW WHY YOU'RE STANDING HERE IN A BLIZZARD WITH THESE THREE IDIOTS...
11-26
I DIDN'T THINK I WAS EVER GOING TO GET A SENSIBLE QUESTION
SCHULZ

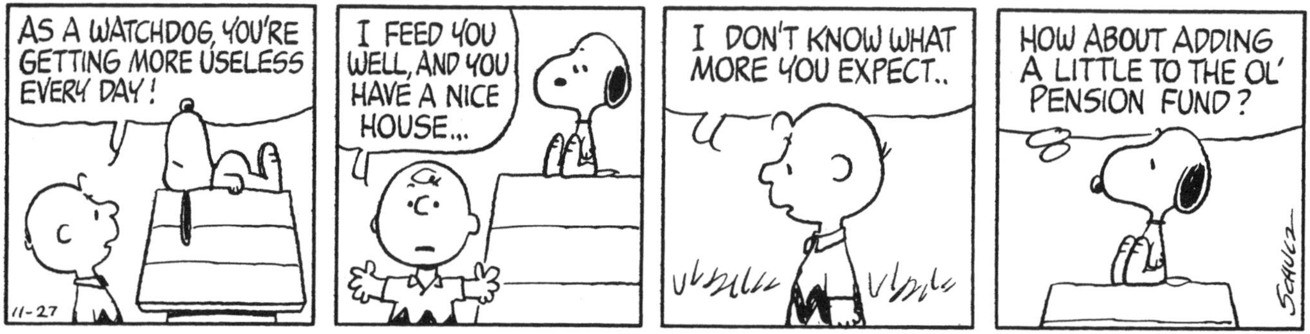
AS A WATCHDOG, YOU'RE GETTING MORE USELESS EVERY DAY!
I FEED YOU WELL, AND YOU HAVE A NICE HOUSE...
I DON'T KNOW WHAT MORE YOU EXPECT..
HOW ABOUT ADDING A LITTLE TO THE OL' PENSION FUND?
11-27
SCHULZ

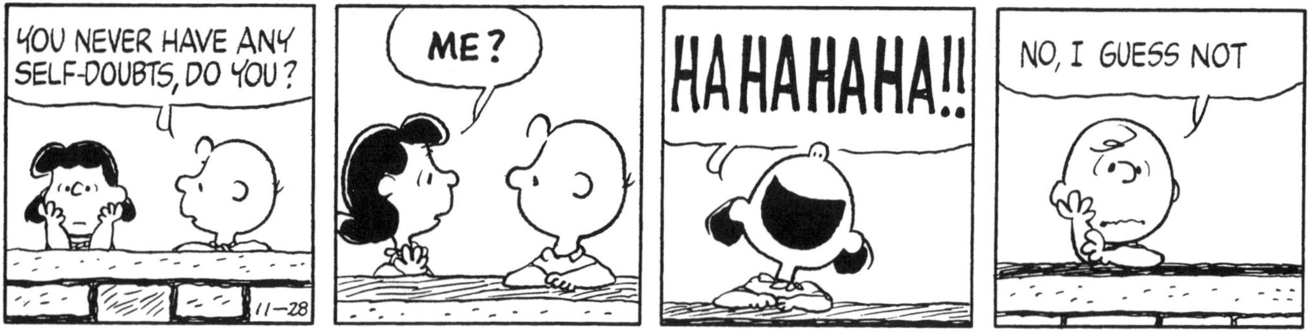
YOU NEVER HAVE ANY SELF-DOUBTS, DO YOU?
ME?
HAHAHAHA!!
NO, I GUESS NOT
11-28

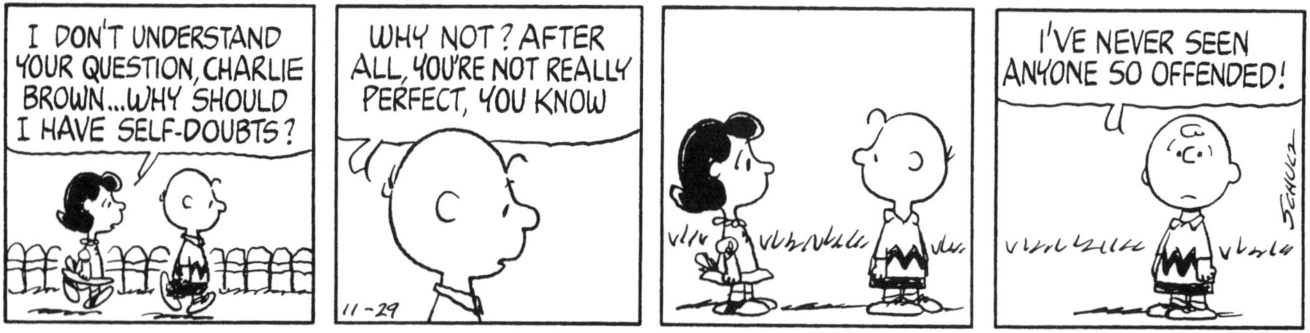
I DON'T UNDERSTAND YOUR QUESTION, CHARLIE BROWN...WHY SHOULD I HAVE SELF-DOUBTS?
WHY NOT? AFTER ALL, YOU'RE NOT REALLY PERFECT, YOU KNOW
I'VE NEVER SEEN ANYONE SO OFFENDED!
11-29
SCHULZ

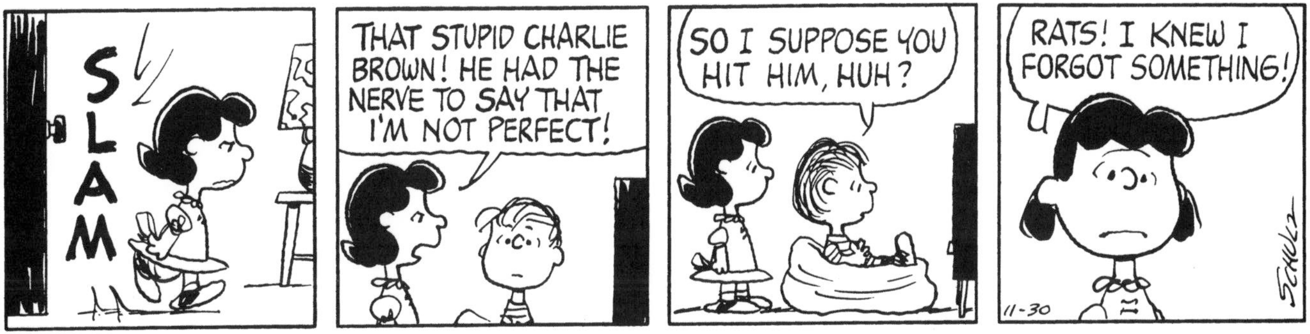
SLAM
THAT STUPID CHARLIE BROWN! HE HAD THE NERVE TO SAY THAT I'M NOT PERFECT!
SO I SUPPOSE YOU HIT HIM, HUH?
RATS! I KNEW I FORGOT SOMETHING!
11-30
SCHULZ

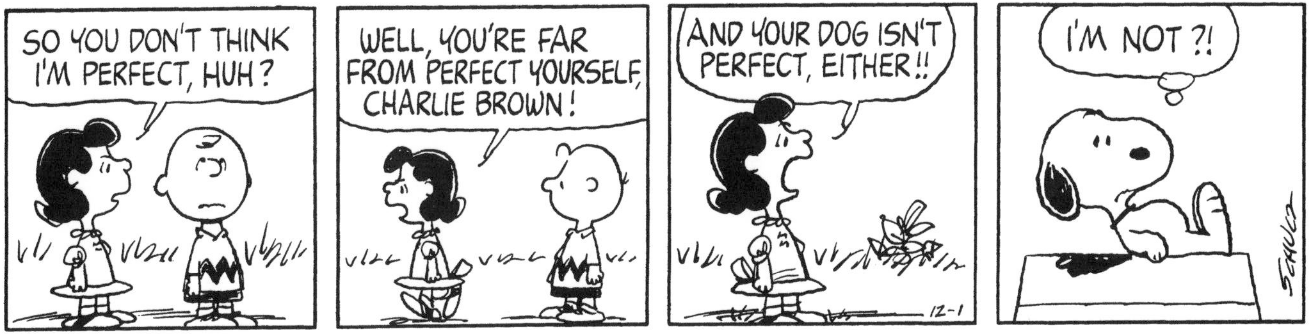
SO YOU DON'T THINK I'M PERFECT, HUH?
WELL, YOU'RE FAR FROM PERFECT YOURSELF, CHARLIE BROWN!
AND YOUR DOG ISN'T PERFECT, EITHER!!
12-1
I'M NOT ?!
SCHULZ

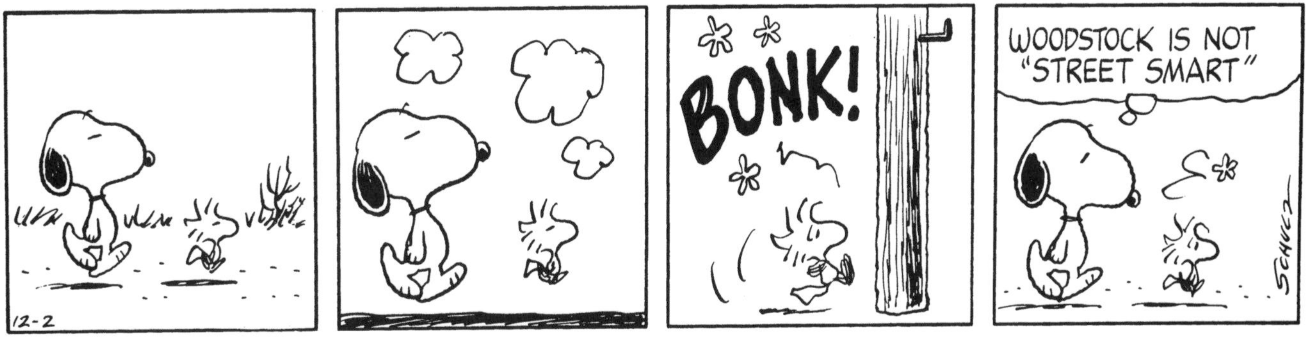
12-2
BONK!
WOODSTOCK IS NOT "STREET SMART"
SCHULZ

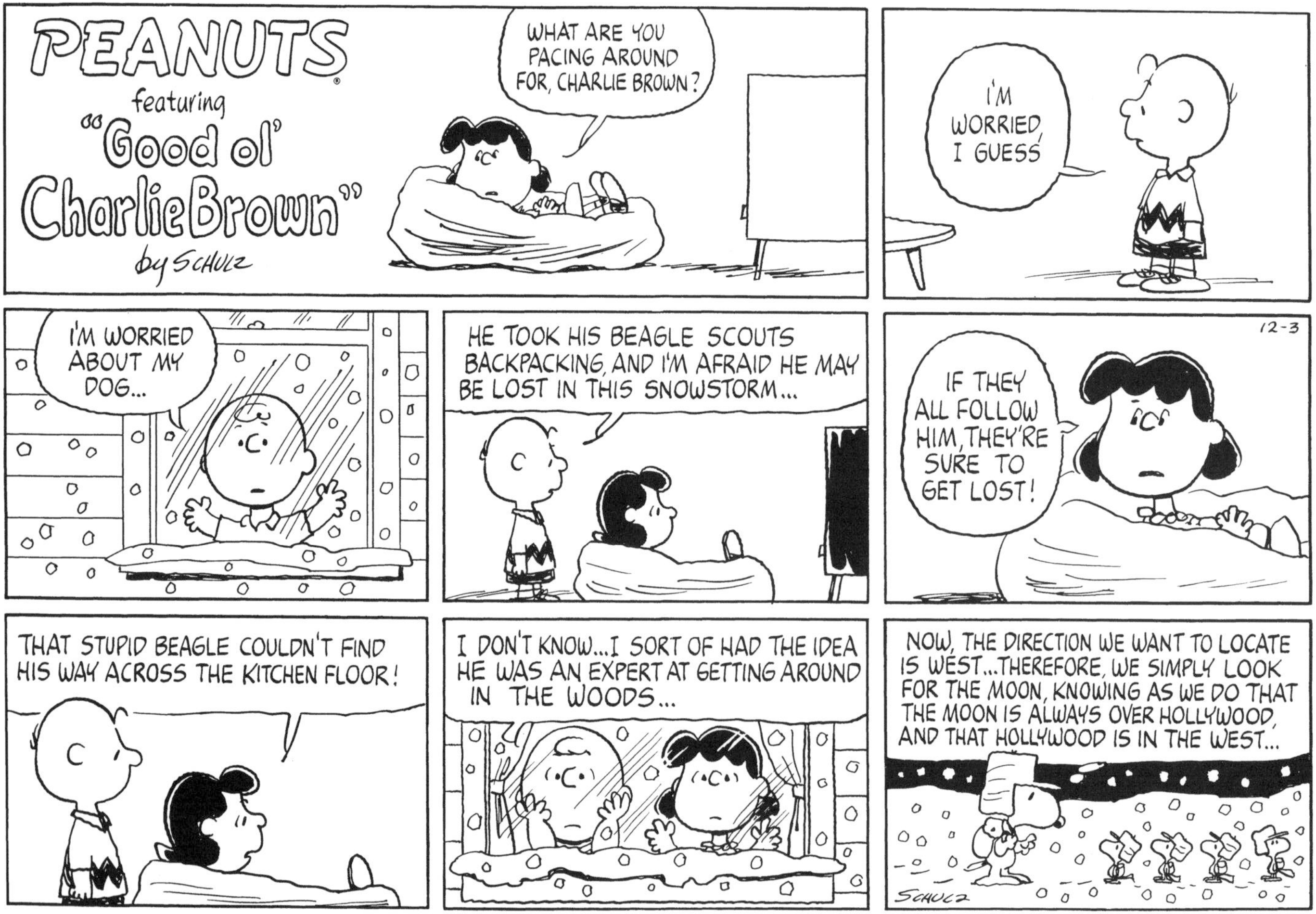
PEANUTS
featuring
"Good ol' Charlie Brown"
by SCHULZ
WHAT ARE YOU PACING AROUND FOR, CHARLIE BROWN?
I'M WORRIED, I GUESS
I'M WORRIED ABOUT MY DOG...
HE TOOK HIS BEAGLE SCOUTS BACKPACKING, AND I'M AFRAID HE MAY BE LOST IN THIS SNOWSTORM...
12-3
IF THEY ALL FOLLOW HIM, THEY'RE SURE TO GET LOST!
THAT STUPID BEAGLE COULDN'T FIND HIS WAY ACROSS THE KITCHEN FLOOR!
I DON'T KNOW...I SORT OF HAD THE IDEA HE WAS AN EXPERT AT GETTING AROUND IN THE WOODS...
NOW, THE DIRECTION WE WANT TO LOCATE IS WEST...THEREFORE, WE SIMPLY LOOK FOR THE MOON, KNOWING AS WE DO THAT THE MOON IS ALWAYS OVER HOLLYWOOD, AND THAT HOLLYWOOD IS IN THE WEST...
SCHULZ

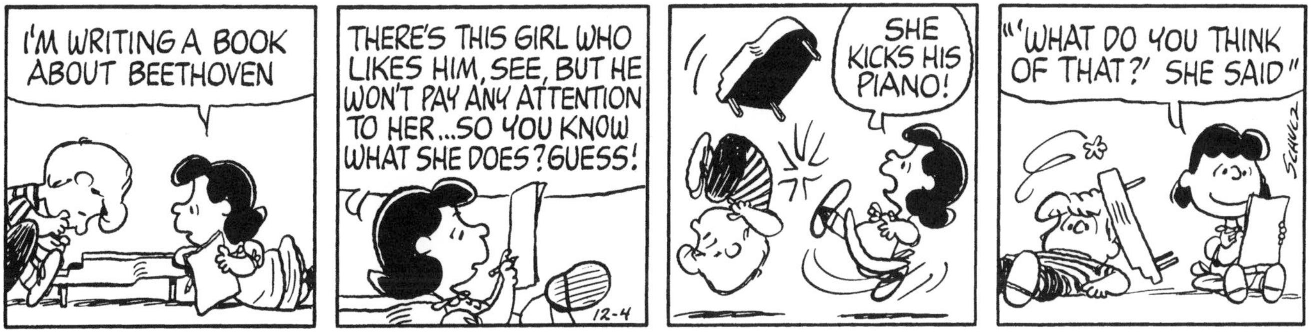
I'M WRITING A BOOK ABOUT BEETHOVEN
THERE'S THIS GIRL WHO LIKES HIM, SEE, BUT HE WON'T PAY ANY ATTENTION TO HER...SO YOU KNOW WHAT SHE DOES? GUESS!
12-4
SHE KICKS HIS PIANO!
"'WHAT DO YOU THINK OF THAT?' SHE SAID"
SCHULZ

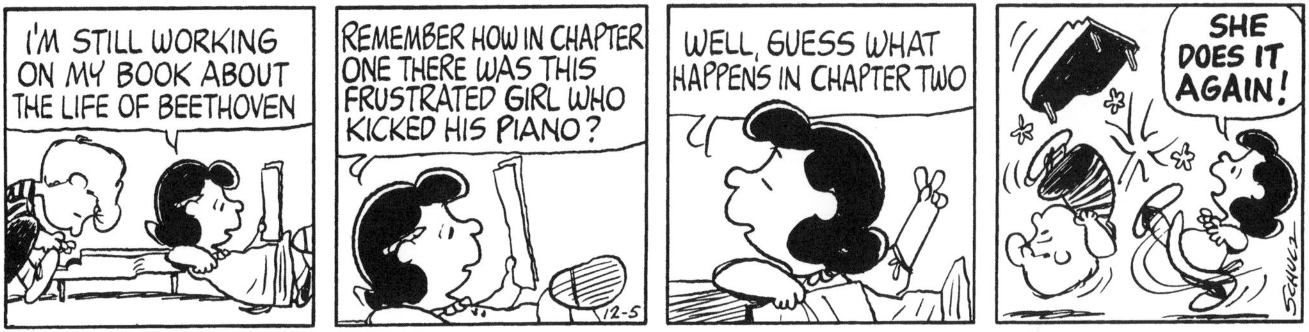
I'M STILL WORKING ON MY BOOK ABOUT THE LIFE OF BEETHOVEN
REMEMBER HOW IN CHAPTER ONE THERE WAS THIS FRUSTRATED GIRL WHO KICKED HIS PIANO?
12-5
WELL, GUESS WHAT HAPPENS IN CHAPTER TWO
SHE DOES IT AGAIN!
SCHULZ

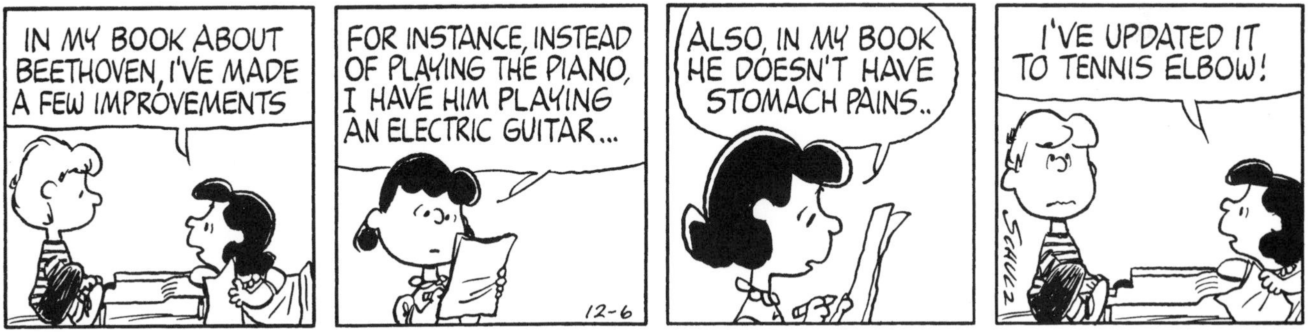
IN MY BOOK ABOUT BEETHOVEN, I'VE MADE A FEW IMPROVEMENTS
FOR INSTANCE, INSTEAD OF PLAYING THE PIANO, I HAVE HIM PLAYING AN ELECTRIC GUITAR...
12-6
ALSO, IN MY BOOK HE DOESN'T HAVE STOMACH PAINS..
I'VE UPDATED IT TO TENNIS ELBOW!
SCHULZ

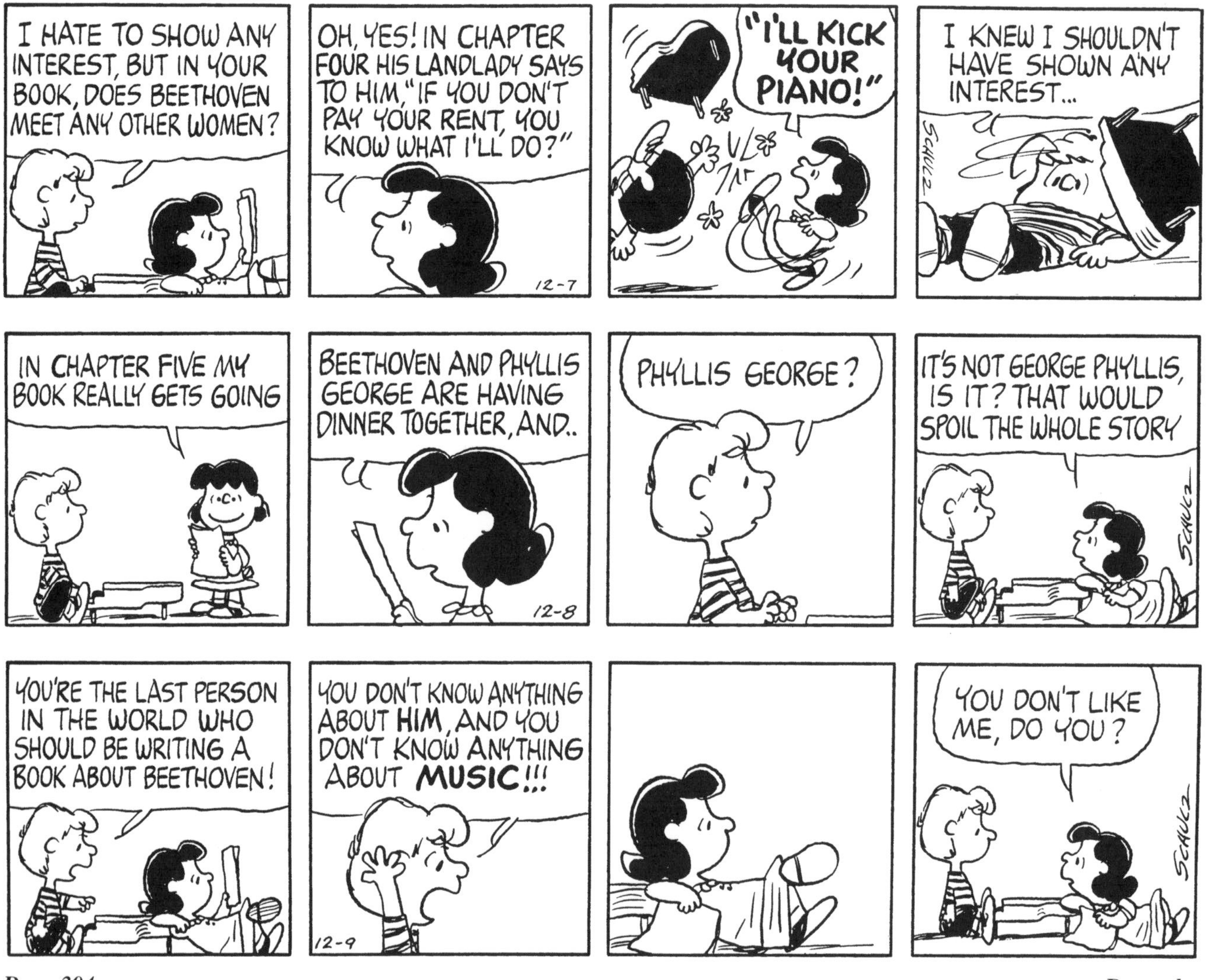
I HATE TO SHOW ANY INTEREST, BUT IN YOUR BOOK, DOES BEETHOVEN MEET ANY OTHER WOMEN?
OH, YES! IN CHAPTER FOUR HIS LANDLADY SAYS TO HIM, "IF YOU DON'T PAY YOUR RENT, YOU KNOW WHAT I'LL DO?"
12-7
"I'LL KICK YOUR PIANO!"
I KNEW I SHOULDN'T HAVE SHOWN ANY INTEREST...
SCHULZ
IN CHAPTER FIVE MY BOOK REALLY GETS GOING
BEETHOVEN AND PHYLLIS GEORGE ARE HAVING DINNER TOGETHER, AND..
12-8
PHYLLIS GEORGE?
IT'S NOT GEORGE PHYLLIS, IS IT? THAT WOULD SPOIL THE WHOLE STORY
SCHULZ
YOU'RE THE LAST PERSON IN THE WORLD WHO SHOULD BE WRITING A BOOK ABOUT BEETHOVEN!
YOU DON'T KNOW ANYTHING ABOUT HIM, AND YOU DON'T KNOW ANYTHING ABOUT MUSIC!!!
12-9
YOU DON'T LIKE ME, DO YOU?
SCHULZ

PEANUTS
featuring
"Good ol' Charlie Brown"
by SCHULZ

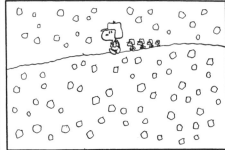

THIS BLIZZARD IS GETTING WORSE, MEN

12-10

ANYONE HAVE ANY SUGGESTIONS?

OKAY, WE'LL ALL FOLLOW WOODSTOCK... HE SAYS HE CAN LEAD US TO THE PERFECT SPOT TO SPEND THE NIGHT...

?

WOODSTOCK IS A BORN LEADER!

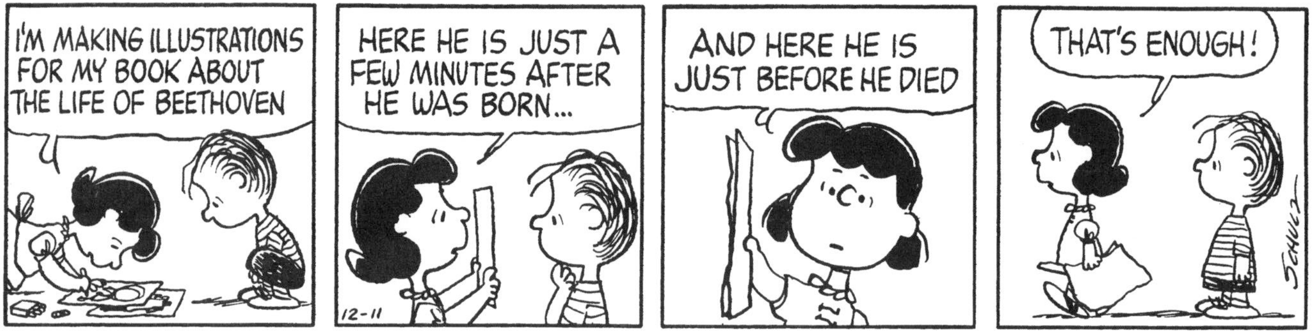
I'M MAKING ILLUSTRATIONS FOR MY BOOK ABOUT THE LIFE OF BEETHOVEN
HERE HE IS JUST A FEW MINUTES AFTER HE WAS BORN...
12-11
AND HERE HE IS JUST BEFORE HE DIED
THAT'S ENOUGH!
SCHULZ

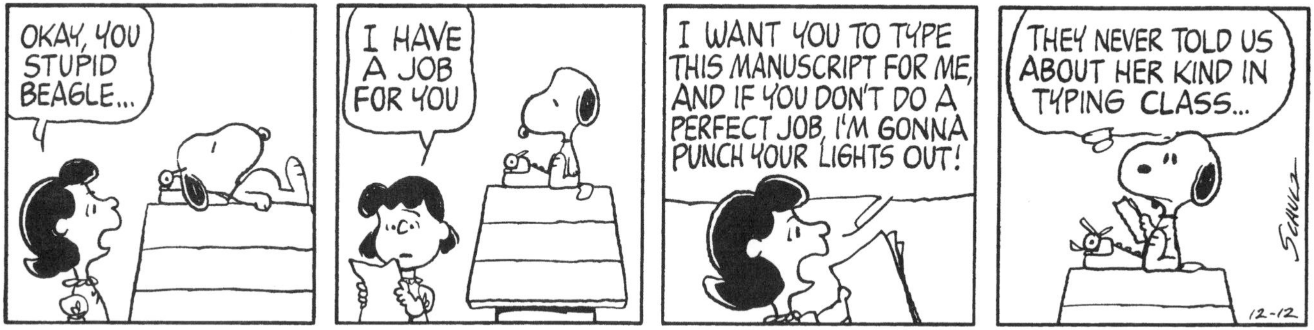
OKAY, YOU STUPID BEAGLE...
I HAVE A JOB FOR YOU
I WANT YOU TO TYPE THIS MANUSCRIPT FOR ME, AND IF YOU DON'T DO A PERFECT JOB, I'M GONNA PUNCH YOUR LIGHTS OUT!
THEY NEVER TOLD US ABOUT HER KIND IN TYPING CLASS...
SCHULZ
12-12

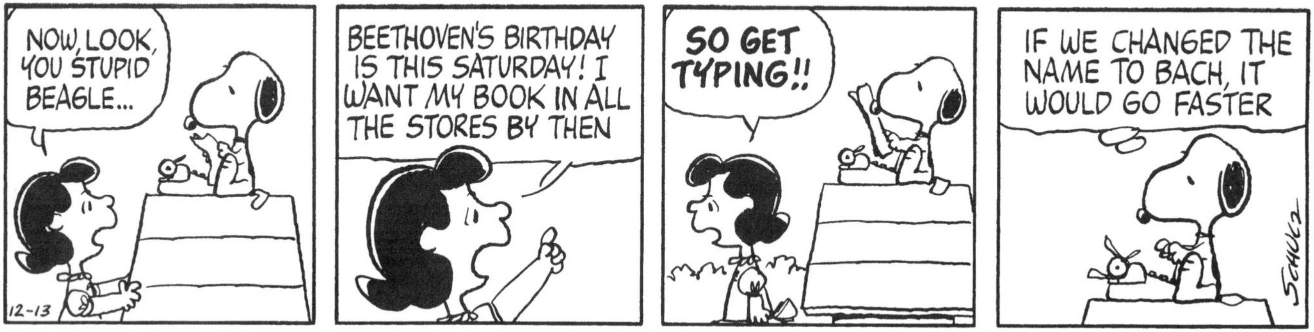
NOW, LOOK, YOU STUPID BEAGLE...
12-13
BEETHOVEN'S BIRTHDAY IS THIS SATURDAY! I WANT MY BOOK IN ALL THE STORES BY THEN
SO GET TYPING!!
IF WE CHANGED THE NAME TO BACH, IT WOULD GO FASTER
SCHULZ

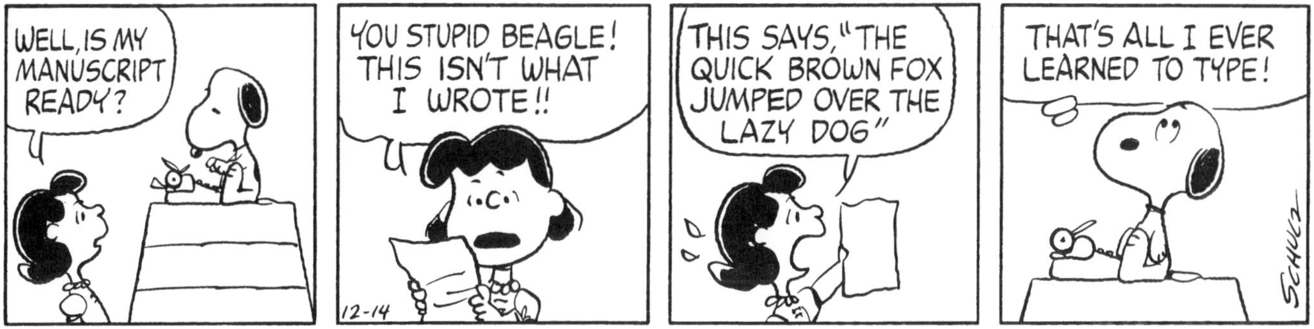

WELL, IS MY MANUSCRIPT READY?
YOU STUPID BEAGLE! THIS ISN'T WHAT I WROTE!!
12-14
THIS SAYS, "THE QUICK BROWN FOX JUMPED OVER THE LAZY DOG"
THAT'S ALL I EVER LEARNED TO TYPE!
SCHULZ

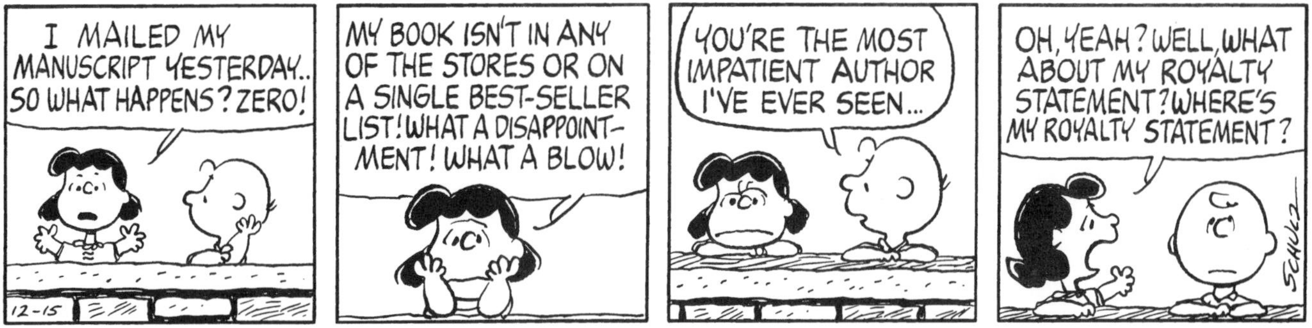

I MAILED MY MANUSCRIPT YESTERDAY.. SO WHAT HAPPENS? ZERO!
12-15
MY BOOK ISN'T IN ANY OF THE STORES OR ON A SINGLE BEST-SELLER LIST! WHAT A DISAPPOINTMENT! WHAT A BLOW!
YOU'RE THE MOST IMPATIENT AUTHOR I'VE EVER SEEN...
OH, YEAH? WELL, WHAT ABOUT MY ROYALTY STATEMENT? WHERE'S MY ROYALTY STATEMENT?
SCHULZ

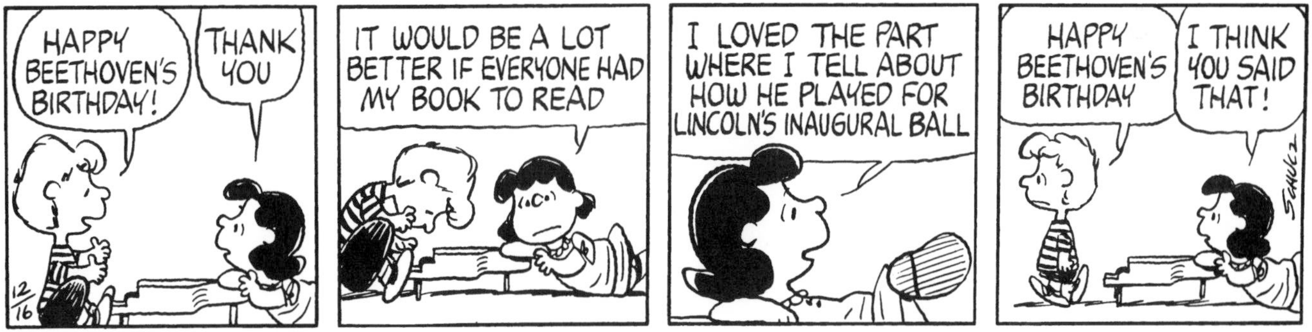

HAPPY BEETHOVEN'S BIRTHDAY!
THANK YOU
12/16
IT WOULD BE A LOT BETTER IF EVERYONE HAD MY BOOK TO READ
I LOVED THE PART WHERE I TELL ABOUT HOW HE PLAYED FOR LINCOLN'S INAUGURAL BALL
HAPPY BEETHOVEN'S BIRTHDAY
I THINK YOU SAID THAT!
SCHULZ

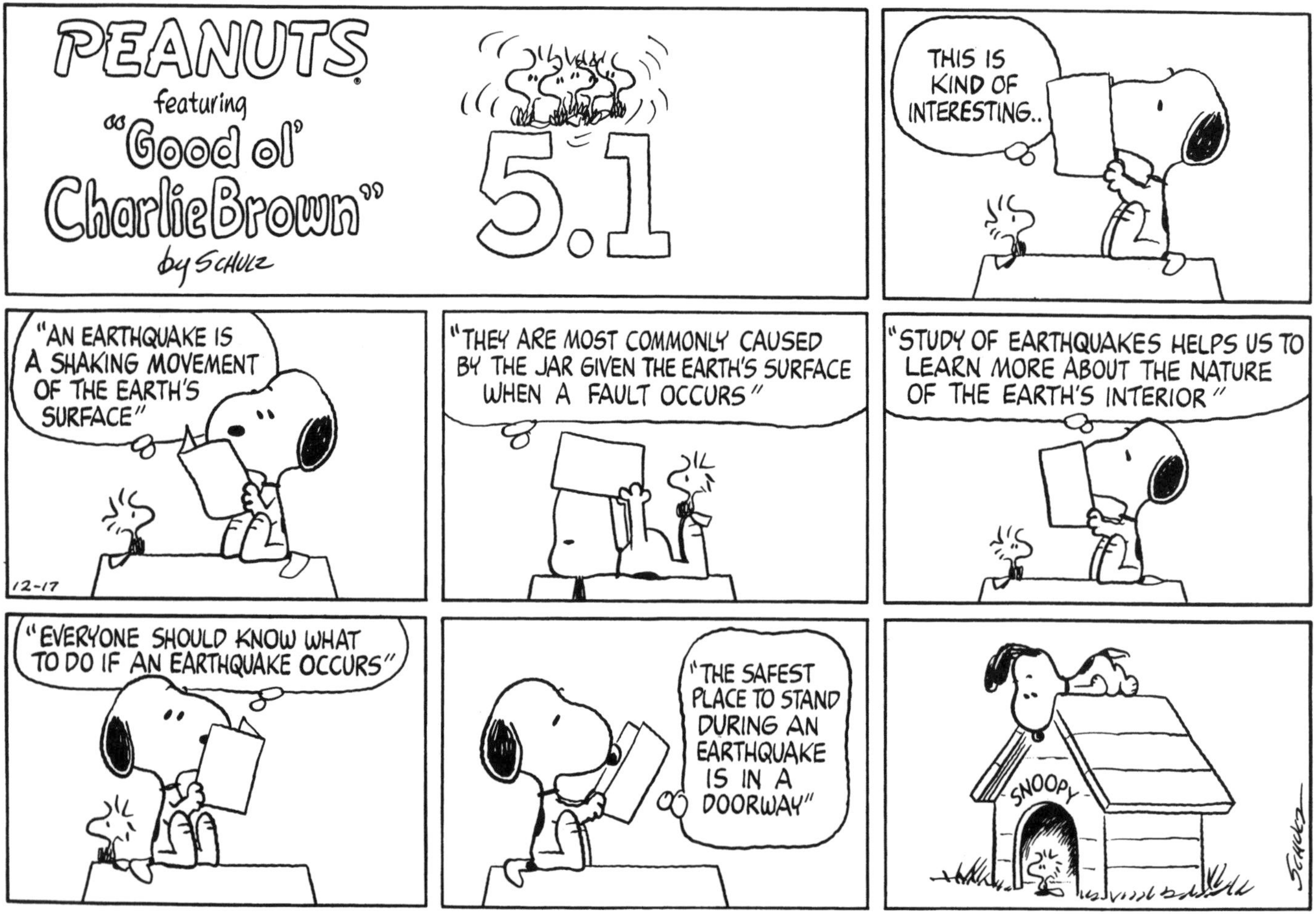
PEANUTS
featuring
"Good ol' CharlieBrown"
by SCHULZ
5.1
THIS IS KIND OF INTERESTING..
"AN EARTHQUAKE IS A SHAKING MOVEMENT OF THE EARTH'S SURFACE"
12-17
"THEY ARE MOST COMMONLY CAUSED BY THE JAR GIVEN THE EARTH'S SURFACE WHEN A FAULT OCCURS"
"STUDY OF EARTHQUAKES HELPS US TO LEARN MORE ABOUT THE NATURE OF THE EARTH'S INTERIOR"
"EVERYONE SHOULD KNOW WHAT TO DO IF AN EARTHQUAKE OCCURS"
"THE SAFEST PLACE TO STAND DURING AN EARTHQUAKE IS IN A DOORWAY"
SNOOPY
SCHULZ

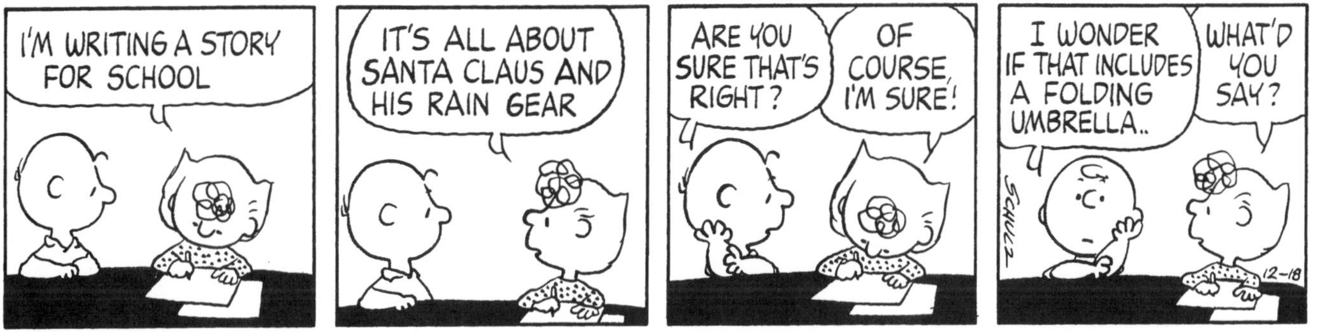
I'M WRITING A STORY FOR SCHOOL
IT'S ALL ABOUT SANTA CLAUS AND HIS RAIN GEAR
ARE YOU SURE THAT'S RIGHT?
OF COURSE, I'M SURE!
I WONDER IF THAT INCLUDES A FOLDING UMBRELLA..
WHAT'D YOU SAY?
SCHULZ
12-18

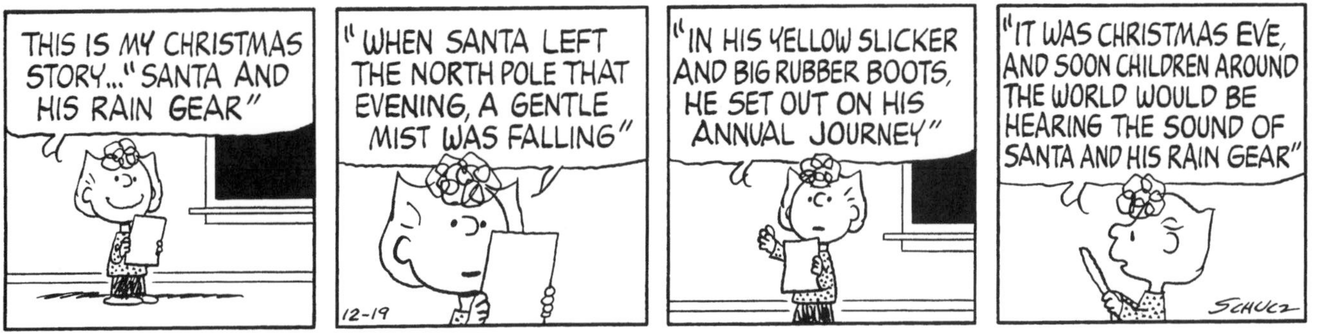
THIS IS MY CHRISTMAS STORY..."SANTA AND HIS RAIN GEAR"
"WHEN SANTA LEFT THE NORTH POLE THAT EVENING, A GENTLE MIST WAS FALLING"
12-19
"IN HIS YELLOW SLICKER AND BIG RUBBER BOOTS, HE SET OUT ON HIS ANNUAL JOURNEY"
"IT WAS CHRISTMAS EVE, AND SOON CHILDREN AROUND THE WORLD WOULD BE HEARING THE SOUND OF SANTA AND HIS RAIN GEAR"
SCHULZ

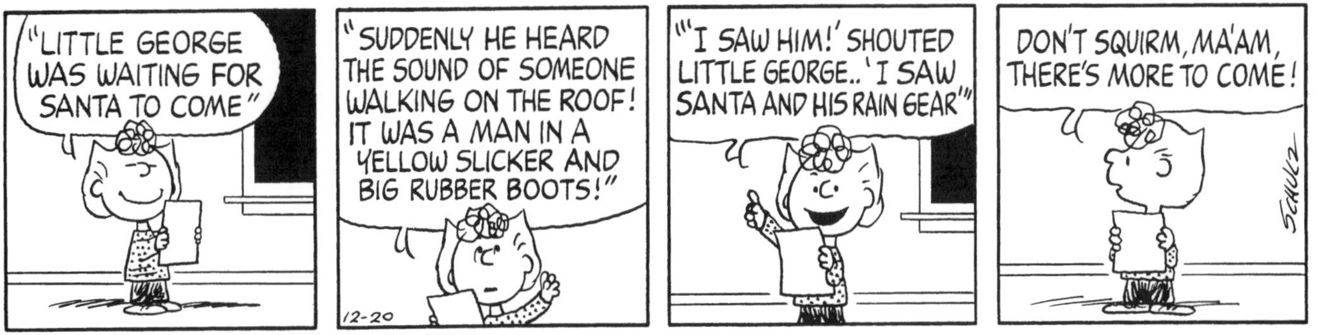
"LITTLE GEORGE WAS WAITING FOR SANTA TO COME"
"SUDDENLY HE HEARD THE SOUND OF SOMEONE WALKING ON THE ROOF! IT WAS A MAN IN A YELLOW SLICKER AND BIG RUBBER BOOTS!"
12-20
"'I SAW HIM!' SHOUTED LITTLE GEORGE..'I SAW SANTA AND HIS RAIN GEAR'"
DON'T SQUIRM, MA'AM, THERE'S MORE TO COME!
SCHULZ

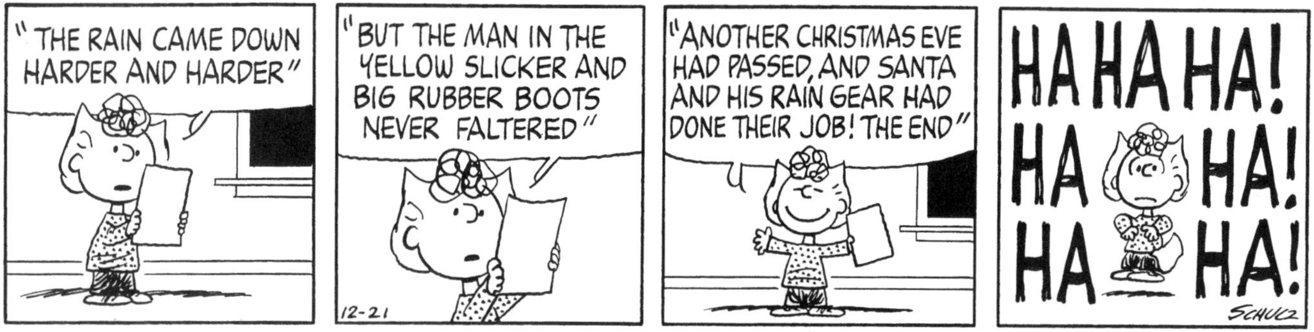

"THE RAIN CAME DOWN HARDER AND HARDER"
"BUT THE MAN IN THE YELLOW SLICKER AND BIG RUBBER BOOTS NEVER FALTERED"
12-21
"ANOTHER CHRISTMAS EVE HAD PASSED, AND SANTA AND HIS RAIN GEAR HAD DONE THEIR JOB! THE END"
HA HA HA HA! HA HA! HA HA!
SCHULZ

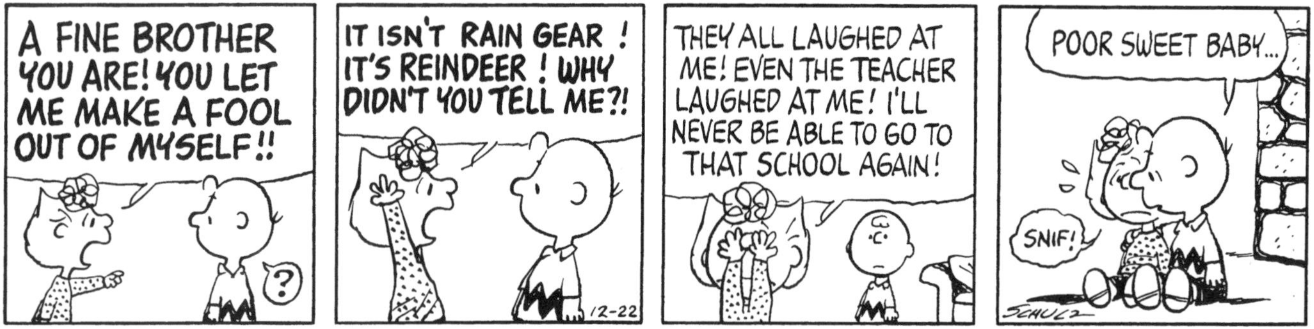

A FINE BROTHER YOU ARE! YOU LET ME MAKE A FOOL OUT OF MYSELF!!
?
IT ISN'T RAIN GEAR! IT'S REINDEER! WHY DIDN'T YOU TELL ME?!
12-22
THEY ALL LAUGHED AT ME! EVEN THE TEACHER LAUGHED AT ME! I'LL NEVER BE ABLE TO GO TO THAT SCHOOL AGAIN!
POOR SWEET BABY...
SNIF!
SCHULZ

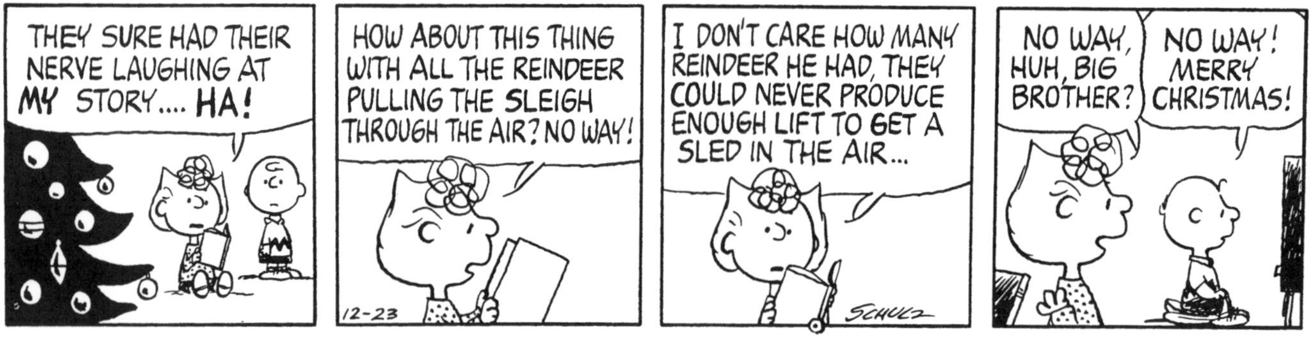

THEY SURE HAD THEIR NERVE LAUGHING AT MY STORY.... HA!
HOW ABOUT THIS THING WITH ALL THE REINDEER PULLING THE SLEIGH THROUGH THE AIR? NO WAY!
12-23
I DON'T CARE HOW MANY REINDEER HE HAD, THEY COULD NEVER PRODUCE ENOUGH LIFT TO GET A SLED IN THE AIR...
SCHULZ
NO WAY, HUH, BIG BROTHER?
NO WAY! MERRY CHRISTMAS!

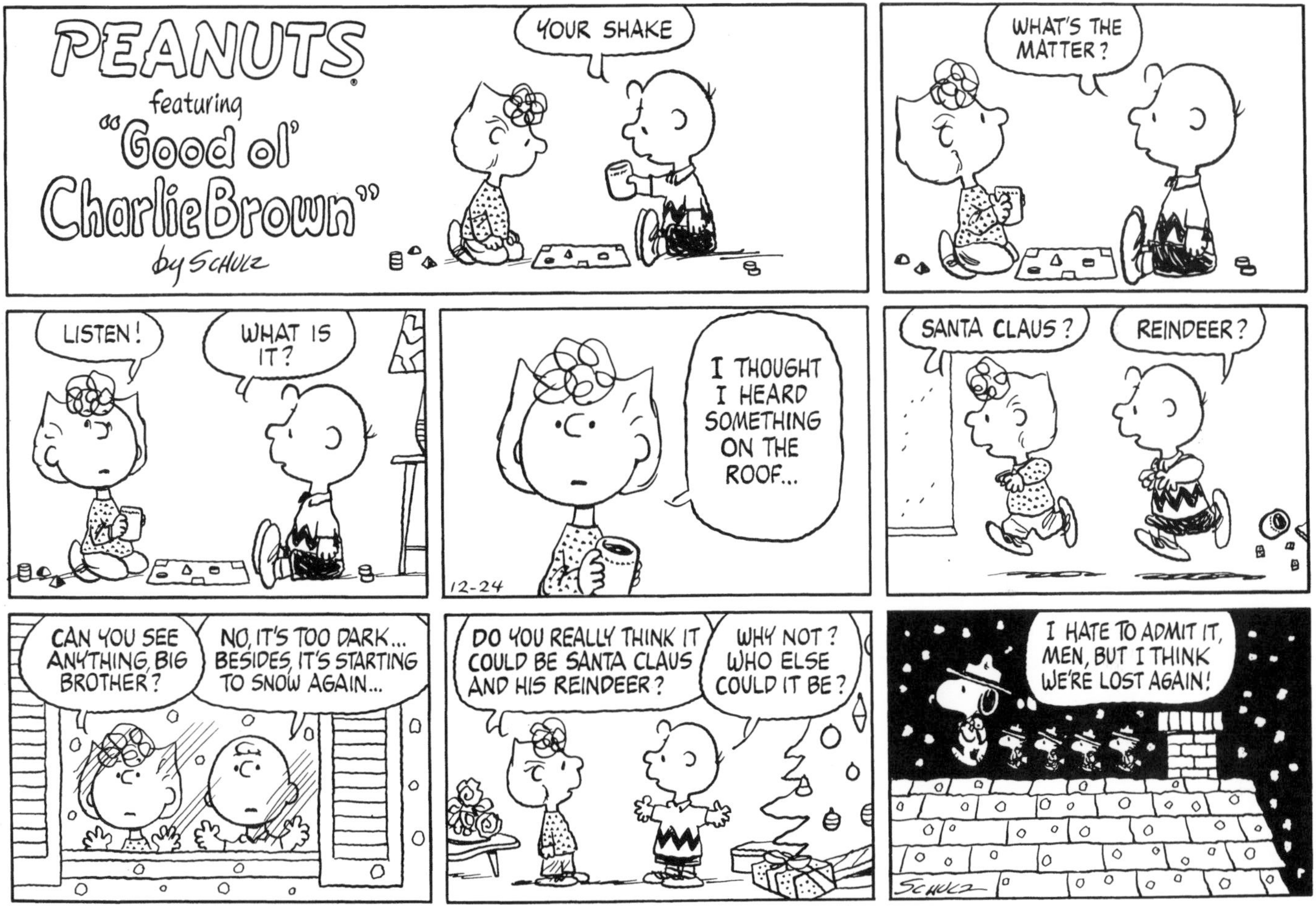
PEANUTS
featuring "Good ol' Charlie Brown"
by SCHULZ
YOUR SHAKE
WHAT'S THE MATTER?
LISTEN!
WHAT IS IT?
I THOUGHT I HEARD SOMETHING ON THE ROOF...
12-24
SANTA CLAUS?
REINDEER?
CAN YOU SEE ANYTHING, BIG BROTHER?
NO, IT'S TOO DARK... BESIDES, IT'S STARTING TO SNOW AGAIN...
DO YOU REALLY THINK IT COULD BE SANTA CLAUS AND HIS REINDEER?
WHY NOT? WHO ELSE COULD IT BE?
I HATE TO ADMIT IT, MEN, BUT I THINK WE'RE LOST AGAIN!
SCHULZ

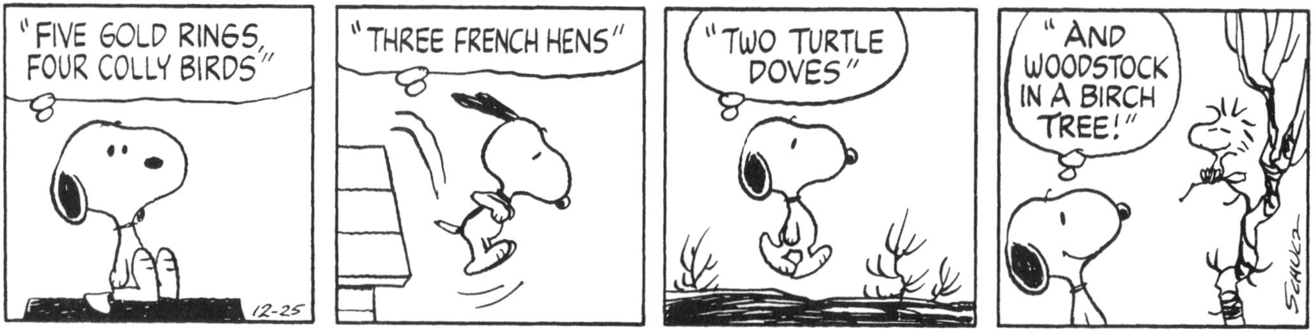
"FIVE GOLD RINGS, FOUR COLLY BIRDS"
12-25
"THREE FRENCH HENS"
"TWO TURTLE DOVES"
"AND WOODSTOCK IN A BIRCH TREE!"
SCHULZ

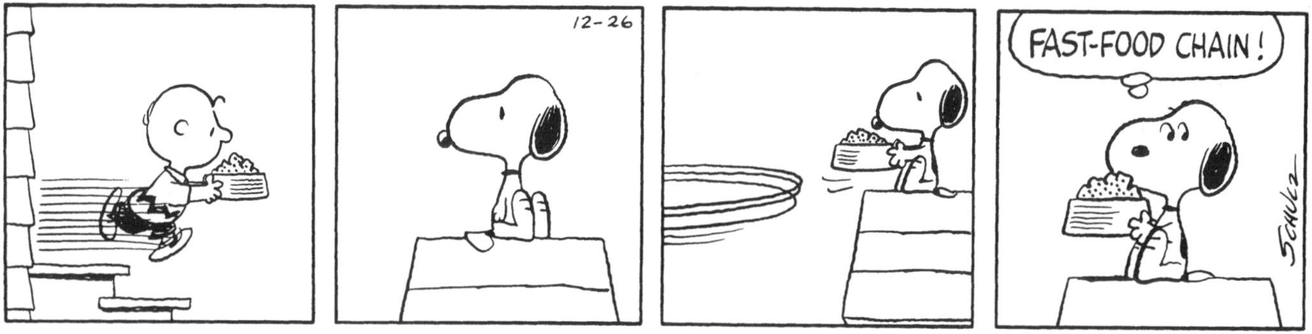
12-26
FAST-FOOD CHAIN!
SCHULZ

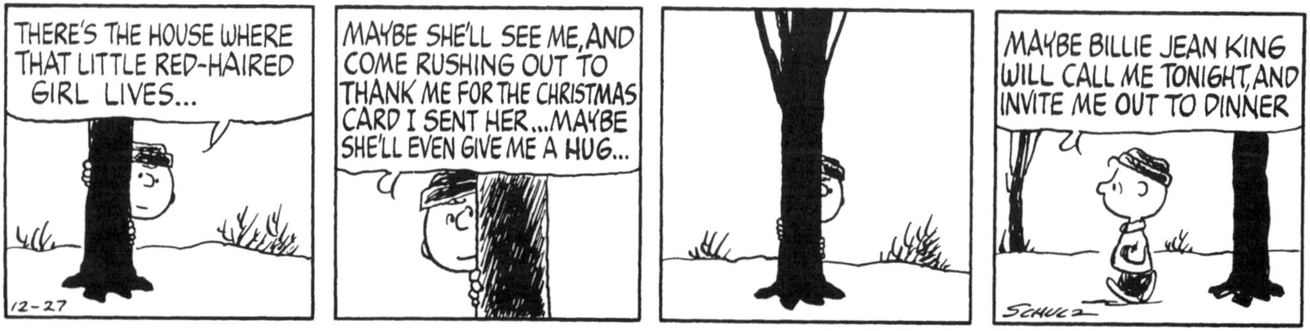
THERE'S THE HOUSE WHERE THAT LITTLE RED-HAIRED GIRL LIVES...
12-27
MAYBE SHE'LL SEE ME, AND COME RUSHING OUT TO THANK ME FOR THE CHRISTMAS CARD I SENT HER...MAYBE SHE'LL EVEN GIVE ME A HUG...
MAYBE BILLIE JEAN KING WILL CALL ME TONIGHT, AND INVITE ME OUT TO DINNER
SCHULZ

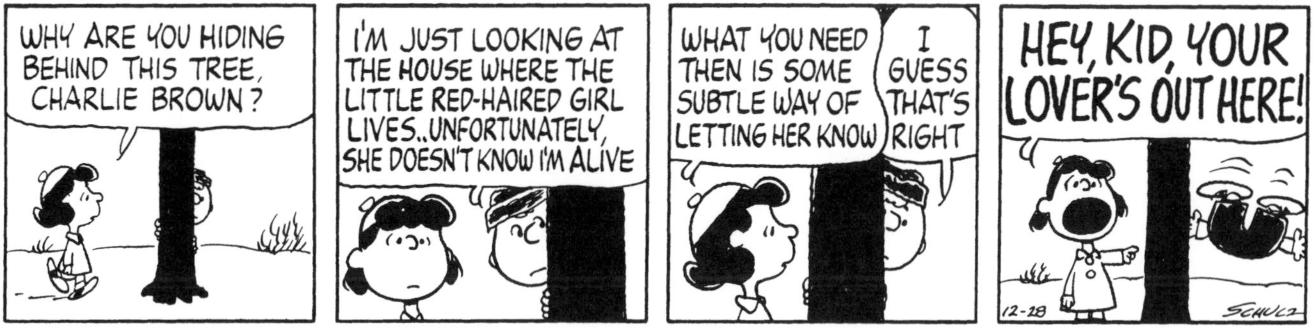
WHY ARE YOU HIDING BEHIND THIS TREE, CHARLIE BROWN?
I'M JUST LOOKING AT THE HOUSE WHERE THE LITTLE RED-HAIRED GIRL LIVES..UNFORTUNATELY, SHE DOESN'T KNOW I'M ALIVE
WHAT YOU NEED THEN IS SOME SUBTLE WAY OF LETTING HER KNOW
I GUESS THAT'S RIGHT
HEY, KID, YOUR LOVER'S OUT HERE!
12-28
SCHULZ

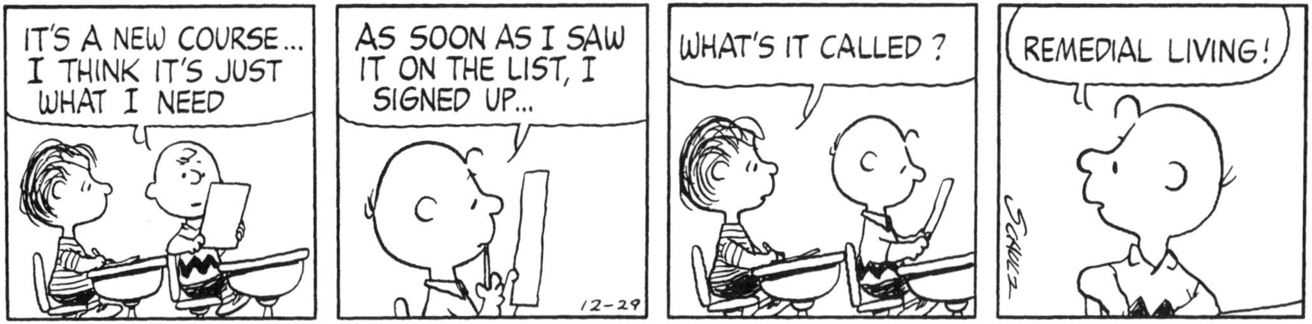
IT'S A NEW COURSE... I THINK IT'S JUST WHAT I NEED
AS SOON AS I SAW IT ON THE LIST, I SIGNED UP...
12-29
WHAT'S IT CALLED?
SCHULZ
REMEDIAL LIVING!

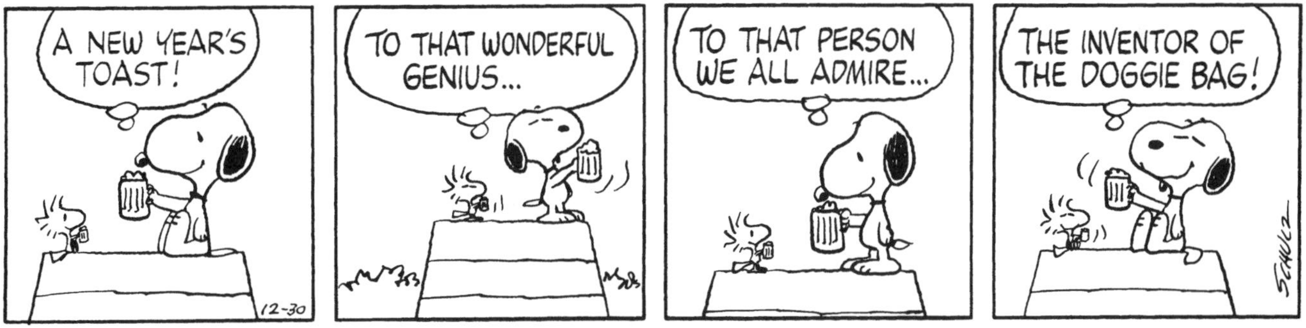
A NEW YEAR'S TOAST!
12-30
TO THAT WONDERFUL GENIUS...
TO THAT PERSON WE ALL ADMIRE...
THE INVENTOR OF THE DOGGIE BAG!
SCHULZ

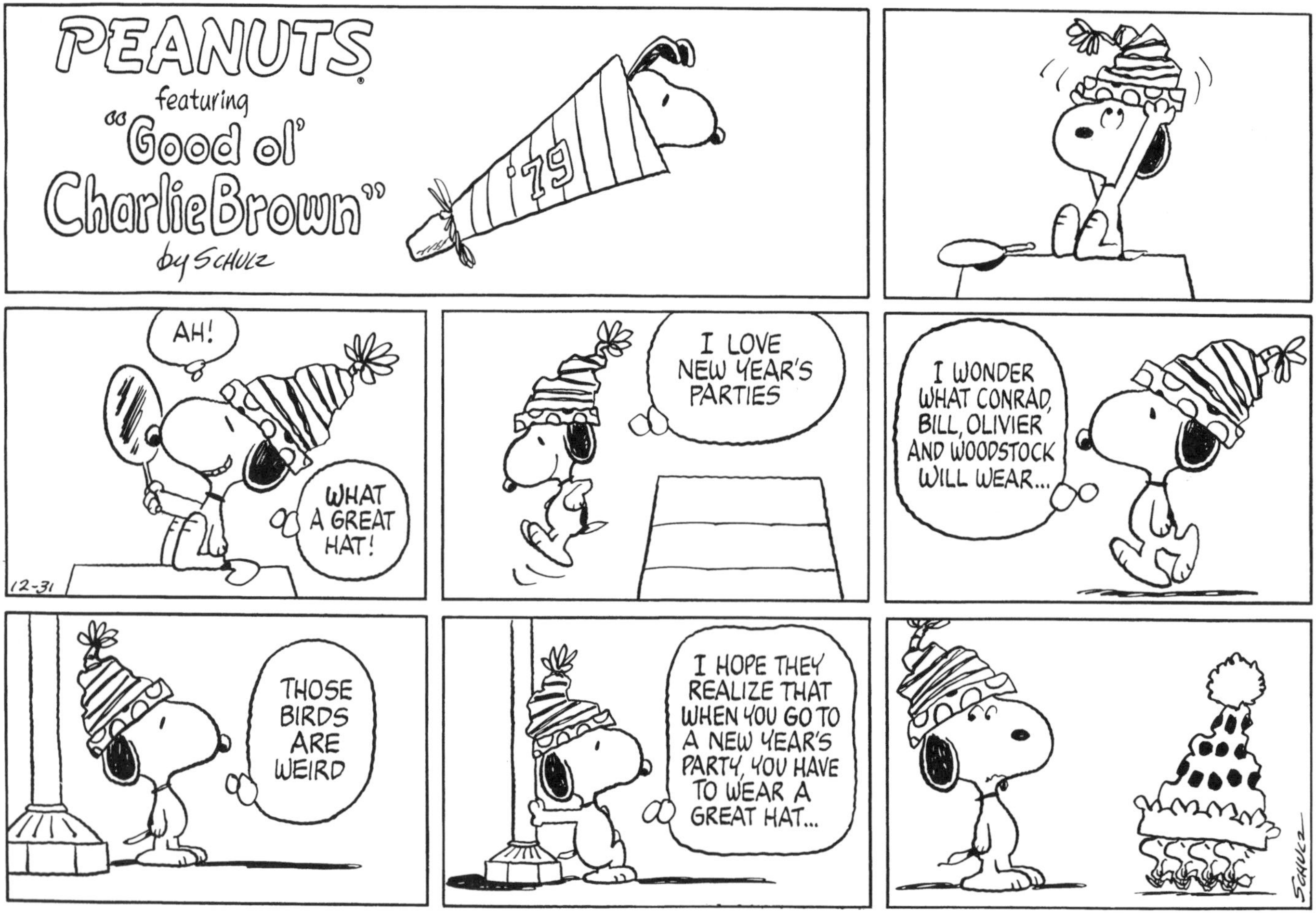
PEANUTS
featuring
"Good ol' Charlie Brown"
by SCHULZ
'79
AH!
WHAT A GREAT HAT!
12-31
I LOVE NEW YEAR'S PARTIES
I WONDER WHAT CONRAD, BILL, OLIVIER AND WOODSTOCK WILL WEAR...
THOSE BIRDS ARE WEIRD
I HOPE THEY REALIZE THAT WHEN YOU GO TO A NEW YEAR'S PARTY, YOU HAVE TO WEAR A GREAT HAT...
SCHULZ

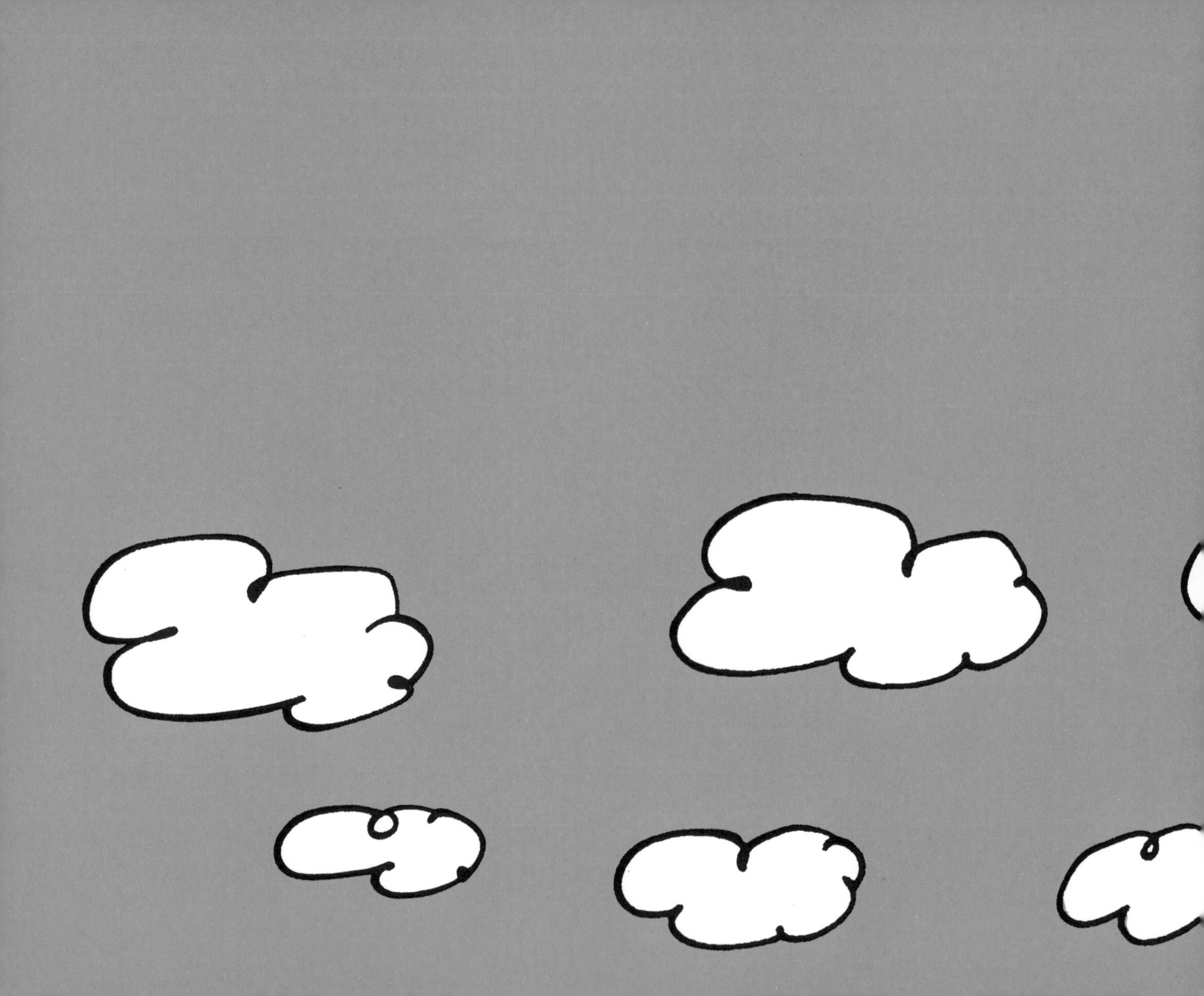

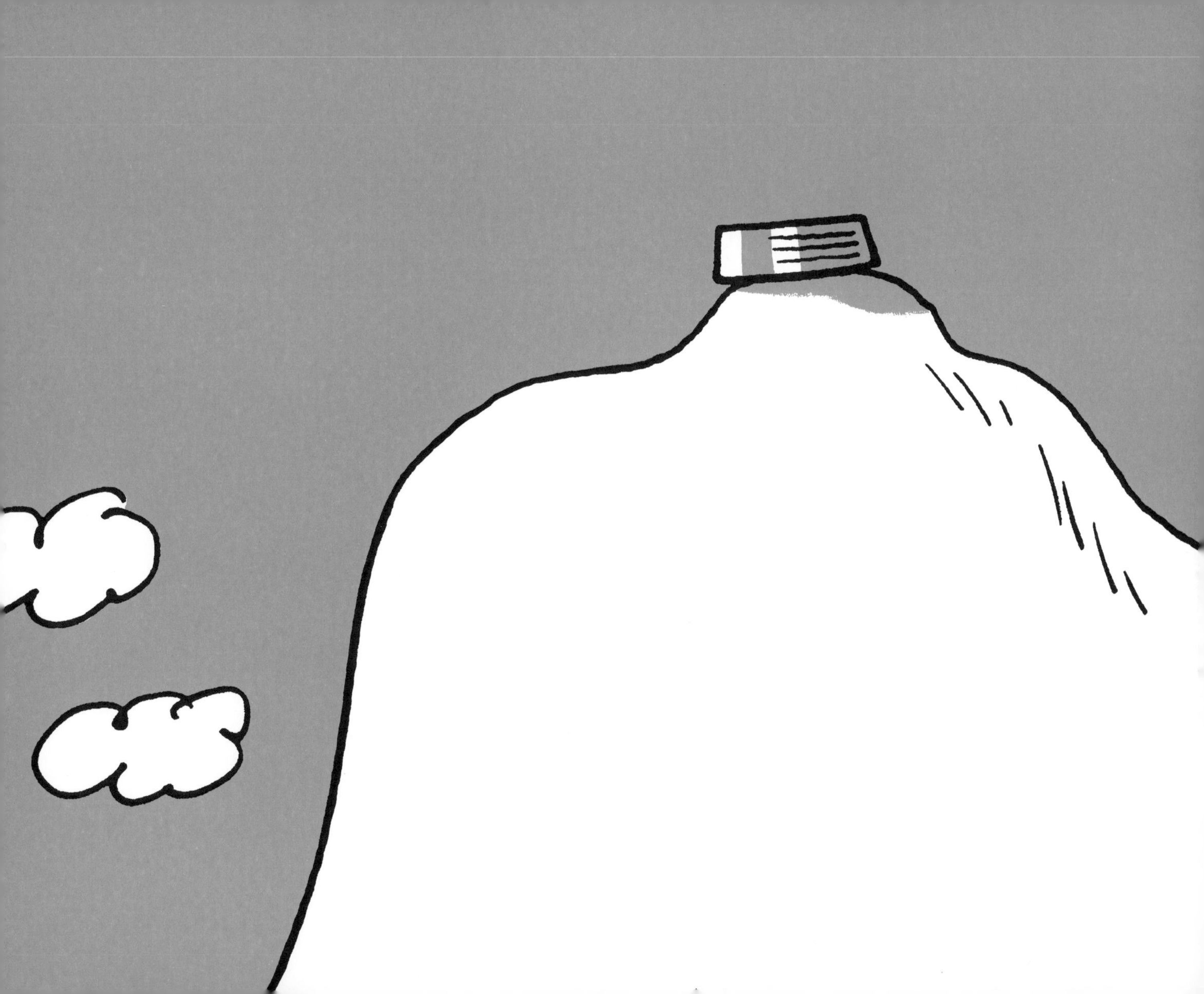

INDEX

Aaron, Hank...87
"Aaugh!"...3, 6, 64, 78, 95, 160, 182, 189, 240, 275
Ace Country Club...72, 73, 75, 76, 78, 79, 81
Albo the Great...8
Alice in Wonderland...5
ampersand...126, 127
Austin...31, 33, 37
backpacking...239, 245, 302
banana...275
baseball...32-34, 37, 40, 47, 59, 77, 84, 87, 109, 193-194, 198, 205, 211, 213-214, 220, 249-250, 298
bean bag...270
bread crumbs...161
Bach, Johann Sebastian...306
Bacon, Francis...46
Beethoven, Ludvig Van...150, 151, 164, 247, 303, 304, 306, 307

Beagle Scout Troop...174-175, 195-196, 200, 242, 245, 255-256, 296, 299, 302, 305, 311, 314
   Bill (*mentioned*)...195-196, 255, 299, 314
   Conrad (*mentioned*)...195-196, 255, 299, 314
   Olivier (*mentioned*)...195-196, 242, 245 (*only shown*), 255, 299, 314
Bethlehem...155
Bible, the...172, 200, 202, 290
birthday...218
"blockhead"...276
"Blues in the Night"...267
Boobie, Bobby...237
Boobie, "Crybaby"...237, 238, 240-241
Book of Genesis, The...100, 103
Book of Jeremiah, The...133
Book of John, The...133
Book of Kings, The...69
Book of Luke, The...133
Book of Matthew, The...133
bowling...193
Bronze Age, The...110
Brown, Charlie...1, 11, 14, 17, 21, 22, 24, 25, 27, 28, 30-37, 39, 40, 42, 43, 47, 48, 54, 55, 57, 59-61, 63, 64, 70, 71, 77, 80, 84, 87, 89, 90, 93, 94, 96-100, 102, 103, 105-107, 109, 111, 112, 117, 121-124, 126, 127, 130, 132, 134, 138, 139, 142, 143, 145, 146, 152-157, 166, 169, 171, 177-179, 181-182, 188-189, 192-194, 197-198, 201, 202, 204-205, 207, 211-214, 216-217, 221, 223-224, 227-228, 234-235, 237, 240, 243-

244, 246-250, 252, 254, 258-262, 264-265, 267-268, 272, 275, 279, 282, 286-288, 290, 298, 300-302, 307, 309-313
Brown, Sally...9, 10, 12-16, 18, 19, 21, 22, 27, 28, 30, 37, 44-46, 69, 80, 84, 85, 106, 108, 109, 114-116, 121, 123, 125-128, 130, 133, 135, 136, 139, 142, 146, 151, 152, 155, 156, 163, 165-166, 168-169, 171-172, 176-180, 192, 199, 202, 204, 207-208, 210-211, 213, 220-221, 227-229, 231-232, 234-235, 243, 244, 257, 260, 262, 264-265, 272, 277-280, 289, 290, 309-311
   reports/essays...165, 168, 202, 204, 207-208, 210-211, 220, 265, 289, 309, 310
caddy master...73, 81
"Caisson Song, The"... 233
camping...174-175, 196, 229, 231, 242

carrier pigeon...225-226
Caterpillar, The...8
cat (neightbor's)...41 (laughing), 66 (first doghouse slash), 89, 97, 129, 135, 149, 158, 164, 169, 204, 209, 283, 285
checkers...138
Cheshire Cat, The...5, 8, 16
chionophobia...136
chocolate sandwich...277
Christmas...149, 151, 154, 155, 299, 309-312
Christo...297
classic cars...230
Cleopatra...135
Colby, Frank Moore...290
Daisy Hill Puppy Farm...264
DiMaggio, Joe...250
disco...217, 282, 283
doughnuts...25, 105, 297
earthquake...308
Easter...44, 194
Easter Island...239
"Eek!"...221
Environmental Protection Agency, The...27
Eudora...228-229, 231-232, 234, 246, 276-277, 279, 282-283
Father's Day...74, 230
"faster than a speeding bullet"...225
Fawcett-Majors, Farrah...116
fishing...142, 232
fleuron...178
football...106, 114, 115, 120, 122 (Lucy pulling ball out), 125, 127, 275 (again), 291, 292
Forest Hills...61
Franklin...144
Frieda...246

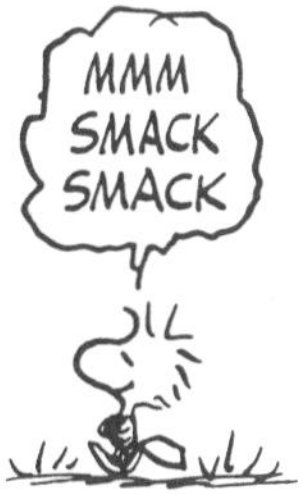
MMM
SMACK
SMACK

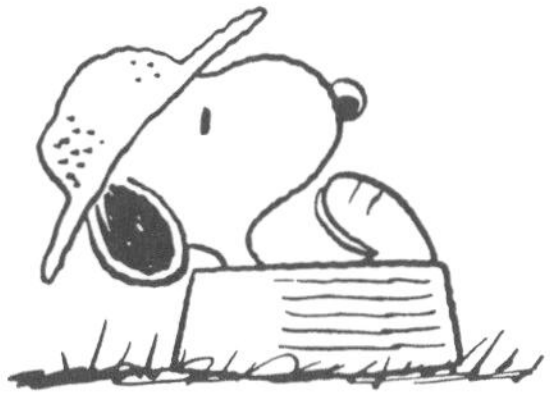

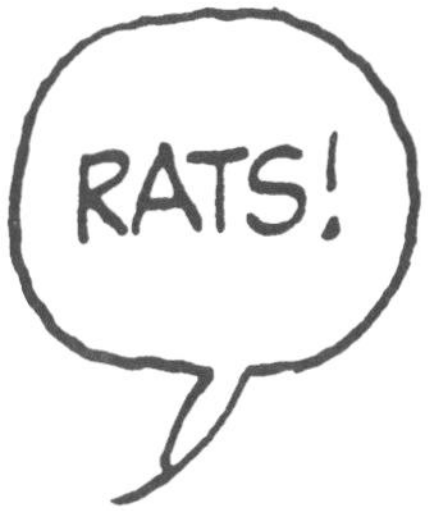
RATS!

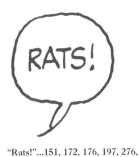

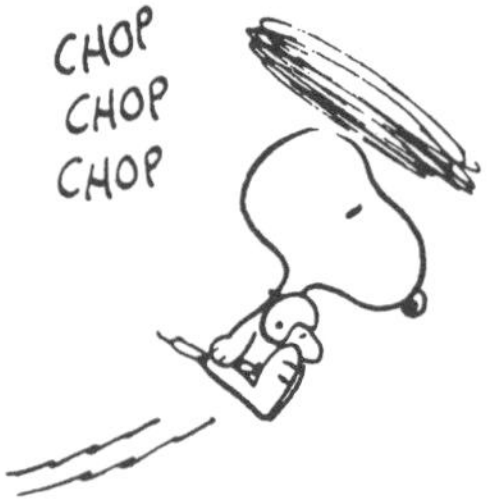
CHOP
CHOP
CHOP

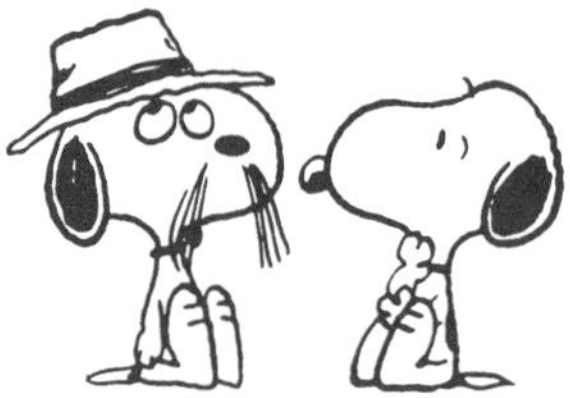

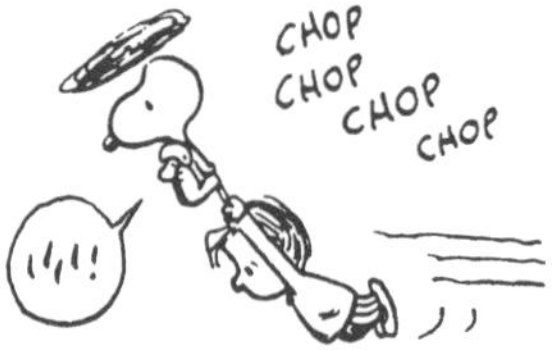
CHOP
CHOP
CHOP
CHOP

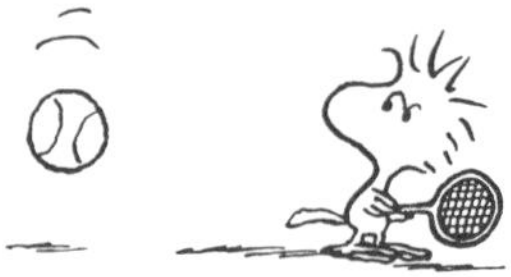

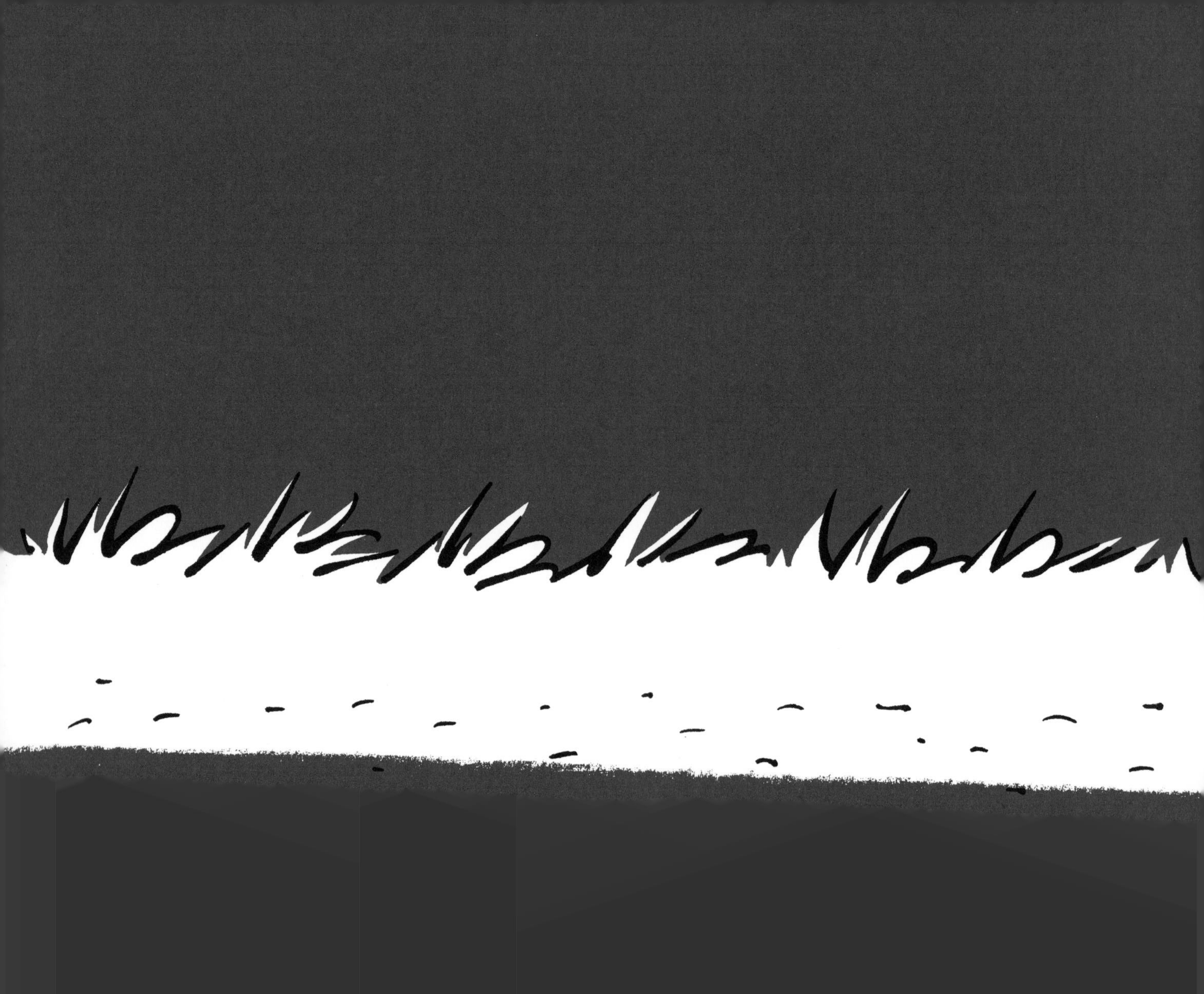

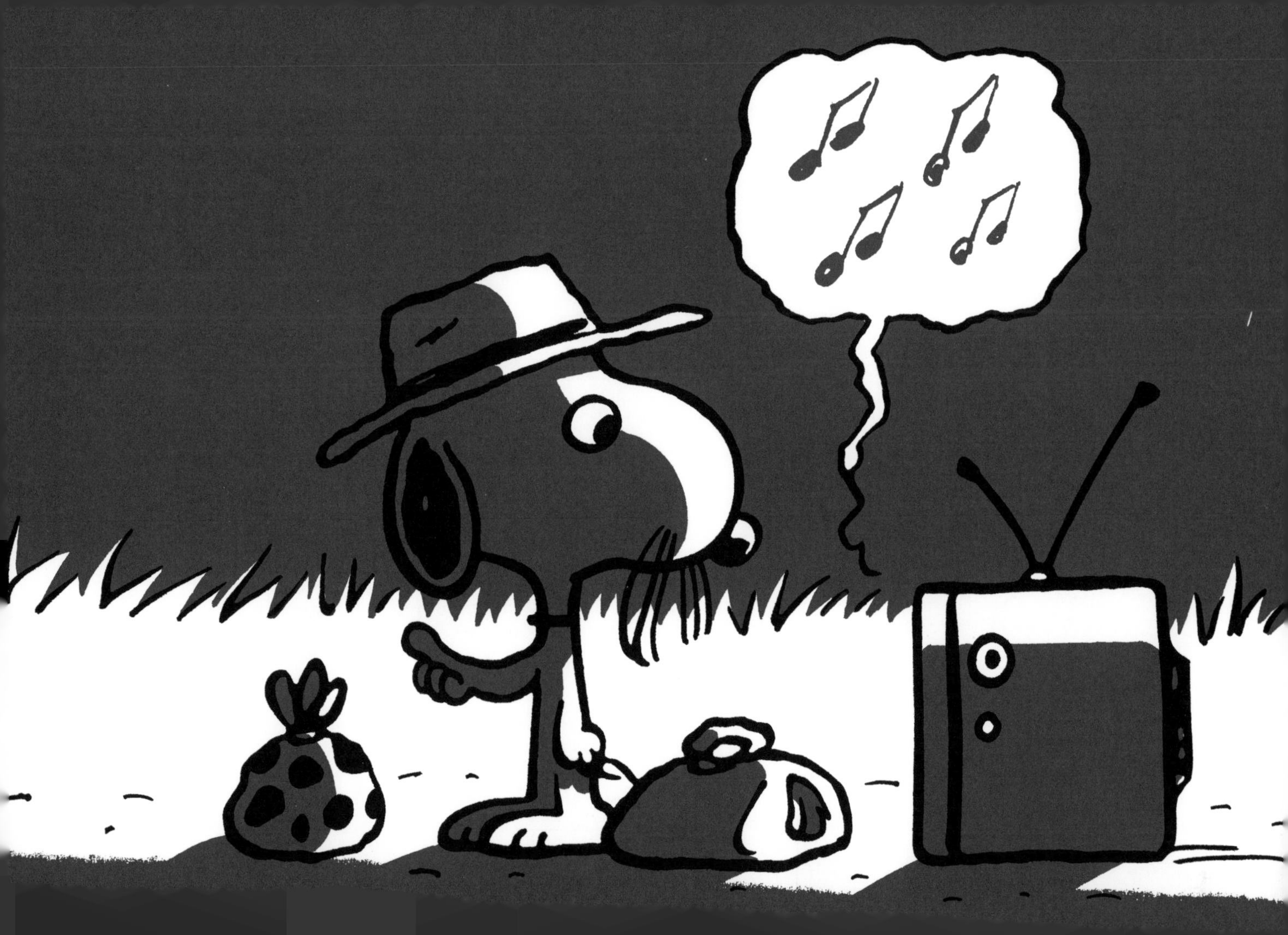

CHARLES M. SCHULZ · 1922 To 2000

Charles M. Schulz was born November 25, 1922 in Minneapolis. His destiny was foreshadowed when an uncle gave him, at the age of two days, the nickname Sparky (after the racehorse Spark Plug in the newspaper strip *Barney Google*).

Schulz grew up in St. Paul. By all accounts, he led an unremarkable, albeit sheltered, childhood. He was an only child, close to both parents, his eventual career path nurtured by his father, who bought four Sunday papers every week — just for the comics.

An outstanding student, he skipped two grades early on, but began to flounder in high school — perhaps not so coincidentally at the same time kids are going through their cruelest, most status-conscious period of socialization. The pain, bitterness, insecurity, and failures chronicled in *Peanuts* appear to have originated from this period of Schulz's life.

Although Schulz enjoyed sports, he also found refuge in solitary activities: reading, drawing, and watching movies. He bought comic books and Big Little Books, pored over the newspaper strips, and copied his favorites — *Buck Rogers*, the Walt Disney characters, *Popeye, Tim Tyler's Luck*. He quickly became a connoisseur; his heroes were Milton Caniff, Roy Crane, Hal Foster, and Alex Raymond.

In his senior year in high school, his mother noticed an ad in a local newspaper for a correspondence school, Federal Schools (later called Art

Instruction Schools). Schulz passed the talent test, completed the course and began trying, unsuccessfully, to sell gag cartoons to magazines. (His first published drawing was of his dog, Spike, and appeared in a 1937 *Ripley's Believe It Or Not!* installment.)

After World War II had ended and Schulz was discharged from the army, he started submitting gag cartoons to the various magazines of the time; his first breakthrough, however, came when an editor at *Timeless Topix* hired him to letter adventure comics. Soon after that, he was hired by his alma mater, Art Instruction, to correct student lessons returned by mail.

Between 1948 and 1950, he succeeded in selling 17 cartoons to the *Saturday Evening Post* — as well as, to the local *St. Paul Pioneer Press*, a weekly comic feature called *Li'l Folks*. It was run in the women's section and paid $10 a week. After writing and drawing the feature for two years, Schulz asked for a better location in the paper or for daily exposure, as well as a raise. When he was turned down on all three counts, he quit.

He started submitting strips to the newspaper syndicates. In the Spring of 1950, he received a letter from the United Feature Syndicate, announcing their interest in his submission, *Li'l Folks*. Schulz boarded a train in June for New York City; more interested in doing a strip than a panel, he also brought along the first installments of what would become *Peanuts* — and that was what sold. (The title, which Schulz loathed to his dying day, was imposed by the syndicate). The first *Peanuts* daily appeared October 2, 1950; the first Sunday, January 6, 1952.

Prior to *Peanuts*, the province of the comics page had been that of gags, social and political observation, domestic comedy, soap opera, and various adventure genres. Although *Peanuts* changed, or evolved, during the 50 years Schulz wrote and drew it, it remained, as it began, an anomaly on the comics page — a comic strip about the interior crises of the cartoonist himself. After a painful divorce in 1973 from which he had not yet recovered, Schulz told a reporter, "Strangely, I've drawn better cartoons in the last six months — or as good as I've ever drawn. I don't know how the human mind works." Surely, it was this kind of humility in the face of profoundly irreducible human question that makes *Peanuts* as universally moving as it is.

Diagnosed with cancer, Schulz retired from *Peanuts* at the end of 1999. He died on February 12th 2000, the day before his last strip was published (and two days before Valentine's Day) — having completed 17,897 daily and Sunday strips, each and every one fully written, drawn, and lettered entirely by his own hand — an unmatched achievement in comics.

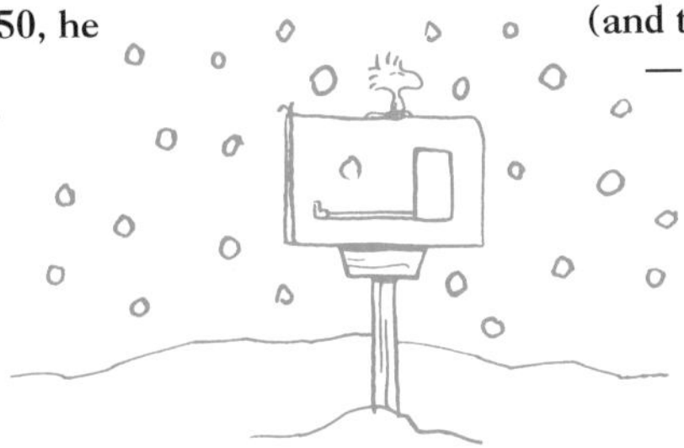

—Gary Groth

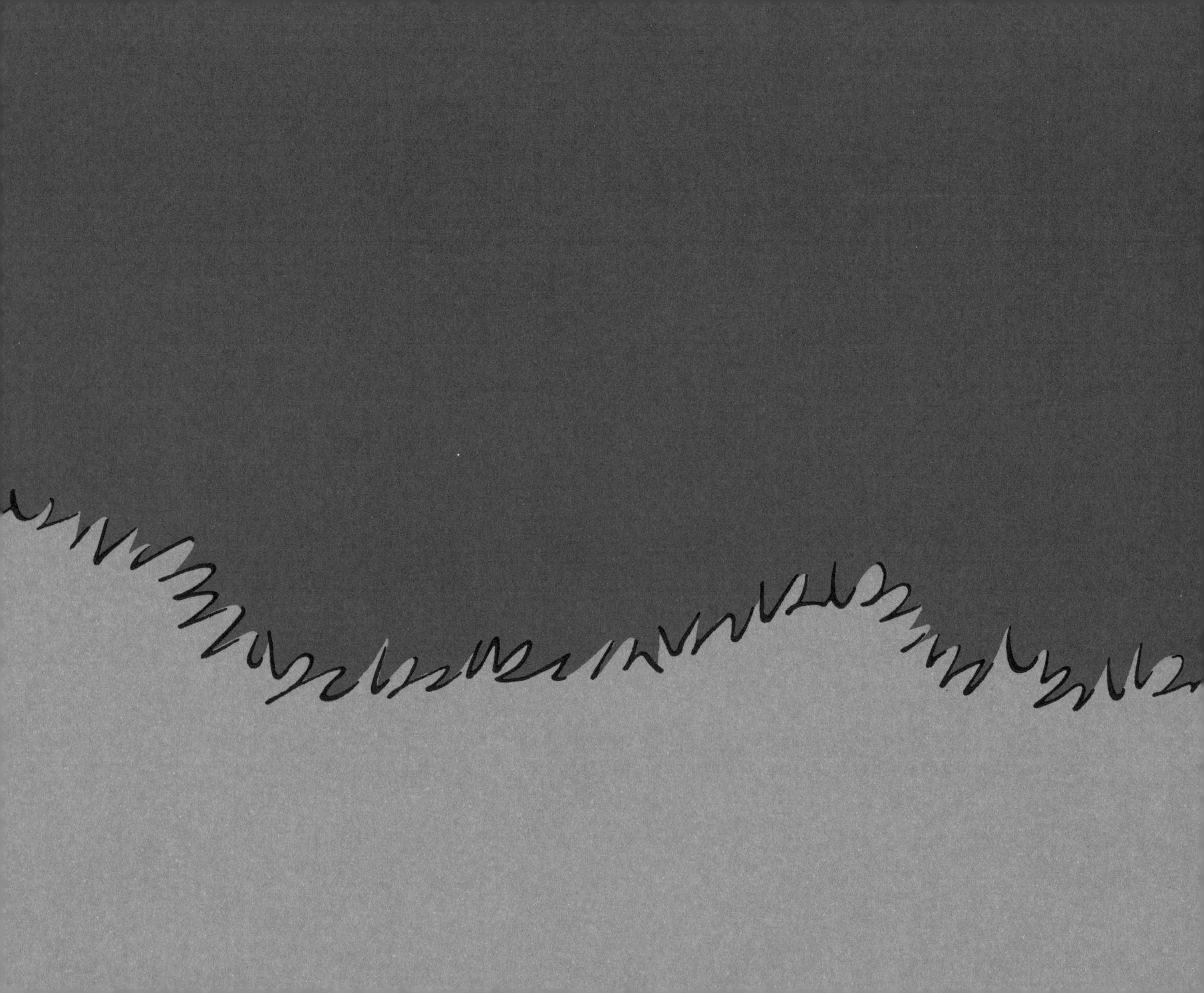

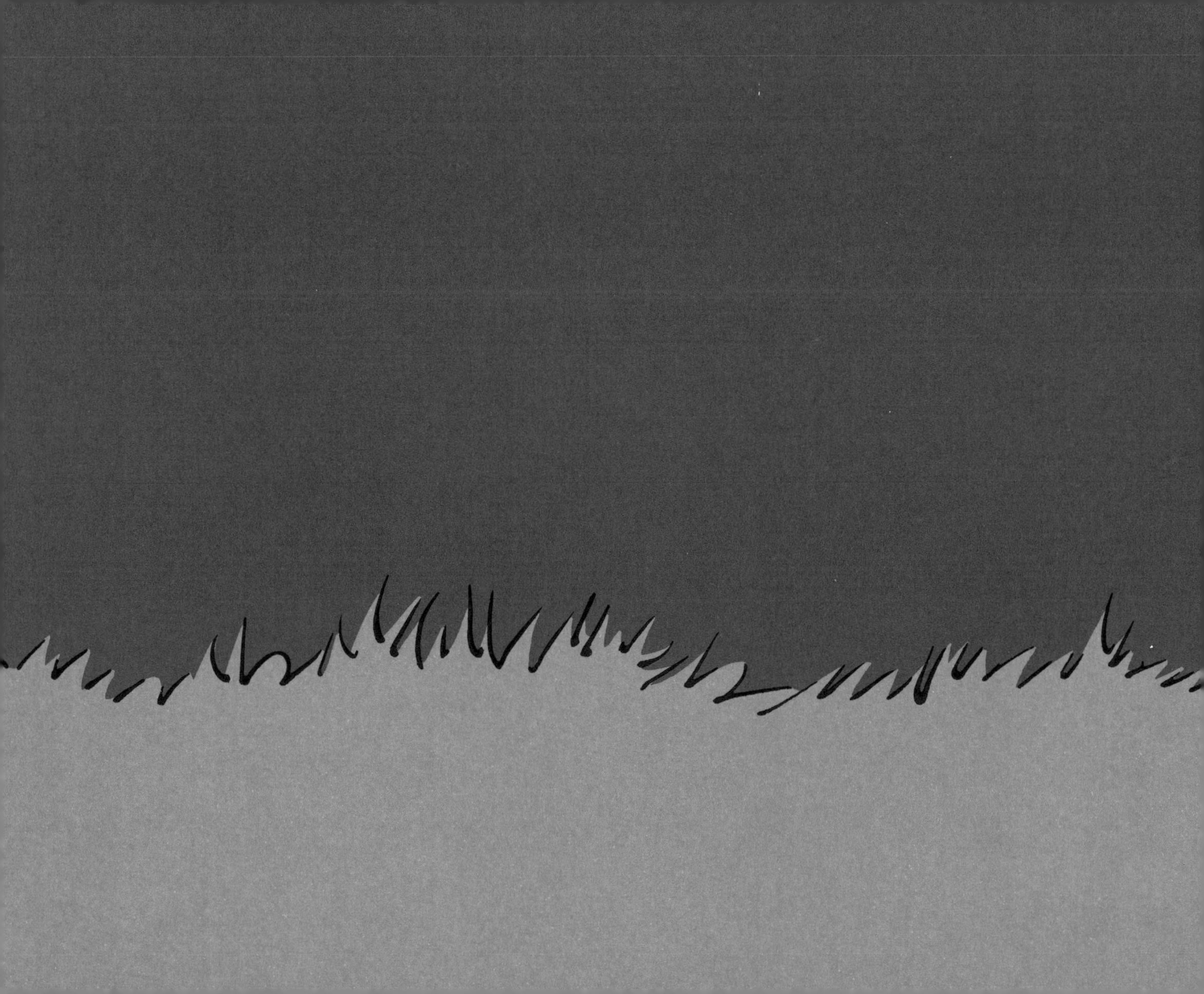

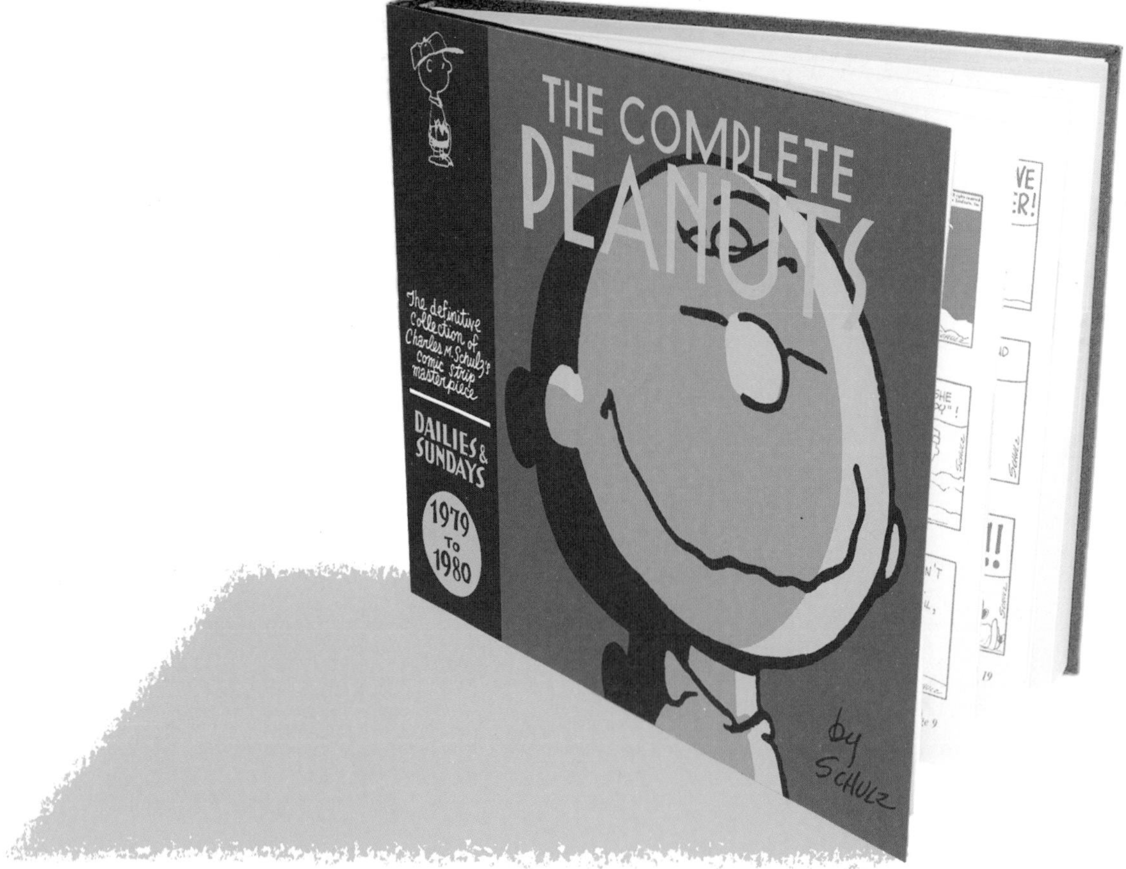
THE COMPLETE PEANUTS
The definitive collection of Charles M. Schulz's comic strip masterpiece
DAILIES & SUNDAYS
1979 TO 1980
by SCHULZ

COMING IN *THE COMPLETE PEANUTS: 1979-1980*

Snoopy flirts with both Eudora and Marcie, in different languages... Peppermint Patty sues her school over a ceiling leak... Charlie Brown ends up in the hospital and thinks he may be dying... Blackjack Snoopy, Riverboat Gambler (plus Snoopy, Census Taker and Snoopy, World Famous Surveyor)... Peppermint Patty and Marcie get militant about equal pay for women... Snoopy's scout troop goes co-ed with the addition of Harriet... and the single most unexpected romance in *Peanuts* history!